# The Use of Force and Internatio

**Second Edition**

Newly-revised, this textbook provides an authoritative conceptual and practical overview of international law governing the resort to force. Following an introductory chapter, which includes coverage of the key issues in identifying the law and actual and potential changes to it, the book addresses the breadth and scope of the prohibition of the threat or use of force and the meaning of 'force' as the focus of this. The book proceeds to address the use of force through the United Nations and regional organisations, the use of force in peacekeeping operations, the right of self-defence and the customary limitations upon this right, the controversial doctrine of humanitarian intervention and forcible interventions in civil conflicts. Updated to include greater focus on aspects such as cyber operations, the threat of force and the 'human element' to the use force, as well as the inclusion of recent developments such as the 2022 Russian invasion of Ukraine, it seeks to address the contemporary legal framework through the prism of contemporary challenges that it currently faces.

**Christian Henderson** is Professor of International Law at the University of Sussex. He has published several books and many peer-reviewed journal articles on the use of force in international law and is co-editor-in-chief of the *Journal on the Use of Force and International Law*.

# The Use of Force and International Law

*Second Edition*

Christian Henderson
*University of Sussex*

CAMBRIDGE UNIVERSITY PRESS

# CAMBRIDGE
UNIVERSITY PRESS

Shaftesbury Road, Cambridge CB2 8EA, United Kingdom

One Liberty Plaza, 20th Floor, New York, NY 10006, USA

477 Williamstown Road, Port Melbourne, VIC 3207, Australia

314–321, 3rd Floor, Plot 3, Splendor Forum, Jasola District Centre, New Delhi – 110025, India

103 Penang Road, #05-06/07, Visioncrest Commercial, Singapore 238467

Cambridge University Press is part of Cambridge University Press & Assessment, a department of the University of Cambridge.

We share the University's mission to contribute to society through the pursuit of education, learning and research at the highest international levels of excellence.

www.cambridge.org
Information on this title: www.cambridge.org/highereducation/isbn/9781108831017

DOI: 10.1017/9781108923057

© Christian Henderson 2018, 2024

This publication is in copyright. Subject to statutory exception and to the provisions of relevant collective licensing agreements, no reproduction of any part may take place without the written permission of Cambridge University Press & Assessment.

First published 2018
Second edition 2024

*A catalogue record for this publication is available from the British Library*

*Library of Congress Cataloging-in-Publication Data*
Names: Henderson, Christian, author.
Title: The use of force and international law / Christian Henderson, University of Sussex.
Description: Second edition. | Cambridge, United Kingdom ; New York, NY : Cambridge University Press, [2024] | Includes bibliographical references and index.
Identifiers: LCCN 2022044125 (print) | LCCN 2022044126 (ebook) | ISBN 9781108831017 (hardback) | ISBN 9781108926256 (paperback) | ISBN 9781108923057 (epub)
Subjects: LCSH: Aggression (International law) | Intervention (International law) | Self-defense (International law)
Classification: LCC KZ6396 .H465 2022 (print) | LCC KZ6396 (ebook) | DDC 341.6/2–dc23/eng/20230105
LC record available at https://lccn.loc.gov/2022044125
LC ebook record available at https://lccn.loc.gov/2022044126

ISBN 978-1-108-83101-7 Hardback
ISBN 978-1-108-92625-6 Paperback

Additional resources for this publication at www.cambridge.org/henderson

Cambridge University Press & Assessment has no responsibility for the persistence or accuracy of URLs for external or third-party internet websites referred to in this publication and does not guarantee that any content on such websites is, or will remain, accurate or appropriate.

# CONTENTS

|  | | |
|---|---|---:|
| | **Introduction** | *page* 1 |
| | Related Frameworks of International Law | 4 |
| | The Sources of the Law on the Use of Force and the Question of Methodology | 6 |
| | Legal and Procedural Issues Associated with the *Jus ad Bellum* | 10 |
| | Subsidiary Means for Determining (and Shaping?) the Law | 14 |
| | Aims, Limitations and Structure of the Book | 16 |
| | Acknowledgements | 18 |
| **PART I** | **The Prohibition of the Threat or Use of Force** | |
| **1** | **The General Breadth and Scope of the Prohibition of the Threat or Use of Force** | 23 |
| 1.1 | Introduction | 23 |
| 1.2 | Historical Attempts at Regulating the Use of Force in International Affairs | 24 |
| 1.3 | The Sources of the Contemporary Prohibition of the Threat or Use of Force | 31 |
| 1.3.1 | The Text of Article 2(4) | 32 |
| 1.3.1.1 | Lack of Express Mention of Exceptions to the Prohibition | 33 |
| 1.3.1.2 | 'against the territorial integrity or political independence of any state' | 33 |
| 1.3.1.3 | 'or in any other manner inconsistent with the purposes of the United Nations' | 35 |
| 1.3.1.4 | The Subjects of the Prohibition: 'International Relations' | 36 |
| 1.3.2 | The Peremptory Status of the Prohibition | 38 |
| 1.4 | The 'Threat' of Force | 40 |
| 1.4.1 | The Element of a Demand or an Ultimatum | 41 |
| 1.4.2 | The Communicative Nature of Threats of Force | 42 |
| 1.4.3 | Threats of Force Not in a Verbal or Written Form | 44 |
| 1.4.4 | The Credibility of a Threat of Force | 47 |
| 1.4.5 | Uses of Force versus Threats of Force: Normative Relativity? | 48 |

| | | |
|---|---|---|
| 1.5 | Accountability, State Responsibility and Responses to a Threat or Use of Force | 48 |
| 1.5.1 | Reparations | 50 |
| 1.5.2 | Countermeasures | 51 |
| 1.5.3 | Self-Defence | 52 |
| 1.5.4 | Institutional Involvement: The United Nations and Regional Organisations | 53 |
| 1.5.5 | Courts and Tribunals | 54 |
| 1.5.5.1 | The Actions of States | 54 |
| 1.5.5.2 | The Actions of Individuals: The Crime of Aggression | 55 |
| 1.5.5.2.1 | An Agreed Definition for the International Criminal Court | 57 |
| 1.5.5.2.2 | The Crime of Aggression as a 'Manifest Violation' of the Charter of the United Nations | 58 |
| 1.5.5.2.3 | The *Mens Rea* Element of the Crime of Aggression | 60 |
| 1.5.5.2.4 | The Potential Impact of the Jurisdiction of the International Criminal Court over the Crime of Aggression | 61 |
| 1.5.6 | Commissions of Inquiry | 65 |
| 1.6 | The Emerging Recognition of a Human Element to the Prohibition of Inter-State Force | 66 |
| 1.6.1 | The UN Human Rights Committee, the Right to Life and the *Jus ad Bellum* | 68 |
| 1.6.1.1 | Objections to the Approach of the UN Human Rights Committee | 69 |
| 1.6.1.2 | Implications of Providing the *Jus ad Bellum* with a Human Element | 70 |
| 1.7 | Questioning the Continued Relevance, Scope and Effectiveness of the Prohibition | 72 |
| 1.7.1 | State Practice and the Claimed 'Death' of the Prohibition of Force | 72 |
| 1.7.2 | Justifications for and Reactions to the Use of Force | 76 |
| 1.7.3 | Reaffirmation of the Prohibition in the Abstract | 78 |
| 1.7.4 | Reaffirmation of the Prohibition in the Context of Cyber Operations | 79 |
| 1.8 | Conclusion | 86 |
| | Questions | 87 |
| | Suggested Further Reading | 88 |
| **2** | **The Meaning of 'Force'** | **89** |
| 2.1 | Introduction | 89 |
| 2.2 | The Principle of Non-intervention | 90 |
| 2.3 | The Type of 'Force' Envisaged in Article 2(4) | 92 |
| 2.4 | The Meaning of 'Armed Force' | 94 |
| 2.4.1 | The Means Used | 95 |
| 2.4.2 | The Effects Created | 97 |
| 2.4.3 | The Indirect Use of Armed Force | 102 |
| 2.5 | The 'Gravity' Element of a Use of Force | 105 |

| | | |
|---|---|---|
| 2.5.1 | Distinguishing 'Use of Force', 'Armed Attack' and 'Aggression' | 105 |
| 2.5.1.1 | 'Armed Attack' | 105 |
| 2.5.1.2 | 'Aggression' | 107 |
| 2.5.2 | 'Minimal' Uses of Force and the Possible Existence of a *De Minimis* Threshold | 109 |
| 2.5.2.1 | The *De Minimis* Gravity Threshold: Of a Quantitative or Qualitative Nature? | 112 |
| 2.6 | The *Mens Rea* Element of the Use of Force | 125 |
| 2.6.1 | Distinguishing General Motives for Action and Intention | 126 |
| 2.6.2 | Mistake | 127 |
| 2.6.3 | Discerning Hostile Intent | 128 |
| 2.7 | Conclusion | 130 |
| | Questions | 130 |
| | Suggested Further Reading | 131 |

## PART II  The Use of Force in the Context of Collective Security

| | | |
|---|---|---|
| **3** | **The Use of Force under the Auspices of the United Nations** | **135** |
| 3.1 | Introduction | 135 |
| 3.2 | The Maintenance of International Peace and Security: The Division of Competence within the United Nations | 137 |
| 3.2.1 | The Security Council | 137 |
| 3.2.2 | The General Assembly | 140 |
| 3.2.3 | The Secretariat | 142 |
| 3.3 | The Forcible Powers of the Security Council in the UN Charter | 143 |
| 3.3.1 | Article 39: The 'Gateway' Provision to Chapter VII | 143 |
| 3.3.1.1 | Threats to the Peace | 144 |
| 3.3.1.2 | Breaches of the Peace and Acts of Aggression | 147 |
| 3.3.2 | Envisaged Measures under Chapter VII | 148 |
| 3.3.3 | Limits to the Forcible Powers of the Security Council | 149 |
| 3.4 | The Chapter VII Powers of the Security Council to Use Force in Practice | 153 |
| 3.4.1 | The Cold War Era (1945–89) | 153 |
| 3.4.2 | The Post-Cold War Era (1989–) | 156 |
| 3.4.2.1 | The Development of the 'Authorisation' Method | 156 |
| 3.4.2.2 | Subsequent Practice in the Use of the Authorisation Method | 158 |
| 3.4.2.3 | Concerns Regarding the Authorisation Method | 161 |
| 3.4.2.4 | The General Assembly and the Use of Force | 165 |
| 3.5 | Chapter VIII and the Authorisation of 'Regional Organisations' | 167 |
| 3.5.1 | The African Union | 169 |
| 3.5.2 | The North Atlantic Treaty Organization | 171 |
| 3.6 | Conclusion | 172 |

|  | Questions | 173 |
|---|---|---|
|  | Suggested Further Reading | 174 |
| **4** | **Issues in Relation to Authorisation by the United Nations Security Council** | **175** |
| 4.1 | Introduction | 175 |
| 4.2 | Striking the Balance between Unilateralism and Multilateralism | 176 |
| 4.3 | The Revival of Past Authorisations | 179 |
| 4.3.1 | The Mandate Contained within Resolution 678 (1990) | 182 |
| 4.3.2 | The Concept of 'Material Breach' in the Practice of the Security Council | 183 |
| 4.3.3 | The Authority to Determine a 'Material Breach' and the Consequences | 185 |
| 4.3.4 | The Legacy of the Revival Argument | 187 |
| 4.4 | Determining the Breadth and Scope of an Authorisation | 189 |
| 4.4.1 | Libya (2011) | 189 |
| 4.4.1.1 | Assistance to Opposition Forces | 191 |
| 4.4.1.2 | Regime Change | 194 |
| 4.4.2 | Côte d'Ivoire (2011) | 195 |
| 4.5 | The Doctrine of 'Implied' Authorisation | 196 |
| 4.5.1 | Unilateral Enforcement of the 'Collective Will' of the UN Security Council | 197 |
| 4.5.1.1 | Iraq (1991–2002) | 197 |
| 4.5.1.2 | Kosovo (1999) | 199 |
| 4.5.1.3 | Assessing Claims to Unilaterally Enforce the 'Collective Will' | 201 |
| 4.5.2 | Retrospective Authorisation or Approval | 202 |
| 4.5.2.1 | Liberia (1990–7) | 203 |
| 4.5.2.2 | Sierra Leone (1996–9) | 204 |
| 4.5.2.3 | Assessing Claims of Retrospective Authorisation or Approval | 206 |
| 4.6 | Implementing the 'Responsibility to Protect' | 207 |
| 4.6.1 | Enforcement of the Secondary Responsibility to Protect | 208 |
| 4.6.2 | R2P: Old Wine in New Bottles? | 211 |
| 4.6.2.1 | Darfur (Sudan) (2003–20) | 212 |
| 4.6.2.2 | Libya (2011) | 213 |
| 4.6.2.3 | Syria (2011–) | 216 |
| 4.7 | Conclusion | 217 |
|  | Questions | 218 |
|  | Suggested Further Reading | 219 |
| **5** | **United Nations Peacekeeping and the Use of Force** | **220** |
| 5.1 | Introduction | 220 |
| 5.2 | Attempting to Define UN Peacekeeping | 222 |
| 5.3 | The Legal Basis for UN Peacekeeping Operations | 224 |
| 5.4 | The Basic Principles of UN Peacekeeping | 226 |
| 5.4.1 | Consent of the Parties | 227 |

| | | |
|---|---|---|
| 5.4.2 | Impartiality | 227 |
| 5.4.3 | Non-use of Force Except in Self-Defence | 228 |
| 5.5 | Peacekeeping Operations: 1945–89 | 230 |
| 5.5.1 | UNEF I (1956–67) | 230 |
| 5.5.2 | ONUC (1960–4) | 232 |
| 5.5.3 | Other Notable Cold War Peacekeeping Operations | 233 |
| 5.6 | Peacekeeping Operations: 1990–2022 | 234 |
| 5.6.1 | UNPROFOR (1992–5) | 235 |
| 5.6.2 | UNOSOM II (1993–5) and AMISON (2007–) | 236 |
| 5.6.3 | UNAMSIL (1999–2005) | 238 |
| 5.6.4 | UNAMID (2007–21) | 239 |
| 5.6.5 | MONUC (2000–10) and MONUSCO (2010–) | 240 |
| 5.6.6 | MINUSMA (2013–) | 242 |
| 5.6.7 | MINUSCA (2014–) | 243 |
| 5.7 | The Evolution in the Use of Force by UN Peacekeeping Operations | 245 |
| 5.7.1 | Non-use of Force Except in Self-Defence | 246 |
| 5.7.2 | Consent | 249 |
| 5.7.3 | Impartiality | 250 |
| 5.7.4 | Peace Observation, Peacekeeping, Peace Enforcement or War Fighting? | 251 |
| 5.8 | Conclusion | 253 |
| | Questions | 255 |
| | Suggested Further Reading | 256 |

## PART III   The Use of Force in Self-Defence

| | | |
|---|---|---|
| 6 | **General Aspects of the Right of Self-Defence** | 259 |
| 6.1 | Introduction | 259 |
| 6.2 | The Concept of an 'Armed Attack' | 261 |
| 6.2.1 | The Perpetrators of an Armed Attack | 262 |
| 6.2.2 | The Targets of an Armed Attack | 267 |
| 6.2.2.1 | The Armed Forces of a State | 267 |
| 6.2.2.2 | State Interests | 269 |
| 6.2.2.3 | Embassies | 269 |
| 6.2.2.4 | Targets within Cyberspace | 271 |
| 6.2.3 | Issues of Proof | 272 |
| 6.2.4 | The *Mens Rea* Element: Does an Armed Attack Need to Be Intended? | 274 |
| 6.2.5 | A Gravity Threshold Distinguishing 'Armed Attacks' from 'Uses of Force'? | 276 |
| 6.2.5.1 | The Threshold in the General Practice of States | 281 |
| 6.2.5.2 | The Gravity Threshold in the Context of Cyber Operations | 285 |
| 6.2.5.3 | The ICJ's Concept of 'Proportional Forcible Countermeasures' | 290 |

| | | |
|---|---|---|
| 6.2.5.4 | Gravity and the 'Accumulation of Events' Theory | 290 |
| 6.3 | The Customary Requirements of Necessity and Proportionality | 296 |
| 6.3.1 | Necessity | 299 |
| 6.3.1.1 | No Reasonable Alternatives to the Resort to Armed Force | 299 |
| 6.3.1.2 | The Use of Force for the Attainment of Defensive Objectives | 305 |
| 6.3.1.2.1 | The Formal Illegality of 'Armed Reprisals' | 306 |
| 6.3.1.2.2 | The Fine Line between Armed Reprisals and Self-Defence | 308 |
| 6.3.2 | Proportionality | 316 |
| 6.3.2.1 | Proportionality and the 'Accumulation of Events' Theory | 321 |
| 6.4 | The Protection of Nationals Abroad | 322 |
| 6.4.1 | Attacks on Nationals as an Armed Attack | 324 |
| 6.4.2 | Attacks or Threats to Nationals by a Foreign Government | 327 |
| 6.4.3 | Attacks or Threats to Nationals that a Foreign Government Is Either Unwilling or Unable to Prevent | 333 |
| 6.4.3.1 | Operations to Extract Nationals | 335 |
| 6.5 | The Right of Collective Self-Defence | 336 |
| 6.5.1 | The Nature of Collective Self-Defence | 337 |
| 6.5.2 | The Regulation of the Right of Collective Self-Defence | 338 |
| 6.6 | The Role of the UN Security Council | 343 |
| 6.6.1 | The Reporting Requirement | 344 |
| 6.6.2 | The 'Until Clause' | 349 |
| 6.7 | Conclusion | 354 |
| | Questions | 355 |
| | Suggested Further Reading | 356 |
| **7** | **Preventative Self-Defence** | 357 |
| 7.1 | Introduction | 357 |
| 7.2 | Intercepting an Armed Attack | 359 |
| 7.3 | Anticipating an Armed Attack: The Concept of 'Imminence' | 360 |
| 7.3.1 | The Academic Debate: 'Expansionists' versus 'Restrictionists' | 361 |
| 7.3.2 | International Jurisprudence | 362 |
| 7.3.3 | Cold War State Practice on the Right of Anticipatory Self-Defence: The 1967 Six-Day War | 363 |
| 7.4 | Pre-empting the Development of a Threat of an Armed Attack: Moving beyond 'Imminence'? | 364 |
| 7.4.1 | Cold War State Practice on the Right of Pre-emptive Self-Defence | 365 |
| 7.4.1.1 | The 1962 Cuban Missile Crisis | 365 |
| 7.4.1.2 | The 1981 Israeli Strike on the Osiraq Nuclear Reactor (Iraq) | 367 |
| 7.4.2 | Attempts to Adapt the Concept of 'Imminence' in the Aftermath of 9/11: The 'Bush Doctrine' | 368 |
| 7.4.2.1 | Test Cases for the Bush Doctrine of Pre-emptive Self-Defence? | 371 |
| 7.4.2.1.1 | Iraq (2003) | 371 |

| | | |
|---|---|---|
| 7.4.2.1.2 | Syria (2007) | 373 |
| 7.4.2.2 | General Reaction to the Bush Doctrine of Pre-emptive Self-Defence | 374 |
| 7.4.2.3 | Pre-emptive Self-Defence and the International Court of Justice | 378 |
| 7.4.3 | The Obama Doctrine of 'Necessary Force' | 379 |
| 7.5 | Reassessing 'Imminence' in the Light of Contemporary Threats: The 'Bethlehem Principles' and Beyond | 381 |
| 7.5.1 | From 'Temporal' to 'Contextual' Imminence | 384 |
| 7.5.1.1 | The Expected Timing of the Attack | 384 |
| 7.5.1.2 | Capabilities of the Potential Attacker | 385 |
| 7.5.1.3 | Gravity of the Threatened Attack | 386 |
| 7.5.1.4 | Intent of the Potential Attacker | 386 |
| 7.5.1.5 | The Occurrence of Previous Attacks | 387 |
| 7.5.2 | Imminence and the Drone Strike on Iranian General Soleimani (2020) | 389 |
| 7.5.3 | The Impact of 'Contextual Imminence' upon the Necessity Criterion | 395 |
| 7.6 | Conclusion | 398 |
| | Questions | 398 |
| | Suggested Further Reading | 399 |
| **8** | **The Use of Force against Non-state Actors** | 400 |
| 8.1 | Introduction | 400 |
| 8.2 | General Considerations of the Right of Self-Defence against Non-state Actors | 401 |
| 8.3 | Self-Defence against Non-state Actors and Their Host State | 404 |
| 8.3.1 | The 'Effective Control' Standard of Attribution | 404 |
| 8.3.2 | The 'Harbouring' Standard of Attribution | 407 |
| 8.4 | Military Action Restricted to the Non-state Actors | 408 |
| 8.4.1 | Lowering the Standard of Attribution | 413 |
| 8.4.2 | The 'Unable or Unwilling' Doctrine | 414 |
| 8.4.2.1 | Theoretical and Practical Problems of the Doctrine | 420 |
| 8.4.2.1.1 | Unable (and Unwilling?) States | 420 |
| 8.4.2.1.2 | Failed States | 422 |
| 8.4.2.1.3 | Unable Yet Willing States | 423 |
| 8.4.2.1.4 | Able Yet Unwilling States | 424 |
| 8.4.2.1.5 | Other Relevant Factors | 426 |
| 8.4.2.1.6 | The Legal Status of the Doctrine | 427 |
| 8.5 | Targeted Killings | 428 |
| 8.6 | Conclusion | 439 |
| | Questions | 440 |
| | Suggested Further Reading | 441 |

## PART IV  Forcible Intervention in Situations of Civil Unrest

| | | |
|---|---|---|
| **9** | **Consent to Intervention and Intervention in Civil Wars** | 445 |
| 9.1 | Introduction | 445 |
| 9.2 | Identifying Authority to Consent | 447 |
| 9.2.1 | The General Framework: Governments and Non-state Actors | 448 |
| 9.2.2 | Effective Control | 452 |
| 9.2.3 | Recognition | 455 |
| 9.2.4 | The Principle of Self-Determination | 459 |
| 9.3 | Intervention in Civil Wars | 461 |
| 9.3.1 | The 'Negative Equality' Principle | 462 |
| 9.3.2 | The Purpose-Based Approach | 466 |
| 9.3.3 | Counter-Intervention | 469 |
| 9.4 | The Form of the Consent or Invitation to Intervene | 472 |
| 9.5 | The Limits of the Consent or Invitation to Intervene | 479 |
| 9.6 | Conclusion | 484 |
| | Questions | 485 |
| | Suggested Further Reading | 485 |
| **10** | **The Doctrine of Humanitarian Intervention** | 486 |
| 10.1 | Introduction | 486 |
| 10.2 | The UN Charter and Humanitarian Intervention | 487 |
| 10.3 | Humanitarian Intervention in the Practice of States | 494 |
| 10.3.1 | Cold War | 494 |
| 10.3.2 | Post-Cold War: From Iraq to Kosovo | 497 |
| 10.3.2.1 | Iraq (1991–2002) | 497 |
| 10.3.2.2 | ECOWAS Intervention in Liberia (1990) | 499 |
| 10.3.2.3 | ECOWAS Intervention in Sierra Leone (1997–8) | 500 |
| 10.3.2.4 | Kosovo (1999) | 501 |
| 10.3.2.5 | Humanitarian Intervention in the Aftermath of Operation Allied Force | 504 |
| 10.3.2.5.1 | Humanitarian Intervention and the 'Thin Red Line' from Legality | 506 |
| 10.3.2.5.2 | Justified by a Failure of the UN Security Council? | 507 |
| 10.3.2.5.3 | Genocide: A Legal Requirement to Save Lives? | 508 |
| 10.3.2.5.4 | The Operation of a Possible Right of Humanitarian Intervention in Practice | 511 |
| 10.4 | The Civil War in Syria and Humanitarian Intervention | 512 |
| 10.4.1 | The Debate Regarding Air Strikes in 2013 | 513 |
| 10.4.2 | The April 2017 Air Strikes | 515 |
| 10.4.3 | The April 2018 Air Strikes | 516 |

| | | |
|---|---|---:|
| 10.5 | Humanitarian Intervention and the Responsibility to Protect | 520 |
| 10.6 | Conclusion | 521 |
| | Questions | 522 |
| | Suggested Further Reading | 522 |

**Concluding Remarks** 523

Index 527

# INTRODUCTION

It is a sad and depressing reality that, for any international lawyer interested and working in the field of international law governing the use of military force by and between states (the '*jus ad bellum*'), business tends to be bad during moments of relative peace and stability. Arguably even more depressing, however, is the fact that this is not often the case.

The adoption of the United Nations (UN) Charter in 1945, at the end of the Second World War, was a landmark moment for this branch of international law, in that a legal prohibition of the 'threat or use of force' had taken the place of the broader – and largely unsuccessful – attempts at regulating the resort to 'war' contained in the Covenant of the League of Nations (1919) and the Kellogg–Briand Pact (1928).[1] According to the Charter regime, states were, therefore, prohibited from resorting to military action against and in the territory of other states unless acting in self-defence or under the authority of the UN Security Council.[2] This regime has so far stood the test of time, at least to the extent that it continues to exist today. However, it is, as this book attempts to demonstrate, subject to constant scrutiny and challenge in terms of its breadth, effectiveness and relevance.

Although the world has not witnessed catastrophic global wars since 1945, the use of force has never been far from our consciousness. This has often been in the form of one or more states taking – or at least threatening – military action against another, which was arguably the type of scenario envisaged by the drafters of the prohibition of force contained within Article 2(4) of the UN Charter, confined as it is to the 'international relations' between states.[3] The military action by the United States, the United Kingdom and Australia against Iraq in 2003, which had the somewhat inevitable result of a regime change, provides a notable example of such action, and one which proved highly controversial and the ramifications of which both Iraq and the broader international community are continuing to face today.[4] Nearly two decades later Russia's invasion of Ukraine in 2022 demonstrates that such large-scale

---

[1] See Section 1.2.   [2] See Chapters 6–8 and 3–5, respectively.   [3] See Section 1.3.1.4.
[4] See Section 4.3.

inter-state uses of force with significant global ramifications have not been eradicated in the UN Charter era.[5] Of course, it cannot go unnoticed that both were perpetrated by permanent members of the UN Security Council, the body ordained with 'primary responsibility for the maintenance of international peace and security'.[6]

Today it is, however, more likely that when a state resorts to force it does so against a non-state actor, often of a perceived terrorist nature. Indeed, just a few years preceding its use of force against Iraq in 2003, the United States responded to the attacks of 11 September 2001 by launching a military campaign against al-Qaida, the terrorist group responsible for the attacks.[7] The rise to prominence of contemporary terrorism, ranging from lone-wolf suicide bombers to groups with aspirations of statehood, has meant that, while new rules of the *jus ad bellum* have not been introduced since 1945, the interpretation provided to existing ones has often been brought into sharp focus.

Further questions have been asked of the law due to the evolution in weaponry, in that, while what may be considered to be relatively conventional weaponry is still very visible – as both the use of force against Iraq in 2003 and the Russian invasion of Ukraine in 2022 vividly demonstrate – weapons of mass destruction, drones, and cyber weaponry have asked questions of the rules in this area, as will be highlighted throughout the chapters of this book. The rapidly occurring and far reaching climate change that the world is currently witnessing is also tentatively beginning to raise certain questions of the law governing the use of inter-state force.[8] In particular, the pressures that will be placed on the international community through, for example, migration and land and water shortages, have already begun to be addressed in terms of their threat to peace and security.[9]

In addressing the various issues and controversies that arise one may question what this branch of international law seeks to do. While the law regulating the use of force is centred upon a broad prohibition of the threat or use of force, there is also a pragmatic realisation that there will be occasions when force will be deemed to be necessary. Indeed, to deny states the possibility of using force would have in the view of some made signing up to and ratifying the UN Charter akin to a suicide pact, something which states, for obvious reasons, would never have agreed to. The law therefore aims to

---

[5] This incident is discussed throughout the book. See, in general, James A. Green, Christian Henderson and Tom Ruys, 'Russia's Attack on Ukraine and the *Jus ad Bellum*' (2022) 9 *Journal on the Use of Force and International Law* 4.
[6] Article 24(1), UN Charter (1945).   [7] See, in particular, Sections 7.4.2 and 8.3.2.
[8] See, for example, Craig Martin, 'Atmospheric Intervention?: The Climate Change Crisis and the *Jus ad Bellum* Regime' (2020) 45 *Columbia Journal of Environmental Law* 331.
[9] Ibid., at 374–8.

minimise to the greatest extent possible the occasions when force will be used, by not only preserving an 'inherent' right of states to engage in self-defence,[10] but also through centralising the collective use of force within the UN, in particular the Security Council in providing it with primary responsibility for the maintenance of international peace and security.[11] Although the existence and functioning of regional organisations is expressly recognised in the UN Charter,[12] it is also clear that, in terms of enforcement measures involving the use of force, the Security Council is to take precedence and possess ultimate control.[13]

However, closely tied to the question of what this branch of the law seeks to do is the question of what it can realistically achieve. The law is to a great extent premised upon reciprocity between states and, although the notion of sovereign equality is preached within the UN Charter,[14] one does not have to look far to see that it is imperfectly practised. As noted in the previous paragraph, the Security Council stands at the apex of the system of collective security and holds potentially great power not only over collective measures but through its oversight of invocations of self-defence.[15] Yet, the Council consists of five permanent members (the United Kingdom, United States, France, Russia and China) that not only have a permanent presence within the Council but also possess a power of veto,[16] providing these member states with notably greater rights and power than other states. This, combined with the pressures of international politics, has meant that the system of collective security, and international law regulating the use of force more generally, has not functioned as arguably intended most of the time, with the collective security system in a state of partial paralysis for most of its existence.[17] That said, however, and in particular with the end of the Cold War, the law can arguably be seen to have played a role in restraining, or at least conditioning, the forcible actions of states.[18] For example, whether or not it is simply a case of saving face, states nonetheless often appear compelled to justify their actions, which can be taken to indicate that the law in this context is not, at least, purely epiphenomenal.

The decision to resort to the use of force is one of the most solemn that a state can take and the international legal regulation of the use of force undoubtedly remains one of the most fundamental areas of international law. Indeed, the prohibition of force contained within Article 2(4) of the UN

---

[10] Article 51, UN Charter (1945). See Chapters 6–8.   [11] Article 24(1), ibid. See Chapters 3–5.
[12] Chapter VIII, UN Charter (1945).   [13] See Section 3.5.
[14] Article 2(1), UN Charter (1945).   [15] See, in particular, Section 6.6.
[16] See Articles 23(1) and 27(3), respectively, UN Charter (1945).
[17] Nigel D. White, *Keeping the Peace: The United Nations and the Maintenance of International Peace and Security*, 2nd ed. (Manchester University Press, 1997), at 7.
[18] See further, in particular, Section 1.7.

Charter is often referred to as the 'cornerstone' provision of what some have described as the 'constitution' of the international community.[19] Furthermore, there can be little of greater importance to a state or the international community than self-preservation and the protection of sovereignty, and this is what much of the law is concerned with. Yet, and partly for these very reasons, the law in this area also remains one of the most controversial within the broader field of international law. A further reason for the controversy regarding this area of the law can be found in its relative simplicity, consisting mainly of just a handful of provisions within the UN Charter.[20] Compared with, for example, the law regulating armed conflicts (the '*jus in bello*' or international humanitarian law), which is comprised of numerous dedicated treaties and conventions, this is legal regulation at its most minimalist.

## RELATED FRAMEWORKS OF INTERNATIONAL LAW

While the branch of international law under focus in this book ostensibly seeks to limit when states resort to the use of inter-state force, there are other related branches and frameworks of international law that will be touched upon.[21] For example, when states resort to armed force, the *jus in bello* will frequently be triggered.[22] It is often said that, whereas the *jus ad bellum*, which is under focus in this volume, seeks to regulate *when* states may resort to force, the *jus in* bello regulates *how* states may use force within the context of an armed conflict. Indeed, the key underlying obligations within this latter branch of international law provide for the distinction between civilians and combatants and civilian objects and military objectives, the balancing of the principles of military necessity with that of humanity, the obligation to take precautions in attacking the opposing party to an armed conflict and the obligation that any military advantage gained in an attack must be proportionate to the collateral civilian harm caused by it. However, the 'when' and 'how' distinction between the *jus ad bellum* and *jus in bello* frameworks is not entirely accurate. As will be seen, the twin criteria of 'necessity' and 'proportionality' within the *jus ad bellum* also have much to say on the 'how'

---

[19] See James L. Brierly, *The Law of Nations*, 6th ed. (rev. Humphrey Waldock) (Oxford University Press, 1963), at 414 and Bardo Fassbender, *The United Nations Charter as the Constitution of the International Community* (Martinus Nijhoff, 2009).

[20] In particular, Articles 2(4), Chapter VII, including Article 51, and Chapter VIII.

[21] There are additional frameworks and areas of international law that are of some relevance, including arms control law, the law of the sea, civil aviation law, disarmament and non-proliferation and the law relating to outer space, although due to limited space they are not covered or given similar attention here.

[22] For an overview of this area of international law, see Emily Crawford and Alison Pert, *International Humanitarian Law*, 2nd ed. (Cambridge University Press, 2020).

question, as well as the where and when questions, and continue to operate in parallel with the operation and application of the *jus in bello*.[23]

A further branch of international law that is increasingly seen as having a role in decisions and actions regarding the inter-state use of force is that of international human rights law.[24] Indeed, although there has long been a debate regarding the relationship between the *jus in bello* and international human rights law and when each will apply or be said to constitute the *lex specialis*, as well as interest in the relationship between the *jus ad bellum* and *jus in bello*, there has been until recently comparatively little interest in the relationship between the *jus ad bellum* and international human rights law, in particular the right to life.[25] There are several possible reasons for this void, including that decisions to resort to inter-state force and war are often perceived as being removed from the obligations that states owe to individual human beings. In addition, although the position is increasingly less common, the idea still lingers that states somehow shed their obligations to protect human rights once they venture outside of their territory and jurisdiction. This book will address the idea that the *jus ad bellum* has a 'human element' and, although international human rights law is arguably of relevance across the spectrum of issues covered in this book, it has been given particular attention in the context of so-called targeted killings, which is arguably where the interaction between the three branches of the *jus ad bellum*, *jus in bello* and international human rights law is particularly pertinent.[26]

In addition, while so often associated more with war crimes and violations of the *jus in bello*, international criminal law is now another framework of relevance in discussions on the *jus ad bellum*, in particular with the emergence of the crime of aggression as a crime the International Criminal Court now has jurisdiction over.[27] Indeed, although the law on the use of force is generally seen at the level of the 'state', the crime of aggression has to an extent 'individualised' the law in this area, so that those individuals engaged in decisions to resort to such inter-state force may be held accountable. The crime might still be perceived as being of restricted utility, with limited possibilities for holding individuals accountable. Yet it is nonetheless arguably a step forward in attempting to achieve the founding purpose of the United Nations of 'saving succeeding generations from the scourge of war'.[28]

---

[23] See, in particular, Section 6.3. See, in general, Keiichiro Okimoto, *The Distinction and Relationship between* Jus ad Bellum *and* Jus in Bello (Hart, 2011).
[24] See, in general, Daniel Moeckli, Sangeeta Shah, Sandesh Sivakumaran, and David Harris (eds.), *International Human Rights Law*, 4th ed. (Oxford University Press, 2022).
[25] Although see Section 1.6.    [26] See Section 8.5.    [27] See Section 1.5.5.2.
[28] Preamble, UN Charter (1945).

## THE SOURCES OF THE LAW ON THE USE OF FORCE AND THE QUESTION OF METHODOLOGY

Ascertaining the contours of the law is in this area is by no means an easy or straightforward task, and several qualifications are called for. The book takes its cue from the sources of international law found within Article 38(1) of the Statute of the International Court of Justice (1945), in particular treaties and customary international law.[29] Both of these main sources of international law are of key relevance to the topic of this book as, while the adoption of the Charter of the United Nations as a treaty in 1945 was a landmark moment in the historical regulation of the threat or use of force, it is broadly accepted that inter-state force is also regulated through customary international law,[30] with extensive similarities, if not total symmetry, in the law as it is contained in both sources.

There is no formal hierarchy between the sources of international law. Yet, in addressing the law this book will start where possible with the text of the UN Charter. Indeed, it is easy to be drawn first to the Charter given its written and tangible nature from which to obtain an understanding of the contours and content of the law. As Bianchi has noted, in this area of international law '[t]he instinct to give priority to the UN Charter provisions is ... understandable in the light of the allegedly more secure character of a written text, particularly as compared with the uncertain process of ascertaining the existence as well as the content of unwritten rules of customary law.'[31] Furthermore, one could argue that 'the sheer fact that something is written down gives it a special authority'.[32] In any case, virtually the entire international community of states is a member of the United Nations, meaning that

---

[29] Article 38(1)(a) and (b), Statute of the International Court of Justice (1945). Treaties are written agreements between states and may take a multilateral form, such as the UN Charter, or be of a bilateral nature between two states. Customary international law, on the other hand, is formed through the practice of states which is underpinned by a general belief (*opinio juris*) that the particular act or omission is either required or prohibited as an international legal norm. Article 38, which also includes in paragraph (d) 'judicial decisions and the teachings of the most highly qualified publicists' as 'subsidiary means for the determination of rules of law', is arguably incomplete or at least does not paint a complete and accurate picture of the sources of international law. For sure, while not fitting squarely under the headings of Article 38, the work of the International Law Commission, resolutions and statements of – as well as debates within – the UN Security Council and General Assembly, as well as documents of other organisations are central to any discussion and analysis of the law.

[30] See *Case Concerning Military and Paramilitary Activities in and against Nicaragua (Nicaragua v. United States of America)*, Merits, (1986) ICJ Reports 14, at para. 34.

[31] Andrea Bianchi, 'The International Regulation of the Use of Force: The Politics of Interpretive Method' (2009) 22 *Leiden Journal of International Law* 651, at 657.

[32] Ibid., at 658.

whatever arguments one may make about the possible nature of, or changes to, the customary source of a particular obligation or right, these would still need to be squared with the obligations and rights states have under the Charter.[33]

A discernible level of agreement exists both between states and between scholars on the core of the law within these sources, and the basic processes and fundamental principles regarding ascertaining the law and the formation, interpretation and modification of both treaties and customary international law. Yet, beyond this we find that any agreement soon begins to dissipate.[34] For example, while there is a core of law that is clear and agreed upon by states – indeed, no state denies that there is a prohibition of the threat or use of force or that all states have a right of self-defence – questions remain regarding its extent and breadth, over which there are sometimes significantly differing views.

Resorting to the Vienna Convention of the Law of Treaties (1969) (VCLT) provides some guidance as to how one should approach interpreting the UN Charter.[35] These rules of interpretation, however, leave a large measure of discretion to the individual interpreter and, in many ways, give rise to more questions than answers. For example, the VCLT provides that '[a] treaty shall be interpreted in good faith in accordance with the ordinary meaning to be given to the terms of the treaty in their context and in the light of its object and purpose'.[36] Yet, in addition to any 'subsequent agreement' between the parties regarding the interpretation of the treaty,[37] the interpreter is also

---

[33] In this respect Bianchi claims that 'it is puzzling to see how there can be state practice on the use of force outside the UN Charter'. Ibid., at 661. Crawford and Nicholson also note that the relevant norms and rules of the *jus ad bellum* 'are first and foremost treaty rules, subject to the law of treaties'. James Crawford and Rowan Nicholson, 'The Continued Relevance of Established Rules and Institutions Relating to the Use of Force', in Marc Weller (ed.), *The Oxford Handbook of the Use of Force in International Law* (Oxford University Press, 2015), 96, at 110. In any event, Article 103 of the UN Charter provides that Member states agree that '[i]n the event of a conflict between the obligations of the Members of the United Nations under the present Charter and their obligations under any other international agreement, their obligations under the present Charter shall prevail.' There does not seem to be a reason for excluding customary international law from coming within the reference here to 'any other international agreement'.

[34] As Bianchi notes, 'the societal consensus on the centrality of the Charter regulatory framework to the use of force evaporates when it comes to interpreting the content and scope of application of its most fundamental provisions.' Ibid., at 658. Bianchi puts this down to a failure 'to agree on the method that must be used for interpreting the law'. Ibid., at 654.

[35] See Articles 31–33, Vienna Convention of the Law of Treaties (1969).

[36] Article 31(1), ibid.

[37] Article 31(3)(a), ibid. While states rarely adopt express 'agreements' on interpretation, as per Article 31 of the Vienna Convention, they have attempted to provide some elaboration on the brief provisions of the UN Charter through the adoption of various general resolutions of the UN General Assembly. These have been declaratory on issues of the *jus ad bellum*, although

8 Introduction

permitted to take into account 'any subsequent practice in the application of the treaty which establishes the agreement of the parties regarding its interpretation'[38] and '[a] special meaning shall be given to a term if it is established that the parties so intended'.[39] However, if after having applied these general rules of interpretation the interpreter still feels the need to 'confirm' a particular meaning,[40] or if the application of the rules has left 'the meaning ambiguous or obscure' or has led 'to a result which is manifestly absurd or unreasonable',[41] they are permitted to have recourse 'to supplementary means of interpretation, including the preparatory work of the treaty and the circumstances of its conclusion'.[42]

All of these aspects of treaty interpretation leave the interpreter with a good degree of interpretative latitude, with the very real possibility of their application leading to diverging interpretations. For example, in the context of the UN Charter the right of self-defence is described as an 'inherent right' in Article 51 and one which arises 'if an armed attack occurs', which has led to much disagreement as to what the drafters of the Charter meant by the inclusion of these terms and what they should mean in the contemporary context, as well as disagreement regarding the impact differing interpretations of them have had on the extent of the contemporary right of self-defence and, therefore, the breadth and scope of the prohibition of force.[43] Furthermore, the Charter does not expressly provide for a right of so-called humanitarian intervention. Yet, questions have been raised as to whether one might be read into the Charter. This is on the basis of the references made

---

the price of consensus has usually been a good degree of ambiguity, meaning that, while representing elaborations on the bare bones of the Charter provisions, these resolutions often simply raise further questions. See Declaration on Principles of International Law concerning Friendly Relations and Co-operation among States in accordance with the Charter of the United Nations, UNGA Res. 2625 (XXV) (1970); Definition of Aggression, UNGA Res. 3314 (XXIX) (1974); Declaration on the Enhancement of the Effectiveness of the Principle of Refraining from the Threat or Use of Force in International Relations, UNGA Res. 42/22 (1987).

[38] Article 31(3)(b), ibid. For example, while formally '[d]ecisions of the Security Council on all [non-procedural] matters shall be made by an affirmative vote of nine members including the concurring votes of the permanent members' (Article 27(3), UN Charter (1945)), the requirement for the 'concurring votes' of the permanent members has been interpreted through the practice of the states on the Council to permit abstentions from voting. See Constantin A. Stavropoulos, 'The Practice of Voluntary Abstentions by Permanent Members of the Security Council under Article 27, Paragraph 3, of the Charter of the United Nations' (1967) 61 *American Journal of International Law* 737. In the context of the *jus ad bellum*, such 'subsequent practice' can be seen in the form of the UN Security Council now 'authorising' individual states and coalitions of states to employ force, something which is not expressly found within the Charter, in particular Article 42. See, further, Chapters 3–5.

[39] Article 31(4), ibid.  [40] Article 32, ibid.  [41] Articles 32(a) and 32(b), respectively, ibid.
[42] Article 32, ibid.  [43] See, further, Chapters 6–8.

in it to human rights and self-determination, or due to the fact that the UN Security Council has not operated in line with its original purposes and functions as set out within the Charter, which has meant that it has been unable to reliably prevent such humanitarian atrocities from occurring, or finally due to the various incidences of armed intervention that have occurred since 1945 and which appeared ostensibly to have a humanitarian purpose.[44]

By contrast, the methodology for understanding the formation and modification of customary international law has emerged largely within the jurisprudence of the International Court of Justice (ICJ)[45] and within scholarship.[46] In essence, in order to confirm both the existence and contours of a rule, or the modification or particular interpretation of one, a general state practice confirming the rule or interpretation should be supported by *opinio juris* (that is, a belief by states that the practice is permitted or prohibited *as a matter of law*). While there is extensive scholarship on customary international law in general, and the International Law Commission has set out its views on aspects of it,[47] there has also been much written specifically on the customary regulation of the use of force and associated methodological issues.[48]

There is, however, no agreed upon method for determining relevant state practice and *opinio juris* for the purposes of identifying customary international law.[49] For example, while the general understanding is that there should be general consistency, rather than complete uniformity, between states in the context of a particular practice,[50] it is difficult to pinpoint when sufficient consistency and agreement has become identifiable. In addition, it is possible that a state that persistently objects to the formation of a customary rule can be excluded from being a subject of it,[51] and the interests of specially affected states may be taken into account in determining the status of

---

[44] For more on these issues see Chapter 10 on the doctrine of humanitarian intervention.
[45] See, for example, *North Sea Continental Shelf Cases* (Federal Republic of Germany/Denmark; Federal Republic of Germany/Netherlands), Judgment, (1969) ICJ Reports 3, at para. 77; *Nicaragua* case, n. 30, at paras. 184, 186.
[46] See, for example, Michael Akehurst, 'Custom as a Source of International Law' (1974–5) 47 *British Yearbook of International Law* 1; Pierre-Marie Dupuy (ed.), *Customary International Law* (Edward Elgar, 2021).
[47] See International Law Commission, Draft Conclusions on Identification of Customary International Law, with Commentaries, UN Doc. A/73/10 (2018), 121. These were adopted by the UN General Assembly in UNGA Res. 73/203 (2018).
[48] See, for example, Enzo Cannizzaro and Paolo Palchetti (eds.), *Customary International Law on the Use of Force: A Methodological Approach* (Martinus Nijhoff, 2005).
[49] See, for example, Daniel H. Joyner, 'Why I Stopped Believing in Customary International Law' (2019) 9 *Asian Journal of International Law* 31.
[50] *Nicaragua* case, n. 30, at para 186.
[51] On this possibility, see James A. Green, *The Persistent Objector Rule in International Law* (Oxford University Press, 2016).

customary rules.[52] Furthermore, some scholars adhere to an 'extensive' approach, which prioritises physical state practice and, in that sense, the actions, views and values of powerful states who are more readily able to engage in it,[53] while others adhere to a more 'restrictive' approach, which focuses rather on *opinio juris*, something which all states are in principle able to participate in.[54] There is also the question of whether a lack of state practice can be compensated for by a strong *opinio juris*, and vice versa, an issue which has never been, and perhaps never can be, fully settled, at least not in the abstract.[55]

Ultimately, regardless as to how thorough and objective one claims to be, interpreting treaties and the meaning and legal significance of state practice and *opinio juris* will always be clouded by at least a measure of selection bias and subjectivity.[56]

## LEGAL AND PROCEDURAL ISSUES ASSOCIATED WITH THE *JUS AD BELLUM*

There are, however, further particular methodological issues in identifying and interpreting international law, several of which are specific to the context of the *jus ad bellum*. For example, whereas states are required under Article 51 of the UN Charter to report their actions taken in self-defence to the UN Security Council,[57] they are not obliged to provide a legal justification as such. When states resort to military action – whether in self-defence or otherwise – they may well offer a legal justification, although they do not

---

[52] See Keven Jon Heller, 'Specially-Affected States and the Formation of Custom' (2018) 112 *American Journal of International Law* 191. Whilst 'specially affected' states might, for example, plausibly include those with a coastline in the context of the formation and interpretation of customary rules regarding the law of the sea, it is more difficult to identify whether such a doctrine exists in the context of the *jus ad bellum*, and if so to which states it would apply to.

[53] For an example of this approach see Abraham D. Sofaer, 'On the Necessity of Pre-emption' (2003) 14 *European Journal of International Law* 209.

[54] For an example of this approach, see François Dubuisson, 'La problématique de la légalité de l'opération "Force alliée" contre la Yougoslavie: enjeux et questionnements', in Olivier Corten and Barbara Delcourt (eds.), *Droit, légitimation et politique extérieure: l'Europe et la guerre du Kosovo* (Bruylant, 2001), 176.

[55] On this possibility, see Frederic L. Kirgis, 'Custom on a Sliding Scale' (1987) 81 *American Journal of International Law* 146.

[56] Indeed, '[l]egal significance must be inferred from primary materials and factual content, which necessarily involves a degree of personal judgment. Identifying relevant state practice and discerning *opinio juris* requires a measure of subjectivity.' Chris O'Meara, *Necessity and Proportionality and the Right of Self-Defence in International Law* (Oxford University Press, 2021), at 16.

[57] See, further, Section 6.6.1.

always do so. While some scholars might attribute a legal justification to the state or label the military action with the most appropriate legal basis, it is important to be guided first and foremost by how states themselves view and justify their own actions, whether or not in express legal terms. When justifications are proffered, whilst on occasion these may be clear and straightforward, they are often vague, ambiguous, or contradictory, or states provide what may be described as a 'shotgun' justification, offering several different bases for the action taken – often including a mix of both legal and non-legal elements – in the hope that at least one may find acceptance, or, alternatively, they will find acceptance when viewed cumulatively.[58] An important key procedural concern in this respect is the lack of accessibility to reports submitted by states under Article 51, and with that a lack of transparency, which has recently been the subject of some concern.[59] There is, in any case, no agreed upon procedure or method for how such justifications and communications should be received, discussed or judged.

Contentious cases have also come before the ICJ in which the states involved have had a chance to advance their views on legal issues connected with the *jus ad bellum*, and when advisory opinions have been requested of the ICJ by another organ of the United Nations on relevant issues all states have the possibility of making submissions to the court.[60] It is apparent that '[t]hese pleadings tend to contain more clearly articulated legal positions on the part of states than might be provided to political organs such as the [UN Security Council] and in other diplomatic fora, where politics and law tend to be intermingled.'[61]

States may also make unilateral statements setting out their positions on particular legal issues connected with the *jus ad bellum* outside of the context of any particular incident and not necessarily within any particular forum for

---

[58] When states provide justifications for their actions in self-defence, they do not often state to be specifically doing so under either the treaty source of the right or as it exists in customary international law. A state may specifically refer to Article 51 in a letter to the UN Security Council reporting its invocation of the right while in the same letter justify the necessity and/or proportionality of the action taken, elements of the right that exist in customary international law. In this sense, the justification will be of relevance both for interpreting the treaty source of the law and in contributing to an understanding of the contours and content of the customary source of the law.

[59] See, for example, Pablo Arrocha Olabuenaga, 'An Insider's View of the Life-Cycle of Self-Defense Reports by U.N. Member States: Challenges posed to the international order', *Just Security*, 2 April 2019, available at: www.justsecurity.org/63415/an-insiders-view-of-the-life-cycle-of-self-defense-reports-by-u-n-member-states/. See, further, Section 6.6.1.

[60] Assertions made by states in written and oral pleadings before courts and tribunals might be relevant for both interpreting the UN Charter and as evidence of *opinio juris* for the purposes of customary international law. In this respect, see paragraph 5 of the commentary to Conclusion 6 and paragraph 4 of the commentary to Conclusion 10, ILC Draft conclusions, n. 47, at 134 and 141 respectively.

[61] O'Meara, n. 56, at 15.

the purposes of doing so. For example, states have issued national security strategies and military manuals,[62] and set out their position on how the *jus ad bellum* should be interpreted in particular contexts, most recently and notably in the cyber context,[63] all of which are of relevance for assessing the status of the rules under focus without any specific weight or significance being able to be attributed to them in the abstract.

A further pertinent consideration in the context of the *jus ad bellum* is that, while states may resort to military action, they equally may refrain or omit from acting, even in circumstances where it may be prudent or legally justifiable. If states refrain from using aggressive force, which is, of course, the default position, the question arises as to whether we are able to attribute this inaction to the existence of a prohibition of the use of force and take it as an implicit affirmation of it, or whether it is not possible to read any particular legal significanc into it, given the varied reasons that a state may have for refraining from taking military action, whether they be political, economic, strategic, etc.[64]

The practice and views of individual states – both in the abstract and in respect to their military actions – are important to ascertain. Yet, interpreting the UN Charter and the formation and modification of the customary source of the law is a collective enterprise involving *all* states. Indeed, when a state uses force, whether or not it provides a justification for doing so, the reaction and response of other states is of particular significance in attempting to ascertain the law on an issue, or its future direction. However, whereas some states may react unilaterally to a state's military action, many do not and, when they do, as is the case with the justifications themselves, the reactions are not always specifically focused on the legal issues involved. Although general condemnation by other states may imply that these states deem the particular action to be unlawful on the basis of the *jus ad bellum*, it equally may not, with the general condemnation instead being indicative of concern in regard to other aspects of the action, for example its geopolitical ramifications. Military action that has been resorted to will occasionally be debated in the UN Security Council amongst the fifteen states that are members at the time,

---

[62] Perhaps most famously in this respect see Office of the White House, *The National Security Strategy of the United States* (2002), available at: https://2009-2017.state.gov/documents/organization/63562.pdf.

[63] See, as just one example of this, UK Attorney General Jeremy Wright, 'Cyber and International Law in the 21st Century', 23 May 2018, available at: www.gov.uk/government/speeches/cyber-and-international-law-in-the-21st-century. See further, Section 1.7.4.

[64] The ILC cautions that, while relevant state practice for the purposes of customary international law 'may, under certain circumstances, include inaction', before attributing any significance to such negative action one must be clear that the state in question 'is conscious of refraining from acting in a given situation'. See paragraph 3 of the commentary to Conclusion 6, paragraph 1, ILC Draft conclusions, n. 47, at 133. See, further, Section 1.7.

and perhaps with a few other interested states present.[65] While the legal issues may be debated within this forum, states rarely move beyond general statements and in any case one should bear in mind that the Council is a political rather than a legal body.

In addition, the fact is that forcible actions are often greeted with silence, at least by a majority of the 193 states that make up the international community.[66] Questions arise here as to whether such silence is to be taken as acquiescence in the actions and their (il)legality or whether it is only to be taken as such if states have notice of them and a reaction would have been called for in the circumstances.[67] There is no uniform and agreed upon method of assessing, weighing, and gauging the reactions of states, whether that be those that respond to the legal issues involved, those who approve or condemn the action but not expressly in legal terms, or those states that remain silent. Added to this is the reality that the voices of certain states are simply more easily heard, either due, for example, to their permanent representation on certain bodies such as the UN Security Council or due to the power of projection of their national and international media outlets. This disparity in the volume and prominence of the voices of states makes gaining a balanced approach to ascertaining the law particularly difficult and something which all legal publications, including this one, have to contend with.

These issues arguably take on a particular significance if we accept that the prohibition in Article 2(4) of the Charter is a *jus cogens*, or peremptory, norm, that is, a norm that is not only impossible to derogate from,[68] but also one that is very difficult to modify – not to mention eradicate altogether – as any modification of the norm would require evidence of the acceptance, or at least acquiescence, of 'the international community of states as a whole'.[69] Even if one is not of the view that the prohibition as contained in the UN Charter is *jus cogens*,[70] given that it is nonetheless widely viewed as representing an important value within the international community the state practice demonstrating such agreement would, while not necessarily needing to be universal and

---

[65] See Articles 23, 31 and 32, UN Charter (1945).
[66] Sutin A. Lewis, Naz K. Modirazdeh and Gabriella Blum, 'Quantum of Silence: Inaction and the *Jus ad Bellum*', *The Harvard Law School Program on International Law and Armed Conflict* (2019), available at: https://dash.harvard.edu/bitstream/handle/1/40931878/Quantum%20of%20Silence%202019.pdf?sequence=1&isAllowed=y.
[67] The ICJ has observed, in a different context, that '[t]he absence of reaction may well amount to acquiescence ... That is to say, silence may also speak, but only if the conduct of the other State calls for a response'. See *Sovereignty over Pedra Branca/Pulau Batu Puteh, Middle Rocks and South Ledge (Malaysia/Singapore)*, Judgment, (2008) ICJ Reports 12, at para. 121.
[68] All treaties conflicting with peremptory norms of general international law are deemed void under Article 53 of the VCLT (1969). In this respect, whereas collective self-defence pacts are permitted as a means of undertaking conduct that falls within an established exception to the prohibition, a pact of aggression, on the other hand, would not be.
[69] Article 53, VCLT (1969).    [70] See Section 1.3.2 on the peremptory status of the prohibition.

absolute, at least arguably need to be general and widespread amongst states with no significant and sustained dissent.

Finally, and aside from these legal and procedural methodological issues associated with the decentralised nature of the international legal system, there are other sites of contestation that make assessments regarding the law and its application difficult. Indeed, even where there is consensus on the interpretation or position of the law on an issue, disagreements often arise over the application of it to the facts of a particular situation or over the facts themselves. Whereas the UN Security Council may wade in on the issue or a commission of inquiry or similar investigative mechanism may be established after the fact, there remains no central arbiter of the facts and certainly not one that can provide anything resembling an assessment prior to the resort to any unilateral military force, although the UN Security Council may provide this function on occasion, for example in providing an implicit determination of the necessity of the resort to force against Iraq by the United States and United Kingdom in 2003.[71] In addition, states may simply assert facts, for example in regards to the occurrence of an incident or a series of incidents without providing any credible evidence or further explanation. The claim that a state faced an 'imminent' threat of attack which justified it resorting to military force in response is sometimes made, with the state refraining from offering any concrete evidence in support. Indeed, this was a key controversy regarding the justification for the drone strike which led to the death of Iranian General Qasem Soleimani by the United States in January 2020.[72]

## SUBSIDIARY MEANS FOR DETERMINING (AND SHAPING?) THE LAW

In aiming to provide an overview of international law pertaining to the use of force state practice, whilst key, is only one element. In addition to state practice – or where practice is either lacking or inconclusive – reference should be made to the 'subsidiary means for the determination of rules of law' as contained within Article 38(1)(d) of the Statute of the ICJ, that is, 'judicial decisions and the teachings of the most highly qualified publicists of the various nations'. Judicial decisions and the jurisprudence of the ICJ, as well of those of other international tribunals and domestic courts, provide a key aid in determining the law in this area. Indeed, the pronouncements of the ICJ in the *Nicaragua* case, for example, continue to reverberate and provide the basis for much discussion – and, it has to be said, disagreement – over key aspects of the *jus ad bellum* nearly 40 years later.[73] In addition, while formally they are

---

[71] See, in general, Section 4.3.   [72] See Section 7.5.2.   [73] See *Nicaragua* case, n. 30.

mere 'subsidiary means' for determining what the law is, courts occasionally go beyond this function by stating the position of the law without providing any evidence in support of the adopted position as well as actively developing the law in a particular direction.[74] Of course, for the purposes of understanding the *jus ad bellum*, the decisions of courts and tribunals are not generally binding and merely reflect the way in which that particular court or judge has viewed an issue.[75] But, and arguably in particular in regards to the ICJ which represents the judicial organ of the United Nations, the views of these courts carry a certain weight and, at the very least, deserve close attention,[76] regardless of whether or not one agrees with either their jurisprudence or the means by which decisions are reached.

In addition, international law scholarship on the *jus ad bellum* is rich and extensive and is key to broadening one's understanding of the position of the law and any emerging directions it is taking, as well as one's perspective on the range of views that have been taken on a certain issue.[77] Some publications that have aimed to set out how an existing legal framework applies within a particular context have become standard reference works. The *Tallinn Manual on the International Law Applicable to Cyber Warfare*,[78] for example, can be seen as representative of such a publication with states themselves making reference to it in setting out their position on various aspects of the law governing the use of force as it applies to cyber operations.[79] Other publications have provided a pivotal focal point for debate between scholars on certain issues. As an example of this, and as explored further in Section 7.5, Daniel Bethlehem's 2013 article on the right of self-defence against attacks by non-state actors, while proving controversial, has undoubtedly provided a key

---

[74] For discussion, see Anthea Roberts and Sandesh Sivakumaran, 'The Theory and Reality of the Sources of International Law', in Malcolm D. Evans (ed.), *International Law*, 5th ed. (Oxford University Press, 2018), 89, at 106–7.

[75] In addition, the jurisprudence of domestic courts may also constitute evidence of the practice of the state in whose jurisdiction it is located. See Anthea Roberts, 'Comparative International Law? The Role of National Courts in Creating and Enforcing International Law' (2011) 60 *International & Comparative Law Quarterly* 57.

[76] Although it is true that '[o]ccasionally, the almost religious deference shown by some commentators towards the ICJ judgments borders on the ridiculous.' Bianchi, n. 31, at 654 (n.9).

[77] See Sandesh Sivakumaran, 'The Influence of Teachings of Publicists on the Development of International Law' (2017) 66 *International & Comparative Law Quarterly* 1.

[78] Michael N. Schmitt (ed.), *Tallinn Manual on the International Law Applicable to Cyber Warfare* (Cambridge University Press, 2013); Michael N. Schmitt (ed.), *Tallinn Manual 2.0 on the International Law Applicable to Cyber Warfare* (Cambridge University Press, 2017).

[79] See Dutch Minister of Foreign Affairs, 'Letter to the Parliament on the International Legal Order in Cyberspace', 5 July 2019, available at: www.government.nl/ministries/ministry-of-foreign-affairs/documents/parliamentary-documents/2019/09/26/letter-to-the-parliament-on-the-international-legal-order-in-cyberspace.

focal point for the debate on the way the law should, and does, apply in this context.[80]

However, it should be kept in mind that '[t]he *interpretive community* that shapes the common understanding of legal rules on the use of force' is wider than national governments, judges and scholars.[81] Indeed, it also includes, for example, non-governmental organisations that may have a particular interest in the issues under focus, the media and UN bodies such as the International Law Commission, as well as the collective voices of the UN Security Council and UN General Assembly.[82] While interpretive communities exist in all legal systems, the decentralised nature of the international legal system gives the community associated with it and its different fragmented regimes a particular significance.[83]

## AIMS, LIMITATIONS AND STRUCTURE OF THE BOOK

The task of writing a book on the use of force in international law is one that could be undertaken in different ways, with different agendas and different focuses. For example, this area of international law has been the focus of international lawyers who have sought to expose its structural and linguistic biases and inconsistencies,[84] as well as those who have approached it from a feminist or third world perspective.[85] This book remains cognisant that the

---

[80] Daniel Bethlehem, 'Principles Relevant to the Scope of a State's Right of Self-Defense against an Imminent or Actual Armed Attack by Nonstate Actors' (2012) **106** *American Journal of International Law* 769.

[81] Bianchi, n. 31, at 653.

[82] As the ILC has stated, '[i]n certain cases, the practice of international organizations also contributes to the formation, or expression, of rules of customary international law.' Conclusion 4, paragraph 2, ILC Draft conclusions, n. 47, at 130. However, this is 'practice that is attributed to international organizations themselves, not practice of States acting within or in relation to them (which is attributed to the States concerned)'. See paragraph 4 of the commentary to Conclusion 4, paragraph 2, ibid. This might arise, for example, should the UN Security Council affirm in a resolution or presidential statement that a state possesses the right of self-defence in relation to a particular situation. By contrast, statements made by states within debates that take place within the Council are positions attributed to the states themselves, and not the Council.

[83] For discussion on the interpretive communities associated with the *jus ad bellum* see Christian Henderson, *The Persistent Advocate and the Use of Force: The Impact of the United States upon the* Jus ad Bellum *in the Post–Cold War Era* (Routledge, 2010), at 7–36; Ian Johnstone, 'Security Council Deliberations: The Power of the Better Argument' (2003) **14** *European Journal of International Law* 437.

[84] See, for example, Martti Koskenniemi, '"The Lady Doth Protest Too Much": Kosovo, and the Turn to Ethics in International Law' (2002) **65** *Modern Law Review* 159.

[85] See, respectively, Gina Heathcote, *The Law on the Use of Force: A Feminist Analysis* (Routledge, 2012) and Ntina Tzouvala, 'TWAIL and the "Unwilling or Unable" Doctrine: Continuities and Ruptures' (2016) **109** *AJIL Unbound* 166.

rules governing the use of force, or the *jus ad bellum*, and the system and structures that underpin it are far from perfect or indeed in many respects fair. However, and notwithstanding the – not insignificant – methodological qualifications discussed in this introduction, the central aim of the book is to attempt to weave together a conceptual picture of the law on the use of force through an exposition and analysis of its sources and the way they have been interpreted and utilised by different actors. It seeks to provide a contemporary overview of how the law operates in theory and in practice, how it is used (and abused) by states in their international relations, the complexities and controversies that underpin its interpretation and application and how it has evolved and may or need to continue to evolve into the future.

The use of and reliance upon different sources in the book will inevitably vary depending upon the circumstances. In some cases, a particular issue will be driven by, and take as its starting point, state practice, while in others it may be a judgment of the ICJ or a particularly significant academic publication, for example. Through an examination of state practice in connection with these sources it may be possible to conclude that a particular novel interpretation of, or movement within, the law appears to have been confirmed or rejected (*lex lata*) or it may be that, while it is not possible to say that a change in the law has occurred, it is nonetheless possible to identify it moving in a particular direction (*lex ferenda*).

It is, however, not possible to be entirely comprehensive in the inclusion of state practice and selections will necessarily have to be made in either demonstrating (what this author considers to be) where the law sits on a particular issue, taking into account the various circumstances or placing a focus on particularly significant or problematic incidences. However, while on certain issues the book takes a definite position on the law where it feels it is warranted it has nonetheless tried to avoid taking an overly categorical or polemic approach and to provide sufficient information and signposts to enable the reader to come to their own judgment, or to at least explore an issue further, in particular where the issue is unsettled. In addition, although an attempt has been made to make the book as up to date as possible, events have inevitably outpaced the production of it.

It is important to note that some examples of state practice have been referred to in more than one chapter of the book, often as a result of a state's 'shotgun' approach to justification or several legal bases perhaps being implicit in its justification. Although attempts have been made to keep factual repetition to a minimum and appropriate cross-references are included where necessary, it is also recognised that readers may dip into the book at various places and so as much detail as possible has been included in each of the chapters to ensure that they allow for an understanding of the issues discussed.

There is considerable literature on the subject and the book has, as with state practice, inevitably had to be selective. Space simply does not permit the depth of detail and discussion that the subject ultimately deserves. Yet, the book provides relevant signposts to further investigation and discussion where appropriate and references to additional sources and academic commentary are contained both within the footnotes and in 'suggested further reading' sections at the end of each chapter. While the current book has attempted to provide reference to works of scholars of the 'various nations' and more broadly than simply the work of Anglo-American authors, it is nonetheless the case that much of the scholarship on the *jus ad bellum* is published in English. Added to this, the author's generally poor proficiency in languages other than English has meant that the book cannot claim to fully represent the breadth and scope of literature on the issues addressed within. However, the book, which is targeted toward students, academics, researchers, practitioners and those working within organisations, has aspired to be challenging yet accessible and as comprehensive as possible while remaining concise.

With this as the background, Part I focuses upon the contemporary prohibition of the threat or use of force. Chapter 1 addresses the general breadth and scope of the prohibition, while Chapter 2 looks more specifically at the meaning of 'force'. Parts II and III address the two main established exceptions to this prohibition. Part II concerns the use of force in the context of collective security. Chapter 3 sets out the general structure of the UN Charter and the ways in which force might be taken under the auspices of the UN and other organisations, and Chapter 4 then takes a closer look at issues in relation to 'authorisation' being granted, or not, by the UN Security Council. Chapter 5 examines peacekeeping and the use of force specifically within peacekeeping operations. Part III focuses on the right of self-defence, with Chapter 6 examining general aspects of the right. Chapters 7 and 8 address particularly controversial aspects of the right in the form of preventative self-defence and the use of force against non-state actors. Finally, Part IV has as its focus forcible intervention in situations of civil unrest, with Chapter 9 examining consent to intervention and intervention in civil wars and Chapter 10 addressing the issue of interventions for humanitarian purposes.

## ACKNOWLEDGEMENTS

I am grateful to the many friends and colleagues who have assisted and offered advice and comments at various stages of the writing and production of both the first and second editions of this book. Furthermore, I am deeply indebted to Cambridge University Press for their continued support and incredible patience, in particular Caitlin Lisle and Laura Blake, as well as to Liz Steel for doing such a super job in copy-editing.

The writing of the two editions of this book has in one form or another spanned the last ten years and, with that, the life-spans of my two daughters

Minttu and Vilja. While it has inevitably meant that time has been spent on it and away from them, the conversations on the topic that we inadvertently engaged in – largely in response to me justifying the use of my time – will forever be etched in my memory and have no doubt made their mark in some way in the book. While my wife, Sanna, no doubt found these conversations amusing, she too has shown unwavering patience over this period of our lives, for which I will be forever grateful. Lastly, and bathing in the brazen optimism that a third edition will be forthcoming at some stage, I would welcome contact from readers of the book notifying me of any omissions or errors that have undoubtedly made their way into the final draft, or on clarifications, suggestions for improvements and any points of disagreement, all of which will aid in improving the text for the future.

# Part I

# The Prohibition of the Threat or Use of Force

# 1 The General Breadth and Scope of the Prohibition of the Threat or Use of Force

## 1.1 INTRODUCTION

Part I of this book provides an examination of the contemporary prohibition of the threat or use of force, as found within Article 2(4) of the United Nations (UN) Charter and in customary international law.[1] Not only is this a pivotal rule within the international legal framework governing the use of force, but it is also a 'cornerstone' provision of the UN Charter[2] and a norm of great importance within international law more generally. Nonetheless, it has given rise to some controversy in regard to both its breadth and scope of application and the specific meaning of 'force', leading to the observation that there is a 'lack of agreed-upon definitions, criteria and thresholds' in its application.[3]

As such, the first of the chapters in this Part of the book provides an exposition of the general breadth and scope of the contemporary prohibition, while Chapter 2 examines more specifically the meaning of 'force' that is the focus of it. Only by understanding this fundamental norm, including its difficulties, can one fully appreciate the actual and proclaimed exceptions to it that are addressed in the subsequent sections of the book. Together, the chapters provide an understanding of the design and function in practice of this fundamental norm of international law. Furthermore, an appreciation of the contours and application of the exceptions to it will provide a greater understanding of the circumstances in which we might be able to conclude that the prohibition has been breached.

The prohibition does not operate in an historical vacuum and, in understanding its breadth and scope, one must first understand where it is

---

[1] *Case Concerning Military and Paramilitary Activities in and against Nicaragua (Nicaragua v. United States of America)*, Merits, (1986) ICJ Reports 14, at para. 34.
[2] James L. Brierly, *The Law of Nations*, 6th ed. (rev. Humphrey Waldock) (Oxford University Press, 1963), at 414; *Case Concerning Armed Activities in the Territory of the Congo (Congo v. Uganda)*, Judgment, (2005) ICJ Reports 168, at 223.
[3] Michael N. Schmitt (ed.), *Tallinn Manual on the International Law Applicable to Cyber Warfare* (Cambridge University Press, 2013), at 42.

positioned along the historical continuum of efforts to regulate inter-state force. Section 1.2 therefore sets the contemporary prohibition in this context. Section 1.3 then examines the sources of the prohibition, as found in Article 2 (4) of the UN Charter and in customary international law, but also its status as a 'peremptory' or '*jus cogens*' norm of international law and the potential meaning of this in terms of the prospects for its adaptation and modification in the future. While much focus has been traditionally placed upon the *use* of force, by comparison relatively little attention has been given to the *threat* of force, despite both coming under the umbrella of the contemporary rule against force. As such, Section 1.4 sets out and provides an examination of the concept of a threat of force. The prohibition is of undoubted importance, yet the decentralised nature of the international legal system means that accountability and responsibility for its violation are uncertain. This is the focus of Section 1.5. The prohibition of the threat or use of force has traditionally been seen in a purely inter-state context, yet there is a growing recognition and understanding of a link between violations of the prohibition and violations of the rights of individuals, in particular their right to life. Section 1.6 looks at this link, while Section 1.7 assesses the continued relevance and effectiveness of the norm prohibiting force.

## 1.2 HISTORICAL ATTEMPTS AT REGULATING THE USE OF FORCE IN INTERNATIONAL AFFAIRS

If there has been one constant feature in the relations of empires, states and peoples, it is the resort to war and force to resolve disputes and in the attainment of certain aims. From early peoples and religious entities, to the rise and dominance of the Roman Empire, and from the emergence of what we might describe as the modern state in the seventeenth century, through to the rise of non-state actors in the form of self-determination fighters, opposition groups and global terrorist groups, war and force have been persistently present. Furthermore, while the contemporary law on the use of force is relatively modern, dating back to the adoption of the UN Charter in 1945, regulation of the resort to force in some form can be traced back to ancient times.[4]

The earliest form of regulation of the use of force can be found in the *bellum justum* or 'just war' doctrines of classical Greek and Roman philosophers, such as Cicero,[5] which were subsequently drawn upon and developed by certain

---

[4] For an account of the history of war from the standpoint of international law see, in general, Stephen C. Neff, *War and the Law of Nations: A General History* (Cambridge University Press, 2005).

[5] Cicero, *De officiis* 1.11.33–1.13.41; Cicero, *De re publica* 3.33.

Christian theologians of the Middle Ages, such as Saint Augustine[6] and Saint Thomas Aquinas.[7] Moralistic instinct led to certain conditions being placed upon the launching of war in an attempt to restrict its prevalence and the human and physical destruction that was a natural result. War could, for example, only have been launched under the authority of a sovereign, it required a just cause (such as a reaction to a prior wrong) and it must also have been launched with a rightful intention (such as doing justice and attaining peace). The just war doctrine became tied in with the Church and the Holy Roman Empire, with the papal court providing a means of discriminating between just and unjust belligerents and handing down the appropriate sanction to the latter. While there were different conceptions of the just war doctrine, the seventeenth-century Dutch humanist, Hugo Grotius,[8] can be said to have brought it closest to being legally regulated in synthesising 'the theological–canonist tradition of just war with the civilian tradition of legal war'.[9] Indeed, future writers on issues of war and peace, such as the eighteenth-century writer Emer de Vattel,[10] continued to adhere to this theological–legalistic synthesis of just war traditions.

The Peace of Westphalia of 1648, which followed an extended period of war in the form of the Thirty Years War (1618–48) within the Holy Roman Empire, is a historical landmark to which the birth of the modern sovereign state – which has come to represent the pre-eminent creator and subject of international law – is often credited. During the following centuries, the dominant doctrine appears to be that 'the *jus ad bellum* withered to the mere recognition that sovereign states had a right to resort to force or war to pursue their claims or protect their security and interests'.[11] Indeed, international law was viewed as having become 'indifferent' to the use of force by states[12] so that 'the decision to go to war was not a matter of law, but one of expediency'.[13] War had, in essence, become an essential instrument of statecraft or 'a pursuit of policy by other means'.[14]

---

[6] Robert A. Markus, 'Saint Augustine's Views of the "Just War"', in William J. Sheils (ed.), *The Church and War* (Blackwell, 1983), 1.

[7] Thomas Aquinas, *Summa Theologiae* IIaIIae 40.1.

[8] Hugo Grotius, *De jure belli ac pacis libri tres* (1625) (contained in James Brown Scott (ed.), *Classics of International Law* (Clarendon Press, 1925), 2.1.2).

[9] Randall Lesaffer, 'Too Much History: From War as Sanction to the Sanctioning of War', in Marc Weller (ed.), *The Oxford Handbook of the Use of Force in International Law* (Oxford University Press, 2015), 35, at 41.

[10] Vattel, *Le Droit des gens* 3.3.24–28 and 3.3.40.    [11] Lesaffer, n. 9, at 46.

[12] Agatha Verdebout, 'The Contemporary Discourse on the Use of Force in the Nineteenth Century: A Diachronic and Critical Analysis' (2014) 1 *Journal on the Use of Force and International Law* 223, at 224. See, further, Agatha Verdebout, *Rewriting Histories of the Use of Force: The Narrative of 'Indifference'* (Cambridge University Press, 2021).

[13] Lesaffer, n. 9, at 46.

[14] See Carl von Clausewitz, *On War*, trans. James J. Graham (Wandsworth, 1977 [1832]), at 22.

Yet, it is arguably the case that '[m]ainstream international legal doctrine does not wholly reflect 19th-century state practice' and '[t]he just war tradition proved somewhat more resilient'.[15] For example, while there were few legal constraints upon a state's right to resort to force at the height of state sovereignty in the eighteenth and nineteenth centuries, states were, nonetheless, expected to proffer a justification for their actions, even if solely for political purposes. A well-known illustration of this is the correspondence between Great Britain and the United States of America following an incident in 1837 involving the sinking of a US ship, the *Caroline*, by British forces on the US–Canada border, in which the importance of being able to justify the actions of the British as self-defence was agreed upon between the parties.[16] As such, 'although ultimately the sovereign states of the 19th century had a right to resort to force, the *jus ad bellum* had not been emptied of all meaning. State practice of the 19th century demonstrated that states still justified or condemned forcible actions under a widely accepted, albeit evolving, framework of reference that partook in the tradition of just war.'[17] Indeed, while there was no legal norm prohibiting the forcible actions of states *per se*, they also did not enjoy an unbridled freedom to act.[18]

In addition, the concept of war emerged as a legal institution in the nineteenth century. This had two consequences. First, war came to denote a formal status and something more than simply the *de facto* engagement of the armed forces of two states. In particular, the rules of belligerency became applicable, which imposed certain restrictions upon the two belligerent states, notably the applicability of the laws of armed conflict, but also for third states, in terms of neutrality.[19] Given that wars now had to be formally declared,[20] states would thus often attempt to avoid the limitations and restrictions of belligerency and neutrality by simply avoiding doing so. In this respect, and secondly, 'the 19th century also saw the rise of "measures short of war" in doctrine and practice. The different types of measures short of war were all rooted in the tradition of just war. The major categories were humanitarian

---

[15] Lesaffer, n. 9, at 46.
[16] 29 *British and Foreign State Papers* 1137–8; 30 *British and Foreign State Papers* 193–5. For more on this incident and the impact of the correspondence upon the right of self-defence see Section 6.3.
[17] Lesaffer, n. 9, at 36.
[18] On this issue see the different perspectives taken in Verdebout, n. 12, and Tom Ruys, 'From Passé *Simple* to *Future Imparfait?* A Response to Verdebout' (2015) 2 *Journal on the Use of Force and International Law* 3.
[19] Quincy Wright, 'When Does War Exist?' (1932) 26 *American Journal of International Law* 362, at 363.
[20] See, in general, Clyde Eagleton, 'The Form and Function of the Declaration of War' (1938) 32 *American Journal of International Law* 19.

and political intervention, self-defence, defence of nationals and reprisal.'[21] This led to the emergence of a self-serving distinction between 'war' and other uses of force.

Furthermore, the nineteenth century witnessed the appearance of the first collective security regime, in the form of the Concert of Europe (1815–1914). This was an alliance between the United Kingdom, Austria, Russia, Prussia and – after the fall of Napoleon – France. However, the Concert was an alliance of political convenience between the great powers of the time and represented more a 'balance of power' as opposed to a collective security regime governed by law. Although still in existence after the Crimean War (1853–6) question marks began to be raised over its continued relevance, given that Britain and France had declared war on Russia.[22] The late nineteenth and early twentieth centuries also witnessed the two Hague Peace Conferences in 1899 and 1907, respectively, and the adoption of the Hague Conventions. While primarily concerned with the laws of war (or the '*jus in bello*'), the Hague Convention I on the Pacific Settlement of International Disputes (1899) did include a promise by the contracting parties 'to use their best efforts to ensure the pacific settlement of international disputes',[23] whereas the Hague Convention III Relative to the Opening of Hostilities (1907) codified the obligation upon states to formally declare war before commencing hostilities.[24]

Although it is debatable whether any legal restraints upon the actions of states would have prevented it, the calamity of the First World War (1914–18) undoubtedly initiated moves towards greater legal regulation of the use of force and serious attempts at collective security. In the ashes of this tragedy, the former president of the United States, Woodrow Wilson, influenced the internationalist and cosmopolitan ideas that led to the development of the League of Nations (1919–46).[25] Indeed:

Wilson refused to adhere to a traditional strategy for peace and pushed his allies at the Paris Peace Conference (1919–20) towards a new world order. At the heart of this stood collective security, a combination of an obligation to settle disputes peacefully by international law, the limitation of the right to wage war, and collective action against

---

[21] Lesaffer, n. 9, at 46. The *Naulilaa* case of 1928, for example, set out the conditions for a lawful reprisal, including the requirement for a prior wrong/breach of international law, that there be an unsuccessful demand for reparation and that any response be proportionate to the wrong suffered. See *Portugal* v. *Germany (The Naulilaa case)*, Special Arbitral Tribunal, 31 July 1928 (1927–8) *Annual Digest of Public International Law Cases* 526.

[22] See Gerry Simpson, *Great Powers and Outlaw States: Unequal Sovereigns in the International Legal Order* (Cambridge University Press, 2004), at 96–102.

[23] Article 1, Hague Convention I on the Pacific Settlement of International Disputes (1899).

[24] Article 1, Hague Convention III Relative to the Opening of Hostilities (1907).

[25] See, in general, M. Patrick Cottrell, *The League of Nations: Enduring Legacies of the First Experiment at World Organization* (Routledge, 2017).

aggression by an organized international community, the League of Nations. The Peace Treaty of Versailles of 28 June 1919 between the Allied and Associate Powers of Germany was an amalgam of Wilson's radical ideas and tradition, but altogether caused a revolution in the *jus ad bellum*.[26]

The League of Nations represented the first permanent international organisation with the principal aim of maintaining world peace as well as the first attempt at a legal regime of collective security. Of significance was the fact that the Covenant of the League of Nations (1919) contained an 'obligation[] not to resort to war',[27] as well as a declaration that '[a]ny war or threat of war' was now 'a matter of concern to the whole League, and the League shall take any action that may be deemed wise and effectual to safeguard the peace of nations'.[28] While this was indeed a significant landmark, the League and its Covenant were, nonetheless, beset with qualifications and loopholes. For example, although members were obliged to submit any dispute likely to lead to a rupture in relations to arbitration, judicial settlement or to the League Council,[29] they agreed not to resort to war only for three months after the decision by the court, the award by the arbitrators or the report by the League Council.[30] Furthermore, if the Council failed to reach a report which was unanimously agreed to, then the members of the League reserved the right to take such action as they considered necessary for the maintenance of right and justice.[31] There was also an obligation upon the court or arbitrators to make their decision or award within a reasonable time and on the Council to issue its report within six months,[32] the implication being that if they failed to do so then members had the right to resort to war. Problems with the League were thus manifold. Indeed, in addition to the United States never becoming a member, it was also clear that '[t]hese clauses from the League's Covenant did not lay down a new, coherent, and all-encompassing *jus ad bellum* ... The League system neither provided for an effective mechanism of collective security nor for a general prohibition to use force'.[33]

However, building upon the 'success' of the Covenant of the League of Nations, the General Treaty for Renunciation of War as an Instrument of National Policy (1928), otherwise known as the 'Kellogg–Briand Pact' (or 'Pact of Paris') after the American Secretary of State and the French Foreign Minister who drafted it, was adopted in 1928, and remains in force today.[34] The Covenant has only three – on the face of it simple – articles, most significantly solemnly declaring that the Contracting Parties 'condemn recourse to war for the solution of international controversies, and renounce

---

[26] Lesaffer, n. 9, at 50. [27] Preamble, Covenant of the League of Nations (1919).
[28] Article 11, ibid. [29] Article 12(1), ibid. [30] Article 12(1), ibid. [31] Article 15(7), ibid.
[32] Article 12(2), ibid. [33] Lesaffer, n. 9, at 51.
[34] See, in general, James L. Brierly, 'Some Implications of the Pact of Paris' (1929) 10 *British Yearbook of International Law* 208.

it as an instrument of national policy in their relations with one another',[35] while also agreeing that the settlement of disputes 'shall never be sought except by pacific means'.[36] On this basis, it might be argued, '1928 was a watershed date in the history of the legal regulation of the use of inter-State force'.[37]

The Pact, however, has four significant weaknesses. First, it still appears to leave open the possibility of war as an instrument of *international* policy. Indeed, 'a war which is a reaction against a violation of international law, and that means a war waged for the maintenance of international law, is considered an instrument of international and hence not of national policy'.[38] Yet, there is still the requirement in Article 2 of the Pact that the settlement of disputes 'shall never be sought except by pacific means'. Secondly, it does not apply to the whole of the international community. The renunciation of war in Article 1 is limited to the Contracting Parties, of which there were sixty-three before the beginning of the Second World War (out of the seventy-two states that existed at that time). Thirdly, self-defence is not specifically addressed, although formal notes reserving the right of self-defence were exchanged between the principal signatories prior to the conclusion of the Pact. The preamble of the Pact does, nonetheless, make it clear that any Contracting Party 'which shall hereafter seek to promote its national interests by resort to war should be denied the benefits furnished by this Treaty', indicating that, while non-contracting parties still possess such a right, other Contracting Parties can also resort to war to defend themselves against an initial breach of the Pact. Lastly, forcible measures 'short of war' are not addressed at all and 'war' is not defined in the Pact. Given the practices at the time it was adopted, it appeared that the application of the Pact might be avoided by simply not declaring war. Ultimately, however, the success of both the League of Nations and the Kellogg–Briand Pact are, along with Japan's invasion of Manchuria in 1931 and Italy's conquest of Abyssinia in 1934, defined by Germany's invasion of Poland in 1939 and, subsequently, the calamities of the Second World War (1939–45).[39]

At the end of the Second World War nations came together under the guidance of Churchill, Stalin and Roosevelt to adopt the United Nations

---

[35] Article 1, General Treaty for Renunciation of War as an Instrument of National Policy (1928).
[36] Article 2, ibid.
[37] Yoram Dinstein, *War, Aggression and Self-Defence*, 6th ed. (Cambridge University Press, 2017), at para. 236. For a detailed and illuminating account, see Oona A. Hathaway and Scott J. Shapiro, *The Internationalists: How a Radical Plan to Outlaw War Remade the World* (Penguin, 2018).
[38] Hans Kelsen, *Principles of International Law*, 1st ed. (Rinehart & Co., 1952), at 43.
[39] Despite being rendered somewhat redundant by subsequent events, the Pact is still in force today.

Charter on 26 June 1945 at the San Francisco Conference.[40] Not only did this establish the United Nations, an organisation with the primary purpose of maintaining international peace and security,[41] but it also led to the world entering the contemporary era of the legal regulation of the use of force. Given how quickly previous attempts at regulating war and force were effectively rendered redundant, the fact that we are still witnessing this era might lead one to argue that, on this basis alone, it can be considered a relative success.

As will be elaborated upon in this and the subsequent chapters of this book, the contemporary prohibition of 'the threat or use of force' is located in its textual form within Article 2(4) of the UN Charter (1945). The major significance of this provision is that it comprehensively prohibits 'force' as opposed to the broader concept of 'war'.[42] In this respect, the provision does not simply prohibit the launching of aggressive wars, but also covers those acts involving the use of force that fall short of war.[43] This, along with the obligation upon members to 'settle their disputes by peaceful means'[44] and the establishment of the collective security system,[45] means that '[t]he UN Charter stands at the end of an evolution by which the right of states to use force was progressively limited'[46] and can thus be seen as a revolutionary moment in the history of the legal framework governing the use of force.[47]

---

[40] See, in general, Stephen C. Schlesinger, *Act of Creation: The Founding of the United Nations* (Westview, 2003).

[41] Article 1(1), UN Charter (1945).

[42] While 'force' replaced 'war' as the focus of the contemporary prohibition contained within the UN Charter, the concept of 'war' is still found within the UN Charter, in that the very opening words of the Charter proclaim that '[w]e the peoples of the United Nations determined to save succeeding generations from the scourge of war ...'.

[43] This is in contrast to the predecessors of the UN Charter – the League of Nations Covenant of 1919 and the Kellogg–Briand Pact of 1928 – where the term 'war' was used instead of 'force'. See Edward Gordon, 'Article 2(4) in Historical Context' (1985) 10 *Yale Journal of International Law* 271, at 273-4.

[44] Article 2(3), UN Charter (1945).

[45] While the UN General Assembly also plays a role in the collective security system contained within the Charter, the most important provisions in connection with this system are included within Chapters VI-VIII of the Charter, which are concerned with the powers and functions of the UN Security Council. See, further, Chapters 3-5.

[46] Lesaffer, n. 9, at 35.

[47] Dinstein claims that Article 2(4) was 'an innovation at the time it was crafted'. Dinstein, n. 37, at para. 243. While the norm as found in Article 2(4) can be seen as revolutionary given that 'force' was now expressly prohibited as opposed to the much broader concept of 'war', Ian Brownlie claimed in 1963 that, by the time of the adoption of the UN Charter, customary international law had, under the influence of the major treaties and state practice, developed to the point whereby the legal regime contained within the Charter might not be seen as such a radical departure. See Ian Brownlie, *International Law and the Use of Force by States* (Clarendon Press, 1963), at 105-11. By contrast, Lesaffer has argued that '[t]his conclusion gives too rosy a picture of how far the prohibition to use force had progressed before its inscription in the UN Charter'. Lesaffer, n. 9, at 53.

## 1.3 THE SOURCES OF THE CONTEMPORARY PROHIBITION OF THE THREAT OR USE OF FORCE

The prohibition of the threat or use of force is contained in its treaty form in Article 2(4) of the UN Charter, which has been described as the 'cornerstone' of the Charter.[48] Following on from Article 2(3) of the Charter, which obliges member states to 'settle their international disputes by peaceful means', Article 2(4) provides that:

All Members shall refrain in their international relations from the threat or use of force against the territorial integrity or political independence of any state, or in any other manner inconsistent with the Purposes of the United Nations.

The prohibition is not only located within the UN Charter. While the wording has differed slightly on occasion, it can also be found recited within, for example, the United Nations Convention on the Law of the Sea,[49] the Rome Statute of the International Criminal Court,[50] the United Nations Declaration on Principles of International Law concerning Friendly Relations and Co-operation among States in accordance with the UN Charter,[51] the Definition of Aggression,[52] the Rio de Janeiro Inter-American Treaty of Reciprocal Assistance,[53] the Helsinki Final Act,[54] as well as several bilateral treaties.

Of perhaps greater significance, however, is that the prohibition of the threat or use of force is also found in customary international law, which is defined as 'a general practice accepted as law'.[55] As the International Court of Justice (ICJ) noted in the *Nicaragua* case, '[t]here can be no doubt that the issues of the use of force . . . are issues which are regulated both by customary international law and by treaties, in particular by the United Nations

---

[48] See n. 2.   [49] Article 301, United Nations Convention on the Law of the Sea (1982).
[50] Article 8bis, para. 2, Rome Statute of the International Criminal Court (1998): '"act of aggression" means the use of armed force by a State against the sovereignty, territorial integrity or political independence of another State, or in any other manner inconsistent with the Charter of the United Nations'. See, further, Section 1.5.5.2, on the crime of aggression.
[51] Principle 1, UNGA Res. 2625 (XXV) (1970).
[52] Article 1, UNGA Res. 3314 (XXIX) (1974): 'Aggression is the use of armed force by a State against the sovereignty, territorial integrity or political independence of another State, or in any other manner inconsistent with the Charter of the United Nations, as set out in this Definition.'
[53] Article 1, Rio de Janeiro Inter-American Treaty of Reciprocal Assistance (1947).
[54] Article 1(a)(II), Final Act of the Conference on Security and Co-operation in Europe (1975).
[55] Article 38(1)(b), Statute of the International Court of Justice (1945). Two elements need to be identified in this respect: state practice and *opinio juris sive necessitatis*. See, further, the section on 'The Sources of the Law on the Use of Force and the Question of Methodology' in the Introduction.

Charter'.[56] Although it is possible for conventional and customary norms to develop autonomously and in divergent ways, because there has now been over sixty years of state practice subsequent to the introduction of the UN Charter and because the addressees of the Charter and those of customary international law almost completely coincide, there has been a 'certain degree of uniformity and coherence in their respective development'[57] so that the two sources of the prohibition 'are substantially identical'.[58] Arguments to the contrary have not been made by states and, when discussing forcible actions, a distinction is not generally made between the two sources. For example, the ICJ noted in the *Nicaragua* case that 'both Parties [in their pleadings] take the view that the principles as to the use of force incorporated in the United Nations Charter correspond, in essentials, to those found in customary international law'.[59] It is, of course, difficult to see how they could be different as, in the absence of an express statement limiting any impact to one source of the law, state practice would be of significance both for (re)interpreting the UN Charter form and modifying the customary form of the prohibition.

### 1.3.1 The Text of Article 2(4)

Despite the formally equal status of the treaty and customary forms of the prohibition, the text of Article 2(4) has historically proven to be the focal point of much debate between commentators and, albeit less frequently, states regarding the breadth and scope of the prohibition. The arguments in this

---

[56] *Nicaragua* case, n. 1, at para. 34. While the prohibition of the *use* of force undoubtedly exists within customary international law, there is some disagreement as to whether the prohibition of the *threat* of force has been sufficiently clearly articulated within the practice of states to constitute a norm of customary international law. See Nicholas Stürchler, *The Threat of Force in International Law* (Cambridge University Press, 2007), at 92–126; James A. Green and Francis Grimal, 'The Threat of Force as an Action in Self-Defence under International Law' (2011) 44 *Vanderbilt Journal of Transnational Law* 285, at 290 (n.17).

[57] Tarcisio Gazzini, 'The Rules on the Use of Force at the Beginning of the XXI Century' (2007) 11 *Journal of Conflict & Security Law* 319, at 320.

[58] Ibid. As will be demonstrated at certain points in this book there has been a certain amount of reciprocal conditioning between the two sources. However, in the case of the right of self-defence, which is also regulated by the UN Charter and customary international law, the two sources of the right more clearly retain their separate existence and identity so that '[o]n a number of points, the areas governed by the two sources of law do not exactly overlap, and the substantive rules in which they are framed are not identical in content'. *Nicaragua* case, n. 1, at para. 175. For example, the requirement of an 'armed attack' before an action in self-defence can commence is found in Article 51 of the UN Charter, whereas the requirement that actions taken in self-defence be 'necessary' and 'proportional' is found within customary international law. In addition, the right of self-defence as found within the Charter contains procedural requirements that do not exist in customary international law. For more on the right of self-defence see Chapters 6–8.

[59] *Nicaragua* case, n. 1, at para. 188.

respect have been both of a textual and contextual nature. While these arguments will be explored more fully in subsequent chapters, attention will be drawn to their central tenets here.

### 1.3.1.1 Lack of Express Mention of Exceptions to the Prohibition

Exceptions to the prohibition of forcible action exist within the UN Charter. Action taken under the auspices of the UN Security Council, as explored in Chapters 3–5 of this book, and in self-defence, as explored in Chapters 6–8, are contained within Chapter VII of the Charter.[60] However, none of these are expressly mentioned or referred to in Article 2(4) itself. Indeed, one has to read much further into the Charter for these exceptions and, even then, they are not labelled expressly as exceptions to the prohibition. Given this lack of attachment to Article 2(4) and the implicitness with which they are read as exceptions, it is possible that other exceptions to Article 2(4) might also be implied or located outside of the parameters of the UN Charter, although there were no agreements to this effect upon the adoption of the Charter. For example, it is often stated that a further exception to the prohibition can be found in the 'consent' or 'invitation' by the authorities of a state for the armed forces of another state to use force upon its territory[61] or, and more controversially, that there is a right of states to engage in humanitarian intervention in the territories of other states.[62] The Charter is a living instrument and it is possible that subsequent practice or agreement will lead to its reinterpretation.[63] In the absence of a formal modification or agreement in regards to interpretation, however, the problem is being able to draw upon sufficient, and sufficiently clear, state practice to claim that such a reinterpretation has occurred.[64]

### 1.3.1.2 'against the territorial integrity or political independence of any state'

Particular emphasis has been placed upon a textual analysis to argue for limited constraints, asserting that use of the phrase 'against the territorial integrity or political independence of any state' in Article 2(4) suggests that force is permitted so long as it does not target these two fundamental elements

---

[60] The now defunct licence to take action against the 'enemy states' of the Second World War is also contained within the Charter (see Articles 53 and 107).
[61] See Chapter 9, although this book takes the view that this is not in fact an exception, as due to the consensual nature of the intervention the prohibition is not engaged *ab initio*.
[62] See Chapter 10.
[63] See Article 31, Vienna Convention of the Law of Treaties (1969). See, further, the section on 'The Sources of the Law on the Use of Force and the Question of Methodology' in the Introduction.
[64] See, further, Section 1.3.2 on the peremptory status of the prohibition.

of statehood.[65] This kind of narrow interpretation, which has the potential to open up some gaping loopholes in the prohibition, was used by Anthony D'Amato, who, in an article regarding the Israeli missile strike against the Iraqi nuclear reactor in Osiraq in 1981, argued that:

> ... it is open to serious question whether Israel's strike was a use of force against either Iraq's territorial integrity or its political independence. No portion of Iraq's territory was taken away from Iraq by the bombardment. A *use* of the territory – namely, to construct a nuclear reactor – was interfered with, but the territory itself remained integral. Nor was Iraq's political independence compromised. Iraq's *power* was undoubtedly lessened, but in what sense was its governmental authority *vis-à-vis* other sovereign governments diminished?[66]

However, many scholars have been critical of this particular reading of Article 2(4). Oscar Schachter, for example, famously rejected this interpretation by commenting that it demands an 'Orwellian' construction of the terms of this provision.[67] Others have also argued for a more water-tight reading of the prohibition.[68] The *travaux préparatoires* of the provision also indicate that the inclusion of this wording was not to be seen as limiting the prohibition of the use of force but instead to provide 'particular emphasis' in it to the protection of these attributes of statehood.[69] Michael Akehurst has stated that 'the *travaux préparatoires* indicate that the reference to territorial integrity, political independence, and the purposes of the United Nations was added to Article 2(4), not in order to limit the prohibition on the use of force, but in a clumsy attempt to strengthen it'.[70]

It is of particular relevance, however, that states themselves have rarely relied upon such textual arguments either to justify their uses of force or, more significantly, in an attempt to place limitations upon the breadth and scope of Article 2(4). Shortly after the adoption of the UN Charter, the United Kingdom argued in the *Corfu Channel* case of 1949 that its military action to retrieve

---

[65] See, for example, Derek Bowett, *Self-Defence in International Law* (Manchester University Press, 1958), at 152.
[66] See Anthony D'Amato, 'Israel's Air Strike Upon the Iraqi Nuclear Reactor' (1983) **77** *American Journal of International Law* 584, at 585. See also Anthony D'Amato, *International Law: Process and Prospect* (Transnational Publishers, 1987), at 58–9.
[67] See Oscar Schachter, 'The Legality of Pro-Democratic Invasion' (1984) **78** *American Journal of International Law* 645, at 649.
[68] See, for example, Brownlie, n. 47, at 267–8.
[69] See Albrecht Randelzhofer, 'Article 2(4)', in Bruno Simma (ed.), *The Charter of the United Nations: A Commentary*, 2nd ed. (Oxford University Press, 2002), 112, at paras. 37–9.
[70] See Michael Akehurst, 'Humanitarian Intervention', in Hedley Bull (ed.), *Intervention in World Politics* (Clarendon Press, 1986), 95. See also Ian Brownlie, *The Rule of Law in International Affairs* (Martinus Nijhoff, 1998), at 198. According to Article 32 of the Vienna Convention of the Law of Treaties (1969), the preparatory works of a treaty are to be employed as a supplementary means of interpretation.

evidence from Albania's territorial waters was lawful in that it did not threaten the territorial integrity or political independence of Albania.[71] However, the ICJ was not receptive to this argument and was instead of the opinion that the UK's arguments were based upon a policy of force:

> such as has, in the past, given rise to most serious abuses and such as cannot, whatever be the present defects in international organization, find a place in international law ... from the nature of things, it would be reserved for the most powerful States, and might easily lead to perverting the administration of international justice itself.[72]

An additional argument occasionally advanced in order to evade the application of Article 2(4) is the irredentist claim that a state is reclaiming territory that is rightfully theirs. This was the basis of the justification for India's invasion of Goa in 1992, Argentina's attempted seizure of the Falkland Islands from the United Kingdom in 1982 and Iraq's invasion and occupation of Kuwait in 1990, all of which received widespread condemnation. Arguably, the reason for this condemnation can be found in the fact that 'border disputes between States are so frequent that any exception to the prohibition of the threat or use of force for territory that is allegedly occupied unlawfully would create a large and dangerous hole in a fundamental rule of international law'.[73]

### 1.3.1.3 'or in any other manner inconsistent with the purposes of the United Nations'

In an attempt to limit the breadth and scope of the prohibition, certain arguments have also been made in regard to Article 2(4)'s requirement that force should not be used 'in any other manner inconsistent with the purposes of the United Nations'. While some have attempted to argue that certain

---

[71] *Corfu Channel Case (United Kingdom v. Albania)*, Merits (1949) ICJ Reports 4.
[72] Ibid., at 35. For further discussion on the *Corfu Channel* case see Section 2.5.2.
[73] Eritrea–Ethiopia Claims Commission – Partial Award: *Jus ad Bellum* – Ethiopia's Claims 1–8, 19 December 2005, at para. 10, available at: https://legal.un.org/riaa/cases/vol_XXVI/457-469.pdf. Quoted with approval in Award in the arbitration regarding the delimitation of the maritime boundary between Guyana and Suriname, award of 17 September 2007, at para. 423, available at: https://legal.un.org/riaa/cases/vol_XXX/1-144.pdf. States have agreed in the UN General Assembly that '[e]very State has the duty to refrain from the threat or use of force ... as a means of solving international disputes, including territorial disputes and problems concerning frontiers of States.' See Principle 1, Declaration on Principles of International Law concerning Friendly Relations and Co-Operation among States in accordance with the Charter of the United Nations (1970). However, although an independent exception to recover territory cannot be said to exist under the prohibition of force, there is a debate between scholars as to whether – and, if so, under what circumstances – states are permitted under the right of self-defence to recover territory that continues to be occupied by another state following an armed attack. See Section 6.3.1.1.

purposes of the UN – such as the promotion of human rights under Articles 1, 55 and 56 of the Charter – trump the prohibition,[74] these arguments are not sustainable on the basis that these purposes contained within the Charter are often promotional or aspirational in nature compared with the obligatory character of the prohibition of force. It is also significant that the preparatory works of the UN Charter demonstrate that the 'intention of the authors ... was to state in the broadest terms an absolute all-inclusive prohibition; the phrase "or in any other manner" was designed to ensure that there should be no loopholes'[75] and states have rarely attempted to justify their actions upon this basis or raised it with the aim of limiting the scope and breadth of the prohibition.[76]

### 1.3.1.4 The Subjects of the Prohibition: 'International Relations'

Given what has been said thus far, the prohibition might well appear to be absolute. Yet, the breadth and scope of the prohibition is limited by Article 2 (4)'s reference to its application in the 'international relations' of member states. Indeed, it applies to the use of force by 'All Members' – membership of the UN being restricted to 'peace-loving states'[77] – and only in their forcible actions against 'any state'. This restriction is hardly surprising given that the Charter was adopted at a time when the primacy of the state as the subject of, and actor within, international law was clearer than it is today.[78] As such, with arguably the exception of what we might describe as 'contested states',[79] non-state actors and armed groups do not fall within the scope of the provision and are, thus, not directly prohibited from threatening or using force under it.[80]

---

[74] See, for example, Fernando R. Tesón, *Humanitarian Intervention: An Inquiry into Law and Morality*, 2nd ed. (Transnational Publishers, 1997), at 151.

[75] Summary Report of Eleventh Meeting of Committee I/1, 4 June 1945, Doc. 784, I/1/27, *Documents of the United Nations Conference on International Organization*, vol. VI, at 334–5.

[76] As a notable exception, the United Kingdom and Belgium attempted to make such an argument in the context of NATO's intervention in Serbia in order to cease the atrocities that were taking place in Kosovo. See, further, Section 10.3.2.4.

[77] Article 4, UN Charter (1945).

[78] If the Charter was to be rewritten today, it is possible that, due to the rise in frequency of internal conflicts and the reality of global terrorism, the use of force between states and non-state entities would be addressed in some form in the provisions regulating the use of force. However, by contrast to Article 2(4), the sole unilateral exception of self-defence to this prohibition contained in Article 51 does not expressly restrict itself to responses to 'armed attacks' by state actors. See, further, Chapters 6 and 8.

[79] For example, it is arguable that it would apply in the relations between China and Taiwan. See, in general, Christian Henderson, 'Contested States and the Rights and Obligations of the Jus ad Bellum' (2013) 21 *Cardozo Journal of International and Comparative Law* 367.

[80] Although see Nicholas Tsagourias, 'Non-State Actors and the Use of Force', in Jean d'Aspremont (ed.), *Participants in the International Legal System: Multiple Perspectives on Non-State Actors in International Law* (Routledge, 2011), 326.

## 1.3 Sources of the Prohibition of Force

It is also clear that the original intention behind the prohibition was for it to apply to *inter*-state situations, and not those of an *intra*-state or domestic nature. It does not, in this respect, expressly prohibit states from using force internally in domestic situations, something that is governed by domestic law, human rights considerations and the law governing non-international armed conflicts. It was noticeable, for example, during the Arab Spring uprisings that began in 2011 that, while the repressive actions undertaken by the police and armed forces of the various states were condemned,[81] this was not as a violation of the prohibition of the use of force norm. Instead, the situations were generally viewed in the context of international human rights law and, subsequently, the law of armed conflict as it applies to non-international armed conflicts.[82]

Although it will generally be a state's military that engages in the type of forcible action that is covered by the prohibition, there is nothing to exclude the actions of a state's police forces from also engaging the prohibition. Indeed, just as the military may be deployed in domestic situations a state's police forces may, on occasion, be deployed to undertake forcible action with an international dimension.[83] In any case, not every state will have a clear dividing line between the military and the police and their respective activities.

Furthermore, the prohibition might be considered as applying only to states individually. Yet, Chapter VIII of the UN Charter, which deals with regional arrangements and organisations, is clear that 'no enforcement action shall be taken under regional arrangements or by regional agencies without the authorization of the Security Council'.[84] This can only be understood upon the basis that these regional arrangements are similarly prohibited from using force. While this issue will be addressed further in Chapter 3, it bears noting at this stage that in reality the actions of other organisations can only be viewed

---

[81] For example, the UN Security Council '[d]*eplor*[ed] the gross and systematic violation of human rights, including the repression of peaceful demonstrators' and 'express[ed] deep concern at the deaths of civilians' in Libya. See UNSC Res. 1970 (2011), preamble.

[82] In the context of the situation in Libya, for example, see Human Rights Council resolution A/HRC/RES/S-15/1 of 25 February 2011. See also Claus Kreß, 'Major Post-Westphalian Shifts and Some Important Neo-Westphalian Hesitations in the State Practice on the International Law on the Use of Force' (2014) 1 *Journal on the Use of Force and International Law* 11, at 25. However, the failure of the contemporary *jus ad bellum* to extend to internal conflicts, which, today, are far more prevalent than inter-state conflicts, has been noted. See, e.g., Mary Ellen O'Connell, 'Energized by War Fatigue' (2014) *ESIL Reflections*, available at: https://esil-sedi.eu/post_name-141/. Furthermore, in drawing upon revisionist just war theory and international human rights law the idea of an 'internal *jus ad bellum*' which would seek to regulate internal resorts to force by both governments and opposition groups has been theorised. See, e.g., Eliav Lieblich, 'Internal *Jus ad Bellum*' (2016) **67** *Hastings Law Journal* 687.

[83] Although this is subject to what is said in Section 2.5.2.1 on the relevance of international relations.

[84] See, further, Section 3.5.

through the prism of the obligations imposed upon the individual member states of which they are comprised, otherwise states would simply club together to do something that they would otherwise be prohibited from doing individually.

Finally, it is notable that the prohibition applies to the actions of the UN Security Council.[85] Indeed, despite action under its auspices providing an exception to the prohibition, the Council must still abide by the principles and purposes of the UN,[86] one being the prohibition of the threat or use of force, and the Council is also bound by *jus cogens* norms,[87] with the prohibition of the threat or use of force arguably being an example of such a norm.[88] As such, the Council is, formally speaking, prohibited from using force unless certain prerequisite procedural requirements are followed, for example by first determining the existence of a 'threat to the peace', 'breach of the peace' or 'act of aggression', which will be discussed further in Part II.

### 1.3.2 The Peremptory Status of the Prohibition

The prohibition of the threat or use of force is generally regarded as a fundamental norm within the international legal framework in that it is often categorised as a peremptory or *jus cogens* (as opposed to *jus dispositivum*) norm. In other words it is perceived as 'a norm that enjoys a higher rank in the international hierarchy than treaty law and even "ordinary" customary rules'.[89] Perhaps the most authoritative definition of peremptory norms is found in Article 53 of the Vienna Convention of the Law of Treaties (1969). This states that:

[a] peremptory norm of general international law is a norm accepted and recognized by the international community of States as a whole as a norm from which no derogation is permitted and which can be modified only by a subsequent norm of general international law having the same character.

Many writers have placed the prohibition of the threat or use of force in this category of legal norms.[90] The International Law Commission also expressed

---

[85] For a discussion on this issue, see Patrick M. Butchard, *The Responsibility to Protect and the Failures of the United Nations Security Council* (Hart, 2020).
[86] Article 24(2), UN Charter (1945).
[87] The International Law Commission, for example, has accepted this in Article 26 of its Draft Articles on the Responsibility of International Organisations: 'Nothing in this Chapter precludes the wrongfulness of any act of an international organization which is not in conformity with an obligation arising under a peremptory norm of general international law.' International Law Commission, Draft Articles on the Responsibility of International Organisations, UNGA Res. 66/10 (2011). See further, for example, Alexander Orakhelashvili, *Collective Security* (Oxford University Press, 2011), at 57–8.
[88] See Section 1.3.2.
[89] *Prosecutor* v. *Furundzija*, Case No IT-95-17/1-T, ICTY, Trial Chamber, 1998, at para. 153.
[90] See, for example, Daniel Costelloe, *Legal Consequences of Peremptory Norms in International Law* (Cambridge University Press, 2017), at 16; James Crawford, *The Creation of States in*

## 1.3 Sources of the Prohibition of Force

the view that 'the law of the Charter concerning the prohibition of the use of force in itself constitutes a conspicuous example of a rule in international law having the character of *jus cogens*'.[91] Furthermore, the ICJ, in the *Nicaragua* case, while not stating that it was itself of the opinion that it constituted a *jus cogens* norm, nonetheless noted that the prohibition of the use of force 'is frequently referred to in statements by *State representatives* as being not only a principle of customary international law but also a fundamental or cardinal principle of such law'.[92] Indeed, this characterisation of the norm is one that is shared by a number of states, with no apparent express dissent.[93]

However, while some scholars have taken issue with the general concept of 'normative hierarchy',[94] others have taken issue with the specific labelling of the prohibition of the threat or use of force as such a norm.[95] For example, it has been claimed that the *jus cogens* prohibition is restricted to *aggressive* force,[96] while others have taken issue with the fact that the prohibition of force has exceptions.[97] Indeed, whereas other peremptory norms, such as the prohibition of torture and genocide, are absolute and have no exceptions, the prohibition of the threat or use of force, on the other hand, has two; individual or collective self-defence and forcible intervention authorised by the UN Security Council. Others, however, do not regard these as constituting derogations from or discrete exceptions to the prohibition of the use of force which would therefore preclude the conferral of *jus cogens* status but rather as elements that are built into the substantive scope of the prohibition.[98]

---

*International Law* (Oxford University Press, 2006), at 146; Lauri Hannikainen, *Peremptory Norms (Jus Cogens) in International Law: Historical Development, Criteria and Present Status* (Finnish Lawyers' Pub. Co., 1988), at 323, 356; Lindsay Moir, *Reappraising the Resort to Force: International Law, Jus ad Bellum, and the War on Terror* (Hart, 2010), at 9; Alexander Orakhelashvili, *Peremptory Norms in International Law* (Oxford University Press, 2006), at 50.

[91] See 'Draft Articles on the Law of Treaties with Commentaries' (1966) 2 *Yearbook of the International Law Commission* 187, at 247

[92] *Nicaragua* case, n. 1, at para. 190 (emphasis added).    [93] See Hannikainen, n. 90, at 324–5.

[94] See, e.g., Dinah Shelton, 'Normative Hierarchy in International Law' (2006) 100 *American Journal of International Law* 291.

[95] See, e.g., James A. Green, 'Questioning the Peremptory Status of the Prohibition of the Use of Force' (2011) 32 *Michigan Journal of International Law* 215.

[96] Hannikainen, n. 90, at 323–56. The UN General Assembly's Definition of Aggression states that 'aggression is the most serious and dangerous form of the illegal use of force'. See UNGA Res. 3314 (XXIX), 14 December 1974, annex, preamble. Article *8bis*, para. 1, or the Rome Statute of the International Criminal Court (1998) states that 'an act of aggression which, by its character, gravity and scale, constitutes a manifest violation of the Charter of the United Nations.'

[97] Green, n. 95, at 229–36.

[98] See, for example, Sondre T. Helmerson, 'The Prohibition on the Use of Force as *Jus Cogens*: Explaining Apparent Derogations' (2014) 61 *Netherlands International Law Review* 167, at 175–6.

Although one cannot shy away from some of the theoretical issues that are associated with labelling the prohibition of force a *jus cogens* norm, given the general weight of opinion that appears to exist as to its *jus cogens* status it can arguably be seen as such a norm, even if of a quirky or *sui generis* nature. However, given that such norms should be seen as accepted and recognised 'by the international community of States as a whole' this does raise the bar somewhat for any proponents of normative change.[99]

## 1.4 THE 'THREAT' OF FORCE

Given the volume of ink that has been spilt over the actual use of force, one might be forgiven for overlooking the fact that the prohibition also covers the *threat* of force. As with the actual use of force, the UN Charter does not provide any elaboration upon what constitutes such a 'threat' and states themselves have not – either through their individual practice or, for example, through the adoption of a UN General Assembly resolution – expressly elaborated upon the legal nature of threats of force and the circumstances in which the prohibition would be infringed. Instead, the ICJ has, again, been the point of focus for discussions on this issue, and declared in its 1996 *Nuclear Weapons* advisory opinion that:

If the envisaged use of force is itself unlawful, the stated readiness to use it would be a threat prohibited under Article 2, paragraph 4 ... The notions of 'threat' and 'use' of force under Article 2, paragraph 4, of the Charter stand together in the sense that if the use of force itself in a given case is illegal – for whatever reason – the threat to use such force will likewise be illegal. In short, if it is to be lawful, the declared readiness of a State to use force must be a use of force that is in conformity with the Charter.[100]

In other words, in the eyes of the ICJ threats of force are prohibited if it would be unlawful to employ actual force in the same circumstances.[101] In this respect, if a threat is made to use force lawfully – that is, in self-defence if a

---

[99] See, further, the section on 'Legal and Procedural Issues Associated with the *Jus ad Bellum*' in the Introduction.

[100] *Legality of the Threat or Use of Nuclear Weapons*, Advisory Opinion (1996) ICJ Reports 226, at para. 47. The reasoning of the ICJ was cited with support by the *Award in the arbitration regarding the delimitation of the maritime boundary between Guyana and Suriname*, award of 17 September 2007, at para. 439, available at: http://legal.un.org/riaa/cases/vol_XXX/1-144.pdf. Dinstein has commented that 'irrefutably it reflects the generally accepted interpretation of Article 2(4)'. Dinstein, n. 37, at para. 250.

[101] As such, when discussing the meaning of 'force' in the following chapters of this book only the 'use' of force will generally be referred to. There are no independent express exceptions to the prohibition of the threat of force, as there are to the actual use of force. It has been claimed, however, that threats of force could be used in self-defence. See Green and Grimal, n. 56, at 239.

state were to suffer an armed attack or if it were to petition the UN Security Council to grant it authorisation to use force – then this would not *per se* fall within the scope of the prohibition.

### 1.4.1 The Element of a Demand or an Ultimatum

This particular manifestation of 'force' has been defined elsewhere as 'a message, explicit or implicit, formulated by a decision maker and directed to the target audience, indicating that force will be used if a rule or demand is not complied with',[102] as well as 'an express or implied promise by a government of a resort to force conditional on non-acceptance of certain demands of that government'.[103] On this basis, the ultimatum given by the United States and the United Kingdom in 2003 prior to the invasion of Iraq for Saddam Hussein to leave the country or be forcibly removed was unlawful.[104] Although the US-led coalition justified its actions upon a 'revival' of the authorisation to use 'all necessary means' that had been issued by the UN Security Council for the forcible eviction of Iraq from Kuwait in 1990–1, this argument was not accepted by other members of the UN Security Council, or indeed large swathes of the broader international community,[105] thereby rendering the threat to use such force upon that basis and at that time unlawful.

However, on the basis of the ICJ's depiction of threats of force in the *Nuclear Weapons* advisory opinion in Section 1.4, while a threat would need to be coercive in nature,[106] there would not seem to be the need for it to be accompanied by a particular demand or ultimatum, despite the fact that this would normally be the case given the very nature of threats.[107] Indeed, all that the ICJ seemed to require was a 'stated' or 'declared' readiness to use force. In this respect, the publication of the UK's legal opinion on the prospective use of force against the Syrian government as a response to the Ghouta chemical weapons attack in August 2013 arguably constituted an unlawful 'declared

---

[102] Romana Sadurska, 'Threats of Force' (1988) **82** *American Journal of International Law* 239, at 242.

[103] Brownlie, n. 47, at 364. While these definitions talk of messages 'formulated by a decision maker' and promises 'by a government', the question arises as to whether threats of force can be made by proxy. For example, amidst tension between Chinese and Indian soldiers at a Himalayan border location, the editor of the state-run Chinese newspaper *The Global Times*, Hu Xijin, Tweeted '[d]on't mess with [the People's Liberation Army] otherwise they will teach you a heavier lesson.' See Lily Kuo, 'Satellite Images Show Chinese Construction Near Site of India Border Clash', *The Guardian*, 25 June 2020, available at: www.theguardian.com/world/2020/jun/25/satellite-images-show-chinese-construction-near-site-of-india-border-clash.

[104] See BBC News, 'Bush Ultimatum to Saddam: Text', 18 March 2003, available at: http://news.bbc.co.uk/1/hi/world/americas/2859269.stm.

[105] See Section 4.3 for more on this particular intervention and arguments regarding the revival of UN Security Council authority to use military force.

[106] See Section 2.2 for more on the element of 'coercion'.

[107] *Tallinn Manual*, n. 3, at 53.

readiness' to use force, seeing as it was premised upon the basis that a legal right of unilateral humanitarian intervention existed, which, as explained in Chapter 10, is a controversial position.[108] As a further example, in 2019 the Chinese president, Xi Jinping, stated in relation to Taiwan that 'we make no promise to renounce the use of force and reserve the option of taking all necessary means', ominously adding that Taiwan's unification with China was inevitable and that China would permit 'no external interference'.[109] Although given the generally accepted 'one China' policy, this may be perceived of as a threat to use force solely within Chinese territory and thereby outside of the scope of the prohibition of the threat or use of force under focus here, given Taiwan's existence as a de facto independent and geographically separate entity it is arguable that the prohibition was, and continues to be, applicable between it and the People's Republic of China.[110]

### 1.4.2 The Communicative Nature of Threats of Force

While so far we have briefly discussed examples of *explicit* verbal or written threats to use force by one state towards another, difficulties arise with regard to characterising threats of force of a more *implicit* nature. Although a prohibited threat may be made implicitly, it would still appear to need to be at least communicated towards a particular state or group of states, as in these examples, in order to distinguish a 'threat of force' in the international relations of states from broader and more general 'threats to the peace'. In this respect, although the circumstances in which a state is willing to resort to force on a particular occasion might be clearly established, it may not be sufficiently directed towards a particular state or group of states. Highlighting this point, the publication by the United States of its 2002 National Security Strategy in which the existence of a right of pre-emptive self-defence was clearly proclaimed cannot, by itself, be seen as an unlawful threat to use force.[111] While, as discussed in Chapter 7, the right of self-defence does not extend to pre-emptive action, the threat of any use of force in this instance was not targeted towards a particular state or entity but towards 'rogue states' and 'terrorism' more generally, although, seen in the context of President Bush's prior announcement of the existence of an 'axis of evil', which

---

[108] See, in general, Christian Henderson, 'The UK Government's Legal Opinion on Forcible Measures in Response to the Use of Chemical Weapons by the Syrian Government' (2015) 64 *International & Comparative Law Quarterly* 179.

[109] Lily Kuo, '"All necessary means": Xi Jinping Reserves Right to Use Force against Taiwan', *The Guardian*, 2 January 2019, available at: www.theguardian.com/world/2019/jan/02/all-necessary-means-xi-jinping-reserves-right-to-use-force-against-taiwan.

[110] For a discussion on this issue, see, further, Henderson, n. 79.

[111] Office of the White House, The National Security Strategy of the United States of America (2002), available at: https://2009-2017.state.gov/documents/organization/63562.pdf.

consisted of Iran, Iraq and North Korea,[112] this might be disputed. None of these states complained at the time, however, that they had been the victim of an unlawful threat to use force.

On the other hand, while animosity may be clearly expressed by one state towards another state, its readiness to resort to forcible measures may not be sufficiently clearly established, although this is a rather difficult issue to assess. For example, tension between the United States and Iran increased following the Trump administration's decision to pull the United States out of the nuclear deal with Iran – the Joint Comprehensive Plan of Action – that was agreed upon by the Obama administration. In one exchange on Twitter in July 2018, Iranian President Rouhani cautioned President Trump against pursuing hostile policies towards Iran, saying 'Mr Trump, don't play with the lion's tail, this would only lead to regret' and that 'war with Iran is the mother of all wars'.[113] In response, President Trump tweeted:

'To Iranian President Rouhani: NEVER, EVER THREATEN THE UNITED STATES AGAIN OR YOU WILL SUFFER CONSEQUENCES THE LIKES OF WHICH FEW THROUHGOUT HISTORY HAVE EVER SUFFERED BEFORE. WE ARE NO LONGER A COUNTRY THAT WILL STAND FOR YOUR DEMENTED WORDS OF VIOLENCE & DEATH. BE CAUTIOUS!'[114]

The animosity expressed by both leaders in this instance clearly raises concerns regarding international peace and security. Yet, both leaders refrained from making any direct reference to the use of force. However, while the initial Tweet by President Rouhani would appear too general to constitute a prohibited threat of force, despite the demand made within it, the response by President Trump, while similarly refraining to expressly speak of the use of military force, would seem to be implicitly threatening the use of disproportionate forcible military action in response to any further *threats* by Iran, something that would appear to engage the prohibition.

The difficulty in assessing threatening language through the prism of the prohibition of the threat of force can be seen in the fact that states often talk of 'all options' remaining 'on the table' in the context of a particular situation. For example, following unrest in Venezuela in January 2019 and the rise of a significant opposition to the rule of President Nicolás Maduro and led by Juan Guaidó, US President Donald Trump, in response to a question as to whether the United States would consider a military option if Maduro refused to cede

---

[112] George W. Bush, 'State of the Union Address', 29 January 2002, available at: https://georgewbush-whitehouse.archives.gov/news/releases/2002/01/20020129-11.html.

[113] Oliver Laughland and Saeed Kamali Dehghan, 'Trump Says Iran Will "Suffer Consequences" after Speech by President Rouhani', *The Guardian*, 12 July 2018, available at: www.theguardian.com/world/2018/jul/23/irans-mafia-elite-amass-fortunes-while-people-suffer-says-mike-pompeo.

[114] Ibid.

power, said: 'We're not considering anything but all options are on the table. All options, always, all options are on the table.'[115] This might be seen as a rather vague reference to the possibility of the United States resorting to the use of military force in what would be unlawful circumstances, given that neither a legal right of unilateral pro-democratic or humanitarian intervention can be said to exist under international law,[116] and neither did Guaidó arguably possess the authority to invite states to intervene in support.[117] However, Trump's words might be interpreted as sufficiently specific to engage the prohibition of the threat of force given that they were spoken in the context of the possibility of military action. US Vice President Mike Pence was, nontheless, more cautious, and in that sense tempered the possibility for the use of force, in stating that '[t]he United States is going to continue to bring the full weight of our *economic and diplomatic pressure* until freedom and democracy and fair elections are restored for the people of Venezuela',[118] something that, although potentially infringing the principle of non-intervention,[119] did not engage the prohibition of the threat or use of force.

### 1.4.3 Threats of Force Not in a Verbal or Written Form

In general terms, and on the basis of the examples already discussed in this section, one might think of a threat being conveyed verbally or in written form. However, the ICJ in the *Nuclear Weapons* advisory opinion did not limit threats in this way and was of the view that '[w]hether a signalled intention to use force if certain events occur is or is not a "threat" within Article 2, paragraph 4, of the Charter depends upon various factors',[120] raising the question as to whether the 'signalled intention to use of force' – or the 'message' or 'promise' – may be conveyed through other means.

Dinstein has observed that, while a demonstration of military capacity might constitute a threat of force, 'such a demonstration would have to be a non-routine operation staged in a provocative manner'.[121] However, mere provocative military exercises or missile tests arguably would not, in and of themselves,

---

[115] Joe Parkin Daniels, Mariana Zuñiga and Julian Borger, 'Trump Says "All Options on the Table" as Venezuela Crisis Deepens', *The Guardian*, 24 January 2019, available at: www.theguardian.com/world/2019/jan/23/enezuela-trump-president-juan-guaido-maduro-recognition-news-latest.

[116] On pro-democratic and humanitarian interventions, see Section 9.2.3 and Chapter 10, respectively.

[117] Federica Paddeu and Alonso Gurmendi Dunkelberg, 'Recognition of Governments: Legitimacy and Control Six Months after Guaidó', *Just Security*, 18 July 2019, available at: http://opiniojuris.org/2019/07/18/recognition-of-governments-legitimacy-and-control-six-months-after-guaido/.

[118] Parkin Daniels et al., n. 115 (emphasis added).

[119] See Section 2.2 for more on the principle of non-intervention.

[120] *Nuclear Weapons* advisory opinion, n. 100, at para. 47.    [121] Dinstein, n. 37, at para. 253.

## 1.4 The 'Threat' of Force

constitute a prohibited threat of force, and some kind of concrete communicative threat towards a particular state or entity would arguably need to be identifiable. In this respect, a distinction can be made between threats of force that are covered by the prohibition and more general threats to peace and security.[122] For example, although North Korea's various tests of nuclear weapons and missiles were often not – in and of themselves – sufficiently specific to constitute a threat of force against South Korea, Japan or the United States,[123] they were, nonetheless, in defiance of resolutions of the UN Security Council and were characterised as a threat to international peace and security.[124]

Things become a little murkier, however, if there have been recent previous military engagements between the state concerned and another state or group of states. Indeed, while no direct verbal threats to invade Ukraine were made, concerns began to mount during a military build-up of 130,000 Russian troops and hardware to the east and south of Ukraine in early April 2021.[125] President Putin continued to deny any prospect of the use of force against Ukraine,[126] and other factors might be considered as pointing away from characterising this as an unlawful threat of force. For example, it was reported that security at the Voronezh staging point was relaxed, with the Russians allowing foreign journalists into the area.[127] In addition, there was speculation that this massing of troops was a flexing of Russian military muscle following US President Joe Biden's arrival at The White House or was an attempted distraction from the situation involving the health of the dissident Alexei Navalny who was currently incarcerated in a Russian prison.[128] Yet, on the other hand, this build-up occurred seven years after the Russian invasion and subsequent annexation of the Crimea peninsula and during Russian involvement in a conflict which continued to simmer in the east of Ukraine, as well as being accompanied by threats of unspecified military action if its security demands were not met.[129] The response of the international community appeared to treat Russia's military build-up and accompanying demands as a threat to use force, despite the fact that they were not generally explicitly categorised as

---

[122] For more on 'threats to the peace', see Section 3.3.1.1.
[123] See, for example, BBC News, 'North Korea Conducts Ballistic Missile Test', 12 February 2017, available at: www.bbc.co.uk/news/world-asia-38947451.
[124] See UNSC Res. 1695 (2006); UNSC Res. 1718 (2006); UNSC Res. 1874 (2009); UNSC Res. 2087 (2013); UNSC Res. 2094 (2013); UNSC Res. 2270 (2016); UNSC Res. 2321 (2016); UNSC Res. 2371 (2017); UNSC Res. 2375 (2017). See also www.un.org/press/en/2016/sc12191.doc.htm.
[125] Dan Sabbagh, 'Military Buildup Near Ukraine Sows Confusion over Russian Intentions', *The Guardian*, 12 April 2021, available at: www.theguardian.com/world/2021/apr/12/military-buildup-near-ukraine-sows-confusion-over-russian-intentions.
[126] Natalia Zinets and Vladimir Soldatkin, 'Putin Accuses U.S. of Trying to lure Russia into War', *Reuters*, 2 February 2022, available at: www.reuters.com/world/europe/ukraine-announces-plan-boost-army-foreign-leaders-rally-2022-02-01/.
[127] Sabbagh, n. 125.   [128] Ibid.   [129] Zinets and Soldatkin, n. 126.

such. The United States was clear, for example, that it would not allow Russia to do anything to disrupt the territorial integrity of Ukraine, implicitly treating the actions of Russia as an unacceptable threat of force.[130]

One of Russia's security demands was that a guarantee be provided that Ukraine would not be admitted into the North Atlantic Treaty Organization (NATO). The question arises then if Ukraine joining NATO would itself constitute a threat of force towards Russia. Indeed, the prospect of Ukraine joining NATO, and the prospect of its eastward expansion, formed the pretext for Russia's invasion in February 2022.[131] While any state joining an organisation potentially has geopolitical ramifications, President Putin's claim that this was a threat to 'the very existence' of the Russian state thereby justifying a forcible response failed to place such an act within the context of the prohibition of threats of force.[132] Indeed, '[i]t must be observed that if a State joins a military alliance (e.g. NATO) – established pursuant to the right of collective self-defence against a potential armed attack, in conformity with the United Nations Charter – such a step cannot be regarded by a non-member (apprehensive of the alliance) as an unlawful threat of force.'[133]

Although having first emerged during the Cold War states continue to possess nuclear weapons as part of a policy of deterrence against possible attack. Yet, while specific treaty commitments exist prohibiting states from possessing such weapons,[134] the mere possession of nuclear weapons does not by itself constitute an unlawful threat to use force and, even if states were to obtain nuclear weapons in violation of these treaty commitments, this would still be insufficient by itself to constitute a threat of force. In the *Nuclear Weapons* advisory opinion the ICJ did not 'pronounce ... upon the practice

---

[130] Olafimihan Oshin, 'Blinken: US Commitment to Ukraine's Territorial Integrity Is "unwavering"', *The Hill*, 2 December 2021, available at: https://thehill.com/policy/international/europe/583980-blinken-us-commitment-to-ukraines-territorial-integrity-is/.

[131] See Address by the President of the Russian Federation', Office of the President of the Russian Federation, 24 February 2022, available at: http://en.kremlin.ru/events/president/transcripts/67843 (official English translation, as published by the Kremlin); Обращение Президента Российской Федерации,ПрезидентРоссии, 24 февраля 2022 года, available at: http://kremlin.ru/events/president/news/67843 (original Russian text, as published by the Kremlin).

[132] Ibid.  [133] Dinstein, n. 37, at para. 254.

[134] Under the 1968 Treaty on the Non-Proliferation of Nuclear Weapons non-nuclear-weapon states pledge to refrain from acquiring such weapons while nuclear weapon states are permitted to retain their nuclear weapons while also pledging to pursue complete disarmament. On 7 July 2017 the UN General Assembly adopted the Treaty on the Prohibition of Nuclear Weapons, which was voted for by 122 states, although the nine states known to possess nuclear weapons (the United States, the United Kingdom, France, China, Russia, Israel, India, Pakistan and North Korea) were ominously absent from the vote. The Treaty provides a comprehensive ban on the development, testing, production, possession, transfer, acquisition, use or stationing of nuclear weapons. See Treaty on the Prohibition of Nuclear Weapons, UN Doc. A/CONF.229/2017/8, 7 July 2017.

known as the "policy of deterrence'",[135] although after surveying the present state of international law the Court was of the view that whether the mere possession of nuclear weapons constituted a threat to use them depended upon, as noted in Section 1.4 and this section, whether there was a 'signaled intention' to use them in circumstances that were unlawful.[136]

### 1.4.4 The Credibility of a Threat of Force

In elaborating upon the policy of deterrence in the *Nuclear Weapons* advisory opinion, the ICJ noted, however, that:

[s]ome States put forward the argument that possession of nuclear weapons is itself an unlawful threat to use force. Possession of nuclear weapons may indeed justify an inference of preparedness to use them. In order to be effective, the policy of deterrence, by which those States possessing or under the umbrella of nuclear weapons seek to discourage military aggression by demonstrating that it will serve no purposes, necessitates that *an intention to use nuclear weapons be credible.*[137]

Assessing the credibility of such an intention can, of course, only be made on a case-by-case basis. In this respect, where a state threatens to use the nuclear weapons it possesses, yet does so in circumstances where it is manifestly clear that it does not intend to carry out the threat, this cannot be seen, upon the jurisprudence of the ICJ, as a threat to use force. Similarly, if a state manifestly lacks the capability to follow through on a threat to resort to nuclear weapons, meaning that the threat is not a credible one, then it is also not one that would appear to be in violation of the prohibition. As an example of such a credible intention, North Korea has threatened South Korea and the United States with indiscriminate nuclear strikes in response to their joint military exercises off the Korean peninsula.[138] While such threats have not been uncommon, in 2017 a series of nuclear and long-range ballistic missile tests were carried out by North Korea at the same time as it made specific threats to target the US territory of Guam in response to provocative remarks made by US President Donald Trump on Twitter.[139] Such threats must be seen as falling within the prohibition of threats of force, given the specificity of the threats made combined with a demonstrated capability to carry them out.

---

[135] *Nuclear Weapons*, advisory opinion, n. 100, at para. 66.  [136] Ibid., at para. 47.
[137] Ibid., at para. 48 (emphasis added).
[138] BBC News, 'North Korea Threatens US and S Korea with Nuclear Strikes', 7 March 2016, available at: www.bbc.co.uk/news/world-asia-35741936.
[139] Will Worley, 'North Korea Threatens Guam with "Salvo of Missiles" if Donald Trump Keeps Up Provocations', *The Independent*, 14 October 2017, available at: www.independent.co.uk/news/world/asia/north-korea-guam-missiles-threat-donald-trump-twitter-a8000276.html.

### 1.4.5 Uses of Force versus Threats of Force: Normative Relativity?

Although Article 2(4) makes no distinction between the *threat* of force and the *use* of force in terms of their significance and importance,[140] it would appear that states demonstrate a higher degree of tolerance towards threats than they do to actual uses of force, and the UN very rarely expresses any condemnation of the former. On the contrary, while the threats of force made in the lead-up to the intervention in Kosovo by NATO in 1999 were arguably unlawful given that the intervening states were not acting in self-defence and there was no prospect of an authorisation to use forcible measures by the UN Security Council,[141] this assessment is clouded to a degree by the comment of the former UN Secretary-General, Kofi Annan, that '[y]ou can do a lot with diplomacy, but with diplomacy backed up by force you can get a lot more done'.[142] In addition, in contrast to the use of force, the threat of force has received far less commentary by international law scholars,[143] and threats are excluded from the recitation of Article 2(4) contained within the Rome Statute of the International Criminal Court in defining the crime of aggression.[144] The reason for this might simply be due to the fact that threats are less destructive than actual uses of force. Alternatively, they may seemingly be more overlooked because when they escalate to an actual use of force there is little need to appraise the preceding threat, and, where they do not so escalate, instead of addressing the threat the international community instead simply feels a collective sense of relief.[145]

## 1.5 ACCOUNTABILITY, STATE RESPONSIBILITY AND RESPONSES TO A THREAT OR USE OF FORCE

Article 1 of the International Law Commission's Draft Articles on Responsibility of States for Internationally Wrongful Acts (2001) (DARSIWA)

---

[140] While the prohibition of the use of force, or perhaps, at least, force of a particularly aggressive nature, is seen by many to be a *jus cogens* norm, the threat of force has not been seen in the same light.

[141] See Section 4.5.1.2.

[142] See Press Release SG/SM/6470, 24 February 1998, available at: https://press.un.org/en/1998/19980224.SGSM6470.html.

[143] Stürchler, n. 56; Sadurska, n. 102; Marco Roscini, 'Threats of Armed Force and Contemporary International Law' (2007) 54 *Netherlands International Law Review* 229; Francis Grimal, *Threats of Force: International Law and Strategy* (Routledge, 2013); Nicholas Tsagouras, 'The Prohibition of Threats of Force', in Nigel D. White and Christian Henderson (eds.), *Research Handbook on International Conflict and Security Law*: Jus ad Bellum, Jus in Bello *and* Jus post Bellum (Edward Elgar, 2013), 67.

[144] Article 8*bis*, para. 2, Rome Statute of the International Criminal Court (1998).

[145] Nigel D. White and Robert Cryer, 'Unilateral Enforcement of Resolution 687: A Threat Too Far?' (1999) 29 *California Western International Law Journal* 243, at 246.

states: 'Every internationally wrongful act of a State entails the international responsibility of that State.'[146] Where a violation of the prohibition of the threat or use of force occurs, the victim state will be able to establish the *prima facie* commission of an internationally wrongful act.[147] It is also notable that, under the DARSIWA, 'States shall cooperate to bring to an end through lawful means' a breach of a *jus cogens* norm,[148] and that '[n]o State shall recognize as lawful a situation ... nor render aid or assistance in maintaining [a] situation' created by a breach of such a norm.[149] This general principle lay behind the collective non-recognition of the Turkish Republic of Northern Cyprus which was declared following the 1974 Turkish invasion of Cyprus,[150] the UN General Assembly '[c]*all*[ing] *upon* all States to desist and refrain from ... any attempts to modify Ukraine's borders through the threat or use of force or other unlawful means' following Russia's forcible annexation of the province of Crimea from Ukraine in 2014,[151] and then the Assembly denouncing in unequivocal terms the 2022 Russian recognition of the Donetsk and Luhansk regions 'as a violation of the territorial integrity and sovereignty of Ukraine and [as] inconsistent with the principles of the Charter'.[152]

Although the law of state responsibility will not be engaged with in any detail here,[153] it is important to be clear on whether, and if so how, responsibility may be invoked in the context of the use of force, a notoriously thorny area of international law. Indeed, while '[t]he characterization of an act of a State as internationally wrongful is governed by international law',[154] the law in this area, while agreed upon in principle, can be difficult to apply in practice, and determining whether 'a breach of an international obligation' has taken place is often open to disagreement.[155] One need only recall the debates over the legality of the use of force against Iraq in 2003 to see that, while some states argued that this was a lawful use of force authorised by the UN Security Council, others interpreted it as a clear-cut act of aggression.[156] In addition, states have not put in place measures of accountability and responsibility in the same way as they have in respect to certain other areas

---

[146] Annexed to UNGA Res. 56/83 (2001).
[147] Such a violation would also constitute an unlawful intervention. See Section 2.2 for more on the principle of non-intervention.
[148] Article 41(1), DARSIWA.   [149] Article 41(2), ibid.   [150] UNSC Res. 541 (1983), para. 7.
[151] UNGA Res. 68/262 (2014), para. 2. The non-acquisition of territory by force was made unlawful in 1945 in the UN Charter, although its roots go back even further to the Stimson Doctrine, which was formulated by the United States in response to Japan's annexation of Manchuria in 1931.
[152] UNGA Res. ES-11/1 (2022), para. 5.
[153] See James Crawford, *The International Law Commission's Articles on State Responsibility: Introduction, Text and Commentaries* (Cambridge University Press, 2002); James Crawford, *State Responsibility: The General Part* (Cambridge University Press, 2014).
[154] Article 3, DARSIWA.   [155] Article 2(b), ibid.   [156] See, further, Section 4.3.

of international life. There is not, for example, a court of arbitration which exists to settle a dispute, or a permanent court of law with the compulsory jurisdiction to hear cases between states. As such, invoking responsibility and gaining accountability for a state that has engaged in an unlawful use of force is fraught with both political and legal difficulties.

### 1.5.1 Reparations

If a violation of the prohibition of the use of force is discernible this will confer upon the victim state the legal right to claim both the cessation of the unlawful act and assurances of non-repetition.[157] Furthermore, the aggressor state may be liable for reparations in the form of restitution, compensation, satisfaction or a combination thereof.[158] Indeed, '[t]he responsible state is under an obligation to make full reparation for the injury caused by the internationally wrongful act'.[159] While full restitution may not be realistically possible, given the death and destruction that is often a result of the use of force, satisfaction, which may take the form of 'an acknowledgement of the breach, an expression of regret, a formal apology, or another appropriate modality',[160] may not be seen to be sufficient. However, after Turkey shot down a Russian fighter jet that was operating on its border with Syria on 24 November 2015 it was reported that, in addition to taking other non-forcible countermeasures against Turkey, Russian President Vladimir Putin was waiting for an apology from his Turkish counterpart, Recep Tayyip Erdogan, before agreeing to speak to him.[161]

In practice, monetary compensation is often the preferred and most practical form of reparation for the losses suffered by a state that finds itself the victim of an unlawful use of force.[162] The Treaty of Versailles (1919), adopted in the wake of the First World War, is a formative example here, in that Germany accepted responsibility 'for causing all the loss and damage to which the Allied and Associated Governments and their nationals have been subjected as a consequence of the war imposed upon them by the aggression of Germany and her allies'.[163] Arguably one of the most important, and certainly most extensive, examples of reparation arising from an unlawful use of force

---

[157] Article 30, DARSIWA.  [158] Article 31, ibid.
[159] Article 31(1), ibid. See also *Case Concerning the Factory at Chorzów (Claim for Indemnity) (Germany v. Poland)*, Merits (A/17, 1928), 1 WCR 646, at 664.
[160] Article 37(2), DARSIWA.
[161] BBC News, 'Turkey's Downing of Russian Warplane – What We Know', 1 December 2015, available at: www.bbc.co.uk/news/world-middle-east-34912581.
[162] This is not to be confused with any liability of a state, whether aggressor or victim, to pay compensation for breaches of the *jus in bello*, as found in Article 3 of Hague Convention (IV) (1907) and Article 91 of Additional Protocol I to the Geneva Conventions (1977).
[163] Article 231, Versailles Treaty of Peace with Germany (1919).

followed Iraq's invasion and occupation of Kuwait in 1990.[164] In Resolution 674 (1990) the UN Security Council stated that 'under international law [Iraq] is liable for any loss, damage or injury arising in regard to Kuwait and third States, and their nationals and corporations, as a result of the invasion and illegal occupation of Kuwait by Iraq'.[165] Subsequently, as part of the 'formal ceasefire' contained in Resolution 687 (1991) following the eviction of Iraq from Kuwait, the Council decided to establish a Compensation Fund out of Iraqi oil reserves to pay compensation[166] and, in Resolution 692 (1991), the Compensation Fund and a Compensation Commission were established.[167] A further, although much more limited, example can be found in the Eritrea–Ethiopia Claims Commission. After finding that Eritrea's actions against Ethiopia had violated Article 2(4) of the UN Charter,[168] the Commission made an award in its 2007 Decision regarding *jus ad bellum* liability.[169]

### 1.5.2 Countermeasures

Countermeasures are acts taken 'in order to induce [another] State to comply with its obligations',[170] but which are 'not in conformity with an international obligation' owed towards that other state.[171] However, the wrongfulness of a countermeasure that is taken in response to a prior internationally wrongful act may be precluded provided that certain conditions are satisfied.[172] In particular, acts taken as a form of countermeasure must be proportionate or, in other words, 'must be commensurate with the injury suffered, taking into account the gravity of the internationally wrongful act and the rights in question'.[173] In addition, before taking countermeasures the injured state should call upon the responsible state to fulfil its obligations,[174] including by specifying 'the conduct that the responsible state should take in order to cease the wrongful act, if it is continuing'[175] and 'what form reparation should take',[176] as well as notifying the responsible state of any decision to take countermeasures and offering to negotiate with that state.[177] They must also 'be terminated as soon as the responsible State has complied with its obligations ... in relation to the internationally wrongful act'.[178] The decision to take countermeasures will most likely be taken

---

[164] See, further, Section 3.4.2.1.    [165] UNSC Res. 674 (1990), para. 8.
[166] UNSC Res. 687 (1991), para. 18.    [167] UNSC Res. 692 (1991), paras. 2 and 3.
[168] Eritrea–Ethiopia Claims Commission – Partial Award: *Jus ad Bellum* – Ethiopia's Claims 1–8, 19 December 2005, at paras. 10–20, available at: http://legal.un.org/riaa/cases/vol_XXVI/457-469.pdf.
[169] Eritrea–Ethiopia Claims Commission – Preliminary Decisions, *Guidance Regarding 'Jus ad Bellum' Liability*, 27 July 2007, available at: http://legal.un.org/riaa/cases/vol_XXVI/1-22.pdf.
[170] Article 49(1), DARSIWA.    [171] Article 22, ibid.    [172] Ibid.    [173] Article 51, ibid.
[174] Article 52(1)(a), ibid.    [175] Article 43(2)(a), ibid.    [176] Article 43(2)(b), ibid.
[177] Article 52(1)(b), ibid.    [178] Article 53, ibid.

in response to ongoing breaches of international law and can take the form of sanctions. For example, following its military intervention in Ukraine and the subsequent annexation of Crimea in early 2014, several governments, led by the United States, imposed sanctions against Russian individuals, businesses and officials,[179] with the Russian government responding in kind, in particular by imposing a total ban on food imports from several countries.[180] Following Russia's invasion of Ukraine in February 2022, the United States, the EU and other countries significantly expanded existing sanctions in addition to introducing new ones, in particular to include Vladimir Putin, other government members, and those of the Russian business and political elite, cutting off selected Russian banks from the SWIFT network, targeting the Russian energy sector, imposing restrictions on trade and transport, and the suspension of the operation of some major international companies located within Russian territory.[181]

However, Article 50(1)(a) of the DARISWA is clear that '[c]ountermeasures shall not affect ... the obligation to refrain from the threat or use of force as embodied in the Charter of the United Nations',[182] while Article 26 states that '[n]othing in this chapter precludes the wrongfulness of any act of a State which is not in conformity with an obligation arising under a peremptory norm of general international law'. Consequently, despite some doubt by members of the ICJ that will be discussed in Chapter 6,[183] 'the possibility of relying on grounds precluding wrongfulness is in principle excluded in relation to the actual use of force'.[184]

### 1.5.3 Self-Defence

It is not to be implied from anything that has been said thus far in this section that forcible measures are not permitted *in toto* as a response to a prior use of

---

[179] See, for example, US Executive Orders 13660, 13661, 13662, 13685.
[180] Jennifer Rankin, 'Russia Responds to Sanctions by Banning Western Food Imports', *The Guardian*, 7 August 2014, available at: www.theguardian.com/world/2014/aug/07/russia-retaliates-western-sanctions-ban-food-imports.
[181] See Elena Chachko and J. Benton Heath, 'A Watershed Moment for Sanctions? Russia, Ukraine, and the Economic Battlefield' (2022) **116** *AJIL Unbound* 135.
[182] Article 50(1)(a), DARSIWA. Article 50(1)(d), ibid., also states that '[c]ountermeasures shall not affect ... other obligations under peremptory norms of general international law'. Mention should also be made here of Article 2(3) of the UN Charter (1945), which contains an obligation to settle disputes through peaceful means.
[183] See Section 6.2.5.3.
[184] Tom Ruys, 'The Meaning of "Force" and the Boundaries of the *Jus ad Bellum*: Are "Minimal" Uses of Force Excluded from UN Charter Article 2(4)?' (2014) **108** *American Journal of International Law* 159, at 162. See also Award in the Arbitration Regarding the Delimitation of the Maritime Boundary between Guyana and Suriname, award of 17 September 2007, at para. 446, available at: http://legal.un.org/riaa/cases/vol_XXX/1-144.pdf ('It is a well established principle of international law that countermeasures may not involve the use of force').

force under the regime of state responsibility. Article 21 of DARISWA states that '[t]he wrongfulness of an act of a State is precluded if the act constitutes a *lawful measure* of self-defence taken *in conformity with the Charter of the United Nations*' (emphasis added). In this sense, and as will be expanded upon much further in Chapters 6–8 of this book, a state may take measures of both individual and collective self-defence under Article 51 of the Charter and customary international law. However, the prior forcible intervention would need to have the characteristics of an 'armed attack',[185] with the forcible measures taken in response in self-defence satisfying the dual customary requirements of necessity and proportionality.[186]

### 1.5.4 Institutional Involvement: The United Nations and Regional Organisations

In all cases the victim state may report the forcible measures it has been the victim of to either a regional organisation of which it is a member or to the UN Security Council, or potentially have them discussed within the UN General Assembly. In particular, the Council is often used as a forum to hear and discuss such allegations, as was the case following the invasion of Iraq by the United States and United Kingdom in 2003[187] and Russia's invasion of Ukraine in February 2022,[188] and can then issue either a presidential statement or a resolution that sets out its position on the situation, with possible demands being made upon particular actors. For example, following an attack by Israel upon the Iraqi Osiraq nuclear installation in June 1981, and after having received a letter of complaint from Iraq, the Council, in recalling Article 2(4) of the UN Charter, '[s]*trongly condemn*[ed] the military attack by Israel in clear violation of the Charter of the United Nations and the norms of international conduct'.[189] The Council may then resort to its powers in regard to the pacific settlement of disputes under Chapter VI of the UN Charter or, if it declares the existence of a threat to the peace or the occurrence of a breach of the peace or act of aggression, resort to enforcement powers under Chapter VII.[190] Measures under Chapter VII may be either of a non-forcible nature, such as a demand for a ceasefire, sanctions or another measure in an attempt to end the dispute, or may involve enforcement action of a forcible nature, such as when it authorised a US-led coalition of states to evict Iraq from

---

[185] For more on this concept, see Section 6.2.
[186] For more on the twin concepts of necessity and proportionality, see Section 6.3.
[187] At the meetings on 26–27 March 2003 over seventy states spoke. See UN Docs. S/PV.4726, 26 March 2003 and S/PV.4726 (Resumption 1), 27 March 2003.
[188] See UN Doc. S/PV. 8980, 27 February 2022. At this meeting the UN Security Council adopted a resolution (UNSC Res. 2623 (2022)) referring the situation to the UN General Assembly.
[189] UNSC Res. 487 (1981), para. 1.   [190] See Part II.

Kuwait in 1990.[191] In either case, action would require the members of the UN Security Council to agree upon the necessity, breadth and scope of such measures, something which, as discussed in Part II, is far from straightforward or free from controversy.

### 1.5.5 Courts and Tribunals

#### 1.5.5.1 *The Actions of States*

There is no permanent international court with compulsory universal jurisdiction to hear disputes arising involving the prohibition of the threat or use of force. Nonetheless, while the docket of the ICJ has not been inundated with requests from states to provide a judicial determination in the case of a use of force by one state against another, the Court has addressed issues of the use of force in four contentious cases[192] and in two advisory opinions.[193] One should be mindful of the fact that the decisions of the Court are not binding except upon the states before it in contentious cases.[194] Yet, the fact that certain issues have been judicially determined by the Court means that they are provided with a particular weight of authority and the jurisprudence from both the contentious cases and the advisory opinions of the Court have undoubtedly contributed to our understanding of, and debates regarding, the various rules and principles of international law concerning the use of force.[195]

The contentious cases, in particular, also provide a means by which to examine the responsibility of one state for a use of force against another, and each member of the UN 'undertakes to comply with the decision of the International Court of Justice in any case to which it is a party'.[196] It is also notable that '[i]f any party to a case fails to perform the obligations incumbent upon it under a judgment rendered by the Court, the other party may have recourse to the Security Council, which may, if it deems necessary, make recommendations or decide upon measures to be taken to give effect to the judgment'.[197]

---

[191] UNSC Res. 678 (1990), para. 2.
[192] See *Corfu Channel* case, n. 71; *Nicaragua* case, n. 1; *Case Concerning Oil Platforms (Islamic Republic of Iran v. United States of America)*, Judgment, (2003) ICJ Reports 161; *Armed Activities on the Territory of the Congo (Democratic Republic of the Congo v. Uganda)*, Judgment, (2005) ICJ Reports 168.
[193] *Nuclear Weapons*, advisory opinion, n. 100; *Legal Consequences of the Construction of a Wall in the Occupied Palestinian Territory*, Advisory Opinion (2004) ICJ Reports 135.
[194] Article 59, Statute of the International Court of Justice (1945).
[195] See Christine Gray, 'The ICJ and the Use of Force', in Christian Tams and James Sloan (eds.), *The Development of International Law by the International Court of Justice* (Oxford University Press, 2013), 237. See, further, the section on 'Subsidiary Means for Determining (and Shaping?) the Law' in the Introduction.
[196] Article 94(1), UN Charter (1945).
[197] Article 94(2), ibid. See Attila Tanzi, 'Problems of Enforcement of Decisions of the International Court of Justice and the Law of the United Nations' (1995) 6 *European Journal of International Law* 539.

The *Nicaragua* case is the most famous of the Court's decisions regarding the use of force.[198] In this case Nicaragua accused the United States of supporting the military and paramilitary actions of the 'contra' forces, who were opposed to the Sandinista regime in Nicaragua, which had toppled the previous government of Anastasio Somoza which, in turn, had been favourable to the United States. This support, Nicaragua claimed, amounted to a sustained use of force on the part of the United States. In addition, Nicaragua claimed that the United States had used force directly against it in the form of the mining of ports and aerial incursions into Nicaraguan territory. However, while the Court found the United States to be, inter alia, 'in breach of its obligation under customary international law not to use force' against Nicaragua, thus incurring a responsibility to make appropriate reparations, not only were no reparations forthcoming but the United States went on to withdraw its general acceptance of the Court's jurisdiction. The Court asserted that the United States was 'under an obligation to make reparation' to Nicaragua,[199] and also decided that 'the form and amount of such reparation, failing agreement between the Parties, w[ould] be settled by the Court, and reserve[d] for this purpose the subsequent procedure in the case'.[200] Yet, in 1991, Nicaragua renounced its right of action, leading the Court to discontinue its proceedings.[201]

Issues of the use of force between states have been examined in other judicial arenas, for example the Eritrea–Ethiopia Claims Commission as well as, on occasion, in domestic courts,[202] although, while it would not affect a state's liability to make reparations, a state would be entitled to jurisdictional immunity for its actions before the domestic courts of other states.[203]

### 1.5.5.2 *The Actions of Individuals: The Crime of Aggression*

Although the prohibition of the use of force in Article 2(4) and customary international law applies to the acts of states, the individuals involved in making the decision to resort to the unlawful use of force may be guilty of the 'crime of aggression'. As far back as 1924, in the Preamble to the Geneva Protocol on the Pacific Settlement of International Disputes, it was recognised that 'a war of aggression constitutes ... an international crime'.[204] Following the Second World War aggressive war was criminalised in the 1945 Charter of

---

[198] *Nicaragua* case, n. 1.   [199] Ibid., at para. 292.   [200] Ibid.
[201] *Case Concerning Military and Paramilitary Activities in and against Nicaragua (Nicaragua v. United States)*, Order (1991) ICJ Reports 47, at 48.
[202] See, for example, *R v. Jones (Appellant)* [2006] UKHL 16; *R (on the Application of Gentle and Another) v. Prime Minister and Others* [2008] UKHL 20.
[203] See, for example, *Jurisdictional Immunities of the State (Germany v. Italy: Greece Intervening)*, Judgment, (2012) ICJ Reports 99.
[204] Preamble, Geneva Protocol on the Pacific Settlement of International Disputes (1924).

the International Military Tribunal, which laid the foundations of the Nuremberg trial of the major German war criminals and which provided the Tribunal with jurisdiction over 'crimes against peace'.[205] However, to avoid accusations of *ex post facto* criminalisation of the acts of the defendants the Tribunal drew upon in its judgment the renunciation of war as an instrument of national policy contained in the Kellogg–Briand Pact of 1928, although it also conceded that the Pact had not expressly proclaimed aggressive war to be a crime.[206] Indeed, attempts by the Tribunal to establish the existence of a crime from a proscribed state activity is not entirely convincing as there are many state acts that are not crimes. However, the Tribunal argued that a 'war of aggression' was different given its enormous and far reaching consequences. Indeed, on this basis it 'is not only an international crime' but 'the supreme international crime'.[207] Despite the Tribunal's efforts it is, however, doubtful whether aggression existed as a crime within customary international law at the time of the Nuremberg trials.[208]

Nonetheless, 'the criminality of aggressive war has entrenched itself since Nuremberg as an impregnable concept of international law'.[209] For example, in the 1970 Friendly Relations Declaration the UN General Assembly proclaimed that 'war of aggression constitutes a crime against peace, for which there is responsibility under international law'.[210] Furthermore, as early as 1947 the General Assembly instructed the International Law Commission to commence work on a Draft Code of Offences against the Peace and Security of Mankind.[211] Despite the fact that work on the Draft Code stuttered owing to a lack of agreement on the definition of aggression, it was revived following the adoption by the General Assembly in 1974 of the Definition of Aggression.[212] Although it was intended that the 1974 Definition would provide guidance to the Security Council in determining when an act of aggression had occurred for the purposes of Article 39 of the UN Charter, it nonetheless again reiterated that a 'war of aggression is a crime against international peace'.[213] Work on the Draft Code was finally completed in 1996, and notably stated that: 'An individual who, as leader or organizer, actively participates in or orders the planning, preparation, initiation or waging of aggression committed by a State

---

[205] Article 6(a), Charter of the International Military Tribunal, Annexed to the London Agreement for the Establishment of an International Military Tribunal (1945). This was reiterated in Article 5(a) of the Charter of the International Military Tribunal for the Far East (1946) which was designed for the trial of the major Japanese war criminals.
[206] *Nuremberg* judgment (International Military Tribunal, 1946), 1 *IMT* 171, at 219–20. See, further, Section 1.2 for more on the Kellogg–Briand Pact.
[207] Ibid., at 186.    [208] Dinstein, n. 37, at para. 367.    [209] Ibid.    [210] See n. 51.
[211] UNGA Res. 177 (II) (1947).    [212] See n. 52.
[213] Article 5(2), Definition of Aggression (1974).

shall be responsible for a crime of aggression.'[214] The momentum behind the interest that had developed through the decades in aggression as a crime was arguably driven by the powerful statement of the Nuremberg Tribunal that: 'Crimes against international law are committed by men, not be abstract entities, and only by punishing individuals who commit such crimes can the provisions of international law be enforced.'[215] In line with this statement it is only if the *individuals* who make the decision to resort to the use of military force are held individually accountable will the obligation upon *states* to refrain from military aggression be of any practical significance and have any real impact in restraining decision-makers.

This premise was arguably the subsequent driving force behind the inclusion of the crime of aggression within the Rome Statute of the International Criminal Court in 1998, two years after the International Law Commission had produced its Draft Code. However, while aggression was included as one of the four crimes in the Rome Statute, the Court did not have jurisdiction over it due, again, to a lack of agreement on a definition amongst the state parties.[216]

#### 1.5.5.2.1 An Agreed Definition for the International Criminal Court

In what was seen as a major achievement, in 2010 the Assembly of the State Parties of the International Criminal Court agreed on a definition of the crime of aggression at a review conference in Kampala, although the Court still did not have jurisdiction over the crime, which was only activated on 17 July 2018 after the amendments to the Rome Statute had received thirty ratifications.[217] The crime, as now set out in Article *8bis* of the Rome Statute, is defined as:

the planning, preparation, initiation or execution, by a person in a position effectively to exercise control over or to direct the political or military action of a State, of an act

---

[214] Article 16, Draft Code of Crimes against the Peace and Security of Mankind, Report of the International Law Commission, 48th Session, [1996] II (2) *ILC Ybk* 17.

[215] *Nuremberg* trial, n. 206, at 223.

[216] This lack of agreement may have raised doubts as to its status as a crime within customary international law. However, in the UK House of Lords in 2006, Lord Bingham, referring back to the Nuremberg tribunal, attempted to respond to such doubts: 'It was suggested, on behalf of the Crown, that the crime of aggression lacked the certainty of definition required of any criminal offence, particularly a crime of this gravity ... [T]he core elements of the crime of aggression have been understood, at least since 1945, with sufficient gravity to permit the lawful trial (and, on conviction, punishment) of those accused of this most serious crime. It is unhistorical to suppose that the elements of the crime were clear in 1945 but have since become in any way obscure.' See *R* v. *Jones and Others (Appellant)* [2007] AC 136, at 157–8.

[217] For discussion on the complicated path for the Court to finally have jurisdiction, see Claus Kreß, 'On the Activation of ICC Jurisdiction over the Crime of Aggression' (2018) **16** *Journal of International Criminal Justice* 1.

of aggression which, by its character, gravity and scale, constitutes a manifest violation of the Charter of the United Nations.[218]

What is clear is that an essential element of the *crime* of aggression is the existence of a *state act* of aggression, and the Rome Statute draws heavily upon the Definition of Aggression and the UN Charter in establishing the scope of the *actus reus* of the crime. In providing a definition for the purposes of the Rome Statute, Article *8bis* continues that an '"act of aggression" means the use of armed force by a State against the sovereignty, territorial integrity or political independence of another State, or in any other manner inconsistent with the Charter of the United Nations'. While excluding 'threats of force' from the definition, it otherwise closely traces the wording of the prohibition of force in Article 2(4) of the UN Charter and the definition of aggression provided in the 1974 Definition of Aggression. There are other noticeable links between the definition of the crime of aggression contained in the Rome Statute and the state act of aggression, in that paragraphs (a)–(g) of Article 3 of the Definition of Aggression, which provides a non-exhaustive list of acts which qualify as acts of aggression, are replicated in the second paragraph of Article *8bis* of the Rome Statute.[219] In addition, neither the state act or the crime represent simple violations of Article 2(4), but instead constitute a violation of a particular scale and gravity.[220] However, Article *8bis* goes further by explicitly requiring that the act of aggression concerned must, 'by its character, gravity and scale, constitute[] a manifest violation of the Charter of the United Nations'.[221]

### 1.5.5.2.2 The Crime of Aggression as a 'Manifest Violation' of the Charter of the United Nations

There is both a quantitative and qualitative dimension to the requirement for a 'manifest' violation of the Charter. The quantitative dimension is located in the fact that such a violation is found in the particularly serious 'gravity and scale' of the use of force. It is unclear, however, how the Court might deal with certain uses

---

[218] Article *8bis*, para. 1, Rome Statute of the International Criminal Court (1998). For the drafting history of the crime of aggression, see Stefan Barriga and Claus Kreß (eds.), *The Travaux Préparatoires of the Crime of Aggression* (Cambridge University Press, 2012).

[219] It has been suggested that this implied that the Kampala review conference believed that these provisions of the Definition of Aggression were declaratory of customary international law. See Dinstein, n. 37, at para. 395.

[220] The preamble to both the Definition of Aggression and Understanding Six adopted at the Kampala review conference provide that 'aggression is the most serious and dangerous form of the illegal use of force'.

[221] Article *8bis*, para. 1, Rome Statute, n. 218. One may wonder whether these criteria are cumulative or disjunctive in nature. However, Understanding 7 is clear that 'in establishing whether an act of aggression constitutes a manifest violation of the Charter of the United Nations, the three components of character, gravity and scale must be sufficient to justify a "manifest" determination. No one component can be significant enough to satisfy the manifest standard by itself.'

## 1.5 Accountability, State Responsibility and Responses

of force that are seen as of lesser scale and effects, such as cyber-attacks, targeted killings of individuals, small-scale counter-terrorist operations, frontier incidents between states, and even what might be described as 'bloodless invasions'.[222]

The qualitative dimension – that the manifest violation is found in the 'character' of the use of force – has been said to 'exclude[] those instances of use of force from the State conduct element of the definition, the legality of which forms the object of genuine disagreement between reasonable international lawyers'.[223] Such 'grey areas' might include, for example, the use of force in self-defence in anticipation of an 'imminent' attack,[224] the use of force in response to attacks by non-state actors which are located in the territory of a state that is 'unable or unwilling' to take the necessary against to prevent further attacks[225] and forcible interventions in the territory of a state for humanitarian purposes.[226]

Whether humanitarian interventions were to be covered by the crime of aggression was said to in particular be 'lurking in the background of the negotiations'[227] and has given rise to much academic interest since.[228] For example, while the ICC's jurisdiction over the crime may indeed deter potential acts of military aggression, there were also concerns raised that it could also have a 'chilling effect' in deterring genuine humanitarian interventions.[229] In this respect, some scholars argued for an exception to the Court's jurisdiction for *bone fide* unilateral humanitarian interventions,[230] while others raised the possibility for an 'opt out' from the Court's jurisdiction in regards to humanitarian interventions under Article 15bis(4) of the Rome Statute.[231]

---

[222] For example, the latter of these might be seen to have occurred in the Russian intervention in Crimea in 2014.

[223] Claus Kreß, 'Aggression', in Robin Geiß and Nils Melzer (eds.), *The Oxford Handbook of the International Law of Global Security* (Oxford University Press, 2021), 232, at 250. See also Carrie McDougall, *The Crime of Aggression under the Rome Statute of the International Criminal Court* (Cambridge University Press, 2013), at 125.

[224] See Chapter 7 for a discussion on the use of force in 'anticipatory' self-defence in such circumstances.

[225] See Chapter 8 for a discussion on the use of force in self-defence in such circumstances under the so-called 'unable or unwilling' doctrine.

[226] See Chapter 10 for a discussion on the doctrine of humanitarian intervention.

[227] Kreß, n. 223, at 250.

[228] See, for example, Jennifer Trahan, 'Defining the "Grey Area" Where Humanitarian Intervention May Not Be Fully Legal, But Is Not the Crime of Aggression' (2015) 2 *Journal on the Use of Force and International Law* 42.

[229] See Michael Reisman, 'Reflections on the Judicialization of the Crime of Aggression' (2014) 39 *Yale Journal of International Law* 66, at 73.

[230] See, for example, Elise Leclerc-Gagne and Michael Byers, 'A Question of Intent: The Crime of Aggression and Unilateral Humanitarian Intervention' (2009) 41 *Case Western Reserve Journal of International Law* 391.

[231] Leslie Esbrook, 'Exempting Humanitarian Intervention from the ICC's Definition of the Crime of Aggression: Ten Procedural Options for 2017' (2015) 53 *Virginia Journal of International Law* 791.

By slight contrast, the United States put forward a draft 'understanding' at the Kampala conference for an exception to jurisdiction in the context of forcible action taken to prevent the commission of the other crimes contained within the Rome Statute, that is, in the case of the commissions of war crimes, crimes against humanity or genocide.[232]

While none of these proposals were ultimately accepted, Understanding 6, regarding the amendments to the Rome Statute on the crime of aggression, stresses that the crime covers only 'the most serious and dangerous form of the illegal use of force' and that a finding of aggression requires consideration 'of all the circumstances of each particular case, including the gravity of the acts concerned and their consequences'.[233] It is, at this stage, difficult to predict whether the ICC would pursue a prosecution for a forcible act that had the consequence of ending genocide or the commission of widespread crimes against humanity in another state and the Kampala amendments suggest that the Court 'has been given very little guidance as to where to draw the line in the sand' in this respect.[234] However, it is safe to conclude that a decision to pursue a prosecution would, at the very least, subject international criminal law 'to a most delicate tension'.[235]

### 1.5.5.2.3 The *Mens Rea* Element of the Crime of Aggression

As with all international crimes, there is a *mens rea* element to the crime of aggression, in that 'the material elements are committed with intent or knowledge'.[236] In other words, it must be established that a person specifically intended to engage in the conduct or bring about the particular consequences, although there is no need for it to be done so with a specifically aggressive intent or purpose. However, it is also clear that '[n]o consideration of whatever nature, whether political, economic, military or otherwise, may serve as a justification for aggression',[237] so in the context of humanitarian interventions, for example, as long it can be demonstrated that an individual intended to use force in the territory of another state the fact that it was done so with the intention of saving lives would be irrelevant. That being said, '[a] mistake of fact shall be a ground for excluding criminal responsibility' but 'only if it negates the mental element required by the crime'.[238] In this respect, if it could be established that the individuals who ordered the military action concerned mistakenly believed that the conduct that was being engaged in was an act of self-defence against an armed attack then this mistake regarding the factual

---

[232] See McDougall, n. 223, at 120.
[233] See RC/Res. 6, 11 June 2010, Annex III, 'Understandings Regarding the Amendments to the Rome Statute of the International Criminal Court on the Crime of Aggression'.
[234] McDougall, n. 223, at 132.   [235] Kreß, n. 223, at 250.
[236] Article 30, Rome Statute, n. 218.   [237] Article 5(1), Definition of Aggression, n. 96.
[238] Article 32(1), Rome Statute, n. 218.

circumstances may be used to exonerate them from individual criminal responsibility. Furthermore, depending on how the Court views cases of what would appear to be genuine humanitarian interventions, a mistake of fact might be relevant in situations in which a decision is taken to launch a military intervention where those taking the decision did so under the genuine but ultimately erroneous belief that a grave humanitarian situation was imminent or unfolding.

However, '[a] mistake of law as to whether a particular type of conduct is a crime within the jurisdiction of the Court shall not be a ground for excluding criminal responsibility' unless, that is, 'it negates the mental element required by such a crime'.[239] Indeed, the Elements of Crime stress that there is 'no requirement to prove that the perpetrator has made a legal evaluation as to whether the use of armed force was inconsistent with the [UN Charter]' or as to whether the action constitutes a manifest violation of it.[240] Nonetheless, while establishing a defence of mistake of law would be difficult, it is arguably not needed 'because the "manifest violation" threshold already excludes cases of *bona fide* legal uncertainty about which a state leader could reasonably be mistaken'.[241]

### 1.5.5.2.4 The Potential Impact of the Jurisdiction of the International Criminal Court over the Crime of Aggression

Although the inclusion of the crime of aggression in the Rome Statute in 1998, its definition in 2010 and the subsequent activation of the ICC's jurisdiction over it in 2018 together 'undoubtedly constitute[] a noteworthy change in the landscape of international criminal justice, its practical significance is yet to be seen',[242] and there is a sense that it may come to represent more 'an act of symbolic international "legislation"'.[243] There are, for example, several impediments to the Court hearing a case of aggression, some of which are specific to the crime of aggression itself and others which are more general within the ICC regime.

To begin with, and unlike the other crimes over which the ICC has jurisdiction, the crime of aggression is restricted *ratione personae* to 'person[s] in a position effectively to exercise control over or to direct the political or military action of a State'.[244] In addition, the '[p]rosecutor's prosecutorial policy is to

---

[239] Article 32(2), ibid.
[240] Kampala Amendments, Annex II: Amendments to the Elements of Crime, paras. 2, 4.
[241] Frances Anggadi, Greg French and James Potter, 'Negotiating the Elements of the Crime of Aggression', in Barriga and Kreß, n. 218, 58 at 73.
[242] Kreß, n. 223, at 253.
[243] Andreas Zimmermann, 'A Victory for International Rule of Law? Or: All's Well that Ends Well? The 2007 ASP Decision to Amend the Kampala Amendment on the Crime of Aggression' (2018) 16 *Journal of International Criminal Justice* 19, at 28.
[244] Article 8*bis*, Rome Statute, n. 218.

focus on those who, having regard to the evidence gathered, bear the greatest responsibility for the crimes'.[245] This of course restricts the crime to senior political and military leaders, and any immunity such individuals might normally possess under customary international law is removed under the ICC regime.[246] Furthermore, and in addition to the specific gravity element of the crime discussed in Section 1.5.5.2.2, a case may be inadmissible if 'not of sufficient gravity to justify further action by the Court'[247] or, alternatively, there are 'substantial reasons to believe that an investigation would not serve the interests of justice'.[248] There is also, in any case, the need for Pre-Trial Chamber authorisation before the prosecutor is able to proceed with an investigation *proprio motu*.[249]

A fundamental aspect of the ICC regime is that it is 'complementary to national criminal jurisdictions'.[250] In other words, the ICC will not have jurisdiction if '[t]he case is being investigated or prosecuted by a State which has jurisdiction over it, unless the State is unwilling or unable genuinely to carry out the investigation or prosecution'.[251] In theory, therefore, unless a state refuses to prosecute, there are attempts to shield an individual from prosecution, or it is simply unable to prosecute, the ICC will not have jurisdiction. A further impediment, albeit a relatively uncontroversial one, can be found in the fact that the Court's jurisdiction is limited *ratione temporis* in that '[t]he Court has jurisdiction only with respect to crimes committed after the entry into force of this Statute'[252] and, in addition, '[n]o person shall be criminally responsible under this Statute for conduct prior to the entry into force of the Statute'.[253]

There are also particular idiosyncrasies associated with the crime of aggression in contrast with the other crimes contained within the Rome Statute regarding the means by which the Court may come to have jurisdiction. Indeed, while the Court may exercise jurisdiction in respect to a crime that has been referred to it by a state party, where the Prosecutor has initiated an investigation *proprio motu* or, in the case of the UN Security Council, having referred a situation to the Prosecutor,[254] the crime of aggression has a specific regime in respect to state referrals and investigations *proprio motu*, with the ultimate result being the limitation of possibilities for the Court to exercise jurisdiction. In particular, the Court may only exercise jurisdiction over a state party that has accepted jurisdiction and also then not subsequently opted

---

[245] Understanding the International Criminal Court, available at: www.icc-cpi.int/iccdocs/pids/publications/uicceng.pdf.
[246] Article 27, Rome Statute, n. 218.   [247] Article 17(1)(d), ibid.   [248] Article 53(1)(c), ibid.
[249] Article 15, ibid.   [250] Preamble and Article 1, ibid.   [251] Article 17(1)(a), ibid.
[252] Article 11(1), ibid.   [253] Article 24(1), ibid.   [254] See Article 13, ibid.

out.[255] Furthermore, and in contrast to the other crimes within the Rome Statute, the Court cannot exercise jurisdiction over the crime of aggression unless the perpetrator is a party to the Rome Statute *and* it takes place upon the territory of a state party.[256] Finally, before proceeding with an investigation in respect to the crime of aggression the Prosecutor must first check to see if the UN Security Council has determined that an act of aggression has taken place.[257] If the Council has made such a determination the Prosecutor can proceed with the investigation.[258] However, if no determination is made by the Council within six months the Prosecutor may proceed with an investigation provided that the Council has not decided otherwise.[259]

A more general reason perhaps for a lack of enthusiasm in respect to the ICC now having jurisdiction over the crime of aggression is that the Court has, in any case, been mostly concerned with non-international armed conflicts in which the crime of aggression has not been an issue. Furthermore, the crime is limited to the actions of a few states that have accepted the amendments to the Rome Statute. A sizeable proportion of states – including the United States, Israel, Russia, North Korea, and China, for example – are not even a party to the ICC statute. In this respect, it is unlikely that many states, including those with a record of foreign interventions, will accept the ICC's jurisdiction over the crime of aggression, although it is noticeable that Belgium, Spain, Poland and the Netherlands have all accepted the jurisdiction of the ICC for the crime of aggression, with all having been involved in controversial uses of force in recent years, in particular the NATO intervention in Kosovo and the intervention in Iraq in 2003.[260]

These impediments to the ICC having a case of aggression before it has, however, rather than dampening efforts to hold individuals accountable for the crime of aggression, led to some creative initiatives. In particular, it was not long following Russia's full-scale invasion of Ukraine in 2022 that proposals were made for the establishment of an ad hoc special tribunal for the punishment of the crime of aggression against Ukraine to try senior Russian and Belarusian leaders.[261] The proposal, while receiving

---

[255] Article 15bis(4), ibid., states that '[t]he Court may … exercise jurisdiction over a crime of aggression, arising from an act of aggression committed by a State Party, unless that State Party has previously declared that it does not accept such jurisdiction by lodging a declaration with the Registrar.'

[256] Article 15bis(5), ibid. [257] Article 15bis(6), ibid. [258] Article 15bis(7), ibid.

[259] Article 15bis(8), ibid. Although '[a] determination of an act of aggression by an organ outside the Court shall be without prejudice to the Court's own findings under this Statute.' Article 15bis(9), ibid.

[260] Tom Ruys, 'Criminalizing Aggression: How the Future of the Law on the Use of Force Rests in the Hands of the ICC' (2018) 29 *European Journal of International Law* 887, at 891.

[261] See 'Combined Statement and Declaration Calling for the Creation of a Special Tribunal for the Punishment of the Crime of Aggression Against Ukraine', 4 March 2022, available at: https://gordonandsarahbrown.com/wp-content/uploads/2022/03/Combined-Statement-and-Declaration.pdf.

criticism,[262] has nonetheless attracted notable support, including the Council of Europe,[263] the European Commission,[264] the NATO Parliamentary Assembly,[265] the European Parliament,[266] as well as support within the academic and practitioner communities.[267]

Some have speculated over the true extent to which the ICC's jurisdiction over this crime will impact upon the law governing the use of force.[268] It is, at this stage, too early to be able to say with any certainty. However, determinations by the Prosecutor as to whether to proceed with a prosecution, and in particular whether certain actions by a state constitute a 'manifest' violation of the UN Charter, may pave the way for a clarification on the breadth and scope of the prohibition of the use of force and the exceptions to it.[269] Indeed, these determinations may have the effect of leading to a broadening or narrowing of the rules governing force. In addition, while the leaders of many states will remain safe from prosecution, the investigation and findings of the Court in respect to the actions of a leader of a state party which was involved in a collective military action involving several states will arguably have ramifications for perceptions regarding the legality of the operation as a whole, with the unintended consequence of an implicit determination of the legality of the actions of *all* states involved, whether or not they have consented to the Court's jurisdiction over the crime of aggression.

---

[262] See, for example, Kevin Jon Heller, 'Creating a Special Tribunal for Aggression against Ukraine Is a Bad Idea', *Opinio Juris*, 7 March 2022, available at: https://opiniojuris.org/2022/03/07/creating-a-special-tribunal-for-aggression-against-ukraine-is-a-bad-idea/.

[263] Council of Europe, 'PACE Calls for an Ad hoc Criminal Tribunal to Hold Account Perpetrators of the Crime of Aggression against Ukraine', 28 April 2022, available at: www.coe.int/en/web/portal/-/pace-calls-for-an-ad-hoc-international-criminal-tribunal-to-investigate-war-crimes-in-ukraine.

[264] European Commission, 'Statement by President von der Leyen on Russian Accountability and the Use of Russian Frozen Assets', 30 November 2022, available at: https://ec.europa.eu/commission/presscorner/detail/en/statement_22_7307.

[265] NATO Parliamentary Assembly, Resolution 479, Article 19(h), available at: www.nato-pa.int/download-file?filename=/sites/default/files/2022-11/RESOLUTION%20479%20-%20%20NATO%20POST%20MADRID%20.pdf.

[266] European Parliament, 'Ukraine War: MEPs Push for Special Tribunal to Punish Russian War Crimes', 19 January 2023, available at: www.europarl.europa.eu/news/en/press-room/20230113IPR66653/ukraine-war-meps-push-for-special-tribunal-to-punish-russian-crimes.

[267] The Combined Statement and Declaration was signed by, amongst others, Professor Dapo Akande, Professor Philippe Sands QC, Sir Nicolas Bratza, Benjamin Ferencz, Richard Goldstone, Baroness Helena Kennedy QC and Professor Helene Ruiz Fabri.

[268] See, for example, ibid.; Tom Ruys, 'The Impact of the Kampala Definition of Aggression on the Law on the Use of Force' (2016) 3 *Journal on the Use of Force and International Law* 187.

[269] Ruys, n. 260, at 917.

## 1.5.6 Commissions of Inquiry

Fact-finding missions or commissions of inquiry (CoIs) may provide a limited form of accountability for both states and individuals following an unlawful use of force.[270] After the *Maine* inquiries of 1898 between the United States and Spain, the Hague Convention I on the Pacific Settlement of International Disputes (1899) attempted to provide some regulation to these bodies of inquiry in settling international disputes, including those involving the use of force. Although the Convention envisaged these inquiries being used for settling disputes of fact and not deciding questions of law, and that their findings were not to be obligatory, 'CoIs have nonetheless generally shifted from pure fact-finding bodies to providing at least some form of legal adjudication, even if not often of a legally binding nature.'[271] Indeed, from as early as the *Dogger Bank* inquiry, which involved a naval dispute between England and Russia in 1904, it became clear that 'legal and factual issues need not always be sharply distinguished'.[272] Furthermore, states began to conclude bilateral treaties which provided for the submission of disputes to an international commission for investigation, such as the Bryan Treaties (1913–14), which also stipulated that the parties to the dispute could not resort to war for a period of twelve months.[273]

Today, CoIs are established in various forms and by various actors, in particular by the UN Human Rights Council, the UN Security Council, regional organisations and individual states. The UN has expressly recognised the benefits of utilising CoIs, with the UN General Assembly adopting a resolution encouraging UN organs to establish them in connection with the international peace and security element of their respective roles and functions.[274] CoIs are also often provided with an express mandate to examine legal issues, most commonly regarding international humanitarian law and international human rights law, but also occasionally issues of the use of force. For example, the European Union's Independent International Fact-Finding Mission on the Conflict in Georgia (2009), which was established to examine the Russian intervention in Georgia in 2008, engaged extensively with the *jus ad bellum* issues of the conflict.[275] The report of the Mission was not legally binding

---

[270] See, in general, Vaios Koutroulis, 'The Prohibition of the Use of Force in Arbitrations and Fact-Finding Reports', in Marc Weller (ed.), *The Oxford Handbook of the Use of Force in International Law* (Oxford University Press, 2015), 605; Christian Henderson (ed.), *Commissions of Inquiry: Problems and Prospects* (Hart, 2017).

[271] Christian Henderson, 'Commissions of Inquiry: Flexible Temporariness or Permanent Predictability?' (2014) 45 *Netherlands Yearbook of International Law* 287, at 290.

[272] John G. Merrills, *International Dispute Settlement*, 5th ed. (Cambridge University Press, 2011), at 44.

[273] See, for example, Treaty between the United States and Austria–Hungary (1914).

[274] See UNGA Res. 46/59 (1991), para. 1.

[275] Report of the Independent International Fact-Finding Mission on the Conflict in Georgia, September 2009, vol. II, 227–95, available at: www.mpil.de/de/pub/publikationen/archiv/

upon either party to the conflict, but exists as the most formal treatment of the legal issues in connection with this particular conflict. Similarly, individual states have established commissions of inquiry that have been expressly mandated to examine the legal basis for a particular intervention, such as the report of the Netherlands government into its involvement in the Iraq war of 2003.[276] Alternatively, CoIs, while not expressly mandated to address legal issues, have produced reports that have nonetheless implicitly provided a judgment on the legal basis of an intervention. For example, the Iraq Inquiry, established by the UK government to investigate the United Kingdom's involvement in Iraq in 2001-9,[277] provided findings that enabled conclusions to be drawn as to the legality of the conflict, even if it did not expressly draw these itself.[278]

## 1.6 THE EMERGING RECOGNITION OF A HUMAN ELEMENT TO THE PROHIBITION OF INTER-STATE FORCE

There has been for some time an interest in – and an acknowledgement of – the relationship between international human rights law (IHRL) and international humanitarian law (IHL), in that, while some claim that during times of armed conflict IHL displaces IHRL as the *lex specialis*,[279] others see the two regimes operating in parallel alongside each other,[280] something that Schabas has described as the 'belt and suspenders' approach.[281] There has, furthermore, been a notable interest in the relationship between IHL and the law governing the use of inter-state force.[282] This interest has not primarily been driven by

---

independent_international_fact.cfm. See Christian Henderson and James A. Green, 'The *Jus ad Bellum* and Entities Short of Statehood in the Report on the Conflict in Georgia' (2010) 59 *International & Comparative Law Quarterly* 129.

[276] See BBC News, 'Dutch Inquiry Says Iraq War Had No Mandate', 12 January 2010, available at: http://news.bbc.co.uk/1/hi/world/europe/8453305.stm.

[277] The Report of the Iraq Inquiry, July 2016, available at: www.iraqinquiry.org.uk/the-report/.

[278] Christian Henderson, 'Reading between the Lines: The Iraq Inquiry, Doctrinal Debates, and the Legality of Military Action against Iraq in 2003' (2017) **87** *British Yearbook of International Law* 105.

[279] See *Legality of the Threat or Use of Nuclear Weapons*, Advisory Opinion, (1996) ICJ Reports 226, at para. 25.

[280] See UN Human Rights Committee, General Comment No. 29: States of Emergency (article 4), UN Doc. CCPR/C/21/Rev.1/Add.11 (24 July 2001), at para. 3.

[281] See William A. Schabas, '*Lex Specialis*? Belt and Suspenders? The Parallel Operation of Human Rights Law and the Law of Armed Conflict, and the Conundrum of *Jus ad Bellum*' (2007) **40** *Israel Law Review* 592.

[282] Notable contributions in this respect are Christopher Greenwood, 'The Relationship between *Jus ad Bellum and Jus in Bello*' (1983) 9 *Review of International Studies* 221; Keiichiro Okimoto, *The Distinction and Relationship between* Jus ad Bellum *and* Jus in Bello (Hart, 2011).

the question as to whether the use of inter-state force regime has a 'human element', as such, but rather by the relationship and interplay between these two legal regimes governing armed conflict.

There has, however, been to date far less attention given to the relationship between the use of inter-state force and IHRL and whether consideration of the legal issues in one have a role to play in assessments made in the other.[283] There are arguably several reasons for the lack of attention in regard to the relationship between the *jus ad bellum* and IHRL. For example, while IHRL and IHL are both very much concerned with the protection of individuals and groups, decisions to resort to inter-state force are seen more as being at the high-end of political decision-making concerning states as collectives and, therefore, somewhat removed from the impact on individuals and their right to life. Furthermore, states might be seen as 'enjoy[ing] rights to resort to war in situations much wider than those that would permit violence in regular, ordinary life, and in complex circumstances that cannot be judged under the supposedly rigid framework of IHRL'.[284] Related to this, and on the basis of the separation of powers doctrine and the often discretionary nature of the power to deploy armed forces abroad, domestic courts have also traditionally been deferential to governments in regard to decisions to resort to war and deploy armed forces abroad.[285]

Ultimately, the two branches of international law may be seen to operate in entirely different 'environments' so that 'armed conflict is a reality of human existence that international human rights law is simply unsuited to address in a comprehensive manner'.[286] At the same time, however, viewing the *jus ad bellum* as having a human element would seem 'to correspond with the revisionist approach that all state action, including quintessential "acts of state" such as resort (or non-resort) to war, should be subject to the same ethical framework that applies in other contexts'.[287]

---

[283] However, see Frédéric Mégret, 'What Is the Specific Evil of Aggression?', in Claus Kreß and Stefan Barriga (eds.), *The Crime of Aggression: A Commentary* (Cambridge University Press, 2016), 1398, at 1445; Erin Pobjie, 'Victims of the Crime of Aggression', ibid., 816, at 825; Eliav Lieblich, 'The Humanization of *Jus ad Bellum*: Prospects and Perils' (2021) 32 *European Journal on International Law* 579; Schabas, n. 281, at 607–12. Schabas has noted that both the *lex specialis* approach and the 'belt and suspenders' approach to the relationship between IHRL and IHL 'overlook a fundamental difference in conception between the two systems, namely the attitude they take to aggressive war'. Indeed, while IHL is, for good reason, indifferent to the origins and causes of the conflict, human rights law, on the other hand, 'has suggestions within it, albeit hesitant and underdeveloped, that aggressive war is itself a violation. Put otherwise, there is a human right to peace.' Schabas, ibid., at 593.

[284] Lieblich, ibid., at 584.

[285] See, for example, *R* v. *Jones (Appellant)* [2006] UKHL 16, at paras. 65–7. However, this is not a consideration that is of relevance to international courts and tribunals or commissions of inquiries in their treatment of inter-state uses of force.

[286] Schabas, n. 281, at 611.   [287] Lieblich, n. 283, at 581.

## 1.6.1 The UN Human Rights Committee, the Right to Life and the *Jus ad Bellum*

Article 6(1) of the International Covenant on Civil and Political Rights (ICCPR) provides that '[e]very human being has the inherent right to life' and that '[n]o one shall be arbitrarily deprived of his life'. The right to life is, therefore, not absolute, with focus being placed on the question of when it can be said to be 'arbitrary' to deprive an individual their life. In a general sense, '*non*-arbitrary killings are only those that can be justified as necessary and proportionate acts of self or other-defense against an imminent threat to life'.[288]

In 2018 the Human Rights Committee, which is the treaty body of the ICCPR, published General Comment 36 (GC 36).[289] While general comments of the Human Rights Committee are not binding per se, they are highly regarded and GC 36 could be seen as something of a landmark moment in the relationship between the right to life and the *jus ad bellum* as, in paragraph 70, it was stated that:

> States parties engaged in acts of aggression as defined in international law, resulting in deprivation of life, violate ipso facto article 6 of the Covenant. At the same time, all States are reminded of their responsibility as members of the international community to protect lives and to oppose widespread or systematic attacks on the right to life, including acts of aggression ..., while respecting all of their obligations under international law. States parties that fail to take all reasonable measures to settle their international disputes by peaceful means might fall short of complying with their positive obligation to ensure the right to life.

This paragraph was said to have three 'pillars',[290] the first being that states have a negative duty under the right to life to refrain from acts of aggression that result in the loss of life.[291] The second pillar provides that states have, as part of their duty to respect the right to life, a positive responsibility to 'oppose' acts aggression which constitute a 'widespread or systematic' attack on the right to life.[292] The final pillar provides that states that fail to settle their disputes peacefully – either through acts or omissions – 'may' fall foul of their positive duty to protect the right to life.[293] While the position of the Human

---

[288] Ibid.
[289] UN Human Rights Committee, General Comment No. 36 (2018) on Article 6 of the International Covenant on Civil and Political Rights, on the Right to Life, UN Doc. CCPR/C/GC/36 (30 October 2018).
[290] Lieblich, n. 283, at 581.
[291] See Section 2.5.1.2 for further discussion on the state act of aggression.
[292] This responsibility should be read in conjunction with GC 36's position that 'States parties must take appropriate measures to protect individuals against deprivation of life by other States.' GC 36, n. 289, at para. 22.
[293] This obligation should be read in light of Article 2(3) of the UN Charter which provides that '[a]ll Members shall settle their international disputes by peaceful means in such a manner that international peace and security, and justice, are not endangered.'

## 1.6 A Human Element to the Prohibition of Inter-State Force

Rights Committee is, in itself, arguably a positive development, there were some notable objections raised to the publication of GC 36. In addition, there are some implications that emerge from viewing the relationship between aggression and the right to life in these ways.

### 1.6.1.1 Objections to the Approach of the UN Human Rights Committee

In regard to the objections that were raised to the approach taken by the Human Rights Committee in GC 36, the United States, in particular, was of the view that human rights obligations simply do not apply extraterritorially.[294] While there has been some academic and judicial support for this view,[295] there have also been notable objections to it within the academic community,[296] and it would appear that the judicial tide has begun to turn against it.[297] In addition, and drawing upon the *lex specialis* approach in the debate regarding the relationship between IHRL and IHL, arguments were made that the *jus ad bellum* is the *lex specialis* in the context of the use of inter-state force.[298] However, and as pointed out by Lieblich, 'there are no convincing reasons to conclude that the prohibition on the use of force, as enshrined in

---

[294] Human Rights Committee, Observations of the United States of America on the Human Rights Committee's Draft General Comment No. 36 on Article 6 – Right to Life, 6 October 2017, at para. 20, available at: www.ohchr.org/Documents/HRBodies/CCPR/GCArticle6/UnitedStatesofAmerica.docx.

[295] See, for example, European Court of Human Rights, *Bankovic v. Belgium*, Appl. no. 52207/99, Decision as to the Admissibility of 12 December 2001, at paras. 67–82. In the *Bankovic* case the Court ruled that aerial bombing does not trigger the jurisdiction of the attacking state over potential victims as during such operations the attacking state does not acquire effective control over the territory in which the victims are located.

[296] See, for example and in general, Marko Milanovic, *Extraterritorial Application of Human Rights Treaties: Law, Principles and Policy* (Oxford University Press, 2011).

[297] See, for example, *Legal Consequences of the Construction of a Wall in the Occupied Palestinian Territory*, Advisory Opinion (2004) ICJ Reports 136, at paras. 102–12; European Court of Human Rights, *Al-Skeini v. UK*, Appl. no. 55721/07, Judgment of 7 July 2011, at paras. 1–3, 9–10, 12, 19, 21, 72, 95, 101, 114, 125, 130–9, 143–50. Although there has been some recent judicial hesitation. See European Court of Human Rights, *Georgia v. Russia (II)*, Appl. no. 38263/08, Judgment of 21 January 2021, at para. 137. See Marko Milanovic, 'Georgia v. Russia No. 2: The European Court's Resurrection of Bankovic in the Contexts of Chaos', *EJIL: Talk!*, 25 January 2021, available at: www.ejiltalk.org/georgia-v-russia-no-2-the-european-courts-resurrection-of-bankovic-in-the-contexts-of-chaos/.

[298] See Observations of the United States of America, n. 294, at para. 20; Human Rights Committee, Draft General Comment No. 36 on Article 6 of the International Covenant on Civil and Political Rights – Right to Life: Comments by the Government of Canada, 23 October 2017, at para. 22, available at: www.ohchr.org/Documents/HRBodies/CCPR/GCArticle6/Canada.docx; Human Rights Committee, Submission of the Australian Government Draft General Comment No. 36 on Article 6 of the International Covenant on Civil and Political Rights: Right to life (2017), at para. 7, available at: www.ohchr.org/Documents/HRBodies/CCPR/GCArticle6/Australia.docx.

Article 2(4) of the UN Charter, excludes – as the *lex specialis* – the application of IHRL to resorts to inter-state force'.[299] Finally, the argument was made that the determination that an act of aggression has occurred is a matter for the UN Security Council and not human rights bodies.[300] Yet, while the Security Council does indeed have a role to play in determining that an act of aggression has occurred,[301] there is nothing to prevent other bodies from making such determinations and, in particular, if it is related to an issue within their particular remit, as would appear to be the case in the context of the Human Rights Committee and the right to life.

### 1.6.1.2 Implications of Providing the Jus ad Bellum with a Human Element

Arguably the primary motive of the Committee in adopting GC 36 was to prevent, or remedy, a situation of 'rightslessness'.[302] Indeed, one of

> the key reasons for not discarding offhand the possible humanization of *jus ad bellum*, is that in its absence, international law can be said to produce the rightslessness of those harmed 'lawfully' in an unlawful war: their deaths might be wrongful, but they are neither recognized as such nor provided with a remedy.[303]

In other words, although the deaths of individuals during a use of inter-state force may be lawful under IHL, and by implication IHRL, this loses sight of the fact that the initiation of the forcible measure was in the first place unlawful. In terms of the provision of remedies in such situations, various categories of victims might be recognised. Of course, the direct victims of aggression may acquire standing to demand individual reparations from other states before human rights bodies. Yet, viewing acts of aggression through the prism of GC 36 may also provide the possibility for individuals to make claims against their *own* state following situations where they have either suffered harm as a result of having been taken to war unnecessarily or because the state has refrained from using force to protect them from acts of aggression, as per paragraph 70.[304]

---

[299] Lieblich, n. 283, at 582.
[300] See Observations of the United States of America, n. 294, at para. 20.
[301] This is in the context of opening up the enforcement mechanism of the Council contained within Chapter VII of the UN Charter (see Section 3.3.1). However, the Council now also has a role to play in determining whether prosecutions for the crime of aggression can proceed at the International Criminal Court (see Section 2.5.5.2).
[302] Lieblich, n. 283, at 586.    [303] Ibid.
[304] Indeed, as Dannenbaum has argued, the primary concern of the crime of aggression is the harm inflicted on individuals, rather than the harms inflicted on states and on state sovereignty. This is, Dannenbaum argues, something which is rooted in the internal logic of the law. Tom Dannenbaum, *The Crime of Aggression, Humanity and the Soldier* (Cambridge University Press, 2018), at 79–93. Furthermore, it is argued that soldiers that are harmed

Connected with this, there are possible institutional implications of the approach taken in GC 36 of both a procedural and substantive nature. In particular, international human rights courts might gain jurisdiction over the decisions of states to resort to the use of inter-state force,[305] and treaty bodies may place a requirement upon states to provide reports of their behaviour in this respect. Finally, commissions of inquiry and procedures such as the UN's Special Rapporteurs might well be mandated to address such questions involving the *jus ad bellum* and indeed have already done so.[306]

However, there are further possible implications of the approach of the Human Rights Committee. For example, paragraph 64 of GC 36 states that '[u]se of lethal force consistent with international humanitarian law and other applicable international law norms is, in general, not arbitrary', a proposition in line with the conventional wisdom of both the *lex specialis* and 'belt and suspenders' approaches discussed earlier in this section. However, under the approach on aggression as set out in Paragraph 70 of GC 36, attacks that are lawful under IHL may still constitute an arbitrary deprivation of the right to life. Indeed, 'one key implication of this approach is the recognition that casualties of attacks that might be lawful under IHL – such as soldiers and civilians caught as "proportionate" collateral damage – may nevertheless be victims of wrongful killings, if they are killed in pursuit of an unjust cause.'[307] The reference in Paragraph 64 to the use of lethal force also having to be consistent with 'other applicable international law norms' would, in any case, include the *jus ad bellum*, thereby providing a qualification to the conventional understanding to the relationship between IHL and IHRL.

A further impact of GC 36 may be that states are seen as having a *positive obligation* to resort to the use of force to protect potential victims of

---

during an aggressive war should be recognised as victims in proceedings before the International Criminal Court. Ibid., at 312–39.

[305] For example, see the concurring opinion of Judge Keller in the recent *Georgia v. Russia (II)* ruling of the European Court of Human Rights, in which GC 36 is cited in making the observation that the Court might be called upon to engage with the *jus ad bellum* in future cases in interpreting and applying the European Convention of Human Rights. *Georgia v. Russia (II)*, n. 297, at paras. 26–31 (concurring opinion of Judge Keller).

[306] As an example of this, the former UN Special Rapporteur on extrajudicial, summary or arbitrary executions, Agnes Callamard, applied GC 36 to the targeted killing of Iranian General Qassem Soleimani. See United Nations Human Rights Council, Report of the Special Rapporteur on Extrajudicial, Summary or Arbitrary Executions, UN Doc. A/HRC/44/38 (2020), Annex., at para. 81.

[307] Lieblich, n. 283, at 600. As Schabas points out, 'if the *lex specialis* approach is followed, once the threshold is crossed from peacetime to a situation of armed conflict, a human rights court examining a complaint based upon allegations of deprivation of the right to life should no longer concern itself with the "legitimate aim" of the state ... This is where the attempts to marry international human rights law and international humanitarian law break down. International human rights law is not indifferent to and does not look favourably upon unjust war.' Schabas, n. 281, at 697.

aggression. The decision as to whether a state resorts to force in self-defence has traditionally been perceived as one that is left to the discretion of the state concerned, with no positive obligation to do so. Indeed, there may be various reasons why a state chooses to refrain from invoking the right, for example due to it lacking the capabilities to do so or due to other considerations of a political or economic nature that tilt the balance against invoking the right. If instead states are seen as having a positive obligation to resort to force to oppose acts of aggression then the approach of GC 36 may in fact have the result of increasing the resort to force within the international community. States may also seize upon what might be seen as the 'securitisation' of human rights in GC 36 as an opportunity to legitimise the use of force, portraying it as a moral and legal necessity to take action. Ultimately, infusing the *jus ad bellum* with a human element may further enable – rather than limit – the legitimation of force.[308]

While 'these concerns require refraining from a celebratory tone when discussing the prospects of the humanization of *jus ad bellum*'[309] it may ultimately not, in any case, have that much of a practical impact. For example, GC 36 refers to 'aggression' specifically and not to unlawful resorts to force more generally. Given the lack of precise clarity over what constitutes an act of aggression, as well as the wariness which states have shown in reaching a definition,[310] there may well be a hesitation in categorising acts as aggression for the purposes of applying GC 36. In addition, the gap between acts of aggression and other unlawful uses of force means that there will be violations of the prohibition of the use of force that do not engage the right to life. In addition, while elements of GC 36 would 'seem to establish that at least in some cases, opposing aggression, as well as threats by non-state actors, might require states to resort to inter-state force', it remains the case that 'like all positive measures, states must only take such measures insofar as they "do not impose on them disproportionate burdens"',[311] meaning that there does not exist an absolute duty to act. Ultimately, each of the pillars of GC 36 is framed 'in a manner that reserves space for significant state discretion'.[312]

## 1.7 QUESTIONING THE CONTINUED RELEVANCE, SCOPE AND EFFECTIVENESS OF THE PROHIBITION

### 1.7.1 State Practice and the Claimed 'Death' of the Prohibition of Force

Despite the widely (although not universally) held view that the prohibition of the threat or use of force is of peremptory status,[313] it has been argued by some

---

[308] Lieblich, ibid. [309] Ibid. [310] See Sections 2.5.1.2 and 3.3.1.2.
[311] Lieblich, n. 283, at 603. See also GC 36, n. 289, at para. 21. [312] Ibid.
[313] See Section 1.3.2.

## 1.7 Continued Relevance, Scope and Effectiveness

scholars that, due to the numerous violations of it that have occurred since 1945, it can be pronounced 'dead'. This argument was first made by Thomas Franck in 1970,[314] but the argument that the norm has fallen into desuetude has since been made, perhaps most vociferously, by Michael Glennon.[315]

It is true that there have been many notable incidences of states ostensibly acting in violation of the norm. Cold War examples can be found in the Soviet Union's interventions in Hungary (1956), Czechoslovakia (1968) and Afghanistan (1979) and the United States' interventions in Grenada (1982) and Panama (1989). In fact, 'for the first 44 years of the United Nations, Member States often violated [the Charter] rules and used military force literally hundreds of times'.[316] More recently, NATO intervened, for example, in Kosovo in 1999, a US-led coalition invaded Iraq in 2003 and Russia intervened in Ukraine and annexed the Crimean peninsula in 2014 followed by a full-scale invasion of Ukraine in 2022, all of which were preceded by a threat to intervene and without a generally accepted legal justification.[317] Taken together, these might seem to suggest that the prohibition of the use of force provides little restraining influence upon the actions of states or that the prohibition may well be claimed to be 'dead' and, with no rule consequently prohibiting force, states are thereby free to do as they wish. It is in this context that the argument has been made that the legal framework governing the use of force should now be formally discarded[318] or at least the prohibition of the threat or use of force should be retained but narrowly interpreted.[319] In both cases, it is argued, the rules would more accurately reflect both what states do and need to do in the contemporary world, both in terms of protecting themselves and furthering 'global welfare'.[320]

Yet, while there have been some notable examples of non-compliance with the prohibition of the threat or use of force, it is not quite as straightforward as

---

[314] Thomas Franck, 'Who Killed Article 2(4)?' (1970) **64** *American Journal of International Law* 809. In response to this claim, see Louis Henkin, 'The Reports of the Death of Article 2(4) Are Greatly Exaggerated' (1971) **65** *American Journal of International Law* 544.

[315] See Michael J. Glennon, 'How International Rules Die' (2005) **93** *Georgetown Law Journal* 939. Thomas Franck also stated that, following the US-led intervention in Iraq in 2003, 'Article 2(4) has died again, and, this time, perhaps for good.' Thomas M. Franck, 'What Happens Now? The United Nations after Iraq' (2003) **97** *American Journal of International Law* 607, at 610.

[316] UN Secretary-General's High-Level Panel on Threats, Challenges and Change, 'A More Secure World: Our Shared Responsibility', UN Doc. A/59/565, 2 December 2004, at para. 186.

[317] See Section 10.3.2.4., Section 4.3, and Section 6.5.2, respectively.

[318] See Michael J. Glennon, 'The Limitations of Traditional Rules and Institutions Relating to the Use of Force', in Marc Weller (ed.), *The Oxford Handbook of the Use of Force in International Law* (Oxford University Press, 2015), 79.

[319] See John Yoo, *Point of Attack: Preventive War, International Law, and Global Welfare* (Oxford University Press, 2014).

[320] On this general point, see ibid. See also, W. Michael Reisman, 'Coercion and Self-Determination' (1984) **78** *American Journal of International Law* 642.

simply concluding that the prohibition has been, or should be, dissolved. Although possibly a trite statement, it is nonetheless true that states more often than not comply with the prohibition. As Louis Henkin famously put it, '[a]lmost all nations observe almost all principles of international law and almost all of their obligations almost all the time',[321] and this holds true for the prohibition of force. Indeed, the period since 1945 has witnessed a significant quantitative and qualitative decline in war and certainly of the inter-state variety that the norm was designed to prevent.

Of course, this cannot be solely attributed to the existence of the norm prohibiting the threat or use of force. It is simply not possible to say that the norm is the sole factor and, as Glennon points out, 'correlation is not causation'.[322] The dramatic decline of war since 1945 'does not demonstrate any causal relationship with the Charter rules'.[323] Actually, '[a] number of factors have been cited to explain the decline of war since 1945, including the nuclear deterrent, democracy, trade, membership of international organizations (including the UN), the vastly greater expense of modern means of warfare, and underlying attitudinal shifts. The decline could be due to some or all of these factors.'[324] Furthermore, '[s]ince states are not unitary entities and we often lack evidence of their internal processes, it can be difficult to determine what ultimately influences their behaviour.'[325] Yet, it is also true that the decline in war 'has been sustained over time and is plainly not a mere statistical aberration. In the circumstances, it is plausible to suggest that it could be at least partly due to a progressively embedded norm of state behaviour, reflected in rules of international law, against the use of force other than for self-defence or collective security.'[326] Indeed, although evidence is not always apparent of the influence of the law on state behaviour, it does on occasion arise. For example, while former US State Department lawyers have written of the influence of international law on decision-making within US government,[327] it also emerged during testimony of the UK Prime Minister's former chief advisor, Dominic Cummings, to a parliamentary committee that the UK government had refused a request by the Trump

---

[321] Louis Henkin, *How Nations Behave* (Columbia University Press, 1979), at 47.
[322] Glennon, n. 318, at 84.
[323] James Crawford and Rowan Nicholson, 'The Continued Relevance of Established Rules and Institutions Relating to the Use of Force', in Marc Weller (ed.), *The Oxford Handbook of the Use of Force in International Law* (Oxford University Press, 2015), 96, at 101.
[324] Ibid., at 102.
[325] Ibid., at 101. See also Christine Gray, *International Law and the Use of Force*, 4th ed. (Oxford University Press, 2018), at 27.
[326] Crawford and Nicholson, n. 323, at 102.
[327] See, e.g., Abram Chayes, *The Cuban Missile Crisis: International Crises and the Role of Law* (Oxford University Press, 1974); Michael P. Scharf and Paul R. Williams, *Shaping Foreign Policy in Times of Crisis: The Role of International Law and the State Department Legal Advisor* (Cambridge University Press, 2010).

administration in the United States to join in a bombing campaign of the group Kataib Hezbollah in Iraq in March 2020 on the basis that it would have been unlawful.[328]

Rigorous and absolute conformity with a rule is not, in any case, required to be able to claim its continued existence. In discussing whether the prohibition of the use of force had been established as a rule of customary international law, the ICJ stated in the *Nicaragua* case that '[i]n order to deduce the existence of customary rules, the Court deems it sufficient that the conduct of States should, *in general*, be consistent with such rules'.[329] Indeed, as the Court also said:

> [i]t is not to be expected that in the practice of States the application of the rules in question should have been perfect, in the sense that States should have refrained, with complete consistency, from the use of force or from intervention in each other's internal affairs. The Court does not consider that, for a rule to be established as customary, the corresponding practice must be in absolutely rigorous conformity with the rule.[330]

While this was discussing the establishment of a rule of customary international law, it is also the case that the continued existence of a rule of law, whether of a treaty or customary nature, does not depend upon complete conformity with it. Such conformity is not required for the continued existence of rules in domestic systems and should not be expected in the international system. Indeed, 'the fact that some individuals commit murder does not prove that domestic laws against it are ineffective. Equally, the fact that some states may unlawfully use force cannot in itself demonstrate the ineffectiveness of the Charter rules.'[331]

It is arguable that one of the key reasons for the perceived trampling upon of the norm since 1945 is that the collective security system that is enshrined within the UN Charter and that was designed to limit the need for states to resort to force unilaterally has simply not operated as intended.[332] Given that the intended purpose of this system was to remove the need for states to resort to force outside of the context of defending themselves against an armed

---

[328] Dan Sabbagh, 'PM Refused Trump's Call to Bomb Iraq after Legal Advice, Cummings Claims', *The Guardian*, 27 May 2021, available at: www.theguardian.com/politics/2021/may/27/pm-refused-trump-call-bomb-iraq-legal-advice-cummings-claims?CMP=Share_iOSApp_Other. Such considerations did not have a similar restraining influence on the United States, however, which carried out the bombing operation, targeting at least five sites around Baghdad linked to Kataib Hezbollah.

[329] *Nicaragua* case, n. 1, at para. 186 (emphasis added). [330] Ibid.

[331] Crawford and Nicholson, n. 323, at 102. In this respect, '[t]he classification as "law" of any system, including international law, does not predetermine its effectiveness or the effectiveness of specific rules: that should be clear from the many ineffective domestic systems that are still treated as "law".' Ibid., at 100.

[332] See, for example, Franck, n. 314, at 810. See further Chapter 3.

attack, the fact that this has not operated as envisaged could be used to raise the doctrine of *rebus sic stantibus* in connection with the prohibition of the use of force as found within the UN Charter.[333] Yet, even if we might be able to claim that for much of its existence the UN Security Council has been dysfunctional and ineffective, it is not possible to claim that '[t]he effect of the change is radically to transform the extent of obligations still to be performed under the treaty'.[334] Not only did the functioning of the Security Council not 'constitute[] an essential basis of the consent of the parties to be bound by the treaty'[335] but there is also no express or implied direct link between the functioning of the collective security system and the general prohibition of the threat or use of force.

It is, in any case, important to note that although a fundamental change of circumstances may theoretically be invoked either as grounds for a state to withdraw from the UN Charter or to terminate the continued existence of the UN Charter in its entirety, no state has indicated its desire for such a course of action. Indeed, regardless as to how one interprets state practice since 1945 and its implications for the rule prohibiting force, one cannot escape the fact that states have generally pledged their allegiance to the prohibition as well as refrained from questioning its relevance or existence, despite occasionally implicitly proffering controversial interpretations of it. This support for the prohibition can be seen in a number of ways, in particular the justifications of states for their actions and the reactions to these by other states, as well as general affirmation of the prohibition in the abstract.

### 1.7.2 Justifications for and Reactions to the Use of Force

States rarely use force without attempting to justify their actions through reference to the established framework and associated terminology governing the use of force. Reflecting this, Louis Henkin commented that, if the norm is dead, 'it rules – not mocks us – from the grave'.[336] The justifications put forward by states for their forcible actions may at times appear to be positioned at the boundaries of plausibility, or the state concerned may offer up a series of justifications either in the hope or expectation that one will find acceptance or, alternatively, taken together the justifications will somehow cross the threshold of acceptability. It might, of course, be argued that these justifications are simply used as a fig leaf for covering up breaches of the prohibition of the use of force or, as Michael Glennon describes them, 'cheap talk'.[337] Yet, it is often difficult – if not, impossible – to know what states are

---

[333] Article 62, Vienna Convention of the Law of Treaties (1969). This doctrine provides for the inapplicability of treaties due to the emergence of a fundamental change in circumstances.
[334] Article 62(1)(b), ibid.    [335] Article 62(1)(a), ibid.    [336] Henkin, n. 314, at 547.
[337] Glennon, n. 318, at 93.

actually thinking, so we have to be guided by what they say and the language and terminology they use in justifying their actions. As Christine Gray points out:

> Simple assertions that this use of language is mere cynical manipulation of the rules, and no more than *ex post facto* rationalization for actions reached on other grounds, are not justified in the absence of empirical evidence that this is in fact the case, and such assertions are no more plausible than the opposite version that states are in fact influenced by the law.[338]

However, the fact that there is a tendency for states to legally justify their actions, regardless as to how plausible they may be, is arguably of significance.[339] As the ICJ noted:

> If a State acts in a way prima facie incompatible with a recognized rule, but defends its conduct by appealing to exceptions or justifications contained within the rule itself, then whether or not the State's conduct is in fact justifiable on that basis, the significance of that attitude is to confirm rather than to weaken the rule.[340]

In this sense, it is not possible simply to equate an apparent 'quantum of violation' with 'the international community as a whole no longer view[ing] the rule as a binding rule of international law'.[341]

Of course, in quantitative terms, this view of the robustness of the prohibition – or indeed any rule of international law – may arguably only extend so far. While 'instances of State conduct inconsistent with a given rule should generally be treated as breaches of that rule, not as indications of the recognition of a new rule',[342] if states widely and regularly resorted to acts of force that were clearly positioned outside of the accepted scope of the exceptions to the prohibition of the use of force, despite offering claims of allegiance to it, then legitimate questions might well be asked as to the restraining effect, or even existence, of any prohibition, or at least its breadth and scope. Indeed, in these circumstances the prohibition might rightly be described as a 'paper' rule,[343] or at the very least have come to be interpreted so broadly as to effectively permit the use of force in a wide range of circumstances. Yet, the burden of proof in claiming that such a threshold has been crossed is onerous and not easily met and, as will be demonstrated in subsequent chapters of this

---

[338] Gray, n. 325, at 30.
[339] As Christine Gray has commented: 'Of course, it is common for states to offer other justifications as well; it is rare for a state to use the language of international law exclusively ... but with only a tiny number of exceptions they take care to offer a legal argument for their use of force.' Gray.
[340] *Nicaragua* case, n. 1, at para. 186.   [341] Glennon, n. 318, at 91.
[342] *Nicaragua* case, n. 1, at para. 186.
[343] Michael Walzer, *Just and Unjust Wars: A Moral Argument with Historical Illustrations*, 4th ed. (Basic Books, 2006), at xxi.

book, has not been met. While states generally refrain from using force, those that do resort to forcible measures normally justify their behaviour upon the basis of accepted exceptions to the prohibition and normally within what might be described as at least plausible – if not always agreeable – interpretations of these exceptions.

Support for the continued existence of the prohibition can also be found in the fact that states often react to, and comment upon, the actions of other states through the utilisation of the language of international law. Despite the fact that this might also be claimed to be cynical manipulation of the law in order to either promote the image of an ally or to cast the actions of another state in a negative light, the use of the law in this way still provides either confirmation of a particular interpretation of the prohibition or a challenge to an interpretation that itself will generate reaction and comment, both by states and the broader interpretive community of international organisations, non-governmental organisations, the media, academics, commentators and the judiciary. While a clear and prevailing interpretation of the precise contours of the prohibition may not always be immediately and clearly discernible, the fact that the law in this area is drawn upon in this way has the effect of at least confirming the existence of the prohibition as a rule.

### 1.7.3 Reaffirmation of the Prohibition in the Abstract

It is also significant that the prohibition of the use of force norm has been continuously reaffirmed in the abstract by states, for example in UN General Assembly resolutions dating back to 1970[344] and more recently in the 2005 World Summit Outcome document,[345] albeit in very general and often vague terms. Although it might be said that obtaining consensus has meant that there has also been ambiguity on some important issues, the existence of the general prohibition as a norm has nonetheless been reaffirmed. Core agreement on the existence of a prohibition of force and a right of self-defence, albeit with the existence of ambiguity, was again exhibited at the UN Security Council on 21 February 2021 during an Arria-formula meeting that had been called to provide states with the opportunity to provide their views on the issue of the use of force in self-defence against the actions of

---

[344] Declaration on Principles of International Law concerning Friendly Relations and Co-operation among States in accordance with the Charter of the United Nations, UNGA Res. 2625 (XXV) (1970); Definition of Aggression, UNGA Res. 3314 (XXIX) (1974); Declaration on the Enhancement of the Effectiveness of the Principle of Refraining from the Threat or Use of Force in International Relations, UNGA Res. 42/22 (1987).

[345] 2005 World Summit outcome, UNGA Res. 60/1 (2005), para. 77.

non-state actors.[346] While there was a spectrum of views exhibited on this issue – from narrow and restrictive to broad and expansive[347] – none of the states present challenged the existence of the prohibition of the threat or use of force or the right of self-defence.

### 1.7.4 Reaffirmation of the Prohibition in the Context of Cyber Operations

Over the last few decades there has been an increasing level of interest in cyber operations and their regulation through international law. Given the lack of any specific treaties in this area,[348] there has been much interest in the question as to whether, and if so how, general international law norms and principles apply in the context of state and state-sponsored operations in cyberspace.

This interest has been taken by states on an individual level and working through the UN, as well as in the academic literature and has been driven by a number of factors. There has, to begin with, been a proliferation in the number and type of cyber operations over the past fifteen years. Although the interest in cyber operations can be dated back earlier,[349] intense global interest began in the aftermath of the 'distributed denial of service' cyber-attacks on Estonia in 2007.[350] These attacks were widely thought to be attributable to the Russian Federation and taken in response to a disagreement over the relocation of a Soviet-era statue within Tallinn. While no physical damage or human injury resulted from the attacks, the disruption caused to Estonian organisations, including banks, newspapers, government bodies, and broadcasters, starkly raised the prospect of the potential for more critical cyber-attacks, as well as the prospect of them having far graver consequences.

This interest has arguably been justified, as in the years that followed cyber-attacks were witnessed during the course of the Russian–Georgian conflict in 2008, an Iranian nuclear enrichment plant was targeted with the Stuxnet worm in 2010, the Sony pictures malware attack took place in 2014, the WannaCry ransomware attacks occurred in 2017, the SolarWinds attack in

---

[346] For the written statements see 'Upholding the Collective Security System of the Charter of the United Nations: The Use of Force in International Law, Non-State Actors and Legitimate Self-Defence', UN Doc. S/2021/247, 16 March 2021, annex II.

[347] See Adil Ahmad Haque, 'The Use of Force against Non-State Actors: All Over the Map' (2021) 8 *Journal on the Use of Force and International Law* 278.

[348] An exception to this is the Council of Europe's Convention on Cybercrime (Budapest Convention) (2001), although this focuses on cybercrime and seeks to harmonise domestic laws, enhance investigation techniques, as well as cross-border cooperation. Whilst the Convention is open to accession by non-member states, neither China, India nor Russia have acceded to it.

[349] See, e.g., Walter G. Sharp, *Cyberspace and the Use of Force* (Aegis Research Corp, 1999).

[350] See, e.g., Samuli Haataja, 'The 2007 Cyber Attacks against Estonia and International Law on the Use of Force: An Informational Approach' (2017) 9 *Law, Innovation and Technology* 159.

2020 penetrated the computer systems of thousands of organisations globally but in particular various parts of the United States government, and the world has witnessed foreign disinformation campaigns during elections in various countries and also during the Brexit referendum in the United Kingdom in 2016. These incidents were accompanied by a fast-paced development in the sophistication and application of 'information and communication technologies', as well as concerns being raised regarding the 'weaponisation' of cyberspace.[351] Indeed, some began to describe cyberspace as the 'fifth domain' of military activities.[352] However, the issue was also of importance due to the clear existence of what might be described as uncontained vulnerability, in that, due to the rapid increase in societal dependence on computer systems, cyber operations were clearly of direct concern to *all* states and organs and institutions of government, in addition to businesses and corporations around the globe, public bodies, and private individuals. Although state practice in the area of cyber-attacks remains relatively limited, these factors have given rise to unprecedented concern and a focus by both states and international lawyers on the categorisation of cyber operations and appropriate (and lawful) responses to them in the context of both cyber-crime but also security issues affecting states, specifically turning their attention in the abstract to the question of whether the rules governing the use of force apply to cyber operations.

In relation to this last question one may reply that international law rules and principles are somewhat 'antiquated' and, therefore, unsuitable to apply to modern developments in the field of information and communication technologies. Indeed, one only has to look outside of the UN General Assembly building in New York to find the 'twisted gun' monument to get a sense of the weaponry and context that the rules of 1945 were intended to apply to. In addition, questions have been asked as to whether the existing frameworks and rules of international law could apply in the cyber 'domain' without first having concrete state practice and *opinio juris* confirming as much.[353] This might be responded to with the argument that there is no cyber 'domain' as

---

[351] Alexander Rossino, 'The Weaponization of Cyberspace', *Deltek*, 2 January 2016, available at: www.deltek.com/en/learn/blogs/b2g-essentials/2016/01/the-weaponization-of-cyberspace.

[352] Larry D. Welch, 'Cyberspace – The Fifth Operational Domain', *Institute for Defense Analyses*, available at: www.ida.org/-/media/feature/publications/2/20/2011-cyberspace–the-fifth-operational-domain/2011-cyberspace–the-fifth-operational-domain.ashx.

[353] Roy Schondorf, 'Israel's perspective on Key Legal and Practical Issues Concerning the Application of International Law to Cyber Operations', *EJIL Talk!*, 9 December 2020, available at: www.ejiltalk.org/israels-perspective-on-key-legal-and-practical-issues-concerning-the-application-of-international-law-to-cyber-operations/.

such, but rather 'cyber space' is in reality simply the connection of computer systems.[354]

The agenda for addressing these issues only really began in the late 1990s when the Russian Federation took the initiative by introducing a draft resolution in the UN General Assembly on '[d]evelopments in the field of information and telecommunications in the context of international security'.[355] No mention was made of international law in this resolution, although states were encouraged to begin the process of 'developing international principles' in response to this issue.[356] Some states, most notably the United States, did not support this resolution at the time, however, on the basis that it believed that existing international law rules and principles could and should apply.

Subsequently in 2003 a Group of Governmental Experts on Advancing Responsible State Behaviour in Cyberspace in the Context of International Security (GGE) was formed under the auspices of the First Committee of the UN General-Assembly.[357] Arguably due to the complexity of the issues involved the GGE failed to adopt a final consensus substantive report. A member of the Russian delegation at the GGE meetings claimed that '[t]he main stumbling block was the question of whether international humanitarian law and international law sufficiently regulate the security aspects of international relations in cases of "hostile" use of information and communication technologies for politicomilitary purposes.'[358]

Nonetheless, the GGE process continued with the establishment of a further five GGEs, which have generated four substantive reports, most recently in 2021.[359] Notable progress was made by the third and fourth GGEs which begun to specifically address international legal issues and the ways in which international law might apply, reaching a level of agreement in their respective reports of 2013 and 2015. Indeed, these reports adopted the view that 'international law, and in particular the United Nations Charter, is applicable

---

[354] Dapo Akande, Antonio Coco and Talita de Souza Dias, 'Old Habits Die Hard: Applying Existing International Law in Cyberspace to and Beyond', *EJIL Talk!*, 5 January 2021, available at: www.ejiltalk.org/old-habits-die-hard-applying-existing-international-law-in-cyberspace-and-beyond/.

[355] UNGA Res 53/70 (1998) (adopted without vote). [356] Ibid., para. 2.

[357] UNGA Res 58/32 (2003), para. 4. The eventual GGE consisted of governmental experts from fifteen States: Belarus, Brazil, China, France, Germany, India, Jordan, Malaysia, Mali, Mexico, the Republic of Korea, Russia, South Africa, the United Kingdom and the United States. They unanimously elected Andrey V. Krutskikh of Russia as its Chairman.

[358] Tim Maurer, 'Cyber Norm Emergence at the United Nations: An Analysis of the Activities of the UN Regarding Cyber-Security' (Belfer Center for Science and International Affairs, Discussion Paper #2011-11 September 2011), at 22, available at: www.belfercenter.org/publication/cyber-norm-emergence-united-nations-analysis-uns-activities-regarding-cyber-security.

[359] UN Doc. A/65/201, 30 July 2010; UN. Doc. A/68/98, 24 June 2013; UN Doc. A/70/174, 22 July 2015; UN Doc. A/76/135, 14 July 2021.

[in cyberspace] and is essential to maintaining peace and stability and promoting an open, secure, peaceful and accessible [information and communications technology] environment'.[360] As well as reaffirming the principles of state sovereignty and sovereign equality,[361] the duty to attempt the peaceful settlement of disputes,[362] the principle of non-intervention,[363] the prohibition of the threat or use of force,[364] respect for human rights, and 'the inherent right of States to take measures consistent with international law and as recognized in the Charter'[365] were also reaffirmed. The GGE adopted the view that states should not allow their territory to be used for hostile cyber operations by non-state actors,[366] as well as insisting that states not 'use proxies to commit international wrongful acts'[367] and emphasising the jurisdiction that states enjoy over cyber infrastructure located on their territory.[368]

What seemed like a forming consensus appeared to rapidly dissipate in the fifth GGE, however, which was unable to adopt a final report in 2017, in particular due to disagreement over the proposed inclusion of the terms 'self-defence' and 'international humanitarian law' and disagreements over the right to take countermeasures. Nonetheless, the sixth GGE in its report of 2021 once again demonstrated a level of agreement between its members, with the above principles again being reaffirmed, in particular the prohibition of the threat or use of force which was singled out for individual treatment.[369]

In addition to the GGE process, the General Assembly established an Open-Ended Working Group on Developments in the field of Information and Telecommunications in the Context of International Security (OEWG) which began its work in 2019.[370] This was an initiative proposed by a number of states, including Russia[371] and, as the name suggests, the Group was open to all UN member states, in contrast to the GGE process which had been restricted to a number of 'experts'. The OEWG produced its report in March 2021,[372] although, while noting the applicability of international law in cyberspace and reaffirming the requirement of states to seek a peaceful settlement of disputes, the international law issues remained relatively untouched. Of importance, however, is that the proceedings of both the OEWG and most recent GGE are

---

[360] UN. Doc. A/68/98, ibid., at para. 19; UN Doc. A/70/174, ibid., at para. 24.
[361] UN Doc. A/70/174, ibid., at para. 26.   [362] Ibid.   [363] Ibid.   [364] Ibid.
[365] Ibid., at para. 28(c).   [366] Ibid., at para. 28(e).   [367] Ibid.   [368] Ibid., at para. 28(a).
[369] UN Doc. A/76/135, n. 359, at paras. 69–73.   [370] UNGA Res. 73/27 (2018).
[371] It has been commented that '[b]y advocating for an OEWG, Russia tried to position itself as an advocate of democratic participation and inclusivity.' Alex Grigsby, 'The United Nations Doubles Its Workload on Cyber Norms, and Not Everyone Is Pleased', *Council on Foreign Relations*, 15 November 2018, available at: www.cfr.org/blog/united-nations-doubles-its-workload-cyber-norms-and-not-everyone-pleased.
[372] UN Doc. A/75/816, 14 July 2021. In 2020, the General Assembly through UNGA Res. 75/240 established a new five-year OEWG on security of and in the use of information and communications technologies. This OEWG will meet regularly until 2025.

based on, and took as their starting point, the report of the 2015 GGE and, therefore, proceeded on the basis that international law, and in particular the UN Charter, as well as the 'norms, rules and principles for the responsible behavior of States' included in the 2015 GGE report were applicable to cyber operations.[373]

However, there remains, by contrast, notable disagreement on *how* international law applies in this context. Indeed, the 2013, 2015 and 2021 reports all noted the need for further study on certain issues. In particular, there remains a good degree of normative ambiguity in regards to the status and applicability of certain norms, terms and concepts of international law, many of which are connected with the *jus ad bellum* and its application.[374] For example, there continues to be some disagreement between states on whether 'sovereignty' constitutes a *principle* upon which other rules and principles – such as that of non-intervention and non-use of force, for example – are based, or whether it constitutes a *rule* in itself which can be violated.[375] Nonetheless, while the United Kingdom stands rather isolated in holding that it is merely a principle,[376] most states have taken the position that it is a rule in and of itself.[377] This is of significance in the cyber context in that many operations will not be coercive for the purposes of the rule against non-intervention but may still be an intrusion into a state's sovereign affairs.[378] In the absence of a rule of sovereignty these would be unchecked by international law.

Notably, and related to the normative position of sovereignty, there is ambiguity on how the principle of non-intervention operates in this context and how *coercive* acts are to be distinguished from those that are merely *influential*.[379] Given the misinformation campaigns that have blighted elections and referendums in recent years this has proved of significance. There is, however, broader disagreement amongst states as to whether 'due diligence' exists as a hard obligation which is violated when states fail to take all reasonable efforts to prevent their territory from being used for offensive

---

[373] UN Doc. A/76/135, n. 359, at para. 2; UN Doc. A/75/816, ibid., at paras. 7–8.

[374] There have also been debates regarding the applicability of important elements of international humanitarian law, for example whether the use of information and communication technologies qualify as 'attacks' for the purposes of IHL and whether data can be seen as a 'civilian object' that attracts specific protections.

[375] Michael Schmitt, The Sixth United Nations GGE and International Law in Cyberspace, *Just Security*, 10 June 2021, available at: www.justsecurity.org/76864/the-sixth-united-nations-gge-and-international-law-in-cyberspace/. See Section 2.2 for more on the principle of non-intervention.

[376] United Kingdom Attorney General Jeremy Wright, 'Cyber and International Law in the 21st Century', 23 May 2018, available at: www.gov.uk/government/speeches/cyber-and-international-law-in-the-21st-century.

[377] Schmitt, n. 375.   [378] See Section 2.2 for more on the principle of non-intervention.

[379] Ibid.

cyber operations, or whether it is rather one of the many voluntary 'non-binding norms' that have been developed in this context of information and communication technology.[380] As in the 2015 report, the 2021 report also noted again 'the inherent right of States to take measures consistent with international law and as recognized in the Charter and the need for continued study on this matter.'[381] While the report, again, refrained from using directly the term 'self-defence', it is arguable that the words employed here provide an implicit reference to it, given that the term 'inherent' right is only found within Article 51 of the UN Charter which provides member states with the right of self-defence.[382]

In addition to the activity at the UN, an endorsement of the general applicability of international law and the *jus ad bellum* to cyber operations has also been made elsewhere. In 2008, NATO established the Cooperative Cyber Defence Centre of Excellence based, aptly, in Tallinn, Estonia.[383] Shortly after its establishment, the Centre drew together an International Group of Experts to explore and assess the international law applicable in cyberspace. In 2013, the Group produced the *Tallinn Manual on the International Law Applicable to Cyber Warfare* which addressed the applicability of the *jus ad bellum* to cyber operations as well as the applicable international humanitarian law.[384]

Furthermore, in 2013, the European Union issued a Cybersecurity Strategy,[385] which was followed up by a report in 2018, which confirmed the applicability of international law to cyberspace, something that was also witnessed in the declarations of the Organization of American States,[386] the Association of Southeast Asian Nations[387] and the Commonwealth Heads of

---

[380] Schmitt, n. 375. The 2015 GGE Report set forth other voluntary, non-binding norms of responsible State behavior that 'aimed at promoting an open, secure, stable, accessible and peaceful [information and communication technologies] environment'. UN Doc. A/70/174, n. 359, para. 13. While there was a distinction made in the report between applicable 'norms, rules and principles' and 'international law', the distinction was not often clear cut, with both primary and secondary rules of international law found within both of the relevant sections of the report.

[381] UN Doc. A/76/135, n. 359, at para. 71(e).    [382] Schmitt, n. 375.

[383] See https://ccdcoe.org/.

[384] *Tallinn Manual*, n. 3. In 2017 a follow up '2.0' manual was produced. See Michael N. Schmitt (ed.), *Tallinn Manual 2.0 on the International Law Applicable to Cyber Warfare* (Cambridge University Press, 2017).

[385] *Cybersecurity Strategy of the European Union: An Open, Safe and Secure Cyberspace*, 7 February 2013, available at: www.europarl.europa.eu/doceo/document/TA-7-2013-0376_EN.html.

[386] The Organization of American States issued a declaration in 2012 on 'Strengthening Cyber-Security in the Americas' and in 2015 on the 'Protection of Critical Infrastructure from Emerging Threats'.

[387] *Asian Leaders' Statement on Cybersecurity Cooperation*, 27 April 2018, available at: https://asean.org/wp-content/uploads/2018/04/ASEAN-Leaders-Statement-on-Cybersecurity-Cooperation.pdf.

## 1.7 Continued Relevance, Scope and Effectiveness

Government.[388] In addition, several states have taken the initiative in issuing individual statements and policy positions on the applicability of international law to cyber operations, indicating the degree to which it is seen as both an issue of importance but also one where further discussion and agreement is needed.[389] However, with very few exceptions, the individual opinions and statements of states have taken a similar position in regards to the applicability of the prohibition of force. For example, Finland 'consider[ed] that public international law creates an essential framework for responsible State behavior in cyberspace',[390] the United States 'continues to be of the view that existing international law applies to State conduct in cyberspace',[391] Estonia has stated that 'existing international law applies in cyberspace',[392] New Zealand is of the opinion that '[t]he United Nations Charter and customary international law rules concerning the use of force apply to state activity in

---

[388] *Commonwealth Cyber Declaration*, 2018, para. 3, available at: https://thecommonwealth.org/commonwealth-cyber-declaration-2018.

[389] See, for example, Ministry for Foreign Affairs, 'Finland Published Its Positions on Public International Law in Cyberspace', 15 October 2020, available at: https://valtioneuvosto.fi/en/-/finland-published-its-positions-on-public-international-law-in-cyberspace; US Department of Defense, 'DOD General Counsel Remarks at U.S. Cyber Command Legal Conference', 2 March 2020, available at: www.defense.gov/Newsroom/Speeches/Speech/Article/2099378/dod-general-counsel-remarks-at-us-cyber-command-legal-conference/; Estonian President Kersti Kaljulaid, 'President of the Republic at the Opening of CyCon 2019', 29 May 2019, available at: https://ceipfiles.s3.amazonaws.com/pdf/CyberNorms/LawStatements/Remarks+by+the+President+of+the+Republic+of+Estonia+at+the+Opening+of+CyCon+2019.pdf; New Zealand Ministry of Foreign Affairs and Trade, 'The Application of International Law to State Activity in Cyberspace', 1 December 2020, available at: www.dpmc.govt.nz/publications/application-international-law-state-activity-cyberspace; Dutch Minister of Foreign Affairs, 'Letter to the Parliament on the International Legal Order in Cyberspace', 5 July 2019, available at: www.government.nl/ministries/ministry-of-foreign-affairs/documents/parliamentary-documents/2019/09/26/letter-to-the-parliament-on-the-international-legal-order-in-cyberspace; The Federal Government of Germany, 'On the Application of International Law to Cyberspace', March 2021, available at: www.auswaertiges-amt.de/blob/2446304/32e7b2498e10b74fb17204c54665bdf0/on-the-application-of-international-law-in-cyberspace-data.pdf; Roy Schondorf, 'Israel's Perspective on Key Legal and Practical Issues Concerning the Application of International Law to Cyber Operations', *EJIL Talk!*, 9 December 2020, available at: www.ejiltalk.org/israels-perspective-on-key-legal-and-practical-issues-concerning-the-application-of-international-law-to-cyber-operations/; République Française, Ministère des Armées, 'Droit International Appliqué aux Operations dans le Cyberspace', 9 September 2019, available at: www.justsecurity.org/wp-content/uploads/2019/09/droit-internat-appliqu%C3%A9-aux-op%C3%A9rations-cyberespace-france.pdf; United Kingdom Attorney General Jeremy Wright, 'Cyber and International Law in the 21st Century', 23 May 2018, available at: www.gov.uk/government/speeches/cyber-and-international-law-in-the-21st-century.

[390] 'Finland Published Its Positions on Public International Law in Cyberspace', ibid.

[391] 'DOD General Counsel Remarks at U.S. Cyber Command Legal Conference', n. 389.

[392] 'President of the Republic at the Opening of CyCon 2019', n. 389.

cyberspace',[393] while the Israeli government is of the view that 'the customary prohibition set out in Article 2(4) of the Charter of the United Nations, on "the threat or use of force" in international relations, is clearly applicable in the cyber domain'.[394]

While a great deal of focus has been placed on the issue by states – both individually and in different fora – the epistemic community has also been heavily involved and has engaged in what has been described as 'scholarly interventionism' in attempting to address problems of cyber operations through existing international legal rules and frameworks, including the prohibition of force.[395] Indeed, in addition to extensive academic treatment of the issue of cyber operations and international law,[396] various groups of experts have formed and produced notable contributions on the issue. As noted, the Group of Experts established by NATO and which produced the *Tallinn Manual* was largely made up of international law scholars, who clearly were of the view that existing frameworks and norms apply,[397] something that individual scholarly contributions have not in general cast doubt on. Indeed, although state practice in the area of cyber-operations is still relatively limited, both states and the epistemic community seem prepared to apply international law, and with that the prohibition of the threat or use of force and the *jus ad bellum* more generally, to such operations, despite some differing positions forming as to how precisely such norms might apply.

## 1.8 CONCLUSION

In this first chapter of this Part of the book we have seen how the contemporary prohibition of the threat or use of force fits within the general landscape of international law. This chapter has set out the broad scope and boundaries of the contemporary prohibition of the threat or use of force in international law, including in general the sorts of response that an unlawful forcible intervention might generate, as well as on occasion addressing in further detail the more specific contours of the norm. Its importance, both within the UN Charter and as a norm of customary international law, has been emphasised and its continued existence and relevance highlighted. Ultimately, 'there is no doubt whatsoever that the prohibition on the use of force remains a binding rule of

---

[393] 'The Application of International Law to State Activity in Cyberspace', n. 389. At paragraph 3 it was stated that '[i]nternational law applies online as it does offline'.
[394] Schondorf, n. 389.
[395] Jean d'Aspremont, 'Cyber Operations and International Law: An Interventionist Legal Thought' (2016) 21 *Journal of Conflict & Security Law* 575.
[396] See, e.g., Marco Roscini, *Cyber Operations and the Use of Force in International Law* (Oxford University Press, 2014).
[397] See *Tallinn Manual*, n. 3.

international law'.[398] Questions arise not so much in regards to the existence of the prohibition but rather in connection with its application and scope and how it applies in particular situations. While these questions will be the focus for subsequent chapters of this book, what can be said here is that '[t]he fact that the outer bounds of concepts such as "threat or use of force" may remain indeterminate is not problematic in itself; the question is whether the rules are *so* indeterminate as to abrogate their effectiveness. The answer is no.'[399] But even if one is left at the end of this book with the belief that the norm *has* either become so indeterminate as to be ineffective or has simply ceased to exist for all intents and purposes, the fact remains that states 'choose to use this language to explain their behaviour and to respond to that of others' so that 'anyone involved in any way in advising states or in assessing their actions will have to be able to engage in this discourse'.[400]

Given that the Charter offers no detail as to the contours of the prohibition of force, other than that there are exceptions to it of self-defence and force employed under the auspices of the UN Security Council, its breadth and scope are affected by the meaning given to 'force', which is the central concern of Chapter 2. Furthermore, mapping out the nature and scope of the exceptions to the prohibition, as well as looking at further possible exceptions to it, will further inform our understanding of the breadth and scope of the prohibition and is the purpose of the remaining chapters of this book.

## QUESTIONS

1 Why was the adoption of the UN Charter in 1945 considered revolutionary?
2 Does the prohibition only exist in the UN Charter? Or does it also exist as a norm of customary international law? How do we know?
3 Who or what are the subjects of the prohibition?
4 In what circumstances does an unlawful threat of force arise? Please give examples.
5 What are the means of redress available to a state that is the subject of an unlawful use of force?
6 To what extent can it be said that the prohibition of the use of force continues to exist today? With many glaring examples of it being violated, is it really possible to defend it against the accusation that it is 'dead'?

---

[398] Crawford and Nicholson, n. 323, at 113.  [399] Ibid., at 106.  [400] Gray, n. 325, at 29–30.

## SUGGESTED FURTHER READING

Thomas Franck, 'Who Killed Article 2(4)? Or the Changing Norms Governing the Use of Force by States' (1970) **64** *American Journal of International Law* 809

James Green, 'Questioning the Peremptory Status of the Prohibition of the Use of Force' (2011) **32** *Michigan Journal of International Law* 215

Oona A. Hathaway and Scott J. Shapiro, *The Internationalists and Their Plan to Outlaw War* (Allen Lane, 2017)

Louise Henkin, 'The Reports of the Death of Article 2(4) Are Greatly Exaggerated' (1971) **65** *American Journal of International Law* 54

Mary Ellen O'Connell, 'The Prohibition on the Use of Force', in Nigel D. White and Christian Henderson (eds.), *Research Handbook on International Conflict and Security Law: Jus ad Bellum, Jus in Bello, and Jus post Bellum* (Edward Elgar, 2013), 89

Marco Roscini 'Threats of Armed Force and Contemporary International Law' (2007) **54** *Netherlands International Law Review* 229

Paulina Starski, 'Silence within the Process of Normative Change and Evolution of the Prohibition of the Use of Force: Normative Volatility and Legislative Responsibility' (2017) **4** *Journal on the Use of Force and International Law* 14

# 2 The Meaning of 'Force'

## 2.1 INTRODUCTION

While Chapter 1 discussed the general breadth and scope of the prohibition of the threat or use of force contained within Article 2(4) of the United Nations (UN) Charter and customary international law, the purpose of this chapter is to provide some focused discussion on the meaning of the 'force' prohibited. As will have become clear from Chapter 1, it is difficult to be categorical when talking about the law in this area, and there is some uncertainty regarding various issues. Indeed, it is true that '[t]here is no authoritative definition of, or criteria for, "threat" or "use of force"'.[1] This chapter will seek to expose the uncertainties in regard to this particular issue, and, in the process, attempt to distil various factors or common elements behind the meaning of 'force'.

Force is a particular kind of intervention, and it is important to first be clear as to the kind of intervention that it represents, which is addressed in Section 2.2. The chapter then moves on in Section 2.3 to look at the type of force that the prohibition is concerned with and, concluding that it is 'armed force', then moves on in Section 2.4 to attempt to distil the key elements of such force, including the possibility for force to be used indirectly. Section 2.5 then addresses the 'gravity' or severity aspects of a use of force, in particular by distinguishing it from an 'armed attack' or act of 'aggression', two other terms that are found within the UN Chapter, but also by examining whether there is a level of force – or *de minimis* threshold – below which an action falls outside of the scope of the prohibition. Finally, and having distilled some key theoretical and practical components of a prohibited use of force, Section 2.6 focuses upon the *mens rea* component.

---

[1] Michael N. Schmitt (ed.), *Tallinn Manual on the International Law Applicable to Cyber Warfare* (Cambridge University Press, 2013), at 46.

## 2.2 THE PRINCIPLE OF NON-INTERVENTION

The principle of non-intervention 'involves the right of every sovereign state to conduct its affairs without outside interference'.[2] Although not expressly found in the UN Charter,[3] the principle has been generally recognised as firmly grounded in customary international law.[4] It is perhaps not difficult to think of incidences where the principle as it is stated here has been *prima facie* violated. Interference in the form of concerns expressed by one state over issues that are occurring in another state, for example, are relatively frequent. However, a distinction must be drawn between common forms of *interference* and prohibited *interventions*. Indeed, while this definition uses the word 'interference', the principle has been repeatedly reaffirmed by states as providing that '[n]o state has the right to *intervene*, directly or indirectly, for any reason whatever, in the internal or external affairs of any other state'.[5] In this respect, 'interference pure and simple is not intervention'.[6] A state would be interfering in the affairs of another state if it were, for example, to criticise its human rights record, as many states did in regard to the situation in Rakhine state in Myanmar in September 2017,[7] or as they did in regards to the Uyghur population in the Xinjiang province of China,[8] but this would not by itself constitute a violation of the legal norm of non-intervention. To be sure, if

---

[2] *Case Concerning Military and Paramilitary Activities in and against Nicaragua* (*Nicaragua v. United States of America*), Merits, (1986) ICJ Reports 14, at para. 202.

[3] Vaughan Lowe, 'The Principle of Non-Intervention: Use of Force', in Colin Warbrick and Vaughan Lowe (eds.), *The United Nations and the Principles of International Law: Essays in Memory of Michael Akehurst* (Routledge, 1994), 66, at 68. Article 2(7) of the UN Charter states that '[n]othing contained in the present Charter shall authorize the United Nations to intervene in matters which are essentially within the domestic jurisdiction of any state'. However, this limitation is directed towards the UN and not individual member states.

[4] *Nicaragua* case, n. 2, at paras. 202 and 246.

[5] See, for example, Declaration on the Inadmissibility of Intervention in the Domestic Affairs of States and the Protection of their Independence and Sovereignty, UNGA Res. 2131 (XX) (1965), at para. 1 (emphasis added); Declaration on Principles of International Law concerning Friendly Relations and Co-operation among States in accordance with the Charter of the United Nations, UNGA Res. 2625 (XXV) (1970), at para. 3 (emphasis added). See also the constituent instruments of the Organisation of American States, The League of Arab States and the Organisation of African Unity.

[6] Robert Jennings and Arthur Watts (eds.), *Oppenheim's International Law*, vol. I: *Peace*, 9th ed. (Oxford University Press, 1992), at 432.

[7] See, for example, 'US Voices Concern over Rohingya Crisis in Myanmar', *The Hindu*, 9 September 2017, available at: www.thehindu.com/news/international/us-voices-concern-over-rohingya-crisis-in-myanmar/article19649526.ece.

[8] BBC News, 'Who Are the Uyghurs and Why Is China Being Accused of Genocide?', 24 May 2022, available at: www.bbc.co.uk/news/world-asia-china-22278037.

these types of intervention were prohibited then the norm would almost certainly be honoured more in the breach.

In the *Nicaragua* case of 1986, the International Court of Justice (ICJ) provided one of the few judicial examinations of the principle of non-intervention.[9] An important element of the ICJ's exposition of this principle is that it is transgressed only once a particular act of interference amounts to 'coercion' and bears 'on matters in which each state is permitted, by the principle of state sovereignty, to decide freely'.[10] Indeed, a state's political, economic, social and cultural choices must remain free ones.[11] Thus, while states regularly comment on situations that are occurring in another state, such as the righteousness of the parties engaged in a civil war, the principle of non-intervention becomes engaged only once the intervening state seeks to *coerce* that state, either directly or indirectly, into making certain choices or taking or being subject to certain actions. The principle would, therefore, be *prima facie* breached if a state were to use political or economic leverage to ensure the political leader of a state was to stand down. Yet, one needs to carefully distinguish between acts which are *coercive*, and therefore breach the principle of non-intervention, and those that are merely *influential*. For example, if true, accusations that Russia hacked into the Democratic Party computer systems and email accounts in the United States and leaked information in an attempt to affect the outcome of the US presidential election in 2016, while influential in the campaign and an intrusion into the sovereignty of the United States,[12] would not constitute a coercive act for the purposes of the principle of non-intervention.[13]

---

[9] *Nicaragua* case, n. 2.

[10] Ibid., at para. 205; Declaration on the Inadmissibility of Intervention, n. 5, at paras. 1–2, 5; Declaration on the Principles of International Law Concerning Friendly Relations, n. 5, at para. 1.

[11] *Nicaragua* case, n. 2, at para. 205.

[12] There has been some debate between states and between scholars as to whether sovereignty represents a discreet rule of international law that can be violated or whether it is rather a principle which underpins other rules and principles of international law, such as that regarding non-intervention. Several states and scholars have come out in support of it representing a rule, as otherwise intrusive acts that fall below the intervention threshold would remain outside of the scope of international law and limit the responses available to states. Other scholars and states, including the United Kingdom and the United States, on the other hand, are unconvinced that sovereignty as yet can be said to constitute a rule of international law. See Michael Schmitt, 'In Defense of Sovereignty in Cyberspace', *Just Security*, 8 May 2018, available at: www.justsecurity.org/55876/defense-sovereignty-cyberspace/.

[13] In January 2017, a US intelligence community assessment stated that it had 'high confidence' that Russian President Vladimir Putin ordered an 'influence campaign' to harm Hilary Clinton's electoral chances. See Intelligence Community Assessment, Assessing Russian Activities and Intentions in Recent US Elections, 6 January 2017, available at: www.dni.gov/files/documents/ICA_2017_01.pdf.

However, a further important aspect to the ICJ's elucidation of the principle of non-intervention is that '[t]he element of coercion, which defines, and indeed forms the very essence of, prohibited intervention, is particularly obvious in the case of an intervention which *uses force*.'[14] Interventions involving such forcible coercion, which constitute a more specific form of intervention, are something that are independently prohibited in Article 2(4) of the UN Charter and in customary international law. It is this 'particularly obvious' form of coercion that this chapter is primarily focused upon.

## 2.3 THE TYPE OF 'FORCE' ENVISAGED IN ARTICLE 2(4)

Article 2(4) omits any qualification as to the type of 'force' that is the intended target of the prohibition, and neither the UN Charter or any instrument subsequently adopted within the UN offers any direct assistance in this regard.[15] In general, 'force' could be described as '[p]ower, violence, or pressure directed against a person or thing'.[16] However, if this were accepted as a definition of the 'force' referred to in Article 2(4) then the prohibition would be provided with broad coverage and would be virtually indistinguishable from the broader concept of intervention, as set out in Section 2.2.

The *travaux préparatoires* of the UN Charter does not indicate that there were discussions during the drafting of Article 2(4) regarding the precise meaning of the term 'force'. However, on one reading of the materials, economic and political force were seemingly excluded from the scope of Article 2(4), regardless of how severe the effects of such force might be or who or what are the intended targets. Indeed, during the drafting of the prohibition, the Brazilian delegation proposed that Article 2(4) should expressly prohibit 'the threat or use of force *and the threat or use of economic measures* in any manner inconsistent with the purposes of the Organization'.[17] Needless to say, this proposal was ultimately vetoed by the drafting committee.[18] Although the decision on this omission might be indicative of the fact that the drafters understood the term 'force' to be sufficient to cover all conceivable types of force, it is more widely believed that it reflected the

---

[14] *Nicaragua* case, n. 2, at para. 205 (emphasis added).
[15] 'The United Nations Charter offers no criteria by which to determine when an act amounts to a use of force.' *Tallinn Manual*, n. 1, at 45.
[16] *Black's Law Dictionary*, 9th ed. (Thomson-West, 2009), at 717.
[17] 'Summary Report of Eleventh Meeting of Committee I/1', Doc. 215, I/1/10, *Documents of the United Nations Conference on International Organization*, 1945, vol. VI, 559 (emphasis added).
[18] Ibid., at 334–9, 405, 609.

## 2.3 The Type of 'Force' Envisaged in Article 2(4)

intention of Western states to exclude economic measures and, by extension, diplomatic and political coercion from the reach of the prohibition.[19]

While at no point within the UN Charter is the concept of 'force' defined, the preamble to the UN Charter clearly states that the overriding purpose of the UN is to 'save succeeding generations from the scourge of war'. This is perhaps not surprising given that the Charter was drafted in the wake of two world wars. However, it also restricts itself to stipulating that it is '*armed* force' (emphasis added) that 'shall not be used, save in the common interest', a qualification of the term 'force' also employed at other points within the Charter.[20] In this respect it could be argued that, as references to 'force' elsewhere in the Charter are to the *armed* variety, then this also holds true for Article 2(4), so that the prohibition of the use of force contained within is restricted to force of an armed nature.

One could perhaps equally argue, however, that, given that the Charter is express in its reference to 'armed force' elsewhere, this is indicative of the fact that the type of 'force' referred to in Article 2(4) is of a different, perhaps broader, variety. Yet, subsequent documents, such as the Declaration on Friendly Relations (1970), the Definition of Aggression (1974) and the Declaration on the Non-Use of Force (1987), which are considered to be reflective of customary law on the basis that they were adopted by consensus, would appear to support a more restrictive view of the provision to applications of 'armed force'.[21] For example, the Declaration on Friendly Relations appears to distinguish political and economic coercion from that of the armed variety. Indeed, political and economic coercion are expressly included under the heading of the 'principle concerning the obligation not to intervene' and not under the 'principle that States shall refrain in their international relations from the threat or use of force'. One might argue on this basis 'that as far as the Declaration is concerned, force is restricted to armed coercion, and that forms of political and economic coercion were to be considered intervention'.[22] In a similar vein, the 1987 Declaration on the Non-Use of Force separates the concepts of 'armed intervention' and 'economic, political or any other type of measures',[23] although neither are referred to expressly as a use of 'force', thereby entirely resolving the issue. In the drafting and adoption of these

---

[19] Marco Roscini, 'World Wide Warfare: *Jus ad Bellum* and the Use of Force' (2010) 14 *Max Planck Yearbook of United Nations Law* 85, at 105.

[20] See Articles 41 and 46, UN Charter (1945).

[21] Declaration on the Principles of International Law Concerning Friendly Relations, n. 5; Definition of Aggression, UNGA Res. 3314 (XXIX) (1974); Declaration on the Enhancement of the Effectiveness of the Principle of Refraining from the Threat or Use of Force in International Relations, UNGA Res. 42/22 (1987). However, it should be noted that the Charter of the Organization of American States and the North Atlantic Treaty both use the term 'force' in an unqualified fashion.

[22] Heather Harrison Dinniss, *Cyber Warfare and the Laws of War* (Cambridge University Press, 2012), at 48.

[23] Articles 7 and 8, Declaration on the Non-Use of Force, n. 21.

resolutions it would thus appear that a degree of ambiguity was the price of consensus.

However, while no 'definitive conclusions' can be drawn,[24] it is perhaps fair to say that the 'prevailing view' amongst the academic community is that it is armed force, as opposed to that of a political or economic nature, that is covered by the prohibition.[25] As Bentwich and Martin elaborate:

> Unfortunately, 'force' itself is a flexible term. Under modern conditions the threat or use of economic retaliation may be as effective against a weaker state as the threat or use of armed force. But it appears that the prohibition of Article 2(4) is directed exclusively at force in the sense of 'armed force'.[26]

In addition to what the *travaux* of the Charter and subsequently adopted instruments might suggest, and in full consciousness of the potential power and effect of economic, political and diplomatic coercive measures, state practice subsequent to the adoption of the Charter would seem to confirm that the prohibition is targeted towards armed force, to the exclusion of the other types of force. The imposition of economic or political pressure has rarely been categorised as a use of force for the purposes of the prohibition of the threat or use of force contained in Article 2(4) of the UN Charter and customary international law.[27]

## 2.4 THE MEANING OF 'ARMED FORCE'

Although the generally accepted interpretation of the term 'force' within Article 2(4) is limited to *armed* force, this still leaves open the question as to what, exactly, constitutes such force? This might be determined by either the *effects* created by an action or, alternatively, the *means* used to create them.

---

[24] Harrison Dinniss, n. 22, at 41.

[25] Albrecht Randelzhofer, 'Article 2(4)', in Bruno Simma, Hermann Mosler, Albrecht Randelzhofer, Christian Tomuschat, Ridiger Wolfrum, Andreas Paulus and Eleni Chaitobu (eds.), *The Charter of the United Nations: A Commentary*, 2nd ed. (Oxford University Press, 2002), 117. See also *Tallinn Manual*, n. 1, at 50–1; Tom J. Farer, 'Political and Economic Coercion in Contemporary International Law' (1985) **79** *American Journal of International Law* 405, at 410; Rosalyn Higgins, *Problems and Process: International Law and How We Use It* (Clarendon Press, 1994), at 248; Yoram Dinstein, *War, Aggression and Self-Defence*, 6th ed. (Cambridge University Press, 2017), at para. 246; Tom Ruys, 'The Meaning of "Force" and the Boundaries of the *Jus ad Bellum*: Are "Minimal" Uses of Force Excluded from UN Charter Article 2(4)?' (2014) **108** *American Journal of International Law* 159, at 163.

[26] Norman Bentwich and Andrew Martin, *A Commentary on the Charter of the United Nations* (Routledge & Paul, 1950), at 12.

[27] For an argument that economic sanctions should be categorised as a use of force, see, in general, Cassandra LaRae-Perez, 'Economic Sanctions as a Use of Force: Re-Evaluating the Legality of Sanctions from an Effects-Based Perspective' (2002) **20** *Boston University International Law Journal* 161.

## 2.4.1 The Means Used

In general, the notion of 'armed' force would seem to denote the use of a weapon of some kind, thus placing the focus more upon the means used. On the basis of dictionary definitions of 'armed' this would appear to be the case, with one definition being '[e]quipped with a weapon' or '[i]nvolving the use of a weapon',[28] while another defining the term more specifically as 'equipped with or involving a firearm'.[29]

No guidance is provided either within the UN Charter itself or any subsequently adopted document as to the *type* of weapon that might be required to transgress the prohibition of the use of force. Of course, the Charter was drafted in the 1940s in an era of the use of conventional weapons, such as bombs, rifles, tanks and fighter aircraft, of the sort employed in the two world wars of the twentieth century, and the deployment of force through the conventional armies of states. The drafters of the UN Charter arguably had these at the forefront of their minds in attempting to protect states from the use of armed force. It might, therefore, be argued that the true application of Article 2(4) is to the use of *kinetic* force – that is, force manifested through the use of weapons that emit an 'explosive effect with shock waves and heat'[30] and instruments intended for the delivery of these weapons, such as tanks and aircraft.

There is no discernible evidence, however, to suggest that the prohibition has been restricted to weaponry of a particular nature. Indeed, such a restrictive interpretation would seem to unreasonably exclude the use of knives and bayonets as well as weapons of a chemical and biological nature. Furthermore, in discussing the provisions of the Charter on the use of force the ICJ was of the view in its *Nuclear Weapons* advisory opinion that '[t]hese provisions do not refer to specific weapons. They apply to any use of force, regardless of the weapons employed. The Charter neither expressly prohibits, nor permits, the use of any specific weapon.'[31] Certain treaty regimes exist that prohibit the use of particular weapons under any circumstances.[32] While the general regime of international law governing the use of force does not, in and of itself, prohibit the use of such weapons, these specific regimes, for those states party to them, constitute the *lex specialis*. In this respect, '[a] weapon that is already unlawful

---

[28] *Black's Law Dictionary*, n. 16, at 123.   [29] *Oxford English Dictionary*.
[30] Ian Brownlie, *International Law and the Use of Force by States* (Oxford University Press, 1963), at 362.
[31] *Legality of the Threat or Use of Nuclear Weapons*, Advisory Opinion, (1996) ICJ Reports 226, at para. 39. The ICJ noted, however, that 'in order correctly to apply to the present case the Charter law on the use of force ... it is imperative for the Court to take account of the unique characteristics of nuclear weapons, and in particular their destructive capacity'. Ibid., at para. 36.
[32] See, e.g., Article 1(1)(b), Chemical Weapons Convention (1993); Article 1(1)(d), Treaty on the Prohibition of Nuclear Weapons (2017).

*per se*, whether by treaty or custom, does not become lawful by reason of it being used for a legitimate purpose under the Charter'.[33]

The use of an object which was designed to be used as a weapon does not appear to be the determining factor as to whether an action constitutes 'force'; rather a weapon is instead 'a thing designed *or used* for inflicting bodily harm or physical damage'.[34] As such, although an F-16 fighter jet or a Tomahawk cruise missile are both clearly designed to be employed in an act of armed force, there are many objects and instruments capable of serving a dual purpose – that is, while not serving a primary purpose as a weapon they nonetheless represent potential weapons. Just as in the domestic context a hammer or a wrench may be both a workman's tool or a weapon of murder, a similar analogy arguably applies in the international context, so that, while commercial aircraft provide one of the most convenient, fastest and safest means of long-distance travel, they can also, as the events of 11 September 2001 horrifically demonstrated, be employed as a lethal weapon with devastating consequences.[35] Similarly, although drones were initially used solely as a highly effective means of surveillance, they have since been used to carry weapons and conduct targeted killings and discussed in the context of the prohibition of force.[36] In an analogous vein, although today the world could not operate in the absence of computers and information technology, both states and academics seem prepared to apply the existing rules on the use of force to attacks using cyber means.[37]

With the means used not being decisive in determining whether an action potentially comes within the scope of the prohibition of the threat or use of force, what appears to be of greater significance are the effects created by the use of the weapon, or indeed the object being used as one. As clearly demonstrated by the use of computers to carry out cyber attacks, while not used in a direct physical way to achieve their destructive effect, as is the case with a hammer, aircraft or drone, they nonetheless clearly have the potential to be used as a means of unleashing dire consequences and mass destruction.

---

[33] *Nuclear Weapons* advisory opinion, n. 31, at para. 39.
[34] *Oxford English Dictionary* (emphasis added). Similarly, *Black's Law Dictionary*, n. 16, defines a 'weapon' as '[a]n instrument *used* or designed to be used to injure or kill someone'.
[35] Although this is not to say that the events of 11 September 2001 constituted a use of force for the purposes of the UN Charter as they were not undertaken by a state. See Section 1.3.1.4. It does not follow, however, that the United States did not have a right of self-defence in response to them. See Chapters 6–8.
[36] See, e.g., Christine Gray, 'Targeted Killing outside Armed Conflict: A New Departure for the UK?' (2016) 3 *Journal on the Use of Force and International Law* 198.
[37] See Section 1.7.4.

## 2.4.2 The Effects Created

An incursion or invasion by the armed forces of a state into the territory of another state may not be accompanied by the discharging of any specific weapons but may nonetheless constitute a prohibited use of force. In 2014, Russian tanks carrying armed Russian troops began to appear in the Ukrainian territory of Crimea without, it was claimed, 'a single shot being fired'.[38] While no shots may have been fired, the fact that the troops' presence was the result of an armed coercive act was sufficient to engage the prohibition of the use of force.[39] Similarly, US military helicopters entered Tehran on 24 April 1980 in an attempt to rescue US hostages.[40] The operation failed without a shot being fired yet Iran complained about the 'military aggression of the United States' and the United States in turn justified its actions as self-defence.[41] Indeed, '[w]hat was at first sight a very limited action, involving a few helicopters illegally crossing the border for the sole purpose of saving nationals was considered by both States as coming within the ambit of article 2(4)'.[42] Although very different in terms of the magnitude of the outcome, what these two examples demonstrate is that it is possible that a state may be subject to an act of armed coercion which engages the prohibition of force without the actual discharging of a particular weapon.

Furthermore, it has been questioned whether a prohibited use of armed force must result in either harm to humans or the destruction of physical property. Christopher Joyner and Catherine Lotrionte, for example, note that the 'fundamental proscription against the use of interstate force is traditionally regarded as being confined to the use or threat of "armed" force, meaning

---

[38] This was how the intervention was described by Russian President Vladimir Putin. See Address by President of the Russian Federation, 18 March 2014, available at: http://en.kremlin.ru/events/president/news/20603.

[39] See, for example, Marc Weller, 'Analysis: Why Russia's Crimea Move Fails Legal Test', *BBC News*, 7 March 2014, available at: www.bbc.co.uk/news/world-europe-26481423. Russian troops also strayed from military naval bases located at Sevastopol and Feodosia, which Ukraine claimed was in breach of agreements between the two countries on the status and conditions of the Russian forces on Ukrainian territory. See Thomas D. Grant, 'Annexation of Crimea' (2015) **109** *American Journal of International Law* 68, at 78–80. Article 3(e) of the Definition of Aggression (see n. 21) states that '[t]he use of armed forces of one State which are within the territory of another State with the agreement of the receiving State, in contravention of the conditions provided for in the agreement or any extension of their presence in such territory beyond the termination of the agreement' shall constitute an act of aggression.

[40] *Keesing's* (1980) 30531–3.

[41] Note verbale dated 28 April 1980 from the Permanent Representative of Iran to the UN addressed to the Secretary-General, UN Doc. S/13915, 29 April 1980, at 2; Letter dated 25 April 1980 from the Permanent Representative of the USA to the UN addressed to the President of the Security Council, UN Doc. S/13908, 25 April 1980, at 1. See Chapter 6 for more on the general aspects of the right of self-defence.

[42] Olivier Corten, *The Law against War: The Prohibition on the Use of Force in Contemporary International Law*, 2nd ed. (Hart, 2021), at 82–3.

the possible resort to a violent weapon that inflicts human injury'.[43] Ian Brownlie, on the other hand, talks of the use of a weapon which is employed for the 'destruction of life and property',[44] while the *Tallinn Manual* observes that '[a]cts that injure or kill persons or damage or destroy objects are unambiguously uses of force'.[45] Yet, it may also be the case that humans have neither been killed nor injured, nor property damaged or destroyed, when the prohibition is engaged. Further to the examples in the previous paragraph, even mere attempts to use force by one state against another might be construed as a use of force in breach of the prohibition. For example, the foiled assassination attempt by Iraqi agents upon former US President George H. W. Bush while on a visit to Kuwait resulted in the United States invoking its right of self-defence, a claim that was generally accepted by other states.[46]

What becomes clear, however, is that in any assessment as to whether a particular action constitutes a use of force, a consideration of the *effects* of the action arguably takes on a greater importance the further one moves away from what we might consider to be the threat or use of conventional weapons. For example, in the view of the Finnish government, 'while there is currently no established definition of a cyberattack that would pass the threshold of "use of force" in the sense of article 2(4) of the UN Charter ... it is widely recognized that such a qualification *depends on the consequences* of a cyberattack.'[47] The Dutch government appears to be of a similar view in that it considers that 'the effects of the operation determine whether the prohibition applies, not the manner in which those effects are achieved'.[48]

In determining whether the effects of a cyber operation can be considered armed force for the purposes of the prohibition, several states have expressly adopted a general equivalence position so that 'cyber operations can fall within the scope of the prohibition of the use of force, particularly *when the*

---

[43] Christopher C. Joyner and Catherine Lotrionte, 'Information Warfare as International Coercion: Elements of a Legal Framework' (2001) 12 *European Journal of International Law* 825, at 845 (emphasis added).

[44] Brownlie, n. 30, at 362.   [45] *Tallinn Manual*, n. 1, at 48.

[46] See Dino Kritsiotis, 'The Legality of the 1993 US Missile Strike on Iraq and the Right of Self-Defence in International Law' (1996) 45 *International & Comparative Law Quarterly* 162. Although this reaction might be seen as *sui generis* given that 'an act against a visiting foreign minister or head of state of a country has always been considered an act of force by the host state'. Harrison Dinniss, n. 22, at 70–1. See further Chapters 6–8 on self-defence.

[47] Finland Ministry for Foreign Affairs, 'Finland Published Its Positions on Public International Law in Cyberspace', 15 October 2020, available at: https://um.fi/documents/35732/0/KyberkannatPDF_EN.pdf/12bbbbde-623b-9f86-b254-07d5af3c6d85?t=1603097522727 (emphasis added).

[48] Dutch Minister of Foreign Affairs, 'Letter to the Parliament on the International Legal Order in Cyberspace', 5 July 2019, available at: www.government.nl/ministries/ministry-of-foreign-affairs/documents/parliamentary-documents/2019/09/26/letter-to-the-parliament-on-the-international-legal-order-in-cyberspace.

## 2.4 The Meaning of 'Armed Force'

*effects of the operation are comparable to those of a conventional act of violence covered by the prohibition.'*[49] In slight contrast, some states have adopted the 'scale and effects' test in this context – a test which was originally introduced by the ICJ in the *Nicaragua* case to distinguish 'uses of force' from 'armed attacks' – to help identify prohibited uses of force in the cyber context.[50] For example, the Netherlands government has contended that '[t]here is no reason not to take the same approach [as the ICJ] when assessing whether an act may be deemed a use of force within the meaning of article 2(4) of the UN Charter.'[51] In this respect, the government endorsed 'the generally accepted position that each case must be examined individually to establish whether the "scale and effects" are such that an operation may be deemed a violation of the prohibition of use of force.'[52]

Yet, while this provides something of a threshold test for determining when a cyber operation might fall within the prohibition of the use of force, it is not clear what 'scale and effects' refers to. In this respect, some have looked towards the possible causation of physical destruction or death or injury to individuals.[53] The New Zealand government, for example, has stated that

[s]tate cyber activity can amount to a use of force for the purposes of international law. Whether it does in any given context depends on an assessment of the scale and effects of the activity. State cyber activity will amount to a use of force if it results in effects of a scale and nature equivalent to those caused by kinetic activity which constitutes a

---

[49] Ibid. (emphasis added). See also, for example, Finland: '[f]or a cyberattack *to be comparable to use of force*, it must be sufficiently serious and have impacts in the territory of the target State, or in areas within its jurisdiction, *that are similar to those of the use of force.*' Finland Ministry for Foreign Affairs, n. 47 (emphasis added).

[50] The application of this test to determining uses of force in the cyber context was originally undertaken in the *Tallinn Manual*, n. 1, at 45 (Rule 11).

[51] Dutch Minister of Foreign Affairs, n. 48. And in linking this in with the equivalence position, the Netherlands also stated that '[a] cyber operation would therefore in any case be qualified as a use of force if its scale and effects reached the same level as those of the use of force in non-cyber operations'.

[52] Ibid. See also The Federal Government of Germany, 'On the Application of International Law to Cyberspace', March 2021, available at: www.auswaertiges-amt.de/blob/2446304/32e7b2498e10b74fb17204c54665bdf0/on-the-application-of-international-law-in-cyberspace-data.pdf.

[53] Buchan notes that in the cyber context 'Article 2(4) is an effects-based prohibition. The generally accepted interpretation of Article 2(4) is that only those interventions that produce physical damage will be regarded as an unlawful use of force.' Russell Buchan, 'Cyber Attacks: Unlawful Uses of Force or Prohibited Interventions?' (2012) **17** *Journal of Conflict & Security Law* 212, at 212. A similar position was expressed much earlier in 1999 by Walter Sharp, who noted that 'any computer attack [perpetrated by a state] that intentionally *causes any destructive effect* within the sovereign territory of another state is an unlawful use of force'. Walter G. Sharp Sr, *Cyberspace and the Use of Force* (Ageis Research Corp., 1999), at 133 (emphasis added). For more on the requirement of intention see Section 2.6.

use of force at international law. Such effects may include death, serious injury to persons, or significant damage to the victim state's objects and/or state functioning.[54]

On the basis of this approach if a cyber operation was to lead to the meltdown in a nuclear plant, the opening of the gates of a dam resulting in death and destruction, or the disabling of air traffic control services which resulted in collisions, this would constitute a prohibited use of force.[55] Yet, question marks remain in regard to operations with more minor physical effects. Indeed, as the Stuxnet cyber-attack on the Natanz nuclear plant in Iran in 2010 demonstrated, which reportedly caused damage to test tubes in a nuclear enrichment facility,[56] cyber capabilities may be employed as a weapon to inflict physical damage of a more minor nature.[57] Although admittedly not a view entirely free from controversy, the use of the Stuxnet worm in 2010 was considered by many to be a use of force, while previous cyber-attacks in Estonia in 2007 and Georgia in 2008 were not, on the basis that the Stuxnet attack led to physical damage in the form of the broken test tubes, while the attacks in Estonia and Georgia resulted in no physical damage, but

---

[54] New Zealand Ministry of Foreign Affairs and Trade, 'The Application of International Law to State Activity in Cyberspace', 1 December 2020, at 7, available at: www.mfat.govt.nz/en/media-and-resources/the-application-of-international-law-to-state-activity-in-cyberspace/. See also the United States: 'Depending on the circumstances, a military cyber operation may constitute a use of force within the meaning of Article 2(4) of the U.N. Charter and customary international law. In assessing whether a particular cyber operation – conducted by or against the United States – constitutes a use of force, DoD lawyers consider whether the operation causes physical injury or damage that would be considered a use of force if caused solely by traditional means like a missile or a mine.' U.S. Department of Defense, 'DOD General Counsel Remarks at U.S. Cyber Command Legal Conference', 2 March 2020, available at: www.defense.gov/Newsroom/Speeches/Speech/Article/2099378/dod-general-counsel-remarks-at-us-cyber-command-legal-conference/. Estonia also noted: 'we already know that cyber operations, which cause injury or death to persons or damage or destruction of objects, could amount to use of force or armed attack under the UN Charter.' 'President Kaljulaid at CyCon 2019: Cyber attacks should not be easy weapon', *ERR News*, 29 May 2019, available at: https://news.err.ee/946827/president-kaljulaid-at-cycon-2019-cyber-attacks-should-not-be-easy-weapon. Similarly, Israel claimed to 'share the support among States for the view that a cyber operation can amount to use of force if it is expected to cause physical damage, injury or death, which would establish the use of force if caused by kinetic means'. See Roy Schondorf, 'Israel's Perspective on Key Legal and Practical Issues Concerning the Application of International Law to Cyber Operations', *EJIL Talk!*, 9 December 2020, available at: www.ejiltalk.org/israels-perspective-on-key-legal-and-practical-issues-concerning-the-application-of-international-law-to-cyber-operations/.

[55] See Harold Koh, 'International Law in Cyberspace' (2012) 54 *Harvard International Law Journal* 1, at 4.

[56] Yaakov Katz, 'Stuxnet May Have Destroyed 1,000 Centrifuges at Natanz', *The Jerusalem Post*, 24 December 2010, available at: www.jpost.com/Defense/Stuxnet-may-have-destroyed-1000-centrifuges-at-Natanz.

[57] See Buchan, n. 53, at 219–21.

rather took the form of distributed denial of service attacks.[58] It is arguable, therefore, that without such physical damage the use of the Stuxnet worm in Iran would not by itself have constituted a prohibited use of force.

Furthermore, the question arises as to how cyber operations that do not have any destructive or injurious consequences, such as those limited to significant economic effects, are to be categorised. Indeed, while there appears to be a level of agreement amongst states and scholars in regard to cyber operations with *physical* effects, states appear to be more hesitant in endorsing a position in regard to those with *non*-physical effects, even if of a severe nature. For example, although the Netherlands has stated the view that 'it cannot be ruled out that a cyber operation with a very serious financial or economic impact may qualify as a use of force',[59] ultimately, and as Israel succinctly noted, '[a]s with any legal assessment relating to the cyber domain, as practice in this field continues to evolve, there may be room to further examine whether operations not causing physical damage could also amount to use of force.'[60]

Rather than setting binary physical/non-physical or severe/non-severe divides, an alternative approach that has been taken is the consideration of relevant factors in determining whether a particular cyber operation constitutes a prohibited use of force. Indeed, as the international group of experts involved in the drafting of the *Tallinn Manual 2.0* was unable to definitively resolve the issue of where the threshold for a prohibited use of force lay in the context of cyber operations, it instead set out a number of factors that state decision-makers are likely to consider when determining whether to characterise a cyber operation as a use of force.[61] These included severity, directness, immediacy, invasiveness, measurability of effects, military character of the operation, degree of state involvement, presumptive legality, prevailing political environment, identity of the attacker and nature of the target. This

---

[58] Ibid., at 218–21; Marco Roscini, *Cyber Operations and the Use of Force in International Law* (Oxford University Press, 2014), at 53–4. A distributed denial of service attack involves multiple connected online devices, collectively known as a botnet, which are used to overwhelm a target website with fake traffic.

[59] Dutch Minister of Foreign Affairs, n. 48. In addition, 'France does not rule out the possibility that a cyber operation without physical effects may also be characterized as a use of force'. Ministère des Armées, 'Droit International Appliqué aux Operations dans le Cyberspace', 9 September 2019, available at: www.justsecurity.org/wp-content/uploads/2019/09/droit-internat-appliqu%C3%A9-aux-op%C3%A9rations-cyberespace-france.pdf.

[60] Schondorf, n. 54. Even more broadly, however, it has been claimed that '[i]n assessing the scale and effects of malicious state cyber activity, states may take into account both the immediate impacts and *the intended or reasonably expected consequential impacts.*' New Zealand Ministry of Foreign Affairs and Trade, n. 54, at 7 (emphasis added).

[61] Michael N. Schmitt, *Tallinn Manual 2.0 on the International Law Applicable to Cyber Operations* (Cambridge University Press, 2017), at 330–7.

'factors' approach has seemingly found favour with a number of states,[62] although they should be seen as indicative, rather than legal, criteria.

### 2.4.3 The Indirect Use of Armed Force

Article 2(4) does not allude to whether it also applies to the use of force through *indirect* means, whereby, as opposed to a state directly employing its armed forces or using its information and communication technologies to carry out a use of force against another state, it instead provides the means to a non-state actor – for example, rebel forces, terrorist groups or computer hackers – to do so and where the assistance rendered is insufficient to attribute the forcible actions to the state itself under the law of state responsibility.[63] An expansive interpretation of Article 2(4) so as to incorporate indirect force finds support in the 1970 Declaration on Friendly Relations, which in many respects elaborates upon this relatively brief provision of the UN Charter.[64] In connection with the principle of non-intervention it states that '[n]o State or group of States has the right to intervene, *directly or indirectly*, for any reason whatever, in the internal or external affairs of any other State'[65] and, under the principle not to threaten or use force, that '[e]very State has the duty to refrain from organizing or encouraging the organization of irregular forces or armed bands including mercenaries, for incursion into the territory of another State'.[66]

Furthermore, the ICJ highlighted in the *Nicaragua* case that forcible intervention does not need to be of a direct nature to constitute a violation of the

---

[62] The Netherlands stated that '[i]t is necessary, when assessing the scale and effects of a cyber operation, to examine both qualitative and quantitative factors. The *Tallinn Manual 2.0* refers to a number of factors that could play a role in this regard, including how serious and far-reaching the cyber operation's consequences are, whether the operation is military in nature and whether it is carried out by a state. These are not binding legal criteria. They are factors that could provide an indication that a cyber operation may be deemed a use of force, and the government endorses this approach. It should be noted in this regard that a cyber operation that falls below the threshold of use of force may nonetheless be qualified as a prohibited intervention or a violation of sovereignty'. Dutch Minister of Foreign Affairs, n. 48. See also The Federal Government of Germany, n. 52; Ministère des Armées, n. 59.

[63] As will be discussed further in Chapters 6–8 in the context of the right of self-defence, while mere assistance by a state to a non-state actor may engage the prohibition of force for that state, the threshold for actually attributing the actions of a non-state actor to a state, thereby making the state responsible for an armed attack if the actions perpetrated by the non-state actors are of sufficient gravity, remains controversial.

[64] Declaration on the Principles of International Law Concerning Friendly Relations, n. 5.

[65] Ibid. (emphasis added), under 'The principle concerning the duty not to intervene in matters within the domestic jurisdiction of any State, in accordance with the Charter.'

[66] Ibid., under 'The principle that States shall refrain in their international relations from the threat or use of force against the territorial integrity or political independence of any State or in any other manner inconsistent with the purposes of the United Nations.'

## 2.4 The Meaning of 'Armed Force'

prohibition of the use of force.[67] Indeed, the Court was of the opinion that while the use of force may be 'in the direct form of military action' using, for example, the armed forces of the intervening state, or other forces under the effective control of the state,[68] it may also be 'in the indirect form of support for subversive or terrorist armed activities within another state'.[69] As such, the Court was of the view that an armed forcible act of a state might not be directly and immediately coercive but instead take the form, as was the case in regard to the actions of the United States vis-à-vis the contras, of assisting others to perpetrate such coercive acts.

The Court was, however, keen to distinguish those acts that would violate the prohibition of the use of force from those that would constitute a more minor infringement of the principle of non-intervention. Nicaragua had claimed that the United States had violated the prohibition of the use of force as it had engaged in 'recruiting, training, arming, equipping, financing, supplying and otherwise encouraging, supporting, aiding, and directing military and paramilitary actions in and against Nicaragua'.[70] Yet, in the view of the Court:

while the arming and training of the *contras* can certainly be said to involve the threat or use of force against Nicaragua, this is not necessarily so in respect of all the assistance given by the United States Government. In particular, the Court considers that the mere supply of funds to the *contras*, while undoubtedly an act of intervention in the internal affairs of Nicaragua ... does not in itself amount to a use of force.[71]

The Court provided no basis or authority for this distinction, and it is one that is difficult to clearly discern in state practice, although it has proved relatively uncontroversial amongst scholars and commentators on the judgement. However, the reasoning of the Court in this case led to it finding that the United States, through its provision of support to the contras, had breached its obligations to refrain from both intervening in the affairs of Nicaragua and using force against it.[72]

Whether the support provided by a state crosses the threshold between intervention and force will need to be determined on a case-by-case basis. However, the judgement of the ICJ on this point would seem to indicate that simply *encouraging* physical coercion through verbal means is insufficient by itself to constitute a prohibited use of force. Instead, the state concerned would need to take some practical steps to facilitate the forcible act that occurs, in particular through providing the means, weapons or training to others to enable them to execute it. Indeed, the armed coercion does not need to take place either through overt means or directly in one causal step, but it must

---

[67] *Nicaragua* case, n. 2, at para. 205.   [68] Ibid.   [69] Ibid.   [70] Ibid., at para. 228.
[71] Ibid.   [72] Ibid., at para. 292(3) and (4).

nevertheless constitute an intentional and material contribution towards others carrying out the direct violence that ensues.[73]

It might be questioned whether the provision of arms by a state to a non-state group that does not ultimately go on to perpetrate an act of armed force would constitute a violation of the prohibition. The ICJ, for its part, adopted a position which 'equates assistance of [an indirect nature] with the use of force by the assisting State *when the acts committed in another State "involve a threat or use of force"*'.[74] As such, it can be argued that unless the non-state group were to make an express threat to use force,[75] then an actual act of armed force by the non-state group would need to occur in order for the supporting state's actions to engage the prohibition of force, rather than merely the non-intervention principle.

While the prohibition of force may be breached as a result of a state using indirect force through its assistance to non-state actors, it is also possible for a violation of the prohibition of force to take place through a state's assistance to another state in pursuance of its forcible actions. In this respect, the permission given by Belarus for Russian forces to utilise its territory in order to facilitate its invasion of Ukraine from the north not only made Belarus complicit in Russia's unlawful use of force but also meant that it was in violation of the prohibition of force itself.[76] Article 16 of the International Law Commission's (ILC) Draft Articles on the Responsibility of States for Internationally Wrongful Acts provides that a state's aid or assistance in another state's wrongful act constitutes a derived but separate wrongful act of the assisting state.[77] This secondary rule regarding responsibility requires that a state provides aid or assistance that facilitates another state's breach of international law, that the assisting state does so knowing the circumstances, and that it is bound by the breached rule itself, all of which would appear to be satisfied in the case of Belarus's assistance to Russia in its invasion of Ukraine.[78] In this respect, while Article 16 is a general secondary rule of responsibility, in its commentary on this provision the ILC was clear that '[t]he obligation not to use force may also be breached by an assisting State through permitting the use of its territory by another State to

---

[73] For more on intention see Section 2.6.
[74] *Nicaragua* case, n. 2, at para. 205 (emphasis added).
[75] See Section 1.4 for more on prohibited threats of force.
[76] Amanda Coakley, 'Lukashenko is Letting Putin Use Belarus to Attack Ukraine', *Foreign Policy*, 24 February 2022, available at: https://foreignpolicy.com/2022/02/24/russia-ukraine-war-belarus-chernobyl-lukashenko/.
[77] The International Court of Justice found this rule to be representative of customary international law in its judgment on the Bosnian Genocide. See *Case Concerning Application of the Convention on the Prevention and Punishment of the Crime of Genocide (Bosnia and Herzegovina v. Serbia and Montenegro)*, Judgment (2007) ICJ Reports 43, at para. 417.
[78] Niklas Reetz, 'Belarus Is Complicit in Russia's War of Aggression', *EJIL Talk!*, 1 March 2022, available at: www.ejiltalk.org/belarus-is-complicit-in-russias-war-of-aggression/.

carry out an armed attack against a third State.'[79] As a result, extensive sanctions by the United States, the European Union and the United Kingdom have also been imposed on entities and individuals in the Belarusian defence and finance sectors.[80]

## 2.5 THE 'GRAVITY' ELEMENT OF A USE OF FORCE

The purpose of this section is to examine what might be viewed as the 'gravity' aspects of a use of force. While this chapter – indeed, book – has as its clear focus the international legal regime governing the use of *force*, other terms and concepts exist, both within the UN Charter and external to it, that are related in some way to the concept of force. Many of these terms and concepts will be addressed in detail in other chapters.[81] However, in attempting to provide a comprehensive definition of force for the purposes of this chapter, this section will provide an overview of the essential distinction between uses of force, armed attacks and acts of aggression. The chapter will then – going the other way on the gravity spectrum – address the issue as to whether *all* uses of force can be said to come within the reach of the prohibition of the use of force as contained within Article 2(4) of the UN Charter and customary international law.

### 2.5.1 Distinguishing 'Use of Force', 'Armed Attack' and 'Aggression'

#### 2.5.1.1 *'Armed Attack'*

Of perhaps greatest significance is the distinction between the concepts of 'use of force', as found in Article 2(4) of the UN Charter, and 'armed attack', as

---

[79] International Law Commission, Draft articles on the Responsibility of States for Internationally Wrongful Acts, with commentaries, UN Doc. A/56/10 (2001), Article 16, para. 8. Furthermore, Article 3(f) of the Definition of Aggression (1974) stipulates that an act of aggression shall occur through '[t]he action of a State in allowing its territory, which it has placed at the disposal of another State, to be used by that other State for perpetrating an act of aggression against a third State'. While it may be contended that Belarus' decision to permit its territory to be used for the commission of an unlawful use of force was not an entirely free one given the influence that Russia had over it, both Article 5(1) of the Definition of Aggression and Article 26 of the ILC's Draft Articles on State Responsibility are clear that nothing, not even the threat of a Russian occupation, would justify Belarus' complicity in the Russian aggression against Ukraine.

[80] See BBC News, 'Ukraine Conflict: UK Sanctions Belarus for Role in Russian Invasion', 1 March 2022, available at: www.bbc.co.uk/news/uk-politics-60580294.

[81] Section 2.2 examined the notion of 'intervention', while Section 1.2 distinguished force from the more general and, in many respects, historical, concept of 'war'. Section 1.5.5.2 addressed the concept of 'aggression' in the context of the crime of aggression. The concepts of 'threat to the peace', 'breach of the peace' and 'act of aggression' as they appear within the sections of the UN Charter that set out the powers of the UN Security Council in engaging in enforcement action are discussed in Chapters 3 and 4 in the context of action undertaken by the Council.

found in Article 51, which is the provision of the Charter providing for the right of self-defence.[82] The distinction is potentially important, as Chapter 6 will examine in further detail, since under Article 51 it is only in the case of an 'armed attack' that a forcible response in self-defence becomes permissible. The UN Charter does not itself resolve the question of what, if anything, is the difference between the two concepts of 'use of force' and 'armed attack'. The ICJ has, however, taken the opportunity to address this distinction and was of the view that it is necessary 'to distinguish the most grave forms of the use of force (those constituting an armed attack) from other less grave forms' so that a distinction based upon 'gravity' should be made by taking into account the 'scale and effects' of the particular use of force.[83]

On the face of it this might seem a sensible and logical way of distinguishing the concepts, although, as discussed in Chapter 6, there are various problems with such a conceptual distinction.[84] For example, whereas it would seem to be commendable in theory, it is not clear if such a distinction based upon gravity has worked, or indeed could work, in practice. While the ICJ's gravity threshold between 'force' and 'armed attack' is not universally accepted in scholarly writings,[85] it is also not clear that states make such a distinction in practice, with arguably much greater focus placed upon the necessity and proportionality of the action taken, which does at least raise question marks over the utility of the conceptual distinction.[86] In any case, it might seem that the difference between the two concepts of force and armed attack is not of much significance given that the ICJ in the *Oil Platforms* case did 'not exclude the possibility that the mining of a single military vessel might be sufficient to bring into play the "inherent right of self-defence"'.[87]

It is also arguable, although a view not entirely free from controversy, that, while the prohibition of the use of force applies only to the acts of states, the right of self-defence exists in order for states to be able to defend themselves, regardless of from whom or what the armed attack emanates. Indeed, even if it was not always a widely-held view, the assumption that non-state actors may be perpetrators of an armed attack is now more broadly, if not universally, accepted.[88]

---

[82] See Chapters 6–8 on self-defence. The equally authentic French version uses the term 'aggression armée'.

[83] *Nicaragua* case, n. 2, at paras. 191 and 195. See also *Case Concerning Oil Platforms (Islamic Republic of Iran v. United States of America)*, Judgment, (2003) ICJ Reports 161, at paras. 51 and 64.

[84] See Section 6.2.5.   [85] See Section 6.2.5.

[86] See Sections 6.2 and 6.3, respectively, on the concepts of armed attack and the customary criteria of necessity and proportionality.

[87] *Oil Platforms* case, n. 83, at para. 72.   [88] See Section 6.2.1 and, in general, Chapter 8.

## 2.5.1.2 'Aggression'

The concept of 'aggression', on the other hand, appears in Article 39 of Chapter VII, along with 'threat to the peace' and 'breach of the peace' as a trigger for unlocking the Security Council's enforcement powers under Chapter VII of the UN Charter, as well as existing as a crime in customary international law and within the Rome Statute of the International Criminal Court.[89] While, as with 'use of force' and 'armed attack', 'aggression' remained undefined, in 1974 the UN General Assembly adopted the Definition of Aggression,[90] believing that providing a definition 'ought to have the effect of deterring a potential aggressor' and 'would simplify the determination of acts of aggression and the implementation of measures to suppress them' by the Security Council.[91] It can be doubted whether these aims were achieved following its adoption, not only due to the fact that we have witnessed incidents – including by permanent members of the Council – that would clearly fit within the Definition but also because the Security Council has never expressly cited the Definition itself or referred directly to the basic principles contained within it.[92]

What is noticeable from the Definition of Aggression, and as repeated in the *crime* of aggression within the Rome Statute,[93] is the distinct echo of Article 2(4) of the UN Charter: 'Aggression is the use of armed force by a State against the sovereignty, territorial integrity or political independence of another State, or in any other manner inconsistent with the Charter of the United Nations.'[94] Of course, and as noted in Section 2.2.1.1, armed attacks have been distinguished by the ICJ from uses of force upon the basis of their 'gravity', in particular their 'scale and effects'. This distinction is similarly made in distinguishing uses of force and aggression whereby 'aggression is the *most serious and dangerous form* of the illegal use of force'.[95] In this respect, although '[t]he First use of armed force by a State in contravention of the Charter shall constitute prima facie evidence of an act of aggression',[96] the

---

[89] See Sections 3.3.1.2 and 1.5.5.2, respectively.  [90] Definition of Aggression, n. 21.
[91] Preamble, ibid.
[92] This is in contrast to the UN General Assembly, which, after having the situation of Russia's invasion of Ukraine in 2022 referred to it by the UN Security Council, adopted a resolution on 'Aggression against Ukraine' in which it both recalled the 1974 Definition of Aggression as well as *Deplore[ing] in the strongest terms* the aggression by the Russian Federation against Ukraine in violation of Article 2(4) of the Charter'. See UNGA Res. ES-11/1 (2022), preamble and para. 2, respectively. The ICJ has also made use of it in its jurisprudence. See *Nicaragua* case, n. 2, at para. 195; *Armed Activities on the Territory of the Congo (Democratic Republic of the Congo v. Uganda)*, Judgment, (2005) ICJ Reports 168, at para. 146.
[93] Article 8*bis*(2), Rome Statute of the International Criminal Court (1998). See also Section 1.5.5.2.
[94] Article 1, Definition of Aggression, n. 21.  [95] Preamble, ibid. (emphasis added).
[96] Article 2, ibid.

Council may decide against determining that an act of aggression has occurred if, upon examining all of the circumstances, it concludes that 'the acts concerned or their consequences are not of sufficient *gravity*'.[97] Similarly, the Rome Statute now holds that an act of aggression for the purposes of the crime of aggression is one that 'by its character, gravity and scale, constitutes a manifest violation of the Charter of the United Nations'.[98]

One may then wonder where the line is to be drawn between a use of force and a serious use of force or one with particular gravity, something that will be addressed further in Chapter 6. However, one may also wonder what the difference is, if any, between acts of aggression and armed attacks. The negotiations within the UN preceding the adoption of the Definition give rise to the impression that a separation between the two was not always clear, and it is fair to say that a clear separation has not emerged in state practice. The ICJ in the *Nicaragua* case appeared to equate them, at least in certain respects.[99] Nonetheless, it is clear that '"[a]ggression" ... is a notion broader than "armed attack", with the latter being a sub-category of the former'.[100] For example, while the acts that are included in Article 3 of the Definition as those which qualify as aggression include '[t]he action of a State in allowing its territory, which it has placed at the disposal of another State, to be used by that other State for perpetrating an act of aggression against a third State',[101] this would

---

[97] Ibid (emphasis added).
[98] Article 8*bis*(1), Rome Statute of the International Criminal Court (1998).
[99] That is, in its use of para. 3(g) of the Definition of Aggression to establish that an armed attack may be perpetrated through 'the sending by a State of armed bands to the territory of another State'. *Nicaragua* case, n. 2, at para. 195.
[100] Roscini, n. 58, at 71.
[101] Article 3(f), Definition of Aggression, n. 21. See Section 2.4.3, where this provision is discussed in relation to the provision of territory by Belarus to aid Russia in its invasion of Ukraine in 2022. The acts contained within Article 3 of the Definition include: (a) The invasion or attack by the armed forces of a State of the territory of another State, or any military occupation, however temporary, resulting from such invasion or attack, or any annexation by the use of force of the territory of another State or part thereof; (b) Bombardment by the armed forces of a State against the territory of another State or the use of any weapons by a State against the territory of another State; (c) The blockade of the ports or coasts of a State by the armed forces of another State; (d) An attack by the armed forces of a State on the land, sea or air forces, or marine and air fleets of another State; (e) The use of armed forces of one State which are within the territory of another State with the agreement of the receiving State, in contravention of the conditions provided for in the agreement or any extension of their presence in such territory beyond the termination of the agreement; (f) The action of a State in allowing its territory, which it has placed at the disposal of another State, to be used by that other State for perpetrating an act of aggression against a third State; (g) The sending by or on behalf of a State of armed bands, groups, irregulars or mercenaries, which carry out acts of armed force against another State of such gravity as to amount to the acts listed, or its substantial involvement therein. The acts enumerated are not exhaustive, however, and the Security Council may determine that other acts constitute aggression under the provisions of the Charter. Article 4, Definition of Aggression, n. 21.

not be sufficient in and of itself to give rise to an armed attack for the purposes of the right of self-defence.[102]

## 2.5.2 'Minimal' Uses of Force and the Possible Existence of a *De Minimis* Threshold

While there is nothing to indicate such in the UN Charter, or the subsequently adopted interpretive resolutions of the UN General Assembly, it has been contended that there is a *de minimis* gravity threshold for Article 2(4) uses of force, meaning that the prohibition does not cover *all* uses of force.[103] Indeed, today there is a growing debate amongst academic commentators on this issue, and Tom Ruys, while generally dismissive of such a *de minimis* threshold, nonetheless concedes that this approach 'appears to be gaining ground in legal doctrine'.[104] For example, one of the leading proponents of this view, Olivier Corten, contends that, from state practice, 'it can be concluded that there is a threshold below which the use of force in international relations, while it may be contrary to certain rules of international law, cannot violate article 2(4)'.[105] In addition, Mary Ellen O'Connell, while conceding that '[t]here is no express authority on the point', goes on to argue that 'Article 2(4) is narrower than it might appear on its face. Minimal or *de minimis* uses of force are likely to fall below the threshold of the Article 2(4) prohibition.'[106]

---

[102] The armed attack may be attributed to the assisting state, and thus provide a victim state with the right of self-defence against it, if the assisting state was either in control of the actions of the attacking state or it acknowledged the attack as its own. See Articles 8 and 11, Draft Articles on the Responsibility of States for Internationally Wrongful Acts, n. 79. However, Article 16 of the Draft Articles treats complicity, which would normally be the case in the provision of territory, as distinct from attribution. If such assistance was to be regarded, in and of itself, as an armed attack it raises questions as to whether other forms of (perhaps lesser) assistance might similarly be classified as an armed attack. Yet, '[a] comprehensive and consistent approach classifying assistance as independent aggression/armed attack is hence still to develop.' See Benjamin Nußberger and Paula Fischer, 'Justifying Self-defense against Assisting States: Conceptualizing Legal Consequences of Inter-State Assistance', *EJIL Talk!*, 23 May 2019, available at: www.ejiltalk.org/justifying-self-defense-against-assisting-states-conceptualizing-legal-consequences-of-inter-state-assistance/.

[103] Corten, n. 42, at 66; Mary Ellen O'Connell, 'The Prohibition of the Use of Force', in Nigel D. White and Christian Henderson (eds.), *Research Handbook on International Conflict and Security Law: Jus ad Bellum, Jus in Bello and Jus post Bellum* (Edward Elgar, 2013), 89, at 102.

[104] Ruys, n. 25, at 158. Ruys notes that 'even if the position may be gaining ground, it is certainly not shared universally in legal doctrine'. Ibid., at 191–2.

[105] Corten, n. 42, at 66.

[106] O'Connell, n. 103, at 102. Furthermore, it is contended that '[s]hooting across the bow of a ship, shooting at the legs of a person evading arrest and dropping a bomb on an oil tanker to prevent coastal pollution are all examples of such minimal or *de minimis* armed force'. Ibid.

In elaborating upon the sorts of actions that might fall below the threshold, the Independent International Fact-Finding Mission on the Conflict in Georgia stated in its report of 2009 that the 'prohibition of the use of force covers all physical force which surpasses a minimum threshold of intensity' and that '[o]nly very small incidents lie below this threshold, for instance the targeted killing of single individuals, forcible abductions of individual persons, or the interception of a single aircraft.'[107] Ruys notes that '[o]ther types of acts that have sometimes been characterized as insufficiently "grave" include operations aimed at rescuing nationals abroad, "hot pursuit" operations, small-scale counterterrorist operations abroad, and localized hostile encounters between military units.'[108]

The ICJ has not discussed this issue directly, although some commentators have argued that it was supportive of a gravity threshold for the use of force in the *Corfu Channel* case.[109] Albania suggested that a minesweeping operation undertaken by a British ship contravened Article 2(4).[110] The United Kingdom responded that, even if coercive, in that it was engaged in the 'sweeping of a strait for mines against the will of Albania',[111] its actions 'did not force on Albania any acceptance of a new state of things'.[112] In a similar tone to the British claims, while the Court ultimately concluded that 'the UK violated the sovereignty of Albania', it did 'not consider that the action of the British Navy was a demonstration of force for the purpose of exercising political pressure on Albania'.[113] Corten argues that '[i]n stating this, the Court suggests that the British operation was not serious enough to come under the prohibition of the use of force set out in the UN Charter'.[114]

In contrast, Ruys is arguably correct in claiming that the statement by the Court is ambiguous and open to multiple interpretations.[115] It might also be seen to be a statement of fact, as the purpose of the UK's minesweeping was indeed not to exercise political pressure, but rather the search for mines.

---

[107] Report of the Independent International Fact-Finding Mission on the Conflict in Georgia, September 2009, vol. II, at 242 and n. 48, available at: www.mpil.de/files/pdf4/IIFFMCG_Volume_II1.pdf.

[108] Ruys, n. 25, at 159.

[109] *Corfu Channel (United Kingdom v. Albania)*, Merits (1949) ICJ Reports 4. Some consider that the Court supported such a gravity threshold. See Corten, n. 42, at 79; O'Connell, n. 103, at 102-3. It is also clear that the ICJ has been more focused upon the distinction between intervention and an indirect use of force and between a use of force and an armed attack than the *de minimis* use of force threshold.

[110] *Corfu Channel (United Kingdom v. Albania)*, Reply submitted by the Albanian Government according to Order of the Court of 28 March 1948, 20 September 1948 (1949) ICJ Pleadings, Oral Arguments, Documents, vol. I, 373, at para. 154.

[111] *Corfu Channel (United Kingdom v. Albania)*, Oral Proceedings (First Part) 18 January 1949 (1950) ICJ Pleadings, Oral Arguments, Documents, vol. III, at 595.

[112] Ibid., at 581.   [113] *Corfu Channel* case, n. 109, at 35.   [114] Corten, n. 42, at 79.

[115] Ruys, n. 25, at 166-7.

## 2.5 The 'Gravity' Element of a Use of Force

Alternatively, Christine Gray argues that 'the Court implicitly upheld the prohibition of the use of force under the new UN Charter'.[116] This is supported by the fact that, while the United Kingdom additionally claimed that its actions were lawful as they did not affect the territorial integrity or political independence of Albania, the Court viewed:

> the alleged right of intervention as the manifestation of a policy of force, such as has, in the past, given rise to most serious abuses and such as cannot, whatever be the present defects in international organisation, find a place in international law. Intervention is perhaps still less inadmissible in the particular form it would take here; for, from the nature of things, it would be reserved for the most powerful States.[117]

However, on balance, it is difficult to attach too much support one way or the other for a *de minimis* threshold upon the basis of the judgement in this case.

One may wonder why marking out the line where acts of force engage the prohibition of the use of force is important, particularly as a violation of the prohibition of the use of force does not *per se* provide a right to respond forcibly: the real distinction comes between a 'use of force' and an 'armed attack'. But there are reasons that make the existence of any threshold level for the engagement of the prohibition important. First, determining whether a forcible act amounts to a use of force for the purposes of the prohibition of the use of force is significant, given the fundamental or 'cornerstone' position that the prohibition has within the UN Charter regime and international law more generally.[118] Secondly, and as discussed in Chapter 1, the prohibition of the use of force arguably represents a *jus cogens* norm, or at least a fundamental one.[119] As such, determining whether a state is responsible for an act of force for the purposes of the prohibition amounts to determining whether that state is responsible for the violation of a *jus cogens* norm.

Thirdly, questions arise as to the responses available to the victim state of a forcible act. A state arguably cannot respond forcibly to a prior act not amounting to an 'armed attack'.[120] In this respect, if certain acts do not constitute a use of force, then they likely will not constitute an armed attack, meaning that self-defence cannot be invoked in response to them. Indeed, this 'in principle rules out the possibility of exercising or invoking the right of self-defense in reaction thereto'.[121] Furthermore, if not all uses of force amount to a use of force for the purposes of the prohibition, then certain forcible responses become permissible regardless of whether or not the initial act was

---

[116] Christine Gray, 'The ICJ and the Use of Force', in Christian Tams and James Sloan (eds.), *The Development of International Law by the International Court of Justice* (Oxford University Press, 2013), 237, at 239.
[117] *Corfu Channel* case, n. 109, at 36.    [118] See Chapter 1, n. 2.    [119] See Section 1.3.2.
[120] This depends on the threshold between a use of force and an armed attack, which was discussed in Section 2.5.1.1 and will be addressed further in Section 6.2.5.
[121] Ruys, n. 25, at 162.

of sufficient gravity to be characterised as an armed attack.[122] For example, while certain 'grounds precluding wrongfulness', such as necessity, countermeasures, reprisals and distress, are available to an aggrieved state, these cannot lawfully take the form of an action that would constitute a transgression of the prohibition of the use of force.[123] However, if there are certain forcible acts that do not transgress the prohibition, then a forcible act might be justifiable as a ground precluding wrongfulness. In this respect, '[o]nce the idea of a *de minimis* threshold gains momentum, it may not take long for states to find new ways to justify controversial operations through a (creative?) application of certain grounds precluding wrongfulness'.[124]

Formally speaking there is no indication that the prohibition of force is restricted to uses of force of a particular gravity.[125] However, while states have not directly addressed this issue – one that might be considered as a rather technical, yet important, point of law – practice does nonetheless seem to indicate that not all uses of force will be caught by the prohibition, although whether a particular incident is treated as falling within its scope will inevitably depend upon the particular circumstances, with states sometimes appearing to be divided, or at least uncommitted, on the issue, as discussed in the following section.

### 2.5.2.1 The *De Minimis* Gravity Threshold: Of a Quantitative or Qualitative Nature?

A *de minimis* threshold might seem to imply that it is one of a quantitative nature, and that determinations as to whether or not it has been crossed are made based upon quantifying the level of force under consideration. Yet, the situation is arguably more complex than that with determinations as to whether an incident falls within the purview of the prohibition of force arguably based upon factors of both a quantitative and qualitative nature.

As Article 2(4) prescribes, and as discussed in Section 1.3.1.4, it is only when events occur in the 'international relations' of states that they are to be evaluated in the context of the prohibition of the use of force. The rule does not, as such, regulate all incidences of the use of force 'that may contain some foreign element'.[126] For example, the shooting and killing by British police officers of a Brazilian national, Jean Charles da Silva e de Menezes, after being

---

[122] Ibid.
[123] Article 50(1)(a), Draft Articles on Responsibility of States for Internationally Wrongful Acts (2001). See, further, Section 10.2.
[124] Ruys, n. 25, at 197.
[125] See also the discussion in Section 2.4.2 on the factors that might be taken into account in determining whether an action will constitute armed force for the purposes of the prohibition of the use of force.
[126] Corten, n. 42, at 86.

## 2.5 The 'Gravity' Element of a Use of Force

incorrectly identified as the perpetrator of a failed bombing attempt in London in 2005,[127] led to a police investigation and negative reaction from Brazil, but at no point was an allegation made that the incident engaged the 'international relations' of the United Kingdom and Brazil for the purposes of the prohibition of the use of force.

Yet, even if a coercive action is undertaken outside of the acting state's territory, and even within the territory of another state, it may not be deemed to fall within the prohibition of force, in particular due to it not employing, at least initially, the use of armed force. This is arguably demonstrated by various abductions that have taken place by one state of civilians located within the territory of another. These are often perceived of as engaging the 'international relations' of the two states to the extent that the abducting state violated the jurisdictional rights of the territorial state,[128] thus potentially engaging the principle of non-intervention, yet, they are generally viewed as falling below or outside of the scope of the prohibition of the use of force. Adolf Eichmann, who was one of the principal perpetrators of the 'final solution' under the Nazi regime, was abducted by Israeli special agents from Argentina in 1960.[129] Although Argentina protested about the act and the 'interference in its internal affairs', it did not claim that it had been the victim of a use of force, and neither did other states during the debates on the incident.[130] The UN Security Council ultimately adopted a resolution claiming such abductions 'affect the sovereignty of a Member State',[131] without any reference to the prohibition of the use of force.

As a further example, on 5 October 2013, the US Army's Delta force entered Libyan territory and seized the alleged al-Qaida leader Nazih Abdul-Hamed al-Ruqai (also known as Abu Anas al-Liby) who was wanted by the United States for the 1998 bombings of the US embassies in Kenya and Tanzania which killed over 220 people. al-Liby was indicted by a federal court in Manhattan in 1998 in connection with the bombings and there were international warrants issued for his arrest. While there was some uncertainty as to the precise legal justification of the United States in this instance for its apprehension of al-Liby,[132] the Libyan

---

[127] 'Police Shot Brazilian Eight Times', *The Guardian*, 25 July 2005, available at: www.theguardian.com/uk/ 2005/jul/25/july7.uksecurity5.

[128] As well as constituting a breach of any possible extradition treaty in force between the two states, not to mention the human rights of the individual concerned.

[129] *Keesing's* (1960) 17489-91. See James E. Fawcett, 'The *Eichmann* Case' (1962) 28 *British Yearbook of International Law* 197.

[130] See UN Doc. S/PV.865, 22 June 1960.   [131] UNSC Res. 138 (1960), para. 1.

[132] See Christian Henderson, 'The Extraterritorial Seizure of Individuals under International Law – The Case of al-Liby: Part I', *EJIL Talk!*, 6 November 2013, available at: www.ejiltalk.org/the-extraterritorial-seizure-of-individuals-under-international-law-the-case-of-al-liby-part-one/; Christian Henderson, 'The Extraterritorial Seizure of Individuals under International Law – The Case of al-Liby: Part II', *EJIL Talk!*, 7 November 2013, available at: www.ejiltalk.org/the-extraterritorial-seizure-of-individuals-under-international-law-the-case-of-al-liby-part-two/.

authorities did not condemn the incursion into its territory as a violation of the prohibition of the use of force but instead formally condemned the action as a 'kidnapping', demanded an explanation from the United States, claimed that they had not been informed in advance of the raid and requested that al-Liby be returned.[133]

However, these operations stand in contrast to the practice of targeted killings, often involving the use of armed drones, that have been resorted to against terrorist suspects, such as the United States' raid against the al-Qaida leader, Osama bin Laden, in Pakistan in 2011,[134] the United Kingdom's drone strike which killed Reyaad Khan in Syria in 2015,[135] Israel's intentional killing of a PLO leader, Khalil Ibrahim al-Wazir, in Tunis in 1988,[136] and the United States' drone strike which led to the death of Iranian General Qassem Soleimani in Iraq in 2020.[137] While the acting states may conceive of these operations broadly as extraterritorial 'law enforcement' or as deaths occurring within the context of an existing armed conflict, the fact that the sovereignty and territorial integrity of a state was impinged through the use of armed force led to the states concerned invariably attempting to justify them as falling within the right of self-defence, with concerns being raised by other states and those within the broader interpretive community regarding their compatibility with the *jus ad bellum* framework.[138]

However, clear-cut conclusions as to the applicability of the prohibition are often not possible to make. On 4 March 2018, Sergei Skripal, a former Russian spy turned defector, and his daughter Yulia were found unconscious on a bench in the city of Salisbury within the United Kingdom.[139] Investigations by British officials and the Organization for the Prohibition of Chemical Weapons found that both were deliberately poisoned with 'a military-grade nerve agent

---

[133] Carlotta Gall and David D. Kirkpatrick, 'Libya Condemns U.S. for Seizing Terror Suspect', *New York Times*, 6 October 2013, available at: www.nytimes.com/2013/10/07/world/africa/american-raids-in-africa.html?hp.

[134] BBC News, 'Osama bin Laden's Death: How It Happened', 7 June 2011, available at: www.bbc.co.uk/news/world-south-asia-13257330.

[135] BBC News, 'Cardiff Jihadist Reyaad Khan, 21, Killed by RAF Drone', 7 September 2015, available at: www.bbc.co.uk/news/uk-wales-34176790.

[136] The UN Security Council specifically invoked Article 2(4) on this occasion. See UNSC Res. 611 (1988), preamble.

[137] This incident is discussed in various places in Chapter 6 on general aspects of the right of self-defence.

[138] See Chapters 6–8 and, in particular, Section 8.5 on targeted killings. See, in general, Nils Melzer, *Targeted Killings in International Law* (Oxford University Press, 2009); Meagan S. Wong, 'Targeted Killings and the International Legal Framework: With Particular Reference to the US Operation against Osama bin Laden' (2012) 11 *Chinese Journal of International Law* 127.

[139] Luke Harding, Steven Morris and Caroline Bannock, 'Former Russian Spy Critically Ill in UK "After Exposure to Substance"', *The Guardian*, 6 March 2018, available at: www.theguardian.com/world/2018/mar/05/salisbury-incident-critically-ill-man-is-former-russian-spy-sergei-skripal.

of a type developed by Russia', known as 'Novichok'.[140] Several individuals who came into contact with the substance were hospitalised, including a police officer, while one individual died in July 2018 after coming into contact with the nerve agent following its disposal after the attack on the Skripals in March.[141]

Following the incident, the UK Prime Minister stated that, absent a satisfactory explanation from Russia, the action would be regarded as an 'unlawful use of force by the Russian State against the United Kingdom'.[142] Jonathan Allen, the UK's Ambassador to the United Nations, also stressed that the attempted murder 'was no common crime. It was an unlawful use of force – a violation of article two of the United Nations charter, the basis of the international legal order.'[143]

While Russia refuted the accusations that it was responsible for the incident, instead accusing Britain of the poisoning,[144] if Russia is considered to be the responsible actor it remains that it involved an attempted assassination by a state against one its own nationals, something that might not immediately be seen to engage the prohibition of the inter-state use of force. Furthermore, actual and attempted assassinations of individuals on foreign soil had not previously often been categorised as a prohibited 'use of force',[145] and this

---

[140] 'Salisbury Attack: Chemical Weapons Watchdog Confirms UK Findings on Nerve Agent', *Deutsche Welle*, 12 April 2018, available at: www.dw.com/en/salisbury-attack-chemical-weapons-watchdog-confirms-uk-findings-on-nerve-agent/a-43358224.

[141] Vikram Dodd, Steven Morris and Caroline Bannock, 'Novichok in Wilshire Death "Highly Likely" from Batch used on Skripals', *The Guardian*, 9 July 2018, available at: www.theguardian.com/uk-news/2018/jul/09/novichok-wiltshire-death-dawn-sturgess-highly-likely-same-batch-used-on-skripals.

[142] See Rt Hon Theresa May MP, 'PM Commons Statement on Salisbury incident response: 14 March 2018', 14 March 2018, available at: www.gov.uk/government/speeches/pm-commons-statement-on-salisbury-incident-response-14-march-2018. Later, in September 2018, British authorities identified two Russian nationals as suspected of the Skripals' poisoning, both of whom were active officers in the GRU, Russia's foreign military intelligence agency. See 'Salisbury Novichok Poisoning: Russian Nationals Named as Suspects', *BBC News*, 5 September 2018, available at: www.bbc.co.uk/news/uk-45421445.

[143] See Statement by Ambassador Jonathan Allen, Chargé d'Affaires, at a UN Security Council Briefing on a nerve agent attack in Salisbury, 14 March 2018, available at: www.gov.uk/government/speeches/the-russian-state-was-responsible-for-the-attempted-murderand-for-threatening-the-lives-of-other-british-citizens-in-salisbury.

[144] Lizzie Dearden, 'Russia Claims It Could Have Been in Interests of Britain to Poison Sergei Skripal', *The Independent*, 2 April 2018, available at: www.independent.co.uk/news/world/europe/sergei-skripal-latest-salisbury-poisoning-attack-russia-nerve-agent-sergei-lavrov-a8284766.html.

[145] For example, the assassination of the North Korean leader's half-brother, Kim Jong-nam, with a VX nerve agent in a Malaysian airport early in 2017 was not discussed in these terms.

incident was discussed by several scholars as a relatively minor incident in the context of any *de minimis* threshold.[146]

However, the fact that Russia intentionally utilised a chemical weapon on the territory of another state which had potentially grave implications for the population and security of that state arguably provide support for the United Kingdom's categorisation of the incident as one constituting a prohibited use of force.[147] Yet, it is unclear whether other states shared the UK's view. For example, although during the debate within the UN Security Council the incident was widely condemned, states refrained from referring to the assassination attempt as a use of force, with many instead describing it as a hostile act, a reckless act, a crime, an attack, an incident or a threat to international peace and security.[148] The United Kingdom itself also described the incident as an 'attack', although it was careful to avoid claiming that it was an 'armed attack', thereby potentially giving rise to the right of self-defence.[149] Indeed, the United Kingdom did not seek to respond using forcible measures, but instead took various non-forcible measures, including the expulsion of twenty-three Russian diplomats.[150] The United Kingdom's response (to what it, at least, sought to depict as a prohibited use of force upon its territory) was, however, supported by twenty-eight other countries which responded similarly, with an unprecedented 153 Russian diplomats being expelled by the end of March 2018.[151] It is, therefore, difficult to draw any firm conclusions as to the categorisation of this incident in terms of the prohibition of force.

A particular incident may, however, not be deemed to fall within the prohibition of force due to it being perceived of as an incident of law enforcement and/or regulated in the first instance by another legal framework. In the context of incidents involving both single and groups of individuals international human rights law and the Basic Principles on the Use of Force

---

[146] See, for example, Marc Weller, 'An International Use of Force in Salisbury?', *EJIL:Talk!*, available at: www.ejiltalk.org/an-international-use-of-force-in-salisbury/; Tom Ruys, '"License to Kill" in Salisbury: State-Sponsored Assassinations and the *Jus ad Bellum*', *Just Security*, 15 March 2018, available at: www.justsecurity.org/53924/license-kill-salisbury-state-sponsored-assassinations-jus-ad-bellum/.

[147] In her statement to parliament, the UK Prime Minister referred to the 'potentially catastrophically damaging nerve agent' that was used (see n. 141), while in the UN Security Council the UK claimed that as many as 100 citizens had been potentially exposed (see n. 142).

[148] See UN Doc. S/PV.8203, 14 March 2018.

[149] This was also shared by the North Atlantic Council. See www.nato.int/cps/en/natohq/news_152787.htm. See, further, Section 2.5.1.1.

[150] See BBC News, 'Russian Spy: UK to Expel 23 Russian Diplomats', 14 March 2018, available at: www.bbc.co.uk/news/uk-43402506.

[151] Alia Chughtai and Mariya Petkova, 'Skripal Case Diplomatic Expulsions in Numbers', *Al Jazeera*, 3 April 2018, available at: www.aljazeera.com/news/2018/4/3/skripal-case-diplomatic-expulsions-in-numbers.

and Firearms by Law Enforcement Officials permit, under stringent conditions, the use of force against both domestic and foreign individuals for the purposes of law enforcement.[152] In addition, an independent and express legal basis exists within the United Nations Convention on the Law of the Sea (1982) (UNCLOS) for certain enforcement action against foreign vessels within the territorial seas and exclusive economic zone of states[153] and, while vessels on the high seas are, in principle, subject to the exclusive jurisdiction of their flag states, enforcement action is possible on the high seas in exceptional circumstances, for example when a ship is engaged in piracy, the slave trade or unauthorised broadcasting.[154] Of significance, however, is that Article 301 of UNCLOS also states that, in exercising their rights and performing their duties under the Convention, states 'shall refrain from any threat or use of force against the territorial integrity or political independence of any State, or in any other manner inconsistent with the principles of international law embodied in the Charter of the United Nations', indicating that forcible measures of a law enforcement nature envisaged in the Convention are of a different type to those covered by Article 2(4) of the Charter and which occur in the 'international relations' of states.[155]

Similarly, Article *3bis*(a) of the Chicago Convention on International Civil Aviation (1944) provides that 'every State must refrain from resorting to the use of weapons against a civil aircraft in flight and that, in case of interception, the lives of persons on board and the safety of the aircraft must not be endangered'. In addition, however, the provision 'shall not be interpreted as modifying in any way the rights and obligations of States set forth in the Charter of the United Nations', thus confirming, as in the law of the sea context, that actions taken under the Convention are to be distinguished from those that come within the realms of the UN Charter, that is, within the 'international relations' of states.[156]

Whether a state complies with its obligations under these frameworks – or indeed any other framework – does not impact upon the legality of the operation under the *jus ad bellum*. Nonetheless, this qualitative distinction in the type of force envisaged in these different legal frameworks can arguably be

---

[152] See Basic Principles on the Use of Force and Firearms by Law Enforcement Officials 112, UN Doc. A/CONF.144/28/Rev.1 (1990) (adopted by the Eighth United Nations Congress on the Prevention of Crime and the Treatment of Offenders, Havana, Cuba 27 August–7 September 1990).

[153] See, for example, Articles 25 and 73(1), UNCLOS (1982).

[154] Articles 107 and 110, ibid. See Douglas Guilfoyle, 'Interdicting Vessels to Enforce the Common Interest: Maritime Countermeasures and the Use of Force' (2007) 56 *International & Comparative Law Quarterly* 69.

[155] Corten, n. 42, at 67.

[156] See, in general, Brian E. Foont, 'Shooting Down Civilian Aircraft: Is There an International Law?' (2007) 72 *Air Law and Commerce* 695.

seen in practice. For example, in 1967, and in the face of a significant oil spillage, the UK authorities bombed the wreck of the *Torrey Canyon*, a Liberian-flagged vessel that had run aground outside of British territorial waters.[157] This was a significant operation which lasted several days and witnessed napalm bombs being dropped on the wreck so as to release and burn the oil that was still inside the tank of the ship. The action of the British authorities was not discussed in the context of the prohibition of the use of force, but focus was rather placed upon its legality as a police measure on the high seas.[158] In addition, while ultimately finding that it did not have jurisdiction to hear the case, the ICJ in the *Fisheries Jurisdiction* case between Spain and Canada did determine that the arrest of a private Spanish fishing vessel and its crew by Canadian authorities on the high seas in accordance with a Canadian Act to prohibit the fishing of straddling stocks was a use of force that 'falls within the ambit of what is commonly understood as enforcement of conservation and management measures' and not within the realms of the prohibition of the use of force in Article 2(4), as had been argued by Spain.[159]

As an example of an air incident being treated as law enforcement as opposed to a use of force for the purposes of the UN Charter, in 1996 the Cuban air force shot down two small civil aircraft of the US-based Brothers to the Rescue group in international airspace as they were returning to Florida after having intentionally violated Cuban airspace, which led to the deaths of four persons.[160] Several states found that the operation contravened the principle in Article 3*bis* (a) of the Chicago Convention, although no reference was made to the prohibition of the use of force.[161] The UN Security Council subsequently adopted a resolution in which it noted that the incident 'violated the principle that States must refrain from the use of weapons against civil aircraft in flight',[162] with no reference to the rules and principles of the *jus ad bellum*.

More recently, on 23 May 2021 the government of Belarus ordered Belarusian MiG-29 fighter jets to intercept and force to land in Minsk Ryanair Flight 4978 which was travelling through Belarussian airspace at the time on its way from Athens to Vilnius.[163] This order was made on the basis of a 'potential security threat' in the form of an alleged bomb on board

---

[157] *Keesing's* (1967) 22002–5.   [158] Corten, n. 42, at 69.
[159] *Fisheries Jurisdiction (Spain v. Canada)*, Jurisdiction of the Court, Judgment (1998) ICJ Reports 432. In addition, Corten notes that 'it seems plain that the arrest of the Spanish vessel by Canadian coastguards was not deemed a problem of the use of force because the Canadian State had no intention of attacking the Spanish State'. Corten, n. 42, at 86. For more on the *mens rea* element of a prohibited use of force see Section 2.6.
[160] *Keesing's* (1996) 40945.   [161] UN Doc. S/PV.3682, 26 July 1996.
[162] UNSC Res. 1067 (1996), para. 2.
[163] Andrew Roth, 'Belarus accused of "hijacking" Ryanair flight diverted to arrest blogger', *The Guardian*, 23 May 2021, available at: www.theguardian.com/world/2021/may/23/belarus-diverts-ryanair-plane-to-arrest-blogger-says-opposition.

the plane.[164] Under Article 3*bis*(b) of the Chicago Convention a state is entitled to require a civilian aircraft flying above within its airspace to land at a designated airport when the latter is flying 'without authority' or 'if there are reasonable grounds to conclude that it is being used for any purpose inconsistent with the aims of this Convention'. While Flight 4978 was flying through Belarussian airspace with authority, a bomb on board may qualify as 'a purpose inconsistent with the aims of the Convention'. Belarus failed, however, to provide any evidence that it had any 'reasonable grounds to conclude' that there was such a bomb threat.[165]

Of importance for the purposes here, however, was that the incident was perceived as falling within the Chicago Convention, not the prohibition of force contained within the UN Charter.[166] The International Civil Aviation Organization was 'strongly concerned by the apparent forced landing of a Ryanair flight and its passengers, which could be in contravention of the Chicago Convention'.[167] Furthermore, the European Commission president, Ursula von der Leyen, described the incident as 'utterly unacceptable' and that 'any violation of international air transport rules must bear consequences',[168] Canada's Foreign Affairs Minister, Marc Garneau, claimed that the incident was 'a serious interference in civil aviation and a clear attack on media freedom',[169] while the United Kingdom's Foreign Secretary, Dominic Raab, stated that the incident was a 'shocking assault on civil aviation'.[170]

---

[164] Ibid.

[165] If a fake bomb threat had been made a crime would have been committed under Article 1 of the Convention for the Suppression of Unlawful Acts against the Safety of Civil Aviation (1971). It is widely believed that the real reason for the forced landing of the plane was the arrest and detention of the journalist Roman Protasevich who was a staunch critic of the regime in Belarus which had declared him to be a terrorist as well as having charged him with a number of crimes under Belarusian law. See Roth, n. 162.

[166] Although Jackson and Tzanakopoulos note that 'the scrambling of fighters to intercept and escort the flight to the airport ... must constitute at least a threat of force ... [w]e note that interception, in particular, will likely entail a threat of force when undertaken by fighters'. Miles Jackson and Antonios Tzanakopoulos, 'Aerial Incident of 23 May 2021: Belarus and the Ryanair Flight 4978', *EJIL Talk!*, 24 May 2021, available at: www.ejiltalk.org/aerial-incident-of-23-may-2021-belarus-and-the-ryanair-flight-4978/. It is not entirely clear whether the authors are speaking here of 'force' in general terms or in the context of the prohibition of force contained within the UN Charter.

[167] See https://twitter.com/icao/status/1396515815248257027?s=20.

[168] David Kaminski-Morrow, 'Political Leaders Outraged as Belarus "Forces" Ryanair 737 Diversion to Minsk', *Flight Global*, 23 May 2021, available at: www.flightglobal.com/safety/political-leaders-outraged-as-belarus-forces-ryanair-737-diversion-to-minsk/143868.article.

[169] 'Belarus Diverts Prominent Critic's Flight, Arrests Him upon Landing', *CBC News*, 23 May 2021, available at: www.cbc.ca/news/world/belarus-arrests-critic-divert-flight-raman-pratasevich-1.6038279.

[170] Mary O'Connor, 'UK Airlines Told to Avoid Belarussian Airspace after Journalist Arrest', *BBC News*, 24 May 2021, available at: www.bbc.co.uk/news/uk-57232988.

However, although a particular action may not start out as one perceived of as engaging the prohibition of force – either because it is not deemed to possess the requisite gravity or due to the fact that it is seen as engaging an alternative legal framework – it is possible that the prohibition subsequently becomes engaged as a result of a particular escalation in the incident. For example, while the abduction of Adolf Eichmann discussed above in this section was not seen as an incident engaging the prohibition, it is arguable that the response and categorisation of the incident may have been different if Argentinian authorities had confronted the Israeli agents and forcibly resisted the abduction, thereby escalating the incident between the two states.

Furthermore, on 19 July 2019, and in a different context, Iran's Revolutionary Guards seized two oil tankers while in the strait of Hormuz,[171] claiming that they were in violation of various environmental and maritime regulations, claims that were rejected by the ships' owners.[172] One of the tankers, the *Mesdar*, was Liberian-flagged but British operated, while the other, the *Stena Impero*, was a Swedish owned and British-flagged vessel. The seizures took place in the context of heightened tensions in the region. For example, on 13 June 2019 two oil tankers – one Norwegian-flagged and the other Japanese-flagged – were struck by mines in the Gulf of Oman.[173] Responsibility for these attacks was placed on Iran.[174] Later, on 4 July 2019, a Panamanian-flagged vessel owned by Iran, known as Grace I, was seized by UK marines in Gibraltar, suspected of attempting to transport oil to Syria in contravention of the EU's sanctions on Syria.[175]

Despite this heightened tension between Iran and the United Kingdom the incident was not primarily depicted as one arising in the 'international relations' of the states and thereby within the context of the prohibition of force, but rather in the context of the freedom of navigation of merchant vessels.[176] The UK Foreign Secretary, Jeremy Hunt, stated that '[i]t is essential that freedom of navigation is maintained and that all ships can move safely and

---

[171] Barbara Starr, Ryan Brown and Kara Fox, 'Iran Announces Capture of British-Flagged Oil Tanker; US Officials Say Two Ships Seized', *CNN*, 19 June 2019, available at: https://edition.cnn.com/2019/07/19/middleeast/british-tanker-seized-iran-intl/index.html.

[172] Julian Borger, Patrick Wintour and Kevin Rawlinson, 'Iran Stokes Gulf Tensions by Seizing Two British-linked Oil Tankers', *The Guardian*, 19 July 2019, available at: www.theguardian.com/world/2019/jul/19/british-tanker-iran-capture-fears-stena-impero-uk-ship-latest.

[173] Patrick Wintour and Julian Borger, 'Two Oil Tankers Attacked in Gulf of Oman', *The Guardian*, 13 June 2019, available at: www.theguardian.com/world/2019/jun/13/oil-tankers-blasts-reports-gulf-of-oman-us-navy.

[174] Ibid.

[175] BBC News, 'Iran Summons UK Ambassador in Tanker Seizure Row', 4 July 2019, available at: www.bbc.co.uk/news/uk-48871462.

[176] This was despite the fact that the vessels may have been targeted as a proxy for the United Kingdom.

freely in the region',[177] while a UK government statement claimed that the United Kingdom 'remain[ed] deeply concerned about Iran's unacceptable actions which represent a clear challenge to international freedom of navigation.'[178] In its letter to the UN Security Council the United Kingdom claimed that '[t]he ship was exercising the lawful right of transit passage in an international strait as provided for under international law' which 'requires that the right of transit passage shall not be impeded, and therefore the Iranian action constitute[d] illegal interference.'[179]

Yet, while the UK Foreign Secretary claimed that the United Kingdom was 'not looking at military options' but rather 'at a diplomatic way to resolve the situation' he was 'absolutely clear that, if this situation is not resolved quickly, there will be serious consequences.'[180] The United Kingdom's letter to the UN Security Council was also clear that '[c]urrent tensions are extremely concerning, and our priority is to de-escalate. We do not seek confrontation with Iran. But it is unacceptable and highly escalatory to threaten shipping going about its legitimate business through internationally recognised transit corridors.'[181]

Subsequently, on 28 July, the Royal Navy ship *HMS Duncan* arrived in the area which, along with another ship, *HMS Montrose*, was to support the safe passage of British-flagged ships through the Strait of Hormuz.[182] While these actions were primarily to enforce international maritime law there was clearly the potential for them to be seen as occurring within the 'international relations' of Iran and the United Kingdom, and therefore engaging the prohibition of force.

However, although forcible measures taken by a state against private individuals, aircraft or marine vessels might be seen as being governed by regimes other than the *jus ad bellum*, if such entities are targeted as a *proxy* for another state, then it is likely that the inter-state prohibition, and the *jus ad bellum* in general, will be engaged. Indeed, a state may use direct and overt

---

[177] The Rt Hon Jeremy Hunt MP, 'Situation in the Gulf: Foreign Secretary Statement to Parliament', 22 July 2019, available at: www.gov.uk/government/speeches/situation-in-the-gulf-foreign-secretary-statement.

[178] Borger, Wintour and Rawlinson, n. 172.

[179] Chargé d'Affaires of the Permanent Mission of the United Kingdom to the United Nations, 'Letter to the United Nations Security Council President about the Strait of Hormuz incident', 21 July 2019, available at: www.gov.uk/government/publications/strait-of-hormuz-incident-uk-government-letter-to-un-security-council-president/letter-to-the-united-nations-security-council-president-about-the-strait-of-hormuz-incident.

[180] The Rt Hon Jeremy Hunt MP, n. 177.

[181] Chargé d'Affaires of the Permanent Mission of the United Kingdom to the United Nations, n. 179.

[182] Ione Wells, 'Second UK Warship Arrives to Guard Ships in Strait of Hormuz', *The Guardian*, 28 July 2019, available at: www.theguardian.com/uk-news/2019/jul/28/second-uk-warship-arrives-to-guard-ships-in-strait-of-hormuz.

forcible means to indirectly attack another state,[183] although such forcible measures would not come within the realms of the prohibition unless there is evidence to suggest that a particular individual or group of individuals, aircraft or vessel had, in fact, been used as a medium to target a particular state. One way this might be evidenced, for example, is if the force used 'directly arises from a dispute between sovereign States'.[184] In this respect:

> if a police officer of state A uses excessive lethal force against a criminal suspect who is a national of state B, this incident undoubtedly does not trigger Article 2(4). But if considerable tension exists between two neighboring states A and B – for example, because of a border dispute – and police officers of state A round up and summarily execute a group of nationals of state B, such actions could be seen as a use of force in the sense of Article 2(4) (and potentially as an armed attack).[185]

To put this into context, on 3 July 1988 the *USS Vincennes* shot down an Iranian civilian airliner.[186] While given that this incident involved a civil aircraft it might be perceived as falling within the specific treaty regimes governing such actions, Iran, in taking the matter to the ICJ, argued that the action was a violation of the prohibition of the use of force due to the 'aggressive actions by the US warships that were themselves operating within the territorial sea'.[187] In turn, the United States justified its action as one of self-defence and claimed that the 'incident occurred in the midst of an armed engagement between US and Iranian forces in the context of a long series of attacks on US and other vessels in the Gulf'.[188] Both states thus accepted that the incident involving the civilian airliner was to be viewed in the context of the *jus ad bellum*.

As a further example, in June 2000, patrol boats from the Surinamese navy entered a disputed maritime zone and ordered an oil rig and drill ship that were operating there under licence from Guyana to withdraw from the disputed area.[189] While Guyana considered the Surinamese actions as falling within the realms of Article 2(4), Suriname considered the measures to be of a law enforcement nature.[190] The arbitral award of 17 September 2007, while accepting that force may be employed in law enforcement activities, was of

---

[183] This is to be contrasted with indirect forcible means which are discussed in Section 2.4.2.
[184] Ruys, n. 25, at 206.   [185] Ibid., at 206–7.   [186] *Keesing's* (1988) 36064.
[187] Letter dated 3 July 1988 from the Acting Permanent Representative of the Islamic Republic of Iran to the United Nations addressed to the Secretary-General, UN Doc. S/19979, 4 July 1988, at 2.
[188] *Case Concerning the Aerial Incident of 3 July 1988 (Islamic Republic of Iran v. United States of America)*, Preliminary Objections Submitted by the United States of America, 4 March 1991 (1996) ICJ Pleadings, Oral Arguments, Documents, vol. II, at 3.
[189] Award in the arbitration regarding the delimitation of the maritime boundary between Guyana and Suriname, award of 17 September 2007, at para. 151, available at: https://legal.un.org/riaa/cases/vol_XXX/1-144.pdf.
[190] Ibid., at paras. 443–4.

the view that the action 'seemed more akin to a threat of military action rather than a mere law enforcement activity'.[191] In other words, given the existing dispute between the parties, the action taken against the private oil rig was seen within the context of the international dispute between the two states.

The distinction between the two qualitatively distinct legal regimes of law enforcement and the *jus ad bellum* is far from clear cut, however, where issues of law enforcement arise in the context of an incident directly concerning two state entities. For example, on 25 November 2018 the Russian Federal Security Service (FSB) coast guard fired upon and captured three Ukrainian Navy vessels as they approached the Kerch Strait during an attempt to transit from the Black Sea port of Odessa into the Sea of Azov on their way to the port of Mariupol.[192] On their approach to the Kerch Strait, Russian Coast Guard boats accused the Ukrainian ships of illegally entering Russian territorial waters, and ordered them to leave.[193] When the Ukrainians refused, citing a 2003 Russo–Ukrainian treaty,[194] under which the Strait and the Azov Sea are intended to be the shared territorial waters of both countries and freely accessible by each state's warships and merchant vessels, the Russian boats attempted to intercept them and rammed one of the boats.[195] Although the Ukrainian vessels managed to continue on their journey the Russian forces placed a large cargo ship under the Crimean Bridge blocking the route into the Sea of Azov.[196] Not being able to progress further the Ukrainian ships turned back to return to port in Odessa, although as they were leaving the area the Russian Coast Guard pursued and fired upon them, ultimately capturing the Ukrainian vessels in international waters off the coast of Crimea.[197]

Given the inter-state and forcible nature of the incident it might prima facie appear to constitute one falling to be regulated and assessed under the *jus ad bellum*. Indeed, several states condemned the Russian acts of 'aggression'.[198]

---

[191] Ibid., at para. 445.
[192] BBC News, 'Ukraine Claims Russia "Rammed Our Tugboat" Off Crimea', 25 November 2018, available at: www.bbc.co.uk/news/world-europe-46333976.
[193] BBC News, 'Tension Escalates after Russia Seizes Ukraine Naval Ships', 26 November 2018, available at: www.bbc.co.uk/news/world-europe-46338671.
[194] Ibid.   [195] Ibid.   [196] Ibid.   [197] Ibid.
[198] Andrew Roth, 'Kerch Strait Confrontation: What Happened and Why Does It Matter?', *The Guardian*, 27 November 2018, available at: www.theguardian.com/world/2018/nov/27/kerch-strait-confrontation-what-happened-ukrainian-russia-crimea. It was, however, also an incident that occurred following Russia's unlawful act of aggression against Ukraine in 2014 which resulted in the highly disputed and unrecognised annexation of Crimea. As such, while several states described the 25 November 2018 incident as an act of aggression, including Ukraine itself, it is difficult to fully discern whether this was a reference to it occurring in the context of a continuing act of aggression or whether the incident was considered in and of itself a specific act of aggression.

Yet, both Ukraine and Russia, as well as the majority of reacting states, placed the incident more firmly within the context of the two state's respective rights and obligations regarding innocent passage in territorial waters and transit through the Kerch Strait under the 2003 treaty as well as UNCLOS.[199] In this respect, there was a clear overlap and interaction between the *jus ad bellum* and UNCLOS regimes as the question arose as to whether Russia had the right to physically coerce the Ukrainian vessels in this instance.[200] On the one hand, given the sovereign immunity of warships under the UNCLOS regime of innocent passage,[201] then even if the Ukrainian vessels were engaging in non-innocent activities in the territorial sea Russia had no legal basis to assert jurisdiction over them as foreign sovereign immune naval ships, let alone shoot at them, with the only lawful measure the coastal state having recourse to being to 'require [them] to leave the territorial sea immediately'.[202] Yet, on the other hand, as already noted, Article 301 of UNCLOS clearly states that any rights and obligations under UNCLOS shall not prejudice those under the UN Charter, including the right of self-defence, leaving the question to an extent open, depending upon whether the acts that constituted 'non-innocent passage' could be equated to an 'armed attack', thereby justifying the use of force as an act of self-defence.[203]

---

[199] However, it has been argued that given that the incident was part of a continuing act of aggression by Russia against Ukraine it occurred during a continuing armed conflict between the two states meaning that the law of the sea regime was displaced by the law of armed conflict, specifically the law of naval warfare, thereby not resulting in a violation of UNCLOS. See James Kraska, 'The Kerch Strait Incident: Law of the Sea or Law of Naval Warfare?', *EJIL Talk!*, 3 December 2018, available at: www.ejiltalk.org/the-kerch-strait-incident-law-of-the-sea-or-law-of-naval-warfare/.

[200] Kraska, ibid.

[201] See Article 32, UNCLOS. Warships are allowed to engage in 'innocent passage' through territorial waters as long as it is not prejudicial to the peace or security of the coastal state.

[202] See Article 30, UNCLOS. If coastal states were permitted to resort to the use of force then this could be seen as an example of the use of an independent legal regime in the form of UNCLOS being used to justify what might otherwise be perceived as a prohibited use of force in the 'international relations' of states. However, as Kraska notes, 'States have been rather reticent to use force against foreign warships in the territorial sea that are not in innocent passage . . . as illustrated by decades of state practice to warn but avoid attacking submarines intruding in the territorial sea.' Kraska, n. 198.

[203] For example, Article 19(2) of UNCLOS includes as 'non-innocent' – or 'acts considered to be prejudicial to the peace, good order or security of the coastal State' – the following: '(a) any threat or use of force against the sovereignty, territorial integrity or political independence of the coastal State, or in any other manner in violation of the principles of international law embodied in the Charter of the United Nations', '(b) any exercise or practice with weapons of any kind' and '(f) the launching, landing or taking on board of any military device'. See, further, Chapter 6 on self-defence and, in particular, Section 6.2.5 on the gravity threshold distinguishing 'uses of force' from 'armed attacks'.

## 2.6 THE *MENS REA* ELEMENT OF THE USE OF FORCE

On the basis of what has been said in the preceding two subsections it might be said that an intention to use force against a state, or an *animus belligerandi*, is required in order to breach the prohibition of the threat or use of force. Indeed, 'when a State takes *even limited military measures* and admits that such measures are *part of a policy conducted against one State*, there is no doubt that article 2(4) is applicable'.[204] This is an element that has often been overlooked in writings on the use of force.[205] This might be for the reason that 'no express authority supports the view that intent is needed to establish a violation of UN Charter Article 2(4)'.[206] Indeed, a *mens rea* element in determining violations of the prohibition of the use of force is not one that can be located within the UN Charter or relevant instruments. Alternatively, a lack of attention provided to this factor might be for the reason that violations are based upon the notion of objective liability. Indeed, state responsibility is predicated on this principle, so that, unless the primary rules indicate otherwise, no intention or *mens rea* is needed to engage the secondary consequences of responsibility.[207] But while there is no express authority or primary rule on the element of *mens rea* in the determination that a prohibited use of force has occurred, it is arguable that an intention to use force is nonetheless required.[208] Indeed, Corten goes as far as to argue that '[s]uch an intention appears to be an *essential characteristic* of the use of force under the Charter'.[209] This is arguably due to two reasons.

First, the use of force is a specific form of intervention, and for an interference to reach the level of intervention it must be coercive.[210] Indeed, an interference, whether forcible or not, 'will constitute an unlawful intervention

---

[204] Corten, n. 42, at 87.

[205] A notable exception to this trend is Olivier Corten, who includes a specific section within his book entitled 'A State's Willingness to Resort to Force Against Another State'. See ibid., at 85–90. In addition, some have rather implicitly given it central importance: 'logic dictates that any incursion that would have warranted deliberate recourse to lethal force (*primarily because it demonstrates a manifest hostile intent*) itself constitutes a use of force in the sense of Article 2(4), irrespective of the actual response of the territorial state'. Ruys, n. 25, at 171 (emphasis omitted).

[206] Ruys, ibid., at 191. Thus, in its case before the ICJ concerning Iran Air Flight 655, Iran argued that the possibility that the United States had acted from a mistake had no impact on the application of Articles 2(4) and 51. Ruys, ibid.

[207] James Crawford, *State Responsibility: The General Part* (Cambridge University Press, 2013), at 61.

[208] Although a lack of intention to use force does not necessarily deny a victim state its right of self-defence, which exists so as to protect itself from attack, regardless of whether it was intended. See Sections 2.5.1.1. and 6.2.1.

[209] Corten, n. 42, at 85 (emphasis added).     [210] See Section 2.2.

126  The Meaning of 'Force'

under customary international law where it can be regarded as the *intentional application of coercion* against a State in relation to a matter that it is freely entitled to determine'.[211] In this respect, an 'unintentional coercion' would seem to be something of a misnomer. More generally, Corten notes that '[t]he criterion of willingness may obviously lend itself to different interpretations, but it implies a first observation that is indisputable: one State's use of force against another presupposes ... that the State in question is *aware* it is undertaking an action against another State'.[212]

Secondly, it is arguable that the requirement for an intention to use force is implicit in the jurisprudence of the ICJ. In the *Nicaragua* case the ICJ was of the view that:

> while the arming and training of the *contras* can certainly be said to involve the threat or use of force against Nicaragua, this is not necessarily so in respect of all the assistance given by the United States Government. In particular, the Court considers that the mere supply of funds to the *contras*, while undoubtedly an act of intervention in the internal affairs of Nicaragua ... does not in itself amount to a use of force.[213]

This could be interpreted to mean that there is an implicit forcible intention to use force if a state is supplying weapons, or the necessary training to use the weapons, to non-state actors, while this intention is missing with the supply of funds, which could be used for purposes other than those of a forcible nature. As Roscini notes, the arming and training of armed groups are 'strictly related to weapons, as they *aim* at enabling someone to use them'.[214]

On this basis, it follows that the simple use of a weapon, such as a missile test, while potentially violating specific rules within treaty regimes and/or customary international law, would also not appear to be sufficient in and of itself to constitute a violation of the prohibition of the threat or use of force, if it is not targeted towards another state.[215]

### 2.6.1 Distinguishing General Motives for Action and Intention

The 1987 Declaration on the Enhancement of the Effectiveness of the Principle of Refraining from the Threat or Use of Force in International Relations states that '[n]o consideration of whatever nature may be invoked to warrant the resorting to the threat or use of force in violation of the Charter'.[216] In this respect, while the motives laying behind a state's decision to use force may be benign, or even altruistic, if the intention is to 'forc[e] the will of another

---

[211] Buchan, n. 53, at 227 (emphasis added).    [212] Corten, n. 42, at 87 (emphasis in original).
[213] *Nicaragua* case, n. 2, at para. 228.    [214] Roscini, n. 58, at 50 (emphasis added).
[215] See Section 1.4 for a discussion on whether the testing of weapons might constitute a threat of force.
[216] UNGA Res. 42/22 (1987), annex, para. 3.

State'[217] through armed coercion then the prohibition is engaged. Indeed, if such an intention is found, the prohibition becomes applicable, regardless of any more general motive for the intervention.[218]

The general motives of a state for taking action, which may be humanitarian, economic, political, strategic, etc., must thus be distinguished from the intentions of that state to force the hand of another in achieving them.[219] For example, while it might be argued that in the *Corfu Channel* case the Court did not envisage the mine sweeping by the Royal Navy in terms of Article 2(4) because the UK's intention was not to conduct military actions against Albania, the Court was nonetheless critical of the UK's 'policy of force'.[220] Similarly, while the North Atlantic Treaty Organization (NATO) states that took action in Kosovo in 1999 did so ostensibly for humanitarian reasons, the intention was to force the hand of Serbia in ending the humanitarian crisis, which led to the conclusion being held by some that that action was unlawful, if legitimate.[221] Lastly, when states take anti-terror action in another state's territory, while the action is not necessarily specifically targeted towards the host state, it is nonetheless taking action which it has deemed that the host state should have taken.[222]

### 2.6.2 Mistake

It is also the case that the use of force may be resorted to by mistake or in error. For example, when the *USS Vincennes* shot down a civilian airliner in 1988 it was claimed that the commanding officer was under the mistaken belief that it was facing an imminent attack from an Iranian military aircraft.[223] In response – and this was arguably tied up with the continuing hostilities between the two states – Iran argued that a mistake by the United States did not mean that it avoided responsibility.[224]

However, while states have not expressly elaborated upon this element, 'state practice reveals that, when faced with territorial incursions ostensibly or allegedly lacking hostile intent, territorial states often refrain from invoking

---

[217] Corten, n. 42, at 86.    [218] Ibid., at 85–6.    [219] Ruys, n. 25, at 172–3.
[220] See Section 2.5.2.    [221] See Chapter 10 on the doctrine of humanitarian intervention.
[222] See Section 6.3 on necessity and proportionality and Section 8.4.2 on the 'unable or unwilling' doctrine, both in respect to the right of self-defence.
[223] Letter dated 6 July 1988 from the Acting Permanent Representative of the United States of America to the United Nations addressed to the President of the Security Council, UN Doc. S/19989, 9 July 1988, at 1 and 2. See, in general, David K. Linnan, 'Iran Air Flight 655 and Beyond: Free Passage, Mistaken Self-Defense and State Responsibility' (1991) 16 *Yale Journal of International Law* 245.
[224] *Case Concerning the Aerial Incident of 3 July 1988* (*Islamic Republic of Iran v. United States of America*), Memorial of the Islamic Republic of Iran, vol. I, 24 July 1990, 244, at para. 4.54 and 274, at para. 5.20.

the language of Article 2(4) or 51'.[225] Indeed, 'States do not make accusations of violation of the prohibition of the use of force in international relations in the exceptionally rare cases where military acts are committed in error.'[226] So accidental shots, or accidental incursions, are not often deemed uses of force for the purposes of the prohibition of the use of force.[227] In May 2020, Polish troops took up positions on the Czech Republic side of the border as a part of measures taken in response to the coronavirus outbreak, but which involved preventing Czech citizens from entering the site.[228] However, after being contacted by the Czech authorities the Polish troops left the site and claimed the incident 'was a result of misunderstanding, not a deliberate act', with no claims of a violation of the prohibition of force being made by the Czech Republic or any other state.[229]

However, perhaps one of the best-known examples of the use of force by mistake is the destruction by NATO forces of the Chinese embassy in Belgrade in May 1999, in which four Chinese nationals were killed and twenty others were injured.[230] NATO and the United States were quick to apologise for what was described as a mistake. However, while Article 2(4) was not even mentioned by China, or any other state, China condemned the action as 'a gross violation of Chinese sovereignty and a random violation of the Vienna Conventions on Diplomatic Relations and the norms of international relations'.[231] As such, in the rare case of a genuine mistake, although a state may escape responsibility for a violation of the prohibition of the use of force, this does not mean that its action is not a violation of state sovereignty. Indeed, '[e]rror seems to have the effect of preventing the characterisation of an action as a use of force by one State against another, which does not mean, as the case may be, that the action may not be characterised as unlawful in respect of other legal principles, such as the observance of State sovereignty'.[232]

### 2.6.3 Discerning Hostile Intent

Hostile intent, however, is not necessarily easy to discern and might seem to require entering the mind of the attacking state. Consequently, being able to discern a 'pure *expression* of intent'[233] or '*manifest* hostile intent'[234] is helpful

---

[225] Ruys, n. 25, at 189.  [226] Corten, n. 42, at 88.  [227] See examples in Ruys, n. 25, at 190.
[228] BBC News, 'Poland "Invades" Czech Republic in "Misunderstanding"', 13 June 2020, available at: www.bbc.co.uk/news/world-europe-53034930.
[229] Ibid.  [230] *Keesing's* (1999) 42955.
[231] BBC News, 'China Condemns Strike', 8 May 1999, available at: http://news.bbc.co.uk/1/hi/world/monitoring/338543.stm.
[232] Corten, n. 42, at 89.  [233] Harrison Dinniss, n. 22, at 70 (emphasis added).
[234] Ruys, n. 25, at 171.

## 2.6 The *Mens Rea* Element of the Use of Force

in determining whether an action constitutes a use of force. Ultimately, this may be found in different ways in different cases.

An expression or manifestation of intent behind an action might, for example, be found in the gravity or magnitude of the attack.[235] Indeed, '[i]f there is such an intention, it shall generally be reflected by military action of a certain degree of gravity'.[236] As Ruys notes:

> absent indications to the contrary, the gravity of the incursion (for example, a large-scale intrusion by tanks or aircraft from a neighboring state) may itself betray the hostile intent, thus permitting the victim state to engage in a forcible reaction without undertaking further preventative steps.[237]

So, for example, and without taking other indictors on board, the pure magnitude of Iraq's invasion and seizure of Kuwait in 1990 portrayed a hostile intent for the purposes of claiming that the prohibition of the use of force applied.[238] On the other hand, 'in relation to more small-scale incursions, the lesser gravity of the acts does not exclude a forcible reaction – on condition, however, that additional elements exist that attest to the intruder's hostile intent'.[239] Such elements might include 'the general geopolitical and security context', the 'repeated nature of the incursions', 'the location of the intrusion', 'the nature of the intruding units' and other 'specific indications', such as the locking on of fire-control radar.[240]

In a similar vein, the report of the Independent International Fact-Finding Mission on the Conflict in Georgia noted that:

> [a]ccording to State practice ... not all militarised acts amount to a demonstration of force and thus to a violation of Art. 2(4) of the UN Charter. Many are routine missions devoid of any hostile intent and are meaningless in the absence of a sizeable dispute. But as soon as they are non-routine, suspiciously timed, scaled up, intensified, geographically proximate, staged in the exact mode of a potential military clash, and easily attributable to a foreign-policy message, the hostile intent is considered present and the demonstration of force manifest.[241]

As such, in the context of cyber-attacks '[t]he binary coding required for a computer network attack contains the instructions for the attack and hence represents an almost *pure expression of the intent* of the attacker'.[242]

---

[235] Corten, n. 42, at 77–85; Buchan, n. 53, at 223–4; Maziar Jamnejad and Michael Wood, 'The Principle of Non-Intervention' (2009) 22 *Leiden Journal of International Law* 345, at 348.
[236] Corten, n. 42, at 86.   [237] Ruys, n. 25, at 175.   [238] See, further, Section 3.4.2.1.
[239] Ruys, n. 25, at 175.   [240] Ibid., at 175–6.
[241] Report of the Independent International Fact-Finding Mission on the Conflict in Georgia, n. 107, at para. 232.
[242] Harrison Dinniss, n. 22, at 70 (emphasis added).

## 2.7 CONCLUSION

From the discussion in this chapter we might be able to conclude that for the purpose of the prohibition of the threat or use of force, the key concept of 'force' can be defined as the intentional coercion by one state of another through the direct or indirect use of an instrument which is at least capable of causing human harm or physical destruction. From this, one can surmise that there are various elements that need to be considered in determining whether an unlawful use of force has occurred. Given the different consequences attached to the use of force depending upon its gravity and scale, it is also important to make such a distinction.

Having sketched out the meaning of 'force' and the breadth and scope of its prohibition, the following Parts of the book examine the different exceptions to it that exist or have been proclaimed to exist. Part II opens the discussion by examining the powers and use of force under the auspices of the UN, in particular the UN Security Council, which, while representing perhaps the clearest exception to the prohibition as set out within the Charter framework, has hardly proved free from controversy. Furthermore, the other established exception of self-defence, which is examined in Part III, has, if anything, proved even more controversial. While the central elements of the right are agreed upon, their application in practice is often not. Lastly, the final part of the book, Part IV, first examines in Chapter 9 consent by one state to another to use force upon its territory, in particular within civil wars, while the final chapter, Chapter 10, provides an examination of a controversial potential exception to the prohibition in the form of humanitarian intervention that has proved a constant presence in one form or another since the inception of the UN era in 1945.

### QUESTIONS

1 What, if anything, distinguishes an unlawful use of force from an unlawful intervention?

2 How might 'force' be defined for the purposes of the prohibition of the threat or use of force? What types of 'force' are covered by the prohibition?

3 How can a 'use of force' be distinguished from an 'armed attack' and an act of 'aggression'? Why, if at all, is it necessary to make these distinctions?

4 Does the prohibition of the use of force have a *de minimis* threshold? Why is this a necessary question to answer?

5 Can law enforcement measures be distinguished from uses of force that come within the prohibition of the threat or use of force?

6 Does the intention of a state matter in determining whether a prohibited use of force has occurred?

## SUGGESTED FURTHER READING

Lianne J. M. Boer, 'Echoes of Times Past: On the Paradoxical Nature of Article 2(4)' (2015) **20** *Journal of Conflict & Security Law* 5

Stuart Ford, 'Legal Processes of Change: Article 2(4) and the Vienna Convention on the Law of Treaties' (1999) **4** *Journal of Armed Conflict Law* 75

Christine Gray, 'The ICJ and the Use of Force', in Christian Tams and James Sloan (eds.), *The Development of International Law by the International Court of Justice* (Oxford University Press, 2013), 237

Vaughan Lowe, 'The Principle of Non-Intervention: Use of Force', in Vaughan Lowe and Colin Warbrick (eds.), *The United Nations and the Principles of International Law* (Routledge, 1994), 66

Mary Ellen O'Connell, 'The Prohibition of the Use of Force', in Nigel D. White and Christian Henderson (eds.), *Research Handbook on International Conflict and Security Law:* Jus ad Bellum, Jus in Bello *and* Jus post Bellum (Edward Elgar, 2013), 89

Tom Ruys, 'The Meaning of "Force" and the Boundaries of the *Jus ad Bellum*: Are "Minimal" Uses of Force Excluded from UN Charter Article 2(4)?' (2014) **108** *American Journal of International Law* 159

# Part II

# The Use of Force in the Context of Collective Security

# 3 The Use of Force under the Auspices of the United Nations

## 3.1 INTRODUCTION

It was discussed in Chapter 1 that there have been various attempts over the centuries to collectivise the security of states, for example through the nineteenth-century Concert of Europe and the League of Nations of 1919. With the formation of the United Nations (UN) in 1945 – which, today, enjoys virtually universal membership – member states agreed to go further and attempted to fully collectivise the use of forcible measures. The UN Charter attempts to do this in two ways. First, in their determination 'to save succeeding generations from the scourge of war',[1] the founding states agreed that 'armed force shall not be used, save in the common interest'.[2] With the backdrop of this underlying aim, the Charter goes beyond simply making the UN a dispute resolution organisation, as was arguably the case with the League of Nations, so as to – perhaps idealistically – provide it with broad powers to use, and threaten to use, force. Indeed, the first purpose of the UN, as spelt out in Article 1(1) of the UN Charter, is '[t]o maintain international peace and security, and to that end: to take effective collective measures for the prevention and removal of threats to the peace, and for the suppression of acts of aggression or other breaches of the peace'.[3] The use of force under the auspices of the UN is, as such, contained within the Charter as an exception to the prohibition of the use of force,[4] as set out and examined in Part I.

However, and secondly, while the Charter also affirmed that member states possess an 'inherent' right of individual and collective self-defence, this is firmly framed within Article 51 of the Charter as being under the ultimate oversight of the Security Council and is contained within Chapter VII of the

---

[1] Preamble, UN Charter (1945).   [2] Ibid.   [3] Article 1(1), ibid.
[4] The chapters in Part II will not examine the full range of powers of the UN in the maintenance of international peace and security but will instead focus on those involving the use of force. For a broader picture of the powers of the UN see, in general, Nigel D. White, *Keeping the Peace: The United Nations and the Maintenance of International Peace and Security*, 2nd ed. (Manchester University Press, 1997).

UN Charter within the context of the enforcement powers of the Council. Whereas the Council's role in states invoking and implementing the right of self-defence will be examined in greater detail in Chapter 6, the purpose of the chapters in Part II is to examine the use of force under the auspices of the UN, in particular the Security Council.

This chapter will first, in Section 3.2, set out and examine the relevant provisions of the UN Charter and the division of competence between the various relevant organs of the UN – the Security Council, the General Assembly and the Secretariat – to provide an understanding as to how force was originally envisaged as being employed under the auspices of the UN. While all three organs have a role and responsibilities in this area, as will be explained, the Security Council has 'primary responsibility'.[5] Given the Security Council's primacy both within the Charter and in practice, Section 3.3 will go on to examine the specific powers of the Council in relation to the use of forcible measures within the Charter and the limitations imposed upon these.

Section 3.4 then examines how these powers and responsibilities have been implemented in practice in both the Cold War and post–Cold War eras. The UN Charter is a 'living instrument', meaning that the way in which these provisions have been realised in practice in the face of political and strategic realities has been quite different from how they were envisaged within the Charter. In particular, there has been a certain decentralisation of the arrangements regarding the use of force so that, rather than the Security Council having a standing army of troops at its disposal ready to be used as and when deemed necessary, it has, instead, developed the practice of 'authorising' states, coalitions of states and regional organisations to use force to implement its mandate. While this method of authorising states to use force has received some criticism, it is not an entirely alien concept within the UN Charter, as Chapter VIII, which is concerned with regional organisations, provides that 'no enforcement action shall be taken under regional arrangements or by regional agencies without the *authorization* of the Security Council'.[6] Section 3.5 thus addresses the relationship between the UN and regional – and, by extension, collective defence – organisations in the context of the use of force.

The method of authorising states and organisations to use force has raised many issues and concerns. Whereas some of these will be addressed in this chapter, the main issues that have arisen in practice will be the focus of Chapter 4. In addition, although not expressly included within the UN Charter, the institution of peacekeeping has evolved from being one based, in theory at least, upon the non-use of force to being more 'muscular' in

---

[5] Article 24(1), UN Charter (1945).  [6] Article 53(1), ibid. (emphasis added).

nature, sometimes extensively so, with the UN Security Council again having a central role in this evolution. This will form the focus of Chapter 5.

## 3.2 THE MAINTENANCE OF INTERNATIONAL PEACE AND SECURITY: THE DIVISION OF COMPETENCE WITHIN THE UNITED NATIONS

### 3.2.1 The Security Council

The primary purpose of the UN is, as noted in Section 3.1, the maintenance of international peace and security. It is, therefore, of significance that the UN Charter confers upon the Security Council '*primary responsibility* for the maintenance of international peace and security'.[7] Furthermore, with the clear aim of the UN being to take 'effective collective measures' for this purpose, the Council is comprised of only 15 of the 193 members of the UN.[8] Although the Council lacks the representativeness of the UN General Assembly, which is comprised of *all* member states of the UN, the Council's small composition was arguably designed '[i]n order to ensure prompt and effective action by the United Nations'[9] in securing its primary purpose.

Ten members of the Council are non-permanent and elected for a two-year term.[10] The remaining five are the permanent members (P5) of the Council.[11] The P5 – China, France, Russia, the United Kingdom and the United States[12] – were selected by the founders of the UN as representing the 'great powers' of the time.[13] Not only do the P5 have a continuous seat on the Council, thus permitting them to have a say on all issues that come before it, but they also, and significantly, possess a veto on votes taken within the Council concerning substantive matters.[14]

---

[7] Article 24(1), ibid. (emphasis added).
[8] The size of the Council was expanded from eleven to fifteen members in 1963.
[9] Article 24(1), UN Charter (1945).
[10] Articles 23(1) and (2), ibid. They are elected with due regard being paid to the contribution they make to the maintenance of international peace and security and to the other purposes of the UN as well as to considerations of equitable geographical distribution.
[11] Article 23(1), ibid.
[12] Ibid. Note that the provision still refers to the 'Republic of China' and the 'Union of Soviet Socialist Republics'.
[13] Nigel D. White, *Democracy Goes to War: British Military Deployments under International Law* (Oxford University Press, 2009), at 62.
[14] Article 27(3), UN Charter (1945). The veto does not apply to votes on procedural matters (Article 27(2), ibid.), such as submission to the General Assembly of any questions relating to the maintenance of international peace and security. Each member of the Security Council has one representative and one vote. See Articles 23(3) and 27(1), ibid. However, a development that occurred relatively early on in the life of the UN was that, whereas Article 27(3) of the Charter requires the 'concurring votes' of the P5 before any measures can be adopted, this was interpreted as meaning merely the absence of a negative vote. See

With the increase in size and shifts in the balance of political leanings of the member states of the UN since 1945, along with question marks over the continued legitimacy of certain of the P5 member states, membership and representativeness have become an issue for the Security Council. As Ramesh Thakur notes:

> The irreducible minimum for any credible system of collective security is that the key actors making and enforcing the coercive decisions in the name and on behalf of the collectivity are the major powers of the day. This is the logic justifying permanent membership with veto rights of the Security Council. This is the criterion on which, more than any other single factor, the Council fails the test comprehensively. Consequently, the Council in particular and the UN in general are experiencing accumulating legitimacy deficits.[15]

There have been discussions regarding the possibility of other states, such as India, Brazil, Germany or Japan, joining the Council on a permanent basis, either in addition to or in place of some of the existing P5, although any reform of the Council has thus far been hampered by the fact that any changes would require the consent of the existing P5.[16] Perhaps understandably, none have expressed a willingness to voluntarily relinquish this status or its associated powers and privileges. Nonetheless, until the Council is reformed, UN member states have continued to 'agree that in carrying out its duties under this responsibility [for the maintenance of international peace and security] the Security Council acts on their behalf'.[17]

In carrying out its duties, the Security Council may take action for the 'pacific settlement of disputes' between states, as set out in Chapter VI of the Charter or, if it determines that there exists a 'threat to the peace', 'breach of the peace' or 'act of aggression', it may decide upon both non-forcible and forcible measures of enforcement, as set out in Chapter VII of the Charter, and as will be expanded upon in this chapter.[18] The Charter adopts an open approach to collective security, in that it acknowledges the existence of 'regional arrangements' in Chapter VIII of the Charter, and recognises and encourages their contribution to the pacific settlement of disputes,[19] although

---

Constantin A. Stavropoulos, 'The Practice of Voluntary Abstentions by Permanent Members of the Security Council under Article 27, Paragraph 3, of the Charter of the United Nations' (1967) 61 *American Journal of International Law* 737.

[15] Ramesh Thakur, 'Reconfiguring the UN System of Collective Security', in Marc Weller (ed.), *The Oxford Handbook of the Use of Force in International Law* (Oxford University Press, 2015), 179, at 200. See also, in general, Thomas G. Weiss, *What's Wrong with the United Nations and How to Fix It* (Polity, 2008); Sabine Hassler, *Reforming the UN Security Council Membership: The Illusion of Representativeness* (Routledge, 2012).

[16] Article 108, UN Charter (1945).  [17] Article 24(1), ibid.  [18] See Section 3.3.

[19] Article 52(2) and (3), UN Charter (1945). See further Section 3.5.

## 3.2 The Division of Competence within the UN

it is clear that any enforcement action requires the 'authorisation' of the Security Council.[20]

While one should always be mindful of the fact that the Security Council is a political body, it possesses a unique function within the context of the UN as being the only organ with the power to adopt legally binding measures of general applicability. Indeed, Article 25 of the Charter states that '[t]he Members of the United Nations agree to accept and carry out the decisions of the Security Council in accordance with the present Charter'.[21] The circumstances under which such a legally binding decision may be adopted by the Council have not been entirely agreed upon and form a 'complex question'.[22] In determining this issue, some authors have focused upon whether a resolution of the Council has been adopted under a particular chapter or article of the Charter,[23] so if a resolution specifies that the Council is 'acting under Chapter VII', which contains the enforcement powers of the Council, then it is binding.[24] Others have instead focused more upon the terminology and language employed in the resolution itself,[25] so that the use of terms such as 'decide', 'demand' and 'shall' is indicative of the resolution being binding in nature, while 'call upon', 'appeal' or 'recommend' suggest that the resolution is non-binding. Neither approach, however, satisfactorily resolves the issue,[26] leaving what might be described as a 'fully contextual' approach to interpretation with the issue to be decided upon a case-by-case basis.[27] In this regard, the International Court of Justice (ICJ) stated in the *Namibia* advisory opinion that

[t]he language of a resolution of the Security Council should be carefully analysed before a conclusion can be made as to its binding effect. In view of the nature of the

---

[20] Article 53, ibid.
[21] The primacy of decisions of the Security Council over other obligations that member states may have is provided for in Article 103 of the Charter which declares that '[i]n the event of a conflict between the obligations of the Members of the United Nations under the present Charter and their obligations under any other international agreement, their obligations under the present Charter shall prevail'.
[22] Christine Gray, *International Law and the Use of Force*, 3rd ed. (Oxford University Press, 2008), at 18. See, further, Michael Wood and Eran Sthoeger, *The UN Security Council and International Law* (Cambridge University Press, 2022), at 31–44.
[23] See, for example, Martin Shaw, *International Law* (Cambridge University Press, 2008), at 1268.
[24] See, for example, UNSC Res. 678 (1990), preamble.
[25] See, for example, Yoram Dinstein, *War, Aggression and Self-Defence*, 6th ed. (Cambridge University Press, 2017), at paras. 157–63.
[26] See Christian Henderson and Noam Lubell, 'The Contemporary Legal Nature of UN Security Council Ceasefire Resolutions' (2013) 26 *Leiden Journal of International Law* 369, at 371–88.
[27] Rosalyn Higgins, 'The Advisory Opinion on Namibia: Which UN Resolutions Are Binding under Article 25 of the Charter?' (1972) 21 *International & Comparative Law Quarterly* 270, at 283.

powers of Article 25, the question is to be determined in each case, having regard to the terms of the resolution to be interpreted, the discussions leading to it, the Charter provision invoked and, in general, all circumstances that might assist in determining the legal consequences of the resolution of the Security Council.[28]

A key consideration in managing expectations of the Security Council in it carrying out its functions is that it was envisaged as a body to enforce the peace, not as a body to enforce the law. The Council does not shoulder any responsibility, as originally envisaged in the UN Charter, to uphold and defend international law, although such an outcome might be the result of its actions. As Kelsen noted, '[t]he purpose of enforcement action ... is not to maintain or restore law, but to maintain and restore peace, which is not necessarily identical with the law'.[29] As such, '[w]hile it is true that the Security Council has over recent decades responded to major breaches of humanitarian law for instance, and responded in ways that have led to the punishment of criminal behaviour, such as by the creation of criminal tribunals, its core concern remains peace and security'.[30] However, if a state does not comply with a judgment of the ICJ, the aggrieved party may turn to the Security Council as a means of enforcement. Under Article 94(2) of the UN Charter the Council is empowered to 'make recommendations or decide upon measures to be taken to give effect to [a] judgment' of the ICJ including, if necessary, forcible measures, although the Council is not obliged to act and has discretion in this respect.[31] The Council has to date not drawn upon this power to enforce a judgment.[32]

### 3.2.2 The General Assembly

The fact that the Security Council has *primary* responsibility for the maintenance of international peace and security suggests that it does not have *exclusive* responsibility in this field. As the ICJ stated in the *Certain Expenses* advisory opinion of 1962, the 'responsibility conferred' on the Security

---

[28] *Legal Consequences for States of the Continued Presence of South Africa in Namibia (South West Africa) Notwithstanding Security Council Resolution 276*, Advisory Opinion (1971) ICJ Reports 16, at 53. This interpretive approach follows, in general, the approach set out in Articles 31–33 of the Vienna Convention on the Law of Treaties (1969).

[29] Hans Kelsen, *The Law of the United Nations* (Frederik A. Praeger, 1950), at 736.

[30] Nigel D. White, 'The Relationship between the UN Security Council and General Assembly in Matters of International Peace and Security', in Marc Weller (ed.), *The Oxford Handbook of the Use of Force in International Law* (Oxford University Press, 2015), 293, at 298.

[31] See Attila Tanzi, 'Problems of Enforcement of Decisions of the International Court of Justice and the Law of the United Nations' (1995) 6 *European Journal of International Law* 539.

[32] Although that is not to say that the Council has not had a role to play in the enforcement of judgments of the ICJ. See, further, Wood and Sthoeger, n. 22, at 168–72.

## 3.2 The Division of Competence within the UN

Council is 'primary' and not 'exclusive'.[33] Furthermore, the Court added, the Charter 'makes it abundantly clear' that the General Assembly is 'also to be concerned with international peace and security'.[34]

In its role in the maintenance of international peace and security the General Assembly, which consists of all members of the UN,[35] may discuss 'any questions or any matters within the scope of the present Charter'[36] and 'may make recommendations to the Members of the United Nations or to the Security Council or to both on any such questions or matters'.[37] Decisions of the General Assembly on important questions, such as recommendations with respect to the maintenance of international peace and security, shall be made by a two-thirds majority of the members present and voting.[38] More specifically the General Assembly 'may discuss any questions relating to the maintenance of international peace and security brought before it by any Member of the United Nations, or by the Security Council, or by a state which is not a Member of the United Nations'[39] and 'may make recommendations with regard to any such questions to the state or states concerned or to the Security Council or to both'.[40] There is, as such, a clear overlap between the jurisdictional functions of the Security Council and General Assembly which was witnessed shortly after the adoption of the UN Charter in both organs being involved in the early 1950s in the situation between North and South Korea as well as the situation in the Middle East. Furthermore, '[t]he General Assembly may call the attention of the Security Council to situations which are likely to endanger international peace and security'[41] and 'may consider the general principles of cooperation in the maintenance of international peace and security ... and may make recommendations with regard to such principles to the Members or to the Security Council or to both'.[42]

Importantly, however, while the General Assembly may have *prima facie* wide discursive and recommendatory powers, both in general and in relation to specific cases, these powers are formally limited in two key respects. First, although the two main organs of the UN were envisaged as having distinct yet complementary roles within the context of the maintenance of international peace and security, in alluding to the primacy of the Security Council within this field, Article 12 states that '[w]hile the Security Council is exercising in respect of any dispute or situation the functions assigned to it in the present Charter, the General Assembly shall not make any recommendation with regard to that dispute or situation unless the Security Council so requests'.[43]

---

[33] *Certain Expenses of the United Nations (Article 17, paragraph 2, of the Charter)*, Advisory Opinion (1962) ICJ Reports 151, at 163.
[34] Ibid. [35] Article 9(1), UN Charter (1945). [36] Article 10, ibid. [37] Ibid.
[38] Article 18(2), ibid. Each member shall have one vote. Article 18(1), ibid.
[39] Article 11(2), ibid. [40] Ibid. [41] Article 11(3), ibid. [42] Article 11(1), ibid.
[43] Although see discussion on the Uniting for Peace resolution (1950) in Section 3.4.1 and the role of the General Assembly in the use of forcible measures in Section 3.4.2.4.

Secondly, any question 'on which action is necessary shall be referred to the Security Council by the General Assembly either before or after discussion'.[44] Whereas the Charter does not elaborate upon what is meant by 'action' in the context of this stipulation, the ICJ, in providing an interpretation of it in the *Certain Expenses* advisory opinion, noted that '[t]he word "action" must mean such action as is solely within the province of the Security Council'[45] – in other words, action that is of a 'coercive or enforcement' nature.[46] The General Assembly was, however, deemed to be competent to 'organize peacekeeping operations, at the request, or with the consent, of the States concerned'.[47] The General Assembly was, therefore, ultimately envisaged as having an active role within the realms of international peace and security, even if of a softer nature than that of the Security Council.

### 3.2.3 The Secretariat

While not being provided with extensive responsibilities for the maintenance of international peace and security, the UN Secretariat is of relevance nonetheless. The key figure within the Secretariat is the UN Secretary-General, who acts as the chief administrative officer of the organisation.[48] In this respect, they have the capacity to sit in on meetings of both the Security Council and General Assembly and shall perform such functions 'as are entrusted to [them] by these organs'.[49] As well as making annual reports to the General Assembly on the work of the organisation,[50] they may also 'bring to the attention of the Security Council any matter which in [their] opinion may threaten the maintenance of international peace and security'.[51]

As will become clear in Section 3.4, the greater functioning of the Security Council in the post-Cold War era has led to the Secretary-General having a greater role in the oversight and co-ordination of the use of forcible measures taken by member states under the auspices of the UN, as well as in peacekeeping operations.[52] The Secretary-General also produces reports which have been influential upon issues governing both international peace and security more generally as well as specifically in connection with the law on the use of force. For example, Boutros Boutros-Ghali produced *An Agenda for Peace* in 1992, in 2005 Kofi Annan produced *In Larger Freedom*, Ban Ki-moon

---

[44] Article 11(2), UN Charter (1945).
[45] *Certain Expenses* advisory opinion, n. 33, at 165. See also Francis A. Vallat, 'The General Assembly and the Security Council of the United Nations' (1952) 28 *British Yearbook of International Law* 63, at 97–100.
[46] *Certain Expenses* advisory opinion, n. 33, at 164.
[47] Ibid. See Chapter 5 for more on peacekeeping operations.
[48] Article 97, UN Charter (1945).   [49] Article 98, ibid.   [50] Ibid.   [51] Article 99, ibid.
[52] See, in general, Ralph Zacklin, *The United Nations Secretariat and the Use of Force in a Unipolar World: Power v. Principle* (Oxford University Press, 2010).

produced numerous reports on developing and implementing the 'Responsibility to Protect', while, most recently, António Guterres has taken the initiative in attempts at reforming the UN[53] and has been provided with a leading role by the Security Council in undertaking reform of peace operations.[54] The Secretary-General also often expresses their views and opinions upon the legality of actions taken by member states, as was the case, perhaps most prominently, following the intervention by the United States and United Kingdom in Iraq in March 2003[55] and that of Russia in Ukraine in February 2022.[56]

## 3.3 THE FORCIBLE POWERS OF THE SECURITY COUNCIL IN THE UN CHARTER

In addition to having primary responsibility for the maintenance of international peace and security, the Security Council was also envisaged as being the sole organ of the UN with the powers to use – or, in the case of regional organisations, authorise the use of – coercive action involving the use of force. The purpose of this section is to set these powers out as they are envisaged within the Charter before examining in Section 3.4 how they have operated in practice, while Section 3.5 addresses the specific issue of the authorisation of regional organisations.

### 3.3.1 Article 39: The 'Gateway' Provision to Chapter VII

As briefly discussed in Section 3.2.1, the powers of the Security Council to resort to enforcement measures, including the use of force, are primarily found within Chapter VII of the UN Charter, which concerns 'Action with Respect to Threats to the Peace, Breaches of the Peace and Acts of Aggression'. The first provision of this chapter of the Charter, Article 39, provides that:

> The Security Council shall determine the existence of any threat to the peace, breach of the peace, or act of aggression and shall make recommendations, or decide what measures shall be taken in accordance with Articles 41 and 42, to maintain or restore international peace and security.

---

[53] See, for example, UN Secretary-General, Remarks at UN Reform Event, 18 September 2017, available at: www.un.org/sg/en/content/sg/speeches/2017-09-18/secretary-generals-reform-remarks.

[54] See UNSC Res. 2378 (2017), para. 10.

[55] Ewan MacAskill and Julian Borger, 'Iraq Was Illegal and Breached UN Charter, Says Annan', *The Guardian*, 16 September 2004, available at: www.theguardian.com/world/2004/sep/16/iraq.iraq. For more on this particular intervention see Section 4.3.

[56] See SG/SM/21158, 24 February 2022, available at: www.un.org/press/en/2022/sgsm21158.doc.htm.

This provision has been termed the 'gateway' to the enforcement powers of the Council.[57] Yet, and as made clear by Article 39, before it can access these powers it first needs to determine the existence of a 'threat to the peace', 'breach of the peace' or 'act of aggression'.[58] Prior to addressing the measures then available to the Council this section will first examine the meaning of these terms or, more accurately, situations.

### 3.3.1.1 Threats to the Peace

Before any enforcement action under Chapter VII may take place, the Security Council must first determine the existence of at least a threat to the peace. No doubt as a result of representing the least serious of the three situations, it is the one that the Council has determined most frequently in unlocking its Chapter VII powers of enforcement. A number of questions arise, however, in connection with this term, in particular its meaning and the circumstances in which one may be determined to exist by the Council.

Article 39 states that the Security Council '*shall*' determine the existence of a threat or breach of the peace, or act of aggression. It is possible to interpret this in two ways. It might, for example, be interpreted to mean that the Council is obliged to make a determination of a threat to the peace, breach of the peace or act of aggression if one can be said to be objectively discernible.[59] Yet, given that there is no definition of a threat to the peace, as there is, for example, for aggression,[60] it is difficult to see how such an obligation upon the Council can exist. The better interpretation of this provision, therefore, would seem to be that it is the responsibility and right of the Security Council, to the exclusion of other organs of the UN, to make such a determination.

Although it is arguable that there must be at least some tangible threat, the Security Council also arguably possesses a wide discretion in making determinations of a threat to the peace under Article 39. Kelsen, for example, suggested that 'it is completely within the discretion of the Security Council to decide what constitutes a "threat to the peace"'.[61] It has also been said that 'a threat to the peace in the sense of Article 39 seems to be whatever the Security Council says is a threat to the peace'.[62] This is perhaps the preferred view given that there is no qualification contained within the Charter in regard to the powers of the Council in this respect or, as noted, a definition of the

---

[57] White, n. 4, at 173; Gary Wilson, *The United Nations and Collective Security* (Routledge, 2014), at 34.
[58] See, in general, Wood and Sthoeger, n. 22, at 63–8.
[59] Antonios Tzanakopoulos, *Disobeying the Security Council: Countermeasures against Wrongful Sanctions* (Oxford University Press, 2011), at 60–4.
[60] See Sections 1.5.5.2, 2.5.1.2 and 3.3.1.2.    [61] Kelsen, n. 29, at 727.
[62] Peter Malanczuk, *Akehurst's Modern Introduction to International Law*, 7th ed. (Routledge, 1997), at 426.

term. Furthermore, no reasons are required for the determination of a threat to the peace, or lack thereof,[63] and such a determination does not need to be explicit. Indeed, the Council may implicitly allude to the existence of a threat to the peace through its explicit invocation of Chapter VII in certain resolutions.[64] For example, Resolution 1973 (2011), which was adopted by the Council in the context of the repression by the Gaddafi regime in Libya during the uprising in 2011, stated that the situation in Libya '*continues* to constitute a threat to international peace and security' (emphasis added) although shortly before, in Resolution 1970 (2011), which was similarly adopted under Chapter VII, the Council made no such explicit Article 39 determination. In addition, and as will be discussed in Section 3.4.2.2, the Council has taken a rather liberal approach to determining threats to the peace so as to provide it with the right to take action in connection with ostensibly internal or domestic situations with potential international ramifications, as was the case with the situation in Libya in 2011.[65]

Although the Security Council has not, to date, determined that an attack on a computer network (or cyber-attack) constitutes a threat to the peace, it is likely that such an attack would have the potential to constitute such a threat 'where it is of sufficient gravity that a state is likely to respond to it with force, regardless of whether it is categorised as an armed attack, or where the type of attack indicates further violence to follow, whether electronically or by kinetic means'.[66] In addition, the Security Council has not as yet characterised climate change or its increasingly severe effects and the impact that these have on issues such as mass migration as a threat to international peace and security. Yet,

---

[63] See Erika de Wet, *The Chapter VII Powers of the UN Security Council* (Hart, 2004), at 134–44; Alexander Orakhelashvili, *Collective Security* (Oxford University Press, 2011), at 155.

[64] Alternatively, the Council may allude to the fact that it is acting under Chapter VII – and thus in the realms of legally binding powers – through its determination of a threat to the peace. See, for example, UNSC Res. 688 (1991), para. 1, which '[c]*ondemns* the repression of the Iraqi civilian population in many parts of Iraq, including most recently in Kurdish populated areas, the consequences of which threaten international peace and security in the region', although which was not explicitly adopted under Chapter VII.

[65] While in Resolution 1973 (2011) the Council was primarily concerned with the deteriorating internal situation and heavy civilian casualties, it also expressed its concern regarding the plight of refugees and foreign workers forced to flee Libya.

[66] Heather Harrison Dinniss, *Cyber Warfare and the Laws of War* (Cambridge University Press, 2012), at 110. See also Michael N. Schmitt, 'The Use of Cyber Force and International Law', in Marc Weller (ed.), *The Oxford Handbook of the Use of Force in International Law* (Oxford University Press, 2015), 1110, at 1117–18. For more on the activity of the UN Security Council, and the UN in general, in regard to cyber-security, see Christian Henderson, 'The United Nations and the Regulation of Cyber-Security', in Nicholas Tsagourias and Russell Buchan (eds.), Research Handbook on International Law and Cyberspace, 2nd ed. (Edward Elgar, 2021), 582.

[g]iven that an increasing number of governments are characterizing climate change as a national security threat, and legislatures at various levels of government are passing declarations of 'climate emergency', it seems only a matter of time before states begin to also characterize the risks and consequences of climate change more precisely as a threat to international peace and security – and to press the Security Council to declare it as such and to take up the issue for deliberation.[67]

Some scholars have also suggested that the Council may deploy its collective security mechanisms in responding to the threat and even to enforce climate change law.[68]

It has been contended that 'there is a direct relationship between the concept of "threat of force" under Article 2(4) and the concept of "threat to the peace" under Article 39'.[69] In other words, '[t]he Security Council's competence would be defined, at its limits, by Article 2(4); and to determine that a situation was a "threat to the peace" when it was not a "threat of force" would be *ultra vires*'.[70] However, the Charter does not make this link and it cannot be presumed that such a precise link was intended, particularly as it has not been witnessed in practice. Furthermore, as White notes, 'the triggers for Chapter VII are not to be equated with breach of Article 2(4) since the concern of the Security Council is with world peace and security, much broader notions than the threat of armed force or the actual use of armed force'.[71] Indeed, the Council has treated as threats to the peace issues such as 'the proliferation in armaments, the spread of terrorism, the disintegration of failed and failing states, massive flows of refugees, egregious violations of human rights' all of which fall outside of the realms of Article 2(4).[72]

Lastly, while nothing short of an 'armed attack' provides states with a right of self-defence,[73] the Security Council is able to resort to forcible action even in the face of a mere '*threat* to the peace'. As such, while forcible action by

---

[67] Craig Martin, 'Atmospheric Intervention?: The Climate Change Crisis and the *Jus ad Bellum* Regime' (2020) 45 *Columbia Journal of Environmental Law* 331, at 376.

[68] See Trina Ng, 'Safeguarding Peace and Security in our Warming World: A Role for the Security Council' (2010) 15 *Journal of Conflict & Security Law* 275, at 278–9; Christopher K. Penny, 'Climate Change as a "Threat to International Peace and Security"', in Shirley V. Scott and Charlotte Ku (eds.), *Climate Change and the UN Security Council* (Edward Elgar, 2018), 25–46. See also Mark Nevitt, 'Is Climate Change a Threat to International Peace and Security?' (2021) 42 *Michigan Journal of International Law* 527.

[69] See White, n. 30, at 297 (although White does not subscribe to this view). See Section 1.4 for a discussion of the meaning of threat of force in the context of the prohibition of the threat or use of force.

[70] Ibid.    [71] Ibid.

[72] Ibid. See Chapters 1 and 2 for further discussion on the prohibition of the threat and use of force.

[73] See the discussion in Section 6.2.5 on the possible existence of a gravity threshold for an armed attack.

states of a preventative nature remains controversial,[74] the Security Council is permitted to engage in such action and, today, has frequently determined situations to be threats to the peace – thus opening up a range of enforcement measures, including those involving the use of force – that had not at the time witnessed any state engaging in forcible action. For example, following the overthrow by a military junta of the government of Haiti in 1993, the Security Council determined that the situation, and in particular the flow of refugees from Haiti, 'threatens international peace and security in the region'[75] and subsequently engaged in enforcement action to remove the military junta from power and reinstall the constitutional government.[76] The Council has also consistently determined the nuclear enrichment and testing activities of North Korea to constitute a threat to the peace.[77] While the Council has not engaged in enforcement action against North Korea beyond sanctions in response, it is clear that it could if it deemed it necessary on the basis of the threat posed by North Korea.

### 3.3.1.2 Breaches of the Peace and Acts of Aggression

In contrast to its activity in respect to threats to the peace, the Security Council has determined the existence of a breach of the peace or act of aggression on far fewer occasions, and the occasions when it has done so do not give rise to any clear meaning to be attached to these concepts. It determined a breach of the peace in the context of North Korea's invasion of South Korea in 1950,[78] Argentina's invasion of the Falkland Islands in 1982[79] and upon Iraq's invasion of Kuwait in 1990,[80] all of which involved the invasion and occupation by one state of the territory of another.

Similarly, the Security Council has only made a determination that an act of aggression has occurred on a handful of occasions, notably Israel's actions against Tunisia in 1985[81] and 1988;[82] South Africa's actions against Angola in 1976[83] and 1985[84] and against Botswana in 1985;[85] and Southern Rhodesia's actions against Zambia in 1979.[86] While the General Assembly adopted the 'Definition of Aggression' in 1974 and 'recommend[ed] that [the Security Council] should, as appropriate, take account of that Definition as guidance in determining, in accordance with the Charter, the existence of an act of

---

[74] See, in general, Chapter 7.  [75] UNSC Res. 841 (1993), preamble.
[76] UNSC Res. 940 (1994), para. 4.  [77] See, for example, UNSC Res. 2375 (2017).
[78] UNSC Res. 82 (1950).  [79] UNSC Res. 502 (1982), preamble.
[80] UNSC Res. 660 (1990), preamble.  [81] UNSC Res. 573 (1985), preamble.
[82] UNSC Res. 611 (1988), preamble.  [83] UNSC Res. 387 (1976), preamble.
[84] UNSC Res. 567 (1985), preamble; UNSC Res. 571 (1985), preamble; UNSC Res. 574 (1985), preamble; UNSC Res. 577 (1985), preamble.
[85] UNSC Res. 568 (1985), preamble.  [86] UNSC Res. 455 (1979), preamble.

aggression',[87] the Council has never made any reference to it.[88] However, the Security Council also has a role in the crime of aggression, in that while it may refer a situation to the Prosecutor of the International Criminal Court the possibility for the Prosecutor to proceed with an investigation is also possibly limited by whether the Council has determined that an act of aggression has taken place.[89]

### 3.3.2 Envisaged Measures under Chapter VII

In addition to the 'recommendations' that it may make under Article 39 and the 'provisional measures' that the Council may take under Article 40 in any attempt 'to prevent an aggravation of the situation', the envisaged enforcement measures of the Security Council – should a threat to the peace, breach of the peace or act of aggression be determined – are found within Chapter VII of the Charter. First, the Council has the power, under Article 41, to resort to non-forcible measures, which 'may include complete or partial interruption of economic relations and of rail, sea, air, postal, telegraphic, radio, and other means of communication, and the severance of diplomatic relations'. However, should the Security Council decide that these measures would be, or have proved to be, inadequate, it may, under Article 42, 'take such action by air, sea, or land forces as may be necessary to maintain or restore international peace and security. Such action may include demonstrations, blockade, and other operations by air, sea, or land forces of Members of the United Nations.' Given that the deployment of such forces might be in response to a threat to the peace, it is, as noted in Section 3.3.1.1, clear that the Council may use force 'in anticipation of a future breach of the peace – figuring only as a threat to the peace at the time of action – a privilege that the Charter withholds from any individual State or group of States acting alone'.[90]

A particularly innovative aspect of Chapter VII, over and above any previous attempts to collectivise security within the international community, is that the Security Council was to have something akin to a 'standing army' ready to be deployed should an Article 39 determination be made and the Council deemed it to be necessary. Under Article 43, all members 'undertake to make available to the Security Council, on its call and in accordance with a special agreement or agreements, armed forces, assistance, and facilities, including rights of passage, necessary for the purpose of maintaining

---

[87] UNGA Res. 3314 (XXIX) (1974), preamble (of the resolution, to which the definition is annexed). See further Sections 1.5.5.2 and 2.5.1.2.
[88] See, further, Section 2.5.1.2.
[89] Articles 13(b) and 15*bis*(6–8), Rome Statute of the International Criminal Court (1998). See, further, Section 1.5.5.2.
[90] Dinstein, n. 25, at para. 878. See the discussion on preventative self-defence in Chapter 7.

international peace and security'.[91] In addition, a 'Military Staff Committee' was to be established, comprising of Chiefs of Staff of the P5,[92] and which was 'to advise and assist the Security Council on all questions relating to the Security Council's military requirements for the maintenance of international peace and security, the employment and command of forces placed at its disposal, the regulation of armaments, and possible disarmament'.[93] However, while there was to be a certain level of control over the forcible actions, exercised primarily through the Military Staff Committee, ultimately the decisions of the Council were to be 'carried out by the Members of the United Nations directly and through their action in the appropriate international agencies of which they are members'.[94] Furthermore, the action was to be taken 'by all the Members of the United Nations or by some of them, as the Security Council may determine'.[95]

### 3.3.3 Limits to the Forcible Powers of the Security Council

It has been said that the powers of the Security Council are 'exceedingly wide' and 'well-nigh unlimited'.[96] Yet, while its discretion in determining the existence of the conditions necessary to open the gateway to forcible powers is wide, they are not unlimited, with limits both within the UN Charter and external to it imposed upon the breadth and scope of the Council's powers.

First, 'neither the text nor the spirit of the Charter conceives of the Security Council as *legibus solutus* (unbound by law)'.[97] Indeed, '[b]road as the Security Council's powers are, they still are grounded in the Charter through which they have been delegated to it by states'.[98] Article 24(2) notes that '[i]n discharging [its] duties the Security Council shall act in accordance with the Purposes and Principles of the United Nations'. In support of this view the International Criminal Tribunal for the former Yugoslavia has noted that 'the determination that there exists [a threat to the peace] is not a totally unfettered discretion, as it has to remain, at the very least, within the limits of the Purposes and Principles of the Charter'.[99] Consequently, while the Security Council may employ forcible measures in a wide range of circumstances to 'maintain international peace and security', it would not be able to do so if its actions were to infringe upon any of the other Purposes and Principles found within Chapter I of the Charter, in particular the principle of self-determination,

---

[91] Article 43(1), UN Charter (1945). See Adam Roberts, 'Proposals for UN Standing Forces: A Critical History', in Vaughan Lowe, Adam Roberts, Jennifer Welsh and Dominik Zaum (eds.), *The United Nations Security Council and War: Evolutions in Thought and Practice since 1945* (Oxford University Press, 2010), 99.
[92] Article 47(1), UN Charter (1945). [93] Article 47(2), ibid. [94] Article 48(2), ibid.
[95] Article 48(1), ibid. [96] Dinstein, n. 25, at para. 875.
[97] *Prosecutor* v. *Tadic*, Case No. IT-94-1, Jurisdiction, ICTY, Appeals Chamber, 1995, at para. 28.
[98] Orakhelashvili, n. 63, at 51. [99] *Tadic*, n. 97, at para. 29.

respect for human rights and fundamental freedoms, or the principle of sovereign equality. As White notes:

> Article 1 includes as a purpose of the UN the maintenance of peace and security by means of collective measures if necessary, but also the promotion and encouragement of respect for human rights. Thus, even within the UN Charter, hard security concerns run alongside human rights, so that when fulfilling its primary purpose, the Council must have regard to human rights.[100]

In addition, as discussed in Section 3.2.1, not only is there a need in adopting a resolution to secure the 'concurring votes' of the five permanent members,[101] but there are also procedural limitations upon the Council set out in Chapter VII of the Charter, such as the fact that the Council is required to make a determination under Article 39.

There has also been some debate as to the meaning of Article 25 of the Charter, which provides that '[t]he Members of the United Nations agree to accept and carry out the decisions of the Security Council *in accordance with the present Charter*' (emphasis added). This could, for example, be understood as a reference to the procedural requirements of Article 27 of the Charter.[102] However, it might also be interpreted as a reference to the substantive standards of Chapter I of the Charter, alluded to in this section, under which decisions of the Council should be adopted. Nonetheless, without any decisive reason to exclude either, it is arguable that it refers to both the procedural and substantive limitations contained within the Charter.[103]

Limitations upon the forcible powers of the Security Council can also be imposed by the other organs of the UN.[104] The General Assembly, for example, might be seen as providing a mechanism of accountability for the actions of the Security Council. Indeed, '[i]f the [Security Council] acts *on behalf* of the general membership of the UN then it is fair to say it is accountable to it. More specifically, the general membership is represented in the Organization by the plenary organ of the [General Assembly].'[105] In particular, the Security Council is obliged to submit annual and, where necessary, special reports to the General Assembly for its consideration[106] which 'shall include an account of the measures that the Security Council has decided upon or taken to maintain international peace and security'.[107] Furthermore, although rare, through its discursive powers the General Assembly might simply express its dissatisfaction with the Council. For example, on 3 August 2012 the Assembly adopted a resolution 'deploring the failure of the Security Council' to take

---

[100] White, n. 30, at 298. [101] Article 27(3), UN Charter (1945). [102] See, further, n. 14.
[103] Tzanakopoulos, n. 59, at 58.
[104] See, in general, Christian Henderson, 'Authority without Accountability? The UN Security Council's Authorisation Method and Institutional Mechanisms of Accountability' (2014) 19 *Journal of Conflict & Security Law* 489.
[105] Ibid., at 502. [106] Article 24(3), UN Charter (1945). [107] Article 15(1), ibid.

effective action during the prevailing crisis in Syria.[108] In addition, while not expressly provided with a power of judicial review in regards to the actions of the other organs of the UN, the ICJ, as 'the principal judicial organ of the United Nations',[109] is also not precluded from casting its opinion on the decisions and actions of the Council, either indirectly through its decisions in contentious cases or directly in the form of advisory opinions.[110]

Secondly, the Council's actions are subject to peremptory norms of international law.[111] Article 26 of the ILC's Draft Articles on the Responsibility of International Organisations, for example, states that '[n]othing in this Chapter precludes the wrongfulness of any act of an international organization which is not in conformity with an obligation arising under a peremptory norm of general international law'. More specifically, the European Court of Justice has stated that *jus cogens* is 'a body of higher rules of public international law binding on all subjects of international law, including the bodies of the United Nations'.[112] The UN is a legal person and thus a subject of international law,[113] at least as far as is necessary in the context of its functions and duties, meaning that it is bound by peremptory norms and could not, as such, authorise the use of force that would constitute an act of genocide or authorise the use of torture in purportedly maintaining international peace and security.

Thirdly, decisions and actions of the Security Council must satisfy the requirements of necessity and proportionality. These principles are, as Chapter 6 highlights, normally seen as limiting principles upon the right of individual and collective self-defence.[114] In this respect, Yoram Dinstein argues against the transposition of these limiting principles because 'the conflation of unilateral self-defence and collective security has no leg to stand on, either in theory or in practice'.[115] Yet, these principles have been applied to the decisions and actions of the Security Council in scholarship,[116] and, as noted in Section 3.2.1, Article 42 refers to the Security Council only taking measures 'as may be *necessary* to maintain or restore international peace and security' (emphasis added).[117]

---

[108] UNGA Res. 66/253 B (2012).
[109] Article 1, Statute of the International Court of Justice (1945).
[110] Henderson, n. 104, at 493.
[111] Wood and Sthoeger, n. 22, at 78–84. See, in general, Alexander Orakhelashvili, *Peremptory Norms in International Law* (Oxford University Press, 2008).
[112] *Kadi v. Council of the European Union and Commission of the European Communities*, Court of First Instance of the European Communities, 2005, at para. 226.
[113] See *Reparations for Injuries Suffered in the Service of the United Nations*, Advisory Opinion (1949) ICJ Reports 174.
[114] See Section 6.3.   [115] Dinstein, n. 25, at para. 876.
[116] Judith Gardam, *Necessity, Proportionality and the Use of Force by States* (Cambridge University Press, 2004), at 188–212.
[117] The Iraq Inquiry, that published its report in July 2016 on the involvement of the United Kingdom in the intervention in Iraq in 2003, was also of the view that, while the military

Finally, following a decision to employ forcible measures, the Security Council will become a more *de facto* party to an armed conflict, whether of an international or non-international character. While international humanitarian law (IHL), as a branch of international law, does not make specific provision for the Council as a subject, the UN is, as noted in this section, recognised as possessing international legal personality.[118] Furthermore, the UN Secretary-General has stated that the UN would be responsible for violations of IHL during peacekeeping operations which are under its command and control.[119] The provisions of Chapter VII are not, however, free from doubt as to whether forces would be under such control of the Council during peace enforcement operations. While the Council was to be able to call upon the armed forces of a state as part of any agreement concluded under Article 43, the Military Staff Committee was there to 'advise and assist' the Council[120] and be responsible for the 'strategic direction of any armed forces placed at the disposal of the Security Council'.[121] The decisions of the Council, however, were to be 'carried out by the Members of the United Nations directly and through their action in the appropriate international agencies of which they are members'[122] and that '[q]uestions relating to the command of such forces [were to] be worked out subsequently'.[123] While the Council was therefore envisaged as having overall or strategic control of the forces at its disposal, it did not appear to be intended under Chapter VII that it would necessarily have the sufficient degree of control – that is, effective control – to make the UN responsible for violations of IHL during enforcement operations,[124] with any

---

action that was justified as authorised by the UN Security Council might have been necessary at some point, it was not at the time the action was launched. The Inquiry did not, however, specifically mention the twin principles of necessity and proportionality as they exist within international law governing the use of force. See 'Statement by Sir John Chilcot,
6 July 2016', available at: www.iraqinquiry.org.uk/media/247010/2016-09-06-sir-john-chilcots-public-statement.pdf; Report of the Iraq Inquiry (Report of a Committee of Privy Counsellors), 6 July 2016, Executive Summary, at para. 338, available at: www.iraqinquiry.org.uk/media/247921/the-report-of-the-iraq-inquiry_executive-summary.pdf. See further Section 4.3 on the 'revival' of Security Council authorisation.

[118] *Reparations for Injuries* advisory opinion, n. 113.
[119] See UN Secretary-General's Bulletin, Observance by United Nations Forces of International Humanitarian Law, UN Doc. ST/SGB/1999/13, 6 August 1999. See Chapter 5 for more on peacekeeping operations.
[120] Article 47(1), UN Charter (1945).   [121] Article 47(3), ibid.   [122] Article 48(2), ibid.
[123] Article 47(3), ibid.
[124] See Article 7, Draft Articles on the Responsibility of International Organizations (2011): 'The conduct of an organ of a State or an organ or agent of an international organization that is placed at the disposal of another international organization shall be considered under international law an act of the latter organization if the organization exercises *effective control* over that conduct' (emphasis added). As Tsagourias and White note: 'As far as authorized military operations are concerned, they do not operate under the UN chain of command and thus the UN exercises neither *de jure* nor *de facto* command and control over

violations being attributable instead to the contributing member states concerned. However, whether the Council itself or the states concerned bear responsibility for violations on the ground, it is clear that the law of armed conflict will operate as a limitation upon the decisions of the Security Council and the mandates provided to forces, so that it could not, for example, order them to target civilians.[125]

## 3.4 THE CHAPTER VII POWERS OF THE SECURITY COUNCIL TO USE FORCE IN PRACTICE

So far this chapter has set out the formal powers of the UN and, in particular, the Security Council, in the realms of the UN's enforcement elements for the maintenance of international peace and security as contained within the Charter and the limitations upon the Council in exercising them. The purpose of this section is to examine how these have worked in practice, both during the Cold War, in the midst of the East–West divisions, and post-1989, when the great divisions between member states eased leading to a 'new world order'. As shall be discussed, there has been a stark contrast, both of a qualitative and quantitative nature, in the forcible actions undertaken under the auspices of the UN within these periods.

### 3.4.1 The Cold War Era (1945–89)

It is fair to say that the Security Council 'began and has lived much of its life as partially paralysed'.[126] The Article 43 'special agreements' that were to provide the Council with an army of troops at its disposal never materialised and the Military Staff Committee has never fully functioned as originally intended. The mutual distrust that stemmed from the East–West rivalry meant that there was a relatively constant use, or threat, of the veto power. Consequently, given that enforcement action under the auspices of the Security Council was not seen as a reliable option from early in the life of the UN, other organisations, such as the North Atlantic Treaty Organization (NATO) and the Warsaw Pact, began to emerge. They were not, however, framed as providing an alternative

---

the troops.' Nicholas Tsagourias and Nigel D. White, *Collective Security: Theory, Law and Practice* (Cambridge University Press, 2013), at 368. The European Court of Human Rights has, however, applied an 'ultimate authority and control' test in examining the responsibility of NATO troops under a UN Security Council resolution. See *Behrami and Behrami v. France; Seramati v. France, Germany and Norway*, Grand Chamber (Admissibility Decision), 2 May 2007 (2007) 45 *European Human Rights Reports* SE10, at paras. 133–6, 140–1.

[125] This is a central aspect of IHL that is prohibited under both treaty and customary international law. See, for example, Article 48, Additional Protocol I to the Geneva Conventions of 1949 (1977).

[126] White, n. 4, at 7.

to the UN, as Chapter VIII of the Charter expressly prohibits regional organisations from taking enforcement action in the absence of authorisation by the Council[127] and the constitutive instruments of the organisations themselves generally expressed allegiance to the UN framework of collective security.[128] Given that any threats to the security of their respective member states were seen to be external in nature they, therefore, classed themselves as collective defence organisations with enforcement action only being envisaged in circumstances where the exercise of the right of collective self-defence would be available.[129]

Upon North Korea's invasion of the Republic of Korea in 1950, the Security Council did not have any forces at its disposal. In what was, with hindsight, firm words from the Council, it '[d]etermined that the armed attack upon the Republic of Korea by forces from North Korea constitute[d] a breach of the peace',[130] with the Council going on to 'recommend that the Members of the United Nations furnish such assistance to the Republic of Korea as may be necessary to repel the armed attack and to restore international peace and security in the area'.[131] This mandate was, however, 'ambiguous'.[132] On the one hand, through its constant reference to the 'armed attack' by North Korea, and by welcoming the support that UN member states had given to assist the Republic of Korea in defending itself against an armed attack,[133] it could be interpreted as a blessing by the Security Council to states in invoking the right of collective self-defence in defence of the Republic of Korea. Furthermore, it only passively 'recommended' assistance and did not do so in an operative paragraph, merely requesting the United States to keep it informed of its progress in a similar fashion to the reporting requirement of Article 51 of the UN Charter.[134]

Alternatively, however, the mandate could by contrast be interpreted as an invocation by the Council of its powers under Chapter VII of the Charter. Indeed, it determined that there had been a breach of the peace and that there was a necessity to restore international peace and security in the area,[135] which is arguably broader than what is necessary to solely repel an armed attack. While only making a recommendation to member states to furnish assistance to the Republic of Korea, 'recommendations' by the Council to

---

[127] Article 53(1), UN Charter (1945).   [128] See, further, Section 3.5.
[129] See Section 6.5 for more on the right of collective self-defence.
[130] UNSC Res. 83 (1950). The Security Council rarely decides that either an 'armed attack' or a 'breach of the peace' has occurred.
[131] Ibid.
[132] Nigel D. White, *The United Nations System: Toward International Justice* (Lynne Rienner, 2002), at 153.
[133] UNSC Res. 84 (1950), para. 1.
[134] Ibid., para. 6. See Section 6.6.1. for more on this requirement in the context of self-defence.
[135] UNSC Res. 83 (1950), preamble.

## 3.4 Chapter VII Powers in Practice

member states are nonetheless envisaged under Article 39. Lastly, the Council permitted the acting forces to use the UN flag during the operations which might be interpreted as indicative of it being a UN operation.[136]

While the operation in Korea was a development in terms of the UN carrying out its mandate to maintain international peace and security, the adoption of these resolutions was only possible through a fortuitous twist of fate, in that the USSR was absent from the Council during the meeting in which the resolution was adopted in protest at the Chinese representation in the UN by the nationalist government in Taiwan. As such, and with the return of the USSR, the Western powers within the UN at the time realised that such operations were unlikely to become the norm. It was in this light that the General Assembly adopted the Uniting for Peace resolution (UfP) on 3 November 1950.[137] The key paragraph of this resolution states that:

> if the Security Council, because of lack of unanimity of the permanent members, fails to exercise its primary responsibility for the maintenance of international peace and security in any case where there appears to be a threat to the peace, breach of the peace, or act of aggression, the General Assembly shall consider the matter immediately with a view to making appropriate recommendations to Members for collective measures, including in the case of a breach of the peace or act of aggression the use of armed force if necessary, to maintain or restore international peace and security.[138]

This resolution appeared to be a breakaway from the restrictions of Article 12 of the UN Charter,[139] in that after a procedural vote of the Council, which is not subject to the veto, the General Assembly may make 'appropriate recommendations'. Indeed, the UfP was novel and 'was envisaged as the main pathway for the General Assembly to address issues of war and conflict'.[140] Yet, the significance of this resolution should not be overstated as in the realms of forcible action the General Assembly was still limited to merely 'recommending' the use of armed force, and this was restricted to cases 'of a breach of the peace or act of aggression',[141] and not when merely a threat to the peace existed. While these two circumstances cannot necessarily be

---

[136] UNSC Res. 84 (1950), para. 5.   [137] UNGA Res. 377 A (1950).   [138] Ibid., para. 1.
[139] See Section 3.2.2.
[140] Dominik Zaum, 'The Security Council, the General Assembly, and War: The Uniting for Peace Resolution', in Vaughan Lowe, Adam Roberts, Jennifer Welsh and Dominik Zaum (eds.), *The United Nations Security Council and War: Evolutions in Thought and Practice since 1945* (Oxford University Press, 2010), 154, at 155. For more on the UN General Assembly's powers and role in the prevention of mass atrocity crimes see Asia-Pacific Centre for the Responsibility to Protect, *The Powers of the UN General Assembly to Prevent and Respond to Atrocity Crimes: A Guidance Document*, April 2021, available at: https://r2pasiapacific.org/files/6710/UNGA_2021%20%283%29.pdf.
[141] This limitation was arguably due to the fact that 'this system of collective security was so potentially dangerous in upsetting the underlying balance of power that existed in the Cold War'. White, n. 30, at 309.

directly equated to an armed attack, it still appears that the UfP is, in all practical senses, limited to essentially recommending that states invoke their right of individual or collective self-defence.[142] In any case, the General Assembly 'has not recommended the use of enforcement measures to this day and is instead traditionally more associated with the establishment of consensual peacekeeping missions, something which the [Security Council] has in any case taken over the administration of'.[143]

During the Cold War the Security Council was, other than in Korea, only really involved in the use of force in the context of enforcing its decisions, including an embargo against Southern Rhodesia in 1966 following the declaration by the Ian Smith regime of independence from the United Kingdom in order to establish white minority rule. On this occasion, the Security Council 'called upon' Great Britain 'to prevent, by the use of force if necessary', oil from reaching Southern Rhodesia in an act to enforce sanctions imposed upon it.[144] The Council did not include any reference to Chapter VII or to any provision of the Charter, although it did determine that a breach of the embargo constituted a threat to the peace.[145] Ultimately, while the Security Council was involved in both situations with the use of force, the full extent of its powers was never fully realised during the Cold War. Indeed, these incidences perhaps only go to highlight the state of partial paralysis that the Council was in.[146]

### 3.4.2 The Post–Cold War Era (1989–)

#### 3.4.2.1 The Development of the 'Authorisation' Method

The end of the Cold War brought with it the possibility for consensus within the Security Council, and thus the potential for the functioning of the collective security system as set out in Chapter VII of the UN Charter. Since 1989 there has been a steep decline in the use of the veto and a general increase in the activity of the Council.[147] That has not meant, however, that it has proceeded to function as envisaged and set out within the Charter.

---

[142] See Dinstein, n. 25, at para. 965.

[143] Christian Henderson, 'The Centrality of the United Nations Security Council in the Legal Regime Governing the Use of Force', in Nigel D. White and Christian Henderson (eds.), *Research Handbook on International Conflict and Security Law: Jus ad Bellum, Jus in Bello, and Jus post Bellum* (Edward Elgar, 2013), 120, at 133. For more on peacekeeping see Chapter 5.

[144] UNSC Res. 221 (1966), para. 5.     [145] Ibid., para. 1.

[146] As discussed elsewhere in this book, various arguments have been made in regard to the breadth of both the prohibition of the use of force and the right of self-defence, as well as the permissibility for a right of humanitarian intervention, in the light of the deadlock of the Council. See, for example, Sections 1.6 and 10.3.2.5.2.

[147] As White notes, since this time '[t]he Security Council has been creative in developing a range of non-forcible measures beyond general and targeted sanctions to include the

## 3.4 Chapter VII Powers in Practice

On 2 August 1990 Iraqi tanks and troops entered Kuwaiti territory, providing the first occasion during the UN era that one state had sought to completely annex another.[148] The Security Council immediately condemned the action as a 'breach of international peace and security',[149] demanded an immediate and unconditional withdrawal of Iraqi forces[150] and imposed economic sanctions.[151] However, on 29 November 1990 the Council adopted what has become one of the most celebrated resolutions to have been adopted by it. In Resolution 678 (1990), which was expressly adopted under Chapter VII of the UN Charter, the Council:

Authorize[d] Member States co-operating with the Government of Kuwait, unless Iraq on or before 15 January 1991, fully implement[ed] ... the foregoing resolutions, to use all necessary means to uphold and implement resolution 660 and all subsequent resolutions and to restore international peace and security in the area.[152]

After the final opportunity to comply that had been afforded to Iraq had passed, a US-led coalition launched a military mission codenamed Operation Desert Storm on 16 January 1991. This was an air offensive that was followed by a ground invasion and which ultimately led to Iraqi forces being forcibly compelled to leave Kuwait.[153]

As with the Council's involvement in Korea, it is possible to argue that this operation could be classified as either Security Council 'blessed' collective self-defence or Security Council enforcement action.[154] However, of importance is that, while the Council refrained from using the words 'use of force', the euphemism 'authorisation' to use 'all necessary means' was virtually unanimously accepted and supported by those within the Council as equating to an authorisation to use forcible measures in achieving the objectives of the resolution.[155] There was also a clear belief amongst many at the time that this action by the Council, coming at the time and within the circumstances that it did at the end of the Cold War, would have precedential value.[156] Indeed, this episode undoubtedly gave birth to the relatively consistent practice of the

---

creation of international criminal tribunals and international territorial administrations'. White, n. 30, at 301–2. However, there have been further problems since 2011 and the disagreements regarding the breadth and scope of the authorisation provided in UN Security Council Resolution 1973 (2011).

[148] *Keesing's* (1990) 37632.
[149] UNSC Res. 660 (1990), preamble. The Council did not condemn the action as a violation of Article 2(4), an act of aggression or an armed attack.
[150] UNSC Res. 660 (1990), para. 2.   [151] UNSC Res. 661 (1990), para. 3.
[152] UNSC Res. 678 (1990), para. 2 (second emphasis added).   [153] *Keesing's* (1991) 37936-9.
[154] See Dinstein, n. 25, at paras. 906–12; Eugene V. Rostow, 'Until What? Enforcement Action or Collective Self-Defense?' (1991) 85 *American Journal of International Law* 506.
[155] See UN Doc. S/PV.2963, 29 November 1990. Only Iraq objected.
[156] Ibid., at 6 (US); 18 (Kuwait); 32 (Yemen); 76 (Malaysia); 59–60 (Cuba).

Council providing its authorisation to states to use 'all necessary means' in order to fulfil the Council's aims and objectives.

### 3.4.2.2 Subsequent Practice in the Use of the Authorisation Method

Since the adoption of Resolution 678 (1990), what might be described as the 'authorisation method' has been regularly employed by the Council, and in varying circumstances. For example, while the Security Council has primary responsibility for *international* peace and security, relatively soon after the eviction of Iraq from Kuwait it began to employ the method in the context of non-international or internal situations. The first of these was in Somalia in 1992. Following the downfall of President Siad Barre in January 1991, fighting broke out between various groups across Somalia, with the most intense fighting taking place within the capital city, Mogadishu. With widespread death and destruction, and with many fleeing their homes and seeking refuge in neighbouring countries, there was an urgent need for humanitarian assistance. In January 1992 the Security Council expressed grave alarm at the rapid deterioration of the situation, the loss of life and the widespread damage and determined that the situation constituted a threat to peace and security.[157]

Efforts at implementing a ceasefire between the parties and in securing the delivery of humanitarian aid, including through the deployment of the United Nations Operation in Somalia (UNOSOM I),[158] were largely unsuccessful. On 29 November 1992, in a letter to the Security Council, the UN Secretary-General laid out five options to ensure the safe delivery of humanitarian aid.[159] After consideration of these options, the Council, on 3 December 1992, unanimously adopted Resolution 794 (1992) under Chapter VII of the UN Charter, which authorised the use of 'all necessary means to establish as soon as possible a secure environment for humanitarian relief operations in Somalia'.[160] Acting under Chapter VII of the Charter, the Council also authorised the Secretary-General and the participating member states to make arrangements for 'the unified command and control' of the military forces and requested them to establish appropriate mechanisms for coordination between the UN and their forces.[161] Furthermore, the Council requested the Secretary-General and the states concerned to report regularly to it on the progress in establishing a secure environment in Somalia.[162]

The first elements of the Unified Task Force (UNITAF), led by the United States, were subsequently deployed in Mogadishu on 9 December 1992 and consisted of over 37,000 troops. However, the force was largely unsuccessful in achieving its mandate and, after the United States decided to terminate its

---

[157] UNSC Res. 733 (1992), preamble. [158] UNSC Res. 751 (1992), para. 3.
[159] UN Doc. S/24868, 30 November 1992. [160] UNSC Res. 794 (1992), para. 10.
[161] Ibid., paras. 12 and 13. [162] Ibid., para. 18.

participation, could no longer continue. The Security Council replaced UNOSOM I and UNITAF with UNOSOM II in March 1993,[163] although this was terminated in March 1995 with civil strife continuing in Somalia.

The Security Council has provided a similar humanitarian assistance mandate in other situations. For example, in Albania in 1997, during a period of widespread civil disorder which led to the toppling of the government, the Council authorised states operating as part of a multinational protection force to facilitate 'the safe and prompt delivery of humanitarian assistance, and to help create a secure environment for the missions of international organizations in Albania, including those providing humanitarian assistance'.[164] Furthermore, the Council has authorised missions to ensure the security and freedom of movement of personnel involved in or associated with the operation concerned, including of humanitarian organisations,[165] as well as to prepare for the introduction of a longer-term UN stabilisation force.[166]

Further involving itself in the domestic affairs of State, the Council has provided its authorisation to use all necessary means to ensure compliance with pre-existing agreements that have been concluded between governments and other relevant parties, most often ceasefire agreements.[167] However, and in what remains a high-water point in the Council's involvement in an ostensibly internal situation, the Council provided authorisation to member states in Haiti in 1994 to 'facilitate the departure from Haiti of the military leadership, consistent with the Governors Island Agreement, the prompt return of the legitimately elected President and the restoration of the legitimate authorities of the government of Haiti',[168] although this authorisation was never fully implemented after a negotiated settlement was reached before the forces arrived. This instance of the authorisation method was particularly significant for two reasons, however. First, it was 'unprecedented in authorizing force to remove one regime and install another (however democratically

---

[163] UNSC Res. 814 (1993), paras. 5 and 6. See Section 5.6.2 for more on this peacekeeping operation.

[164] UNSC Res. 1101 (1997), paras. 2 and 4. See, in general, Dino Kritsiotis, 'Security Council Resolution 1101 (1997) and the Multinational Protection Force of Operation Alba in Albania' (1999) 12 *Leiden Journal of International Law* 511. A similar mandate was also provided, for example, to the European Union (EU) in Chad and the Central African Republic in UNSC Res. 1778 (2007), para. 6(a)(ii) and to 'multinational forces' in Liberia in UNSC Res. 1497 (2003), para. 1 and East Timor in UNSC Res. 1264 (1999), para. 3.

[165] See, for example, UNSC Res. 1778 (2007), para. 6(a)(iii) (Chad and the Central African Republic); UNSC Res. 1511 (2003), para. 13 (Iraq); UNSC Res. 1101 (1997), paras. 2 and 4 (Albania).

[166] See, for example, UNSC Res. 1497 (2003), para. 1 (Liberia); UNSC Res. 1529, paras. 2, 3 and 6 (Haiti).

[167] See, for example, UNSC Res. 1305 (2000), para. 11 (Bosnia and Herzegovina); UNSC Res. 1386 (2001), paras. 1 and 3 (Afghanistan); UNSC Res. 1497 (2003), para. 1 (Liberia).

[168] UNSC Res. 940 (1994), para. 4.

elected) within a Member state',[169] and, secondly, it 'was the first time that the United States sought the imprimatur of the United Nations to use force within its own hemisphere'.[170]

More recently, the Council has provided its authorisation to employ all necessary means in the protection of civilians.[171] This was the mandate provided to NATO for its operations in Libya and to the United Nations Operation in Côte d'Ivoire (UNOCI)/French forces in Côte d'Ivoire in 2011.[172] On both occasions the mandate was controversial in that it was used to support opposition forces in their fight for regime change.[173] The protection of civilians is also a common mandate underpinning authorisations that have been provided in 'muscular' peacekeeping missions.[174]

While some of these mandates are broad in nature, and thus provide the possibility for liberal interpretations and flexibility in implementing them depending upon developments on the ground, the Council has also provided authorisations for achieving what could be seen as narrower objectives, such as enforcing no-fly zones[175] and arms embargos[176] as well as for repressing acts of piracy and armed robbery.[177] The Council has employed both the phrases 'all necessary measures' and 'all necessary means' in its various authorisations. There does not, however, seem to be any substantive difference between them, and 'the choice between these words seems to depend on the coincidental outcome of the negotiations preceding the adoption of the relevant resolution'.[178]

Although it is accepted that 'all necessary measures/means' includes the use of force, it bears thinking about what this may mean in practice, given the nature of the scope of 'force' as discussed in Chapters 1 and 2. For example, and as discussed further in Chapter 4, the mandate to use 'all necessary measures' to 'protect civilians' might be interpreted as providing for a right of states to provide weapons to non-state actors on the ground in the state concerned.[179] Furthermore, in 2010 a uranium enrichment plant in Iran was

---

[169] David Malone, *Decision Making in the UN Security Council: The Case of Haiti, 1990–1997* (Clarendon Press, 1998), at 110.

[170] Simon Chesterman, *Just War or Just Peace?: Humanitarian Intervention and International Law* (Oxford University Press, 2002), at 152.

[171] See, for example, UNSC Res. 1671 (2006), para. 8(b) (DRC); UNSC Res. 1778 (2007), para. 6(a)(i) (Chad and the Central African Republic).

[172] UNSC Res. 1973 (2011), para. 4 (Libya); UNSC Res. 1975 (2011), para. 6 (Côte d'Ivoire) (this was recalled from UNSC Res. 1464 (2004)).

[173] See Section 4.4.   [174] See Chapter 5.   [175] UNSC Res. 1973 (2011), para. 8 (Libya).

[176] Ibid., para. 13.   [177] UNSC Res. 1816 (2008), para. 7(b) (Somalia).

[178] Niels Blokker, 'Outsourcing the Use of Force: Towards More Security Council Control of Authorized Operations?', in Marc Weller (ed.), *The Oxford Handbook of the Use of Force in International Law* (Oxford University Press, 2015), 202, at 213.

[179] See, further, Section 4.4.1.1. See also Section 2.4.2 for more on the concept of indirect force.

targeted by a Stuxnet worm that led to test tubes being damaged.[180] In Resolution 1929 (2010), which had been adopted prior to this attack in response to Iran's lack of compliance with Council resolutions on ensuring the peaceful nature of its nuclear programme, the Security Council imposed a series of measures, including additional sanctions, and expanded an arms embargo.[181] While it also specifically stressed that it did not authorise any measures exceeding the scope of the resolution, including the threat or use of force,[182] had the resolution authorised the use of 'all necessary means' to enforce the suspension of enrichment-related activities it is arguable at least that the Stuxnet worm would have proved an efficient way of achieving this particular mandate.[183]

### 3.4.2.3 Concerns Regarding the Authorisation Method

The development and implementation of the authorisation method might be considered a positive step in that it provides the Security Council with a practical means of enforcement that had long been lacking. Nonetheless, concerns have been expressed in regard to it. For example, Nicholas Tsagourias has commented that 'the Charter contains specific enforcement procedures. The [Security Council] has no choice in enforcement mechanisms and indeed authorisations as a practice cannot be assumed from either the letter or the purposes of the intentions of the UN members.'[184] Indeed, some see the Article 43 agreements as a condition precedent to the taking of collective military action by the Security Council under Article 42.[185] Yet, at the same time, 'no explicit language in Article 42 or in Articles 43, 44 and 45 ... precludes states from voluntarily making armed forces available to carry out the resolutions of the Council adopted under Chapter VII'.[186] Furthermore, '[w]hile the Charter appears to envisage the Council taking military action through forces under its own command, nothing in the Charter precludes the Council authorizing military action by others and Articles 48 and 53 clearly envisage it'.[187] As Olivier Corten has noted, '[e]ven if the authorisation given to States to use force is not explicitly taken

---

[180] See Section 2.4.   [181] UNSC Res. 1929 (2010).   [182] Ibid., preamble.
[183] Harrison Dinniss, n. 66, at 113.
[184] Nicholas Tsagourias, 'The Shifting Laws on the Use of Force and the Trivialization of the UN Collective Security System: The Need to Reconstitute It' (2003) 34 *Netherlands Yearbook of International Law* 55, at 63–4.
[185] Kelsen, n. 29, at 756.
[186] Oscar Schachter, 'United Nations Law in the Gulf Conflict' (1991) 85 *American Journal of International Law* 452, at 464.
[187] Christopher Greenwood, 'Humanitarian Intervention: The Case of Kosovo' (1999) 10 *Finnish Yearbook of International Law* 141, at 154.

up in [the provisions of the UN Charter], it seems difficult to contest that such a mechanism is consistent with both their spirit and their letter'.[188]

Yet, others have also looked beyond the specific wording of Chapter VII in attempting to provide an effective interpretation of the Charter based upon its 'spirit' and have thus argued that the authorisation method represents a necessary incremental shift in the powers of the Security Council. In this vein, the ICJ in the *Certain Expenses* advisory opinion rejected the proposition that authorisation for the use of armed force by the Security Council must be based upon Article 42, and in fact it could not assume such 'a limited ... view of the powers of the Security Council'.[189] Indeed, it concluded that '[i]t cannot be said that the Charter has left the Security Council impotent in the face of an emergency situation when agreements under Article 43 have not been concluded'.[190] As Alexander Orakhelashvili notes, '[i]n the *Certain Expenses* Opinion the International Court admitted the exercise of implied powers by principal organs to the extent that this serves the purposes of the UN'.[191] The ICJ in the *Reparations for Injuries* advisory opinion also noted that 'the Organization must be deemed to have those powers which though not expressly provided for in the Charter, are conferred upon it by necessary implication as being essential to the performance of its duties'.[192] As such, '[w]hen the Organization takes action which warrants the assertion that it was appropriate for the fulfilment of one of the stated purposes of the United Nations, the presumption is that such an action is not *ultra vires*'.[193] As already noted in Section 3.1, Article 1(1) of the UN Charter clearly states that '[t]he Purposes of the United Nations are ... [t]o maintain international peace and security, and to that end: to take *effective collective measures* for the prevention and removal of threats to the peace, and for the suppression of acts of aggression or other breaches of the peace' (emphasis added). Given that the Security Council has primary responsibility for fulfilling this purpose of the UN,[194] if the measures contained within the Charter for it to do so have not proved effective, there is on this basis arguably a duty upon the Council to develop a mechanism that will.[195]

---

[188] Olivier Corten, *The Law against War: The Prohibition on the Use of Force in Contemporary International Law*, 2nd ed. (Hart, 2021), at 321.
[189] *Certain Expenses* advisory opinion, n. 33, at 167.   [190] Ibid.
[191] Orakhelashvili, n. 63, at 51.
[192] *Reparations for Injuries Suffered in the Service of the United Nations*, Advisory Opinion (1949) ICJ Reports 174, at para. 182
[193] *Certain Expenses* advisory opinion, n. 33, at 168.
[194] The ICJ in the *Namibia* advisory opinion noted that 'the Members of the United Nations have conferred upon the Security Council powers commensurate with its responsibility for the maintenance of peace and security'. *Namibia* advisory opinion, n. 28, at 52.
[195] The implied powers doctrine has its limits though as '[i]mplied powers can only be those that correspond to the overall character of an organ under the constituent instrument and enable

## 3.4 Chapter VII Powers in Practice

A further, and broader, criticism of the Council's practice of authorisation is that it has essentially led to a 'privatisation' of the collective security system.[196] Yet, as discussed in more detail in Section 3.5, the authorisation practice already exists in connection with regional organisations. While an authorisation of states by the Council is arguably based more upon a 'liberal construction of [the Council's] authority derived from its general powers to maintain and restore international peace and security'[197] than on the strict wording of the provisions of Chapter VII, in both cases states and regional organisations are acting under the Council's general authority and overall strategic control.[198] Indeed, even within the express provisions of the UN Charter as set out in Sections 3.3.2 and 3.3.3, despite provision being made for troops to be at the disposal of the Council, the actual control of these forces was not to fall to the Security Council. Chapter VII does not, therefore, provide for the Security Council to have any more command over the forces at its disposal than as has transpired under the authorisation mechanism.[199] Indeed, while command of the authorised forces of member states has thus far been by the authorised states or international organisations themselves, this is something that was also the case under the system envisaged within the Charter.

Thus, while we can see that, ultimately, the authorisation mechanism and associated practice does not fall squarely within Article 42 and the Chapter VII provisions on collective security as envisaged, and we can identify a practice distinct from the Security Council merely providing its blessing to states to act in collective self-defence of a victim state, a settled interpretation of the UN Charter and the competence of the Security Council appears to have emerged. Indeed, as Simon Chesterman has noted, '[e]arly questions about the procedural legality of this adaptation of the Council's role now appear moot in light of state practice',[200] while Olivier Corten has observed that '[e]ven if it is not covered by explicit regulations in the UN Charter, no one contests the lawfulness of the principle of military intervention authorised by the Security Council'.[201] Furthermore, it is undeniable that while the practice of

---

it to carry out functions conferred on it'. Orakhelashvili, n. 63, at 51. See Section 3.3.3 on the limitations upon the forcible powers of the Security Council.

[196] See John Quigley, 'The "Privatization" of Security Council Enforcement Action: A Threat to Multilateralism' (1996) 17 *Michigan Journal of International Law* 249.

[197] Schachter, n. 186, at 461.   [198] See Section 3.3.3.

[199] See Section 4.2 on correcting the balance between multilateralism and unilateralism.

[200] Chesterman, n. 170, at 164.

[201] Corten, n. 188, at 316. Marcelo Kohen has also noted that 'the practice of Security Council authorizations to member states to use force is today too well established to be contested'. Marcelo G. Kohen, 'The Use of Force by the United States after the End of the Cold War, and its Impact on International Law', in Michael Byers and Georg Nolte (eds.), *United States Hegemony and the Foundations of International Law* (Cambridge University Press, 2003), 206, at 215.

authorisation may not be an ideal solution,[202] and the idea of the Security Council possessing a standing army of troops at its disposal has given way to the emergence of 'coalitions of the willing', each with their own motives for acting, it arguably nonetheless 'provides the Organization with an enforcement capacity it would not otherwise have and is greatly preferable to the unilateral use of force by Member States without reference to the United Nations'.[203]

However, in carrying out its responsibility for the maintenance of international peace and security, the Security Council must still determine at least a 'threat to the peace' either expressly or by issuing the authorisation within a resolution adopted under Chapter VII of the UN Charter. Questions arise as to how those authorisations – in the context of what might be seen as internal situations within a state, such as Haiti in 2004 – might be reconciled with this requirement. Indeed, it has been argued that internal situations do not come within the ambit of Article 39 as they do not constitute a 'threat of force' against another state as found in Article 2(4),[204] and the Charter is concerned with threats to or breaches of international peace, and not to internal peace.

Article 2(7) of the Charter is clear that '[n]othing contained in the present Charter shall authorize the United Nations to intervene in matters which are essentially within the domestic jurisdiction of any state'. However, this provision goes on to qualify this principle by stating that it 'shall not prejudice the application of enforcement measures under Chapter VII'. Furthermore, it might be argued the interventions that have taken place under the auspices of the Council represent a 'redefinition of international peace to include the more positive aspects of common interests of humanity'.[205] Indeed:

the practice of the Security Council is rich with cases of civil war or internal strife which it classified as a 'threat to the peace' and dealt with under Chapter VII . . . [i]t can thus be said that there is a common understanding, manifested by the 'subsequent practice' of the membership of the United Nations at large, that the 'threat to the peace' of Article 39 may include, as one of its species, internal armed conflicts.[206]

To be sure, the interventions noted in Section 3.4.2.2 elicited very little in the way of general condemnation and subsequent practice would seem to validate the claim that '[a] threat to the peace may by determined by the Security Council even in the face of mere violations of human rights not entailing the

---

[202] See Chapter 4 for issues that have arisen in connection with the authorisation method.
[203] Report of the UN Secretary-General, 'Supplement to an Agenda for Peace', UN Doc. A/50/60, 3 January 1995, at para. 80.
[204] Joachim Arntz, *Der Begriff der Friedensbedrohung in Satzung und Praxis der Vereinten Nationen* (Duncker & Humblot, 1975), at 63–4.
[205] Robert Cryer, 'The Security Council and Article 39: A Threat to Coherence?' (1996) 1 *Journal of Armed Conflict Law* 161, at 188.
[206] *Tadic*, n. 97, at para. 30. See also White, n. 30, at 299.

use of force'.[207] Finally, it bears noting that missions authorised by the Security Council have often been undertaken with the consent of, or even at the request of, the territorial state.[208]

### 3.4.2.4 The General Assembly and the Use of Force

There is no clear separation of powers between the organs of the UN, as might be found in domestic political systems between the executive, the legislature and the judiciary. In this respect there has been a 'sometimes fraught relationship between the General Assembly and the Security Council in matters of peace and security'.[209] Given the greater representative legitimacy of the General Assembly, some have argued that it possesses a broad competence in the field of international peace and security. Nigel White, for example, argues that a reading of Articles 10 and 14 of the UN Charter provides broad powers for the Assembly to 'recommend military measures'.[210] Referring back to the envisaged powers of the organs of the UN as set out in Sections 3.2 and 3.3, White argues that 'since the UN has the power to order military action, then it must have the lesser power to *recommend* military action, and once this recommendatory power is recognized there is nothing in the Charter which prohibits the Assembly as well as the Council from exercising it'.[211] Furthermore, although Article 12 of the Charter provides that while the Council is 'exercising in respect of any dispute or situation the functions assigned to it in the present Charter' the 'General Assembly shall not make any recommendations with regard to that dispute or situation', it is true that '[i]n practice, the Assembly often adopts resolutions on a matter at the same time at which the Security Council is considering the question'[212] so that 'the Assembly decides for itself whether the Council was functioning within the meaning of Article 12(1), thereby instituting a crude form of political accountability in the organization'.[213] This was the case, for example, during the civil

---

[207] Dinstein, n. 25, at para. 889. Wood and Sthoeger add 'situations internal to a single state, international terrorism, including the refusal to hand over terrorist suspects, proliferation of weapons of mass destruction and their means of delivery, ... protection of civilians and violations of international humanitarian law, piracy, organized crime, illicit trafficking in small arms and light weapons, overturning of democratic principles, health crises, and the effects of climate change on conflict.' Wood and Sthoeger, n. 22, at 66–7. Article 39 only talks of a threat to the peace, and not *international* peace. The relevance of this is not often asserted.

[208] See Corten, n. 188, at 318.   [209] White, n. 30, at 301.   [210] Ibid., at 305.   [211] Ibid.

[212] Ibid., at 302.

[213] Ibid., at 303–4. See *Legal Consequences of the Construction of a Wall in the Occupied Palestinian Territory*, Advisory Opinion (2004) ICJ Reports 136, at paras. 27–8.

war in Syria which witnessed the UN General Assembly positively urging the Security Council to take action to ensure accountability.[214]

Yet, it has to be acknowledged that the Council's power to 'authorise' the use of force is different from a power to 'recommend' such measures. As noted in Sections 3.2.1 and 3.3, incidences when the Council has authorised the use of force have been underpinned by a Chapter VII decision of the Council. Such decisions are generally legally binding upon all states which means that the aggressor state is compelled to accept the measures to be taken against it. The same power does not exist in the Charter, and neither has it been developed, in the context of the General Assembly. The text of the Charter alludes to this fact, in that Article 14 expressly limits the powers of the General Assembly to 'recommend measures for the *peaceful* adjustment of any situation' (emphasis added), while Article 11(2) states that 'any such question on which *action* is necessary shall be referred to the Security Council by the General Assembly either before or after its discussion'.[215] In any case, and as White acknowledges, 'the power to recommend military measures [by the General Assembly] has not been utilized in the full sense, and in the current post–Cold War climate, has become more a theoretical rather than a practical issue'.[216] Indeed, no clear practice exists to demonstrate that member states have wished to provide the Assembly with such coercive powers.

Such powers have, however, been discussed by some scholars in the context of the deadlock which has gripped the Council during the Syrian civil war since 2011, with the prospect of the UfP resolution being relied upon to provide the Assembly with a role in recommending forcible action.[217] Yet, as noted in Section 3.4.1, UfP provides the Assembly with no role in connection with the use of force unless a 'breach of the peace' or 'act of aggression' has been expressly identified, presumably by the Council, with these concepts appearing to remain within the inter-state or international setting. White argues that 'despite the wording of the Uniting for Peace resolution, there appears to be no cogent argument against allowing the Assembly to recommend military measures to combat a threat to the peace'.[218] Yet, on balance, the physically coercive nature of the action recommended, the texts of both the Charter and the UfP resolution and state practice appear to suggest otherwise. Indeed, practice has been limited to the General Assembly recommending peacekeeping operations such as in the Suez crisis in 1956 and

---

[214] See UNGA Res. 72/191 (2017), para. 34.
[215] The ICJ has interpreted such 'action' to mean enforcement action. See *Certain Expenses*, advisory opinion, n. 33, at 165.
[216] White, n. 30, at 305.
[217] See Andrew J. Carswell, 'Unblocking the UN Security Council: The Uniting for Peace Resolution' (2013) 18 *Journal of Conflict & Security Law* 453.
[218] White, n. 30, at 310.

Congo in 1960, with the UfP resolution forgotten about in the context of the crises in Kosovo in 1999 and Syria from 2011.

The UfP procedure was, however, invoked by the Security Council in the context of the Russian invasion of Ukraine in February 2022.[219] Yet, despite the fact that this incident represented a clear breach of the peace and thus potentially provided the General Assembly with the opportunity to recommend the use of force to repel Russian forces and restore international peace and security the General Assembly instead opted to '[d]*eplore*[]' in the strongest terms the aggression by the Russian Federation against Ukraine in violation of Article 2(4) of the Charter'.[220] In addition, it made several demands upon Russia including 'immediately cease[ing] its use of force against Ukraine',[221] 'immediately and unconditionally revers[ing] the decision related to the status of certain areas of the Donetsk and Luhansk regions of Ukraine',[222] as well as '[d]*emand*[ing] that all parties fully comply with their obligations under international humanitarian law'.[223] The risk of escalation that such a recommendation to use direct force would give rise to ultimately tempered the General Assembly's response, with states similarly preferring to support Ukraine through the provision of military assistance rather than through direct military means.

## 3.5 CHAPTER VIII AND THE AUTHORISATION OF 'REGIONAL ORGANISATIONS'

The UN Charter did not attempt to establish a system of collective security which begins and ends with the UN, and in particular the Security Council. As a result, regional organisations are given specific attention in Chapter VIII of the Charter and are seen as an essential element in the overall scheme of collective security that the Charter attempted to establish. Article 52(1) of Chapter VIII, for example, states that:

Nothing in the present Charter precludes the existence of regional arrangements or agencies for dealing with such matters relating to the maintenance of international peace and security as are appropriate for regional action, provided that such arrangements or agencies and their activities are consistent with the Purposes and Principles of the United Nations.

This recognition of various organisations operating within the realms of collective security raises questions as to how the various competences are allocated between them and the UN. There is no instrument or treaty providing for a regime of competence allocation between organisations within the field of international peace and security. An argument can, therefore, be made that

---

[219] See UNSC Res. 2623 (2022).   [220] UNGA Res. ES-11/1 (2022), para. 2.
[221] Ibid., para. 3.   [222] Ibid., para. 6.   [223] Ibid., para. 12.

in determining such issues resort should be made in the first instance to the constitutive instruments of the organisations concerned.[224] In this respect, an analysis of the provisions of the UN Charter alone arguably provides a sufficiently clear picture.

In the context of disputes or conflicts which develop as, and remain, peaceful, regional organisations possess concurrent competence with the UN.[225] Chapter VI of the UN Charter, concerning the 'Pacific Settlement of Disputes', establishes the framework for the Security Council's involvement with states in peacefully settling disputes. Yet, Article 52(2) of Chapter VIII also notes that '[t]he Members of the United Nations entering into [regional] arrangements or constituting such agencies shall make every effort to achieve pacific settlement of local disputes through such regional arrangements or by such regional agencies *before* referring them to the Security Council' (emphasis added). This reinforces the perception that other organisations were envisaged as having a security and dispute settlement mandate, and that in certain circumstances they should be a state's primary point of contact. Indeed, the Charter is clear that the Security Council shall 'encourage' the pacific settlement of local disputes through such regional arrangements,[226] indicating a presumption in favour of regional organisations over the Security Council in settling such disputes.[227]

If, however, either at the inception of the dispute or through its evolution, enforcement measures become necessary then the competence of the Security Council becomes exclusive. This emerges from a reading of Article 53(3) of Chapter VIII of the Charter which provides that '[t]he Security Council shall, where appropriate, utilize such regional arrangements or agencies for enforcement action under its authority. But no enforcement action shall be taken under regional arrangements or by regional agencies without the authorization of the Security Council.' In this respect, '[t]he primary responsibility of the Security Council necessarily includes its primacy over regional organizations in the area of enforcement'.[228] However, the fact that regional organisations may undertake enforcement action, albeit under the authorisation of the Security Council, highlights an important distinction in that it is not the use of enforcement action itself in which the Security Council has exclusive competence, but rather in making the decision that such measures are necessary.[229]

---

[224] Orakhelashvili, n. 63, at 109.   [225] Ibid., at 107.   [226] Article 52(3), UN Charter (1945).
[227] Orakhelashvili, n. 63, at 124. In addition, '[t]he Security Council shall at all times be kept fully informed of activities undertaken or in contemplation under regional arrangements or by regional agencies for the maintenance of international peace and security'. Article 54, UN Charter (1945).
[228] Orakhelashvili, n. 63, at 120; see also Tsagourias and White, n. 124, at 132.
[229] Henderson, n. 143, at 127.

The majority of organisations, both in terms of their constitutive instruments and practice, do not conflict with this regime of competence allocation.[230] The Arab League, for example, does not consider itself to possess autonomous powers of enforcement and, in its constitutive instrument, reaffirms the primacy of the Security Council.[231] Similarly, both the EU and the Organization of American States submit to the overarching authority of the UN.[232] Some, however, appear to have challenged the authority of the Security Council, either through their constitutive instruments or in practice.[233]

### 3.5.1 The African Union

In its Constitutive Act (2000), the African Union (AU), although reaffirming the principle of the 'peaceful resolution of disputes' and the 'prohibition of the use of force or the threat to use force',[234] also affirmed 'the right of the Union to intervene in a Member State pursuant to a decision of the Assembly in respect of grave circumstances, namely war crimes, genocide and crimes against humanity'.[235] While acknowledging 'the right of Member States to request intervention from the Union in order to restore peace and security',[236] Ademola Abass has argued that, under the Constitutive Act the absence of a request will not prevent the AU from intervening should it consider it necessary to do so.[237] It would thus appear, at least, that the AU has claimed autonomy to make decisions regarding enforcement action in its member states in the light of grave circumstances, namely war crimes, genocide and crimes against humanity.[238] Christine Gray refers to this as 'a regional right of humanitarian intervention'.[239] One might argue that there is nothing objectionable in this arrangement, given that accession to the AU's Constitutive Act

---

[230] See the survey in Orakhelashvili, n. 63, at 64–88.

[231] Article 11, Treaty of Joint Defense and Economic Cooperation between the States of the Arab League (1950).

[232] Article 42 of the EU's Lisbon Treaty (1999) notes that it shall act 'in accordance with the principles of the United Nations Charter'; see the preamble, Articles 1 and 5, Inter-American Treaty of Reciprocal Assistance (1947).

[233] See also the discussion in Chapter 4 on ECOWAS's intervention in Liberia and Sierra Leone which are depicted as receiving retrospective legitimisation by the Council.

[234] Articles 4(e) and 4(f), Constitutive Act of the African Union (2000). [235] Article 4(h), ibid.

[236] Article 4(j), ibid.

[237] Ademola Abass, *Regional Organisations and the Development of Collective Security: Beyond Chapter VIII of the UN Charter* (Hart, 2004), at 165.

[238] Jeremy Levitt, 'The Peace and Security Council of the African Union and the United Nations Security Council: The Case of Darfur, Sudan', in Niels Blokker and Nico Schrijver (eds.), *The Security Council and the Use of Force* (Martinus Nijhoff, 2005), 211, at 229.

[239] Christine Gray, *International Law and the Use of Force*, 4th ed. (Oxford University Press, 2018), at 53. See Chapter 10 for more on the use of force for humanitarian purposes.

ultimately flows from the consent of its member states who are, therefore, simply providing their prior, as opposed to *ad hoc*, consent to intervention.[240] Yet, upon this interpretation there is a clear normative conflict between the Constitutive Act of the AU and the UN Charter.

States freely assent to the UN Charter. In doing so, however, they are submitting to the collective security system contained within it and, with that, the possibility that enforcement action might be taken against them. Regardless of whether they agree or not with such action at the time, the fact remains that they have provided their prior consent to the possibility that it might occur at some point in the future. Organisations set up on the same basis, albeit along regional lines, clearly conflict with the exclusive competence that the Security Council possesses in this respect in the realms of enforcement action.[241] To date, however, the AU has not implemented these particular provisions of its Constitutive Act. It is also perhaps telling as to its willingness to do so that it was only with the consent of the Sudanese government that it was willing to intervene in Darfur during the humanitarian crisis that engulfed the region from 2003.[242]

Arguably a deciding factor in any normative conflict between the obligations of states contained within the UN Charter and those contained in regional arrangements is Article 103 of the UN Charter, which provides that '[i]n the event of a conflict between the obligations of the Members of the United Nations under the present Charter and their obligations under any other international agreement, their obligations under the present Charter shall prevail'. States are under an obligation, in acting through a regional organisation for enforcement purposes, to do so with the authorisation of the Security Council, an obligation that appears to be in conflict with the obligation under the Constitutive Act to permit the AU to forcibly intervene. It might, however, be argued that Article 103 is only binding upon member states and not other organisations.[243] Yet, the rights and obligations of an organisation have to be appreciated through the prism of the rights and obligations applicable to their member states in order that states do not avoid their international obligations simply by establishing, and then acting through, a regional organisation.

---

[240] See Chapter 9 for more on consent to intervention.
[241] This also needs to be distinguished from *ad hoc* consent by one government to another to intervene within its territory. See, further, Chapter 9.
[242] Gray, n. 239, at 61.
[243] This 'systemic inconsistency' was essentially endorsed by the European Court of Justice in the *Kadi* case. See Joined Cases C-402/05 P and C-415/05 P *Yassin Abdullah Kadi and Al Barakaat International Foundation* v. *Council of the European Union and Commission of the European Communities*, Judgement of the European Court of Justice (Grand Chamber), 3 September 2008.

## 3.5.2 The North Atlantic Treaty Organization

While Chapter VIII is concerned with 'regional organisations' not every organisation, expressly at least, falls within this categorisation. It is arguable that NATO is one such organisation, in that in the North Atlantic Treaty NATO is expressly categorised as a collective defence alliance as opposed to a regional organisation.[244] In contrast to the AU, NATO is more concerned with external threats to its members, rather than the internal affairs of a geopolitical area. In this respect, '[t]he Article 5 commitment to collective defence remains the principle *raison d'être* of NATO'[245] and outside of these circumstances the North Atlantic Treaty recognises that the Security Council has primary responsibility for the maintenance of international peace and security.[246] Yet, collective self-defence organisations, such as NATO, are also kept under the wing of the Council through Article 51 of the Charter, whereby any measures taken in self-defence are to be reported to the Council and may only continue until the Council takes measures necessary to maintain international peace and security.[247]

Following the end of the Cold War, NATO adopted a new strategic direction, when it sought to redefine its role.[248] While in 1991 the Alliance still perceived itself to be 'purely defensive in purpose'[249] its role within the conflict in Yugoslavia 1991–5 provided the appearance of it shifting away from its role as a purely external defensive alliance to one concerned with internal crisis management. Following its intervention in Kosovo in 1999, NATO began to expand its role so as to incorporate maintaining peace and security within the 'Euro-Atlantic region'.[250] Indeed, it was said that the Alliance 'not only ensures defence of its members but contributes to peace and stability in the region'.[251] This was, as Orakhelashvili points out, a new field of competence and represents 'a consensually agreed expansion to cover tasks qualitatively different from those set out in Article 5'.[252] These core tasks of collective

---

[244] Preamble and Article 5, The North Atlantic Treaty (1949). The self-labelling as such might arguably have been to avoid the constraints of Chapter VIII. See Dick Leurdijk, 'The UN and NATO: The Logic of Primacy', in Michael Pugh and W. P. S. Sidhu (eds.), *The United Nations and Regional Security: Europe and Beyond* (Lynne Rienner, 2003), 32, at 57.

[245] Orakhelashvili, n. 63, at 80. See Section 6.5 on collective self-defence on NATO's role in the context of Russia's invasion of Ukraine in February 2022.

[246] Article 7, The North Atlantic Treaty (1949).

[247] See, further, Section 6.6 on the role of the Security Council in the right of self-defence.

[248] See Bruno Simma, 'NATO, the UN and the Use of Force: Legal Aspects' (1999) 10 *European Journal of International Law* 1, at 14–21.

[249] 1991 NATO Strategic Concept, at para. 35, available at: www.nato.int/cps/en/natohq/official_texts_23847.htm.

[250] The 1999 NATO Strategic Concept makes thirty-nine references to its operations in the Euro-Atlantic region. See 1999 NATO Strategic Concept, available at: www.nato.int/cps/en/natohq/official_texts_27433.htm.

[251] Ibid., at para. 6.    [252] Orakhelashvili, n. 63, at 80–1.

defence and crisis management were maintained in the 2010 Strategic Concept,[253] and further elaborated upon in the 2022 Strategic Concept in the wake of Russia's invasion of Ukraine.[254] As such, the Alliance remains prepared to act in collective self-defence but now also operates in missions with a crisis management function both within and outside of the Euro-Atlantic region, such as the International Security Assistance Force in Afghanistan and the NATO mission in Libya in 2011, both of which received a mandate from the Security Council.[255]

When the Kosovo crisis in 1999 occurred, some, particularly within the United States, began to argue that NATO had autonomy in the realms of enforcement action and was not to be subordinated to any other organisation, including the UN.[256] Arguments were made in regard to the Security Council having primary but not exclusive authority to act in the face of a humanitarian crisis. In the Security Council, Slovenia, for example, argued that '[t]he responsibility of the Security Council for international peace and security is a primary responsibility ... not an exclusive responsibility' and the Council's authority depended 'on its ability to develop policies that will make it worthy of the authority it has under the Charter'.[257] Yet this did not seem to be shared by other NATO member states, and has been countered in several declarations by NATO which have affirmed the primacy of the UN Security Council in matters of enforcement.[258]

## 3.6 CONCLUSION

The high ambition and formal powers of both the Security Council and General Assembly in terms of maintaining international peace and security were quickly beset with problems stemming from Cold War deadlock. Yet, since 1945, it has also been demonstrated that 'the Charter is a living

---

[253] See, in general, 2010 NATO Strategic Concept, available at: www.nato.int/cps/ic/natohq/topics_82705.htm.

[254] See, in general, 2022 NATO Strategic Concept, available at: www.nato.int/nato_static_fl2014/assets/pdf/2022/6/pdf/290622-strategic-concept.pdf.

[255] See UNSC Res. 1386 (2001) and UNSC Res. 1973 (2011), respectively.

[256] See Orakhelashvili, n. 63, at 143; Marten Zwanenburg, 'NATO, Its Member States, and the Security Council', in Niels Blokker and Nico Schrijver (eds.), *The Security Council and the Use of Force* (Martinus Nijhoff, 2005), 197, at 204.

[257] UN Doc. S/PV.3988, 24 March 1999, at 19.

[258] See Final Communiqué, Brussels Ministerial Meeting, 17 December 1992, at paras. 4–5; Declaration of the Heads of State and Government, Ministerial Meeting of the North Atlantic Council/North Atlantic Cooperation Council, NATO Headquarters, Brussels, 10–11 January 1994, at para. 7; Founding Act on Mutual Relations, Cooperation and Security between NATO and the Russian Federation, Paris, 27 May 1997, Section III; 1999 NATO Strategic Concept, n. 249, at para. 31; 2010 NATO Strategic Concept, n. 253, at para. 2. Interestingly, such a reaffirmation was absent in the 2022 NATO Strategic Concept. See n. 254.

instrument – it evolves and develops – thereby enabling it to keep pace with developments in the international order'.[259] While the UfP resolution demonstrated this as far back as 1950, the institution of UN peacekeeping – something not expressly provided for within the Charter, and which will be discussed further in Chapter 5 – emerged shortly afterwards. At the end of the Cold War, the Security Council, free from the Cold War restraints imposed upon it, also found a way to revitalise, albeit imperfectly, its exclusive powers of enforcement contained within the UN Charter. Today, the 'authorisation method' is an established and, in principle, relatively uncontroversial part of the repertoire of powers at the disposal of the Council. There have, however, been many notable issues and problems specifically concerning the implementation of the authorisation method, some of which have caused major ripples for the UN and crises within the international community, which are the focus of Chapter 4.

While long-running talks of reform of the UN's architecture for the maintenance of international peace and security have stagnated, they have to an extent been revived under the leadership of UN Secretary-General António Guterres.[260] If, and how, any reforms might affect each of the organ's roles within the maintenance of international peace and security and, in particular, the use of forcible measures, is unclear at this stage, although Russia's invasion of Ukraine in 2022 has once again shown the hierarchical structure of the Security Council and the possession of the veto power of the P5 to be a stumbling block towards a meaningful and consistent operation of the Council.[261]

## QUESTIONS

1 In what ways do the formal powers provided to the UN Security Council within the UN Charter for the maintenance of international peace and security operate and, in particular, those concerning the use of forcible measures?

2 In what ways, and why, was the Security Council prevented from exercising its powers contained within the UN Charter during the Cold War?

3 What was the significance of UN Security Council Resolution 678 (1990), and what has been its legacy?

---

[259] White, n. 30, at 296.
[260] See UN News Centre, 'UN Chief Guterres Announces Steps towards Reforming Organization's Peace and Security Architecture', 14 February 2017, available at: https://news.un.org/en/story/2017/02/551502-un-chief-guterres-announces-steps-towards-reforming-organizations-peace-and.
[261] See Kemal Dervis and José Antonio Ocampo, 'Will Ukraine's Tragedy Spur Security Council Reform?', *Brookings Institution*, 3 March 2022, available at: www.brookings.edu/opinions/will-ukraines-tragedy-spur-un-security-council-reform/.

4 Is the authorisation method of the UN Security Council a positive development in the realisation of the effective maintenance of international peace and security?

5 Does the UN General Assembly have a role in the use of force in the maintenance of international peace and security? If so, in what way?

6 What role do regional and collective defence organisations have within the maintenance of international peace and security? Do they have autonomous powers to use forcible measures?

## SUGGESTED FURTHER READING

Niels M. Blokker, *Saving Succeeding Generations from the Scourge of War: The United Nations Security Council at 75* (Brill Nijhoff, 2020)

Andrew J. Carswell, 'Unblocking the UN Security Council: The Uniting for Peace Resolution' (2013) 18 *Journal of Conflict & Security Law* 453

Danesh Sarooshi, *The United Nations and the Development of Collective Security: The Delegation by the UN Security Council of Its Chapter VII Powers* (Clarendon Press, 1999)

Christian Walter, 'Security Council Control over Regional Action' (1997) 1 *Max Planck Yearbook of UN Law* 151

Nigel D. White, 'From Korea to Kuwait: The Legal Basis of United Nations' Military Action' (1998) 20 *International History Review* 5

Nigel D. White and Ozlem Ulgen, 'The Security Council and the Decentralised Military Option: Constitutionality and Function' (1997) **44** *Netherlands International Law Review* 378

Michael Wood and Eran Sthoeger, *The UN Security Council and International Law* (Cambridge University Press, 2022)

# 4 Issues in Relation to Authorisation by the United Nations Security Council

## 4.1 INTRODUCTION

Chapter 3 set out the collective security framework of the United Nations (UN) and the development of the practice of the Security Council 'authorising' states and organisations to use force in the implementation of its mandate. While this practice has a clear grounding within the Charter, and in many ways is not controversial *per se*, there are numerous issues and concerns that have come to light since 1990 when it was first employed in Resolution 678 (1990) in the eviction of Iraq from Kuwait.[1] In some cases these have been resolved or are no longer relevant. In others, however, great division and mistrust has resulted. Indeed, the problems regarding the relative inactivity of the Security Council during the Cold War have been replaced by problems regarding the breadth and legitimacy of states and organisations acting under the auspices of the Council in the post-Cold War era.

This chapter first examines some of the initial ways the Council has attempted to obtain a balance between multilateralism and unilateralism in the design and implementation of its resolutions which have contained an authorisation to use 'all necessary means'. One issue that has not been resolved, and is apparent in many sections of this chapter, is the authority to interpret resolutions of the Security Council. In this respect, Section 4.3 addresses the possibility of 'reviving' past authorisations, something that has thus far been restricted to the use of force in Iraq between 1991 and 2003. Section 4.4, on the other hand, examines the issue of determining the breadth and scope of an authorisation, while Section 4.5 looks at the issue of 'implied' authorisation, in particular in attempts to enforce what might be perceived as the 'collective will' of the Council as well as the Council providing what might be seen as retrospective or *ex post facto* authorisation or approval for military action. Finally, Section 4.6 addresses the issue of the forcible implementation

---

[1] See Section 3.4.2.1.

of the 'Responsibility to Protect' concept which has found its way into the debates regarding the powers and responsibilities of the Council.

## 4.2 STRIKING THE BALANCE BETWEEN UNILATERALISM AND MULTILATERALISM

There was notable controversy regarding the lack of UN oversight and control over Operation Desert Storm to evict Iraq from Kuwait in 1991. For example, Yemen was of the view that Resolution 678 (1990) was 'broad and vague' so that 'the Security Council will have no control over those forces ... the command of those forces will have nothing to do with the United Nations', which leads to a situation of 'authority without accountability'.[2] In a similar tone, Cuba claimed that this was 'equivalent to giving the United States and its allies *carte blanche* to use their enormous sophisticated military capability'.[3] Some scholars expressed similar concerns in regard to some of the other early resolutions of the Council authorising the use of force.[4] In uncompromising terms, Berns Weston was of the view that the Security Council 'eschewed direct UN responsibility and accountability for the military force that ultimately was deployed, favouring, instead, a delegated, essentially unilateralist determination and orchestration of world policy, coordinated and controlled almost exclusively by the United States'.[5] John Quigley claimed that this state of affairs was akin to the 'privatization' of enforcement action by the Security Council.[6]

Subsequently, however, the Council has in general increased the level of control and oversight it possesses over the operations, in particular through greater involvement of the Secretary-General, greater clarity of the breadth and scope of the mandates, and the time limits upon them, and through increasing the reporting requirements upon the acting states and organisations.[7] For example, the authorisation to use force in Somalia in

---

[2] UN Doc. S/PV. 2963, 29 November 1990, at 33.   [3] Ibid., at 58.
[4] Djiena Wembou, 'Reflexions sur la validité et la portée de la Résolution 678 du Conseil de Securité' (1993) 5 *African Journal of International and Comparative Law* 34; Nigel D. White, *Keeping the Peace: The United Nations and the Maintenance of International Peace and Security*, 2nd ed. (Manchester University Press, 1997), at 115–28; Danesh Sarooshi, *The United Nations and the Development of Collective Security: The Delegation by the Security Council of Its Chapter VII Powers* (Oxford University Press, 2000), at 179–80.
[5] Burns H. Weston, 'Security Council Resolution 678 and Persian Gulf Decision Making: Precarious Legitimacy' (1991) 85 *American Journal of International Law* 516, at 517.
[6] John Quigley, 'The "Privatization" of Security Council Enforcement Action: A Threat to Multilateralism' (1996) 17 *Michigan Journal of International Law* 249. See also Helmut Freudenshuß, 'Between Unilateral and Collective Authorisations for the Use of Force by the UN Security Council' (1994) 5 *European Journal of International Law* 492.
[7] See Niels Blokker, 'Is the Authorization Authorized? Powers and Practice of the UN Security Council to Authorize the Use of Force by "Coalitions of the Able and Willing"' (2000) 11 *European Journal of International Law* 541, at 560–7; Niels Blokker, 'Outsourcing the Use of

1992 witnessed greater oversight by the Security Council, including a more limited mandate[8] and an obligation upon both the participating states and the Secretary-General to report to the Security Council, and in the first instance 'no later than fifteen days after the adoption of [Resolution 794 (1992)]'.[9] However, the mission as a whole was to be undertaken very much in coordination with the Secretary-General.[10] This increased overall control and oversight by the Security Council was welcomed.[11] Zimbabwe, for example, noted, at the meeting where Resolution 794 (1992) was adopted, that it:

attache[d] a lot of importance to the idea that in any international enforcement action the United Nations must define the mandate, the United Nations must monitor and supervise its implementation, and the United Nations must determine when the mandate has been fulfilled ... This [resolution] sets an important precedent for future operations under equally unique circumstances.[12]

Furthermore, in marking the progress that had been made in this respect following the adoption and implementation of Resolution 678 (1990), Hungary noted that it was:

pleased that this new type of action has been planned and formulated in such a way as to establish an organic link with our world Organization. It also demonstrates how far the United Nations has come since adopting Resolution 678 (1990) on the Gulf crisis. The distance we have covered eloquently demonstrates the more effective and dynamic role the United Nations can play in the creation of a new international environment.[13]

Similarly, in Resolution 929 (1994), which provided authorisation to France and Senegal to intervene in Rwanda following the genocide that had tragically unfolded within the country, particular mention was made by member states

---

Force: Towards More Security Council Control of Authorized Operations?', in Marc Weller (ed.), *The Oxford Handbook of the Use of Force in International Law* (Oxford University Press, 2015), 202, at 214–19.

[8] The Security Council authorised member states *and* the Secretary-General to 'use all necessary means to establish as soon as possible a secure environment for humanitarian relief operations in Somalia', UNSC Res. 794 (1992), para. 10. This limited mandate was welcomed by members of the Security Council. See, for example, UN Doc. S/PV. 3145, 3 December 1992, at 13 (Ecuador). See Section 3.4.2.2 for more on the situation in Somalia.

[9] UNSC Res. 794 (1992), para. 18. This was welcomed by France (29–30) and Japan (43), UN Doc. S/PV. 3145, 3 December 1992.

[10] UNSC Res. 794 (1992), para. 10. The oversight and involvement of the Secretary-General was welcomed by Ecuador (13), China (16–17), France (29–30), Belgium (24), Austria (32), UN Doc. S/PV. 3145, 3 December 1992.

[11] UN Doc. S/PV. 3145, ibid., Ecuador (14), China (17), France (29–30) and Belgium (24).

[12] Ibid., Zimbabwe (7–8).    [13] Ibid., Hungary (48).

of the clear mandate[14] and time limits,[15] in that the operation was to be 'limited to a period of two months following the adoption of the present resolution',[16] as well as the importance of conducting this operation in an impartial and neutral manner.[17] The authorisation was, again, provided to member states 'cooperating with the Secretary-General'.[18] The involvement of the Secretary-General was important, particularly as it was unlikely that the acting states would report having acted outside of, or abused, the mandate provided. Indeed, the Council has, on occasion, only required that the Secretary-General report back to it, for example as part of the authorisation to the United Nations Operation in Côte d'Ivoire (UNOCI) and the French forces operating in Côte d'Ivoire in 2011.[19] Greater oversight and control can also be found, in general, in the authorisations provided in Haiti,[20] Albania,[21] the Central African Republic,[22] East Timor,[23] Côte d'Ivoire,[24] Liberia[25] and Somalia[26] and many other subsequent resolutions of the Council.

As Blokker has noted, '[i]t is clear from these examples that the Security Council after the adoption of Resolution 678 has chosen to define more precisely the purpose for which the authorization to use force is given ... In doing so, the Security Council reduces the risk that the objectives of the coalition or of coalition members diverge from the Council.'[27] The increase in control and oversight by the Council of operations taken in its name also meant that there was less of a marked difference between the post–Cold War operations and the operations as envisaged within the Charter.[28] However, '[w]hile this may be welcomed from a legal point of view – as a development which is in line with the thrust of the relevant Charter provisions and with general principles of delegation',[29] there may be a limit as to how far greater oversight and control by the Council can go, seeing as 'the precise reason why

---

[14] This was to '[c]ontribute to the security and protection of displaced persons, refugees and civilians at risk in Rwanda, including through the establishment and maintenance, where feasible, of secure humanitarian areas' and to '[p]rovide security and support for the distribution of relief supplies and humanitarian relief operations'. See UNSC Res. 929 (1994), para. 3 and UNSC Res. 925 (1994), para. 4(a) and (b). See also UN Doc. S/PV. 3392, 22 June 1994, USSR (2) and Spain (8).
[15] UN Doc. S/PV. 3392, ibid., USSR (2) and Oman (11).   [16] UNSC Res. 929 (1994), para. 4.
[17] UN Doc. S/PV. 3392, n. 14, Spain (8), Oman (11), Czech Republic (9), Argentina (10) and USSR (2).
[18] UNSC Res. 929 (1994), para. 3.   [19] UNSC Res. 1975 (2011), para. 6.
[20] UNSC Res. 940 (1994).   [21] UNSC Res. 1101 (1997); UNSC Res. 1114 (1997).
[22] UNSC Res. 1125 (1997); UNSC Res. 1136 (1997); UNSC Res. 1152 (1998); UNSC Res. 1155 (1998); UNSC Res. 1159 (1998).
[23] UNSC Res. 1264 (1999).   [24] UNSC Res. 1464 (2003).   [25] UNSC Res. 1497 (2003).
[26] UNSC Res. 1816 (2008).   [27] Blokker, 'Is the Authorization Authorized?', n. 7, at 562.
[28] Ibid., at 565. See Section 3.3.2.   [29] Ibid.

the model of authorizations has become so popular is the *lack* of full UN control and the avoidance of micromanagement by the Security Council'.[30] Yet, the following sections of this chapter demonstrate both that while the developments that have occurred following Resolution 678 (1990) are to be welcomed, it is arguable that the Council still does not have sufficient control, at least on a consistent basis, over when and how force is to be used under its auspices.[31]

## 4.3 THE REVIVAL OF PAST AUTHORISATIONS

It will be recalled from Chapter 3 that the Security Council 'authorised' states to use 'all necessary means' in Resolution 678 (1990) 'to uphold and implement Resolution 660 and all subsequent relevant resolutions and to restore international peace and security in the area'.[32] Following the cessation of military hostilities on 28 February 1991, the Security Council adopted Resolution 687 (1991) on 3 April 1991. This resolution, which was the most extensive resolution adopted in the history of the Council, proclaimed a 'formal ceasefire'[33] and contained extensive provisions on the disarmament of Iraq and an accompanying inspection regime.[34] However, it became clear shortly after the adoption of the resolution that Iraq was failing to provide complete and unconditional cooperation and compliance with the disarmament obligations imposed upon it.[35]

While small-scale operations in response to Iraq's non-compliance were undertaken mainly by the United States and United Kingdom throughout the following decade, it was after Iraq's inclusion in former US President George W. Bush's 'axis of evil', as set out in his State of the Union address on 29 January 2002,[36] that its disarmament obligations came firmly on to the agenda of not just the United States but also the international community. Subsequently, Congress approved a resolution which authorised the president to enforce existing Security Council resolutions against Iraq and to defend the national security interests of the United States against the threat posed by it.[37]

---

[30] Ibid.
[31] For proposals as to how such oversight may be increased, see Karine Bannelier and Théodore Christakis, 'Between Flexibility and Accountability: How Can the Security Council Strengthen Oversight of Use-of-Force Measures?', in Jeremy Farrall and Hilary Charlesworth (eds.), *Strengthening the Rule of Law through the UN Security Council* (Routledge, 2016), 209.
[32] See Section 3.4.2.1.   [33] UNSC Res. 687 (1990), paras. 1 and 33.   [34] Ibid., paras. 7–14.
[35] See Marc Weller, *Iraq and the Use of Force in International Law* (Oxford University Press, 2010), at 106.
[36] President George W. Bush, 'State of the Union Address', 29 January 2002, available at: https://georgewbush-whitehouse.archives.gov/news/releases/2002/01/20020129-11.html.
[37] 'Authorization for Use of Military Force Against Iraq', 10 October 2002, Pub. L. No. 107–243.

However, while the Bush administration subsequently prepared the ground for war in Iraq with the development of its 'Bush doctrine' of pre-emptive self-defence, with Iraq in many respects providing the perfect test case for the invocation of the doctrine,[38] the Congressional resolution also made it clear that before force could be employed for such purposes attempts to work through the UN and other reasonable diplomatic channels needed to be exhausted.[39] In addition, UK Prime Minister Tony Blair had expressed the United Kingdom's commitment to the United States in any action that was to take place but wanted the matter to be taken first to the UN. As a result, the Security Council unanimously adopted Resolution 1441 (2002) on 8 November 2002, which declared that Iraq 'ha[d] been and remains in material breach of its [disarmament] obligations'[40] and that a 'failure by Iraq at any time to comply with, and cooperate fully in the implementation of, this resolution [would] constitute a further material breach'.[41] If Iraq failed to take the 'final opportunity' to comply it was to face 'serious consequences'.[42] The resolution required Iraq to submit a declaration of its weapons programmes[43] and also set up an enhanced weapons inspection regime.[44] While the inspection agencies – the United Nations Monitoring, Verification and Inspection Commission (UNMOVIC) and the International Atomic Energy Agency (IAEA) – reported certain irregularities and incomplete cooperation on the part of the Iraqi authorities, neither reported a 'smoking gun',[45] or that Iraq was in further 'material breach' of its obligations.

However, on 20 March 2003, and with no prospect of the United Kingdom and United States obtaining a second resolution that would have either declared Iraq to be in material breach, confirm that it had failed to take the final opportunity provided to it or, more directly, authorised the use of 'all necessary means',[46] and with themselves declaring that Iraq was in further 'material breach' of its obligations,[47] the United States, the United Kingdom and Australia launched Operation Iraqi Freedom, an air and ground offensive against Iraq that ultimately led to the overthrow of Iraqi President Saddam Hussein and his Batthist regime.[48] This was, significantly, justified upon the

---

[38] See Christian Henderson, 'The Bush Doctrine: From Theory to Practice' (2004) 9 *Journal of Conflict & Security Law* 3. See, further, Section 7.4.2.
[39] See n. 35.   [40] UNSC Res. 1441 (2002), para. 1.   [41] Ibid., para. 4.
[42] Ibid., paras. 2 and 13.   [43] Ibid., para. 3.   [44] Ibid., paras. 5–7.
[45] A term used by UNMOVIC's chief weapons inspector, Hans Blix. See Notes for Briefing the Security Council, 9 January 2003, available at: www.un.org/Depts/unmovic/bx9jan.htm.
[46] Weller, n. 35, at 176–82; Dominic McGoldrick, *From '9/11' to the Iraq War 2003: International Law in an Age of Complexity* (Hart, 2004), at 65–6.
[47] See UN Doc. S/2003/350, 20 March 2003 (UK); UN Doc. S/2003/351, 20 March 2003 (US); UN Doc. S/2003/352, 20 March 2003 (Australia).
[48] *Keesing's* (2003) 45315.

## 4.3 The Revival of Past Authorisations

'revival' of authority to use force contained within Resolution 678 (1991).[49] The 'revival' argument, in the form provided to the UK Parliament on 17 March 2003, deserves setting out in full:[50]

Authority to use force against Iraq exists from the combined effects of resolutions 678, 687 and 1441. All of these resolutions were adopted under Chapter VII of the UN Charter which allows the use of force for the express purpose of restoring international peace and security:

1. In resolution 678 the Security Council authorized force against Iraq, to eject it from Kuwait and to restore peace and security in the area.
2. In resolution 687, which set out the ceasefire conditions after Operation Desert Storm, the Security Council imposed continuing obligations on Iraq to eliminate its weapons of mass destruction in order to restore international peace and security in the area. Resolution 687 suspended but did not terminate the authority to use force under resolution 678.
3. A material breach of resolution 687 revives the authority to use force under resolution 678.
4. In resolution 1441 the Security Council determined that Iraq has been and remains in material breach of resolution 687, because it has not fully complied with its obligations to disarm under that resolution.
5. The Security Council in resolution 1441 gave Iraq 'a final opportunity to comply with its disarmament obligations' and warned Iraq of the 'serious consequences' if it did not.
6. The Security Council also decided in resolution 1441 that, if Iraq failed at any time to comply with and cooperate fully in the implementation of resolution 1441, that constitutes a further material breach.
7. It is plain that Iraq has failed so to comply and therefore Iraq was at the time of resolution 1441 and continues to be in material breach.
8. Thus, the authority to use force under resolution 678 has revived and so continues today.
9. Resolution 1441 would in terms have provided that a further decision of the Security Council to sanction force was required if that had been intended. Thus, all that resolution 1441 requires is reporting to and discussion by the Security Council of Iraq's failures, but not an express further decision to authorize force.

---

[49] See n. 47 for the letters sent to the UN Security Council by the United States, the United Kingdom and Australia. While the majority of the letter by the United States was used to justify the intervention upon the basis of the revival of authority, it also tentatively relied upon self-defence at the end, although did not invoke Article 51 of the UN Charter. See further Section 7.4.2.1.1.

[50] As reproduced in 'The Use of Force against Iraq' (2003) 52 *International & Comparative Law Quarterly* 811.

On the face of it this was a detailed and serious attempt at providing a legal justification for what was, and still is, a controversial use of force. There were, however, many notable problems with the argument and the invocation of all three Security Council resolutions: 678, 687 and 1441. Resolution 678 (1990) was, in particular, vital to the revival argument as it contained the authorisation that the intervening states were attempting to revive. The key issue was, however, whether it was possible to revive an authorisation nearly thirteen years after it had been initially provided.

### 4.3.1 The Mandate Contained within Resolution 678 (1990)

The mandate contained within Resolution 678 (1990) was 'to uphold and implement Resolution 660 and all subsequent relevant resolutions and to restore international peace and security in the area'.[51] The sole demand made in Resolution 660 (1990) was to ensure that 'Iraq withdraw immediately and unconditionally all its forces to the position in which they were located on 1 August 1990',[52] which had been achieved through Operation Desert Storm. While the argument was seemingly being made that '*all* subsequent resolutions', including 687 (1991) and 1441 (2002), could be enforced under this authorisation, it would seem implausible that the Security Council was, in 1990, providing authorisation to implement *all* resolutions following the adoption of Resolution 660 (1990), regardless of at which point in the future they were adopted and what their content was. While the resolutions adopted between 660 (1990) and 678 (1990) were in connection with the eviction of Iraq from Kuwait, it was only after this objective had been achieved that attention shifted towards permanently disarming Iraq. As such, while it is true that there were no express time limits placed upon the authorisation in the resolution itself – a practice of imposing time limits only having developed subsequent to the adoption of this resolution[53] – the revival argument relied upon not only the Security Council having provided authorisation to enforce resolutions that had not yet been adopted, but also those that were adopted in a different context and for a different purpose from forcing Iraq from Kuwait.[54]

It might thus be argued, and as appeared to be relied upon in the revival argument, that this particular intervention was more about enforcing the

---

[51] UNSC Res. 678 (1990), para. 2.   [52] UNSC Res. 660 (1990), para. 2.
[53] See, further, Section 4.2.
[54] Jules Lobel and Michael Ratner, 'Bypassing the Security Council: Ambiguous Authorizations to Use Force, Ceasefires and the Iraqi Inspection Regime' (1999) 93 *American Journal of International Law* 124, at 129; Sean D. Murphy, 'Assessing the Legality of Invading Iraq' (2004) 92 *Georgetown Law Journal* 173, at 181; Tarcisio Gazzini, *The Changing Rules on the Use of Force in International Law* (Manchester University Press, 2005), at 67.

second part of the mandate contained in Resolution 678 (1990) – that is, 'restoring international peace and security in the area'. Yet, this part of the mandate also needs to be read in the light of the context pertaining at the time of its adoption and the goal of securing Iraq's exit from Kuwait. Indeed, 'Resolution 678 clearly authorized force to oust Iraq from Kuwait, but the broad provision on restoring international peace and security ought to be read in the context of that purpose.'[55] Upon the adoption of Resolution 678 (1990) not a single member of the Council made reference to disarmament and James Baker, US Secretary of State at the time, confirmed in his memoirs that 'the U.N. resolutions did not authorize coalition forces to undertake anything beyond the liberation of Kuwait'.[56] Nonetheless, the revival argument advanced in 2003 by the coalition states clearly saw the elimination of Iraq's weapons of mass destruction as falling within the mandate to restore international peace and security in the area and that a 'material breach' of the obligations contained within Resolution 687 (1991) led to a revival of the authorisation provided in Resolution 678 (1990). As Jules Lobel and Michael Ratner noted, '[t]his position assumed that Resolution 678's authorization to use force remained valid, albeit temporarily suspended – a loaded weapon in the hands of any member nation to use force whenever it determined Iraq to be in material breach of the cease-fire'.[57]

### 4.3.2 The Concept of 'Material Breach' in the Practice of the Security Council

While originating in the law of treaties, the terminology of 'material breach' was employed in the resolutions of the Security Council concerning the disarmament of Iraq. Prior to the invasion of 2003, the United States and the United Kingdom had previously used force against Iraq, ostensibly upon the basis of determinations made by the Council that Iraq was in material breach of its obligations contained within Resolution 687. The first notable incident was on 17 January 1993 when, just six days after the Security Council had condemned Iraq's non-compliance and stated it to be in 'material breach',[58] the United States launched several Tomahawk cruise missiles at a nuclear facility on the outskirts of Baghdad.[59] The United States justified its actions on this occasion as being 'designed to help achieve the goals of United Nations Security Council Resolutions 687, 707 and 715'.[60] Several strikes were

---

[55] Lobel and Ratner, ibid., at 129.
[56] James A. Baker, *The Politics of Diplomacy* (Putnam, 1995), at 436.
[57] Lobel and Ratner, n. 54, at 124–5.   [58] UN Doc. S/25091, 11 January 1993.
[59] *Keesing's* (1993) 39291–2.
[60] 'US Press Release: Attack Shows U.S. Fully Backs U.N. Mandate', 17 January 1993, reprinted in Marc Weller (ed.), *Iraq and Kuwait: The Hostilities and Their Aftermath* (Grotius, 1993), at 746.

made against Iraq at this time, with some taken to enforce the no-fly zones that had been established.[61] However, while it was only the strike on 17 January that was taken in response to Iraq's non-compliance with the disarmament regime, confusingly the UN Secretary-General stated on 14 January 1993, in commenting on a strike that had occurred the previous day, that:

> the forces that carried out the raid have received a mandate from the Security Council, according to resolution 678, and the cause of the raid was the violation by Iraq of resolution 687 concerning the ceasefire. So, as Secretary-General of the United Nations, I can say that this action was taken and conforms to the resolutions of the Security Council and conforms to the Charter of the United Nations.[62]

Despite the confusion, this statement was problematic for those opposing the use of the revival argument in 2003, as this was the Secretary-General of the UN effectively stating that non-compliance by Iraq of its Resolution 687 (1991) obligations had the effect of reviving the mandate contained in Resolution 678 (1990).[63] Furthermore, and arguably in light of this comment, the bombings were neither discussed nor condemned by the Security Council, perhaps raising the argument that the Council had provided an 'informal blessing' for the strikes.[64] Indeed, after the commencement of Operation Iraqi Freedom in 2003 the Legal Adviser and Assistant Legal Adviser to the US State Department at the time, William Taft and Todd Buchwald, used the inclusion of the 'material breach' language in Resolution 707 (1993), and in a Security Council presidential statement in 1993 which preceded the use of force by the United States,[65] to argue that these had created an 'understanding that such a determination authorized resort to force'.[66]

The second notable incident when coalition forces used force against Iraq took place in 1998. After a report by the United Nations Special Commission (UNSCOM) Chief, Richard Butler, on 15 December 1998, which outlined a series of obstructions that had been encountered by the inspectors,[67] the

---

[61] See Section 4.5.1.1.
[62] Reprinted in 'UK Materials in International Law' (1993) 65 *British Yearbook of International Law* 736.
[63] For more on the role of the UN Secretariat, see Section 3.2.3.
[64] Murphy, n. 54, at 232. For more on 'informal blessings' by the Security Council see Section 4.5.2.
[65] See UN Doc. S/25091, 11 January 1993.
[66] William H. Taft and Todd F. Buchwald: 'Preemption, Iraq, and International Law' (2003) **97** *American Journal of International Law* 557, at 559. See also Michael Matheson, 'Legal Authority for the Possible Use of Force against Iraq' (1998) **92** *Proceedings of the American Society of International Law* 136, at 141.
[67] See UN Doc. S/1998/1172, 15 December 1998. UNSCOM, established after the adoption of UNSC Res. 687 in 1991, was the predecessor to UNMOVIC which was established in 2002 and led by Dr Hans Blix.

United States and the United Kingdom launched air strikes against Iraqi military capabilities on 20 December 1998, codenamed Operation Desert Fox, during the course of which ninety-seven Iraqi sites were attacked.[68] On this occasion the United States more clearly justified its use of force upon the basis of a 'revival' of authority contained within Resolution 678 (1991) following Iraq's 'material breach' of the ceasefire conditions contained in Resolution 687 (1991).[69] However, the material breach terminology had not been included in the resolutions of the Security Council condemning Iraq's failure to comply with the disarmament regime. Although Resolution 1154 of 2 March 1998 stressed that any 'any violation would have severest consequences for Iraq',[70] which was followed up in Resolution 1205 of 5 November 1998 with the Council '[c]ondemn[ing] the decision by Iraq of 31 October 1998 to cease cooperation with the [UN] Special Commission as a flagrant violation of resolution 687 (1991) and other relevant resolutions',[71] no agreement had coalesced around this choice of language permitting a revival of authority contained within Resolution 678 (1991) and the use of force was condemned by many as a violation of international law.[72] Nonetheless, in Resolution 1441 (2002) the language of 'material breach' had, as set out in Section 4.3, found its way back into Security Council parlance. Furthermore, in its letter to the Security Council upon the launching of Operation Iraqi Freedom, the United States stated that:

[i]t has been long recognized and understood that a material breach of [the] obligations removes the basis of the ceasefire and revives the authority to use force under resolution 678 (1990) ... Iraq continues to be in material breach of its disarmament obligations under resolution 687 (1991) ... In view of Iraq's material breaches, the basis for the ceasefire has been removed and use of force is authorized under resolution 678 (1990).[73]

The three episodes therefore raised the issue as to where the authority lay in determining the existence of a material breach.

### 4.3.3 The Authority to Determine a 'Material Breach' and the Consequences

The question as to who was to determine that there had been a further material breach can be divided into two distinct parts: first, who was to determine that a further material breach had occurred and, secondly, who was to decide upon the consequences of such a breach. Neither of these issues was free from

---

[68] *Keesing's* (1998) 42697–9.
[69] UN Doc. S/1998/1181, 16 December 1998, and UN Doc. S/PV 3955, 16 December 1998, at 9.
[70] UNSC Res. 1154 (1998), para. 3.   [71] UNSC Res. 1205 (1998), para. 1.
[72] See UN Doc. S/PV. 3955, 16 December 1998, Iraq (2), Russia (4), China (5), Costa Rica (7), Sweden (10) and Brazil (11).
[73] UN Doc. S/2003/351, 20 March 2003.

ambiguity. While from November 2002 UNMOVIC and the IAEA were 'to report immediately to the Council any interference by Iraq with inspection activities'[74] – neither of which reported such a material breach – member states were also not expressly precluded from making such a report. Paragraph 3 of Resolution 1441 (2002) had also requested Iraq to 'provide to UNMOVIC, the IAEA, and the Council, ... a currently accurate, full, and complete declaration of all aspects of its [weapons] programmes'. In paragraph 4 of the resolution the Security Council '[d]*ecid*[ed] that false statements or omissions in the declarations submitted by Iraq pursuant to this resolution and failure by Iraq at any time to comply with, and cooperate fully in the implementation of, this resolution *shall constitute a further material breach* of Iraq's obligations' (emphasis added). The position of the United States appeared to be that 'whether there had been a material breach was an *objective fact*, and it was not necessary for the Council to so determine or state'.[75] In addition, as part of the revival argument set out in Section 4.3 it was claimed that 'it is plain' that Iraq had failed to comply and was therefore in further material breach.[76] Indeed, paragraph 4 of Resolution 1441 (2002) appeared to leave open the possibility for states to make such a determination.

Yet, paragraph 4 of Resolution 1441 (2002) also stated that any material breaches 'will be reported to the Council for assessment'. The real question, then, was what form the 'assessment' should take. Paragraph 12 stated that the Security Council '[d]*ecid*[ed] to convene immediately upon receipt of a report ... in order to *consider* the situation and the need for full compliance with all of the relevant Council resolutions in order to secure international peace and security' (second emphasis added). This did not, then, expressly require a 'decision' by the Council to authorise force, a fact that was a central element in the revival argument. Indeed, while simultaneously claiming that there was no 'automaticity' within the resolution, the United Kingdom also claimed that '[i]f there is a further Iraqi breach of its disarmament obligations, the matter will return to the Council for *discussion* as required in paragraph 12. We would expect the Security Council then to meet its responsibilities.'[77]

However, it was clear that the majority of states within the Council took a different view of the meaning of both 'assessment' and, more broadly, 'automaticity', with the general view seeming to be that as it was a Security Council resolution and disarmament regime that was under consideration it should be

---

[74] UNSC Res. 1441 (2002), para. 11.   [75] Taft and Buchwald, n. 66, at 560 (emphasis added).
[76] An issue that was singled out for condemnation in the report of the Iraq Inquiry, which was published in July 2016, was the basis upon which UK Prime Minister Tony Blair arrived at the conclusion that Iraq was in material breach in the absence of a consensus on this issue within the UN Security Council. The Report of the Iraq Inquiry (Report of a Committee of Privy Counsellors), 6 July 2016, vol. 5, Section 5, at para. 775, available at: www.iraqinquiry.org.uk/media/247894/the-report-of-the-iraq-inquiry_section-50.pdf.
[77] UN Doc. S/PV.4644, 8 November 2002, at 5 (UK).

for the Council itself to decide if force was necessary in the circumstances for its implementation.[78] As paragraph 12 clearly stated, the Security Council 'shall remain seized of the matter'. Furthermore, while, '[b]y its terms, Resolution 687 of April 1991 neither expressly suspended nor expressly terminated Resolution 678',[79] the ceasefire contained within Resolution 687 (1991) 'was not a classical one between states, but was embedded in the collective security system of the United Nations'.[80] Indeed, Iraq only had to accept the ceasefire and report its acceptance directly to the Security Council, leading one to conclude that, despite the terminology used, it was more than a ceasefire and, instead, represented a Security Council peacebuilding instrument.[81] Ultimately, while the use of force was never ruled out by the Council, the clear consensus was for a continuation of the inspection process at the time Operation Iraqi Freedom was launched. As it turned out, if the consensus of the Council on this occasion had been respected, the force that was ultimately employed would have proved unnecessary given the absence of WMD in Iraq.

### 4.3.4 The Legacy of the Revival Argument

The intervention in Iraq called into question the relevance and restraining power of the UN. Even before it was launched, President Bush stated that '[t]he conduct of the Iraqi regime is a threat to the authority of the United Nations, and a threat to peace' and posed the question of whether the UN would 'serve the purpose of its founding' or whether it would be 'irrelevant'?[82] After the Iraq invasion, the UN Secretary-General, while claiming that the intervention was unlawful,[83] also spoke of 'a fork in the road' for the UN and declared that 'this may be a moment no less decisive than 1945 itself, when the UN was founded'.[84] Subsequently, the Secretary-General established the High-Level Panel on Threats, Challenges and Change[85] and issued his own report in

---

[78] This becomes clear from a reading of the statements made in the Security Council upon the adoption of UNSC Res. 1441 (2002). See UN Doc. S/PV. 4644, 8 November 2002.

[79] Murphy, n. 54, at 186.

[80] Nico Krisch, 'Unilateral Enforcement of the Collective Will: Kosovo, Iraq, and the Security Council' (1999) 3 *Max Planck Yearbook of United Nations Law* 59, at 71.

[81] Christine Gray, *International Law and the Use of Force*, 3rd ed. (Oxford University Press, 2008), at 144; Murphy, n. 54, at 200.

[82] Statement by President Bush, UN General Assembly, 12 September 2002, available at: www.un.org/webcast/ga/57/statements/020912usaE.htm.

[83] Ewan MacAskill and Julian Borger, 'Iraq Was Illegal and Breached UN Charter, Says Annan', *The Guardian*, 16 September 2004, available at: www.theguardian.com/world/2004/sep/16/iraq.iraq.

[84] The Secretary-General, Address to the General Assembly, 23 September 2003, available at: www.un.org/webcast/ga/58/statements/sg2eng030923.htm.

[85] Report of the High-Level Panel on Threats, Challenges and Change, A More Secure World: Our Shared Responsibility, UN Doc. A/59/565, 2 December 2004.

response.[86] Perhaps unsurprisingly, neither denied or even questioned the continuing relevance of the UN or, indeed, the prohibition of the use of force.

The intervention also proved hugely controversial outside of the UN. The Iraq intervention generated a huge amount of scholarship from various disciplines, and perhaps most notably within the field of international law.[87] The ultimate restraining power of international law was called into question,[88] with some (again) proclaiming the 'death' of the prohibition of the use of force.[89] It was also questioned whether Resolution 1441 (2002) had been intentionally ambiguously drafted,[90] thereby permitting all sides to claim the upper hand over its interpretation. Public inquiries were established to examine the intelligence failings,[91] while others examined the legality of the intervention.[92] The United Kingdom established the Iraq Inquiry, which examined the UK's entire involvement in Iraq and the lessons to be learnt from it, between 2001 and 2009.[93]

There also appeared to be more caution in the wording of resolutions of the Security Council, with Resolution 1718 (2006) on North Korea's nuclear testing expressly stating that 'further decisions will be required should additional measures be necessary'.[94] Yet, despite this, and despite the fact that the circumstances giving rise to the Iraq crisis were arguably *sui generis*, questions remain as to what should happen when the Council is divided and allegations are made that it is failing in its responsibility to maintain peace and security.

---

[86] Report of the UN Secretary-General, In Larger Freedom: Towards Security, Development and Human Rights for All, UN Doc. A/59/205, 21 March 2005.

[87] See, just as a sample, 'Agora: Future Implications of the Iraq Conflict' (2003) **97** *American Journal of International Law* 553 (for a range of opinions on the legality of the military action against Iraq in 2003); Dino Kritsiotis, 'Arguments of Mass Confusion' (2004) **15** *European Journal of International Law* 233; Nigel D. White, 'The Will and Authority of the Security Council after Iraq' (2004) **17** *Leiden Journal of International Law* 645; Lindsay Moir, *Reappraising the Resort to Force: International Law, Jus ad Bellum and the War on Terror* (Hart, 2010), at 73–106; Weller, n. 35 at 132–88; McGoldrick, n. 46, at 47–86; Murphy, n. 54 (in general); Christine Gray, *International Law and the Use of Force*, 4th ed. (Oxford University Press, 2018), at 367–77.

[88] See, for example, Michael J. Glennon, 'Why the Security Council Failed' (2003) May/June *Foreign Affairs* 16.

[89] See Thomas M. Franck, 'What Happens Now? The United Nations after Iraq' (2003) **97** *American Journal of International Law* 607.

[90] Michael Byers, 'Agreeing to Disagree: Security Council Resolution 1441 and Intentional Ambiguity' (2004) **10** *Global Governance* 165.

[91] See, for example, the Review of Intelligence on Weapons of Mass Destruction, Report of a Committee of Privy Counsellors, 14 July 2004, HC 898.

[92] See BBC News, 'Dutch Inquiry Says Iraq War Had No Mandate', 12 January 2010, available at: http://news.bbc.co.uk/1/hi/world/europe/8453305.stm.

[93] Iraq Inquiry, n. 76. See Christian Henderson, 'Reading between the Lines: The Iraq Inquiry, Doctrinal Debates, and the Legality of Military Action against Iraq in 2003' (2017) **87** *British Yearbook of International Law* 105.

[94] UNSC Res. 1718 (2002), para. 16.

This has been prominent in connection with implementing the 'Responsibility to Protect' concept, which is addressed in Section 4.6. However, while it was relevant in the context of the decisions as to the continuing validity of an authorisation, as in the case of Iraq in 2003, it has also been relevant in the context of interpretations as to the breadth and scope of an authorisation, as addressed in Section 4.4.

## 4.4 DETERMINING THE BREADTH AND SCOPE OF AN AUTHORISATION

The fact that the Security Council employs the euphemism 'all necessary means' instead of 'use of force' to indicate that forcible measures may be resorted to alludes to the potential for ambiguity in regard to the interpretation of the resolutions, and in particular their breadth and scope. This, combined with the fact that the force is undertaken by so-called coalitions of the willing – that is, states voluntarily implementing the mandate of the Council where individual motives are ever present – means that problems in determining the breadth and scope of the mandate provided have arisen. Indeed, while the revival argument, addressed in Section 4.3, arose in regard to the length of time an authorisation may remain open – and if it does remain open who possesses the authority to revive it and in what context – this section looks more at the issues regarding the *type* of force authorised as well as the *scope* of the authorisation, including the purpose of the actions that may be taken under it. Questions of this nature have arisen on a number of occasions. For example, it might be questioned whether the mandate provided to coalition forces in Resolution 678 (1990) could have been used at the time to go further than simply evicting Iraq from Kuwait.[95] In addition, it could be questioned whether the mandate provided to the Unified Task Force (UNITAF) in Somalia in Resolution 794 (1992) extended to taking action against specific individuals.[96] More recently, however, stark questions have been raised in regard to the extent of the mandate to protect civilians in the context of a civil disturbance or a civil war, arguably most notably in Libya and Côte d'Ivoire, which will be the focus of this section.

### 4.4.1 Libya (2011)

In February 2011, anti-government protests in Libya were met with repression by Colonel Gaddafi's regime, which used force against the unarmed

---

[95] Although see Baker, n. 56.
[96] Paragraph 10 of this resolution provided authorisation 'to use all necessary means to establish as soon as possible a secure environment for humanitarian relief operations in Somalia'. See, further, Section 3.4.2.2.

protesters.[97] Events soon demonstrated that the country was in a state of civil war,[98] with Gaddafi proclaiming that no mercy would be shown to his opponents.[99] Many died or were displaced from their homes. The Security Council responded by unanimously adopting Resolution 1970 (2011) on 26 February 2011 which 'condemn[ed] the violence and use of force against civilians',[100] deplored 'the gross and systematic violation of human rights, including the repression of peaceful demonstrators',[101] rejected 'unequivocally the incitement to hostility and violence against the civilian population made from the highest level of the Libyan government'[102] and welcomed the establishment by the Human Rights Council of an independent commission of inquiry.[103] Although it did not expressly determine the situation in Libya to be a threat to international peace and security under Chapter VII of the Charter, Resolution 1970 (2011) was nevertheless 'mindful of the primary responsibility of the Security Council for the maintenance of international peace and security', and expressly stated that the Council was acting under Chapter VII of the Charter in taking measures under Article 41.[104] These measures included demanding an immediate end to violence,[105] referring the situation to the International Criminal Court,[106] imposing an arms embargo,[107] as well as a travel ban and assets freeze.[108]

In the light of the continuing violence, however, the Security Council went on to adopt Resolution 1973 (2011) on 17 March 2011. After determining that the situation in Libya 'continued to be a threat to international peace and security'[109] the Council then, acting under Chapter VII, authorised the use of 'all necessary measures ... to protect civilians and civilian protected areas under threat of attack in the Libyan Arab Jamarihiya, including Benghazi, while excluding a foreign occupation force of any form on any part of Libyan territory'.[110] Subsequently, military action by the United States,

---

[97] *Keesing's* (2011) 50309, 50365.
[98] See UN Doc. S/PV. 6505, 24 March 2011; UN Doc. S/PV. 6509, 4 April 2011; UN Doc. S/PV. 6527, 3 May 2011; UN Doc. S/PV. 6530, 9 May 2011; UN Doc. S/PV. 6541, 31 May 2011; *Keesing's* (2011) 50366.
[99] *Keesing's* (2011) 50365.     [100] UNSC Res. 1970 (2011), preamble.     [101] Ibid.     [102] Ibid.
[103] Ibid.
[104] Ibid. Article 41 of the UN Charter provides for the taking of measures of a non-forcible nature.
[105] UNSC Res. 1970 (2011), preamble, para. 1.
[106] Ibid., para. 4. The Court subsequently issued warrants for the arrest of Colonel Gaddafi, his son, Saif al Islam Gaddafi, and the Head of Intelligence for crimes against humanity. See *The Prosecutor v. Muammar Gaddafi, Saif Al-Islam Gaddafi and Abdullah Al-Senussi*, ICC-01/11-01/11, 27 June 2011.
[107] UNSC Res. 1970 (2011), preamble, para. 9.     [108] Ibid., paras. 15–21.
[109] UNSC Res. 1973 (2011), preamble.
[110] Ibid., para. 4. The resolution also reaffirmed and extended various measures adopted in UNSC Res. 1970 (2011), such as the arms embargo (paras. 13–16) and the asset freeze (paras. 19–21). In addition, the resolution established a no-fly zone over Libya and authorised

## 4.4 Determining the Breadth and Scope of an Authorisation

France and the United Kingdom, with assistance from Canada, Denmark, Norway, Belgium, Spain and Italy, commenced on 19 March 2011, with the North Atlantic Treaty Organization (NATO) taking over command on 31 March 2011.[111]

Under the cover of NATO bombing, the rebel forces fighting the Gaddafi regime entered Gaddafi's compound in Tripoli on 23 August 2011, graphically marking the end of the Gaddafi regime in Libya, after which many states began to recognise the Transitional National Council as the legitimate representatives of the Libyan people, with the UN General Assembly accrediting delegates from the Transitional National Council on 16 September.[112] The NATO operation came to an end in October 2011 after the rebels had seized control of the city of Sirte, the birthplace of Colonel Gaddafi.[113] The Security Council subsequently unanimously terminated its authorisation of the use of force in Resolution 2016 (2011) on 27 October 2011.[114]

There was, however, a dispute between states regarding the interpretation of the mandate provided by the Council to protect citizens. In particular, questions were posed as to whether this included assistance to the rebels fighting the Gaddafi regime. Furthermore, the issue arose as to whether the mandate permitted regime change, either through forcibly imposing an exile upon Gaddafi or directly targeting him, in order to secure the long-term protection of the Libyan people. Upon the adoption of the resolution the abstaining states expressed doubts about the wide scope of the authorisation to use force.[115] These concerns manifested themselves when, after operations had begun, many states and organisations, including the Arab League, the African Union, Russia and China, seemed to cast doubt on the aims of the intervening states and their actions on the ground.

### 4.4.1.1 Assistance to Opposition Forces

Questions first arose as to whether the targets chosen by the intervening forces were selected for the protection of civilians or for assisting the opposition

---

member states to take all necessary measures to enforce compliance with it. Ibid., paras. 6–12.

[111] NATO, 'NATO Takes Command in Libya Air Operations', 31 March 2011, available at: www.nato.int/cps/ en/natolive/news_71867.htm. Among Arab states, Qatar and the UAE took part in the operations. See *Keesing's* (2011) 50366.

[112] UN Press Release GA/11137, 16 September 2011.

[113] See, for example, NATO, 'NATO Strikes Protect Civilians in Sirte', 24 September 2011, available at: www.nato.int/cps/en/natolive/news_78493.htm; NATO, 'Operational Media Update: NATO and Libya', 25 October 2011, available at: www.nato.int/cps/en/natolive/news_71994.htm. See also 'NATO Chief Hails End of Military Operation in Libya', *The Guardian*, 1 November 2011, at 1. On the death of Gaddafi, see *Keesing's* (2011) 50735.

[114] UNSC Res. 2016 (2011), paras 5 and 6.    [115] UN Doc. S/PV. 6498, 17 March 2011.

forces in winning a civil war, with NATO acting as the air and intelligence arm of the rebel forces.[116] Indeed, while the air strikes began by destroying the regime's air defences, which might be seen as having an immediate positive impact upon NATO's ability to protect civilians from the air, they were subsequently directed at a wider range of targets, including communications and command-and-control centres.[117] Whereas these are usually acceptable targets under the law of armed conflict – where the aim is generally to overpower the opposition's armed forces in a bid for victory – this was not a typical armed conflict, but rather enforcement action under a specific Security Council mandate provided by the Security Council which was restricted to protecting civilians and civilian-populated areas, thus arguably limiting the choice of targets.

Furthermore, a comprehensive arms embargo precluding the transfer of arms into the whole of the territory was imposed in paragraph 9 of Security Council Resolution 1970 (2011).[118] However, Resolution 1973 (2011) '[a]uthorize[d] Member States ... to take all necessary measures, *notwithstanding paragraph 9 of resolution 1970 (2011)*, to protect civilians and civilian populated areas under threat of attack in the Libyan Arab Jamahiriya'.[119] As such, and in this context, the question arose as to whether 'all necessary measures' really meant *all* necessary measures, including the provision of arms to the opposition forces.[120] The text alone provided no express indication that the arming of rebels was permitted. This was of importance as it became clear that some of the intervening states were doing just that.[121] Others, however, were of the view that the authorisation had been provided so as to protect civilians, not arm the opposition involved in a civil war.[122]

---

[116] Christine Gray, 'The Use of Force for Humanitarian Purposes', in Nigel D. White and Christian Henderson (eds.), *Research Handbook on International Conflict and Security Law: Jus ad Bellum, Jus in Bello, and Jus post Bellum* (Edward Elgar, 2013), 229, at 250. Richard Falk, 'Preliminary Libyan Scorecard: Acting Beyond the UN Mandate', *Foreign Policy Journal*, 8 September 2011, available at: www.foreignpolicyjournal.com/2011/09/08/preliminary-libyan-scorecard-acting-beyond-the-u-n-mandate/.

[117] NATO, 'Operation Unified Protector: Protection of Civilians and Civilian-Populated Areas', June 2011, available at: www.nato.int/nato_static_fl2014/assets/pdf/pdf_2011_06/20110608_Factsheet-UP_Protection_Civilia.pdf.

[118] UNSC Res. 1970 (2011), para. 9.

[119] UNSC Res. 1973 (2011), para. 4 (second emphasis added).

[120] See Section 2.4.3 for more on indirect force. The argument by the intervening states in Libya, however, was that the provision of arms to the opposition forces was covered by the authorisation provided by the UN Security Council.

[121] BBC News, 'French Arming of Libya's Rebels Strategic', 29 June 2011, available at: www.bbc.co.uk/news/world-africa-13966976.

[122] For example, Russia's Foreign Minister, Sergei Lavrov, was of the view that the coalition did not have the right to arm the opposition and should confine their actions to protecting civilians. See BBC News, 'Libya: Council Divided on Arming Rebels', 29 March 2011, available at: www.bbc.co.uk/news/world-africa-12900706.

## 4.4 Determining the Breadth and Scope of an Authorisation

While the question of whether the provision of arms was permitted is not immediately answered upon a textual reading of the resolutions, no statements were made in reference to this point within the Security Council prior to their adoption. Nonetheless, what is clear is that, whatever the force ultimately used, it needed to be directed exclusively towards the protection of 'civilians or civilian populated areas'.[123] In this respect, it could plausibly be argued that the provision of arms to those rebels defending areas particularly targeted by the Gadaffi regime such as Benghazi contributed towards the protection of a civilian populated area. In this sense, it might be that the protection of civilians had, on the ground, been delegated to the opposition forces.

Yet, although arms might originally be provided to opposition forces for *defensive* purposes, they may eventually end up being used for *offensive* purposes. If circumstances meant that the weapons that had been provided to the opposition forces in Libya were subsequently being used offensively against civilians, then Resolution 1973 (2011) would have provided NATO with the authority to use force against the opposition forces and thus have faced staring down the barrels of the very weapons that they had supplied.

Furthermore, even if one was to argue that the provision of arms was unlawful, did this extend to the supply of *non-lethal equipment*, such as body armour and satellite telephones? Indeed, UK Prime Minister David Cameron expressly argued that Resolution 1973 permitted the supply of such equipment. Whilst on the one hand this might seem to be permissible, given their purely protective non-offensive nature, objections might nonetheless be raised due to the fact that they still had the effect of aiding opposition forces fighting in the civil war. Similarly, while the acting states refrained from sending in ground troops, and did not have sufficient numbers in the country to constitute an 'occupation force' - something that was specifically precluded in Resolution 1973 (2011)[124] - some of the coalition members decided to send military personnel to the eastern rebel stronghold of Benghazi to 'advise' the rebels on logistics and intelligence training.[125]

---

[123] Christian Henderson, 'International Measures for the Protection of Civilians in Libya and Côte d'Ivoire' (2011) 60 *International & Comparative Law Quarterly* 767, at 771.

[124] UNSC Res. 1973 (2011), para. 4.

[125] This was principally the UK, France and Italy. See BBC News, 'MPs' Concern Over Mission Creep Grow', 20 April 2011, available at: www.bbc.co.uk/news/uk-politics-13142441 and BBC News, Libya: 'France and Italy to Send Officers to Aid Rebels', 20 April 2011, available at: www.bbc.co.uk/news/ world-africa-13143988. There were reports that CIA and British Special Forces had been in Libya long before this announcement. See BBC News, 'Obama Authorises Covert Aid to Libyan Rebels - Reports', 31 March 2011, available at: www.bbc.co.uk/news/world-us-canada-12915401. The arms embargo in UNSC Res. 1970 (2011) also specifically precluded 'technical assistance, training, financial or other assistance, related to military activities'. See UNSC Res. 1970 (2011), para. 9.

### 4.4.1.2 Regime Change

The support by NATO and its member states to the rebels also led to questions as to whether the ultimate aim of the intervention was not just to assist them in prevailing in a civil war but to result more broadly in a regime change in Libya. Indeed, Resolution 1973 (2011) expressly permitted the use of all necessary measures to protect civilians and civilian-populated areas against the 'threat of attack'. As Christine Gray has highlighted 'this could conceivably be interpreted as flexible enough to cover NATO's use of force so long as pro-Gaddafi forces continued to fight and even to overthrow Gaddafi if this was necessary to protect civilians from the threat of attack'.[126] In addition to forcibly removing Gaddafi from power it was at least arguable that, if attempts to force him into exile proved fruitless, directly targeting him would be lawful given that, ultimately, civilians would only ever be protected if he was no longer in the position of commander of the Libyan forces due to his open hostility to sections of the Libyan population.[127]

In an attempt to clarify the extent of the mandate contained within Resolution 1973 (2011), the leaders of the United States, the United Kingdom and France published a joint letter on 14 April 2011 in which they declared that '[o]ur duty and our mandate under UN Security Council Resolution 1973 is to protect civilians, and we are doing that. It is not to remove Gaddafi by force.'[128] However, it went on to state that 'it is impossible to imagine a future for Libya with Gaddafi in power' meaning that as 'long as Gaddafi is in power, NATO and its coalition partners must maintain their operations so that civilians remain protected and the pressure on the regime builds'. As with Operation Iraqi Freedom in 2003, the message seemed to be that regime change was the only method of achieving the aims of the resolutions of the Security Council, as opposed to being the aim itself.[129] Indeed, while the use of the phrase 'regime change' was too toxic to be mentioned directly, this was the clear implication of the actions on the ground, and in this letter of the leading states taking action. Such broad interpretations of the authorisation were a concern for many other members of the Security Council at the time of the adoption of Resolution 1973 (2011)[130] and have arguably

---

[126] Gray, n. 116, at 250.
[127] See Henderson, n. 123, at 775. It has, however, been argued that '[i]t was no answer to insist that getting rid of Gaddafi was necessary to protect civilians. Rightly or wrongly, the Security Council rejected that logic by refusing to authorize regime change.' See Michael J. Glennon, 'The Limitations of Traditional Rules and Institutions Relating to the Use of Force', in Marc Weller (ed.), *The Oxford Handbook of the Use of Force in International Law* (Oxford University Press, 2015), 79, at 89.
[128] Barack Obama, David Cameron and Nicolas Sarkozy, 'Libya's Pathway to Peace', *New York Times*, 14 April 2011, available at: www.nytimes.com/2011/04/15/opinion/15iht-edlibya15.html.
[129] Henderson, n. 123, at 777.   [130] See UN Doc. S/PV. 6498, 17 March 2011.

had a negative impact upon finding agreement within the Council ever since. Indeed, the disputes regarding the interpretation of UN Security Council resolutions that arose during the intervention in Libya were never resolved and arguably prevented any action from being taken in response to the civil war in Syria.

### 4.4.2 Côte d'Ivoire (2011)

At the same time as the situation in Libya was occurring similar issues regarding the interpretation of Security Council resolutions arose in connection with a mandate of the Council concerning the situation in Côte d'Ivoire. On 30 March 2011, the Security Council recalled, in Resolution 1975 (2011), an authorisation to use all necessary means it had previously provided in the context of the political turmoil in Côte d'Ivoire.[131] This was recalled, however, in the context of civil unrest that had emerged in the country following the disputed result of an election that had taken place there in November 2010 in which the incumbent president, Laurant Gbagbo, refused to hand over power to Alassane Ouattara, who had been widely recognised as the winner of the election.[132] After urging Gbagbo to hand power over to Ouattara in accordance with the election result,[133] the Security Council:

> *Recall*[ed] its authorisation and *stresse*[d] its full support given to [United Nations Operation in Côte d'Ivoire (UNOCI)], while impartially implementing its mandate, to use all necessary means to carry out its mandate to protect civilians under imminent threat of physical violence, within its capabilities and areas of deployment, including to prevent the use of heavy weapons against the civilian population.[134]

Similar questions arose under the mandate to protect civilians contained within Resolution 1975 (2011) as arose in connection with Resolution 1973 (2011) in Libya. Indeed, both mandates provided for the possibility that preventative action be taken. Whereas in Libya NATO had been provided with authorisation to use force to protect 'civilian populated areas under threat of attack', in Côte d'Ivoire UNOCI and the French forces operating there were authorised to 'prevent the use of heavy weapons'. Both appeared to support the use of force in response to more remote or indirect threats.[135]

However, while regime change was never formally stated to be an aim in Libya, this appeared to be precisely the ultimate aim of Resolution 1975 (2011) in Côte d'Ivoire.[136] The mandate to use all necessary means to protect civilians

---

[131] See UNSC Res. 1528 (2004), para. 16.   [132] UNSC Res. 1975 (2011), para. 6.
[133] Ibid., paras. 1–4.
[134] Ibid., para. 6. The authorisation recalled was that originally granted in UNSC Res. 1528 (2004), paras. 6 and 16 to the UNOCI and French forces operating in the country.
[135] Henderson, n. 123, at 773.   [136] UNSC Res. 1975 (2011), paras. 1–4.

also expressly required those implementing it to do so 'impartially'. Yet, this would be difficult, given that action was mandated by the Council in respect of the troubles that had been caused by Laurent Gbago refusing to cede power. It therefore appears that, while the Council wished to see a peaceful transition in power, the forcible protection of civilians, which was to be implemented impartially, would be maintained until the transition in power had occurred.

As in the situation in Libya, if we are to take '*all* necessary means' to its logical conclusion, then, given the situation, regime change was necessary for the continued protection of civilians. Neither UNOCI nor the French forces expressly stated that either support for Alassane Ouattara or regime change was the intended outcome of their forcible actions. Indeed, both the UNOCI and the French forces were keen not to be perceived to be assisting forces loyal to Ouattara. For example, during the 'final assault' on Gbagbo's compound, which ultimately led to his arrest, while forces loyal to Ouattara directly targeted Gbagbo's compound, UNOCI and French attack helicopters restricted their actions to targeting a store of heavy weapons being used by Gbagbo's forces.[137] As they were mandated by the Security Council to 'prevent the use of heavy weapons' they were not, strictly speaking, overstepping their mandate to remain impartial. However, 'there is little doubt that the outcome of the airstrikes against the compound was the en masse surrender and defection of many pro-Gbagbo generals and a substantial contribution to Ouattara's forces' attempts to forcibly remove Gbagbo from power'.[138]

Ultimately, the interventions in both Libya and Côte d'Ivoire demonstrate the uncertainties that may exist in interpreting mandates contained within resolutions of the UN Security Council and the margin of appreciation that those implementing the mandates on the ground arguably possess.

## 4.5 THE DOCTRINE OF 'IMPLIED' AUTHORISATION

The issues in Sections 4.3 and 4.4 have revolved around implementing prior authorisations of the Security Council. This section, however, considers the problem of implied authorisation that has arisen in the light of states and organisations either taking it upon themselves to unilaterally implement what they perceive to be the will and/or aims of the Council in the absence of any express authorisation to do so or, alternatively, taking action for which the Council subsequently provides its retrospective approval, if not express authorisation.

---

[137] See BBC News, 'Ivory Coast: Gbagbo Held after Assault on Residence', 11 April 2011, available at: www.bbc.co.uk/news/world-africa-13039825.

[138] Antonios Tzanakopoulos, 'The UN/French Use of Force in Abidjan: Uncertainties Regarding the Scope of UN Authorizations', *EJIL Talk!*, 9 April 2011, available at: www.ejiltalk.org/the-un-use-of-force-in-abidjan/. See also BBC News, 'Did UN Forces Take Sides in Ivory Coast?', 7 April 2011, available at: www.bbc.co.uk/news/world-africa-13004462.

## 4.5.1 Unilateral Enforcement of the 'Collective Will' of the UN Security Council

The two cases which provide the clearest examples of the unilateral enforcement of the collective will are the coalition enforcement of the safe havens and no-fly zones in Iraq between 1991 and 2002 and the NATO intervention in Kosovo in 1999.

### 4.5.1.1 Iraq (1991-2002)

Following the Gulf War in 1991, the Shias in the south of Iraq and the Kurds in the north were persecuted by the regime of Saddam Hussein.[139] In Resolution 688 (1991), adopted on 5 April 1991, the Security Council condemned and demanded an end to the 'repression of the Iraqi civilian population in many parts of Iraq ... the consequences of which threaten international peace and security'.[140] The resolution also called upon Iraq to 'allow immediate access by international humanitarian organizations to those in need of assistance'[141] and appealed to all member states and to all humanitarian organisations 'to contribute to these humanitarian relief efforts'.[142] It was not, however, expressly adopted under Chapter VII of the UN Charter and did not authorise states to use 'all necessary means' in its implementation. The possible use of force to enforce the terms of the resolution was not something that members of the Council appeared to be too concerned about at the time of its adoption. Instead, the debate within the Council chamber focused more upon whether such an internal human rights situation could be said to constitute a threat to international peace and security.[143]

However, on 16 April 1991, US President George H. W. Bush announced that a coalition force would enter northern Iraq to establish safe havens there.[144] Although the United States stated that the action was 'consistent with' Resolution 688 (1991),[145] the United Kingdom claimed to be acting 'in support of [UN Security Council resolution] 688'[146] and France claimed that 'in all instances involving France, her action in this respect has been strictly confined by the texts of the United Nations and we do not operate outside

---

[139] *Keesing's* (1991) 38081. For a historical account of the crisis see Peter Malanczuk, 'The Kurdish Crisis and Allied Intervention in the Aftermath of the Second Gulf War' (1991) 2 *European Journal of International Law* 114, at 114–23.
[140] UNSC Res. 688 (1991), preamble   [141] Ibid., para. 3.   [142] Ibid., para. 6.
[143] See UN Doc. S/PV.2982, 5 April 1991.
[144] President George H. W. Bush, 'The United States President's News Conference', 16 April 1991, Weekly Compilation of Presidential Documents, 716, quoted in Weller, n. 60.
[145] Ibid.
[146] 'Statement in the House of Commons by the UK Secretary of State', 18 January 1993, quoted in ibid., at 748–9.

of the framework of the United Nations',[147] none of the contributing states provided a legal justification for their actions. This operation came to be known as Operation Provide Comfort and was shortly followed by an air exclusion zone (no-fly zone), codenamed Operation Poised Hammer. On 26 August 1992, a similar no-fly zone was established in southern Iraq.[148] This operation – Operation Southern Watch – was established ostensibly due to Iraq 'failing to meet its obligations under UN Security Council resolution 688'.[149] Action against Iraq in the enforcement of these no-fly zones took place regularly over the course of the next ten years and appeared to be based upon implied authorisation by the Security Council. For example, after a strike in 1998 the United Kingdom stated that:

> a limited use of force was justifiable *in support of purposes laid down by the Security Council but without the Council's express authorization* when that was the only means to avert an immediate and overwhelming humanitarian catastrophe. Such cases ... would depend ... on the terms of relevant decisions of the Security Council bearing on the situation in question.[150]

While there was a clear absence of protest from other states during the earlier years of this military action against Iraq, this began to change, particularly after the United States launched Operation Desert Strike on 3–4 September 1996, which consisted of cruise missile attacks on military targets in southern Iraq following the entry of Iraqi forces into the northern no-fly zone to intervene in a conflict between two rival Kurdish groups.[151] At this time, '[t]he international community clearly viewed the situation differently from the United States'.[152] Indeed, although no meeting was held in either the UN Security Council or General Assembly to discuss the military action, several states condemned it. Russia, for example, denounced the action as a violation of international law and 'an inappropriate and unacceptable reaction to the latest events in northern Iraq'.[153] Other states, such as China,[154] the Arab League and normally pro-US states in the Arab world, such as Egypt,

---

[147] 'Official Declaration issued by the Ministry of Foreign Affairs of France', 21 January 1993, quoted in ibid., at 752.
[148] 'US Press Release: Coalition to Impose "No-Fly" Zone in Southern Iraq', 26 August 1992, quoted in ibid., at 725–5.
[149] Ibid.
[150] Baroness Symons, Hansard HL Debates, WA 1390140, 16 November 1998 (1998) **69** *British Yearbook of International Law* 593 (emphasis added).
[151] *Keesing's* (1996) 41246.
[152] Gavin A. Symes, 'Force without Law: Seeking a Legal Justification for the September 1996 US Military Intervention in Iraq' (1997–8) **19** *Michigan Journal of International Law* 581, at 601.
[153] Craig R. Whitney, 'From Allies, U.S. Hears Mild Applause or Silence', *New York Times*, 4 September 1996, at A1.
[154] Ibid.

Jordan and Saudi Arabia, disagreed with the action that had been undertaken on this occasion.[155] In essence, the United States and United Kingdom had moved 'from unity to polarization' in their claims to enforce the collective will of the Security Council against Iraq.[156]

### 4.5.1.2 Kosovo (1999)

In response to the killing of four Serb police officers by the Kosovo Liberation Army (KLA) in the disputed province of Kosovo in February 1998, violence was launched by Serb forces against the Kosovo Albanians. The Security Council subsequently adopted three resolutions in 1998 – 1160, 1199 and 1203 – all of which were adopted under Chapter VII of the UN Charter. However, while they condemned the excessive force by the Serbian authorities and acts of terrorism by the KLA, and Resolutions 1199 (1998) and 1203 (1998) stated that the situation constituted a threat to peace and security in the region,[157] none of them provided authorisation for the use of 'all necessary means' to prevent the humanitarian situation from worsening.

Furthermore, the stance of several members of the Council made it clear not only that the resolutions had not authorised the use of force but also that such measures were not going to be authorised. For example, at the meeting in which Resolution 1199 was adopted, Russia made it clear that it favoured a 'settlement of the conflict in Kosovo exclusively through peaceful and political means' and that '[n]o use of force and no sanctions [were] being imposed by the Council at the present stage'.[158] Similarly, during the meeting where Resolution 1203 (1998) was adopted, Russia confirmed that '[e]nforcement elements have been excluded from the draft resolution, and there are no provisions in it that would directly or indirectly sanction the automatic use of force',[159] while China stressed its belief 'that the resolution just adopted does not entail any authorization to use force or to threaten to use force against the Federal Republic of Yugoslavia, nor should it in any way be interpreted as authorizing the use of force or threatening to use force against the Federal Republic of Yugoslavia'.[160] By contrast, the United States asserted prior to the adoption of Resolution 1199 (1998) that '[p]lanning at the North Atlantic Treaty Organization for military operations if these efforts do not succeed is nearing completion. The international community will not stand

---

[155] Adel Darwish, 'Arabs Refuse to Back US Strike', *The Independent*, 4 September 1996, at 22.
[156] Christine Gray, 'From Unity to Polarization: International Law and the Use of Force against Iraq' (2002) 13 *European Journal of International Law* 1.
[157] UNSC Res. 1199 (1998), preamble; UNSC Res. 1203 (1998), preamble.
[158] UN Doc. S/PV. 3930, 23 September 1998, at 3.
[159] UN Doc. S/PV. 3937, 24 October 1998, at 11.    [160] Ibid., at 14.

idly by as the situation in Kosovo deteriorates'[161] and, prior to the adoption of Resolution 1203 (1998), that '[t]he NATO allies, in agreeing on 13 October to the use of force, made it clear that they had the authority, the will and the means to resolve the issue'.[162] The attention of the acting states had clearly moved towards NATO and, following the tragedy in the market town of Racak when 45 civilians were killed and 5,500 fled their homes, Operation Allied Force was launched on 24 March 1999 by NATO forces against military targets within the Federal Republic of Yugoslavia with the aim of halting President Slobodan Milošević's repression of the Kosovo Albanians and forcing the withdrawal of Serb troops from Kosovo.[163] A suspension of the seventy-eight-day operation was announced on 10 June 1999.[164]

While, as highlighted in Chapter 3,[165] NATO had begun to move from solely a collective defence organisation to one involved also in crisis management issues, a clear legal justification was never advanced by NATO or its member states for the action, with many of them basing it upon a necessity to respond to a humanitarian crisis.[166] A recurring element of the justifications, however, was reliance upon the resolutions that had been adopted by the Council. Indeed, France stated that '[t]he actions that have been decided upon are a response to the violation by Belgrade of its international obligations, which stem in particular from the Security Council resolutions adopted under Chapter VII of the United Nations Charter',[167] while Slovenia claimed that 'the action which is being undertaken will be carried out strictly within the substantive parameters established by the relevant Security Council resolutions'.[168] Despite the fact that there appeared to be some understanding amongst states for the operation, it also received condemnation, with several states referring to the lack of authorisation by the Security Council. Indeed, Russia was adamant that it was 'carried out in violation of the Charter of the United Nations and without authorization of the Security Council'.[169] Yet, on 26 March 1999 a draft resolution sponsored by Russia condemning the use of force by NATO as a 'flagrant violation' of the UN Charter and which called for an immediate return to negotiations was heavily defeated,[170] with only three

---

[161] UN Doc. S/PV. 3930, 23 September 1998, at 5.
[162] UN Doc. S/PV. 3937, 24 October 1998, at 15. On 13 October 1998, the North Atlantic Council, NATO's decision-making body, issued activation orders for a phased campaign in the Federal Republic of Yugoslavia.
[163] *Keesing's* (1999) 42845–9.   [164] UN Doc. S/1999/663, 10 June 1999.
[165] See Section 3.5.2.
[166] Although only the United Kingdom and Belgium expressly justified it upon a legal doctrine of 'humanitarian intervention'. See Section 10.3.2.4 and, in general, Chapter 10 on the doctrine of humanitarian intervention.
[167] UN Doc. S/PV. 3988, 24 March 1999, at 9.   [168] Ibid., at 7.   [169] Ibid., at 2.
[170] UN Doc. S/1999/328, 26 March 1999.

states (China, Namibia and Russia) voting in favour and the remaining twelve states voting against.

### 4.5.1.3 Assessing Claims to Unilaterally Enforce the 'Collective Will'

It is clear that in both Iraq and Kosovo 'despite different ways of justification in detail, the acting states in principle claimed a right to unilateral enforcement of [the] collective will'.[171] Indeed, 'the intervening states ... invoked the argument that they are acting on behalf of the "international community". The Security Council resolutions represent the will of the international community and the states are enforcing that will.'[172] They were, in essence, claiming that upon the basis of the Council resolutions and in the light of events on the ground, they possessed implicit authorisation to carry out a forcible operation.

Yet, while '[t]hese claims to a right to use force in order to ensure compliance with Security Council resolutions imply the rejection of a legal necessity to obtain clear authorization' they also similarly reject 'a purely unilateral right of action'.[173] Many have, as discussed in Chapter 10, used these interventions in support of the claim that a right of 'humanitarian intervention' exists under international law. It is arguable that the operations had humanitarian aims, but the clear weight given to the Security Council resolutions that had been adopted does raise the question, at least, as to whether they would have been undertaken in the absence of the resolutions adopted by the Security Council.

The interventions are, however, in direct conflict with the practice of authorisation that had emerged after the Gulf War in 1991 whereby, when deemed necessary, the Security Council has provided its express authorisation to use 'all necessary means'. In this respect:

as long as there was no express authorization by the Council to take enforcement action, no State or group of States was entitled to resort to forcible measures in response to a mere threat to the peace. It is the exclusive prerogative of the Security Council to decide or recommend when and how to respond to a threat to the peace. And ... when authorization of enforcement action is issued by the Security Council, the mandate allowing States or regional organizations to take action must be clear and not merely implicit.[174]

As in the case of Kosovo, and as seen for much of the Cold War, the Council is unable to take action, even if widely perceived to be necessary, in the face of a

---

[171] Krisch, n. 80, at 60.
[172] Nigel D. White, 'The Legality of Bombing in the Name of Humanity' (2000) 5 *Journal of Conflict & Security Law* 27, at 34.
[173] Krisch, n. 80, at 91.
[174] Yoram Dinstein, *War, Aggression and Self-Defence*, 6th ed. (Cambridge University Press, 2017), at para. 955; Krisch, ibid., at 86-9.

veto, or threat thereof, by one or more of the permanent member states. Yet, even '[a]ssuming that the Security Council was being blocked by an illegitimate threat of the veto in a situation that clearly warranted Security Council authorized military action, it is still not legally permissible for states to take it upon themselves, whether in the forum of another organization or not, to enforce those resolutions'.[175] While, as we have seen, the UN Charter can, through the practice of the Council, be interpreted and adapted to meet geopolitical realities, there has been no agreement that a practice of states or organisations taking it upon themselves to enforce Council objectives is acceptable. That is not to say that, on occasion, such unilateral enforcement will not be overlooked or even tolerated by the Council and the broader international community, as appeared to be the case for the early years of action in Iraq[176] and following NATO's intervention in Kosovo, but it has not become a practice that has in any sense impacted upon the legal regime governing the use of force.[177] This is to be welcomed as, suggests Michael Wood, 'there is surely a risk that, if this were accepted, the Council's work could be inhibited because of fears that if it laid down a "common purpose" this could be interpreted as indirectly sanctioning the unilateral use of force'.[178]

### 4.5.2 Retrospective Authorisation or Approval

Section 4.5.1 addressed the situation whereby once a threat to the peace has been determined by the Security Council, expressly or implicitly, an argument is made that states have the possibility of enforcing the collective will expressed within the particular resolutions. However, the argument has also been made, either in addition or as an alternative, that action taken without express authorisation, or even a determination that a threat to the peace exists, can subsequently be approved by the Security Council. In other words, it has been contended that a state, a coalition of states or a regional organisation may employ forcible measures and then have these measures subsequently approved or authorised by the Security Council, thereby giving them a veneer of legality.

The Security Council has not to this day provided express retrospective 'authorisation' for action, and it would be extraordinary if it were to adopt a

---

[175] White, n. 172, at 41.
[176] See Christian Henderson, *The Persistent Advocate and the Use of Force: The Impact of the United States upon the* Jus ad Bellum *in the Post-Cold War Era* (Ashgate, 2010), at 100–5.
[177] Although see Monica Hakimi, 'The *Jus ad Bellum's* Regulatory Form' (2018) 112 *American Journal of International Law* 151.
[178] Michael Wood, 'The Law on the Use of Force: Current Challenges' (2007) 11 *Singapore Yearbook of International Law* 1, at 10.

resolution containing such an authorisation. Yet, it has been questioned whether this is strictly necessary, and whether the Council simply commending or condoning an action, or the outcome of it, is sufficient.[179] The interventions by the Economic Community of West African States (ECOWAS) in Liberia and Sierra Leone arguably provide the clearest examples of the Council endorsing prior unauthorised military action in this way.[180]

### 4.5.2.1 Liberia (1990–7)

During 1989 there was an uprising in Liberia against President Doe following an intervention from Côte d'Ivoire of a rebel force (the National Patriotic Front of Liberia – NPFL) under the leadership of Charles Taylor. The country subsequently became embroiled in civil war. Due to the chaotic situation, the mounting loss of human life and following failed appeals to the United States and the UN to intervene,[181] ECOWAS forces entered Liberia in August 1990 to enforce a truce.[182] These forces consisted of troops, tankers and bombers from five ECOWAS member states and acted under the guise of the ECOWAS Monitoring Group (ECOMOG). Although the force mainly consisted of troops from Nigeria, it also included troops from Ghana, Gambia, Guinea and Sierra Leone.

The aim of the intervention was to halt the fighting and to assist in installing an interim government in the capital, Monrovia. Despite attempts at establishing a ceasefire and settling the dispute, fighting between the parties continued. Following an attack by the NPFL on Monrovia in 1992, ECOMOG forces engaged in extensive action and took territory that had previously been occupied by the group. The Cotonou Peace Agreement was adopted in 1993,[183] but did not end the fighting, which only came to an end finally in 1996, followed by an election which was won by Charles Taylor who subsequently became the president of Liberia in 1997.

There was little condemnation of the action undertaken by ECOMOG, with the Security Council, in a general statement in 1991, 'commend[ing] the

---

[179] See Monica Hakimi, 'To Condone or Condemn? Regional Enforcement Actions in the Absence of Security Council Authorization' (2007) 40 *Vanderbilt Journal of Transnational Law* 643.

[180] See, in general, Jeremy Levitt, 'Humanitarian Intervention by Regional Actors in Internal Conflicts: The Cases of ECOWAS in Liberia and Sierra Leone' (1998) 12 *Temple International and Comparative Law Journal* 333.

[181] The United States stated that the problem required an 'African solution' while the Security Council refused to even discuss the situation. See David Wippman, 'Enforcing the Peace: ECOWAS and the Liberian Civil War', in Lori Damrosch (ed.), *Enforcing Restraint: Collective Intervention in Internal Conflicts* (Council on Foreign Relations Press, 1993), 157, at 159.

[182] On this intervention see, in general, Marc Weller (ed.), *Regional Peacekeeping and International Enforcement: The Liberian Crisis* (Cambridge University Press, 1994).

[183] See www.refworld.org/docid/3ae6b5796.html.

efforts made by the ECOWAS Heads of State and Government to promote peace and normalcy in Liberia' and encouraging all parties to cooperate with ECOWAS and the ceasefire agreement.[184] Later, and in recalling Chapter VIII of the UN Charter, the Council again commended ECOWAS for 'its efforts to restore peace, security and stability in Liberia'[185] and, following the adoption of the Cotonou Peace Agreement in 1993, repeated its approval in further resolutions.[186]

It may be relevant to note that '[m]ost delegates treated ECOMOG as a peacekeeping force and avoided awkward questions about its initial authority to intervene'.[187] Nonetheless, 'it is hard to read the Council's statements as anything other than tacit approval of ECOWAS military action'.[188] Indeed, '[i]t appears that Council members, while not wishing to get drawn into the conflict themselves, felt relieved that ECOWAS had taken responsibility for one of the many costly and protracted conflicts then multiplying around the world'.[189] As Thomas Franck noted, '[i]t seemed to signal that the Council, in appropriate circumstances, could retroactively sanitize an action that may have been of doubtful legality at the time it was taken'.[190] The legality of the action was, indeed, doubtful as, while consent is normally required for the deployment of any peacekeeping action or external forces,[191] the existence of this was far from clear at the time ECOMOG was initially deployed. In any case, while there were some reports that President Doe had provided his consent, Charles Taylor and the NPFL which controlled 90 per cent of the country had not done so.

### 4.5.2.2 Sierra Leone (1996–9)

In 1996, after years of instability and conflict, Ahmad Tejan Kabbah was elected president through internationally monitored elections.[192] Just six months later, power was seized from him through a coup by the Armed Force Revolutionary Council (AFRC) which led, again, to great instability and conflict.[193] There was widespread condemnation of the coup and demands that Kabbah be reinstated as president.[194]

---

[184] UN Doc. S/22133, 22 January 1991.   [185] UNSC Res. 788 (1992), para. 1.
[186] See UNSC Res. 866 (1993), UNSC Res. 950 (1994), UNSC Res. 1014 (1995), UNSC Res. 1020 (1995) and UNSC Res. 1041 (1996).
[187] David Wippman, 'Pro-Democratic Intervention', in Marc Weller (ed.), *Regional Peacekeeping and International Enforcement: The Liberian Crisis* (Cambridge University Press, 1994), 797, at 804.
[188] Ibid.   [189] Ibid.
[190] Thomas Franck, *Recourse to Force: State Action against Threats and Armed Attacks* (Cambridge University Press, 2002), at 156.
[191] On the issue of consent see Sections 5.4.1 and 5.7.2, and, in general, Chapter 9.
[192] Wippman, n. 187, at 807.   [193] *Keesing's* (1997) 41625.   [194] Wippman, n. 187, at 807.

## 4.5 The Doctrine of 'Implied' Authorisation

Without prior authorisation from the Security Council and following an appeal from the Organisation of African Unity (OAU) 'to help the people of Sierra Leone to restore the constitutional order',[195] ECOWAS imposed and enforced an embargo upon Sierra Leone, and launched attacks through ECOMOG forces against the AFRC. However, the Security Council welcomed the efforts of ECOWAS to obtain 'a peaceful resolution' to the crisis.[196] In addition, and acting under Chapter VIII of the Charter, the Council subsequently imposed economic sanctions and provided express authorisation to ECOWAS to enforce them, in particular by 'halting inward maritime shipping in order to inspect and verify their cargoes and destinations'.[197] It was notable that only Russia expressed doubts about the legality of the initial action in that 'enforcement measures should not be taken by regional organizations without Security Council authorization'.[198] While a peace plan had been agreed upon in October 1997,[199] this subsequently broke down with ECOWAS again stepping in to take action. In February 1998, after a period of intense conflict, ECOMOG forces seized Freetown without either seeking or receiving authorisation from the Security Council to do so, ousted the junta from power and reinstalled the democratically elected president.[200]

The precedential value of such action should not, however, be overemphasised, as while ECOWAS used force extensively it variously claimed to be acting in self-defence, in enforcement of the oil and arms embargoes and pursuant to a mutual assistance treaty with Sierra Leone.[201] Yet, it has been argued, nonetheless, that 'ECOMOG's failure even to seek Security Council authorization transferred decision-making authority from the Council to a sub-regional organization, leaving the Council with limited options.'[202] However, the Council did not condemn the action taken. On the contrary, it subsequently 'welcome[d] the fact that the rule of the military junta had been brought to an end' as well as commending ECOWAS for its contributions to a 'peaceful resolution of th[e] crisis'.[203] As David Wippman points out, '[i]n short, the Council, and most states, tacitly approved or at least acquiesced in ECOMOG's decision, treating it more or less as another instance of an acceptable – or at least accepted – breach'.[204]

---

[195] Quoted in Franck, n. 190, at 159.  [196] UN Doc. S/PRST/1997/42, 6 August 1997.
[197] UNSC Res. 1132 (1997), para. 8.
[198] Security Council Press Release 6425, 8 October 1997.
[199] This was welcomed by the Security Council. See S/PRST/1997/52, 17 November 1997.
[200] *Keesing's* (1998) 41992 and 42048.   [201] Wippman, n. 187, at 807-8.   [202] Ibid., at 808.
[203] UN Doc. S/PRST/1998/5, 26 February 1998. See also UNSC Res. 1156 (1998); UNSC Res. 1181 (1998); UNSC Res. 1231 (1999); UNSC Res. 1260 (1999).
[204] Wippman, n. 187, at 808.

### 4.5.2.3 *Assessing Claims of Retrospective Authorisation or Approval*

In the long-term the Security Council may have created problems for itself in taking the position it did in both Liberia and Sierra Leone, due to the fact that it has opened the door to reinterpretations of the UN Charter so as to provide, in effect, for retrospective authorisation of military enforcement action. Indeed, the 'Council and the international community seem willing to tolerate and even welcome interventions seen as genuinely or at least predominantly pro-democratic and/or humanitarian, particularly if they are undertaken by multilateral organizations in areas that do not implicate critical strategic interests of major powers.'[205] Yet, while there was no argument by members of the Council or the UN more broadly that Chapter VIII had been, or should be, modified or reinterpreted to permit such a procedure, it has been contended, nonetheless, that the practice of the Council amounts, in effect, to a reinterpretation of Article 53 of the Charter.[206]

It is difficult to go this far, however, as it must be kept in mind that the Council is a political body and, in this sense, must balance conformity with legal procedures with doing what is in the best interests of international peace and security, and there will be occasions when they do not precisely overlap and coincide. Furthermore, any claims that these interventions have set a clear precedent are countered by the fact that such a practice has not been witnessed since.[207] While it might be argued that the Council was in effect providing retrospective authorisation or approval in Resolution 1244 (1999), following NATO's intervention in Kosovo, and in Resolution 1483 (2003), following the US-led coalition's intervention in Iraq,[208] the Security Council was, on these occasions, pragmatically picking up the pieces following two highly controversial interventions and attempting to move on, with the resolutions being carefully drafted so as to avoid any arguments of retrospective authorisation.

Regardless, '[m]any legal scholars now accept that, at least in certain circumstances, the Security Council may retroactively authorize a regional enforcement action'.[209] Furthermore, and on the back of the ostensibly humanitarian missions of the ECOWAS operations in Liberia and Sierra Leone, retrospective authorisation was an option discussed in the report on the 'Responsibility to Protect' by the International Commission on

---

[205] Ibid., at 805.   [206] Franck, n. 190, at 162.
[207] This is arguably with the exception of the intervention by ECOMOG forces in The Gambia in January 2019 which was subsequently welcomed by the Security Council in Resolution 2337 (2019). This intervention took place following a clear invitation by the newly-elected president, Adama Barrow, and is therefore addressed further in Chapter 9 on the topic of consent to interventions.
[208] See UNSC Res. 1244 (1999) and UNSC Res. 1483 (2003), respectively.
[209] Simon Chesterman, *Just War or Just Peace?: Humanitarian Intervention and International Law* (Oxford University Press, 2002), at 123.

Intervention and State Sovereignty.[210] As Section 4.6 highlights, given the problems that have been witnessed in implementing this concept through prospective Security Council authorisation, the notion of retrospective authorisation is not likely to completely recede any time soon.

## 4.6 IMPLEMENTING THE 'RESPONSIBILITY TO PROTECT'

The atrocities that occurred in Rwanda in 1994, which resulted in approximately one million Rwandans losing their lives over a period of three months, shocked the conscience of the world and, in the aftermath, raised serious questions regarding the willingness and ability of the UN, and the international community, to intervene when necessary.[211] Undoubtedly a major factor behind this failure to intervene and take the necessary action had been the preceding failure of the UN and, in particular, the United States to quell the unrest in Somalia which led to the subsequent withdrawal of the mission.[212]

It was not long after the horrors of Rwanda that the notion of sovereignty as a *responsibility*, as opposed to it being viewed as a power or right, began to emerge.[213] However, it was after the unauthorised NATO intervention in Kosovo in 1999 that the reshaping of sovereignty began to become more prominent, with the UN Secretary-General, in particular, placing question marks over whether sovereignty was inhibiting the protection of those at grave risk of harm.[214] The contemporary concept of a 'Responsibility to Protect' (R2P) then emerged in December 2001 in the report of the International Commission on Intervention and State Sovereignty (ICISS).[215] The central idea behind R2P was 'that sovereign states have a responsibility to protect their own citizens from avoidable catastrophe – from mass murder and rape, from starvation – but when they are unwilling or unable to do so, that responsibility must be borne by the broader community of states.'[216] Framing

---

[210] International Commission on Intervention and State Sovereignty, The Responsibility to Protect, December 2001, at para. 6.35, available at: www.globalr2p.org/resources/the-responsibility-to-protect-report-of-the-international-commission-on-intervention-and-state-sovereignty-2001/.

[211] See, in general, Philip Gourevitch, *We Wish to Inform You That Tomorrow We Will Be Killed Along with our Families* (Picador, 2000).

[212] See Section 3.4.2.2 for more on the intervention in Somalia. For a particularly revealing account, see Michael Barnett, *Eyewitness to a Genocide: The United Nations and Rwanda* (Cornell University Press, 2002).

[213] See Francis M. Deng, Sadikiel Kimaro, Terrence Lyons, Donald Rothchild and I. William Zartman, *Sovereignty as Responsibility: Conflict Management in Africa* (Brookings Institution Press, 1996).

[214] See, for example, Kofi Annan, 'Two Concepts of Sovereignty', *The Economist*, 18 September 1999.

[215] See n. 210.   [216] Ibid., at VIII.

the protection in this way – that is, implicitly making the sovereignty of a state conditional upon its willingness and ability to protect those within its borders – had a certain resonance and acceptability that the doctrine of humanitarian intervention, as discussed in Chapter 10, lacked. The concept of R2P was, as such, subsequently given attention in reports issued by various bodies and individuals. For example, it was highlighted in the report of the High-Level Panel on Threats, Challenges and Change of December 2004.[217] In particular, in its report 'A More Secure World' the High-Level Panel claimed that there was an emerging norm of a collective responsibility to protect in cases of genocide, ethnic cleansing or serious violation of international humanitarian law.[218] The Secretary-General then considered the issue in his report of March 2005, 'In Larger Freedom', which also expressly recognised the R2P principle[219] and claimed to be 'aware of the sensitivities involved in this issue',[220] no doubt a reference to the sensitive issues raised in attempting to reconcile intervention with state sovereignty. He further claimed that, despite the disagreements of the past, states should now accept the responsibility to protect in cases where the territorial state was unwilling or unable to act.[221] However, an important aspect in the concept's emergence was the tepid welcome it received by states themselves at the UN World Summit in 2005 where it was unanimously accepted in the World Summit Outcome Document that there was a primary responsibility upon each state to protect its own population from genocide, war crimes, ethnic cleansing and crimes against humanity and that, importantly, a secondary responsibility rested with the international community.[222]

### 4.6.1 Enforcement of the Secondary Responsibility to Protect

While the existence of such a secondary responsibility to protect had been widely acknowledged, there was at that stage some uncertainty as to exactly upon whom such a responsibility rested and in what circumstances it would either require action or could be relied upon in justification for it. Indeed, the emphasis that the doctrine put on the primary responsibility of states to protect those within their borders was not the controversial part of the doctrine. Instead, the major controversy focused on the contours and meaning in practice of the secondary responsibility upon the international community. In particular, was this to be exercised only by the UN through the Security Council? Or could regional organisations or individual states also invoke the

---

[217] A More Secure World, n. 85, at para. 203.   [218] Ibid., at paras. 199–203.
[219] In Larger Freedom, n. 86, at para. 135.   [220] Ibid.   [221] Ibid., at paras. 132–5.
[222] 2005 World Summit Outcome Document, UN Doc. A/60/L.1, 15 September 2005, at paras. 138–9.

## 4.6 Implementing the 'Responsibility to Protect'

responsibility if they identified that a state was failing to live up to its responsibility to protect those within its borders?[223]

In this respect, it is interesting to observe how the doctrine was initially framed in the report of the ICISS. While stressing that the 'Security Council should be the *first port of call* on any matter relating to military intervention for human protection purposes',[224] the ICISS then left open whether an 'intervention not authorized by the Security Council or [the] General Assembly' would be lawful.[225] Carsten Stahn suggests that '[t]he report of the Commission managed to gather broad support because it avoided taking a final stance on the question of the legality/legitimacy of unauthorized interventions',[226] while Christine Gray goes further in stating that the 'Commission envisaged unilateral action if the Security Council failed to act'.[227] However, through a reading of the ICISS's exploration of the options in the absence of Security Council authorisation it becomes clear that the Commission set out only two options in this context: consideration of the matter with a possible subsequent recommendation to use force by the UN General Assembly in an Emergency Special Session under the Uniting for Peace resolution,[228] or by regional organisations acting within their sphere of activity with the proviso that retrospective approval be sought from the Security Council.[229]

What is clear, however, is that the High-Level Panel, the Secretary-General, and states at the World Summit took a more conservative line, placing the R2P concept and its secondary responsibility firmly within the existing paradigm of Security Council collective security. The High-Level Panel, for example, saw this responsibility within the context of strengthening the collective security system of the UN Charter.[230] More expressly, it acknowledged:

the emerging norm that there is a collective international responsibility to protect, *exercisable by the Security Council authorizing military intervention as a last resort*, in the event of genocide and other large-scale killing, ethnic cleansing or serious violations of international humanitarian law which sovereign Governments have proved powerless or unwilling to prevent.[231]

As Chapter 3 demonstrated, the practice of the Security Council in determining the existence of a threat to international peace and security in such

---

[223] For an interesting discussion of these questions, see James Pattison, *Humanitarian Intervention & the Responsibility to Protect: Who Should Intervene?* (Oxford University Press, 2010).
[224] The Responsibility to Protect, n. 210, at para. 6.28 (emphasis added).
[225] Ibid., at para. 6.37.
[226] Carsten Stahn, 'Responsibility to Protect: Political Rhetoric or Emerging Legal Norm?' (2007) 101 *American Journal of International Law* 99, at 104.
[227] Gray, n. 116, at 242.   [228] See, further, Sections 3.4.1 and 3.4.2.4.
[229] See The Responsibility to Protect, n. 210, Principles for Military Intervention 3(E), at xiii.
[230] Stahn, n. 226, at 105.   [231] A More Secure World, n. 85, at para. 203 (emphasis added).

circumstances and then authorising the use of forcible measures has already become an embedded part of Security Council practice in the post–Cold War era.[232] It was in regards to the question of unilateral action that the Panel took a clearer line than the ICISS, stating that, while it recognized 'the possibility of individual Member States bypassing the Security Council',[233] it 'did not envisage that an international responsibility to protect could be invoked by coalitions of the able and willing or regional organizations in the absence of Security Council authorization'.[234]

The UN Secretary-General's report 'In Larger Freedom' 'did not expressly rule out the possibility of unilateral action in any circumstances (e.g. where the veto is used to block action in a case of genocide)'.[235] Yet, in rubberstamping the already developed authorisation method embedded within Security Council practice, the Secretary-General posed the rhetorical question as to whether 'genocide, ethnic cleansing and other such crimes against humanity, are ... not also threats to international peace and security, against which humanity should be able to look to the Security Council for protection?'[236] The position adopted was, therefore, and like that of the High-Level Panel, concerned more with strengthening the collective security system than endorsing any unilateral rights to action.[237]

This faith in the existing system was finally stressed at the UN World Summit in 2005. The relevant paragraphs of the World Summit Outcome Document warrant being read in their entirety:

**138.** Each individual State has the responsibility to protect its populations from genocide, war crimes, ethnic cleansing and crimes against humanity. This responsibility entails the prevention of such crimes, including their incitement, through appropriate and necessary means. We accept that responsibility and will act in accordance with it. The international community should, as appropriate, encourage and help States to exercise this responsibility and support the United Nations in establishing an early warning capability.

**139.** The international community, through the United Nations, also has the responsibility to use appropriate diplomatic, humanitarian and other peaceful means, in accordance with Chapters VI and VIII of the Charter, to help to protect populations from genocide, war crimes, ethnic cleansing and crimes against humanity. In this context, *we are prepared to take collective action, in a timely and decisive manner, through the Security Council, in accordance with the Charter, including Chapter VII, on a case-by-case basis and in cooperation with relevant regional organizations as appropriate, should peaceful means be inadequate and national authorities are manifestly failing to protect their populations from genocide, war crimes, ethnic cleansing and crimes against humanity.* We stress the need for the General Assembly to continue

---

[232] See Chapter 3. See also A More Secure World, n. 85, at para. 202.
[233] Ibid., at paras. 206, 196 and 197.   [234] Stahn, n. 226, at 106.   [235] Ibid., at 107.
[236] In Larger Freedom, n. 86, at para. 125.   [237] Henderson, n. 176, at 127.

consideration of the responsibility to protect populations from genocide, war crimes, ethnic cleansing and crimes against humanity and its implications, bearing in mind the principles of the Charter and international law. We also intend to commit ourselves, as necessary and appropriate, to helping States build capacity to protect their populations from genocide, war crimes, ethnic cleansing and crimes against humanity and to assisting those which are under stress before crises and conflicts break out. (emphasis added)

It is true that the text of the various reports and documents do not 'firmly state that UN collective security action constitutes the *only* option for responding to mass atrocities through the use of force'.[238] Nevertheless, through the direct references to action under the auspices of the Security Council without any mention whatsoever of unilateral action, it appears that this was the favoured approach.

### 4.6.2 R2P: Old Wine in New Bottles?

Given that in all practical senses the various reports envisaged the forcible element of the secondary responsibility existing in the form of the Security Council taking collective action, not states or regional organisations, it has been questioned whether the R2P doctrine is really anything new, or whether it is simply reformulating the existing position under international law.[239] It does, at least on the face of it, seem to be doing just that, an impression confirmed by both the Secretary-General and the former Special Adviser on R2P, Edward Luck, both of whom underscored that the concept is not a new concept but is based on well-established international law, including the provisions of the UN Charter.[240]

However, what these reports and subsequent debates highlighted was that, while the doctrine had become a firm piece of rhetoric, its normative legal status was far from clear, in particular as to whether it had impacted upon the law that existed at the time. As Peter Hilpold has observed:

the norm creation process leading to R2P can be compared with that characterizing the development of the law of self-determination. In both cases, at the beginning we have a political slogan of uncertain meaning. Nonetheless, as the case of self-determination demonstrates, political rhetoric can solidify to legal principles and even if they remain

---

[238] Stahn, n. 226, at 109 (emphasis added).
[239] Gray, n. 116, at 241. See General Assembly Plenary Debates, 63rd session, 97th–101st meetings, UN Press Releases GA/10848, GA/10849, GA/10850, 23, 24, 28 July 2009; General Assembly Annual General Debate, 66th session, 11th–24th meetings, UN Press Releases GA/11147–GA/11153, 21–24 September 2011.
[240] 'Delegates Seek to End Global Paralysis in Face of Atrocities as General Assembly Holds Interactive Dialogue on Responsibility to Protect', UN Press Release, GA/10847, 23 July 2009, available at: https://press.un.org/en/2009/ga10847.doc.htm.

vague and prone to be abused by opposed camps some consensual lines will emerge over time.[241]

For those that argue that R2P has impacted upon the law and that 'consensual lines' have emerged, questions still remain as to how and to what extent this is the case. In particular, if the secondary responsibility was only to be invoked by the Security Council, is there now an obligation upon it to act in clear cases of R2P, or for the permanent members of the Security Council to refrain from casting a veto?[242] Or if the Security Council fails to act in such clear cases is the secondary responsibility to be invoked by other states and/or organisations? Light is perhaps shone upon these issues through an examination of the doctrine in practice.[243]

### 4.6.2.1 *Darfur (Sudan) (2003-20)*

Although not referring directly to R2P in its resolutions regarding the situation in Darfur (Sudan), the Security Council has, on a number of occasions, '[r]ecall[ed] that the Sudanese Government bears the primary responsibility to protect its population within its territory',[244] although it did not make a direct reference to R2P or who might bear the secondary responsibility. From 2003, the Janjaweed Arab-African militia, supported by the government of Sudan, killed at least 200,000 black Africans (although also Muslim) in Darfur and also displaced more than 2 million.[245] This was in order to suppress a rebellion by some of Darfur's agricultural tribes who had risen up against the Sudanese

---

[241] Peter Hilpold, 'Intervening in the Name of Humanity: R2P and the Power of Ideas' (2012) 17 *Journal of Conflict & Security Law* 49, at 79.

[242] The Secretary-General had in his report urged the five permanent members of the Security Council not to use or threaten to use the veto in situations where a state had manifestly failed to meet its obligations with regard to R2P. Some states supported the Secretary-General's call, with some also doing so by taking this opportunity to call for reform of the composition of the Security Council, as well as bringing up the issue as to whether it should be the Security Council or the General Assembly which should authorise action in the context of R2P.

[243] R2P has been discussed in connection with natural disasters and relief operations, in particular in the aftermath of Cyclone Nargis in Burma in May 2008. This discussion has revolved around whether states are free to refuse assistance in the aftermath of such tragedies in the light of the emergence of the R2P doctrine. See Rebecca Barber, 'The Responsibility to Protect the Survivors of Natural Disasters: Cyclone Nargis, a Case Study' (2009) 14 *Journal of Conflict & Security Law* 3. See also Craig Allen and Therese O'Donnell, 'A Call to Alms?: Natural Disasters, R2P, Duties of Cooperation and Unchartered Consequences' (2012) 17 *Journal of Conflict & Security Law* 337.

[244] UNSC Res. 1556 (2004); UNSC Res. 1564 (2004); UNSC Res. 1706 (2006); UNSC Res. 1755 (2007); UNSC Res. 1784 (2007).

[245] Report of the UN Secretary-General, UN Doc. S/2004/703, 30 August 2004.

government in February 2003.[246] However, 'states were not willing to intervene through the Security Council in the absence of [Sudan's] consent, nor did they assert the right of any unilateral action'.[247] The Security Council subsequently set out proposals for a hybrid AU/UN force in Resolution 1706 (2006) but again merely invited Sudan's consent for such a deployment.[248] It was only at the end of 2007 that consent was given for such a force.[249] Significantly, the AU did not rely on its Constitutive Act of 2000 to justify taking action, which had, controversially, asserted the right of the AU to intervene within its member states.[250] As Christine Gray persuasively concludes, '[t]he problems involved in the implementation of the "responsibility to protect", whether through the UN or, more controversially, through regional or unilateral humanitarian intervention, were all too apparent with regard to the humanitarian catastrophe in Darfur (Sudan)'.[251] Things appeared to look different, however, in connection with the crisis in Libya in 2011.

### 4.6.2.2 Libya (2011)

While not making direct reference to the R2P doctrine, Security Council Resolution 1970 (2011) of March 2011 did expressly '[r]ecall[] the Libyan authorities' responsibility to protect its population'.[252] The Security Council had thus seemingly made an indirect reference to the R2P doctrine in the preamble of a Chapter VII resolution. However, some commentators have made much of the fact that it only referred to the responsibility of *Libya*, omitting any express reference to any responsibility by the international community.[253]

NATO similarly exhibited concern at the situation but laid down three conditions before any forcible intervention could occur:[254]

- a demonstrable need;
- broad regional support; and
- a clear legal basis.

Importantly, with regard to the last of these conditions NATO Secretary-General, Anders Fogh Rasmussen, insisted that, unlike in Kosovo in 1999,[255] an authorising resolution from the Security Council was necessary before any

---

[246] See (2004) UNYB 233. [247] Gray, n. 87, at 61. [248] UNSC Res. 1706 (2006), para. 1.
[249] See UN Doc. SG/SM/10945, 16 April 2007. [250] See Section 3.5.1.
[251] Gray, n. 87, at 61. [252] UNSC Res. 1970 (2011), preamble. [253] Gray, n. 116, at 247.
[254] 'NATO Ready to Support International Efforts on Libya', 10 March 2011, available at: www.nato.int/cps/en/natolive/news_71446.htm; 'Libya's War Intensifies as the West Holds Fire', *The Guardian*, 10 March 2011, at 24.
[255] For more on the Kosovo crisis, see Section 4.5.1.2.

military action could take place.[256] In this respect, '[i]t speaks volumes about the new state of mind prevailing in NATO ... that there was no dissent from the view that any humanitarian intervention in Libya, in early 2011 ... must be firmly embedded in Security Council authorization'.[257] However, some individual member states did not appear to entirely agree with this position. Indeed, the United Kingdom, for example, claimed that there was already a clear legal basis for action as 'in cases of great overwhelming humanitarian need nations are able to act under international law, even without a resolution of the Security Council'.[258] This position reflected one that was long held by the United Kingdom,[259] and perhaps reflected its views on where the secondary responsibility to protect lay, but was not reflective of views on this issue more broadly or of those of NATO more specifically. Indeed, the general position placed the Security Council at the heart of any decision to deploy forcible measures in the light of the Libyan government's failure to protect its citizens.

The regional support which NATO appeared to require before launching military action could be witnessed in the form of support from the League of Arab States, which called on:

the Security Council, in view of the deterioration in the situation, to *shoulder its responsibilities* and take the measures necessary to immediately impose a no-fly zone on Libyan military aircraft and establish safe havens in areas that are exposed to bombardment, as precautionary measures that will provide protection for the Libyan people ... while respecting the sovereignty and territorial integrity of neighbouring States.[260]

Somewhat surprisingly, given its Constitutive Act which equivocally provided for intervention in certain circumstances,[261] the AU was not forthcoming in its support for a military option, urging those involved to instead pursue a negotiated solution.[262]

---

[256] 'No-Fly Zone Plan Goes Nowhere as US, Russia and NATO Urge Caution', *The Guardian*, 2 March 2011, at 10.
[257] Dinstein, n. 174, at para. 958.
[258] BBC News, 'G8 Leaders Consider Libya No-Fly Zone', 14 March 2011, available at: www.bbc.co.uk/news/ world-africa-12735491.
[259] See Chapter 10 on the doctrine of humanitarian intervention.
[260] See UN Doc. S/2011/137, 15 March 2011 (emphasis added). The call to establish a no-fly zone was supported by the Organization of the Islamic Conference and the Gulf Cooperation Council. See 'NATO Prepares the Case for a No-Fly Zone', *The Guardian*, 9 March 2011, at 17.
[261] See Section 3.5.1.
[262] African Union Peace and Security Council, 265th meeting, AU Doc. PSC/PR/COMM.2 (CCLXV), 10 March 2011, available at: www.peaceau.org/uploads/265th-communique-en.pdf. Gray has noted that this is surprising given that the International Criminal Court had found the Libyan authorities responsible for crimes against humanity, which is a trigger for action by the AU in its Constitutive Act. See Gray, n. 116, at 246.

Nevertheless, in the light of general support for the Security Council to be positioned at the forefront of action to implement the secondary responsibility to protect, the Council adopted Resolution 1973 (2011) on 17 March 2011. In this resolution the Council, acting under Chapter VII of the UN Charter, '[r]*eiterat*[ed] the responsibility of the Libyan authorities to protect the Libyan population'.[263] Again, as with Resolution 1970, Resolution 1973 only referred to the responsibility of *Libya*. As discussed in Section 4.4.1, this resolution then provided authorisation for the use of 'all necessary means' to protect civilians and civilian-populated areas.[264]

Upon the launching of military action on 19 March 2011 it was notable that the UK's legal justification was not based upon the right of humanitarian intervention, but instead relied on the authorisation provided in Resolution 1973 (2011), although it did not refer to the R2P doctrine in its justification.[265] While it similarly did not directly refer to R2P in its Statement Regarding Use of Force in Libya, the United States nonetheless stated that 'Qaddafi has forfeited his responsibility to protect his own citizens, and created a serious need for immediate humanitarian assistance and protection' and that the operation was legally based upon the authorisation of the Security Council provided in Resolution 1973 (2011).[266]

Nevertheless, there were those who claimed that the use of force on this occasion was, indeed, specifically an implementation of the R2P doctrine. The new government of Libya, for example, claimed that '[f]or the very first time, we witnessed in Libya the operationalization of the responsibility to protect, which was carried out in a reasonable manner, saving the lives of thousands of Libyans and maintaining the sovereignty and territorial integrity of Libya'.[267] It seems then that, while the R2P doctrine did not impact upon the established legal bases for military action, it may come to have an impact when members of the international community, particularly those within the Security Council, feel morally obliged to intervene if the state concerned is clearly not living up to its responsibility to protect those within its borders. Question marks are, however, thrown upon this conclusion in the light of the absence of action by the Security Council in the context of the continuing crisis in Syria.

---

[263] UNSC Res. 1973 (2011), preamble.
[264] UNSC Res. 1973 (2011), para. 4. The resolution also reaffirmed and extended various measures adopted in UNSC Res. 1970 (2011), such as the arms embargo (paras. 13–16) and the asset freezes (paras. 19–21). See also Chapter 3 on the powers of the Security Council to authorise the use of force.
[265] See HM Government's Note on Legal Basis for Deployment of UK Forces and Military Assets, 21 March 2011, available at: www.guardian.co.uk/law/2011/mar/21/government-legal-military-action-libya.
[266] US Department of State Legal Advisor, 'Statement Regarding Use of Force in Libya', 26 March 2011, available at: https://2009-2017.state.gov/s/l/releases/remarks/159201.htm.
[267] See UN Doc. S/PV. 6620, 16 September 2011, at 7 (Libya).

### 4.6.2.3 Syria (2011–)

As in Libya, the uprising in Syria against the leader of the country, Bashar al-Assad, led to violent repression.[268] However, in terms of the response of the international community, in particular the Security Council, this is where the similarities end. Indeed, while in Resolution 1970 (2011) the Council was quick to apparently invoke R2P, the backlash from the ways in which the authorisation to use force in Resolution 1973 (2011) was interpreted and implemented, as set out earlier,[269] meant that condemnation of the Assad regime by the Council did not appear quickly, and even then only in the form of a non-binding presidential statement as opposed to a formal resolution.[270]

The divisions between members of the Security Council, in particular Russia and the United States, meant that forcible intervention with the authorisation of the Security Council was always a distant possibility, at best. Although Russia appeared to finally acknowledge the fact that the fate of the Assad regime was not certain,[271] this was by no means followed with any loosening within the chamber of the Security Council as to the adoption of a resolution which even imposed sanctions, let alone formally invoked the R2P doctrine or authorised military action. However, collective intervention outside of the Security Council also appeared distant, with NATO not drawing up any plans. Indeed, it would have been difficult for NATO to justify any unilateral action after its insistence in Libya on securing the authorisation of the Security Council.

Various states raised the prospect of intervening militarily against the Assad regime, particularly following the Ghouta attack in August 2013, but did not do so, and did not refer to R2P in setting out the legal basis for any possible action.[272] This was, arguably, a consequence of the development of R2P thus far having been firmly located within the realms of authorisation by the Security Council.

The reaction of the international community to the tragedies that have unfolded in Syria raises stark questions over the significance of the R2P

---

[268] BBC News, 'Middle East Unrest: Three Killed at Protest in Syria', 18 March 2011, available at: www.bbc.co.uk/news/world-middle-east-12791738.

[269] See Section 4.4.1.

[270] In this statement the Security Council stated that it 'condemns the widespread violations of human rights and the use of force against civilians by the Syrian authorities' and that it 'calls on the Syrian authorities to alleviate the humanitarian situation in crisis areas by ceasing the use of force against affected towns'. See SC/10352, 3 August 2011.

[271] BBC News, 'Syrian Government "Losing Control" – Russian Official', 13 December 2012, available at: www.bbc.co.uk/news/world-middle-east-20710561.

[272] See, for example, Chemical Weapon Use by Syrian Regime – UK Government Legal Position, 29 August 2013, available at: www.gov.uk/government/publications/chemical-weapon-use-by-syrian-regime-uk-government-legal-position/chemical-weapon-use-by-syrian-regime-uk-government-legal-position-html-version.

doctrine, in particular as to whether it is a legal norm or mere political rhetoric,[273] and raises questions again regarding the selectivity in its application. Furthermore, while the primary responsibility is placed upon the state concerned to protect its citizens and a secondary responsibility has been placed upon the international community – which has come to be interpreted as being represented by the Security Council – there is now the question of whether there could be a *tertiary* responsibility, or at least an alternative reading to the secondary responsibility, to enable action to be taken in the face of a failure by a state to invoke its responsibility to protect.[274] Indeed, as Carlo Focarelli notes, while 'some consensus on the principle does exist, ... disagreement is still considerable on the specific question of a general legal regime allowing military intervention'.[275] In other words, if the Security Council does not authorise military action under the auspices of the R2P doctrine, can other states or organisations do so? There were claims by the Arab League in the light of the prospect of a veto in the Security Council that it had a 'special responsibility', but it is unclear what this meant.[276] Given that in terms of procedure the R2P doctrine has not, legally speaking, provided anything significantly novel, this is the next question that needs to be addressed at the state level if the doctrine is to advance to being a distinctive legal norm, or of any real value in any practical sense.[277]

## 4.7 CONCLUSION

The authorisation method has undoubtedly provided the Security Council, and the UN collective security system more broadly, with a new lease of life. Yet, and as has been discussed in this chapter, it has also led to some notable issues arising in its implementation that have proved divisive.

At a general institutional level, the fact that the Council has five permanent members in itself determines to a degree the situations that are placed on the Council's agenda. The fact that they also possess a veto power means that condemnation is often selective from the Council. This is significant when one considers the argument that has been made that a lack of condemnation by the

---

[273] See the discussion in Hilpold, n. 241.
[274] See, for example, Christian Henderson, 'R2P: Room for a Tertiary Responsibility?', in Vasilka Sancin and Maša Kovič Dine (eds.), *Responsibility to Protect in Theory and Practice* (GV Založba, 2013), 204.
[275] Carlo Focarelli, 'The Responsibility to Protect Doctrine and Humanitarian Intervention: Too Many Ambiguities for a Working Doctrine' (2008) 13 *Journal of Conflict & Security Law* 191, at 210.
[276] See BBC News, 'Syria Unrest: Arab League "Seeks Peacekeeping Mission"', 12 February 2012, available at: www.bbc.co.uk/news/world-middle-east-17004530.
[277] For a scholarly analysis of this issue see Patrick M. Butchard, *The Responsibility to Protect and the Failures of the United Nations Security Council* (Hart, 2020).

Council equates to acquiescence.[278] But it also leads to selectivity as to not only the situations that are formally determined to be a threat to the peace, but also those in response to which the Council authorises the use of forcible measures.

While a clear method of the Council adopting resolutions containing an authorisation has developed, there is no similar method in connection with ending an authorisation. In this respect, not only do the five permanent member states have a greater control over when an authorisation is granted, they have also greater control over when one ends, an issue described by David Caron as the 'reverse veto'.[279] This has not often caused problems in practice and has to an extent been minimised by the practice of the Council imposing time limits upon authorisations.

A more significant practical issue, however, has been the lack of a clear method or practice in determining how such institutional resolutions should be interpreted. This is at the heart of the problems addressed in this chapter. Indeed, many of the problems have arisen due to a lack of clarity regarding the interpretation of resolutions of the Security Council, whether it be regarding the revival of an authorisation, the actions that can be said to fall within the scope of the mandate provided or whether there has been any authorisation or, at least, approval of the action taken at all. It is arguable that an element of intentional ambiguity is often found within the resolutions in order to permit states to make differing claims concerning the Council's intent. However, while member states are expected to interpret Security Council resolutions in good faith, it is the Security Council as a collective body that ultimately has the final say on interpreting its own resolutions. In this respect, if it is clear that there is a consensus against certain action being taken in the name of the Council or a mandate of the Council being implemented in a particular way then that must be respected and act as a decisive limitation upon the way a resolution is interpreted and, ultimately, any military action undertaken.

## QUESTIONS

1 In what ways has the authorisation method changed, or been adapted, since its original use in Resolution 678 (1990)?

2 Was the intervention in Iraq in 2003 lawful?

3 What types of action came within the UN Security Council mandate regarding the 'protection of civilians and civilian populated areas' in Libya in 2011?

---

[278] Franck, n. 190.
[279] David Caron, 'The Legitimacy of the Collective Authority of the Security Council' (1993) 87 *American Journal of International Law* 552, at 577.

4 What is meant by the concept of 'implied' authorisation?

5 To what extent, if any, can states and organisations take action and then seek retrospective approval from the Security Council?

6 Is the R2P concept an 'emerging norm'?

## SUGGESTED FURTHER READING

Niels Blokker, 'Is the Authorization Authorized? Powers and Practice of the UN Security Council to Authorize the Use of Force by "Coalitions of the Able and Willing"' (2000) 11 *European Journal of International Law* 541

Niels Blokker and Nico Schrijver (eds.), *The Security Council and the Use of Force: Theory and Reality: A Need for Change?* (Martinus Nijhoff, 2005)

P. M. Butchard, *The Responsibility to Protect and the Failures of the United Nations Security Council* (Hart, 2020)

Monika Hakimi, 'To Condone or Condemn: Regional Enforcement Actions in the Absence of Security Council Authorization' (2007) 40 *Vanderbilt Journal of International Law* 643

Jules Lobel and Michael Ratner, 'Bypassing the Security Council: Ambiguous Authorizations to Use Force, Cease-Fires, and the Iraqi Inspection Regime' (1999) 93 *American Journal of International Law* 124

Vaughan Lowe et al. (eds.), *The United Nations Security Council and War: The Evolution of Thought and Practice since 1945* (Oxford University Press, 2008)

Sean D. Murphy 'Assessing the Legality of Invading Iraq' (2004) 92 *Georgetown Law Journal* 173

Yasmine Nahlawi, *The Responsibility to Protect in Libya and Syria: Mass Atrocities, Human Protection and International Law* (Routledge, 2019)

Ramesh Thakur (ed.), *The Responsibility to Protect: Norms, Laws and the Use of Force in International Politics* (Routledge, 2011)

# 5 United Nations Peacekeeping and the Use of Force

## 5.1 INTRODUCTION

The previous chapters in Part II addressed the use of force under the auspices of the United Nations (UN), in particular the development of the 'authorisation method' as a means of overcoming the fact that forces that were envisaged as existing under the wings of the UN Security Council, as part of the Article 43 agreements, had never been realised. Of course, even if they had been, agreement within the Council would still have been required for their deployment, which, as has been seen, cannot be guaranteed. The authorisation method has proved far from perfect, but nonetheless revitalised the enforcement powers of the Security Council following years of Cold War deadlock. However, it was the early deadlock within the Council that also gave rise to the institution of peacekeeping.[1] Indeed, '[t]he concept of UN peacekeeping developed as a response to failure of the collective security system envisaged in the Charter',[2] and it is true to say that '[f]rom its modest beginnings ... UN peacekeeping has become a central and indispensable activity of the organization and is now an accepted part of UN law and practice'.[3] Today, there are twelve peacekeeping operations around the world.[4] Yet, while it is possible to make a relatively direct link between the UN Charter and the authorisation method, in that the concept of force being employed with the authorisation of the Security Council is also found within Chapter VIII, the concept of peacekeeping forces, on the other hand, is not specifically provided for anywhere in the UN Charter.

---

[1] Nigel D. White, 'Peacekeeping or War-Fighting?' in Nigel D. White and Christian Henderson (eds.), *Research Handbook on International Conflict and Security Law: Jus ad Bellum, Jus in Bello and Jus post Bellum* (Edward Elgar, 2013), 572, at 573.
[2] Scott Sheeran, 'The Use of Force in United Nations Peacekeeping Operations', in Marc Weller (ed.), *The Oxford Handbook of the Use of Force in International Law* (Oxford University Press, 2015), 347, at 350.
[3] Ibid., at 347–8.   [4] See https://peacekeeping.un.org/en/where-we-operate.

## 5.1 Introduction

Peacekeeping forces have traditionally been deployed to observe and facilitate the implementation of either a ceasefire or a peace agreement. Given the general principles of peacekeeping that were developed early on – consent, impartiality and the non-use of force except in self-defence – the institution of peacekeeping may not seem particularly controversial and may be seen as falling squarely within the UN's purpose of the maintenance of international peace and security. Yet, very early on it became clear that, given the complexity of the situations that peacekeeping forces were established to deal with, in particular the situation in the Congo in the 1960s, these principles were to be tested to – and, arguably, beyond – their limits. It was, therefore, perhaps a natural consequence that peacekeeping operations became more 'robust' or 'muscular' and now regularly resort to forcible measures. As the institution of peacekeeping is not specifically provided for in the UN Charter it perhaps goes without saying that neither is the possibility for peacekeeping operations to use force. However, today '[t]he use of force by UN peacekeepers is an everyday reality and is integral to mission success and failure'[5] and, at the same time, '[w]hether characterized by excess or timidity, the use of force has been central to all the major crises of UN peacekeeping'.[6] While peacekeeping has undoubtedly become more robust, such *peacekeeping* should be seen to be different to peace *enforcement*, which was discussed in Chapters 3 and 4, and judged accordingly.

This chapter has as its focus not the institution of peacekeeping *per se*, but more specifically the *use of force* within, and arguably as an integral part of, peacekeeping.[7] Furthermore, '[a]lthough other organisations such as the African Union ... and the Economic Community of West African States ... have undertaken peacekeeping tasks, the UN dominates practice in this area and UN peacekeeping doctrine and principles have contributed greatly to the development of peacekeeping law'.[8] As such, while the chapter acknowledges the role played by peacekeeping forces from other organisations, the focus will be on the institution of UN peacekeeping. This chapter traces the development and deployment of peacekeeping operations and their drift towards more robust forms, in particular their evolution to include the use of force in defence of their mandate, the protection of civilians, and in stabilisation operations. It also addresses the constitutional issues raised by their existence and the developments that have taken place, whether such developments undermine

---

[5] Sheeran, n. 2, at 348.    [6] Ibid.
[7] See Peter Nadin (ed.), *The Use of Force in UN Peacekeeping* (Routledge, 2018). For extended work on peacekeeping as an institution, see Nigel D. White, *Keeping the Peace: The United Nations and the Maintenance of International Peace and Security*, 2nd ed. (Manchester University Press, 1993).
[8] White, n. 1, at 572.

the legitimacy of peacekeeping operations and whether they have impacted upon the effectiveness of the operations.

Section 5.2 begins by attempting to define UN peacekeeping, given its absence from the UN Charter, while Section 5.3 addresses the legal basis for peacekeeping operations. Section 5.4 sets out the basic principles of peacekeeping, while Sections 5.5 and 5.6 trace the development of peacekeeping, from the early UN Charter-era operations, which saw the establishment of the basic principles, through to the challenges to these principles, which did not take long to manifest themselves, in particular through the use of forcible measures by peacekeeping forces.[9] Finally, Section 5.7 examines the evolution of the use of force within peacekeeping missions, from simple self-defence to the implementation and enforcement of robust mandates, and assesses not only whether the various forms of forcible peacekeeping can be reconciled with the fundamental principles of peacekeeping, but also whether peacekeeping forces have now taken on a war-fighting role.

## 5.2 ATTEMPTING TO DEFINE UN PEACEKEEPING

As already noted, the term 'peacekeeping' is not found within the UN Charter. However, in 1990 it was defined in a UN report as:

an operation involving military personnel, but without enforcement powers, undertaken by the United Nations to help maintain or restore international peace and security in areas of conflict. These operations are voluntary and are based on consent and co-operation. While they involve the use of military personnel, they achieve their objectives not by force of arms, thus contrasting them with the 'enforcement action' of the United Nations.[10]

What has emerged over the years, and arguably as a response to what was happening on the ground, is a variety of interpretations of the term.[11] Some scholars, for example, simply accept as 'peacekeeping' whatever the UN Secretary-General or the UN Department of Peacekeeping Operations (DPKO) say is peacekeeping.[12] Others, however, find such an approach problematic

---

[9] Space in the book does not permit an overview of all peacekeeping missions that have been established since the inception of the UN in 1945. Instead, these sections contain an overview of some of the more prominent operations and their contribution to the development of forcible measures by peacekeeping forces.

[10] United Nations, *The Blue Helmets: A Review of United Nations Peacekeeping*, 2nd ed. (UNDPI, 1990), at 4.

[11] James Sloan, *The Militarisation of Peacekeeping in the Twenty-First Century* (Hart Publishing, 2011), at 12.

[12] James Sloan, 'The Use of Offensive Force in UN Peacekeeping: A Cycle of Boom and Bust?' (2007) 30 *Hastings International & Comparative Law Review* 385, at 389.

due to the UN Secretariat and Secretary-General having been somewhat changeable regarding what, in their view, were the essential aspects of peacekeeping and peacekeeping operations.[13] Yet, while peacekeeping is open to a variety of definitions, there is arguably no single one 'correct' definition.[14] This is no doubt due to the fact – as will become clear in the subsequent sections of this chapter – that since 1945, and in particular since the end of the Cold War, UN peacekeeping has gone through considerable changes, which have been reflected in the attempts to define it. Ultimately, each operation can be distinguished by the environment in which it operates, the functions with which it has consequently been mandated and the methods it ultimately utilises to fulfil its mandate.

There are, however, two notable changes to peacekeeping operations, particularly since the end of the Cold War, that will ultimately affect the definition one gives to 'peacekeeping' today. First, while peacekeeping operations initially began as relatively simple unarmed observers of the peace between two parties which formerly had been in a state of armed conflict, today peacekeeping operations are often significantly more complex and multidimensional – including military, political and civilian elements – in order to both facilitate the ending of conflict and create the conditions for a lasting peace.[15] This kind of operation was, for example, established by the UN Security Council and deployed in Kosovo in June 1999 following the bombing campaign by the North Atlantic Treaty Organization (NATO) in the Federal Republic of Yugoslavia,[16] and is reflected in the 2008 United Nations Peacekeeping Operations: Principles and Guidelines, otherwise known as the 'Capstone Doctrine', where 'peacekeeping' was defined as:

[a] technique designed to preserve the peace, however fragile, where fighting has been halted, and to assist in implementing agreements achieved by the peacemakers. Over the years, peacekeeping has evolved from a primarily military model of observing cease-fires and the separation of forces after inter-state wars, to incorporate a complex model of many elements – military, police and civilian – working together to help lay the foundations for sustainable peace.[17]

---

[13] Ibid.
[14] Rosalyn Higgins, *United Nations Peacekeeping 1946–1967: Documents and Commentary*, 4 vols. (Oxford University Press, 1969–81), vol. I, at ix; Sloan, n. 11, at 13.
[15] Muzaffer Ercan Yilmaz, 'UN Peacekeeping in the Post–Cold War Era' (2005) 22 *International Journal on World Peace* 13, at 15.
[16] See, in general, Richard Caplan, 'United Nations Interim Administration Mission in Kosovo (UNMIK)', in Joachim A. Koops, Thierry Tardy, Norrie MacQueen and Paul D. Williams (eds.), *The Oxford Handbook of United Nations Peacekeeping Operations* (Oxford University Press, 2015), 617.
[17] United Nations, United Nations Peacekeeping Operations: Principles and Guidelines (DPKO/DFS, 2008), at 18.

A second aspect of contemporary peacekeeping operations that will influence the way one might define 'peacekeeping' is that they now routinely use force, both reactively in self-defence but also proactively to fulfil their particular mandates.[18] As a consequence, peacekeeping operations have been characterised as being increasingly 'robust'.[19] This chapter will set out the ways in which this has occurred, with reference back to the original principles of peacekeeping, and will, in particular, address the issue of the extent to which they might still be characterised as of a *peacekeeping*, as opposed to of a peace *enforcement*, nature.

## 5.3 THE LEGAL BASIS FOR UN PEACEKEEPING OPERATIONS

Though peacekeeping is not specifically provided for within the UN Charter, the constitutional basis of UN peacekeeping operations may, arguably, be found within the broad provision of Article 1 of the Charter, which includes, as one of the main purposes of the UN, the maintenance of international peace and security and 'to bring about by peaceful means ... adjustment or settlement of international disputes or situations'. Nonetheless, there has been much speculation as to the precise legal basis within the Charter providing for the establishment of UN peacekeeping operations.

As discussed in Chapter 3, the General Assembly has a role in the maintenance of international peace and security,[20] and consensual peacekeeping operations, unlike enforcement measures, can be established by the General Assembly. It has, however, only established such operations on two occasions: the United Nations Emergency Force (UNEF I), which was established in 1956 to secure the withdrawal of troops from Egyptian territory and to serve as a buffer between Egypt and Israel,[21] and the United Nations Security Force (UNSF), which was created in 1962 to maintain peace and security in the territory of West New Guinea (West Irian).[22] However, as all other peacekeeping operations have been established by the Security Council, attention naturally turns to the powers under which the Council acts in doing so.

---

[18] Marrack Goulding, 'The Evolution of United Nations Peacekeeping' (1993) 69 *International Affairs* 451, at 455; Sloan, n. 11, at 15.

[19] Thierry Tardy, 'A Critique of Robust Peacekeeping in Contemporary Peace Operations' (2011) 18 *International Peacekeeping* 152.

[20] See Section 3.4.2.4.

[21] See, in general, Paul F. Diehl, 'First United Nations Emergency Force (UNEF I)', in Joachim A. Koops, Thierry Tardy, Norrie MacQueen and Paul D. Williams (eds.), *The Oxford Handbook of United Nations Peacekeeping Operations* (Oxford University Press, 2015), 144.

[22] See, in general, Norrie MacQueen, 'United Nations Security Force in West New Guinea (UNSF)', in Joachim A. Koops, Thierry Tardy, Norrie MacQueen and Paul D. Williams (eds.), *The Oxford Handbook of United Nations Peacekeeping Operations* (Oxford University Press, 2015), 171.

The UN Security Council's primary responsibility for the maintenance of international peace and security might give rise to the impression that it is the organ within which the legal powers to establish peacekeeping operations reside. The provisions of Chapter VI of the UN Charter, entitled 'The Pacific Settlement of Disputes', make no reference at all for any sort of military operations, although some scholars have adopted the view that traditional peacekeeping missions fall under Chapter VI due to its broad provisions that refer to a solution through 'other peaceful means'.[23] Yet, it is arguable that the framers of the Charter did not intend Chapter VI to provide for either a political, strategic or operational framework for UN military operations but, rather, the pacific measures noted in Chapter VI were envisaged to exist purely within the realms of peaceful or diplomatic means. While international lawyers can argue *ad nauseam* the relative merits of locating peacekeeping operations within this particular chapter of the Charter, from a functional point of view these remain theoretical possibilities because, in practice, there has been no express reference to it in the resolutions establishing peacekeeping operations.[24]

It is Chapter VII of the Charter – in which the Council receives its powers of enforcement in regards to 'Action with Respect to Threats to the Peace, Breaches of the Peace, and Acts of Aggression' – that arguably provides a more appropriate home for peacekeeping operations. Of course, the operations based purely on consent do not need to be underpinned by such powers of enforcement, although in the *Certain Expenses* advisory opinion the International Court of Justice (ICJ) observed that the Security Council has the legal capacity to establish operations that are not necessarily 'enforcement measures' within the domain of Chapter VII of the Charter.[25] However, as noted in Section 5.1 and as set out further in this chapter, a trend has emerged in UN peacekeeping practice whereby the line between peacekeeping and enforcement has blurred.[26] As James Sloan observes, '[peacekeeping missions have become progressively more forceful, more proactive and, in some cases, have been authorised to use "all necessary means" to achieve their objectives'.[27] As such, Chapter VII is now usually considered the general legal basis for UN peacekeeping operations, even though they are not Chapter VII enforcement measures *per se* and the precise source of the legality within

---

[23] See Bruno Simma, Hermann Mosler, Albrecht Randelzhofer, Christian Tomuschat, Ridiger Wolfrum, Andreas Paulus and Eleni Chaitobu (eds.), *The Charter of the United Nations: A Commentary*, 2nd ed. (Oxford University Press, 2002), 648.
[24] Christine Gray, *International Law and the Use of Force*, 4th ed. (Oxford University Press, 2018), at 270.
[25] *Certain Expenses of the United Nations (Article 17, paragraph 2, of the Charter)*, Advisory Opinion (1962) ICJ Reports 151, at 167.
[26] Sloan, n. 12, at 385.  [27] Ibid., at 385–6.

Chapter VII has not been agreed upon.[28] Indeed, 'to date, the Security Council has never indicated which article of Chapter VII it relies on in adopting peacekeeping resolutions, leading to an abundance of scholarly hypothesis but little legal certainty.'[29]

Ultimately, in fulfilling its primary responsibility for the maintenance of international peace and security, the Council may adopt a range of measures, including the establishment of a UN peacekeeping operation. Indeed, UN Secretary-General Dag Hammarskjöld famously observed that the legal basis for UN peacekeeping may be found at 'Chapter VI and a Half' of the UN Charter[30] while, in 1990, the UN itself stated that peacekeeping operations 'fall short of the provisions of Chapter VII [but] at the same time go beyond purely diplomatic means or those described in Chapter VI'.[31] However, the debate regarding the constitutional basis of peacekeeping operations seems to be without practical significance as the institution has evolved through the practice of the UN without its legality having been the subject of significant or sustained challenge by either states or scholars.[32]

### 5.4 THE BASIC PRINCIPLES OF UN PEACEKEEPING

While the practice of UN peacekeeping has evolved significantly since the inception of the UN in 1945, there are three basic principles of peacekeeping – often referred to as the 'trinity'[33] – which are interlinked and mutually reinforcing.[34] These principles – consent of the parties, impartiality and non-use of force except in self-defence – were initially articulated by former UN Secretary-General Hammarskjöld at the time of the first peacekeeping operation in 1956 (UNEF I), but continue to be relied upon in setting UN peacekeeping operations apart – primarily from peace enforcement – as a tool for maintaining international peace and security. Indeed, these principles have been constantly reaffirmed and are now contained within

---

[28] Katherine E. Cox, 'Beyond Self-Defense: United Nations Peacekeeping Operations & the Use of Force' (1998–9) 27 *Denver Journal of International Law & Policy* 239, at 248–9.
[29] Patryk I. Labuda, 'UN Peacekeeping as Intervention by Invitation: Host State Consent and the Use of Force in Security Council-Mandated Stabilisation Operations' (2020) 7 *Journal on the Use of Force and International Law* 317, at 333. See further, Russell Buchan and Nicholas Tsagourias, *Regulating the Use of Force in International Law: Stability and Change* (Hart, 2021), at 196–9.
[30] Sloan, n. 12, at 385. [31] The Blue Helmets, n. 10, at 5. [32] Gray, n. 24, at 339.
[33] White, n. 1, 574.
[34] Trevor Findlay, 'The Use of Force by Peacekeepers beyond Self-Defence: Some Politico-Legal Implications' in Alex Morrison, Douglas A. Fraser and James D. Kiras (eds.), *Peacekeeping with Muscle: The Use of Force in International Conflict Resolution* (Canadian Peacekeeping Press, 1997), 51, at 52–3.

numerous documents,[35] as well as Status of Force Agreements and rules of engagement.[36]

### 5.4.1 Consent of the Parties

The primary principle in distinguishing peacekeeping operations from peace enforcement is that they are deployed with the consent of the main parties to the conflict,[37] in particular the host state. Under Article 2(7) of the UN Charter the Security Council is prohibited from intervening 'in matters which are essentially within the domestic jurisdiction of any state'. This shall not, however, 'prejudice the application of enforcement measures under Chapter VII' of the Charter where a threat to the peace has been identified or, alternatively, in situations where prior consent has been provided. Therefore, in the absence of the consent of the parties involved, whether absent initially or after having subsequently been withdrawn, any peace operation must be deployed with a Chapter VII enforcement mandate, thereby blurring the lines between peacekeeping and peace enforcement. Given its lack of enforcement powers, consent would be necessary for all peacekeeping operations established by the General Assembly. In addition, whereas consent is, formally speaking, only required of the state(s) upon whose territory the peacekeeping operation is situated, in the absence of consent from all parties involved – whether the government of a state or non-state actors – the operation risks becoming a party to the conflict and moving away from its founding purpose of keeping the peace.[38] In doing so it also risks infringing the second of the basic principles: impartiality.

### 5.4.2 Impartiality

The principle of impartiality requires that a peacekeeping operation 'must not be used either to protect certain positions of one of the parties or to oblige one

---

[35] See, for example, An Agenda for Peace: Preventive Diplomacy, Peacemaking and Peacekeeping, UN Doc. A/47/277-S/24111, 17 June 1992, at paras. 11–12; Supplement to an Agenda for Peace, UN Doc. A/50/60-S/1995/1, 1 January 1995, at para. 33; Report of the Panel on United Nations Peace Operations of 21 August 2000 (Brahimi Report), UN Doc. A/55/305-S/2000/809, 21 August 2001, at para. 48; United Nations Peacekeeping Operations, n. 17, chapter 3; Report of the Independent High-Level Panel on Peace Operations, Uniting our Strengths for Peace: Politics, Partnership and People, UN Doc. A/70/95-S/2015/446, 17 June 2015, at paras. 121–6; Report of the Special Committee on Peacekeeping Operations, UN Doc. A/71/19, 20 March 2017, at para. 28.

[36] Rules of engagement originate in many ways from the 'fighting instructions' of the eighteenth and nineteenth centuries. The rules specify the circumstances in which armed force may be used by a military unit and its authorised extent and degree. See Hilaire McCoubrey and Nigel D. White, *The Blue Helmets: Legal Regulation of United Nations Military Operations* (Dartmouth Publishing, 1996), at 146.

[37] United Nations Peacekeeping Operations, n. 17, at 31.   [38] Ibid., at 32.

party to accept a certain political result or to influence the political balance'.[39] The purpose of the principle of impartiality is in this sense to ensure that UN peacekeepers implement their mandate without favour towards, or prejudice against, any of the parties involved. Furthermore, adhering to the principle of impartiality might also be seen as important in maintaining the consent and cooperation of all parties concerned and, in this sense, any peacekeeping operation must be cautious so as to avoid engaging in activities that might compromise its *image* of impartiality. Indeed, the use of offensive forcible measures against one of the parties not only raises questions regarding the truly consensual nature of the operation but also jeopardises the impartiality of the operation as it appears to infringe the third of the 'trinity' of peacekeeping principles: the non-use of force except in self-defence.

### 5.4.3 Non-use of Force Except in Self-Defence

The basic principles provide for the non-use of force, *except in self-defence*.[40] But what type of self-defence does this refer to? For example, does it refer to individual self-defence in a domestic criminal law sense, 'unit' self-defence of the peacekeepers or the international right of self-defence, as per Article 51 of the UN Charter and as found in customary international law?[41] This is not clear from either the practice of the UN, contributing states or the documents that have sought to set out and develop peacekeeping doctrine and it is not normally spelt out in the mandates provided to peacekeeping operations, although the Capstone Doctrine stated that it should be.[42] Indeed, on the occasions when self-defence has been expressly stated, for example in Resolution 467 (1980) in the context of the United Nations Interim Force in Lebanon (UNFIL) mission or Resolution 918 (1994) in the context of the United Nations Assistance Mission for Rwanda (UNAMIR), there is merely the recognition of the right of self-defence as opposed to any attempt at establishing what kind of right is being recognised.[43]

---

[39] Marianne von Grunigen, 'Neutrality and Peacekeeping', in Antonio Cassese (ed.), *United Nations Peacekeeping: Legal Essays* (Sijthoff & Noordhoff, 1978), at 137–8.
[40] United Nations Peacekeeping Operations, n. 17, at 34.
[41] See Section 6.2.2 for more on the distinction between 'unit' self-defence and the national right of self-defence in international law.
[42] United Nations Peacekeeping Operations, n. 17, at 34.
[43] UNSC Res. 467 (1980), preamble, notes that the Force 'will not use force except in self-defence' and that self-defence 'includes resistance to attempts by forceful means to prevent it from discharging its duties under the mandate of the Security Council'; UNSC Res. 918 (1994), para. 4, '[r]ecognizes that UNAMIR may be required to take action in self-defence against persons or groups who threaten protected sites and populations, United Nations and other humanitarian personnel or the means of delivery and distribution of humanitarian relief'.

In locating the basis and nature of the right of self-defence, Trevor Findlay looks towards the right of self-defence of both the individual peacekeeper *and* the troop-contributing state.[44] On the one hand, the notion of an individual UN peacekeeper defending themself upon being attacked would appear uncontroversial, and even the observer units of the early peacekeeping missions were armed with light weaponry to enable them to do just that. On the other hand, however, the soldiers are provided by individual states all of which in principle possess a right of self-defence should their troops be attacked.[45] Yet, and as Scott Sheeran notes, such a dualistic interpretation is potentially problematic, in particular when considering both 'the hierarchy of international law and national law and consistency among different national laws of the contributing peacekeeping forces'.[46]

Adding to this debate, the UN's Office of Legal Affairs stated in 1993 that the international right of self-defence is not 'limited to States and applies as an inherent right also to the United Nations'.[47] However, as Nigel White notes, '[t]here is potentially a vast difference between recognising that peacekeepers have the right to personal self-defence and equating the UN's right to self-defence with states under Article 51'.[48] While, given the UN's international personality, an argument that it possesses a right of self-defence can be supported, 'this does not mean that it necessarily has the same rights and duties as those of a state when defending its territorial integrity and political independence, existential elements the UN manifestly does not have'.[49] White does, nonetheless, concede that 'if the UN deploys forces around the world then such an international actor should have the right to defend its functionality as a security organisation as well as defend the components of the peace operation',[50] although in practice this perhaps provides the organisation with a potentially very broad right of self-defence which is much broader in scope than that provided to its member states.

Regardless of which of the actors involved within a peacekeeping operation the right of self-defence is bestowed upon, it has traditionally been interpreted narrowly, so as to encompass a peacekeeper using force in defence of her their life, their 'comrades and any person entrusted in [their] care, as well as defending [their] post, convoy, vehicle or rifle'.[51] Furthermore, '[c]ommentators and scholars have tended not to go beyond general descriptions of the scope of self-defence, including that it should be exercised as a matter

---

[44] Trevor Findlay, *The Use of Force in UN Peace Operations* (Oxford University Press, 2002), at 237.
[45] Although the protection of a states' nationals falls within its right of self-defence this may be subject to certain qualifications. For more on this see Section 6.4.
[46] See Sheeran, n. 2, at 362.   [47] *United Nations Juridical Yearbook* (1993), at 371–2.
[48] White, n. 1, at 589.   [49] Ibid.   [50] Ibid.
[51] General Guidelines for Peace-keeping Operations, UN Doc. UN/210/TC/CG95 (1995).

of last resort and must conform to rules on self-defence under international law (which stipulate that it can only be exercised in a manner proportionate to the existing threat)'.[52] However, when one examines the operations, which the remainder of this chapter seeks to do, it becomes clear that there has been something of a 'quiet revolution' in regard to self-defence within UN peacekeeping operations,[53] so that '[w]hat the concept has evolved to mean today bears little resemblance to the common or legal understanding of self-defence, including in Article 51, or national criminal law'.[54]

## 5.5 PEACEKEEPING OPERATIONS: 1945–89

Recognising the importance of peacekeeping operations in realising some minimum level of peace and security,[55] the UN early on turned to deploying basic peacekeeping forces in Kashmir, Yemen and Palestine in the late 1940s. These were generally unarmed observer forces mandated simply to provide the UN with a reliable account of the facts on the ground in these troubled areas. In this sense they did not engage in using forcible measures in any way, although the peacekeepers arguably had the right to engage in self-defence if attacked. However, things began to change from the 1950s when events on the ground gave rise to a necessity for peacekeeping forces to resort to such measures and which also gave rise to the crystallisation of the 'trinity' of basic principles of peacekeeping discussed in Section 5.4.

### 5.5.1 UNEF I (1956–67)

What has become recognised as the first peacekeeping operation was established by the United Nations General Assembly in 1956.[56] Moving on from simple observation, the United Nations Emergency Force (UNEF I) was deployed to secure the peace by acting as a buffer between Israel and hostile nations in an attempt to diffuse the Suez crisis following the French, British and Israeli intervention in Suez in 1956.[57] At the time, peacekeeping 'represented a functional adjustment by the organization to an international political system shaped by deep-seated rivalry and overshadowed by the threat of wider war'.[58] Reflective of this, and in the light of French and British vetoes cast within the Security Council in order to protect their involvement with Israel to secure the Suez Canal from Egypt, UNEF I was established by the UN

---

[52] Sheeran, n. 2, at 364. See Chapter 6 on self-defence.   [53] Ibid., at 363.   [54] Ibid., at 365.
[55] White, n. 1, at 573.   [56] UNGA Res. 1001 (ES-I) (1956).   [57] Diehl, n. 21.
[58] Mats Berdal, 'The Security Council and Peacekeeping' in Vaughan Lowe, Adam Roberts, Jennifer Welsh and Dominik Zaum (eds.), *The United Nations Security Council and War* (Oxford University Press, 2008), 175, at 180.

General Assembly under the Uniting for Peace resolution.[59] In the space of just a few days, the General Assembly had called for a ceasefire and for the Secretary-General to establish the emergency force to secure the ceasefire and to supervise the withdrawal of Israeli, French and British forces from Egyptian territory.[60] Despite the objections of certain parties, '[t]his mission of lightly armed UN peacekeepers was successfully deployed with the consent of all the states engaged to supervise the peace and withdrawal of foreign forces and act as a buffer'.[61] Indeed, UNEF was described as 'acting like a plate-glass window' and as a 'lightly armed barrier that all see and tend to respect'.[62] Following Egypt's withdrawal of its consent for it to continue the force was withdrawn in 1967, preceding the Six Day War.[63]

The significance of this particular peacekeeping operation, however, was that the trinity of peacekeeping principles – consent, impartiality and the non-use of force except in self-defence – were set out by UN Secretary-General Dag Hammarskjöld in his final report on UNEF I in 1958.[64] In particular, and in relation to the last of these, in his report Secretary-General Hammarskjöld stated that:

The rule is applied that men engaged in the operation may never take the initiative in the use of armed force, but are entitled to respond with force to an attack with arms, including attempts to use force to make them withdraw from positions which they occupy under orders from the Commander, acting under the authority of the Assembly and within the scope of its resolutions. The basic element involved is clearly the prohibition against any initiative in the use of armed force.[65]

This essentially recognised both the inherent right of a soldier to defend themselves as an individual against attack, but also the right of the mission to defend itself against any attack 'and was a practical precondition for deployment of military forces'.[66] However, while force was prohibited unless in self-defence, Hammarskjöld perceptively warned that 'a wide interpretation of the right of self-defence might well blur the distinction between [peacekeeping] operations ... and combat operations, which would require a decision under Chapter VII of the Charter'.[67]

Although the rationale for this novel development of UN peacekeeping was not fully considered at the time, it seems clear that '[t]he use of force in simple

---

[59] See the discussion of the Uniting for Peace procedure in Section 3.4.2.4.  [60] Ibid.
[61] Sheeran, n. 2, at 351.
[62] Finn Seyersted, *United Nations Forces in the Law of Peace and War* (Sijthoff, 1966), at 48.
[63] See, in general, Michael B. Oren, *Six Days of War: June 1967 and the Making of the Modern Middle East* (Countrysport Press, 2003).
[64] UN Secretary-General, Summary Study of the Experience Derived from the Establishment and Operation of the Force, UN Doc. A/3943, 9 October 1958, at para. 127.
[65] Ibid., at para. 179.   [66] Sheeran, n. 2, at 351.
[67] UN Secretary-General, n. 64, at paras. 178–9.

self-defence was a natural corollary of a purely consent-based and impartial mission for the maintenance of international peace and security, in which the main tasks were monitoring and observation of peace agreements and cease-fires'.[68] As such, '[t]he use of force in peacekeeping was initially very limited and missions focused on self-defence'.[69]

### 5.5.2 ONUC (1960–4)

It did not take long, however, for these seemingly benign and straightforward principles to be shaken up, with the establishment and deployment of the United Nations Operation in the Congo (ONUC) in 1960.[70] This operation, which was established by the Security Council at the request of the Congo,[71] initially supervised the withdrawal of Belgian colonial forces. While ONUC originally possessed a mandate similar in nature to UNEF I, and based upon the basic principles of peacekeeping, it was the conditions on the ground, including the refusal of Belgium to withdraw from the province of Katanga, that led the Security Council to declare that ONUC would enter Katanga but would 'not be a party to or in any way influence the outcome of any internal conflict'.[72] However:

[c]learly ONUC was fighting on the side of the government so not falling fully on the Chapter VII enforcement side of the line where coercive action is taken against a government, but was clearly not a classical peacekeeping force either. Such interventions are more akin to intervention at the request of the government, when outside states send forces to prop up a beleaguered government.[73]

A worsening of conditions, however, meant that in February 1961 the Security Council widened ONUC's mandate considerably to 'take immediately all appropriate measures to prevent the occurrence of civil war in the Congo, including arrangement for cease-fires, the halting of all military operations, the prevention of clashes and the use of force, if necessary in the last resort'.[74]

The move from supervising the withdrawal of troops to being asked to proactively prevent a civil war was stark and established, as White describes, '[t]he dialectic between consensual peacekeeping and its more belligerent variant'.[75] However, just seven days later in November 1961 the Security Council again strengthened the mandate of this 'peacekeeping' operation 'to include maintaining the integrity of the Congo, to assist the central

---

[68] Sheeran, n. 2, at 351.  [69] Ibid., at 350.
[70] See Jane Boulden, 'United Nations Operation in the Congo (ONUC)', in Joachim A. Koops, Thierry Tardy, Norrie MacQueen and Paul D. Williams (eds.), *The Oxford Handbook of United Nations Peacekeeping Operations* (Oxford University Press, 2015), 160; Sloan, n. 11, at 128–42.
[71] UNSC Res. 143 (1960).  [72] UNSC Res. 146 (1960), para. 4.  [73] White, n. 1, at 579–80.
[74] UNSC Res. 161 (1961), para. 1.  [75] White, n. 1, at 574.

government to restore order, to prevent the occurrence of a civil war, and to secure the withdrawal of foreign forces and mercenaries'.[76] Furthermore, it authorised the operation to 'take vigorous action, including the use of the requisite measure of force, if necessary, for the immediate apprehension, detention, pending legal action and/or deportation of all foreign military and paramilitary personnel and political advisers not under United Nations Command, and mercenaries'.[77] It is apparent that 'at the outset of the operation, the [Secretary-General] clearly viewed ONUC's right to use force as being the same as UNEF's, that is, being based on self-defence'.[78] However, it was also clear that '[w]hile the UN maintained, throughout the operation and escalating conflict, that force was being used only in self-defence, or "active" self-defence, ONUC's actions in practice became indistinguishable from a war-fighting role and standard military campaign'.[79] The robust mandate of ONUC, which also included civilian protection,[80] and how it was being implemented 'went well beyond the "basic principles" of UN peacekeeping from UNEF I'.[81] The operation was withdrawn in 1964.

### 5.5.3 Other Notable Cold War Peacekeeping Operations

Although '[f]or the rest of the Cold War, the UN peacekeeping operations were traditional and did not significantly engage the requirement for use of force beyond simple self-defence',[82] the UN principle of non-use of force except in self-defence was widened beyond individual and mission defence to also expressly incorporate defence of the mandate. This extension could be witnessed in the mandates of several Cold War operations. For example, with the establishment of the United Nations Peacekeeping Force in Cyprus (UNFICYP) in 1964, the UN Secretary-General stated that the UN peacekeepers in Cyprus could use force in self-defence either where 'specific arrangements accepted by both communities [ie the parties] have been or ... are about to be violated, thus risking a recurrence of fighting or endangering law and order' or where there were 'attempts by force to prevent them from carrying out their responsibilities as ordered by their commanders'.[83]

---

[76] Ibid., at 579. See UNSC Res. 169 (1961).   [77] UNSC Res. 169 (1961), para. 4.
[78] White, n. 1, at 588.
[79] Sheeran, n. 2, at 352. This gave rise to the *Certain Expenses* advisory opinion of the ICJ.
[80] For more on this see Section 5.7.1.
[81] Sheeran, n. 2, at 352. See also Derek W. Bowett, *United Nations Forces: A Legal Study of United Nations Practice* (Stevens & Sons, 1964), at 213; Sloan, n. 11, at 131.
[82] Sheeran, n. 2, at 353.
[83] UN Secretary-General, Aide Memoire of the Secretary-General Concerning Some Questions Relating to the Function and Operation of the United Nations Peacekeeping Force in Cyprus, UN Doc. S/5653, 10 April 1964, at paras. 17(c)–18(c). See Jan Asmussen, 'United Nations Peacekeeping Force in Cyprus', in Joachim A. Koops, Thierry Tardy, Norrie MacQueen and

The broadened concept of self-defence was also present in UNEF II, which was established in 1973.[84] As part of UN Secretary-General Kurt Waldheim's proposals for this force, which were accepted by the Security Council, it was stated that while the Force 'shall not use force except in self-defence' this would 'include resistance to attempts by forceful means to prevent it from discharging its duties under the mandate of the Security Council'.[85] The Secretary-General made exactly the same proposal in regard to the use of force in self-defence by the United Nations Interim Force in Lebanon (UNIFIL),[86] which was established in 1978,[87] a proposal which was again approved by the Security Council.[88]

## 5.6 PEACEKEEPING OPERATIONS: 1990–2022

At the end of the Cold War the number of UN peacekeeping operations rapidly expanded. Between 1988 and 1993 more operations were established than during the previous forty years.[89] However, it was not just the number of operations that expanded, but also the situations in which they were requested to use force beyond simple personal and mission self-defence, in particular to proactively defend the mandate of the operation, to protect civilians and to assist governmental forces in the stabilisation of a situation within a state. The UN Security Council has also begun to regularly provide peacekeeping operations with authorisation to use 'all necessary means',[90] thus raising questions as to how far they have strayed into the realms of peace enforcement. Indeed, given these developments it might reasonably be said that in the post–Cold War era the principles of peacekeeping have been 'strained to breaking point'.[91]

---

Paul D. Williams (eds.), *The Oxford Handbook of United Nations Peacekeeping Operations* (Oxford University Press, 2015), 197.

[84] UNSC Res. 340 (1973). See Paul F. Diehl, 'Second United Nations Emergency Force (UNEF II)', in Joachim A. Koops, Thierry Tardy, Norrie MacQueen and Paul D. Williams (eds.), *The Oxford Handbook of United Nations Peacekeeping Operations* (Oxford University Press, 2015), 229.

[85] UN Secretary-General, Report of the Secretary-General on the Implementation of Security Council Resolution 340, UN Doc. S/11052/Rev.1, 27 October 1973, at para. 4(d).

[86] UN Secretary-General, Report of the Secretary-General on the Implementation of Security Council Resolution 425, UN Doc. S/12611, 19 March 1978, at para. 4(d).

[87] UNSC Res. 425 (1978). See Alexandra Novosseloff, 'United Nations Interim Force in Lebanon (UNIFIL I)', in Joachim A. Koops, Thierry Tardy, Norrie MacQueen and Paul D. Williams (eds.), *The Oxford Handbook of United Nations Peacekeeping Operations* (Oxford University Press, 2015), 248.

[88] UNSC Res. 426 (1978).    [89] Sheeran, n. 2, at 353.

[90] See Section 3.4.2 for more on the significance of this phrase within resolutions of the UN Security Council.

[91] Shashi Tharoor, 'The Changing Face of Peace-Keeping and Peace-Enforcement' (1995) 19 *Fordham International Law Journal* 408, at 426.

## 5.6.1 UNPROFOR (1992-5)

The use of force in self-defence was a prominent feature of the United Nations Protection Force (UNPROFOR), which was a peacekeeping operation positioned within the former Yugoslavia between 1992 and 1995 'to create the conditions of peace and security required for the negotiation of an overall settlement of the Yugoslav crisis',[92] which had erupted following declarations of independence by Slovenia and Croatia from the Socialist Federal Republic of Yugoslavia in 1991. While, as this mandate suggests, there was not really a peace to keep at the time of the deployment of UNPROFOR, the Secretary-General was strongly of the view that the 'normal rules in United Nations peace-keeping operations for the bearing and use of arms' should apply.[93] As such, in September 1992 the Security Council authorised the operation, in a non-Chapter VII resolution, to use force in self-defence, including where armed persons attempted by force to prevent it from carrying out its mandate, including the delivery of humanitarian aid.[94] However, while the first sixteen Security Council resolutions on UNPROFOR made no reference to Chapter VII, in the face of Bosnian Serb intransigence and increasing violence in 1992-3, the UN Security Council began to invoke Chapter VII in its instructions to UNPROFOR, for example in Resolution 807 (1993) in which the Council called for the 'unimpeded freedom of movement' of UNPROFOR in order for it to carry out its mandate and functions.[95]

Although the Bosnian government agreed to the presence of UNPROFOR in Bosnia in 1992, the Bosnian Serbs did not, which led to problems in the delivery of humanitarian aid and in the protection of the safe areas. In the light of this, the mandate of UNPROFOR was stepped up in UN Security Council Resolution 836 (1993), which was again a Chapter VII resolution, to include an authorisation to take:

necessary measures, including the use of force, in reply to bombardments against the safe areas by any of the parties or to armed incursion into them or in the event of any deliberate obstruction in and around those areas to the freedom of movement of UNPROFOR or of protected humanitarian convoys.[96]

---

[92] UNSC Res. 743 (1992), para. 5.
[93] UN Secretary-General, Further Report of the Secretary-General Pursuant to Security Council Resolution 721 (1991), UN Doc. S/23592, 15 February 1992, at 6.
[94] UNSC Res. 776 (1992), para. 2 (approving a report of the UN Secretary-General which included this proposal).
[95] UNSC Res. 807 (1993), para. 4.
[96] UNSC Res. 836 (1993), para. 5. NATO, which was operating in the air above Bosnia and Herzegovina, had received a mandate to take 'all necessary measures in the airspace of the Republic of Bosnia and Herzegovina ... to ensure compliance with the ban on flights' in UNSC Res. 816 (1993), para. 4.

With the adoption of this resolution 'the nature of the mission had become more militarised than any previous peacekeeping mission since ONUC'.[97] However, despite what seemed like a Chapter VII authorisation, UNPROFOR was to implement its mandate through the use of force 'in self-defence'.[98] The failure of UNPROFOR to implement the mandate properly and to protect the Security Council-designated Muslim safe areas in Bosnia led to the massacre of approximately 8,000 unarmed men and boys by the Bosnian Serbs in Srebrenica in July 1995.[99] This then led to the deployment of a more coercive Security Council-mandated Rapid Reaction Force to enable it to implement its mandate.[100] NATO, which was operating militarily in the skies above Bosnia and Herzegovina and concurrently with UNPROFOR on the ground, and was acting under the authority of the UN Security Council, carried out bombardments of Bosnian Serb positions.[101] Other peacekeeping operations were subsequently established for various former Yugoslav states and, after the Dayton Peace Agreement had come into effect in Bosnia and Herzegovina in late 1995, UNPROFOR ceased to exist.[102]

### 5.6.2 UNOSOM II (1993–5) and AMISON (2007–)

The United Nations Operation in Somalia (UNOSOM II), which followed on from the largely unsuccessful UNISOM I and Unified Task Force (UNITAF) operations, was deployed in Somalia between 1993 and 1995 with the continued aim of creating a secure environment for humanitarian operations to be carried out.[103] While self-defence was the primary focus of the forcible measures in the mandate of UNPROFOR, the Secretary-General was clear that UNOSOM II 'will not be able to implement [its] mandate unless it is endowed with *enforcement* powers under Chapter VII of the Charter'.[104] Self-defence was not mentioned at any time in regards to its mandate, which included preventing 'any resumption of violence and, if necessary [taking] appropriate action against any faction' violating the ceasefire, securing the disarmament

---

[97] Sloan, n. 11, at 144.
[98] UNSC Res. 836 (1993), para. 9. Sheeran notes that this was based upon an 'ambitious and strained interpretation' of self-defence. Sheeran, n. 2, at 353.
[99] UN Secretary-General, Report of the Secretary-General pursuant to General Assembly Resolution 53/35: The Fall of Srebrenica, UN Doc. A/54/549, 15 November 1999.
[100] UNSC Res. 998 (1995), para. 9.
[101] See Tarcisio Gazzini, 'NATO Coercive Military Activities in the Yugoslav Crisis (1992–1999)' (2001) 12 *European Journal of International Law* 391, at 403.
[102] See 'General Framework Agreement for Peace in Bosnia and Herzegovina', (1996) 35 *International Legal Materials* 89.
[103] UNSC Res. 814 (1993).
[104] UN Secretary-General, Further Report of the Secretary-General Submitted in Pursuance of Paragraphs 18 and 19 of Resolution 794 (1992), UN Doc. S/25354, 3 March 1993, at para. 58 (emphasis added).

of the factions, and taking 'such forceful action as may be required to neutralize armed elements that attack or threaten to attack' UN personnel or property or that of other agencies and organisations.[105]

Following an ambush in June 1993 that resulted in the deaths of twenty-four Pakistani peacekeepers and which left fifty-seven wounded, the Security Council authorised UNOSOM II under Chapter VII to take 'all necessary measures against those responsible', including 'their arrest and detention for prosecution, trial and punishment'.[106] This move, which replicated in many ways the mandate given to ONUC,[107] led to a serious escalation in the conflict, including the number of casualties, a state of affairs that led Lieutenant General Michael Rose, the Force Commander in UNPROFOR, to speak of crossing the 'Mogadishu line'.[108] In other words, the forcible measures that an operation was engaging in had shifted from peacekeeping to those resembling peace enforcement.[109] In the context of the measures undertaken by UNOSOM II, this included the use of substantial military force in attempting to capture or kill General Aideed, the leader of one of the main factions in the civil war.[110]

With the United States no longer willing to participate following an incident in October 1993 which led to the deaths of eighteen US soldiers, UNOSOM II was gradually disbanded and had been completely withdrawn by the end of March 1995 before completing its mission.[111]

Since 2007, the Security Council has authorised a joint African Union (AU)/UN force in Somalia (AMISOM).[112] While designated as a regional peacekeeping force to support transitional governmental structures and to assist in creating a secure environment for the delivery of humanitarian aid, it has actively fought alongside the Somali National Army against factions opposing the transitional federal government, including al-Shabab, although it continues to struggle to fulfil its mandate. However, in March 2022 the Security Council, while '[r]*ecognising* that the security situation in Somalia ha[d] changed significantly since AMISOM was first authorised, and not[ed]

---

[105] UNSC Res. 814 (1993), paras. 5 and 57.   [106] UNSC Res. 837 (1993), paras. 5 and 33.
[107] See Section 5.5.2.
[108] 'The Crossing of the Mogadishu Line', *The Economist*, 13 January 1996.
[109] Sheeran, n. 2, at 354.   [110] Findlay, n. 44, at 192.
[111] The problems with UNOSOM II, especially the blurred line between peacekeeping and peace enforcement, ultimately led to the hesitancy that occurred in regards to offering protection in Rwanda preceding the genocide that took place. A UN peacekeeping force (UNAMIR) proved unsuitable and incapable of preventing a genocide which consumed the lives of over 800,000 people, mainly Tutsis. See Report of the Independent Inquiry into the Actions of the United Nations during the 1994 Genocide in Rwanda, UN Doc. S/1999/1257, 16 December 1999. Subsequently, in 1994 the UN Security Council authorised a French force to intervene in Rwanda under Chapter VII but, in doing so, stressed its humanitarian purposes be conducted in an 'impartial and neutral fashion'. UNSC Res. 929 (1994), preamble and paras. 2 and 3.
[112] UNSC Res. 1744 (2007), para. 4.

improvements in Somalia's capacity and capability to respond to security challenges',[113] also endorsed the AU's decision to reconfigure AMISON into the African Union Transition Mission in Somalia (ATMIS)[114] and authorized it for an initial period of twelve months to use all necessary means to undertake a number of stabilisation objectives in coordination with the Somali authorities,[115] such as 'jointly planned and targeted operations with Somali security forces to degrade Al-Shabaab and affiliates linked to ISIL'.[116]

### 5.6.3 UNAMSIL (1999-2005)

A coup in Sierra Leone in 1997 led to widespread unrest and the establishment of the United Nations Observer Mission in Sierra Leone (UNOMSIL) which was to work alongside the Military Observer Group which had been established under the wings of the Economic Community of West African States (ECOWAS).[117] However, following violence against the operations by rebels and an unstable security situation, UNOMSIL was replaced by a more robust operation in the form of the United Nations Mission in Sierra Leone (UNAMSIL) in October 1999.[118]

It was in connection with UNAMSIL's operations that 'protection of civilians' mandates under Chapter VII began to emerge. Indeed, UNAMSIL was the first operation to be given a 'protection of civilians' mandate in which peacekeepers were authorised under Chapter VII to take the necessary action to protect 'civilians under imminent threat of physical violence', in addition to 'ensur[ing] the security and freedom of movement of its personnel'.[119] This has now become virtually a standard mandate under Chapter VII for UN peacekeepers to use force and, in 2009, the General Assembly endorsed the 'protection of civilians' concept in its annual peacekeeping resolution.[120]

During the following years the operation expanded both in terms of the number of troops, reaching 17,500 in March 2001, and the breadth and forcefulness of its mandate.[121] These changes were a response not only to events on the ground, including attacks against UNAMSIL, but also both the withdrawal of the ECOWAS Monitoring Group (ECOMOG) forces and the deployment of a separate UK force, which was deployed ostensibly to allow for the safe evacuation of British nationals but which actually assisted

---

[113] UNSC Res. 2628 (2022), at preamble.  [114] Ibid., at para. 22.  [115] Ibid., at para. 23.
[116] Ibid., at para. 23(1).
[117] UNSC Res. 1181 (1998). This was an observer mission with the function of monitoring the security situation and respect for international humanitarian law.
[118] UNSC Res. 1270 (1999).
[119] UNSC Res. 1270 (1999), para. 14. The situation in Sierra Leone was also determined as constituting 'a threat to international peace and security in the region'. Ibid., para. 9.
[120] UNGA Res. 63/280 (2009), para. 2.
[121] See UNSC Resolutions 1289 (2000), 1299 (2000), 1313 (2000) and 1346 (2001).

UNAMSIL in fulfilling its mandate and stabilising the situation on the ground.[122] Indeed, the UK's intervention 'gave UNAMSIL breathing space to regroup, recover credibility and reassert its presence'[123] and permitted it to engage in 'robust' military operations.[124] Following elections in May 2002, and with a general improvement in the situation on the ground, the operation was fully withdrawn by December 2005.

### 5.6.4 UNAMID (2007–21)

Most of the operations in the post-Cold War era have been in situations involving a state and a non-state group. All of these operations were deployed with the consent of the government and where forcible action has been taken this has normally been against the non-state actors involved. However, a joint AU/UN force (UNAMID) was established in Darfur in July 2007, taking over from an AU-led force (AMIS), in the face of a humanitarian crisis and crimes against humanity being committed by government-backed militia.[125]

A previous proposal to modify and broaden the mandate of the existing United Nations Mission in Sudan (UNMIS) to cover the situation in Darfur did not receive the consent of the government of Sudan, something that was of importance to many states within the UN Security Council,[126] and so was never deployed.[127] It was, as such, only with the consent of the government that UNAMID was able to deploy, despite being authorised to 'take the necessary action, in the areas of deployment of its forces and as it deems within its capabilities' in order to protect civilians 'without prejudice to the responsibility of the Government of Sudan'.[128] However, UNAMID immediately found it difficult to implement its mandate and was subject to several attacks, meaning that 'almost from the start, [it] was criticised for not meeting its civilian protection mandate',[129] including by the Security Council itself.[130] On 22 December 2020, the UN Security Council unanimously adopted

---

[122] Sloan, n. 11, at 170.
[123] United Nations Best Practices Unit (DPKO), Lessons Learned from the United Nations Peacekeeping Experiences in Sierra Leone, September 2003, at 13.
[124] Fifth Report of the Secretary-General on the United Nations Mission in Sierra Leone, UN Doc. S/2000/751, 31 July 2000, at para. 26.
[125] UNSC Res. 1679 (2006), paras. 3 and 5.  [126] See UN Doc. S/PV.5519, 31 August 2006.
[127] UNSC Res. 1706 (2006), para. 1.
[128] UNSC Res. 1769 (2007), para. 15(a). The operation had only 7,000 troops by January 2008, far short of the 26,000 required, although expanded to 15,000 by the end of 2008 and to 18,000 by 2011.
[129] Sloan, n. 11, at 270. See Darfur Consortium, 'Putting People First: The Protection Challenge Facing UNAMID in Darfur', 28 July 2008, available at: https://archive.globalpolicy.org/images/pdfs/0728unamid.pdf.
[130] See UNSC Res. 1935 (2010), para. 1.

Resolution 2559 (2020) to end the UNAMID mandate on 31 December 2020, with full withdrawal completed on 30 June 2021.[131]

### 5.6.5 MONUC (2000–10) and MONUSCO (2010–)

Conflict in the Democratic Republic of Congo (DRC) arose following the overthrow of the government by Laurent Kabila in May 1997, who was supported by forces from Uganda and Rwanda. However, these two states subsequently turned against Kabila, and forces were later sent from Zimbabwe, Namibia and Angola at his request. The states involved then subsequently signed the Lusaka Ceasefire Agreement in 1999[132] and the United Nations Observer Mission in the DRC (MONUC) was deployed in 2000 once stability had been restored to most of the country.[133]

The ceasefire did not hold and the MONUC force of 5,500 was wholly inadequate and unable to prevent violence in various regions of the country, particularly in Bunia, despite a mandate that contained a provision under Chapter VII authorising necessary action to be taken to protect 'civilians under imminent threat of physical violence'.[134] Indeed, '[t]he Security Council's decision to grant the operation a civilian protection mandate in the circumstances proved to be nothing more than a paper exercise, an empty gesture'.[135] A temporary European Union (EU) force (Operation Artemis), which had been authorised by the Security Council to 'take all necessary measures to fulfil its mandate', instead tackled the violence in the region of Bunia in 2003.[136] Having restored 'a measure of security to the town',[137] it was withdrawn on 1 September 2003, although another EU force was authorised in 2006 to support MONUC during elections being held in the state.[138] MONUC was gradually increased from 5,500 to 16,700, and eventually became involved in fighting rebels alongside government troops.[139] Indeed, although protection of civilians mandates are supposed to be implemented neutrally and impartiality, these mandates are, as demonstrated here, also implemented 'almost never against the host state's forces but rather against non-state actors such as militia and armed groups'.[140] As White points out, 'in implementing its increasingly widely drawn mandate to protect civilians from attacks by

---

[131] UNSC Res. 2559 (2020), paras. 1 and 2. [132] See UN Doc. S/1999/815, 10 July 1999.
[133] UNSC Res. 1279 (1999), para. 4. [134] UNSC Res. 1291 (2000), para. 8.
[135] Sloan, n. 11, at 193. See also Katerina Månsson, 'Use of Force and Civilian Protection: Peace Operations in the Congo' (2005) 12 *International Peacekeeping* 503.
[136] UNSC Res. 1484 (2003), para. 4.
[137] Fourteenth Report of the Secretary-General on the United Nations Organization Mission in the Democratic Republic of the Congo, UN Doc. S/2003/1098, 17 November 2003, at para. 6.
[138] UNSC Res. 1671 (2006). [139] See UNSC Res. 1856 (2008). [140] Sheeran, n. 2, at 355.

nonstate actors MONUC, like its predecessor (ONUC), also ended up fighting on the government's side'.[141]

While the UN had authorised operations that sat somewhere between peacekeeping and peace enforcement, even if in a more veiled way, the peace enforcement element of the operations became much more explicit with the establishment of the United Nations Stabilization Mission in the Democratic Republic of the Congo (MONUSCO), which replaced MONUC in 2010.[142] This was explicitly a 'stabilisation mission' and established to work alongside the governmental institutions of the DRC, in particular in response to the activities of rebel groups in Eastern Congo which had continued to foment insecurity and commit violations of human rights and humanitarian law. As a result, in April 2013 the Security Council decided 'on an exceptional basis and without creating a precedent or any prejudice to the agreed principles of peacekeeping' to authorise an '"Intervention Brigade" ... with the responsibility of neutralising [these] armed groups'.[143] The Brigade was authorised to use force and 'to take all necessary measures to perform ... tasks' which included carrying out 'targeted offensive operations through the Intervention Brigade ... to prevent the expansion of all armed groups, neutralize these groups, and to disarm them'.[144] This operation, which had a Chapter VII 'protection of civilians' mandate, was controversial at the time given the extent and nature of its forcible mandate.[145] While the United Kingdom and France provided their support, both Russia and China expressed reservations, with Russia drawing attention to the fact that the traditional principles were mentioned in the resolution, while China stressed that the operation should not set a precedent.[146] The DRC's armed forces defeated the M23 rebel group in November 2013 with the support of MONUSCO, although the operation continues to operate in the DRC.

In 2016 the Intervention Brigade was, however, folded into MONUSCO's general protection of civilians mandate in UN Security Council Resolution 2277 (2016) which continues under the current mandate contained in Resolution 2502 (2019). On 20 December 2021 the UN Security Council '[d]ecide[d] to extend until 20 December 2022 the mandate of MONUSCO in the DRC, including, on an exceptional basis and without creating a precedent or any prejudice to the agreed principles of peacekeeping, its Intervention

---

[141] White, n. 1, at 581.   [142] UNSC Res. 1925 (2010), para. 1.
[143] UNSC Res. 2098 (2013), para. 9.   [144] Ibid., para. 12(b).
[145] It has been noted that '[t]he mandate of the Intervention Brigade was viewed by many as unprecedented and a shift from "peacekeeping" to "peace enforcement"'. Haidi Willmot and Ralph Mamiya, 'Mandated to Protect: Security Council Practice on the Protection of Civilians', in Marc Weller (ed.), *The Oxford Handbook of the Use of Force in International Law* (Oxford University Press, 2015), 375, at 393.
[146] See UN Doc. S/PV. 6943, 28 March 2013.

Brigade'.[147] The strategic priorities of MONUSCO are to continue to protect civilians and stabilise and strengthen state institutions in the DRC.[148]

### 5.6.6 MINUSMA (2013–)

In 2012 there was an uprising by separatist and Islamist groups, including AQIM (al-Qaida in the Islamic Maghreb), in north Mali, with the armed groups seizing control of two-thirds of the state.[149] In Security Council Resolution 2085 (2012) the Council '[u]rge[d] Member States, regional organizations and international organizations to provide ... any necessary assistance in efforts to reduce the threat posed by terrorist organizations'.[150] In the same resolution the Council authorised an African-led International Support Mission to Mali (AFISMA) to protect civilians and to 'support the Malian authorities in recovering the areas in the north of its territory under the control of terrorist, extremist and armed groups and in reducing the threat posed by terrorist organizations' among other tasks.[151]

In early January 2013, before AFISMA had deployed, France began airstrikes against the rebels and deployed troops to Mali in response to AQIM seizing the town of Konna and an invitation by the incumbent and recognised Malian government.[152] On 25 April 2013, in Resolution 2100 (2013), the Council welcomed 'the swift action by the French forces, at the request of the transitional authorities of Mali, to stop the offensive of terrorist, extremist and armed groups towards the south of Mali'.[153] The Security Council also, and acting under Chapter VII, established a multidimensional UN peacekeeping mission in Mali (MINUSMA) which was to assume authority from AFISMA and to operate alongside the French forces that had been deployed.[154] In reaffirming the traditional principles of peacekeeping,[155] the Council authorised MINUSMA to 'use all necessary means' to carry out its mandate[156] which, in addition to the protection of civilians 'under imminent threat of physical violence',[157] included, 'support[ing] ... the transitional authorities of Mali ... to stabilize the key population centres, especially in the north of Mali and, in this context, to deter threats and take active steps to prevent the return

---

[147] UNSC Res. 2612 (2021), para. 22.   [148] Ibid., para. 24.
[149] Afua Hirsch, 'Islamist Rebels Vow Assault on Malian Capital if International Forces Attack', *The Guardian*, 29 October 2012, available at: www.theguardian.com/world/2012/oct/29/mali-africa.
[150] UNSC Res. 2085 (2012), para. 14. It also demanded that Malian rebels sever all ties to terrorists. Ibid., para. 2.
[151] Ibid., para. 9.
[152] BBC News, 'France Confirms Mali Military Intervention', 11 January 2013, available at: www.bbc.co.uk/news/world-africa-20991719.
[153] UNSC Res. 2100 (2013), preamble.   [154] Ibid., para. 7.   [155] Ibid., preamble.
[156] Ibid., para. 17.   [157] Ibid., para. 16(c)(i)).

of armed elements to those areas'.[158] The French forces that remained in Mali were authorised to use 'all necessary means' to support the mission in times of crisis and upon request by the Secretary-General.[159]

Concerns were raised by some states about the UN operating in close connection with French forces undertaking counterterrorism activities and about the appropriateness of a UN peacekeeping operation potentially undertaking such activity itself, with Russia stressing that MINUSMA's mandate did not include offensive or counterterrorism operations as such actions would be contrary to the basic principles of peacekeeping.[160] Following the adoption of the MINUSMA mandate, the Under-Secretary-General for Peacekeeping, Hervé Ladsous, stated that MINUSMA was not an enforcement mission or an anti-terrorist operation, but 'it is clear at the same time that in an environment which will certainly see asymmetric attacks, the stabilization mission will have to defend itself and its mandate, depending on the circumstances'.[161]

Mali continues to experience instability and violence, with continued fighting between rebel groups and a lack of commitment by all parties to implement a peace agreement that was signed in June 2015.[162] The UN Security Council adopted Resolution 2584 on 29 June 2021,[163] which renewed the authorization for MINUSMA to use 'all necessary means' to carry out its mandate for another year until 30 June 2022,[164] to continue with its priorities of supporting the implementation of the Agreement for Peace and Reconciliation in Mali by the Malian parties and other relevant Malian actors and to facilitate the implementation by Malian actors of a comprehensive politically-led strategy to protect civilians, reduce intercommunal violence and re-establish state authority, state presence and basic social services in Central Mali.[165]

### 5.6.7 MINUSCA (2014–)

The government of the Central African Republic (CAR) had for a long time faced disruption and attacks by rebel forces and challenges to state authority, including in 2013 when the capital was seized, and there was continuous violence and retaliation between different religious and ethnic groups.[166]

---

[158] Ibid., para. 16(a)(i).   [159] Ibid., para. 18.   [160] UN Doc. S/PV.6952, 25 April 2013.
[161] Michelle Nichols, 'U.N. Security Council Approves Creation of Mali Peacekeeping Force', *Reuters*, 25 April 2013, available at: www.reuters.com/article/us-mali-crisis-un-idUSBRE93OOR420130425.
[162] Jean-Hervé Jezequel, 'Mali's Peace Deal Represents a Welcome Development, but Will It Work This Time?', *The Guardian*, 1 July 2015, available at: www.theguardian.com/global-development/ 2015/jul/01/mali-peace-deal-a-welcome-development-but-will-it-work-this-time.
[163] UNSC Res. 2584 (2021).   [164] Ibid., paras. 17 and 20.   [165] Ibid., para. 21.
[166] See Report of the UN Secretary-General, UN Doc. S/2013/677, 15 November 2013.

Following a long period of widespread disorder in the country and the ineffectiveness of an AU mission operating in the country, on 10 April 2014 the UN Security Council established the United Nations Multidimensional Integrated Stabilization Mission in the Central African Republic (MINUSCA).[167] This mission had the protection of civilians as its 'upmost priority' and was established for an initial period until 30 April 2015,[168] although its mandate also included support for implementation of the transition process 'including efforts in favour of the extension of State authority and preservation of territorial integrity', the facilitation of humanitarian assistance, the promotion and protection of human rights, support for justice and the rule of law, and disarmament, demobilization, reintegration and repatriation.[169]

Acting under Chapter VII of the Charter of the United Nations, and after determining that the situation in the CAR constituted a threat to international peace and security in the region and reaffirming the basic principles of peacekeeping, including consent of the parties, impartiality, and non-use of force, except in self-defence and defence of the mandate,[170] the Security Council authorized MINUSCA to take 'all necessary means' to carry out its mandate, within its capabilities and its areas of deployment.[171] Despite the adoption of a more robust mandate in 2016,[172] violence within the CAR continued, mainly as the result of power struggles between various groups and the competition for the wealth of natural resources within the country.[173]

Consequently, over the years MINUSCA's mandate has become increasingly robust, with the mission engaged in various operations that have seen it working alongside the CAR armed forces in stabilising various locations within the country. For example, in February 2017 it launched Operation Bekpa against armed groups located in the town of Bambari in order to stabilise it, using armed helicopters in engaging armed groups which were attempting to re-enter the town.[174] MINUSCA has undertaken further operations of a robust nature, including to 'expel' the Front démocratique group from roads between Baboua and Beloko,[175] as well as a 'joint disarmament

---

[167] UNSC Res. 2149 (2014).
[168] See Report of the UN Secretary General, UN Doc. S/2014/142, at paras. 53–86.
On 15 September 2014, the African-led International Support Mission in the Central African Republic (MISCA) transferred its authority over to MINUSCA, in accordance with Resolution 2149 (2014).
[169] UNSC Res. 2149 (2014), para. 30.   [170] Ibid., preamble.   [171] Ibid., para. 29.
[172] See UNSC Res. 2301 (2016).
[173] See Report of the UN Secretary-General, UN Doc. S/2017/94, 1 February 2017.
[174] U.N. Air Strikes in Central African Republic Kill Several Militia', *Reuters*, 13 February 2017, available at: www.reuters.com/article/us-centralafrica-violence/u-n-air-strikes-in-central-african-republic-kill-several-militia-idUSKBN15R0WC.
[175] See Report of the UN Secretary-General, UN Doc. S/2015/576, 29 July 2015, at para. 23.

and arrest operation' alongside the CAR armed forces against certain criminal groups in a Bangui neighbourhood.[176]

In November 2019 MINUSCA's mandate was extended, including 'to support ... the sustainable reduction of the presence of, and threat posed by, armed groups through a ... proactive and robust posture without prejudice to the basic principles of peacekeeping, with it being implemented by way of joint operations with Central African security forces.'[177] In March 2021 the UN Security Council voted to increase the size of the MINUSCA force by an additional 2,750 troops and 940 police officers,[178] and in November 2021 extended the mandate until 15 November 2022.[179]

## 5.7 THE EVOLUTION IN THE USE OF FORCE BY UN PEACEKEEPING OPERATIONS

The reality of force as a central part of peacekeeping operations, as with the very existence of peacekeeping missions, has not in itself been disputed. In order to fulfil its functions in maintaining or restoring peace and security, the UN would appear to have both the legal competence and legitimacy to create peacekeeping forces with the ability to both defend themselves and their mandates as well as to authorise military enforcement actions either alongside peacekeeping forces or as an integral part of them.[180] However, 'there are significant problems with understanding the legal authority of UN peacekeepers to use force'.[181] Indeed, what becomes clear from the operations discussed in Sections 5.5 and 5.6 is that '[a]s a major constitutional adaptation of the UN, from its beginnings to the present day there has not been a clear legal doctrine for application of force in UN peacekeeping operations'.[182]

It is open to question how far many of the peacekeeping operations that have been established during both the Cold War and post–Cold War eras can be reconciled with the 'trinity' of peacekeeping principles set out in Section 5.4. Indeed, it has, on the contrary, been argued that 'the contention that the "fundamental principles" serve to constrain the Security Council's peacekeeping practice in a meaningful way is largely misleading'.[183] Instead, a 'diffuse and opaque' legal framework has seemingly emerged combining elements of

---

[176] UN Security Council, 'Situation in the Central African Republic', 18 June 2018, UN Doc. S/2018/611, at paras. 16, 17. Following these raids, the UN Independent Expert on the situation of human rights in the Central African Republic, Marie-Thérèse Keita Bocoum, called for a strategy on the 'neutralisation' of armed groups in the CAR, although this has to date not been included in MINUSCA's mandate. See 'UN Expert Calls for Calm, Protection of Civilians in Central African Republic', 3 May 2018, available at: https://minusca.unmissions.org/en/un-expert-calls-calm-protection-civilians-central-african-republic.
[177] UNSC Res. 2499 (2019), paras. 29 and 33(a)(iv).  [178] UNSC Res. 2566 (2021), para. 1.
[179] UNSC Res. 2605 (2021), para. 29.  [180] White, n. 1, at 573.  [181] Sheeran, n. 2, at 348.
[182] Ibid.  [183] Sloan, n. 11, at 9.

the 'trinity' of principles and the Security Council's Charter-based and implied powers.[184] The purpose of this section of the chapter is to use the 'trinity' principles as a vehicle to assess how far peacekeeping has strayed beyond what have traditionally been widely seen as its bedrock, potentially into peace enforcement or what we might term as 'war fighting' and whether this might be seen as a positive development.

### 5.7.1 Non-use of Force Except in Self-Defence

As discussed in Sections 5.4.3 and 5.5.1, the principle of non-use of force except in self-defence dates back to the first deployment of armed UN peacekeepers (UNEF I) in 1956.[185] At this time, the scope of self-defence appeared to be very narrow in that it only included a right for UN personnel to protect themselves if under personal attack. However, while it might be considered that peacekeepers were not permitted to go beyond this at this stage in the development of peacekeeping doctrine, in a sense any action taken in personal defence might be considered as defending the mandate of the operation, albeit in a purely personal and reactive way. If individual peacekeepers were required to allow themselves to be harmed or eliminated, then the mission itself would rest on shaky ground and would likely quickly fail. Yet, as this chapter has demonstrated, the use of force by peacekeeping operations in self-defence has gone beyond the simple defence of lightly armed individual peacekeepers.

By the mid-1970s the notion of self-defence had widened to include resistance by forceful means to attempts to prevent the peacekeeping operation from implementing the mandate it had been provided with by the Security Council.[186] In highlighting the continued relevance of self-defence as a bedrock principle of peacekeeping operations, albeit an expanded one, UN Secretary-General Kurt Waldheim offered some guidelines in 1973 which stated that 'self-defence would include resistance to attempts by forceful means to prevent the force from discharging its duties under the mandate of the Security Council'.[187]

Self-defence is a well-established and accepted concept within international law.[188] In this respect, and '[i]n light of the "basic principles" and the Security Council's silence on use of force in most situations, it is not surprising that "self-defence" became a conceptual vehicle for the expansion of use of force'.[189] Yet, the problem is that clinging to a rather restricted form of self-defence in theory but often going far beyond this in practice has meant that

---

[184] Sheeran, n. 2, at 356.   [185] United Nations Peacekeeping Operations, n. 17, at 34.
[186] Report of the Secretary-General on the Implementation of Security Council Resolution 340 (1973), UN Doc. S/11052/Rev.1, 27 October 1973, at paras. 4(d) and 5.
[187] Ibid.   [188] See Chapters 6-8.   [189] Sheeran, n. 2, at 365.

the current scope of self-defence has become 'both unclear and conceptually incoherent' and seemingly with few boundaries.[190]

On the one hand, being provided with a mandate to protect may require an operation to resort to what might be seen as reactive force. For example, it has been claimed that in UNPROFOR 'self-defence became almost unidentifiable, as it justified using force for the protection of freedom of movement, safe areas, and humanitarian aid convoys'.[191] Yet, this defence of the mandate was still generally *reactive* in nature, just as was the case with the personal self-defence of UN peacekeepers, and thus relatively uncontroversial in that respect.

Similarly, and in particular since UNAMSIL in 1999, peacekeeping operations have begun to receive mandates to protect civilians under threat of physical attack.[192] This was a development that appeared to be championed in the Brahimi Report of 2000 and, later, in the 2015 Uniting our Strengths for Peace Report where there was dissatisfaction with the inability of peacekeepers to prevent violence and protect civilians, and which argued for most, if not all, peace operations in the future to have both a protection mandate and the ability to carry it out.[193] As White notes, '[o]riginating in ideas of human security and the Responsibility to Protect, the protection of civilians has become the focus of attention in peace operations at the turn of the century'.[194] Indeed, the protection of civilians is a key part of the mandate in seven of the UN's on-going missions: DRC (MONUSCO), Mali (MINUSMA), CAR (MINUSCA), Sudan (UNAMID), South Sudan (UNMISS), Abyei (UNISFA) and Lebanon (UNIFIL). Furthermore, this significant conceptual development has arguably created an expectation that peacekeepers are deployed to protect civilians rather than solely to keep the peace and it has come to be considered inherent in the very concept of peacekeeping that peacekeepers should be permitted to protect civilians from harm regardless of their mandate.[195] The 2015 Uniting our Strengths for Peace Report was, in particular, clear that tasks falling under defence of the mandate 'should always include the responsibility to protect civilians'.[196]

---

[190] Ibid., at 363.   [191] Ibid., at 365. See Section 5.6.1.   [192] See Section 5.6.3.
[193] Brahimi Report, n. 35, at paras. 62–3 and 108–9.
[194] White, n. 1, at 592. As a concept, protection of civilians has, however, been more influential and utilised in the mandates of the Security Council than Responsibility to Protect. For more on the Responsibility to Protect concept see Chapters 4 and 10.
[195] White argues that this expectation was arguably created through the adoption of Resolutions 1296 (2000) and 1674 (2006). White, ibid., at 592.
[196] Uniting our Strengths for Peace, n. 35, at para. 125 (emphasis in original). In his follow-up report, the UN Secretary-General also stated that 'protection of civilians' mandates have 'been defined to mean preventative, preemptive and tactical use of force to protect civilians under threat of physical violence'. Secretary-General's Report, The Future of United Nations Peace Operations: Implementation of the High-Level Independent Panel on Peace Operations, UN Doc. S/2015/682, 2 September 2015, at para. 18.

Yet, on the other hand, defence of the mandate may require an operation to resort to more controversial proactive force and '[t]he problems associated with the sheer breadth of such active self-defence have been borne out in UN peacekeeping practice'.[197] These were seen as far back as the ONUC mission in the early 1960s, during which time the conceptual vehicle of self-defence was used 'as practically the sole justification for bringing down the [secessionist] Katangan regime'.[198]

Furthermore, in certain volatile situations, in particular after the end of the Cold War in conflicts in the DRC, Mali and the CAR, but also in the ONUC mission in the 1960s, the Security Council provided UN peacekeeping operations with particularly 'robust' or 'muscular' stabilisation mandates, to, *inter alia*, deter forceful attempts to disrupt the political process, assist the national authorities in maintaining law and order and, most notably, to carry out targeted offensive operations. In this respect, peacekeeping missions have arguably become more regularly *proactive* and *offensive* in nature, and less reactive and defensive, in that they have moved almost entirely away from the defence of peacekeepers, the protection of civilians, the defence of an operation as a whole, or the defence of an operation's mandate, to working alongside governmental authorities within a state to attain or enforce a particular outcome or mandate. While through these developments it might seem that the right of self-defence has been 'stretched and ultimately broken',[199] the right has also arguably become unclear in substance and, as a result, has potentially lost its normative power both to authorise and to constrain.[200] In this respect, it was unsurprising that the 2015 report stated that while '*[s]elf-defence* is a well-recognized concept and well-catered for in UN rules of engagement ... the concept of *defence of the mandate* requires clarity as to which tasks within the mandate may require the use of force'.[201]

It might arguably be this decisive – if not often expressly acknowledged – shift away from the use of force by peacekeeping operations being of a cognizable defensive nature that has led to them now regularly receiving Chapter VII mandates, despite the UN Security Council continuing to often acknowledge the principles of peacekeeping in the respective resolutions of the operations. Today, reliance upon self-defence arguably obscures the true legal basis for proactive forcible action within peacekeeping operations,[202] and 'if peacekeepers' right to

---

[197] Sheeran, n. 2, at 365.    [198] Findlay, n. 44, at 356. See Section 5.5.2.    [199] Ibid., at 356.
[200] Sheeran, n. 2, at 365.
[201] Uniting our Strengths for Peace, n. 35, at para. 125 (emphasis in original).
[202] Sheeran, n. 2, at 365.

use force was based solely on self-defence there would be no need for the mandate of modern peace operations to contain Chapter VII elements'.[203]

Yet, regardless of whether these operations fall under self-defence or authorisation by the UN Security Council questions may be asked regarding the necessity of identifying such a legal basis if they are established with the consent of the parties concerned, a further important peacekeeping principle.

### 5.7.2 Consent

A constant theme of the earlier Cold War peacekeeping operations is that they were established with the consent of, or occasionally with an invitation by, the states between which they were attempting to keep the peace or the host state upon which the operation was located in the case of a conflict between a state and non-state actors. Regardless of how 'muscular' or 'robust' the peacekeeping operations became or how extensive the mandates were which they were provided with it is arguably this factor which makes one hesitant in describing them as full-fledged peace *enforcement* operations, which remain an exception to the international prohibition of the use of force and which has at its core the element of coercion.[204]

In the context of a peacekeeping operation that has been established to keep the peace *between states*, the consent of both or all parties is necessary for the positioning of the operation on the soil of one or all of the parties. If any of the states withdraws its consent, as Egypt did in regard to UNEF in 1967,[205] the peacekeeping force must be withdrawn, repositioned or re-mandated, possibly with a Chapter VII mandate. While if any party to the conflict, in particular the host state, withdraws its consent, the operation may ultimately resort to action that resembles more traditional enforcement action, in this case it is no longer possible to consider the operation as one of peacekeeping, but rather as one of enforcement.[206]

However, in the case of those operations established more in the post–Cold War era *between governmental forces of a state and non-state actors* operating

---

[203] White, n. 1, at 590 and Nicholas Tsagourias, 'Consent, Neutrality/Impartiality and the Use of Force in Peacekeeping' (2006) 11 *Journal of Conflict & Security Law* 465, at 473. Gray notes that '[t]here seem to be various explanations for the choice to create an operation under Chapter VII', including 'to indicate that it has a mandate going beyond mere observation', to allow it 'to regulate matters that would normally be within the domestic jurisdiction of the state concerned', to ensure that it is 'clear that the operation does not depend on the consent of that state', as well as emphasising 'that there is a duty on all parties to cooperate with the UN force'. Gray, n. 24, at 313.

[204] See Section 2.2.    [205] See Section 5.5.1.

[206] As Tsagourias has noted, 'states cannot be compelled to accept the [continued] deployment of a PKO' because '[i]f this is the case, then it is an enforcement action'. Tsagourias, n. 203, at 469.

within the state it is not entirely accurate to say that they are based entirely upon consent. Most often, while the state in which the operation is deployed has consented, the non-state actors involved, for example the Bosnian Serbs during the crisis in Yugoslavia or the rebel groups in the Eastern Congo, have not consented to the deployment of the operation. Indeed, '[c]ontrary to traditional peacekeeping doctrine, the UN increasingly limits itself to obtaining consent from the host state only. This reflects the realities of complex internal conflicts, where securing consent from myriad non-state actors would be difficult, if not impossible.'[207]

Although consent is still of relevance in these situations as it has been provided by the government of the host state – without which the operation would be one of coercive enforcement – it is, in this sense and in the context of the conditions in which many modern peacekeeping operations are deployed, difficult to say that the principle has quite the relevance it once did. In addition, to be fully effective as a *peacekeeping* operation the consent of all parties is a necessary precondition, as the parties are, in essence, giving their word that they will respect the operation to which they have consented. Without such consent from all concerned there will often be no peace to keep, meaning that a robust peacekeeping force with a heavy enforcement or counterterrorism element, as with MINUSMA in Mali or MONUSCO in the DRC, has been deployed.

The rise of stabilisation missions, such as that of MINUSCA in the Central African Republic, highlights, in particular, the absence of this universal consent and the fact that for the non-state parties in the situation, at least, the operation is very much one of enforcement. In this respect, given that such contemporary peacekeeping operations are now very often aligned with and tied to the operations of host governments it does call into question if, and, if so, how far, they can be reconciled with the third of the classic 'trinity' peacekeeping principles, that of impartiality.[208]

### 5.7.3 Impartiality

States may offer an invitation to other states and organisations to operate and resort to forcible measures upon their territory.[209] In this respect, a state may actively request that an impartial peacekeeping operation be established upon its territory. While an operation is located within a state with the consent of the government this need not necessarily throw its impartiality into question

---

[207] Labuda, n. 29, at 346.   [208] Ibid., at 347.
[209] See Chapter 9 for more on the issuing of an invitation to intervene as a legal basis for the use of force upon the territory of another state.

and the operation may resort to force against the governmental forces in defence of its mandate including for the protection of civilians should it be deemed necessary. That being said, 'it is well known that peacekeepers are more reluctant to use force against government troops than non-state actors'[210] and one may question, therefore, whether a peacekeeping operation established with the consent of the host state can ever be fully impartial in implementing its mandate and, in turn, facilitating the broader peace process.

However, the evolution of peacekeeping operations towards the development of stabilisation mandates – which means that troops of peacekeeping missions are regularly witnessed operating in conjunction with, or even in place of, the forces of the host state government to restore state authority and conduct military operations against armed groups – places serious question marks over the current status of the principle of impartiality. Indeed, '[s]tabilisation mandates constitute a more radical departure from peacekeeping norms than is commonly acknowledged. Mandated by the Security Council to support host governments, stabilisation missions have more in common with the *jus ad bellum* doctrine of intervention by invitation than traditional or robust peacekeeping (the latter two still premised on the impartial application of force).'[211] Indeed, certain operations that have received authorisation by the Security Council, in particular UNOSOM in 1993 and the FIB of MONUSCO in 2013, not only involved the clear designation of an enemy but also purposely did not treat all parties equally.[212] This raises the question as to how far we can continue to say that UN peacekeeping operations are still within the realms of keeping the peace or even peace enforcement, or whether they have, alternatively, moved more into the realms of war fighting? Indeed, these so called 'stabilisation missions' are 'one sided interventions on behalf of host states, where joint operations comprising UN troops and national armies turn peacekeepers into parties to an underlying conflict'.[213]

### 5.7.4 Peace Observation, Peacekeeping, Peace Enforcement or War Fighting?

Whichever way one views the legality and legitimacy of the various occasions upon which the UN has deployed peacekeeping operations, there has been an undeniable evolution, from unarmed forces deployed simply as observation units, to lightly armed soldiers acting as a buffer, to troops acting under a more specific mandate, often with the underlying authority to enforce it, to simply intervening at the invitation of – and fighting alongside – a

---

[210] Labuda, n. 29, at 350. [211] Ibid., at 355.
[212] See Sections 5.6.2 and 5.6.5, respectively. [213] Labuda, n. 29, at 318.

governmental regime. There have been times, however, when it may have seemed that an operation has moved beyond any logically conceived notion of peacekeeping, or even peace enforcement, but instead can more easily be placed within the realms of war fighting.

The MONUSCO 'Intervention Brigade' in the DRC, which appears to be at the high-water mark of the 'robust' form of peacekeeping in the post–Cold War era, would seem to be directly contrary to the basic principles of peacekeeping discussed here. Indeed, its 'military operations are designed around eliminating particular parties to the conflict. This potentially goes beyond peace enforcement and into the realms of war-fighting, albeit that this is in respect to one component and aspect of the overall MONUSCO mission.'[214] It is arguably for this reason that the resolution establishing the Brigade stated that the mandate was provided 'on an exceptional basis and without creating a precedent or any prejudice to the agreed principles of peacekeeping'.[215] This represented an implicit recognition that, while the principles of peacekeeping continue to be valid, the MONUSCO operation was – while not wishing to be portrayed as peace enforcement – an exception to them. The precedential impact of the Security Council attempting to make such an exception is, at the time of writing, unclear.

What is clear, however, is that mandates for this kind of particularly robust use of force by a peacekeeping operation have the potential of turning the peacekeepers into a *de facto* (if not *de jure*) party to the conflict. As Brian Urquhart, former Under-Secretary-General for Special Political Affairs in the UN, has pointed out, 'the moment a peacekeeping force starts killing people it becomes a part of the conflict it is supposed to be controlling, and therefore a part of the problem'.[216] In particular, if peacekeeping operations use offensive force, then the protections afforded to them are put into jeopardy. UN peacekeepers are non-combatants and have a protected status under the law of armed conflict,[217] although they may lose their protected status upon engaging in military activities.[218] In this respect, Sloan argues that 'where a peacekeeper uses force beyond self-defence, he or she becomes a combatant [under the law of armed conflict] and, as such, a legitimate target'.[219] This has the consequence of leaving UN forces more broadly open to being targeted. Indeed, this would appear to have been a factor in attacks that have occurred against UN forces, for example in Somalia in 1993, in the former Yugoslavia in 1995, in Sierra Leone in 2000 and in February 2005 when nine MONUC

---

[214] Sheeran, n. 2, at 366–7.   [215] UNSC Res. 2098 (2013), para. 9.
[216] Brian Urquhart, *A Life in Peace and War* (Harper and Row, 1987), at 178–9.
[217] See Article 7, Convention on the Safety of UN Personnel (1994).
[218] Daniel S. Blocq, 'The Fog of UN Peacekeeping: Ethical Issues Regarding the Use of Force to Protect Civilians in UN Operations' (2006) 5 *Journal of Military Ethics* 201, at 208.
[219] Sloan, n. 12, at 451.

peacekeepers were killed in the Ituri region in what was described as a retaliatory attack.[220]

Ultimately, the increased use of force in peacekeeping operations may bring heightened risk to populations in the areas of operation. As Jonathan Fink has observed, the 'blurring of peacekeeping "guiding principles" and peace enforcement standards for use of force ... jeopardizes the safety of the peacekeepers and hampers the effectiveness of the mission'.[221] Furthermore, if UN peacekeeping forces not only conduct offensive missions but are viewed as a party to a particular conflict this has the potential of undermining the perceived impartiality of UN actors in general, and consequently their ability to deliver on their mandate, in particular their ability to keep or obtain any sort of peace as well as offer effective protection to civilians on the ground.[222]

## 5.8 CONCLUSION

The basic principles that emerged during the early stages of peacekeeping doctrine have, on paper at least, stood the test of time. However, what can be said is that, while they are generally accepted, they 'have not really guided the Security Council's work'[223] and 'the fit of contemporary operations with the principles is therefore strained'.[224] Peacekeeping operations have often had to rub up against at least one of the principles. For example, on many occasions, while a peacekeeping operation has been operating with the consent of the host state, it has also effectively fought alongside, or in place of, the government, meaning that not only has the operation lost its impartiality, but that it is also simply no longer possible to sensibly claim that the use of force takes place within the realms of self-defence. As discussed in Section 5.7.4, this warfighting role for peacekeeping operations has potentially serious implications.

However, it is also possible to argue that, on occasion, 'strict adherence to the principles, regardless of the hostility of the mission's environment or need for civilian protection, can prevent more forceful options from being considered when they are appropriate'.[225] Indeed, in Darfur, for example, where the government itself was wholly or partially responsible for attacks on civilians, 'the legal and conceptual basis of peacekeeping and peace operations

---

[220] Ibid., at 449.

[221] Jonathan E. Fink, 'From Peacekeeping to Peace Enforcement: The Blurring of the Mandate for the Use of Force in Maintaining International Peace and Security' (1995) 19 *Maryland Journal of International Law & Trade* 1, at 31. See also Supplement to An Agenda for Peace, n. 35, at para. 35.

[222] Haidi Willmot and Scott Sheeran, 'The Protection of Civilians Mandate in UN Peacekeeping Operations: Reconciling Protection Concepts and Practices' (2013) 95 *International Review of the Red Cross* 517, at 536.

[223] Sheeran, n. 2, at 357.   [224] Ibid., at 358.

[225] Sheeran, n. 2, at 358–9. See also Berdal, n. 58, at 197.

is undermined, since to protect civilians in these circumstances is to confront the government and the state. In these circumstances enforcement action is necessary; a robust peace operation is insufficient both legally and practically.'[226] As was witnessed, however, the UN was not willing to undertake enforcement action and was only prepared to intervene with the consent of the Sudanese government.

A number of possible solutions become apparent. The first is to build upon the general call made in both the Brahimi Report and the 2015 Uniting our Strengths for Peace Report that greater clarity be provided in regards to both the applicable legal frameworks and the ways in which they are applied in each mission.[227] One of the reasons for requiring clarity is that '[a]ll states, not only the host state and the troop contributing nations ..., need to know when a force is benign and impartial and when it is coercive and belligerent'.[228] In addition, other states, the UN and, perhaps most importantly, peacekeeping troops and civilians on the ground affected by the operation need to know what is to be expected of the peacekeepers.

Related to this, the Brahimi Report and the 2015 Uniting our Strengths for Peace Report stressed that peacekeeping forces should, on a practical and strategic level, be equipped to effectively fulfil the mandate they have been provided with. As the 2015 report states, for too long there has been a credibility gap.[229] However, with the continued determination on the part of the UN to authorise peacekeeping operations under Chapter VII of the UN Charter with ever more robust and ambitious mandates the question arises as to whether UN peacekeeping – based, as it continues to be, on the trinity of peacekeeping principles – is in danger of getting 'out of its depth' and biting off more than it can, or indeed should, chew, if indeed it has not done so already.

An alternative to this approach would be to maintain a clear separation between peacekeeping and peace enforcement forces and what they are trying to achieve and equipped as well as able to do. There are, of course, problems with both types of peace mission operating in the same space, in particular in coordinating the operations so as to avoid friendly-fire incidents, as well as them being seen as one and the same and thus generating mistrust amongst the warring parties and leading to reprisals against those engaged purely in peaceful or humanitarian tasks. However, given the continued need for robust peace missions on the ground this not only enables peacekeeping to be reconciled with its core principles but also provides some measure of clarity in the peacekeeping/peace enforcement divide. It was notable in this respect

---

[226] White, n. 1, at 596.   [227] Uniting our Strengths for Peace, n. 34, at x.
[228] Sheeran, n. 2, at 356.
[229] Uniting our Strengths for Peace, n. 34, at para. 36. However, in September 2015 a 'Leader's Summit on Peacekeeping' was held in New York where new commitments were pledged by over fifty states. See https://peacekeeping.un.org/en/leaders-summit-peaceekeeping.

that, while the 2015 Uniting our Strengths for Peace Report called for a flexible and progressive interpretation of the traditional principles of peacekeeping in the context of the use of force in defence of the mandate, including the protection of civilians in the context of which the core principles should not be used as an excuse for inaction, '[it] was not ready to take a radical approach on peace enforcement and counter-terrorism operations'.[230] Indeed, the report was, on the contrary, clear that 'as a rule these were still not suitable for UN peacekeeping forces'[231] and so should, instead, be left to 'first responders', such as regional organisations or *ad hoc* coalitions of UN member states.[232] The problem, however, and as ever, is finding the political will to establish the peace enforcement mission (often led by, or at least involving, Western states) to accompany the peacekeeping operation, which will often predominantly consist of troops contributed by developing countries.

## QUESTIONS

1 How might we define 'peacekeeping'? How does it differ from 'peace enforcement'?

2 Does peacekeeping have a basis within the UN Charter? If not, where is its legal basis located?

3 What are the basic principles of peacekeeping and do they permit peacekeeping forces to use force?

4 Do modern peacekeeping operations still operate within the bounds of the traditional principles?

5 To what extent have peacekeeping operations become focused upon protecting civilians or aiding the stability of a government as opposed to simply keeping the peace?

---

[230] Christine Gray, 'The 2015 Report on Uniting Our Strengths for Peace: A New Framework for UN Peacekeeping?' (2016) *Chinese Journal of International Law* 193, at 213. By contrast, the Cruz Report of 2017 argued that peacekeeping operations need to be more robust – even aggressive – to fulfil their mandates. Indeed, because '[t]he era of "Chapter VI-style" peacekeeping is over', 'the United Nations needs to be strong and not fear to use force when necessary', 'use overwhelming force and be proactive and preemptive', and 'take the initiative, using all the tactics, to neutralize or eliminate' threats. Carlos Alberto Dos Santos Cruz, William Philipps and Salvator Cusimano, 'Improving Security of United Nations Peacekeepers: We need to Change the Way We Are Doing Business' (19 December 2017), available at: https://peacekeeping.un.org/sites/default/files/improving_security_of_united_nations_peacekeepers_report.pdf. Yet, taking this approach has, again as discussed in this section and Section 5.7.4, potentially serious implications for all those working on the ground whether involved in the fighting or not.

[231] Ibid.   [232] Uniting our Strengths for Peace, n. 35, at para. 115.

## SUGGESTED FURTHER READING

Yasushi Akashi, 'The Use of Force in a United Nations Peace-Keeping Operation: Lessons Learnt from the Safe Areas Mandate' (1995) 19 *Fordham International Law Journal* 312

Mats Berdal, 'Lessons Not Learned: The Use of Force in "Peace Operations" in the 1990s' (2000) 7 *International Peacekeeping* 55

Hanna Bourgeois, '"All Necessary Means" to Protect Civilians: The Interpretation and Implementation of UN Security Council Mandates Authorising the Protection of Civilians' (2020) 24 *International Peacekeeping* 53

Jacob Katz Cogan, 'Stabilization and the Expanding Scope of the Security Council's Work' (2015) 109 *American Journal of International Law* 324

Katherine E. Cox, 'Beyond Self-Defense: United Nations Peacekeeping Operations and the Use of Force' (1998–9) 27 *Denver Journal of International Law and Policy* 239

Alexander Gilder, 'The Effect of "Stabilization" in the Mandates and Practice of UN Peace Operations' (2019) 66 *Netherlands International Law Review* 47

Aditi Gorur, *Defining the Boundaries of UN Stabilization Missions* (Stimson Center, 2016)

Joachim A. Koops et al. (eds.), *The Oxford Handbook of United Nations Peacekeeping Operations* (Oxford University Press, 2015)

Peter Nadin (ed.), *The Use of Force in UN Peacekeeping* (Routledge, 2018)

Alexander Orakhelashvili, 'The Legal Basis of the United Nations Peacekeeping Operations' (2003) 43 *Virginia Journal of International Law* 485

James Sloan, *The Militarisation of Peacekeeping in the 21st Century* (Hart, 2011)

Dale Stephens, 'The Lawful Use of Force by Peacekeeping Force: The Tactical Imperative' (2007) 14 *International Peacekeeping* 157

# Part III

# The Use of Force in Self-Defence

# 6 General Aspects of the Right of Self-Defence

## 6.1 INTRODUCTION

The three chapters of this Part of the book have as their focus the right of self-defence, which constitutes the only established exception to the prohibition of the use of force outside of action undertaken under the auspices of the United Nations (UN) Security Council. Consequently, it is of no surprise that the justification of self-defence is the one that is most commonly resorted to by states and the one that has arguably given rise to the greatest controversy in both theory and practice.

The textual source of the right of self-defence is contained within Article 51 of the UN Charter, which provides that:

Nothing in the present Charter shall impair the inherent right of individual or collective self-defence if an armed attack occurs against a Member of the United Nations, until the Security Council has taken measures necessary to maintain international peace and security. Measures taken by Members in the exercise of this right of self-defence shall be immediately reported to the Security Council and shall not in any way affect the authority and responsibility of the Security Council under the present Charter to take at any time such action as it deems necessary in order to maintain or restore international peace and security.

This right was not one that was to be originally included within the Charter and was not a right included in any of the previous attempts at regulating the use of force, including within the Covenant of the League of Nations or the Kellogg–Briand Pact.[1] Yet, it was included within the UN Charter at the insistence of certain South American states – that had previously entered into the collective self-defence arrangement found in the Act of Chapultepec – in order to protect the right of collective self-defence.[2]

---

[1] For more on these attempts at regulating the use of force see Section 1.2.
[2] This was later formalised in the Inter-American Treaty of Reciprocal Assistance (1947).

The general consensus appears to be that the adoption of the UN Charter did not establish a completely novel right of self-defence.[3] In this respect, the reference in Article 51 to the right of self-defence being 'inherent' might be viewed as an acceptance of the right existing as an innate element of statehood, meaning that 'the right *inheres* in, and is thus inseparable from, the right-holder which in this instance would be the state'.[4] This, in the view of some, takes the meaning of the right above positive international law and places it within the realms of natural law.[5]

Alternatively, and in giving the 'inherent' nature of the right a more positivist interpretation, the International Court of Justice (ICJ) took the view in the *Nicaragua* case that this phrasing represents a reference to the right as it exists within customary international law. As the Court noted:

> On one essential point, [the UN Charter] itself refers to *pre-existing customary international law*; this reference to customary law is contained in the actual text of Article 51, which mentions the 'inherent right' (in the French text the 'droit naturel') of individual or collective self-defence, which 'nothing in the present Charter shall impair' *and which applies in the event of an armed attack*. The Court therefore finds that Article 51 of the Charter is only meaningful on the basis that there is a 'natural' or 'inherent' right of self-defence, *and it is hard to see how this can be other than of a customary nature, even if its present content has been confirmed and influenced by the Charter.*[6]

In addition to the right existing in general within customary international law, there are two specific requirements contained within the customary source of the right – that is, that any military action taken in self-defence be both 'necessary' and 'proportionate' – which have a pedigree that stretches back to the events of the *Caroline* incident that occurred in the United States/Canada in the nineteenth century,[7] and which will be addressed further

---

[3] See the debate in Yoram Dinstein, *War, Aggression and Self-Defence*, 6th ed. (Cambridge University Press, 2017), at paras. 523–7. This is a point that both Ian Brownlie and Derek Bowett agree upon. See Ian Brownlie, *International Law and the Use of Force by States* (Clarendon Press, 1963), at 251–7; Derek Bowett, *Self-Defence in International Law* (Manchester University Press, 1958), at 182–4.

[4] Dino Kritsiotis, 'A Study of the Scope and Operation of the Rights of Individual and Collective Self-Defence under International Law', in Nigel D. White and Christian Henderson (eds.), *Research Handbook on International Conflict and Security Law: Jus ad Bellum, Jus in Bello and Jus post Bellum* (Edward Elgar, 2013), 170, at 174.

[5] M. A. Weightman, 'Self-Defense in International Law' (1951) 31 *Virginia Law Review* 1095, at 1108.

[6] *Case Concerning Military and Paramilitary Activities in and Against Nicaragua* (*Nicaragua v. United States of America*), Merits, (1986) ICJ Reports 14, at para. 176 (emphasis added). An essential aspect of the *Nicaragua* case was that the rules on the use of force in general are contained not just within the UN Charter but also within customary international law. See ibid., at para. 34. See also Section 1.3.

[7] See, in particular, Section 6.3.

throughout the chapters of this Part of the book. While the right of self-defence was therefore formalised in Article 51 – in particular, with the inclusion of the formal requirement of an 'armed attack' – it is implicit in the jurisprudence of the Court that during the seventy years since the UN Charter came into being there has been what might be termed a reciprocal conditioning between the two sources of the right.[8] The right of self-defence today can therefore be seen as a fusion between the treaty and customary sources of international law.

Against this background, the first chapter in this Part of the book provides an overview of the right of self-defence. Section 6.2 examines the concept of an 'armed attack' as found in Article 51, with the aim of shedding some light on the difficult issues and questions raised by this prerequisite for the invocation of the right of self-defence,[9] including how this concept is to be viewed in the context of cyber operations. Section 6.3 goes on to provide an examination of the twin customary principles of necessity and proportionality, including taking a specific look at the controversial concept of armed reprisals and their relationship with the right of self-defence. A particular aspect of the right of self-defence that has been asserted is that it extends to military action for the protection of nationals who are located abroad. Section 6.4 provides an examination of the practice that has occurred in regard to this aspect of the right of self-defence. What is clear from a reading of Article 51 as just set out is that the right of self-defence exists in both individual and collective forms, and Section 6.5 takes a specific look at the right of collective self-defence. Finally, Section 6.6 examines the role of the UN Security Council in the invocation and implementation of the right of self-defence, an aspect of the right which is prominent throughout the text of Article 51.

The scene is then set for a detailed examination in the following two chapters of two applications of the right of self-defence that have proved particularly controversial in recent years: the use of force in preventative self-defence (Chapter 7) and that used against non-state actors (Chapter 8).

## 6.2 THE CONCEPT OF AN 'ARMED ATTACK'

Of all the elements of Article 51, perhaps the one that has generated most discussion is the requirement of an 'armed attack'.[10] The requirement remains, formally at least, the only prerequisite for the invocation of the right of self-

---

[8] There is no formal hierarchy between these sources of international law, as discussed in 'The Sources of the Law on the Use of Force and the Question of Methodology' section within the Introduction to this book and in Section 1.3.
[9] This was touched upon in Section 2.5.1.1.
[10] See, in general, Tom Ruys, *'Armed Attack' and Article 51 of the UN Charter: Evolutions in Customary Law and Practice* (Cambridge University Press, 2010).

defence and the ICJ has confirmed that nothing short of an armed attack will be sufficient to trigger the right.[11] Indeed, '[t]he text of Article 51 hinges on the expression "armed attack". This is the threshold requirement: recourse to self-defence under the Article is not vindicated by any violation of international law which falls short of an armed attack.'[12] In this respect, '[w]hile controversy exists in relation to certain aspects of the right of self-defence under international law, there is nevertheless a considerable degree of agreement regarding its core nature'.[13]

Yet, the apparently simple phrase 'if an armed attack occurs' nonetheless masks disagreement as to, inter alia, the sort of actions that might constitute such an attack, the possible perpetrators of an armed attack, how and when states may respond to such an attack, when one begins and ends and whether the threat of an imminent, or even more temporally remote, armed attack is sufficient to justify the invocation of the right of self-defence. The problems with finding answers to these questions are exacerbated by the Charter itself being generally 'silent as to what constitutes an armed attack and when it can be said to commence and terminate'.[14] Indeed, as with the term 'force', a definition of this concept 'is not provided [for] in the Charter, and is not part of treaty law',[15] although some of the subsequent instruments, such as the Definition of Aggression, might be seen as providing some assistance in this regard.[16] This section will first discuss some general elements of the concept of an armed attack, followed by a specific focus on the question as to whether an attack needs to be of a particular gravity to constitute an 'armed attack' for the purposes of the right of self-defence.

### 6.2.1 The Perpetrators of an Armed Attack

The first – although not uncontroversial – issue is whether the definition of 'armed attack' in Article 51 of the UN Charter and related customary international law requires the perpetrator to be a state.[17] To be sure, whereas Article 2(4) obliges member states of the UN to refrain from threatening or using force

---

[11] *Nicaragua* case, n. 6, at para. 176; *Case Concerning Oil Platforms (Islamic Republic of Iran v. United States of America)*, Judgment (2003) ICJ Reports 161, at para. 51.
[12] Dinstein, n. 3, at para. 542.
[13] Terry D. Gill, 'When Does Self-Defence End?', in Marc Weller (ed.), *The Oxford Handbook of the Use of Force in International Law* (Oxford University Press, 2015), 737, at 738.
[14] Ibid., at 738.   [15] *Nicaragua* case, n. 6, at para. 176.
[16] For example, the ICJ drew upon para. 3(g) of the Definition of Aggression in establishing that an armed attack may be perpetrated through 'the sending by a State of armed bands to the territory of another State'. See ibid., at para. 195.
[17] See Kimberley N. Trapp, 'Can Non-State Actors Mount an Armed Attack?', in Marc Weller (ed.), *The Oxford Handbook of the Use of Force in International Law* (Oxford University Press, 2015), 679.

against 'any state', thus firmly placing it within the inter-state context,[18] Article 51 does not expressly require that an 'armed attack' be perpetrated by, or be attributed to, a state. Indeed, while, as discussed in Chapter 2, Article 2(4) expressly arises in the context of 'international relations', Article 51 contains no such stipulation. As such, there are two pertinent and interlinked questions that call to be addressed here.

The first is whether the actions of non-state actors are able to constitute an armed attack for the purposes of the right of self-defence. There is, as noted in the previous paragraph, nothing in Article 51 restricting the invocation of the right to attacks by state actors.[19] In addition, and as will be explored further in Section 6.3, while taking place in the nineteenth century and before force was legally regulated, the (in-)famous *Caroline* incident, which has been described as the *locus classicus* of self-defence,[20] was itself an example of an action in self-defence against the activities of non-state actors. However, academic opinion is to an extent divided on this issue. Some scholars have maintained what may be described as the traditional view that the right of self-defence only exists in connection with an attack by a state actor.[21] This would appear to be the consistent line taken by the ICJ. For example, while different interpretations have been put on its statement on this issue, the Court nonetheless stated in the *Wall* advisory opinion that 'Article 51 of the Charter ... recognizes the existence of an inherent right of self-defence in the case of armed attack *by one State against another State. However, Israel does not claim that the attacks against it are imputable to a foreign State.*'[22] Given this apparent need for the author of an armed attack to be in the form of a state, much ink has been spilt over the issue as to whether attribution to a state is required for the actions of non-state actors, including terrorist groups, to constitute an armed attack.[23] Indeed, this issue was before the ICJ in the *Nicaragua* case, in which it appeared at least to claim that such attribution was in fact required.[24]

---

[18] See the discussion in Section 1.3.1.4.

[19] Judge Higgins was correct in pointing out in her separate opinion in the *Wall* advisory opinion that '[t]here is, with respect, nothing in the text of Article 51 that ... stipulates that self-defence is available only when an armed attack is made by a State'. See *Legal Consequences of the Construction of a Wall in the Occupied Palestinian Territory*, Advisory Opinion (2004) ICJ Reports 136, Separate Opinion of Judge Higgins, at 33.

[20] Robert Y. Jenning, 'The Caroline and McLeod Cases' (1938) 32 *American Journal of International Law* 82, at 92.

[21] See, for example, Alexander Orakhelashvili, 'Changing *Jus Cogens* through State Practice? The Case of the Prohibition of the Use of Force and Its Exceptions', in Marc Weller (ed.), *The Oxford Handbook of the Use of Force in International Law* (Oxford University Press, 2015), 157, at 171–3.

[22] *Wall* advisory opinion, n. 19, at para. 139 (emphasis added).    [23] See Sections 8.3 and 8.4.

[24] *Nicaragua* case, n. 6, at para. 195. Although see the discussion in Section 8.4.

However, today, it is perhaps fair to say that many states and scholars are of the view that non-state actors are qualified in their own right to perpetrate an armed attack under international law.[25] This view arguably crystallised following the invocation of the right of self-defence by the United States in response to the attacks of 11 September 2001 (9/11).[26] Not only was self-defence specifically invoked in the face of attacks by the non-state terrorist group al-Qaida, but the justification of self-defence appeared to be not simply passively tolerated but rather widely accepted within the international community, with very few dissenting states.[27] The UN Security Council adopted

---

[25] See, for examples, Ruth Wedgwood, 'Responding to Terrorism: The Strikes against bin Laden' (1999) 24 *Yale Journal of International Law* 559; Thomas M. Franck, 'Terrorism and the Right of Self-Defense' (2001) 95 *American Journal of International Law* 839; Sean D. Murphy, 'Terrorism and the Concept of "Armed Attack" in Article 51 of the UN Charter' (2002) 43 *Harvard Journal of International Law* 41; Carsten Stahn, 'Terrorist Attacks as "Armed Attack": The Right to Self-Defense, Article 51(1/2) of the UN Charter, and International Terrorism' (2003) 27 *Fletcher Forum of World Affairs* 35; Sean D. Murphy, 'Self-Defense and the Israeli Wall Advisory Opinion: An Ipse Dixit from the ICJ?' (2005) 99 *American Journal of International Law* 62; Ruth Wedgwood, 'The ICJ Advisory Opinion on the Israeli Security Fence and the Limits of Self-Defense' (2005) 99 *American Journal of International Law* 52; Elizabeth Wilmshurst, 'The Chatham House Principles of International Law on the Use of Force in Self-Defence' (2006) 55 *International & Comparative Law Quarterly* 963; Kimberley N. Trapp, 'Back to Basics: Necessity, Proportionality, and the Right of Self-Defence against Non-State Terrorist Actors' (2007) 56 *International & Comparative Law Quarterly* 141; Constantine Antonopoulos, 'Force by Armed Groups as Armed Attack and the Broadening of Self-Defence' (2008) 55 *Netherlands International Law Review* 159. See Chapter 8 for more on this issue.

[26] See UN Doc. S/2001/946, 7 October 2001.

[27] NATO, for the first time in its history, invoked Article 5, which is the collective self-defence provision of The North Atlantic Treaty (1949). See Statement by NATO Secretary-General, Lord Robertson, 2 October 2001, available at: www.nato.int/docu/speech/2001/s011002a .htm. The Organisation of American States determined that the attacks on the United States were an attack on 'all American States' and that member states shall provide 'effective reciprocal assistance'. See Terrorist Threat to the Americas, Twenty-Fourth Meeting of Consultation of Ministers of Foreign Affairs, OEA/Ser.F/II.24RC.24/RES.1/01, 21 September 2001, available at: www.oas.org/oaspage/crisis/rc.24e.htm. The European Union declared its 'wholehearted support for the action that is being taken in self-defence'. See UN Doc. S/2001/967, 8 October 2001. Australia invoked the 1951 ANZUS treaty in contributing land, air and naval units to the US. See UN Doc. S/2001/1104, 23 November 2001. Many other states, including Canada, France, Germany, the Netherlands, Czech Republic, Italy, Japan, Turkey, the United Kingdom and New Zealand offered ground troops, while states such as Georgia, Oman, Pakistan, the Philippines, Qatar, Saudi Arabia, Tajikistan, Turkey and Uzbekistan provided airspace and facilities. China, Egypt, Mexico and Russia expressed approval of the response of the United States. See *Keesing's* (2001) 44335-6. Only Iraq expressly challenged the legality of the military action. See Brian Whitaker, 'Attack on Afghanistan: Iraqi Reaction', *The Guardian*, 8 October 2001, at 6. For more on the reaction to the attacks and support for the response of the United States see Lindsay Moir, *Reappraising the Resort to Force: International Law*, Jus ad Bellum *and the War on Terror* (Hart, 2010), at 41-6.

Resolution 1368 on 12 September 2001 and Resolution 1373 on 28 September 2001. While at the time of their adoption it was not entirely clear who the perpetrators of the attacks were, both resolutions reaffirmed the right of self-defence in the light of the attacks.[28] This reaction could, of course, be interpreted as recognition that, due to the scale of the attacks that had taken place, contemporary terrorist groups now have a global reach and possess the capabilities to use force on an equivalent scale to that used by states, employing weapons with incredibly destructive potential. In this respect, if a state is the victim of a horrific attack, and there is the potential for further attacks, it should not make a difference, in principle, as to whether it was perpetrated by a state or non-state actor, as in either case there is a necessity for the state in question to defend itself.

States had the opportunity to put forward their positions on this issue in the Arria-formula meeting of the Security Council on the theme 'Upholding the collective security system of the Charter of the United Nations: the use of force in international law, non-State actors and legitimate self-defence', held on 24 February 2021.[29] From the statements of the various participating states the majority appeared to be supportive of the position that non-state actors could perpetrate armed attacks for the purposes of the right of self-defence, albeit certain states (e.g., Brazil) nonetheless remained firmly of the view that armed attacks may only be perpetrated by state actors. In this respect, while there has clearly been a swing in support of the view that the right of self-defence applies in the context of non-state actors, it is not possible to say that this is a universally held one.

This is also an issue that has been identified as being of relevance in the cyber context, with some notable disagreement between states within their various position papers. Some states, for example Israel, the Netherlands, the United Kingdom and Germany, have been clear that in their view the right of self-defence applies to armed attacks by both state and non-state actors.[30] However, while Finland was clear that in its view 'the conditions for the exercise of the right of self-defence apply in cyberspace as they do with regard

---

[28] UNSC Res. 1368 (2001), preamble; UNSC Res. 1373 (2001), preamble.

[29] See Letter dated 8 March 2021 from the Permanent Representative of Mexico to the United Nations addressed to the Secretary-General and the President of the Security Council, UN Doc. S/2021/247, 16 March 2021, Annex II.

[30] Dutch Minister of Foreign Affairs, 'Letter to the Parliament on the International Legal Order in Cyberspace', 5 July 2019, available at: www.government.nl/ministries/ministry-of-foreign-affairs/documents/parliamentary-documents/2019/09/26/letter-to-the-parliament-on-the-international-legal-order-in-cyberspace; United Kingdom Attorney General Jeremy Wright, 'Cyber and International Law in the 21st Century', 23 May 2018, available at: www.gov.uk/government/speeches/cyber-and-international-law-in-the-21st-century; The Federal Government of Germany, 'On the Application of International Law to Cyberspace', 9 March 2021, available at: www.auswaertiges-amt.de/blob/2446304/32e7b2498e10b74fb17204c54665bdf0/on-the-application-of-international-law-in-cyberspace-data.pdf.

to the use of armed force',[31] it also required that an armed attack 'be attributed to a particular State' before the right of self-defence would become available.[32] Similarly, France has rejected the premise that cyber armed attacks can be perpetrated by non-state actors unless attributable to another state as a result of them being conducted pursuant to the instructions or direction or control of that state.[33] Interestingly, however, in its position paper France also qualified this by stating that in 'exceptional' cases self-defence is available against armed attacks conducted by a so-called quasi-State, for example the Islamic State,[34] as well as acknowledging that there appears to be a general trend, as noted, in the direction of endorsing a general right of self-defence against non-state actors.[35]

Nevertheless, while it might in general be argued that the right of self-defence has been recognised by states as existing for them to protect themselves, regardless of the identity of the perpetrators of the attack, the fact remains that non-state actors do not reside on the high seas or in outer space, but instead upon the territory of another state, or across the territories of several states. This gives rise to the second, and more problematic, issue of whether, and under what conditions, a state is able to respond in self-defence. The events of 9/11 and their aftermath – which involved the United States using force in self-defence against al-Qaida upon the territory of Afghanistan – may again be used to demonstrate that a response in self-defence is possible under these circumstances. Furthermore, while certain states such as Brazil, China, Mexico and Sri Lanka took the view in the Arria-formula meeting of the UN Security Council in February 2021 that the positive consent of the territorial state was required before the use of force was permissible against non-state actors located there, the majority of states appeared to accept that self-defence in the absence of such consent was possible on the territory of other states under certain circumstances.[36] However, several complicated issues arise in regard to the implementation of the right of self-defence against non-state actors and the conditions under which it might be invoked, and these will be addressed in more detail in Chapter 8, which examines the implementation of the right of self-defence specifically in response to attacks by such actors.

---

[31] Finland Ministry for Foreign Affairs, 'Finland Published Its Positions on Public International Law in Cyberspace', 15 October 2020, available at: https://um.fi/documents/35732/0/KyberkannatPDF_EN.pdf/12bbbbde-623b-9f86-b254-07d5af3c6d85?t=1603097522727.
[32] Ibid.
[33] Ministère des Armées, 'Droit International Appliqué aux Operations dans le Cyberspace', 9 September 2019, available at: www.justsecurity.org/wp-content/uploads/2019/09/droit-internat-appliqu%C3%A9-aux-op%C3%A9rations-cyberespace-france.pdf. See, further, Chapter 8 on the right of self-defence against non-state actors.
[34] Ibid.   [35] Ibid.   [36] See UN Doc. S/2021/247, n. 29.

## 6.2.2 The Targets of an Armed Attack

Although the perpetrator of an armed attack need not be a state, it is generally accepted that the entity invoking the right of self-defence under international law will be.[37] Indeed, Article 51 talks of the occurrence of an armed attack 'against a Member of the United Nations', members being restricted to 'peace-loving states'.[38] However, the issue arises as to how we define the manifestations of a 'state' that, if attacked, give rise to the right of self-defence. In other words, what are the possible targets of an armed attack and the location of them that provide the victim state with the right of self-defence? There is no distinction in the *jus ad bellum*, for example, between combatants and civilians, or between military objectives and civilian objects, as found in international humanitarian law.[39]

### 6.2.2.1 The Armed Forces of a State

While attacks that occur upon the territory of the victim state are naturally covered by the right of self-defence, there is nothing in Article 51 requiring the attacks to occur upon a state's territory. Although, as discussed in Section 2.5.1., 'armed attack' and 'aggression' are not synonymous, Article 1(d) of the Definition of Aggression includes as an act of aggression '[a]n attack by the armed forces of a State on land, sea or air forces, or marine and air fleets of another State'.[40] As an example of such an attack forming the basis for the invocation of the right of self-defence, in her statement to the UN Security Council on 9 January 2020 the US Ambassador to the UN, Kelly Craft, stated that the decision taken by President Trump to invoke the right of self-defence for the drone strike that led to the death of Iranian General Qassem Soleimani on 2 January 2020 'was in direct response to an escalating series of armed attacks in recent months by Iran and Iranian supported militias *on U.S. forces and interests in the region*'.[41] In this respect, the fact that the United States was

---

[37] There exists some debate as to whether certain non-state actors in the form of 'contested states' possess a right of self-defence under international law. See Christian Henderson, 'Contested States and the Rights and Obligations of the *Jus ad Bellum*' (2013) 21 *Cardozo Journal of International and Comparative Law* 367.

[38] Article 4(1), UN Charter (1945).

[39] See, for example, Article 48, Additional Protocol I to the Geneva Conventions of 1949 (1977).

[40] See UNGA Res. 3314 (XXIX) (1974).

[41] United States Mission to the United Nations, Remarks at a UN Security Council Debate on Upholding the UN Charter, 9 January 2020, available at: https://usun.usmission.gov/remarks-at-a-un-security-council-debate-on-upholding-the-un-charter/ (emphasis added). General Soleimani was one of the most significant members of the Iranian leadership and, since 1998, commander of Iran's Quds force of the Islamic Revolutionary Guard Corps, a part of Iran's armed forces responsible for extraterritorial military and clandestine operations. Also among the dead was Abu Mahdi al-Mouhandis, who, while holding a formal position within the Iraqi

in part responding to the targeting of military 'bases where U.S. forces in Iraq [were] located' was not in itself controversial.[42]

Arguably more controversial, however, was the fact that in its letter to the UN Security Council on 8 January 2020 the United States also made reference to 'a threat to the amphibious ship USS BOXER on July 18, 2019 ... by an Iranian unmanned aerial system'[43] as well as 'an armed attack on June 19, 2019, by an Iranian surface-to-air missile on an unmanned U.S. Navy MQ-4 surveillance aircraft on a routine surveillance mission monitoring the Strait of Hormuz in international airspace'.[44] Putting aside issues such as whether a state may respond to such a 'threat' on one of its military vessels, not to mention one that occurred so much earlier in time, and whether an attack on an unmanned drone could be of sufficient gravity to constitute an 'armed attack', Article 1(d) of the Definition of Aggression also arguably provides support for the claim that these were targets of attack that, in principle at least, and subject to the other elements of the right discussed in subsequent sections of this chapter, may give rise to the right of self-defence. In this respect, the ICJ in the *Oil Platforms* case could 'not exclude the possibility that the mining of a single military vessel might be sufficient to bring into play the "inherent right of self-defence"'.[45]

In discussing self-defence in response to attacks on the armed forces of a state some academic commentators have drawn a distinction between 'national', 'unit' and 'personal' self-defence, with the latter two undertaken 'on the spot' by those soldiers who come under fire from across a border.[46] However, attacks on units and individual soldiers may, subject to the gravity of the attack and the defending state satisfying the twin requirements of necessity and proportionality,[47] provide for the possibility of invoking the right of national self-defence. Indeed, self-defence in all three situations would appear to be covered by the right of self-defence under international law without distinction.[48]

---

military, was also leader of Kata'ib Hezbollah, a militia with close ties to Iran but also officially part of Iraq's security forces. See Crispin Smith, 'United States Killed Iraqi Military Official and Iraqi Military Personnel in the Two Recent Attacks', *Just Security*, 5 January 2020, available at: www.justsecurity.org/67917/united-states-killed-iraqi-military-official-and-iraqi-military-personnel-in-the-two-recent-attacks/.

[42] Letter dated 8 January 2020 from the Permanent Representative of the United States of America to the United Nations addressed to the President of the Security Council, UN Doc. S/2020/20, 9 January 2020.

[43] Ibid. [44] Ibid. [45] *Oil Platforms* case, n. 11, at para. 72.

[46] See Dinstein, n. 3, at paras. 685–90. [47] See Sections 6.2.5 and 6.3, respectively.

[48] See Chris O'Meara, 'The Relationship between National, Unit and Personal Self-Defence in International Law: Bridging the Disconnect' (2017) 4 *Journal on the Use of Force and International Law* 273.

### 6.2.2.2 State Interests

Of potentially greater controversy in relation to the killing of General Soleimani, however, was the invocation by the United States of self-defence in the defence of its 'interests'.[49] This claim was inserted into several of the justifications that emerged from the Trump administration, although it remained relatively undefined. One can perhaps accept certain physical or human manifestations or interests of a state – such as, for example, its territory or armed forces, as discussed in Section 6.2.2.1, or its embassies or nationals, as discussed in Sections 6.2.2.3 and 6.4, respectively – as constituting the 'state' for the purposes of the right of self-defence. Yet, this is arguably far more difficult to establish in connection with broader 'interests' of a state and incorporating such interests under the right would open it up so as to permit military action in an almost unlimited range of circumstances, providing that a claim is made that a state's 'interests' were in one way or another at stake. As the ICJ framed it in the *Armed Activities* case, Article 51 of the Charter 'does not allow the use of force by a State to protect perceived security interests … Other means are available to a concerned State, including, in particular, recourse to the Security Council.'[50] Fortunately, however, and as seen throughout this chapter and Chapters 7 and 8, states are a little more specific when invoking the right of self-defence than doing so, without more, to protect their general interests.

### 6.2.2.3 Embassies

Through the justificatory discourse of the Trump administration in the United States following the drone strike which led to the death of General Soleimani the nature of the 'interests' that were being referenced as the basis for the invocation of the right of self-defence began to become clear. Indeed, in addition to the military targets discussed in Section 6.2.2.1, the interests being referred to appeared to include the US embassy in Baghdad which had been attacked on 31 December 2019.[51] President Trump also made reference to the

---

[49] Remarks at a UN Security Council Debate on Upholding the UN Charter, n. 41.
[50] *Case Concerning Armed Activities on the Territory of the Congo (Democratic Republic of Congo v. Uganda)*, Judgment, (2005) ICJ Reports 168, at para. 148.
[51] Supporters of Kata'ib Hezbollah who had been attending a funeral service for those killed in US airstrikes on 29 December 2019 marched into Baghdad's secure Green Zone and attacked the US Embassy, including breaching the main gate and setting alight fires, before Iraqi security forces finally intervened. See Falih Hassan, Ben Hubbard and Alissa J. Rubin, 'Protestors Attack U.S. Embassy in Iraq, Chanting "Death to America"', *New York Times*, 31 December 2019, available at: www.nytimes.com/2019/12/31/world/middleeast/baghdad-protesters-us-embassy.html.

invocation of self-defence on this occasion being in response to a threat to four US embassies.[52]

Steven Ratner has claimed that the question of whether an embassy of a state is covered by the term 'armed attack' in Article 51 is 'contentious'[53] and this would seem to be borne out in the range of views taken by scholars on this issue. On the one hand there are scholars that contend that only attacks mounted against the actual territory of a state can be considered as 'armed attacks' and they must have an 'across-the-border' character.[54] Attacks against troops and warships located outside of a state's territory are viewed as permissible targets of an armed attack as they 'are instruments of safeguarding political independence',[55] or because they have a 'quasi-territorial' nexus with a state,[56] while attacks against embassies and diplomatic missions should be excluded from the triggering of the right of self-defence given that attacks on them do not threaten the existence or security of the state.[57]

However, on the other hand there are scholars who are more open to attacks against embassies constituting 'armed attacks' for the purposes of the right of self-defence. While some appear to take this view in general terms,[58] others are of the view that such attacks might constitute armed attacks in 'special circumstances',[59] such as where the gravity of the attack is particularly severe.[60] There appeared to be, for example, general acceptance of the US' qualification of the attacks upon its embassies in Nairobi and Dar es Salaam in

---

[52] Ben Gittleson, 'Trump Offers New Iran Account, Now Says 4 Embassies Targeted but Still Few Specifics', *ABC News*, 10 January 2020, available at: https://abcnews.go.com/Politics/trump-offers-iran-account-now-embassies-targeted-specifics/story?id=68196851. However, Secretary of Defense Mark Esper stated that he had not seen any specific piece of intelligence information that Iran was planning an attack on four American embassies. See Peter Baker and Thomas Gibbons-Neff, 'Esper says he saw no evidence Iran targeted 4 embassies, as story shifts again', *New York Times*, 12 January 2020, available at: www.nytimes.com/2020/01/12/us/politics/esper-iran-trump-embassies.html?te=1&nl=morning-briefing&emc=edit_MBE_p_20200113&section=topNews?campaign_id=51&instance_id=15140&segment_id=20272&user_id=612ba96aa233942c06819c798ec67875&regi_id=99749597tion=topNews.

[53] See Steven R. Ratner, 'Self-Defence Against Terrorists: The Meaning of Armed Attack', in Larissa van den Herik and Nico Schrijver (eds.), *Counter-Terrorism Strategies in a Fragmented International Legal Order: Meeting the Challenges* (Cambridge University Press, 2013), 334, at 339.

[54] Theodor Schweisfurth, 'Operations to Rescue Nationals in Third States Involving the Use of Force in Relation to the Protection of Human Rights' (1980) 23 *Germany Yearbook of International Law* 159, at 164.

[55] Georg Nolte and Albrecht Randelzhofer, 'Article 51', in Bruno Simma, Daniel-Erasmus Khan, Georg Nolte, and Andreas Paulus (eds.), *The Charter of the United Nations: A Commentary*, 3rd ed. (Oxford University Press, 2012), 1397, at 1403.

[56] Schweisfurth, n. 54.   [57] Nolte and Randelzhofer, n. 55, at para. 28.

[58] See, Wilmshurst, n. 25, at 965.

[59] See Tom Ruys, 'The "Protection of Nationals" Doctrine Revisited', (2008) 13 *Journal of Conflict & Security Law* 233, at 245–6.

[60] Ibid.

August 1998, which led to the destruction of the embassies and the deaths of 224 people including 12 US citizens, as 'armed attacks' as well as of the subsequent invocation of the right to self-defence in response.[61] Indeed, the categorisation of these embassy attacks as 'armed attacks' was not refuted by any state.[62]

To date, the United States has been the only state to invoke its right of self-defence in response to attacks against its embassies,[63] beginning with its aborted 'Eagle Claw' military rescue mission in response to its embassy coming under siege in Tehran in 1979 which, it was claimed, was an 'Iranian armed attack'.[64] While in the majority of incidences in which attacks against embassies have taken place the right of self-defence has not been specifically invoked – or the language of the *jus ad bellum* more generally – this in itself does not automatically exclude such attacks from being categorised as 'armed attacks'. Indeed, the general lack of reference to the right of self-defence may equally be due to the circumstances of the attacks that have occurred, such as their often small scale nature,[65] or the lack of a necessity to respond in self-defence.[66]

### 6.2.2.4 Targets within Cyberspace

While following the adoption of the 2021 report of the United Nations Group of Government Experts divisions remained between certain states on the role and functioning of the *jus ad bellum* and *jus in bello* in regard to cyber operations,[67] the report noted that 'the Charter applies in its entirety' to cyber operations and reiterated the applicability of 'the inherent right of States to take measures consistent with international law and as recognized in the Charter'.[68] As Michael Schmitt notes, '[t]his can only be a reference to self-defense, for the term "inherent right" is drawn directly from Article 51 of that

---

[61] See Letter dated 20 August 1998 from the Permanent Representative of the United States of America to the President of the Security Council, UN Doc. S/1998/780, 20 August 1998. See also Wedgwood, 'Responding to Terrorism', n. 25, at 559.

[62] See Wedgwood, ibid., at 564.

[63] Gábor Kajtár and Gergö Barna Baláza, 'Beyond Tehran and Nairobi: Can Attacks against Embassies Serve as a Basis for the Invocation of Self-Defence?' (2021) 32 *European Journal of International Law* 863, at 873.

[64] Letter dated 25 April 1980 from the Permanent Representative of the United States of America to the United Nations Addressed to the President of the Security Council, UN Doc. S/13908, 25 April 1980.

[65] Tom Ruys, 'Can Attacks against Embassies Serve as a Basis for the Invocation of Self-Defence? A Reply to Gábor Kajtár and Gergö Barna Baláza' (2021) 32 *European Journal of International Law* 889. See, further, Section 6.2.5 on the possibility of a gravity threshold existing an armed attacks.

[66] See Section 6.3 on the twin requirements of necessity and proportionality.

[67] See, further, Section 1.7.4.    [68] UN Doc. A/76/135, 14 July 2021, at para. 71(e).

instrument, the provision on self-defense, and appears in no other Charter article.'[69] Furthermore, various states in their individual position papers have confirmed that, in their view, the right of self-defence as enshrined in Article 51 of the UN Charter applies in principle to cyber operations,[70] a position that would seem to be shared by several scholars.[71] In this respect, the direct target of an armed attack need not be a tangible manifestation of a state, but may be one that exists within cyber space, although, as discussed in Section 6.2.5.2, the attack would need to result in effects and consequences akin to an armed attack of a kinetic nature to be considered an armed attack for the purposes of the right of self-defence.

In conclusion, while there is no specific requirement for an armed attack to occur in the 'international relations' of states, as is the case with a use of force under Article 2(4),[72] for the purposes of the invocation of the right of self-defence the attack should nonetheless be directed against a manifestation of a state, although there is no comprehensive definitive list of possible targets. However, in addition to the specific targets articulated for discussion in this section there is, and as will be discussed later, general agreement that, under certain circumstances, a state may invoke self-defence in the protection of its nationals abroad.[73] It should also be noted that the right of collective self-defence, again as discussed later, gives rise to the possibility for a state to use force in self-defence when it has not been directly physically attacked itself.[74]

### 6.2.3 Issues of Proof

In the context of self-defence, the burden of proving that an armed attack has occurred falls upon the defending state. As the ICJ stated in the *Oil Platforms*

---

[69] Michael N. Schmitt, 'The Sixth United Nations GGE and International Law in Cyberspace', *Just Security*, 10 June 2021, available at: www.justsecurity.org/76864/the-sixth-united-nations-gge-and-international-law-in-cyberspace/.

[70] See, for example, Roy Schondorf, 'Israel's Perspective on Key Legal and Practical Issues Concerning the Application of International Law to Cyber Operations', *EJIL Talk!*, 9 December 2020, available at: www.ejiltalk.org/israels-perspective-on-key-legal-and-practical-issues-concerning-the-application-of-international-law-to-cyber-operations/; U.S. Department of Defense, 'DOD General Counsel Remarks at U.S. Cyber Command Legal Conference', 2 March 2020, available at: www.defense.gov/Newsroom/Speeches/Speech/Article/2099378/dod-general-counsel-remarks-at-us-cyber-command-legal-conference/.

[71] For example: '[t]he premise that the right of self-defence applies in the cyber context is indisputable. It would defy logic to assert that a State could suffer widespread destruction or death produced by cyber means, but not enjoy the right of individual or collective self-defence against a State or non-State actor launching the attack'. Michael N. Schmitt, 'Cybersecurity and International Law', in Robin Geiß and Nils Melzer (eds.), *The Oxford Handbook of the International Law of Global Security* (Oxford University Press, 2021), 661, at 675.

[72] See Sections 1.3.1.4 and 2.5.2.1.   [73] This is the subject of Section 6.4.

[74] See Section 6.5 on the right of collective self-defence.

case, it is for the state acting in self-defence to prove that it has been the victim of an armed attack.[75] In the context of traditional kinetic attacks by states and terrorist actors it may not be difficult for a state to prove that it has been the victim of an attack, in the sense that it is an observable reality. However, while in the context of more contemporary forms of attack, such as those of a cyber nature, the effects are similarly often an observable reality that can be demonstrated by the victim state, the often more pressing issue is proving the identity of the perpetrator and whether the attacks can be attributed to another state.[76] Furthermore, although the burden of proof rests upon the state invoking self-defence, it is unclear how one is to determine whether the burden has been discharged, with it falling, in most cases, to the international community to make such a judgement. Reacting states rarely engage, however, with the issue of whether the attack the victim state is responding to is an 'armed attack' for the purposes of the right of self-defence.

It is also apparent that there is no clear standard of proof in the context of the use of force and self-defence.[77] Evidential issues have been addressed in cases before the ICJ, but with no clear resolution as to what, if any, the required standard of proof is.[78] The United States has appeared to suggest that 'clear and compelling' evidence is required before embarking upon actions in self-defence,[79] but this is by no means settled in state practice and even the United States has apparently resorted to what might appear to be differing evidentiary standards in the context of the right of self-defence.[80] And even then, it is not entirely understood what is meant by 'clear and compelling' and how it can be distinguished from other potential standards of proof, such as 'convincing', 'beyond reasonable doubt' or 'on the balance of probabilities'. While the international community will often require more than mere assertions, exactly what standard of proof regarding the existence of an armed attack, or the threat of one, and the identity of the perpetrator of it will be required will depend to a large degree upon the individual circumstances in which the right of self-defence is being invoked.

---

[75] *Oil Platforms* case, n. 11, at para. 57.  [76] On the issue of attribution, see Section 8.3.
[77] See, in general, James A. Green, 'Fluctuating Evidentiary Standards for Self-Defence in the International Court of Justice' (2009) 58 *International & Comparative Law Quarterly* 163; Mary Ellen O'Connell, 'Evidence of Terror' (2002) 7 *Journal of Conflict & Security Law* 19.
[78] See, for example, *Oil Platforms* case, n. 11, at para. 61.
[79] See UN Doc. S/2001/946, 7 October 2001. See also O'Connell, n. 77, at 21–8 (who argues for a 'clear and convincing' standard).
[80] In invoking its right of self-defence following the African embassy attacks in 1998, for example, the United States claimed in its letter to the Security Council that it had 'obtained convincing information from a variety of reliable sources' that al-Qaida was behind the attacks. See UN Doc. S/1998/780, 20 August 1998.

### 6.2.4 The *Mens Rea* Element: Does an Armed Attack Need to Be Intended?

Given what was said in Chapter 2 about the importance of discerning intention in determining whether a use of force has taken place, it may be considered equally important that an armed attack be intended, given that it is a use of force, albeit arguably one with a particular gravity.[81] It has been claimed, in broad terms, that '[t]he term "armed attack" requires the attacker to have the intention to attack'.[82] Indeed, this requirement might be inferred from the ICJ's statements in the *Oil Platforms* case that, for Iran's actions to have constituted an armed attack, it had to have had the 'specific intention' of harming US vessels.[83] This case arose in the context of military action taken by the US Navy against offshore Iranian oil production complexes situated in the Persian Gulf. The United States first struck, and completely destroyed, the Reshadat complex on 19 October 1987, which it claimed was an action in self-defence in response to Iran firing a 'Silkworm' missile at a Kuwaiti-owned US-flagged vessel, the *Sea Isle City*, on 16 October 1987. The United States subsequently engaged in military action again on 18 April 1988 which led to the destruction of two further installations, the Salman and the Nasr, which the United States again justified as self-defence in response to the mining of the USS *Samuel B. Roberts* on 14 April 1988. While these strikes formed part of a broader operation codenamed Operation Praying Mantis, the Court restricted itself to addressing these two specific attacks, finding that the claims by the United States that it was acting in self-defence were not justified due to the fact that they were not 'aimed specifically at the United States'.[84]

However, a specific *mens rea* element of intention to commit an armed attack is not included within Article 51 of the UN Charter, and it is difficult to both discern such a requirement in customary international law and to reconcile it with the basic right of self-defence, which exists for states to take necessary action to defend themselves, regardless of whether the attack was intended or not.[85] If intention is a necessary *mens rea* element of an armed

---

[81] See further, Section 6.2.5 on the possibility of a 'gravity' threshold distinguishing uses of 'force' from 'armed attacks'.
[82] The Chatham House Principles, n. 25, at 966. See also Dinstein, n. 3, at para. 655.
[83] *Oil Platforms* case, n. 11, at para. 64.
[84] Ibid. In instituting proceedings before the ICJ, Iran alleged that the attacks amounted to a violation of provisions of the Treaty of Amity, Economic Relations and Consular Rights between the United States and Iran (1955) and, in particular, that there had been a breach by the United States of Article X(1) of the Treaty which guaranteed 'freedom of commerce and navigation' between the two states. In addressing the justification of self-defence, the Court therefore considered whether such actions satisfied Article XX(1)(d) of the Treaty which permitted action 'necessary to protect its essential security interests'. The incidents also took place during the Iran–Iraq war which began in 1980.
[85] During the negotiations on the UN General Assembly's Definition of Aggression, hostile intent was also not generally seen as a necessary ingredient for an act of aggression. This was

attack it would require a state in grave peril to wait and prove that an attack had actually been intentionally taken against it prior to being able to invoke the right of self-defence, resulting in a *reductio ad absurdum*.

Intention is not, however, entirely irrelevant for the purposes of identifying the occurrence of an armed attack and whether the invocation of the right of self-defence is necessary in the circumstances. Indeed, a hostile intention may be of clear probative value. For example, if the military vehicles of one state were to cross into the territory of a bordering state then – and in the absence of any clearly identifiable hostile intent – the territorial state would be expected to first determine whether the incursion was a mistake or not before confirming whether military action in self-defence might be necessary. In this respect, when Russian military vessels rolled over the border into Ukrainian territory first in Crimea in 2014 and then in northern and eastern Ukraine in 2022, Ukraine did not have to wait to invoke its right of self-defence given the clear hostile intent shown by Russian President Vladimir Putin towards the state of Ukraine.[86] Furthermore, the presence of hostile intent may be viewed as a relevant factor in establishing whether an attack is imminent[87] or whether an attack that has taken place is a discrete attack or whether it rather constitutes part of a 'concerted pattern of continuing armed activity'.[88]

Yet, aside from the probative value of identifying intention in these circumstances a general requirement of proving intention is neither possible nor desirable. It is sometimes difficult, if not impossible, to ascertain state intention. While non-state actors may be open about their intentions – indeed, an intention to attack a state may represent the very raison d'être for a terrorist group – this is not necessarily the case with state actors and intention may be far more problematic to identify. Furthermore:

[i]f the intention of the attacking state *is* relevant to whether it has committed an armed attack, this could preclude a state from responding in self-defence to indiscriminate attacks, even attacks of a high degree of gravity. Such a position is surely

---

not without exception, however, as the United States stated that a 'criterion of intent could help in distinguishing between an act of aggression and less serious forms of the use of force'. Special Committee on the Question of Defining Aggression, UN Doc. A/AC.134/SR.68, 31 July 1970, at 23. By contrast, in connection with the crime of aggression 'it follows from Article 30 of the International Criminal Court's Rome Statute and from the "Amendments to the Elements of Crimes" annexed to the 2010 resolution on aggression that the perpetrator of aggression must have intended to plan, prepare, initiate, or execute an act of aggression'. Ruys, n. 10 at 191.

[86] See 'Russia Is Stoking Tension with Ukraine and the EU', *The Economist*, 14 November 2021, available at: www.economist.com/europe/2021/11/14/russia-is-stoking-tension-with-ukraine-and-the-eu.

[87] See Section 7.5.

[88] Daniel Bethlehem, 'Principles Relevant to the Scope of a State's Right of Self-Defense against an Imminent or Actual Armed Attack by Non-State Actors' (2012) **106** *American Journal of International Law* 769, Principle 4. See Section 7.5 on 'contextual imminence'.

undesirable, as it could potentially encourage states to launch indiscriminate attacks, as no victim would possess a right to respond to them.[89]

Ultimately, it can be concluded that a state that is the victim of a military action may, regardless of the intent of those behind it, take appropriate military measures in response to ensure its own safety and security.[90] This is subject to any military measures in self-defence satisfying the twin customary requirements of necessity and proportionality, as discussed in Section 6.3, as well as satisfying any gravity threshold requirements which are discussed in the following section.

### 6.2.5 A Gravity Threshold Distinguishing 'Armed Attacks' from 'Uses of Force'?

Based upon the wording alone, the concepts of 'force' (as found in Article 2(4) and other places of the Charter) and 'armed attack' (as found in Article 51, which is solely concerned with the right of self-defence), would appear to be different. However, the distinction between them, if any, is not clear from a reading of the Charter alone. While the right of self-defence as found in Article 51 is universally considered an exception to the prohibition of the use of force as found in Article 2(4), the two are not expressly linked at any point in the Charter. As such, although Article 2(4) prohibits the use of force, the question arises as to whether a use of force equates to an armed attack, thus providing the victim state with the possibility of defending itself under international law. Or, alternatively, are there differences that exist between them of either a qualitative or quantitative nature?

The issue of whether there is a *de minimis* threshold distinguishing uses of 'force' from 'armed attacks' has given rise to a significant level of debate and discussion between scholars and commentators and the ICJ has also had the opportunity to explore and elucidate upon this distinction. In the *Nicaragua* case the Court made it clear that it was necessary 'to distinguish the most grave forms of the use of force (those constituting an armed attack) from other less grave forms', thus distinguishing uses of force from armed attacks upon the basis of their 'gravity', which was to be measured in terms of 'scale and effects'.[91] Beyond distinguishing between an armed attack and a 'mere frontier

---

[89] James A. Green, 'Self-Defence: A State of Mind for States?' (2008) 55 *Netherlands International Law Review* 181, at 205.

[90] See also Olivier Corten, *The Law against War: The Prohibition on the Use of Force in Contemporary International Law*, 2nd ed. (Hart, 2021), at 89.

[91] *Nicaragua* case, n. 6, at paras. 191 and 195. On this issue see Christine Gray, *International Law and the Use of Force*, 4th ed. (Oxford University Press, 2018), at 153–7. Article 2 of the Definition of Aggression (1974) states that forcible acts may not constitute acts of aggression due to 'the fact that the acts concerned or their consequences are not of sufficient gravity'.

incident' the Court did not expressly elaborate further on this distinction in the abstract.[92] The Eritrea–Ethiopia Claims Commission also excluded 'border encounters' from the purview of armed attack when it stated that '[l]ocalized border encounters between small infantry units, even those involving the loss of life, do not constitute an armed attack for the purposes of the Charter'.[93] The Commission, as such, concluded that the clashes between the Ethiopian and Eritrean forces were 'relatively minor incidents ... not of a magnitude to constitute an armed attack by either State against the other within the meaning of Article 51 of the U.N. Charter',[94] meaning that the Commission did not have to settle this particular element of the dispute.

This distinction between 'armed attacks' for the purposes of the right of self-defence and 'frontier incidents' or 'border encounters' was also arguably at play in the incident between China and India on the Himalayan Line of Control between Tibet and Ladakh in June 2020.[95] Despite the fact that 20 Indian troops lost their lives (China refused to say how many of their troops had been killed) neither India or China, or any other state, depicted this incident, which involved shouting, stone throwing, and fist fights, within the context of the *jus ad bellum* and the dispute led to a diplomatic rather than military confrontation between the two states.

In elucidating upon the distinction the ICJ in *Nicaragua* did, however, determine that 'assistance to rebels in the form of the provision of weapons or logistical or other support' by the Nicaraguan Sandanista government to the rebel groups in El Salvador was insufficient, by itself, to constitute an armed attack,[96] although in general '[s]uch assistance may be regarded as a threat or use of force, or amount to intervention in the internal or external affairs of other States'.[97] The Court provided no authority or support for this distinction and it was controversial, as discussed later in this section, for certain members of the Court.

Some claim that the distinction based on gravity was made by the Court as part of a conscious attempt to increase the divergence between the two concepts, thereby limiting the possibility for the escalation in violence and all-out war between states.[98] Indeed, 'it was thought that requiring a minimum gravity for acts to amount to "armed attacks" triggering the right of self-

---

[92] *Nicaragua* case, n. 6, at para. 195.
[93] Eritrea-Ethiopia Claims Commission – Partial Award: *Jus Ad Bellum* – Ethiopia's Claims 1–8, 19 December 2005, at para. 11, available at: http://legal.un.org/riaa/cases/vol_XXVI/457-469 .pdf. See, in general, Christine Gray, 'The Ethiopia/Eritrea Claims Commission Oversteps Its Boundaries: A Partial Award?' (2006) 17 *European Journal of International Law* 69.
[94] Ibid., at para. 12.
[95] BBC News, 'India–China Clash: 20 Indian Troops Killed in Ladakh Fighting', 16 June 2020, available at: www.bbc.co.uk/news/world-asia-53061476.
[96] *Nicaragua* case, n. 6, at para. 195.  [97] Ibid. See Section 2.4.3 on the indirect use of force.
[98] Ruys, n. 10, at 139–49; Gray, n. 91, at 156.

defense would strengthen the stability of the international order by avoiding rapid escalation of conflicts into an unstoppable cycle of force and counter-force'.[99] Gray adds that the Court's concern was, in particular, with *collective* self-defence; it wanted to limit *third state* involvement and '[i]f there was no armed attack, there could be no collective self-defence'.[100] Limiting the response of states that have been subject to a 'mere' use of force to non-forcible countermeasures would avoid the possible unnecessary escalation of what was a relatively minor infringement of the norm prohibiting the use of force.[101] If we are to take the Court's conception of armed attack as correct, in terms of the general relationship between Article 2(4) and Article 51 it would thus appear that self-defence is not an exception *in toto* to the prohibition of the use of force found in Article 2(4), but only certain, particularly serious, violations of it.

Yet, some scholars and commentators have argued against such a distinction, with many finding it artificial. Joseph Kunz, for example, argued that '[i]f "armed attack" means illegal armed attack, it means ... any illegal armed attack, even a small border incident'.[102] Yorum Dinstein, on the other hand, and in more moderate tones, admits of a *de minimis* or gravity threshold in this context and accepts that there will be occasions when a use of force will have occurred but which should not qualify as an armed attack justifying the invocation of the right of self-defence,[103] although is also of the view that the assumption by the ICJ 'that "a mere frontier incident" can have no "scale and effects" is quite bothersome'.[104]

There was, however, even disagreement within the Court itself on this issue. In his dissenting opinion, Judge Schwebel, the judge on the Court from the United States, was of the view that the reference in Article 3(g) of the Definition of Aggression to the 'substantial involvement' of states in the sending of armed bands was a reference to financial and logistical support.[105]

---

[99] Tom Ruys, 'The Meaning of "Force" and the Boundaries of the *Jus ad Bellum*: Are "Minimal" Uses of Force Excluded from UN Charter Article 2(4)?' (2014) **108** *American Journal of International Law* 159, at 178.

[100] Gray, n. 91, at 156. See Section 6.5 for more on collective self-defence.

[101] See Section 1.5.2 on countermeasures as a response to a prior use of force.

[102] Joseph L. Kunz, 'Individual and Collective Self-Defence in Article 51 of the Charter of the United Nations' (1947) **41** *American Journal of International Law* 872, at 878. See also John Hargrove, 'The *Nicaragua* Judgment and the Future of the Law of Force and Self-Defense' (1987) **81** *American Journal of International Law* 135, at 139. More recently, the Chatham House Principles stated that '[a]n armed attack means any use of armed force, and does not need to cross some threshold of intensity'. See the Chatham House Principles, n. 25, at 966.

[103] Dinstein, n. 3, at para. 543. An example provided by Dinstein is one state breaking into the diplomatic bag of another state, although it is doubtful whether such an action could qualify as a use of force.

[104] Ibid., at 210.

[105] *Nicaragua* case, n. 6, Dissenting Opinion of Judge Schwebel, at para. 166. Article 3(g) of the Definition of Aggression provides that '[t]he sending by or on behalf of a State of armed bands, groups, irregulars or mercenaries, which carry out acts of armed force against another

## 6.2 Concept of an 'Armed Attack'

While the Court had used Article 3(g) to demonstrate the situation when non-state actors may perpetrate an armed attack under the control of a state, it had also ruled out financial and logistical support as insufficient to constitute such an armed attack.[106] In addition, in the view of Judge Schwebel, the Court's narrow conception of 'armed attack' would mean that governments would more easily be able to overthrow weaker governments in that they would more broadly be denied the right of self-defence.[107] In similar tones, the British judge on the Court, Judge Jennings, focused upon the unrealistic nature of the Court's conception of 'armed attack', particularly given the nature of the conflicts occurring during the Cold War, which did not generally witness large-scale armed attacks.[108] In addition, the lack of functioning of the Chapter VII collective security system during this period meant that the right of self-defence, and the definition of armed attack, should not be read too restrictively. Indeed:

> [i]t may readily be agreed that the mere provision of arms cannot be said to amount to an armed attack. But the provision of arms may nevertheless be an important element in what might be thought to amount to an armed attack where it is coupled with other kinds of involvement.[109]

However, as Gray notes, '[n]either Schwebel nor Jennings adduced any evidence that in state practice mere provision of weapons and logistical support in isolation had been treated as an armed attack (as opposed to unlawful intervention) in cases of self-defence',[110] and it appears their arguments may also have been concerned more with policy than legal doctrine. It is true that, while the issue has rarely been addressed directly, the supply of arms and other support has never been expressly identified, either by states or the Security Council, as an armed attack. However, there have occasionally been 'hints of such a position',[111] notably by the United States and Lebanon in 1958 who, despite not directly referring to 'armed attack', suggested that the infiltration of arms and supplies from Syria into the United Arab Republic gave rise to the right of self-defence.[112]

Other members of the Court have subsequently taken issue with the distinction. Although writing in her personal capacity, former president of the ICJ

---

State of such gravity as to amount to the acts listed [in Sections 3(a-f)], or its substantial involvement therein' shall qualify as an act of aggression. For more on substantial involvement see Section 8.4.

[106] *Nicaragua* case, ibid., para. 195.
[107] Dissenting Opinion of Judge Schwebel., ibid., at para. 177.
[108] Dissenting Opinion of Judge Jennings, Ibid., at 543.
[109] Ibid., at 543. A similar position was taken by (mainly US) scholars following the Court's judgment in *Nicaragua*. See, for example, John Norton Moore, 'The Nicaragua Case and the Deterioration of World Order' (1987) 81 *American Journal of International Law* 151, at 154.
[110] Gray, n. 91, at 138.   [111] Ibid., at 176.   [112] See UN Doc. S/PV. 827, 15 July 1958.

Dame Rosalyn Higgins has claimed that 'is not *any* use of force by a foreign army entitled to be met by sufficient force to require it to withdraw? ... Is the question of *level* of violence by regular armed forces not really an issue of *proportionality*, rather than a question of determining what is "an armed attack"?'[113] This was a similar position to that adopted by Ian Brownlie in 1963.[114] Indeed, the gravity issue was only seen as 'relevant in so far as the minor nature of the attack is prima facie evidence of an absence of intention to attack, of honest mistake, or simply the limited objectives of the attack'.[115] The question as to whether the particular use of force constitutes lawful self-defence was thus to be determined more by its compliance with the twin requirements of necessity and proportionality,[116] which are addressed further in Section 6.3.

If one subscribes to the Court's gravity threshold it is, as may have already become clear, 'almost impossible to fix the threshold of force employed to define the notion of armed attack',[117] something which is particularly difficult given the spectrum of contexts in which it is of relevance. This might be seen in the jurisprudence of the Court itself, as it has not seemingly been entirely clear or consistent in its pronouncements as to where or at which point the threshold may be located. Indeed, in the *Oil Platforms* case, the Court did 'not exclude the possibility that the mining of a single military vessel might be sufficient to bring into play the "inherent right of self-defence"'.[118] From this alone it might appear that the difference in gravity between the two concepts is small, or even non-existent, although while not clear from the judgments of the Court the requirement of 'scale and effects' does not appear to be cumulative, so while the scale of the attack may be small, the significance or gravity of its effects may alter how it is perceived, and vice versa. The Court itself has, nonetheless, persisted with the gravity threshold in subsequent decisions and opinions.[119] However, regardless as to where one stands in principle in regard to the existence of a gravity threshold to distinguish uses of force from armed

---

[113] Rosalyn Higgins, *Problems and Process: International Law and How We Use It* (Clarendon Press, 1994), at 250–1. For more on the requirement of proportionality see Section 6.3.2.
[114] Brownlie, n. 3, at 366.
[115] Ibid. However, see Section 6.2.4 on *mens rea* and Section 2.6 on *mens rea* in connection with the prohibition of force.
[116] Ibid.
[117] Natalino Ronzitti, 'The Expanding Law of Self-Defence' (2006) 11 *Journal of Conflict & Security Law* 343, at 351.
[118] *Oil Platforms* case, n. 11, at para. 72.
[119] Ibid., at paras. 51 and 64. An argument by Uganda in the *DRC* v. *Uganda* case that the provision of logistical support to armed bands with knowledge of the objectives would be sufficient to constitute an armed attack was not adopted by the Court. See *Armed Activities on the Territory of the Congo (Democratic Republic of the Congo v. Uganda)*, Counter-Memorial Submitted by the Republic of Congo, vol. 1, 21 April 2001, at para. 350.

attacks, there are nonetheless a number of problems with such a threshold in practice that potentially limit its practical utility.

### 6.2.5.1 The Threshold in the General Practice of States

Following the decision of the ICJ in the *Nicaragua* case the government of the United States denied that a gravity threshold existed.[120] Indeed, '[t]he United States has long taken the position that the inherent right of self-defense potentially applies against *any* illegal use of force.'[121] While this was – and remains – the formal stated position of the United States, its position in practice has however been more nuanced and inconsistent. For example, on 31 December 2019 supporters of Kata'ib Hezbollah, who had been attending a funeral service for those killed in the US airstrikes of 29 December, marched into Baghdad's secure Green Zone and attacked the US Embassy, including breaching the main gate and setting alight fires.[122] Given its position regarding the lack of a gravity threshold, along with the fact that it was an attack on one of its embassies, this incident might arguably have been sufficient by itself for the United States to have invoked the right of self-defence in responding with a drone strike in Iraq on 2 January 2020 which led to the death of Iranian General Qassem Soleimani. Yet, the Trump administration clearly felt the need to bolster the gravity of the situation by not only taking time within its letter to the UN Security Council to set out all of the attacks it was ostensibly responding to by Iran and Iranian supported militias, but also by describing some of these expressly as 'armed attacks'.[123]

The following year, after a rocket attack on Erbil airport in Iraq on 15 February 2021,[124] President Biden launched the first use of military force since entering the White House.[125] Ten days after the attack on the airport

---

[120] Abraham D. Sofaer, 'International Law and the Use of Force' (1988) 82 *American Society of International Law Proceedings* 420, at 422.

[121] Department of Defense, Law of War Manual, June 2015, at 47 (emphasis added). See also William Taft IV, 'Self-Defense and the *Oil Platforms* Decision' (2004) 29 *Yale Journal of International Law* 295, at 299–302; Harold Koh, 'International Law in Cyberspace' (2012) 54 *Harvard International Law Journal Online* 1, at 7.

[122] Luke Harding, 'Trump Accuses Iran over Storming of US Embassy Compound in Baghdad', *The Guardian*, 31 December 2019, available at: www.theguardian.com/world/2019/dec/31/us-embassy-stormed-in-baghdad.

[123] See Letter dated 8 January 2020 from the Permanent Representative of the United States of America to the United Nations addressed to the President of the Security Council, UN Doc. S/2020/20, 9 January 2020.

[124] BBC News, 'US "Outraged" by Deadly Rocket Attack on Irbil', 16 February 2021, available at: www.bbc.co.uk/news/world-middle-east-56078980.

[125] Bethan McKernan, 'Airstrikes in Syria Kill 22 in Joe Biden's First Military Act as President', *The Guardian*, 26 February 2021, available at: www.theguardian.com/world/2021/feb/25/us-airstrike-syria-iran-militia.

two US F-15 fighter jets dropped seven 500-pound bombs on a group of buildings at a Syria–Iraq border crossing which, the Biden administration claimed, were being used by Iranian-backed militant groups.[126] The incident reportedly led to the deaths of 22 militiamen.[127] In its letter to the UN Security Council the Biden administration stated that '[t]he United States took this action pursuant to the United States' inherent right of self-defense as reflected in Article 51 of the United Nations Charter.'[128] By contrast to the Trump administration the year before, however, the Biden administration did not appear to feel the need to bolster the gravity of the rocket attack on the airport in Erbil which, while resulting in the death of a Filipino contractor, merely led to the wounding of four US contractors and a US soldier. In addition, it was further notable that, unlike with the Trump administration's justification for the strike killing General Soleimani, the Biden administration refrained from depicting the attack on Erbil airport at any point as an 'armed attack', but rather made reference exclusively to this as an 'attack' *simpliciter*. However, although these strikes were justified as self-defence, the Biden administration's justification, as with that of the Trump administration a year before, raised question marks over the meaning of, and even the requirement for, an 'armed attack' in the form the ICJ had set out.[129]

While the United States' general position regarding the absence of a distinction between a 'use of force' and an 'armed attack' represents the view of a single state, and while the United States is often painted as an outsider in terms of its position on this issue,[130] the difference between its position and the position of other states can often appear marginal. The strike against General Soleimani of 2 January 2020 generated extensive reaction from states, with some condemning the action in legal terms, others supporting the action in legal terms, while positions demonstrating ambiguity in regards to the legal position were also discernible.[131] There was, by contrast, far less reaction to the strikes on 25 February 2021. Yet, whether or not implicit in their reaction,

---

[126] Ibid.   [127] Ibid.

[128] Letter dated 27 February 2021 from the Permanent Representative of the United States of America to the United Nations addressed to the President of the Security Council, UN Doc. S/2021/202, 3 March 2021.

[129] See Christian Henderson, 'The 25 February 2021 Military Strikes and the "Armed Attack" Requirement of Self-Defence: From "Sina Qua Non" to the Point of Vanishing?' (2022) 9 *Journal on the Use of Force and International Law* 55.

[130] See Adil Ahmad Haque, 'U.S. Legal Defense of the Soleimani Strike at the United Nations: A Critical Assessment', *Just Security*, 10 January 2020, available at: www.justsecurity.org/68008/u-s-legal-defense-of-the-soleimani-strike-at-the-united-nations-a-critical-assessment/.

[131] See Mehrnusch Anssari and Benjamin Nußberger, 'Compilation of States' Reactions to U.S. and Iranian Uses of Force in Iraq in January 2020', *Just Security*, 22 January 2020, available at: www.justsecurity.org/68173/compilation-of-states-reactions-to-u-s-and-iranian-uses-of-force-in-iraq-in-january-2020/.

states did not raise as problematic the fact that none of the incidents specifically represented an armed attack,[132] although this was something that was raised in the waves of reaction by scholars and commentators to these incidents.[133]

However, the broader reality is that states do not often distinguish between 'uses of force' and 'armed attacks' and often omit to speak of 'armed attacks' specifically in the abstract or depict attacks that they are responding to – or that other states have responded to – as 'armed attacks'. Instead, the general focus is upon the necessity and proportionality of the response taken,[134] thus perhaps raising question marks over the existence of a conceptual distinction between a use of force and armed attack.[135] Even attacks that have resulted in no human harm or physical damage have been classed as armed attacks for the purposes of the right of self-defence. For example, the United States took action against Iraq, which included bombing an intelligence headquarters on the outskirts of Baghdad, in response to an assassination attempt upon former

---

[132] It was also interesting that, while initially categorising the killing of Soleimani as a 'terrorist attack', an 'assassination' and as a 'criminal act', Iran did not categorise the strike as an 'armed attack'. Although it did reserve its right to exercise its inherent right of self-defence it at the same time called upon the UN Security Council to uphold its responsibilities. See Letter dated 3 January 2020 from the Permanent Representative of the Islamic Republic of Iran to the United Nations addressed to the Secretary-General and the President of the Security Council, UN Doc. S/2020/13, 3 January 2020. Later, on 7 January 2020, the Iranian Foreign Minister described the strikes as both an 'armed attack' and an 'act of aggression'. See Fred Pleitgen, 'Iranian Foreign Minister Accuses US of "State Terrorism" as Country's Parliament Votes to Designate US Forces as Terrorists', *CNN*, 7 January 2020, available at: https://edition.cnn.com/2020/01/07/middleeast/iran-zarif-united-states-intl/index.html. Repeating these accusations in a separate interview, the Foreign Minister also stated that Iran would 'respond according to [its] own timing and choice'. See 'Transcript: NPR's Full Interview with Iran's Foreign Minister', *NPR*. 7 January 2020, available at www.npr.org/2020/01/07/794175782/transcript-nprs-full-interview-with-iran-s-foreign-minister?t=1598536745689.

[133] For a range of views, see, for example, Mary Ellen O'Connell, 'The Killing of Soleimani and International Law', *EJIL Talk!*, 6 January 2020, available at: www.ejiltalk.org/the-killing-of-soleimani-and-international-law/; Marko Milanovic, 'The Soleimani Strike and Self-Defence against an Imminent Armed Attack', *EJIL Talk!*, 7 January 2020, available at: www.ejiltalk.org/the-soleimani-strike-and-self-defence-against-an-imminent-armed-attack/; Michael J. Glennon, 'The Irrelevance of Imminence', *Lawfare*, 15 January 2020, available at: www.lawfareblog.com/irrelevance-imminence; Stefan Talmon and Miriam Heipertz, 'The U.S. Killing of Iranian General Qasem Soleimani: Of Wrong Trees and Red Herrings, and Why the Killing May Be Lawful after All', *German Practice in International Law*, 23 January 2020, available at: https://gpil.jura.uni-bonn.de/2020/01/the-u-s-killing-of-iranian-general-qasem-soleimani-of-wrong-trees-and-red-herrings-and-why-the-killing-may-be-lawful-after-all/; Henderson, n. 129.

[134] See Section 6.3 for more on the necessity and proportionality criteria.

[135] Indeed, 'customary evidence ... makes clear that the gravity threshold should not be set too high and that even small-scale attacks involving the use of (possibly) lethal force may trigger Article 51'. Ruys, n. 10, at 155.

President George H. W. Bush during a visit to Kuwait in 1993.[136] President Clinton described the attempt as an 'armed attack,'[137] while the Secretary of State, Madeleine Albright, described it as an 'attempted attack' giving rise to the right of self-defence.[138] Other states did not expressly describe the assassination attempt as an 'armed attack' but did make reference to Article 51, thereby implying acceptance of the attempt as an 'armed attack' or at least an incident which justified the invocation of the right of self-defence.[139]

While the concept of 'armed attack' potentially alludes to the actual use of a weapon, it would appear that if either or both the scale or the consequential effects of an action are sufficiently significant then an armed attack may occur without the actual discharging of such a weapon.[140] For example, if the tanks and jeeps of a state were to violate the territorial sovereignty of another state through rolling across its border with apparent hostile intent despite no shots being fired, as initially occurred with Russia's invasion and occupation of Crimea in 2014,[141] a state would be entitled to treat this as an armed attack and take immediate steps to forcefully repel it.[142] As Dinstein notes, '[w]hen one State sends armed formations across an international frontier, without the consent of the local Government, it must be deemed to have triggered an armed attack even if no shots have been fired'.[143] Furthermore, and as was also the case in Crimea, if one state has an agreement with the territorial state for the positioning of its troops within the territory of that state but which subsequently moves its troops outside of the agreed location or they remain beyond the length of any agreed upon time for their presence, then this represents what has been termed a 'constructive armed attack'.[144] In the latter situation, however, there would arguably be an obligation to pursue non-forcible measures first on the basis that an immediate armed response in self-defence might be perceived to be unnecessary, particularly in light of the prior

---

[136] *Keesing's* (1993) 39531. See, in general, Dino Kritsiotis, 'The Legality of the 1993 US Missile Strike on Iraq and the Right to Self-Defence under International Law' (1996) **45** *International & Comparative Law Quarterly* 162.

[137] Kritsiotis, ibid., at 171–2.   [138] UN Doc. S/26003, 26 June 1993.

[139] See UN Doc. S/5657, 27 June 1993.

[140] See Section 2.4.1 on whether the use of a weapon is required to constitute a use of force.

[141] See Annie Gowen and Karoun Demirjian, 'Ukraine Says Russian Forces Cross Border in Tanks, Armored Vehicles', *The Washington Post*, 25 August 2014, available at: www.washingtonpost.com/world/europe/ukraine-says-russian-forces-cross-border-in-tanks-armored-vehicles/2014/08/25/8cb7d1d4-2c3f-11e4-994d-202962a9150c_story.html?utm_term=.e7ee34eb2404.

[142] See Marco Roscini, 'Russia Has Not Breached the *Jus ad Bellum* in 2022; It Did in 2014', *voelkerrechtsblog*, 7 March 2022, available at: https://voelkerrechtsblog.org/russia-has-not-breached-the-jus-contra-bellum-in-2022-it-did-in-2014/.

[143] Dinstein, n. 3, at para. 602.

[144] Ibid. Such action amounts to an act of aggression under Article 3(e) of the General Assembly's Definition of Aggression (1974) and Article *8bis* of the Rome Statute of the International Criminal Court (1998).

cooperation between the states and in the absence of any discernible hostile intent.[145]

Furthermore, Israel launched an extensive military campaign in Lebanon in July 2006 in response to several missiles being launched into Israeli territory and the kidnapping of two Israeli soldiers by Hezbollah.[146] In its letter to the Security Council, Israel described the acts as a 'belligerent act of war' and reserved its 'right to act in accordance with Article 51 of the Charter of the United Nations and exercise its right of self-defence when an armed attack is launched against a Member of the United Nations',[147] both of which implied that Israel considered the acts to be armed attacks justifying the invocation of the right of self-defence as opposed to constituting, in the ICJ's terminology, a mere 'frontier incident'. It is perhaps arguably also of significance that although Israel received condemnation, this was mainly due to concerns regarding the proportionality of the response as opposed to the invocation of the right of self-defence to what were relatively minor attacks.[148]

Ultimately, and while acknowledging that these are but a handful of examples, it is possible to infer that '[i]n the end, customary practice suggests that, subject to the necessity and proportionality criteria, even small-scale bombings, artillery, naval or aerial attacks qualify as "armed attacks" activating Article 51 of the UN Charter, as long as they result in, or are capable of resulting in destruction of property or loss of lives'.[149] Nonetheless, 'a considerable grey area remains'.[150]

### 6.2.5.2 The Gravity Threshold in the Context of Cyber Operations

This debate regarding a gravity threshold has been particularly strong in the context of cyber operations and has been something states have expressed their views on. In their various statements on the applicability of international law to cyber operations states have generally adopted the position advanced by the ICJ in the *Nicaragua* case that an armed attack is the 'most grave form' of a use of force.[151] The Netherlands has been quite clear, for example, that

---

[145] See Section 6.3.1 on the criterion of necessity and Section 6.2.4 on the *mens rea* element of intention.

[146] Greg Myre and Steven Erlanger, 'Israelis Enter Lebanon after Attacks', *New York Times*, 13 July 2006, at A1. See, in general, Tom Ruys, 'Crossing the Thin Blue Line: An Inquiry into Israel's Recourse to Self-Defence Against Hezbollah' (2007) **45** *Stanford Journal of International Law* 265; Michael N. Schmitt, '"Change Direction" 2006: Israeli Operations in Lebanon and the International Law of Self-Defence' (2008) **29** *Michigan Journal of International Law* 127.

[147] UN Doc. S/2006/515-A/60/937, 12 July 2006.

[148] See UN Doc. S/PV. 5489, 14 July 2006.   [149] Ruys, n. 10, at 155.

[150] Ibid. See also Heather Harrison Dinniss, *Cyber Warfare and the Laws of War* (Cambridge University Press, 2012), at 79–80.

[151] See Sections 1.7.4, 2.4.2 and 6.2.5.

'[a]n armed attack is not the same as the use of force within the meaning of article 2(4) of the UN Charter'.[152] Similarly, in measuring the 'gravity' of a use of force for the purposes of identifying an armed attack in the context of the right of self-defence, most states have similarly adopted the general position of the ICJ that this can be measured by the 'scale and effects' of the forcible act.[153]

However, and as discussed in Section 6.2.5, '[i]nternational law is ambiguous on the precise scale and effects an operation must have in order to qualify as an armed attack'.[154] It is also arguably even more difficult to determine scale and effects in the context of cyber-operations as the possible effects of computer network attacks 'span the spectrum of consequentiality'.[155] It appears, however, that there is a level of agreement that for a cyber operation to qualify there must be some equivalence in terms of the scale and effects to those of a traditional kinetic armed attack and, in particular, that the operation has caused serious damage, serious physical injury or death.[156] Indeed, while each attack must be assessed individually '[i]t seems certain ... that where a computer network attack causes destruction and fatalities on a par with a conventional attack, a state will have a right to respond in self-defence'.[157]

To put this into context, '[i]f a [computer network attack] were to cause severe damage to property or even human fatalities (as a result, e.g., of the shutdown of computers controlling waterworks and dams, leading to the flooding of inhabited areas), it would qualify as an armed attack'.[158] Furthermore, and as expressed by New Zealand, 'cyber activity that disables

---

[152] Dutch Minister of Foreign Affairs, n. 30.
[153] The *Tallinn Manual* experts and most states that have spoken to the issue are in accord (e.g., Germany, Australia, Finland France, Israel, Netherlands, New Zealand, United Kingdom, United States). No state has yet expressed opposition to this general point. Interestingly, Finland also notes that 'most commentators agree that when the scale and effects of a cyberattack correspond to those of an armed attack responding to the cyberattack is justifiable as self-defence'. See Finland Ministry for Foreign Affairs, n. 31.
[154] Dutch Minister of Foreign Affairs, n. 30.
[155] Michael Schmitt, 'Computer Network Attack and the Use of Force in International Law: Thoughts on a Normative Framework' (1999) **37** *Columbia Journal of Transnational Law* 885, at 912.
[156] Finland stated that '[i]t is obvious that the attack must have caused death, injury or substantial material damage, but it is impossible to set a precise quantitative threshold for the effects, and other circumstantial factors must be taken into account in the analysis, as well'. Finland Ministry for Foreign Affairs, n. 31.
[157] Harrison Dinniss, n. 150, at 80. As Harrison Dinniss expands: 'A state is ... permitted to respond in self-defence when it is the victim of a computer network attack causing damage to property or persons of sufficient scale and effect to elevate it beyond the equivalent of a frontier incident.' Ibid., at 81. On the notion of a 'mere frontier incident' see Section 6.2.5.
[158] Dinstein, n. 3, at para. 579.

the cooling process in a nuclear reactor, resulting in serious damage and loss of life, would constitute an armed attack',[159] while the United Kingdom noted that '[i]f it would be a breach of international law to bomb an air traffic control tower with the effect of downing civilian aircraft, then it will be a breach of international law to use a hostile cyber operation to disable air traffic control systems which results in the same, ultimately lethal, effects'.[160]

On the other hand, however, it would seem that an intrusion into public systems or systems containing sensitive national security data would be treated 'as simple espionage, an act not prohibited under international law'.[161] In this respect, neither states or scholars at the time treated the distributed denial of service attacks against Estonia in 2007 and Georgia in 2008 as armed attacks so as to permit the victim states to resort to force in self-defence or third states to invoke the right of collective self-defence.[162] By contrast, the 2010 Stuxnet worm purportedly resulted in destruction of property, in that Iran needed to replace 1,000 of the 9,000 IR-1 centrifuges at the Natanz nuclear fuel enrichment facility.[163] While this was arguably of sufficient 'scale and effects' to constitute a use of force,[164] it is perhaps difficult to conclude that it constituted sufficiently serious damage, and was therefore of sufficient gravity, to constitute an armed attack.[165] This assessment would arguably be different, however, if the attack on the nuclear fuel enrichment facility had instead led to nuclear radiation harming humans, the facility or surrounding area, or the natural environment. Speaking to this point, Finland recently expressed the view that

[a]ny interpretation of the use of force in cyberspace should respect the UN Charter and not just the letter of the Charter but also its object and purpose, which is to prevent the escalation of armed activities. This would mean, for instance, that the distinction

---

[159] New Zealand Ministry of Foreign Affairs and Trade, 'The Application of International Law to State Activity in Cyberspace', 1 December 2020, at 8, available at: www.mfat.govt.nz/en/media-and-resources/the-application-of-international-law-to-state-activity-in-cyberspace/.

[160] United Kingdom Attorney General Jeremy Wright, 'Cyber and International Law in the 21st Century', 23 May 2018, available at: www.gov.uk/government/speeches/cyber-and-international-law-in-the-21st-century.

[161] Harrison Dinniss, n. 150, at 81. Cf. Walter G. Sharp, *Cyberspace and the Use of Force* (Aegis Research Corp., 1999), at 129. However, see Section 2.2 on the principle of non-intervention.

[162] Nicholas Tsagourias, 'Cyber Attacks, Self-Defence and the Problem of Attribution' (2012) 17 *Journal of Conflict & Security Law* 229, at 232.

[163] See Section 2.4.2.

[164] Russell Buchan, 'Cyber Attacks: Unlawful Users of Force or Prohibited Interventions?' (2012) 17 *Journal of Conflict & Security Law* 212, at 232.

[165] Tsagourias, for example, claims that only a cyber-attack that 'causes *substantial* human and/or material destruction can be equated to an armed attack for the purposes of the right of self-defence. That would be the case, for example, when a cyber-attack on an air traffic control system, or a cyber attack on a nuclear reactor, caused substantial material or human destruction'. Tsagourias, n. 162, at 231 (emphasis added).

between armed attack as a particularly serious violation of the Charter, on the one hand, and any lesser uses of force, on the other, is preserved.[166]

Interestingly, in its position paper Finland also noted that '[a] widely discussed question is, to what extent the definition of a cyberattack comparable to an armed attack should take account of *the indirect and long-term impacts* of the attack.'[167] In a sense, the physical impacts of any cyber-attack are in general *indirect* in nature, in that the attack would, for example, strike the computer system which controls a dam or a nuclear reactor, rather than the dam or nuclear reactor directly. Although this stands in contrast to kinetic attacks in which the impacts of any attack would occur through more direct means, the distinction is largely inconsequential if the impacts of the cyber-attack are sufficiently proximate in time to the attack which led to their occurrence.

However, whether the *longer-term* impacts of a cyber operation should be considered is a more open question. If, as the Netherlands has suggested, there is a 'serious disruption with long-lasting consequences' then the nature of the serious disruption – in terms of scale and effects – might in itself justify a response in self-defence. Yet, it might be that the attack is not in itself serious, or at least of the gravity and 'scale' of an armed attack, but that the long-lasting consequences or 'effects' prove to be of a serious nature. In these situations, a victim state would therefore arguably not be able to invoke the right of self-defence at the time of the attack on the basis of the attack being of insufficient gravity in terms of both its scale and effects, meaning that any response would be limited to non-forcible measures. This must, however, be without prejudice to the possibility of a state invoking its right of self-defence in the future, should the effects of an attack that may have occurred in the past take a significant turn, leaving the state with a necessity of invoking proportionate measures in self-defence.[168]

A different issue is whether *non-physical* effects can be considered in gauging the scale and effects of an attack. However, '[a]t present there is no international consensus on qualifying a cyberattack as an armed attack if it does not cause fatalities, physical damage or destruction yet nevertheless has very serious non-material consequences.'[169] In this respect, the type of 'non-material' consequences that have most often been raised in the context of cyber operations are '*significant economic effects* such as the collapse of a State's financial system or parts of its economy'.[170] While those states that

---

[166] Finland Ministry for Foreign Affairs, n. 31.  [167] Ibid. (emphasis added).
[168] See Section 6.3 on the customary requirements of necessity and proportionality.
[169] Dutch Minister of Foreign Affairs, n. 30.
[170] Finland Ministry for Foreign Affairs, n. 31 (emphasis added).

have raised these types of effects in their position papers have left this question open, several have expressly noted that it is one that 'merits further consideration'.[171]

Given the emphasis placed on the serious physical nature of any effects stemming from a cyber operation in terms of justifying a response in self-defence, combined with the general response to the distributed denial of service attacks against Estonia in 2007 and Georgia in 2008, it might seem doubtful that economic effects would be deemed to be of a nature to constitute an armed attack. However, certain states have been clear that they consider such non-physical effects as potentially constituting an armed attack for the purposes of the right of self-defence. For example, the Netherlands has stated that 'if a cyber-attack targets the entire Dutch financial system' or even 'if it prevents the government from carrying out essential tasks such as policing or taxation' then, in its view, 'it would qualify as an armed attack ... and ... trigger a state's right to defend itself even by force'.[172] In similar, albeit arguably more expansive tones, France has suggested that an attack on critical infrastructure with substantial consequences, an attack that causes a technological or ecological disaster, a major attack against the French economy or one that otherwise would paralyze whole swathes of the country's activities, would, in its view, constitute an armed attack.[173] While this remains an open and in many respects controversial issue, some have predicted that the position of states will, in general, 'move in the general direction of the French stance over time'.[174] Indeed, while attacks which are limited to financial effects are one thing, those that while not manifesting themselves in terms of physical effects nonetheless lead to a state's virtual paralysis are another, and something that states are unlikely to view so benevolently.

---

[171] Ibid.

[172] Ank Bijleveld, Dutch Minister of Defence, 'Keynote Address: We Have to Steer the Cyber Domain before It Steers Us' (Diplomacy and Defense in Cyber Space Cyber Seminar, The Hague, 21 June 2018), available at: https://puc.overheid.nl/mrt/doc/PUC_248478_11/1/.

[173] Ministère des Armées, n. 33.

[174] Michael Schmitt, 'France's Major Statement on International Law and Cyber: An Assessment', *Just Security*, 16 September 2019, available at: www.justsecurity.org/66194/frances-major-statement-on-international-law-and-cyber-an-assessment/. Elsewhere Schmitt has commented that '[u]nquestionably, a cyber operation resulting in significant death, injury, physical damage, or destruction would be an armed attack. Whether States will be willing to characterize those causing lesser damage or injury – as in the case of a loss of functionality of cyber infrastructure that does not result in significant destructive or injurious knock-on effects, or no damage or injury at all – as an armed attack remains to be seen. It is, however, likely that victim-States would consider some such operations as activating their right to self-defence.' Schmitt, n. 71, at 675.

### 6.2.5.3 The ICJ's Concept of 'Proportional Forcible Countermeasures'

In contributing to this 'grey area' the ICJ in the *Nicaragua* case appeared to leave open the question as to whether a state may resort to proportional forcible countermeasures 'in reaction to measures which do not constitute an armed attack but may nevertheless involve a use of force'.[175] In other words, the question appeared to be left open as to whether it might be permissible to use force in response to a prior use of force that does not possess the 'scale and effects' to constitute an armed attack. If one adopts the position that a gravity threshold for an armed attack is positive from a policy perspective, in that it limits the potential for a forcible response and the prospects for all-out war, then the possibility that uses of force even below this gravity threshold give rise to a lawful forcible response is troubling.

However, along similar lines, Judge Simma, in the ICJ's *Oil Platforms* case, also claimed that proportional countermeasures involving the use of armed force may be resorted to in response 'smaller-scale uses of force' that do not reach the gravity of an 'armed attack'.[176] This position appeared to be adopted upon the basis of the Court's statement in *Nicaragua* that 'States do not have a right of "collective" armed response to acts which do not constitute an "armed attack"'.[177] Indeed, it has been argued that the Court appeared to have left open a loophole here, in that, while it had excluded the possibility of forcible countermeasures by third states, it omitted to do the same for the victim state of the use of force.[178] Ruys goes as far as to say that 'it is rather flabbergasting that the Court flags a crucial *potential* gap in the rules on the use of force, which would seem to be prima facie incompatible with the comprehensive regime established by Articles 2(4) and 51 of the UN Charter, without providing any further guidance or supporting arguments'.[179] Yet, given the significance otherwise paid to the distinction between uses of force and armed attacks in its judgment in *Nicaragua*, and the fact that the Court specifically stated an armed attack to be a *sine qua non* of the right of self-defence,[180] it is arguably unlikely that the Court was undermining this distinction and the permissible rights under it in the very same judgment.

### 6.2.5.4 Gravity and the 'Accumulation of Events' Theory

While viewing attacks through the gravity threshold would mean that a single small-scale use of force would not necessarily permit a forcible reaction, the question arises as to whether a state is able to respond in self-defence if

---

[175] See *Nicaragua* case, n. 6, at para. 210.
[176] *Oil Platforms* case, n. 11, Separate Opinion of Judge Simma, at para. 12.
[177] *Nicaragua* case, n. 6, at para. 211. Hargrove claims that this was an 'arbitrary announcement' by the Court. Hargrove, n. 102, at 141.
[178] Ruys, n. 10, at 141.   [179] Ibid.   [180] *Nicaragua* case, n. 6, at para. 237.

presented with multiple low-level – or 'pin prick' – uses of force which might, if viewed cumulatively, give rise to an armed attack. Indeed, it could be argued that the gravity threshold encourages states and non-state actors to engage in such small-scale military attacks in the expectation that they can do so without being subjected to armed defensive measures by the victim state. In this respect, some would argue that although each attack would not possess the requisite gravity sufficient to constitute an armed attack, they might collectively constitute an armed attack for the purposes of the right of self-defence under what has come to be known as the 'accumulation of events theory'.[181]

The ICJ has continuously alluded to the existence of such a possibility. In the *Nicaragua* case, for example, the Court queried whether incursions 'may be treated for legal purposes as amounting, singly *or collectively*, to an "armed attack"'.[182] Furthermore, in the *Oil Platforms* case it was noted that 'the question is whether the attack, either in itself *or in combination with the rest of the "series of attacks"* cited by the United States can be categorized as an "armed attack" on the United States justifying self-defence',[183] while in the *Armed Activities* case the Court appeared to accept that a 'series of deplorable attacks could be regarded as cumulative in character'.[184] There is relatively little dedicated academic treatment of the theory, although it has been acknowledged and discussed in the work of scholars.[185]

Of perhaps most significance, however, is that the accumulation of events theory has also been implicitly, although often tentatively, witnessed in the practice of states. For example, in 1964 the Southern Arab Federation (SAF), which had military links with the United Kingdom, complained of an armed attack by Yemen which consisted of a 'series of aggressions'. In invoking collective self-defence at the SAF's request, the United Kingdom launched an air strike in Yemen which destroyed a fort. However, in viewing the UK's response as more of an act of reprisal than a legitimate claim in self-defence based upon the accumulation of events theory, the Security Council issued a statement condemning reprisals as 'incompatible with the principles and purposes of the UN'.[186] There was, however, also arguably an implicit rejection

---

[181] Dinstein, n. 3, at paras. 554–6; Ruys, n. 10, at 168–75. This also raises the question as to the level, and aims, of any armed response, that will be addressed in Section 6.3.2.1.
[182] See *Nicaragua* case, n. 6, at para. 231 (emphasis added).
[183] *Oil Platforms* case, n. 11, at para. 64 (emphasis added).
[184] *Armed Activities* case, n. 50, at para. 146.
[185] See, for example, Chris O'Meara, *Necessity and Proportionality and the Right of Self-Defence in International Law* (Oxford University Press, 2021), at 79; Dinstein, n. 3, at paras. 554–6; James A. Green, *The International Court of Justice and Self-Defence in International Law* (Hart Publishing, 2009), at 42–4.
[186] UNSC Res. 188 (1964). See Section 6.3.1.2 for more on the nature of armed reprisals.

of the accumulation of events theory by the Council in this statement given its overall condemnation of the operation.

More recently, the theory has been of relevance in the context of rockets launched from the Gaza strip into Israel which have been fired in resistance to Israel's continued control over Gaza's external existence.[187] These increased following Hamas's forcible assumption of control of Gaza in 2007, which led to Israel declaring it to be hostile territory.[188] Israel has conducted numerous raids into Gaza, justified as self-defence, in response to the launching of these rockets. The most significant operations were Operation Cast Lead (2008-9), Operation Pillar of Defense (2012), Operation Protective Edge (2014) and Operation Guardian of the Walls (2021). Regarding these operations, the question has arisen as to whether the missile attacks, either individually or cumulatively, amount to an armed attack for the purposes of Article 51. Of course, taken individually the rocket attacks might be characterised as 'mere frontier incidents' not giving rise to the right of self-defence.[189] Israel, however, appears to have implicitly argued that, for the purposes of its right of self-defence, the rocket attacks should not be seen in isolation but should, instead, be assessed cumulatively. For example, on the morning of the launching of Operation Cast Lead in December 2008, Gabriela Shalev, Israel's Permanent Representative to the United Nations, sent a letter to the UN Security Council stating that 'after a long period of utmost restraint, the Government of Israel has decided to exercise, as of this morning, its right to self-defense'.[190]

Unsurprisingly, the interventions have given rise to a significant level of controversy and the expression of a range of views amongst states, with some condemning Israel's actions as aggression and others expressing understanding of the need to respond in self-defence.[191] It was, however, significant that while Israel received condemnation for its various operations, few denied that it had, in principle, a right of self-defence. Israel also carried out air strikes against Iranian targets in Syria in June 2019, with Prime Minister Benyamin

---

[187] See, in general, Christian Henderson, 'Israeli Military Operations against Gaza: Operation Cast Lead (2008-2009), Operation Pillar of Defense (2012), and Operation Protective Edge (2014)', in Tom Ruys, Olivier Corten and Alexandra Hofer (eds.), *The Use of Force in International Law: A Case-Based Approach* (Oxford University Press, 2018), 729.

[188] Israel Ministry of Foreign Affairs, 'Behind the Headlines: Israel Designates Gaza a "Hostile Territory"', 24 September 2007, available at: www.mfa.gov.il/mfa/foreignpolicy/issues/pages/gaza%20designated%20a%20"hostile%20territory"%2024-sep-2007.aspx.

[189] *Nicaragua* case, n. 6, at para. 195. See also Eritrea-Ethiopia Claims Commission, n. 93, at para. 11.

[190] See UN Doc. S/2008/816, 27 December 2008.

[191] These views were expressed during various meetings in the UN Security Council: UN Doc. S/PV.6060, 31 December 2008; UN Doc. S/PV.6061, 6 January 2009; UN Doc. S/PV.6863, 14 November 2012; UN Doc. S/PV.7214, 10 July 2014; UN Doc. S/PV.7220, 18 July 2014; UN Doc. S/PV.7222, 22 July 2014; UN Doc. S/PV.8782, 27 May 2021.

Netanyahu stating that '[t]he accumulation of recent attacks proves that we are determined more than ever to take action against Iran in Syria, just as we promised'.[192]

As a further prominent incident that arguably falls within the purview of the accumulation of events doctrine, the Trump administration of the United States seemingly attempted to justify its strike in January 2020 which led to the death of Iranian General Qassem Soleimani upon an accumulation of prior incidents. In its letter to the UN Security Council, the US claimed to have 'been the target of a series of escalating threats and armed attacks by the Islamic Republic of Iran', including 'a threat to the amphibious ship USS BOXER on July 18, 2019' and 'an armed attack on June 19, 2019, by an Iranian surface-to-air missile on an unmanned U.S. Navy MQ-4 surveillance aircraft'.[193] Furthermore, it was claimed that 'Qods Force-backed militias have engaged in a series of attacks against U.S. forces. Qods Force-backed militia groups in Iraq, including Kata'ib Hizballah, have conducted a series of indirect fire attacks targeting bases where U.S. forces in Iraq are located'.[194]

The Trump administration, while never expressly contradicting the established US position that *any* use of force will be sufficient to trigger self-defence, also did not attempt to paint any of these past events as individually sufficient to justify the invocation of the right of self-defence and the killing of General Soleimani. On the contrary, a key part of the US' strategy on this occasion was to claim that its military action was 'in response to an escalating series of armed attacks'[195] and to paint a picture of a 'string of attacks'[196] and generally 'bad behaviour'[197] that might, taken together, be seen as sufficient to constitute the conditions required for the invocation of the right of self-defence, rather than to pinpoint a single discrete incident that could be said to provide the trigger. However, it was perhaps of little surprise, given the differences between – and imprecision of – the various justifications proffered by the Trump administration for the strike, that only on one occasion was it claimed that '[a]lthough the threat of further attack existed, *recourse to the*

---

[192] See https://twitter.com/IsraeliPM/status/1084427850697068544.
[193] See Letter dated 8 January 2020 from the Permanent Representative of the United States of America to the United Nations addressed to the President of the Security Council, UN Doc. S/2020/20, 9 January 2020.
[194] Ibid.   [195] Ibid.
[196] U.S. Department of Defense, 'Statement of Secretary of Defense Dr. Mark T. Esper as Prepared', 2 January 2020, available at: www.defense.gov/Newsroom/Releases/Release/Article/2049227/statement-by-secretary-of-defense-dr-mark-t-esper-as-prepared/.
[197] U.S. Department of Defense, 'Press Gaggle by Secretary Esper and Chairman Milley', 2 January 2020, available at: www.defense.gov/Newsroom/Transcripts/Transcript/Article/2049496/press-gaggle-by-secretary-esper-and-chairman-milley/.

*inherent right of self-defense was justified sufficiently by the series of attacks that preceded the January 2 strike*'.[198]

Similarly, while the attack on Erbil airport was clearly of prominence in the justification of the Biden administration for its strike in Syria on 25 February 2021,[199] there also appeared to be an attempt by the administration to increase the perceived gravity of what it was responding to in that it was stressed in its report to Congress that the non-state militia groups behind the Eribil attack were also involved in other 'recent attacks against United States and Coalition personnel in Iraq'.[200] Yet, unlike with the Trump administration, the Biden administration did not elaborate on the nature of these 'recent attacks' thereby denying the possibility for objective verification and assessment of the claim of self-defence.

In assessing gravity some states – notably France – seem to accept the applicability of the 'accumulation of events' doctrine in the context of cyber operations,[201] an approach also adopted in the *Tallinn Manual 2.0*.[202] Whether this would mean that a series of attacks of the nature and consequence of the Stuxnet worm attack would have entitled Iran to invoke its right of self-defence is open to question,[203] although to the extent that this doctrine is accepted in the context of kinetic attacks there would not seem to be a cogent reason for excluding its applicability in the context of cyber operations.

If we are to accept in principle, however, that an armed attack can be constituted by a string of smaller attacks, various questions of both a theoretical and practical nature nonetheless remain regarding the invocation of the right of self-defence and how it operates in practice. To begin with, even if the somewhat ambiguous claims in the examples above that a series of attacks sufficiently justified the invocation of the right of self-defence are in fact references to the accumulation of events theory, it is not clear to what extent these references are sufficient to push the accumulation of events doctrine

---

[198] See 'Notice on the Legal and Policy Frameworks Guiding the United States Use of Military Force and Related National Security Operations', 14 February 2020 (emphasis added), available at: www.justsecurity.org/wp-content/uploads/2020/02/notice-on-the-legal-and-policy-frameworks-guiding-the-united-states-use-of-military-force-and-related-national-security-operations.pdf.

[199] See Section 6.2.5.1 for more on this incident.

[200] The White House, 'A Letter to the Speaker of the House and President Pro Tempore of the Senate Consistent with the War Powers Resolution', 27 February 2021, available at: www.whitehouse.gov/briefing-room/statements-releases/2021/02/27/a-letter-to-the-speaker-of-the-house-and-president-pro-tempore-of-the-senate-consistent-with-the-war-powers-resolution/.

[201] Ministère des Armées, n. 33.

[202] Michael N. Schmitt (ed.), *Tallinn Manual 2.0 on the International Law Applicable to Cyber Operations* (Cambridge University Press, 2017), at 342.

[203] See Sections 2.4.2 and 6.2.5.2.

beyond being a 'theory' so as to firmly locate it as an established *lex lata* aspect of the right of self-defence.

It is, in any case, not clear how one is to gauge whether there has been a sufficient quantity of low-level incidents and attacks to cross the gravity threshold for an armed attack, assuming of course that such a gravity threshold exists. From the incidents discussed above it appears that while it is not possible to determine in the abstract at what point, if at all, a series of attacks may have occurred to such a degree that, taken together, they constitute an armed attack, it is also difficult to do so in specific cases. For example, even if we could envisage the threshold of an armed attack as one that could be crossed through an accumulation of smaller attacks it is unclear whether the rocket attacks by Hamas or the string of claimed attacks by the Trump and Biden administrations crossed this threshold. In addition, questions arise as to whether the various attacks need to emanate from the same location or source, or whether it is sufficient that they can be broadly attributed to a single group or actor.

Furthermore, even if the *actual* effects of the various attacks may not be sufficient to constitute an armed attack, should we instead make such an assessment through their *potential* effects?[204] In the context of the Hamas rocket attacks, for example, while their actual effects – taken individually or cumulatively – might have been relatively minor, their potential effects, along with the constant fear of attack, were arguably of far greater severity.

A further issue arises in terms of the temporal frequency or density required of attacks to enable them to move from being seen as isolated individual attacks to being able to be accumulated to form a single *armed* attack. And when, after a series of attacks have occurred, is the 'legal clock' reset,[205] so that a state loses its right to respond in self-defence with any armed response constituting an unlawful armed reprisal? If there is a pause in attacks should the next attack be seen as contributing to the accumulation of the prior attacks, or should it be seen as an isolated attack which perhaps begins a new accumulation? How long would the pause in attacks need to be? Some have argued, for example, that such a reset takes place in the absence of a truly imminent further attack,[206] but, as Chapter 7 demonstrates, there is a notable lack of agreement amongst states as to what 'imminence' means, particularly in the contemporary context.

Of course, while this analysis has been focused upon the accumulation of events theory in the context of the gravity issues involved, any response would also need to be both necessary and proportionate, as is the case with

---

[204] See Henderson, n. 187, at 745.
[205] Human Rights Council, 'Report of the Special Rapporteur on Extrajudicial, Summary or Arbitrary Executions', UN Doc. A/HRC/44/38, 29 June 2020, annex, at para. 61.
[206] See, for example, ibid.; O'Meara, n. 185, at 80.

singular armed attacks. These customary principles of the right of self-defence are discussed next in Section 6.3.

## 6.3 THE CUSTOMARY REQUIREMENTS OF NECESSITY AND PROPORTIONALITY

The *Caroline* was a merchant ship which had been taking arms, men and other supplies from the territorial waters of the United States to Navy Island on the Canadian side of the border to assist the rebels positioned there in their fight against British rule in Canada.[207] On the night of 29 December 1837, it was set on fire whilst on the US side of the border by British forces and sent over the Niagara Falls, destroying the ship and killing several individuals.[208] Given that the incident had taken place upon US territory, the US government was outraged. In particular, during the course of correspondence between Great Britain and the United States over this incident, US Secretary of State, Daniel Webster, asserted what has come to be known as the 'Webster formula':

It will be for [the British government] to show a necessity of self-defense, instant, overwhelming, leaving no choice of means, and no moment for deliberation. It will be for it to show, also that [it], – even supposing the necessity of the moment authorized them to enter the territories of the United States at all, – did nothing unreasonable or excessive; since the act justified by the necessity of self-defense, must be limited by that necessity, and kept clearly within it.[209]

This point was accepted by Lord Ashburton, special envoy of Great Britain to the United States. Of significance, however, is the fact that neither war nor the use of force were prohibited at the time of the incident.[210] In that sense, the question was not whether Britain had lawfully exercised its right of self-defence, but rather whether it 'could use forcible measures of self-defence within American territory without plunging the two countries into war'.[211] The issue was of a political nature rather than a legal one.

---

[207] For an account of the incident and how it has impacted upon the right to resort to force, see Craig Forcese, *Destroying the Caroline: The Frontier Raid that Reshaped the Right to War* (Irwin Law Inc., 2018).

[208] Jenning, n. 20, at 84.

[209] W. R. Manning, *Diplomatic Correspondence of the United States, Canadian Relations, 1784–1860, III: 1836–1848, Documents 1193–1853* (Carnegie Endowment for International Peace, 1943), at 145 (Doc. No. 1269) (letter of Daniel Webster, US Secretary of State, to Lord Ashburton, special envoy of Great Britain to the United States of 27 July 1842).

[210] Confusingly in this respect Lord Ashburton admitted that 'exceptions growing out of the great *law* of self-defence do exist'. Letter from Mr Webster to Lord Ashburton, Department of State, Washington, 6 August 1842, available at: http://avalon.law.yale.edu/19th_century/br-1842d.asp (emphasis added).

[211] Dinstein, n. 3, at para. 589.

That the incident took place in the absence of a prohibition of force makes it difficult to say that, by itself, it generated customary international law on the right of self-defence.[212] Nonetheless, the incident 'has attained a mythical authority'[213] and has come to represent the *locus classicus* of the law of self-defence.[214] In particular, the twin criteria of 'necessity' and 'proportionality' that represent defining features of the correspondence referred to in this section are certainly central to the customary form of the right as it exists today.[215] Indeed, while Article 51 is a relatively detailed provision, at least in the context of the UN Charter, it is not exhaustive and only paints a part of the picture, with much of the rest completed by customary international law, and in particular these twin criteria. As the ICJ noted in the *Nicaragua* case:

> the Charter, having itself recognized the existence of [the inherent right of self-defence], does not go on to regulate directly all aspects of its content. For example, it does not contain any specific rule whereby self-defence would warrant only measures which are proportional to the armed attack and necessary to respond to it, a rule well established in customary international law.[216]

Since the Court did not find Nicaragua responsible for an armed attack – the condition *sine qua non* for the lawful exercise of the right of self-defence – it did not go into the necessity and proportionality of the US response in collective self-defence, although it did regard these criteria as potentially providing 'an additional ground of wrongfulness'.[217] These criteria were also reaffirmed on other occasions by the ICJ as customary limitations upon the invocation and exercise of both individual and collective self-defence,[218] although similarly treated as somewhat 'marginal considerations'.[219] Furthermore, when it has applied them it has done so in a rather confusing manner and 'has offered only minimal insight into their scope and content'.[220]

However, while the Court has placed greater emphasis upon identifying an armed attack than it has on assessing the necessity and proportionality of state action, it is possible to argue that it is these twin customary requirements that are given more prominence in state practice.[221] As James Green notes, 'in terms of the actual practice of states, *these criteria represent the fundamental aspect in the determination of the lawfulness of state claims*'.[222] Indeed, they

---

[212] For more on the historical development of the *jus ad bellum* see Section 1.2.
[213] Christine Gray, *International Law and the Use of Force*, 3rd ed. (Oxford University Press, 2008), at 149.
[214] Jenning, n. 20, at 92.  [215] Green, n. 185, at 64–76.
[216] *Nicaragua* case, n. 6, at para. 176.  [217] Ibid., at para. 237.
[218] The ICJ has also spoken of '[t]his dual condition' of necessity and proportionality. *Legality of the Threat or Use of Nuclear Weapons*, Advisory Opinion (1996) ICJ Reports 226, at para. 141; *Oil Platforms* case, n. 11, at paras. 43, 51, 73–7; *Armed Activities* case, n. 50, at para. 147.
[219] Gray, n. 91, at 160.  [220] O'Meara, n. 185, at 4–7.  [221] Green, n. 185, at 108.
[222] Ibid. (emphasis in original). See also Ruys, n. 10, at 93–4; Gray, n. 91, at 163.

have proved to be key in assessing the lawfulness of armed reprisals,[223] the protection of nationals abroad,[224] the use of force in preventative self-defence,[225] self-defence against non-state actors[226] and the validity of self-defence in the context of measures taken by the Security Council.[227] Furthermore, with the specific requirement for an 'armed attack' coming under significant strain in the context of contemporary threats,[228] they have arguably played a more decisive role in assessing actual or proposed uses of force than that provided to them by the ICJ,[229] as well as in determining possible modifications in the law or the way its existing boundaries are interpreted.[230]

The principles can be seen as having a dual role, in that they act as a condition governing the availability of the right of self-defence,[231] but also as a restraint or limitation upon the exercise of the right.[232] Not only do the principles play a decisive role in the question as to *when* the right of self-defence might be invoked and *when* it ceases, but also *where* it is permissible to take action and against *whom* or *what*.[233] They also, however, shape the objectives to be attained in any action, how – and in what form – the right of self-defence is to be exercised and the permissible outcomes. Nonetheless, and as will become clear both in this chapter and the following two chapters, given that these principles of the right of self-defence 'permit a substantial uncertainty, and consequently a considerable latitude, in application'[234] they can also often be seen today as *enabling*, rather than merely *restricting* and *conditioning*, actions in self-defence.[235] The purpose of this section is to attempt to provide some clarity as to the relevant factors in connection with each of the principles, before addressing them further throughout both this chapter and Chapters 7 and 8.

---

[223] See Sections 6.3.1.2.1 and 6.3.1.2.2.     [224] See Section 6.4.     [225] See Chapter 7.
[226] See Chapter 8.     [227] See Section 6.6.
[228] For example in the context of preventative self-defence and 'contextual' imminence, on which see Chapter 7.
[229] See Sections 6.3.1. and 6.3.2 on the way the necessity and proportionality criteria have operated in practice.
[230] In particular, in regard to the concept of imminence and the use of force against non-state actors, see Chapters 7 and 8, respectively.
[231] Dapo Akande and Thomas Liefländer, 'Clarifying Necessity, Imminence and Proportionality in the Law of Self-Defence' (2013) **107** *American Journal of International Law* 563, at 564.
[232] Christian J. Tams, 'The Necessity and Proportionality of Anti-Terrorist Self-Defence', in Larissa Van Den Herik and Nico Schrijver (eds.), *Counter-Terrorism Strategies in a Fragmented International Legal Order: Meeting the Challenges* (Cambridge University Press, 2013) 373, at 374.
[233] Chris O'Meara divides necessity into the two aspects of 'general' and 'specific' necessity. O'Meara, n. 185, at chapter 2.
[234] Robert W. Tucker, 'Reprisals and Self-Defense: The Customary Law' (1972) **66** *American Journal of International Law* 586, at 588.
[235] See, in particular, Sections 7.5.3 and 8.4.2.1.

## 6.3.1 Necessity

The *jus ad bellum* principle of necessity was a prominent one in the correspondence of the *Caroline* affair of 1837 and, today, plays an important role in self-defence, including the effect any action taken by the Security Council has upon the continuing validity of a claim to self-defence.[236] As a starting point, however, it is necessary to distinguish the principle of necessity as it is found within the *jus ad bellum* and the principle of necessity which exists as a 'circumstance precluding wrongfulness' in general international law.[237] While the latter has been perceived by some as providing an additional basis for the use of force within international law,[238] the former is, as noted in the previous section, a conditioning factor upon existing exceptions to the prohibition of the use of force, most notably the right of self-defence. A distinction should also be drawn between necessity as found within the *jus ad bellum* and the principle of 'military necessity' within international humanitarian law, the function of which is to permit a state to achieve its military objectives but 'with the minimum expenditure of life and resources'.[239] While this particular principle thus shares similarities with the operation of *jus ad bellum* necessity and proportionality, it operates in respect to each individual military operation undertaken during an armed conflict as opposed to the armed conflict as a whole.

There are no clear-cut rules determining how states will regard the necessity of any military action taken in self-defence, and much will inevitably depend upon the individual circumstances. Yet, it is possible to isolate two clear elements of the criterion, that is, that there be no reasonable alternatives to the use of military force and that any military force that is undertaken is done so in the pursuit of defensive – as opposed to retaliatory or punitive – objectives.

### 6.3.1.1 No Reasonable Alternatives to the Resort to Armed Force

In the context of self-defence, necessity has traditionally been interpreted as a requirement that there be no alternatives to resorting to the use of force.[240]

---

[236] See Section 6.6 on the role of the Security Council in self-defence.
[237] Necessity as a circumstance precluding wrongfulness is found in Article 25 of the International Law Commission's Draft Articles on Responsibility of States for Internationally Wrongful Acts (2001).
[238] See, for example, Andreas Laursen, 'The Use of Force and (the State of) Necessity' (2004) 37 *Vanderbilt Journal of Transnational Law* 485. See also the discussion in Olivier Corten, 'Necessity', in Marc Weller (ed.), *The Oxford Handbook of the Use of Force in International Law* (Oxford University Press, 2015), 861, at 863–7. This is doubted by the current author. See, further, Section 10.2.
[239] UK Ministry of Defence, *The Manual of the Law of Armed Conflict* (Oxford University Press, 2005), section 2.2.
[240] In US President Barack Obama's State of the Union address in January 2015, for example, the president mentioned that the American people expected the use of force only as a last resort.

Special Rapporteur Robert Ago, in his Eighth Report on State Responsibility to the International Law Commission, stated that

> the state attacked ... must not, in the particular circumstances, have had any means of halting the attack other than recourse to armed force. In other words, had it been able to achieve the same result by measures not involving the use of armed force, it would have no justification for adopting conduct which contravened the general prohibition against the use of armed force.[241]

Yet, this requirement is softened by the incorporation of a level of reasonableness in the alternatives sought. Indeed, a further part of the correspondence from the US Secretary of State in the *Caroline* affair stated that it would have to be shown that other non-forcible measures were 'impracticable, or would have been unavailing'.[242] To put this differently, it would need to be demonstrated that no reasonable non-forcible measures were available to a state before resorting to the use of force in self-defence, or that there was a reasonable expectation that recourse to such measures would not have been effective. In support of this view, Ruys notes that the principle 'implies that a State can only resort to armed force against another State when there are no realistic alternative means of redress available. In other words, self-defence is permissible only when peaceful means have reasonably been exhausted, or when diplomatic enterprises would clearly be futile'.[243] Such non-forcible alternatives might include a complaint to the perpetrator of the armed attack.[244] In the *Oil Platforms* case, the ICJ considered the issue of whether actions carried out by the United States against Iranian oil platforms on 19 October 1987 and 18 April 1988 were necessary and proportionate to the attacks on the *Sea Isle City* and the mining of the *Samuel B. Roberts* that had taken place earlier on 16 October 1987 and 14 April 1988, respectively.[245] The Court was not satisfied that the attacks on the platforms that were ostensibly taken in self-defence were necessary, in particular due to the fact that there was no evidence that the United States had explored non-forcible measures, such as complaining to Iran of the military activities of the platforms, as it did

---

See White House, 'Remarks by the President in State of Union Address', 20 January 2015, available at: https://obamawhitehouse.archives.gov/the-press-office/2015/01/20/remarks-president-state-union-address-january-20-2015.

[241] Roberto Ago, 'Addendum to the Eighth Report on State Responsibility' (1980) 2 *Yearbook of the International Law Commission* 13, at 69.

[242] Manning, n. 209, at 145 (Doc. No. 1269). Albeit in a different context, it will be recalled from Chapter 3 that the Security Council is able to resort directly to forcible measures should it 'consider that [non-forcible measures] *would be inadequate or have proved to be inadequate*'. Article 42, UN Charter (1945) (emphasis added).

[243] Ruys, n. 10, at 95. See also James A. Green, 'The Ratione Temporis Elements of Self-Defence' (2015) 2 *Journal on the Use of Force and International Law* 97, at 101.

[244] See, further, Section 1.5.1 on reparations.

[245] *Oil Platforms* case, n. 11, at paras. 73–6. See Section 6.2.4 for more on the facts of this case.

## 6.3 Customary Requirements of Necessity and Proportionality

in relation to other events that had occurred, such as minelaying and attacks on neutral shipping.[246] This, in the Court's view, '[did] not suggest that the targeting of the platforms was seen as a necessary act'.[247]

Alternatively, injured states may have recourse to non-forcible countermeasures as a means to implement the responsibility of the state concerned, enforce international law more generally and enforce their legal rights.[248] However, as discussed in Section 1.5.2, the taking of countermeasures, such as sanctions, may not be effective in putting an end to any unlawful use of force against the victim state. In that respect, and in particular if there has been a threat to or breach of international peace and security or an act of aggression, recourse may be had to the UN Security Council which has the power to adopt measures of both a diplomatic and enforcement nature, or indeed the state may have recourse to a regional organisation in the first instance.[249]

Recourse to such non-forcible alternatives will depend upon the urgency of the particular situation, with any requirement that non-forcible measures attempted, or even that a state turns to them in the first place, be reasonable in the circumstances. Furthermore, it is important to note that neither state practice or the case law of the ICJ provide any indication that a legal obligation exists upon states to first prove that they have exhausted non-forcible alternatives before invoking the right of self-defence.[250]

The question then turns on what is 'reasonable', something that can only be ultimately answered in relation to the facts of each case. Whether a state has available reasonable non-forcible measures is not, for example, of any practical relevance in the moment when a state finds itself under direct physical armed attack, as it would be illogical to assume that there is any legal obligation upon it to attempt to negotiate or resort to, let alone exhaust, peaceful alternatives before resorting to forcible measures to protect itself.[251] Indeed, in these situations there will almost certainly be 'a necessity of self-defense, instant, overwhelming, leaving no choice of means, and no moment

---

[246] Ibid., at para. 76
[247] Ibid. In addition, the United States had admitted that one of the attacks on the oil platforms had, in its words, been a 'target of opportunity'. Ibid.
[248] See, further, Section 1.5.2 on the taking of countermeasures.
[249] See, further, Section 1.5.4 and Chapters 3 and 4 more generally. See also Section 6.6 on state obligations to, and the role of, the Security Council in the context of invocations of the right of self-defence.
[250] Corten, n. 90, at 478; O'Meara, n. 185, at 52 ('It is difficult to identify a case where there is a general consensus amongst states that the *sole* reason for condemnation was that the necessity of using force was absent because reasonable alternatives to force were available to resolve a situation.')
[251] See Ruys, n. 10, at 98; O'Meara, ibid., at 57.

for deliberation' and there would 'be an almost irrebuttable presumption ... that such a use of force in self-defense would pass the test of necessity'.[252]

However, defensive action may be considered necessary where a state, or a manifestation of it,[253] is the victim of an armed attack and there is a delay in the launching of the defensive action, thus potentially providing the opportunity to pursue non-forcible alternatives. For example, following the invasion of the Falkland Islands by Argentina on 2 April 1982 a period of twenty-three days passed before the United Kingdom launched an action in self-defence.[254] No sustained claims were made that the United Kingdom should have resorted to peaceful means before having done so.[255] That this was generally perceived as an acceptable delay was arguably due to the continued occupation of the islands by Argentinian forces, the scale of the response necessary and the geographical location of the islands from the United Kingdom.[256] The refusal of Argentina to comply with the demands of the UN Security Council arguably led to an increase in the general acceptance of the necessity of the action in the circumstances, and in the absence of any specific demands upon the United Kingdom made by the Security Council or effective action by the Council to end the continuing armed attack manifested in the occupation.[257]

Whilst in this case Argentina's occupation of the Falkland Islands was perceived as an ongoing armed attack giving rise to a necessity to act in self-defence, questions arise as to whether – and, if so, for how long – a necessity to act in self-defence continues to exist in these situations. During July–September 2020 military clashes took place along the Line of Contact border between Armenia and Azerbaijan in the Nagorno-Karabakh conflict zone, with both states accusing the other of ceasefire violations.[258] However, on 27 September 2020 intense fighting broke out between the two states, with each state again accusing the other of initiating the hostilities. After claiming

---

[252] Akande and Lieflander, n. 231, at 564.
[253] See Section 6.2.2 on the targets of an armed attack.
[254] See (1982) United Nations Yearbook 1320–46.
[255] Judith Gardam, *Necessity, Proportionality and the Use of Force by States* (Cambridge University Press, 2004), at 151. On the general acceptance by other states of the legality of the actions of the United Kingdom, see Michael J. Levitin, 'The Law of Force and the Force of Law: Grenada, the Falklands, and Humanitarian Intervention' (1986) **27** *Harvard International Law Journal* 621, at 638.
[256] Incidentally, the UN Security Council also determined that the Argentine invasion was a 'breach of the peace'. See UNSC Res. 502 (1982), preamble. For more on Security Council determinations of breaches of the peace, see Section 3.3.1.2.
[257] See Section 6.6 on the relationship between the right of self-defence and the UN Security Council.
[258] 'Armenia, Azerbaijan trade blame for new ceasefire violations', *Al Jazeera*, 23 September 2022, available at: www.aljazeera.com/news/2022/9/23/armenia-azerbaijan-trade-blame-for-fresh-ceasefire-violations.

that Armenia had engaged in 'military aggression' against it, Azerbaijan stated that it had taken 'counter-offensive measures within the right of self-defence',[259] while Armenia, in similar tones, accused Azerbaijan of 'aggression' and of wishing to resolve the Nagorno-Karabakh conflict through the use of armed force.[260] Armed hostilities lasted for forty-four days,[261] with a cessation of hostilities only emerging following the agreement of a peace deal on 9 November 2020 between Armenia, Azerbaijan and Russia.[262] Some states supported Azerbaijan's claim of self-defence,[263] whereas most of the international reaction expressed more general concern over the escalation in hostilities and called for calm and a cessation of fighting.[264]

While Azerbaijan claimed to have taken 'counter-offensive measures' a significant part of Nagorno-Karabakh that had long been controlled by Armenia had effectively been recovered by Azerbaijan in its action in self-defence.[265] Indeed, the incident substantially modified the territorial status

---

[259] Letter dated 27 September 2020 from the Permanent Representative of Azerbaijan to the United Nations addressed to the Secretary-General, UN Doc. A/75/357–S/2020/948, 28 September 2020, Annex.

[260] Letter dated 28 September 2020 from the Permanent Representative of Armenia to the United Nations addressed to the Secretary-General, UN Doc. A/75/366-S/2020/955, 29 September 2020, Annex.

[261] The conflict claimed the lives of 5,000 soldiers and at least 140 civilians, with more than 130,000 civilians displaced by the fighting, and hundreds of homes and vital infrastructure such as schools and hospitals destroyed.

[262] Letter dated 10 November 2020 from the Permanent Representative of the Russian Federation to the United Nations addressed to the President of the Security Council, UN Doc. S/2020/1104, 11 November 2020, Annex. As part of the agreement, Russia would deploy 'peacemaking forces' along the Nagorno-Karabakh Line of Contact and along the Lachin Corridor (connecting the region to Armenia). Ibid., at para. 3. The agreement largely held throughout the rest of 2020, with Armenia withdrawing troops as per the deal and returning territory to Azerbaijan. See, for example, 'Azerbaijani Forces Raise Flag in Last District Handed Back by Armenia', *The Defense Post*, 1 December 2020, available at: www.thedefensepost.com/2020/12/01/azerbaijani-last-district-armenia/.

[263] See Letter dated 16 October 2020 from the Permanent Representative of Turkey to the United Nations addressed to the Secretary-General, UN Doc. A/75/525–S/2020/1024, 19 October 2020, at 1–2; Pakistan, Ministry of Foreign Affairs, 'Renewed Tension in Nagorno-Karabakh', 27 September 2020, available at: http://mofa.gov.pk/renewed-tension-in-nagorno-karabakh/.

[264] See, for example, UK Foreign Commonwealth and Development Office, 'Nagorno-Karabakh: UK and Canada Joint Statement in Response to Continued Military Clashes', 6 October 2020, available at: www.gov.uk/government/news/nagorno-karabakh-uk-and-canada-joint-statement-in-response-to-continued-military-clashes; 'Nagorno-Karabakh Consultations', Security Council Report, 19 October 2020, available at: www.securitycouncilre-port.org/whatsinblue/2020/10/nagorno-karabakh-consultations.php.

[265] Prior to the conflict the Nagorno-Karabakh region was widely regarded as belonging de jure to Azerbaijan, but as being unlawfully occupied for more than twenty-five years by Armenia. ECtHR, *Chiragov* v. *Armenia*, Appl. No. 13216/95, Judgment of 16 June 2015, at para. 186; UNGA Res. 62/243, 25 April 2008. The self-proclaimed 'Republic of Artsakh' was

quo that had existed in the region ever since the 1994 Bishkek Protocol.[266] The question therefore arose as to whether a state can have lawful recourse to military force to recover a part of its territory that has been occupied by another state for such a prolonged period of time.

Arguably a key aspect to answering this question is a consideration of the necessity criterion of self-defence, a central tenet of which is that any military response be as immediate as possible in the circumstances.[267] In other words, there must be 'a temporal link between attack and defence'.[268] In this respect, one might adopt the position that the right of self-defence 'ceases to apply when a new territorial status quo is established, whereby the occupying state peacefully administers the territory concerned for a prolonged period',[269] as was the case with Armenia's long-held control over the territory of Nagorno-Karabakh.

A contrasting view, however, is that occupations of any duration constitute a *continuing* armed attack, thus permitting the right of self-defence to be exercised for as long as the occupation continues, even if this results in challenging a long-held territorial status quo.[270] Under this view rather than questioning whether immediate action has been taken by a victim state what seems to be of importance in determining the necessity of forcible action is whether non-forcible alternatives have been reasonably exhausted by the victim state in achieving the objective of defending itself and reclaiming its lost territory. There remains a temporal link, however, in that 'the passage of time may actually show that there are no other reasonable means of bringing the armed attack and occupation to an end, rendering the use of force in self-defence the *ultima ratio* – which is precisely the point of the necessity requirement'.[271] There is, therefore, a judgement call to be made under each

---

seen as nothing but a puppet regime under the control of Armenia. Indeed, it has not been recognised by any member of the United Nations, including Armenia.

[266] Bishtek Protocol, 5 May 1994, available at: https://peacemaker.un.org/sites/peacemaker.un.org/files/Bishkek%20Protocol.pdf.

[267] Some have claimed that a third discrete criterion of 'immediacy' or 'imminence' can be distilled from the correspondence of the *Caroline* incident, but it can also be seen as an aspect of necessity. Indeed, '[n]ecessity is a threshold, and the criterion of imminence can be seen to be an aspect of it, in as much as it requires that there be no time to pursue non-forcible measures with a reasonable chance of averting or stopping the attack'. Chatham House Principles, n. 25, at 967.

[268] O'Meara, n. 185, at 72.

[269] Tom Ruys and Felipe Rodríguez Silvestre, 'Illegal: The Recourse to Force to Recover Occupied Territory and the Second Nagorno-Karabakh War', (2022) 32 *European Journal of International Law* 1287, at 1289.

[270] Dapo Akande and Antonios Tzanakopoulos, 'Legal: Use of Force in Self-Defence to Recover Occupied Territory', (2021) 32 *European Journal of International Law* 1299, at 1303; Marco Longobardo, *The Use of Armed Force in Occupied Territory* (Cambridge University Press, 2019), at 121.

[271] Akande and Tzanakopoulos, ibid., at 1306.

view as, on the one hand, it is difficult to identify the moment which self-defence ceases to apply and the principle of the non-use of force takes over, whilst, on the other hand, it is difficult to define precisely when peaceful alternatives have been exhausted thus making the use of force in self-defence necessary.

Of course, states are under a 'duty to refrain from the threat or use of force ... as a means of solving ... territorial disputes and problems concerning the frontiers of States' as well as being under an obligation to settle their 'international disputes with other States by peaceful means in such a manner that international peace and security and justice are not endangered'.[272] Yet, this is arguably not conclusive as it is possible to draw a distinction between a territorial dispute, on the one hand, and to which the above provisions were arguably intended to apply, and a situation of armed attack resulting in the continuing occupation of territory, on the other hand, in determining whether the right of military action is an option.[273] Of course, the application of the principle of necessity in the latter situation would require the reasonable exhaustion of non-forceful alternatives, despite the fact that it may not always be easily – and objectively – determined when such exhaustion has been reached.

### 6.3.1.2 The Use of Force for the Attainment of Defensive Objectives

A second key element of any military action taken in self-defence is that it constitutes 'a genuinely defensive measure'.[274] While any measures taken in self-defence should be 'genuinely' defensive in nature, this does not rule out the pursuit of other intermediate objectives in pursuit of the 'main or ultimate aim' of defence.[275] In this respect, in meeting the overall defensive objective of the acting state even the overthrowing of a government may, in certain circumstances, be deemed a necessary and proportionate intermediate objective. This can be seen in the removal of the Taliban regime in Afghanistan in

---

[272] See Declaration on Principles of International Law concerning Friendly Relations and Cooperation among States (1970), UNGA Res. 2625 (XXV), 24 October 1970. See also Article 2(3), UN Charter (1945).

[273] Akande and Tzanakopoulos, n. 279, at 1301–2.

[274] Corten, n. 90, at 480. This can be contrasted with Buchan and Tsagourias who claim that 'States must consider whether diplomatic or legal options can be employed to *resolve the dispute* before resorting to self-defence action.' Russell Buchan and Nicholas Tsagourias, *Regulating the Use of Force in International Law: Stability and Change* (Edward Elgar, 2021), at 67 (emphasis added). See also O'Meara, n. 185, at 76. A clear distinction is needed here, in that, although non-forcible measures may be resorted to for the purposes of resolving a dispute, the failure of these to achieve such a resolution does not mean that resort may then be had to forcible measures to achieve it, as these are strictly limited to what is required for the *defence* of the state concerned.

[275] Corten, ibid., at 481.

2001 by the United States as part of its defensive operation following the attacks of 11 September 2001.[276] In addition, the objectives of the acting state do not have to be exclusively defensive, in the sense that the defensive objective is invalidated if there are other discernible objectives of the state present. The fact that a state may be pursing different objectives in its military action may be apparent from the 'shotgun' nature of justificatory discourse that states often engage in, whereby they offer up several justifications for their actions in the hope that one will find acceptance from other states.[277] Furthermore, the fact that states may not be acting for exclusively defensive purposes has found some support within the jurisprudence of the ICJ. In the *Nicaragua* case the Court was faced with the claim by Nicaragua that the United States was merely acting under the 'pretext' of self-defence with its real objective being 'to impose its will upon Nicaragua and force it to comply with United States demands'.[278] In the Court's view, however, providing that any support that Nicaragua had been giving to the armed opposition in El Salvador constituted an armed attack on El Salvador,[279] then 'collective self-defence could be legally invoked by the United States, even though there may be the possibility of an additional motive, one perhaps even more decisive for the United States'.[280] Indeed, '[t]he existence of an additional motive, other than that officially proclaimed' does not necessarily deprive the acting state of its right to resort to individual or collective self-defence.[281] With these qualifications in mind, however, one must be cognisant of the distinction between 'genuinely defensive measures' from those constituting what are described as 'armed reprisals'.

### 6.3.1.2.1 The Formal Illegality of 'Armed Reprisals'

In general, reprisals 'are a traditional act of self-help under international law, consisting of a breach of international law in response to a prior violation by another state and undertaken for the purpose of enforcing compliance'.[282] In this respect, *armed* reprisals are 'acts of forcible self-help, involving an unlawful use of force falling short of war, by one state in response to a prior violation of international law by another'.[283] While on the basis of this definition it might be said that the main purpose of armed reprisals is law enforcement[284] – that is, measures of coercion intended to impose a return to legality – other aims, such as protection of a state's interests, retaliation,

---

[276] See, further, Section 8.3.2.
[277] See 'Legal and Procedural Issues Associated with the *Jus ad Bellum*' in the Introduction.
[278] *Nicaragua case*, n. 6, at para. 127.   [279] see Section 6.2 on the concept of 'armed attack'.
[280] *Nicaragua* case, n. 6, at para. 127.   [281] Ibid.
[282] Shane Darcy, 'Retaliation and Reprisal', in Marc Weller (ed.), *The Oxford Handbook of the Use of Force in International Law* (Oxford University Press, 2015), 879, at 879.
[283] Ibid., at 881.   [284] Ibid., at 882.

deterrence, the prevention of future wrongs and even punishment,[285] have all been included under the banner of armed reprisals.

Despite the fact that no prohibition of force existed prior to 1945, certain criteria emerged regulating the use of armed reprisals. In 1914, the governor of German South-West Africa ordered reprisal attacks on Portuguese forts and posts after two German officers and an official were killed by Portuguese soldiers. Germany and Portugal subsequently established a Special Arbitral Tribunal, which set out the following criteria:

> Reprisals are illegal if they are not preceded by a request to remedy the alleged wrong. There is no justification for using force except in cases of necessity ... Reprisals which are altogether out of proportion with the act that prompted them are excessive and therefore illegal. This is so even if it is not admitted that international law requires that reprisals should be approximately of the same degree as the injury to which they are meant to answer.[286]

The significance of this is that, as with the 'Webster formula' emerging from the *Caroline* incident of 1837,[287] necessity and proportionality were vital elements for the acceptability, if not legality *per se*, of armed reprisals.[288]

A key question that arises is the extent to which the gradual legal restrictions upon the resort to forcible measures in international law – culminating in the prohibition of the threat or use of force and the express sole exception of self-defence 'if an armed attack occurs' in 1945 – have had an impact upon the legality of armed reprisals. Despite the fact that '[t]he doctrine [of reprisal] does not seem to have even been discussed at either Dumbarton Oaks or San Francisco, even though the proposed rules on the use of force were obviously subjected to detailed negotiations',[289] it is undeniable that the UN Charter is 'largely viewed as having prohibited resort to the doctrine of armed reprisals'.[290] Indeed, today armed reprisals are widely perceived as unlawful,[291] with Derek Bowett declaring in 1972 that 'few propositions about international law have enjoyed more support than the proposition that, under

---

[285] Ibid. Antonio Cassese claimed that armed reprisals 'were aimed at either impelling the delinquent state to discontinue the wrongdoing, or at punishing it, or both'. Antonio Cassese, *International Law*, 2nd ed. (Oxford University Press, 2005), at 299. Armed reprisals are to be distinguished from the concept of belligerent reprisals found within the law of armed conflict. On this topic see Frits Kalshoven, *Belligerent Reprisals* (Martinus Nijhoff, 1971).

[286] *Portugal v. Germany (The Naulilaa case)*, Special Arbitral Tribunal, 31 July 1928 (1927–8) *Annual Digest of Public International Law Cases* 526, at 527.

[287] See Section 6.3 for more on the 'Webster formula'.

[288] Schwarzenberger also noted that reprisals 'receive their legality from the unredressed prior wrong'. Georg Schwarzenberger, *International Law as Applied by International Courts and Tribunals, II: The Laws of Armed Conflict* (Stevens & Sons, 1968), 39, at 48.

[289] Darcy, n. 282, at 887.   [290] Ibid., at 886.

[291] See, for example, Brownlie, n. 3, at 281; Ruys, n. 10, at 95; Corten, n. 90, at 234–4; *Nuclear Weapons* advisory opinion, n. 218, at para. 46.

the Charter of the United Nations, use of force by way of reprisal is illegal'.[292] Not only is the use of force prohibited in Article 2(4) but a 1946 Commentary on the Charter states that the obligation in Article 2(3) to settle disputes by peaceful means effectively 'rules out recourse to certain measures short of war which involve the use of force, such as armed reprisals'.[293] As such, while armed reprisals were not exactly a hot topic at the negotiation of the Charter in 1945, this is perhaps not surprising given that the emphasis of the moment was on limiting inter-state force to the greatest extent possible, which meant that it arguably 'seemed unnecessary to specifically issue a death sentence on the old reprisal doctrine'.[294]

In substantiating this view, in 1964 the Security Council adopted Resolution 188 concerning British military action in Yemen in which it 'condemn[ed] reprisals as incompatible with the purposes and principles of the United Nations'.[295] In addition, the General Assembly's 1970 Declaration on Principles of International Law Concerning Friendly Relations and Co-operation among States is clear that 'states have a duty to refrain from acts of reprisal involving the use of force'.[296] The Final Act of the Conference on Security and Cooperation in Europe similarly obliges participating states to 'refrain in their mutual relations from any act of reprisal by force'.[297] As for the ICJ, 'it appears that one of the guiding considerations of the [Court in the *Nicaragua* case] was the *function* of the right of self-defence as a defensive (rather than punitive) measure of action taken by states',[298] while in the *Nuclear Weapons* advisory opinion the ICJ considered reprisals to be unlawful.[299]

### 6.3.1.2.2 The Fine Line between Armed Reprisals and Self-Defence

With what was discussed in Section 6.3.1.2.1 as a background, a central question that remains is the extent to which actions in self-defence are distinguishable from armed reprisals. In particular, although the necessity of

---

[292] Derek W. Bowett, 'Reprisals Involving Recourse to Armed Force' (1972) 66 *American Journal of International Law* 1, at 1.

[293] Leland M. Goodrich and Edvard Hambro, *Charter of the United Nations: Commentary and Documents* (World Peace Foundation, 1946), at 67.

[294] Michael J. Kelly, 'Time Warp to 1945 – Resurrection of the Reprisal and Anticipatory Self-Defense Doctrines in International Law' (2003) 13 *Journal of Transnational Law and Policy* 1, at 12.

[295] UNSC Res. 188 (1964), para. 1.

[296] Declaration on Principles of International Law concerning Friendly Relations and Cooperation among States, n. 272 (1970), principle 1. See also the Declaration on the Inadmissibility of Intervention and Interference in the Internal Affairs of States, UNGA Res. 36/103, 9 December 1981, Section II(c).

[297] Final Act, Conference on Security and Cooperation in Europe, 1 August 1975.

[298] Kritsiotis, n. 4, at 215.   [299] *Nuclear Weapons* advisory opinion, n. 218, at para. 46.

responding while an armed attack is physically occurring is clear, questions arise as to the true necessity of responding *after* an armed attack would seem to have come to an end. For example, the United Kingdom resorted to force in Yemen in 1964, Israel resorted to forcible measures on various occasions against targets of the PLO and other organisations in Lebanon and other states in the Middle East, and the United States invoked its right of self-defence in Libya in 1986, in Iraq in 1993, in Sudan and Afghanistan in 1998 and in Afghanistan in 2001, on each occasion after the respective attacks to which the state was responding to being ostensibly over. The question thus arises whether such *post facto* responses can be reconciled with the defensive nature of self-defence or whether they are to be viewed as having additional or ulterior motives, perhaps of a retaliatory, punitive, deterrent or preventative nature? If not immediately necessary to defend the state invoking its right of self-defence from an armed attack, can they legitimately be classed as self-defence or are they to be more appropriately classed as armed reprisals?

The International Law Commission, during the preparatory work of the Draft Articles on the Responsibility of States for Internationally Wrongful Acts, which addressed countermeasures,[300] dismissed the suggestion that armed reprisals might be legitimate or lawful as a form of self-defence. Instead, the Commission stated:

The contrary trend, aimed at justifying the noted practice of circumventing the prohibition by qualifying resort to armed reprisals as self-defence, does not find any plausible legal justification and is considered unacceptable by the Commission. Indeed, armed reprisals do not present those requirements of *immediacy and necessity* which would only justify a plea of self-defence.[301]

While an aspect of necessity is that there should be at least some proximate temporal link to the armed attack,[302] whether self-defence needs to be 'immediate' – or, as stated in the *Caroline* formula, 'instant' so that there is 'no moment for deliberation' – can be questioned. To begin with, Article 51 permits the invocation of the right of self-defence 'if an armed attack occurs' and is not restricted in a textual sense solely to those moments during which an armed attack, or its physical manifestation, is occurring. Furthermore, if it is accepted, as set out in the previous section, that necessity requires that some recourse to, or at least consideration of, non-forcible means is made before having recourse to means of a forcible nature, it is then somewhat paradoxical to expect an immediate forcible reaction in the heat of the moment.[303]

---

[300] Article 50(1)(a) of the Draft Articles states that the obligation to refrain from the threat or use of force is not affected by the general right to take countermeasures, which are, in any case, limited to injured states.
[301] ILC, Summary Record of the 2424th Meeting, 21 July 1995 (1995) 1 *Yearbook of the International Law Commission* 297 (emphasis added and footnotes omitted).
[302] O'Meara, n. 185, at 72–4.    [303] Corten, n. 90, at 483.

Delayed actions in self-defence have occasionally been implicitly or expressly condemned as constituting unlawful reprisal action. In the *Nicaragua* case the ICJ condemned the military action undertaken by the United States on the basis that even if the supply of arms by Nicaragua to the opposition force in El Salvador had amounted to an armed attack, measures in self-defence 'were only taken, and began to produce their effects, several months after the major offensive of the armed opposition in El Salvador had been completely repulsed'.[304] While the actions of the United States were therefore condemned on the basis of the delay, '[w]here the Court draws the line between lawful self-defence and unlawful reprisal remains unclear.'[305] Condemnation on the basis of a delay can also be seen in the case of the United Kingdom's actions in Yemen in 1964, the bombing in Libya by the United States in 1986 and with various actions undertaken by Israel.[306]

However, of significance is that many delayed military responses that would appear to be of the nature of an armed reprisal occur without receiving condemnation, or at least they are not condemned for the specific reason that they have taken place with some delay after an armed attack has ceased.[307] Indeed, '[i]n some cases the reaction of the international community towards armed reprisals has been surprisingly restrained and has failed to call the child by its name'.[308] For example, when the United States responded forcibly to the assassination attempt against former US President George H. W. Bush while on a visit to Kuwait, a two-month delay due to an intensive investigation into the assassination plot did not seem to lead to accusations of illegality, despite it not being exactly clear what the United States was then defending against. Indeed, while it was 'difficult not to see the operation as a classical punitive expedition', it was clear that 'the US self-defence claim gained wide support among [UN Security] Council members'.[309] Similarly, the delay of thirteen days between the bombings of US embassies in Nairobi and Dar es Salaam in 1998 and the forcible response in self-defence by the United States in Sudan and Afghanistan did not generally lead to accusations of reprisal or illegality.[310] Furthermore, a delay of nearly a month between the attacks of 9/11 on the territory of the United States and its response in Afghanistan on 7 October 2001 did not lead to claims of illegality, and no questions were asked regarding the clearly expressed justification of self-defence.[311] On the

---

[304] *Nicaragua* case, n. 6, at para. 237.   [305] O'Meara, n. 185, at 73.
[306] Darcy, n. 282, at 893. For example, UN Doc. S/PV.1502, 18 August 1969, at para. 74.
[307] David Kretzmer, 'The Inherent Right to Self-Defence and Proportionality in *Jus ad Bellum*' (2013) 24 *European Journal of International Law* 235, at 252.
[308] Ibid., at 258.   [309] Ruys, n. 10, at 107.
[310] Christian Henderson, *The Persistent Advocate and the Use of Force: The Impact of the United States upon the* Jus ad Bellum *in the Post–Cold War Era* (Ashgate, 2010), at 150–1.
[311] Ibid., at 154–6.

contrary, the action and the justification for it were clearly accepted by virtually the entire international community of states.[312]

The extent of the delay in responding may, nonetheless, be of significance as '[w]hile a use of force in self-defence need not be contemporaneous with the armed attack to which it responds, there must be sufficient temporal proximity to the attack to distinguish self-defence from mere retaliation'.[313] Indeed, subject to what was said in Section 6.3.1.1 regarding occupations, it is arguable that the further in time from an armed attack that a response is taken the more punitive, and less defensive, it will appear to be.[314]

If the armed response is taken after the attack has been completed, however, then regardless as to how proximate in time the response is to the original attack, its defensive objective would seem to be inherently future oriented in nature. In this respect, while not constituting a part of the same initial attack *per se*, the prospect of further attacks may prevent a delayed response from being perceived as an unlawful punitive armed reprisal, while the fact that the defending state has already been the victim of an attack will seemingly prevent the response from being seen as unlawful preventative self-defence.[315] The United States has, for example, resorted to the use of force in self-defence with the express aim of 'preventing and deterring' future attacks following, as set out immediately above, the assassination attempt on former President George H. W. Bush by Iraqi agents while on a visit to Kuwait in 1993,[316] following the bombing of its embassies in Nairobi and Dar Es Salaam in 1998,[317] and following the terrorist attacks of 9/11.[318] The future oriented objectives of 'prevention' and 'deterrence' would, in general, take an element of time to prepare for, by contrast to situations where there is an 'instant' and 'overwhelming' necessity to act in self-defence leaving 'no

---

[312] Ibid., at 155.
[313] Michael N. Schmitt, 'The Use of Cyber Force and International Law', in Marc Weller (ed.), *The Oxford Handbook of the Use of Force in International Law* (Oxford University Press, 2015), 1110, at 1127; Ruys, n. 10, at 101; O'Meara, n. 185, at 72; Buchan and Tsagourias, n. 274, at 66.
[314] O'Meara, n. 185, at 76.  [315] For more on preventative self-defence, see Chapter 7.
[316] 'It is the sincere hope of the United States Government that such limited and proportionate action may frustrate future unlawful actions on the part of the Government of Iraq and discourage or preempt such activities.' See UN Doc. S/26003, 26 June 1993.
[317] 'In response to these attacks, and to prevent and deter their continuation, United States armed forces today struck at a series of camps and installations used by the bin Laden organisation ... [t]he United States ... had no choice but to use armed force to prevent these attacks from continuing ... [i]t is the sincere hope of the United States Government that these limited actions will deter and prevent the repetition of unlawful terrorist attacks.' See UN Doc. S/1998/780, 20 August 1998.
[318] 'In response to these attacks, and in accordance with the inherent right of individual and collective self-defence, United States armed forces have initiated actions designed to prevent and deter further attacks on the United States.' See UN Doc. S/2001/946, 7 October 2001.

moment for deliberation'.[319] However, these objectives can at the same time be seen to possess at least a plausible defensive purpose, rather than simply a punitive one, particularly given that the state has already demonstrably been the victim of an attack by the actor against whom the action is taken.

Some scholars have adopted the position that a defensive necessity in self-defence only arises in these situations where there is 'convincing proof' of further attacks.[320] Others have, however, taken the view that there should be '*a good reason to expect* a series of armed attacks from the same source',[321] or that there be 'the *probability of a new attack* further to a number of others'.[322] Such a prediction might indeed be based on the fact that the defending state has been the victim of a series of prior attacks from the particular actor, or a 'concerted pattern of continuing armed activity',[323] providing, therefore, a sufficient evidential basis to conclude that a further attack is forthcoming, and that a riposte in self-defence is necessary regardless as to whether the next attack can be seen to be imminent in the temporal sense.[324] In highlighting the defensive necessity of any action in self-defence these latter situations have sometimes been portrayed as a continuous or ongoing armed attack,[325] meaning that, unless there is evidence to suggest otherwise, the next instalment of the attack is just around the corner.[326] If a recent attack is demonstrably one in a series of attacks from the particular actor it demonstrates the behavioural trait of a propensity to attack, which arguably reduces the evidential burden on the defending state, and may impact upon the way the temporal nature of any military response in self-defence, and ultimately its necessity, is received.[327]

---

[319] As provided for in the *Caroline* correspondence, set out in Section 6.3.
[320] Ruys, n. 10, at 102.   [321] O'Meara, n. 185, at 78 (emphasis added).
[322] Corten, n. 90, at 483.
[323] Daniel Bethlehem, 'Principles Relevant to the Scope of a State's Right of Self-Defense against an Imminent or Actual Armed Attack by Nonstate Actors' (2012) 106 *American Journal of International Law* 769, principle 8.
[324] See Chapter 7 for more on the concept of imminence.
[325] For an example of this, see the discussion in Section 7.5.2 on the justificatory discourse engaged in by the United States following the drone strike that killed Iranian General Qassem Soleimani in January 2020.
[326] Indeed, Corten is of the view that 'the "immediate" character of self-defence must not be taken in too narrow a sense: it is a matter of requiring that the riposte is aimed at behaviour that is still current, even if the material effects of its latest manifestation have already disappeared. It will be important to check therefore on a case by case basis whether the purpose of the act of self-defence is indeed to put an end to an aggression that is "underway", which may perfectly well be reflected by the probability of a new attack further to a number of others.' Corten, n. 90, at 483. See, further, the discussion on 'contextual imminence' in Section 7.5.
[327] Ago has stated that '[i]f ... the attack in question consisted of a number of successive acts, the requirement of the immediacy of the self-defensive action would have to be looked at in the light of those acts as a whole.' Ago, n. 241, at 70.

A greater tolerance for delayed armed actions under the guise of self-defence may also be due to the nature of the perpetrators of the armed attack, that is, it may depend upon whether defensive action is subsequently contemplated against a state or a non-state actor.[328] In responding to terrorist acts the identity and location of the perpetrators is not always as apparent as in the case with conventional attacks by states, with more limited possibilities for negotiation and non-forcible measures. Furthermore, a delay may be necessary to enable evidence to be collected in identifying the attacker and because negotiations with the state upon whose territory the non-state actors are located will be necessary to either obtain its consent for the proposed military action or to determine whether it is able and willing to take the necessary action itself to end any continuing threat presented by the actors.[329] Following the attacks of 11 September 2001, for example, and having identified al-Qaida as responsible, the Taliban regime rejected US demands that it unconditionally close al-Qaida training camps in Afghanistan, surrender the group's leader, Osama bin Laden, to the United States and open Afghanistan to inspections.[330] The Taliban's refusal to comply meant that upon the launching of Operation Enduring Freedom on 7 October 2001 the United States claimed that '[d]espite every effort by the United States and the international community, the Taliban regime has refused to change its policy'.[331] While one may question the legitimacy of such demands, the international community broadly accepted the invocation of the right of self-defence by the United States on this occasion.[332] In this light there have been calls by certain scholars for a reconsideration of the legal position on reprisals in the context of forcible measures taken in response to terrorist attacks.[333]

In addition, making the case that further attacks are anticipated is arguably less onerous with terrorist groups than with states, as it is often the very raison d'être of such groups to perpetrate attacks against one or more states. In this respect, while a terrorist group may target a particular state, terrorism is something that many states face in one form or another, particularly with the advent of global terrorist groups, meaning that they may be more benevolent in terms of the responses permitted.

---

[328] See Chapter 8 for more on self-defence against non-state actors.
[329] See Section 8.4.2 for more on the so-called unwilling or unable doctrine. Similarly, while necessity in the context of a response to cyber-attacks, or the threat thereof, is determined in the same way as with traditional attacks, evidential issues in terms of identifying the attacker and any potential connection with a state would appear to be even more critical.
[330] *Keesing's* (2001) 44337.   [331] UN Doc. S/2001/946, 7 October 2001.
[332] See n. 27 for the general reaction to the United States' response to the attacks taken in self-defence.
[333] See William O'Brien, 'Reprisals, Deterrence and Self-Defense in Counterterror Operations' (1990) 30 *Virginia Journal of International Law* 421.

Finally, over and above any obligations a state may have under international humanitarian law, it would appear that defensive force in the context of the *jus ad bellum* should in principle either be directed against the source of the armed attack(s) or a target directly connected to the original attack.[334] Whilst not always overly clear on the issue, the ICJ has seemingly placed emphasis on this defensive element of necessity. In the *Oil Platforms* case, for example, the Court advanced as a relevant consideration 'the nature of the target of the force used avowedly in self-defence',[335] and on this basis was critical of the US' claim that the oil platforms targeted in self-defence performed a military function, with the targeting of them therefore not seen as necessary in responding to either the missile attack on the *Sea Isle City* or the mining of the *USS Samuel B. Roberts*.[336] In this case '[w]hat is clear, is that it viewed force used against targets that had no direct connection with the armed attacks as being punitive or retaliatory acts, thereby constituting reprisals'.[337] In a similar vein, in the *Armed Activities* case, the Court could not 'fail to observe ... that the taking of airports and towns many hundreds of kilometres from Uganda's border would not seem proportionate to the series of transborder attacks it claimed had given rise to the right of self-defence, nor to be necessary to that end'.[338]

However, the selection of targets that have a direct connection with the defensive objective of the acting state is also a relevant factor that can be identified in state practice, where there are examples of states stressing that the targets of the action in self-defence were directly connected to the attack to which they were responding to. For example, this was the case with the United States' military action in Libya in 1986 following the attack on its military personnel in Berlin,[339] and its targeting of a military headquarters in Iraq following the attempted assassination of former President Bush whilst on a visit to Kuwait in 1993.[340] Interestingly, in January 2020 Iran responded in self-defence to the US' killing of General Soleimani (which was also justified in self-defence),[341] in doing so stressing that it had specifically targeted the military base in Iraq from which the attack on General Soleimani had emanated.[342] States are also increasingly keen to stress that, in responding in self-defence to terror attacks by non-state armed groups, their response is limited to the terrorists themselves rather than state infrastructure.[343]

---

[334] O'Meara, n. 185, at 90. (who labels this as 'specific necessity'). See also Ruys, n. 10, at 108–9.
[335] *Oil Platforms* case, n. 11, at para. 74.   [336] Ibid., at paras. 74–7.
[337] O'Meara, n. 185, at 91.   [338] *Armed Activities* case, n. 50, at para. 147.
[339] UN Doc. S/PV.2674, 15 April 1986, at 13–15.
[340] UN Doc. S/PV.3245, 27 June 1993, at 6.
[341] This incident is discussed throughout this chapter and Chapter 7.
[342] Letter dated 8 January 2020 from the Permanent Representative of the Islamic Republic of Iran to the United Nations, addressed to the Secretary-General and the President of the Secretary Council, UN Doc. S/2020/19, 8 January 2020.
[343] See Section 8.4, and in particular the discussion on the unable or unwilling doctrine.

## 6.3 Customary Requirements of Necessity and Proportionality

What becomes clear from the above discussion in this section is that in practice there is 'no clear-cut distinction between "premeditated" reprisals and "spontaneous" self-defence'.[344] Some have therefore commented that there remains something of a 'credibility gap' between the clear norm prohibiting reprisals and state practice.[345] Derek Bowett, as far back as 1972, advanced the idea of 'reasonable' reprisals, in that 'certain reprisals will, even if not accepted as justified, at least avoid condemnation',[346] while Yoram Dinstein has introduced the concept of 'defensive armed reprisals'[347] under which 'the responding State strikes at a time and a place different from those of the original armed attack'.[348] However, while these are in some ways accurate terms to describe many of the actions that have occurred, they have not taken a place within the vernacular of states and many scholars, who continue to justify such actions under the guise of self-defence and condemn, in principle, armed reprisals. This is arguably reflective of the fact that states 'are aware of the illegality of their conduct if it is described in any other way'.[349]

Given that these military strikes often avoid condemnation, this raises the question as to the impact of this practice on the interpretation of Article 51 and the contours of the customary right of self-defence.[350] In this respect, can the express or implicit acceptance the actions, or at least silence regarding their legality, be interpreted as acceptance of them as self-defence or that armed reprisals are in fact, in certain circumstances, acceptable? Bowett was perhaps correct in observing that 'while reprisals remain illegal *de jure*, they [have] become accepted *de facto*'.[351] Indeed, although there is nothing to indicate that states have begun to expressly accept the lawfulness of armed reprisals or defensive armed reprisals under the guise of self-defence, their lawfulness, at least in certain circumstances, has arguably seeped in through the backdoor. Furthermore, as there appears to be some recognition of a defensive necessity in many of these cases of the invocation of self-defence,[352] it would seem that at the very least there is an acceptance of an elongation of the 'if an armed attack occurs' stipulation contained within Article 51, and

---

[344] Ruys, n. 10, at 100. See also Kretzmer, n. 307, at 253; in general, Tucker, n. 236.
[345] Bowett, n. 292, at 1.   [346] Ibid., at 10, 20.   [347] Dinstein, n. 3, at paras. 691–5.
[348] Ibid.
[349] Roberto Barsotti, 'Armed Reprisals', in Antonio Cassese (ed.), *The Current Legal Regulation of the Use of Force* (Martinus Nijhoff, 1986), 79, at 91.
[350] Ruys talks of 'an inevitable blurring of the distinction between self-defence and unlawful reprisals'. Ruys, n. 10, at 107.
[351] Bowett, n. 292, at 10–11.
[352] However, armed reprisals have also occurred outside of the context of self-defence. For example, in response to the alleged use of chemical weapons by the Assad regime against civilians the United States justified its strikes in April 2017 against a Syrian government airbase at Shayrat, near Homs, as deterrence against the further use of chemical weapons, and as enforcement of the prohibition of their use. See Section 10.4.2.

more flexibility in understanding the necessity requirement so that it is clearly not strictly equated to an 'instant, overwhelming' necessity for military action.[353]

### 6.3.2 Proportionality

The connected principle of proportionality exists principally 'to serve as a constraint on the scale and effects of defensive action',[354] and is, again, a constraint that is 'inherent in the very concept of self-defence'.[355] It is arguably also the criterion for a lawful act of self-defence that is most often referenced by states, both in justifying their own actions and in appraising the actions of others.

The notion of proportionality differs depending upon whether one is discussing action taken under the *jus ad bellum* or the *jus in bello*, a distinction that is not always clearly identified in assessments of proportionality of military action. For example, 'whereas the former intends to measure the force used in an operation of self-defence in its entirety, the latter considers the force applied as against a specific military target as defined by international law at any given point during that operation'.[356] In other words, in the *jus ad bellum* 'it is the forceful response as a whole that must be scrutinized, instead of singling out specific attacks, implying that one should often look at strategic and political decisions at the highest levels of command' in making assessments as to the proportionality of an action.[357]

Furthermore, while the concept of proportionality arises in the context of all forcible actions, the way it applies differs depending upon whether the action is taken in self-defence or under the authority of the United Nations. For example, Operation Desert Storm in 1991 involved the eviction of Iraqi forces from Kuwait by a US-led coalition of forces. Yet, an assessment under the proportionality criterion would differ depending upon whether the operation is perceived as taken in collective self-defence or collective security.[358] More specifically, 'the operation of the principle of proportionality would define the permissible amount of force in self-defence in a much more limited and constraining manner than had the same operation been undertaken with the

---

[353] This is taken from the 'Webster formula'. For more on this, see Section 6.3.
[354] Ruys, n. 10, at 110.   [355] *Nuclear Weapons* advisory opinion, n. 218, at para. 40.
[356] Kritsiotis, n. 4, at 211–12.
[357] Ruys, n. 10, at 110. See also The Chatham House Principles, n. 25, at 969. Kritsiotis notes that 'the principle of proportionality would stand to measure all of the force that ensues in the name of self-defence – where it would measure the quantum of force in its totality'. Kritsiotis, n. 4, at 211.
[358] Christopher Greenwood, 'New World Order or Old? The Invasion of Kuwait and the Rule of Law' (1992) 55 *Modern Law Review* 153, at 162. See Section 3.4.2.1 for further discussion as to whether this invasion was one of collective self-defence or collective security.

authorization of the Security Council'.[359] Indeed, while if viewed as an operation of self-defence the coalition forces would arguably have been limited to halting and repelling the Iraqi aggression against Kuwait, Resolution 678 (1990) contained the arguably broader aim of the restoration of international peace and security in the area.[360]

As with the principle of necessity, the principle of proportionality is not underpinned or supported by concrete guidelines in terms of its application. In this respect, while it has been claimed that the precise parameters of the principle of proportionality cannot be 'configured exactly or with the kind of precision that would be expected from the law',[361] it has also been said that 'the principle is shrouded in uncertainty'.[362] There are, in this respect, several ways in which it might be viewed. First, the response in self-defence might be required to be *quantitatively* the same as the prior attack in terms of the overall force used, damage caused or casualties suffered.[363] This conception of proportionality was seemingly advanced, for example, by Russia in stressing that the force used against Georgia in self-defence in 2008 did not go beyond the scale of the attacks it had been subjected to.[364] More recently, in June 2019 former US President Trump called off a strike against Iran in response to its destruction of an unmanned US surveillance drone as it would have resulted in the deaths of 150 people and therefore would have not been proportional.[365] There also appears to be some support for this form of proportionality from the ICJ in the *Nicaragua* case:

[W]hether or not the assistance to the *contras* might meet the criterion of proportionality, the Court cannot regard the United States activities ... relating to the mining of the Nicaraguan ports and the attacks on ports, oil installations, etc., as satisfying that criterion. *Whatever uncertainty may exist as to the exact scale of the aid received by the Salvadoran armed opposition from Nicaragua, it is clear that these latter United States activities in question could not have been proportionate to that aid.*[366]

Furthermore, the ICJ in the *Oil Platforms* case did not find the attacks by the United States of 18 April 1988 upon the Salman and Nasr complexes to be proportionate to the mining of the USS *Samuel B. Roberts*. Oddly, while the Court on the one hand claimed that it was 'solely the action against the

---

[359] Kritsiotis, n. 4, at 216.  [360] See, further, Sections 3.4.2.1 and 4.3.
[361] Kritsiotis, n. 4, at 213.  [362] Kretzmer, n. 307, at 237.
[363] Barry Levenfeld, 'Israeli Counter-Fedayeen Tactics in Lebanon: Self-Defence and Reprisal under Modern International Law' (1982–3) 21 *Columbia Journal of Transnational Law* 1, at 41.
[364] UN Doc. S/2008/545, 11 August 2008.
[365] This was relayed through the medium of a Tweet. See Marko Milanovic, 'President Trump Admits US Strike against Iran Would Have Been Illegal', *EJIL Talk!*, 21 June 2019, available at: www.ejiltalk.org/president-trump-admits-us-strike-against-iran-would-have-been-illegal/.
[366] *Nicaragua* case, n. 6, at para. 237 (emphasis added).

Salman and Nasr complexes' that was before it, it also said that it could not 'close its eyes to the scale of the whole [Operation Praying Mantis]', including 'the destruction of two Iranian frigates and a number of other naval vessels and aircraft' in assessing the proportionality of the attacks.[367] Consequently:

[a]s a response to the mining, by an unidentified agency, of a single United States Warship [the *Samuel B. Roberts*], which was severely damaged but not sunk, and without loss of life, neither 'Operation Praying Mantis' as a whole, nor even that part of it that destroyed the Salman and Nasr platforms, can be regarded, in the circumstances of this case, as a proportionate use of force in self-defence.[368]

Adopting this quantitative approach to assessing proportionality, however, would mean that a state might be permitted to do far more than is actually required to defend itself or, alternatively, it might not in the circumstances be able to take the action necessary to effectively defend itself. It has also found little support, by itself, amongst the majority of states, scholars and commentators.[369]

Alternatively, the principle of proportionality might require that the response in self-defence be *qualitatively* equivalent to the prior attack or threat, for example in terms of the weapons used or the nature of the armed attack. Similarly, however, this approach would mean that in many situations the victim state might be permitted to be either overly destructive in its response or instead be deprived of the opportunity to effectively defend itself. Furthermore, it is not one that appears to have found acceptance in state practice. For example, the United States has expressly reserved the right to respond to cyber-attacks using conventional military means:

Just as our military is prepared to respond to hostile acts on land, air and sea, we must be prepared to respond to hostile acts in cyberspace. Accordingly, the United States reserves the right ... to respond to serious cyberattacks, with a proportional and justified military response, at the time and place of its choosing.[370]

In addition, while Finland is tentatively of the view that '[i]t is reasonable to think that a State victim to such a [cyber-]attack can respond with either cyber means or armed action',[371] Israel is, more affirmatively, of the view that 'the

---

[367] *Oil Platforms* case, n. 11, at para. 77.    [368] Ibid.
[369] For rejection of this conception of proportionality see Sina Etezazian, 'The Nature of the Self-Defence Proportionality Requirement' (2016) 3 *Journal on the Use of Force and International Law* 260, at 264–70; Ruys, n. 10, at 111; Gray, n. 91, at 159. Green notes, however, that 'some equivalence of scale must be taken into account, meaning that attacks that are wholly disproportionate in terms of scale (such as regime change) are unlikely to be legally proportional'. Green, n. 185, at 96.
[370] Anna Fifield and Joseph Menn, 'US Prepared for Military Response in Cyberwar', *Financial Times*, 14 July 2011, available at: www.ft.com/content/61b1d2aa-ae34-11e0-8752-00144feabdc0.
[371] Finland Ministry for Foreign Affairs, n. 31.

## 6.3 Customary Requirements of Necessity and Proportionality

use of force in accordance with the right of self-defense, against an armed attack conducted through cyber means, may be carried out by either cyber or kinetic means; just as use of force in self-defense against a kinetic armed attack may be conducted by kinetic or cyber means'.[372]

Lastly, proportionality might be interpreted as providing that the defending state should do no more than achieve the specific *defensive objective*, so that it may only take measures that are necessary to be able to effectively halt and repel the armed attack. In support of this view, Special Rapporteur Robert Ago stated that:

> The action needed to halt and repulse [an] attack may well have to assume dimensions disproportionate to those of the attack suffered. What matters in this respect is the result to be achieved by the 'defensive' action, and not the forms, substance and strength of the action itself.[373]

This approach is the one arguably best reflected in state practice. So, for example, while the events immediately preceding the initiation by Israel of Operation Change Direction in Lebanon in 2006 included the launching of missiles and the abduction of two Israeli soldiers by Hezbollah, the actions of Israel in self-defence, which involved the bombing of Hezbollah targets in order to 'secure the release of the kidnapped soldiers and bring an end to the shelling that terrorizes our citizens',[374] appeared to be generally accepted.[375] It was in this respect notable that condemnation of Israel's actions, specifically on the basis of their proportionality, was made in regard to its targeting of Lebanese infrastructure – strikes that were not deemed necessary in countering the threat posed by Hezbollah and therefore deemed disproportionate – as opposed to restricting its force to targets belonging to Hezbollah.[376]

This conception of proportionality has also attracted arguably the greatest scholarly support,[377] with several factors having been advanced that are

---

[372] Schondorf, n. 70.    [373] Ago, n. 241, at 69–70.    [374] UN Doc. S/2006/515, 12 July 2006.

[375] See UN Doc. S/PV. 5489, 14 July 2006. See also Frederic L. Kirgis, 'Some Proportionality Issues Raised by Israel's Use of Force in Lebanon' (2006) 10 *American Society of International Law Insights*; Enzo Cannizzaro, 'Contextualizing Proportionality: *Jus ad Bellum*, and *Jus in Bello* in the Lebanese War' (2006) **864** *International Review of the Red Cross* 779.

[376] See UN Doc. S/PV. 5489, 13 July 2006; UN Doc. S/PV. 5493, 21 July 2006.

[377] See, for example, Christopher Greenwood, 'Self-Defence and the Conduct of International Armed Conflict', in Yoram Dinstein and Mala Tabory (eds.), *International Law at a Time of Perplexity: Essays in Honour of Shabtai Rosenne* (Brill, 1989), 273, at 274; Tarcisio Gazzini, *The Changing Rules on the Use of Force in International Law* (Manchester University Press, 2005), at 148; Keiichiro Okimoto, *The Distinction and Relationship between* Jus ad Bellum *and* Jus in Bello (Hart, 2011), at 60; Gray, n. 91, at 159; Green, n. 185, at 88–9; Kretzmer, n. 307, at 282; Etezazian, n. 369, at 267–8. See also *Nicaragua* case, n. 6, Separate Opinion of Judge Schwebel, at para. 212; *Nuclear Weapons* advisory opinion, n. 218, Dissenting Opinion of Judge Higgins, at para. 5.

perceived as relevant in assessing proportionality upon this basis, such as target selection, effects on civilians, geographical scope and temporal scope.[378]

However, if we are to view proportionality in this way then the concepts of necessity and proportionality largely merge into one another, as proportionality is, in essence, equated to defensive necessity in each case. There will, however, often be a lack of clarity as to what ends the defensive necessity permits and 'in the absence of agreement on these ends it is obviously impossible to agree on the necessary means to achieve them'.[379] Irrespective of such disagreement, '[i]t is not clear how far the two concepts can operate separately. If a use of force is not necessary it cannot be proportionate and, if it is not proportionate, it is difficult to see how it can be necessary'.[380]

This conception of proportionality is, however, also linked in the view of some to the concept of quantitative proportionality identified earlier in that '[a] response that is disproportionate in scale to the initial attack is also likely to be disproportionate to the goal of abating that attack'.[381] It is interesting to note in this respect that the ICJ in the *Nuclear Weapons* advisory opinion was of the view that '[t]he proportionality principle [does] not in itself exclude the use of nuclear weapons in self-defence in all circumstances',[382] in particular in the extreme circumstances where a state's 'very survival would be at stake'.[383]

However, in light of the fact that most actions in self-defence do not occur while an actual specific armed attack is in progress, this view of proportionality might permit the state acting in self-defence to defend itself against *further* armed attacks in the future. For example, and as discussed in Section 6.3.1.2.2, the justification for the response of the United States to the attacks of 9/11 was portrayed as being 'to *prevent and deter further attacks* on the United States'[384] an objective which was seemingly accepted by the majority of other states. Of course, the fact that this intervention resulted in regime change raises questions regarding the proportionality of such an outcome in relation to the unclear future threat posed to the United States by al-Qaida and the support it was receiving from the Taliban regime. Furthermore, in its letter to the Security Council, the United States also stated that '[w]e may find that our self-defence requires further actions with respect to other organisations and other states'.[385] This claim, which raises questions in relation to the doctrine of

---

[378] Ruys, n. 10, at 118–23; Etezazian, n. 369, at 277–88; Okimoto, n. 377, at 62–75.
[379] Kretzmer, n. 307, at 282. [380] Gray, n. 91, at 159.
[381] Green, n. 185, at 94–5. As Green goes on to note: 'Therefore, the question is not merely one of balancing the response with the legitimate defensive aims of responding: it would seem that there is also a need for states to ensure a level of equivalence in terms of the scale of their activity to that of the initial attack.' Ibid., at 95.
[382] *Nuclear Weapons* advisory opinion, n. 218, at para. 42. [383] Ibid., at para. 97.
[384] UN Doc. S/2001/946, 7 October 2001 (emphasis added). [385] Ibid.

preventative self-defence,[386] is controversial from a proportionality perspective as, upon any of the ways of viewing proportionality noted, it would be difficult to gauge in either quantitative or qualitative terms the level of force required in self-defence, as well as raising questions of an evidentiary nature.

One, of course, has to consider that the success of claims of self-defence are very much context-specific. In this respect, 'the most important reason why the proportionality standard is so difficult to handle is its inherently contextual nature. Indeed, a magical template applicable to all instances of defensive action simply does not exist, since so much resides in the contingencies of the situation.'[387] Ultimately, the principle of proportionality does not provide exact parameters by which to guide states in their actions or in the judgement of the actions of others, but rather provides 'a space for "second opinions" to which claims of disputants can be referred'.[388]

### 6.3.2.1  *Proportionality and the 'Accumulation of Events' Theory*

A further aspect of the accumulation of events theory, which has already been addressed in connection with determining the *gravity* of an armed attack,[389] is the question of gauging the proportionality of a response to individual smaller attacks that may cumulatively amount to an armed attack. Indeed, under this theory the proportionality of the response would be seen in the context of the entirety of the previous cumulative attacks and not simply the one immediately preceding it, thereby potentially justifying a larger response.

Again, this has arguably come into sharpest focus in connection with Israel's various raids into Gaza. Despite the rockets having resulted in a handful of Israeli deaths, the Israeli operations in response were extensive, with Operation Cast Lead alone resulting in the death of approximately 1,400 Palestinians,[390] while Operation Protective Edge, which lasted for seven weeks, led to the deaths of over 2,000 Palestinians.[391] Both operations also resulted in the extensive destruction of, or severe damage to, Gazan infrastructure, including homes, schools and mosques.[392]

---

[386] See Chapter 7 for more on preventative self-defence.  [387] Ruys, n. 10, at 111.
[388] Thomas M. Franck, 'On Proportionality of Countermeasures in International Law' (2008) 102 *American Journal of International Law* 715, at 717.
[389] See Section 6.2.5.4.
[390] Human Rights Council, 'Human Rights in Palestine and Other Occupied Arab Territories: Report of the United Nations Fact Finding Mission on the Gaza Conflict', UN Doc. A/HRC/12/48, 15 September 2009, at paras. 352–61.
[391] Human Rights Council, 'Report of the Independent Commission of Inquiry Established Pursuant to Human Rights Council Resolution S-21/1', UN Doc. A/HRC/29/52, 24 June 2015, at para. 20.
[392] See Henderson, n. 187, at 729–32.

Israel justified the operations upon the basis of self-defence, making clear at the beginning of Operation Cast Lead, for example, that '[i]t is about ensuring the end of terrorism from Gaza and the end of smuggling weapons into Gaza, so that there is no longer a need for Israeli defensive operations'.[393] Indeed, Israel was clear that it intended its actions not to result merely in a 'band aid' solution.[394] However, while the views of states commenting upon the operations were mixed, the condemnation and accusations of aggression did not appear to be based upon the fact that Israel had no right to use force in the first place, due to the absence of either an armed attack or defensive necessity, but more on the basis of the disproportionate nature of the respective operations.[395]

Given the persistent and cumulative nature of the rocket attacks from Gaza, the proportionality of Israel's response might be viewed in light of Israel's aim of permanently preventing further rocket attacks. In this respect, the scale and effects of the rocket attacks would not be viewed upon the basis of their actual effects, with the question then becoming whether the operation as a whole was proportionate in halting the attacks and the continuing threat they posed. However, given that there were several major operations by Israel, all with the stated goal of permanently halting the attacks yet with none having that result and, at the same time, leading to significant death and destruction, it is arguable that, if not at the time of Operation Cast Lead in 2008, then certainly by Operation Protective Edge in 2014 and Operation Guardian of the Walls in 2021, the operations were ineffective in achieving this defensive aim and thus represented an unnecessary and disproportionate response. Indeed, while conceding that a proportionate response in self-defence may well be of a larger scale than the attack(s) preceding it if required by defensive necessity, it is difficult to view these operations in response to the preceding rocket attacks as proportionate.

## 6.4 THE PROTECTION OF NATIONALS ABROAD

During the nineteenth century, states possessed a right to intervene in other states to protect both their nationals and property located there.[396] Some continue to argue that there is a discrete and independent right of states to intervene to protect their nationals.[397] The problem with this position is that it

---

[393] UN Doc. S/PV/6060, 31 December 2008, at 7 (Israel).
[394] UN Doc. S/PV.7214, 10 July 2014, at 6–7 (Israel).
[395] See n. 191 for the meetings within the UN where the incidents were discussed.
[396] Brownlie, n. 3, at 289. See Section 1.2 for more on the historical regulation of the use of forcible measures.
[397] In attempting to provide a framework to assess claims of force for the protection of nationals abroad, Sir Humphrey Waldock stated that states possess such a right providing that three conditions are satisfied: 'There must be (1) an imminent threat of injury to nationals, (2) a failure or an inability on the part of the territorial sovereign to protect them and (3) measures of protection strictly confined to the object of protecting them against injury.' 'The

would appear to add an additional right to use unilateral force under international law – alongside self-defence and authorisation by the UN Security Council – which is not something that has been generally accepted in the practice of states or in the work of scholars.[398] In this respect, the more widely held position is that military action for the protection of nationals abroad in fact falls to be assessed under the general right of self-defence.[399]

The initial justification provided by the Trump administration for the drone strike in January 2020 which led to the death of Iranian General Qassem Soleimani was that the United States was taking defensive action 'to protect U.S. personnel abroad'.[400] At no point did any of the justificatory discourse engaged in by the United States make reference to the 'protection of nationals' doctrine, either as a standalone doctrine or as an aspect of the right of self-defence. Yet, given the relatively consistent line of self-defence in the discourse it can be assumed that the Trump administration was – wittingly or not – positioning this as an underpinning basis for its recourse to the legal right of self-defence under Article 51. This is supported by the fact that the United States has relatively consistently maintained the position that '[a] State's right to use force in self-defense may be understood to include the right to use force to protect its nationals abroad.'[401]

The protection of nationals has not generally been expressly advanced in justification or adopted by states as an aspect of the right of self-defence. Indeed, the various statements by the Trump administration following the killing of General Soleimani is about as close to an invocation of the protection of nationals under the right of self-defence as one is likely to find. However, there have nonetheless been several incidences in which attacks

---

Regulation of the Use of Force by Individual States in International Law' (1952) **81** *Recueil des Cours* 451, at 467. Others have relied upon the 'Webster formula' from the *Caroline* incident as providing appropriate guidelines. See Malcolm Shaw, *International Law*, 8th ed. (Cambridge University Press, 2017), at 872.

[398] On the protection of nationals, see, in general, Natalino Ronzitti, *Rescuing Nationals Abroad through Military Coercion and Intervention on the Grounds of Humanity* (Martinus Nijhoff Publishers, 1985); Tom Ruys, 'The "Protection of Nationals" Doctrine Revisited' (2008) 13 *Journal of Conflict & Security Law* 233; Mathias Forteau, 'Rescuing Nationals Abroad', in Marc Weller (ed.), *The Oxford Handbook of the Use of Force in International Law* (Oxford University Press, 2015), 947.

[399] As discussed in Section 2.5.2.1, attacks upon individuals do not necessarily fall to be assessed under the *jus ad bellum*. Yet, if an attack or a threat of attack on the nationals of one state occurs at the hands of, or through an inability to protect by, the state in which they are located, in particular if it is clear that they are being attacked due to their nationality, the prohibition of the use of force potentially becomes engaged. It arguably follows, then, that if the attacks are sufficiently grave, they also potentially give rise to the right of self-defence.

[400] U.S. Department of Defense, 'Statement by the Department of Defense', 2 January 2020, available at www.defense.gov/Newsroom/Releases/Release/Article/2049534/statement-by-the-department-of-defense/.

[401] Department of Defense, Law of War Manual, December 2016, at para. 1.11.5.3.

on a state's nationals have been utilised as one of several underpinning rationales for the invocation of the right of self-defence and states have not, as set out in this section, generally objected to this on a point of principle.

Questions remain, however, regarding the types of situations in which – and conditions required before – self-defence in the protection of a states' nationals may be invoked. For example, is a single attack on, or threat to, a single individual sufficient, or is there a threshold of harm to a state that must be met? Are there any limitations on which nationals may receive protection? And at what point may a state invoke and implement its right of self-defence? There is also the issue of the purpose of the action in self-defence, in that questions arise as to whether there is a distinction to be made between missions to rescue or evacuate nationals from perilous situations, military action in direct response to attacks on nationals, and then broader military interventions with the aim of ensuring the continued protection of a state's nationals within the state in which they are located. These issues essentially revolve around the armed attack criterion of self-defence, along with the necessity and proportionality of any action taken, which are addressed in Sections 6.4.1–6.4.3.

### 6.4.1 Attacks on Nationals as an Armed Attack

It was notable that US Ambassador to the UN, Kelly Craft, was clear following the drone strike that led to the death of General Soleimani in January 2020 that the United States 'will act decisively in the exercise of [its] inherent right of self-defense to protect Americans when necessary, *as is recognized under the Charter*'.[402] However, the right of self-defence in the protection of nationals is not, as would seem to be asserted here, expressly recognized within the UN Charter. Yet, there is also nothing that would appear to limit the concept of 'armed attacks' to attacks that take place against a state's territory,[403] meaning that there is nothing *per se* to prevent the right being invoked in response to attacks on manifestations of a state that are located outside of its territory, territorial waters or airspace, including its nationals. Indeed, 'the protection of nationals can be assimilated without great strain to the right of self-defence explicitly contained in the text of the Charter'.[404] As eloquently stated by Christopher Greenwood:

---

[402] United States Mission to the United Nations, Remarks at a UN Security Council Debate on Upholding the UN Charter, 9 January 2020, available at: https://usun.usmission.gov/remarks-at-a-un-security-council-debate-on-upholding-the-un-charter/ (emphasis added).

[403] Indeed, if states were restricted to invoking self-defence in response to attacks that take place on their territory, then this might seem to render the right of self-defence as an exception to the prohibition of the use of force somewhat redundant.

[404] Tom J. Farer, 'Panama: Beyond the Charter Paradigm' (1990) **84** *American Journal of International Law* 503, at 505.

While it has often been argued that the notion of an armed attack is confined to attacks upon the territory and, perhaps, the ships and aircraft, of a State, the better view is that an attack upon a State's nationals outside its territory also constitutes an armed attack, or at least amounts to a use of force sufficient to allow the victim State to invoke the right of self-defence. There is little doubt that customary international law in the period before 1945 recognized a right to use force in defence of nationals who were attacked abroad and there is no indication that Article 51 [of the Charter] was intended to remove that aspect of the customary right. On the contrary, Article 51 refers to an armed attack upon a member State; since population is one of the attributes of statehood, an attack upon a State's population would seem to be just as much an attack upon that State as would an attack upon its territory. There is something inherently unattractive about a view of self-defence which would allow a State to use force to protect uninhabited territory but not in defence of its nationals. State practice in protecting nationals abroad since 1945 also supports this interpretation of Article 51.[405]

One problematic issue with this view, however, is the generally minor gravity of the attacks or threats involved in cases of the protection of nationals abroad, despite the fact that it is somewhat unclear how widespread or severe the attacks or threat would need to be to justify invoking the right of self-defence.[406] While Russia claimed that the deaths of 1,500 of its citizens in South Ossetia and attacks on Russian peacekeepers in 2008 was of a 'scale' to justify its invocation of the right of self-defence under Article 51 of the UN Charter,[407] in many of the situations where states have intervened it is questionable whether an armed attack can be said to have occurred, particularly if we are, of course, to take the ICJ's conception of such an attack being of a certain gravity.[408] Following the strike which killed General Soleimani, the United States made a host of claims in its justificatory discourse in regards to the past behaviour of – and threats by – Iran. However, much focus, at least at the outset, was placed on the specific death of a US civilian contractor which resulted from an attack of 27 December 2019 involving a series of rocket attacks against an Iraqi military base outside of the Iraqi city of

---

[405] Christopher Greenwood, 'International Law and the United States' Air Operation against Libya' (1986-7) 89 *West Virginia Law Review* 933, at 940-1.
[406] If, however, one is of the view that the response in self-defence is to be assessed more on the basis of the proportionality of the armed response to the prior attack and any continuing threat, as opposed to whether the attack giving rise to action has met a particular threshold of gravity, then the protection of nationals arguably falls more easily within the confines of the right of self-defence. Indeed, in acknowledging the fact that there is a widely perceived 'gravity threshold' for an armed attack, Greenwood, ibid., in the quote here, appears to note that while an attack on nationals might not constitute an armed attack it might 'at least amount[] to a use of force sufficient to allow the victim State to invoke the right of self-defence'.
[407] See UN Doc. S/2008/515, 11 August 2008. [408] See Section 6.2.5.

Kirkuk.[409] Even for those, like the United States, who claim that there is no gravity threshold for the invocation of the right of self-defence, it would be difficult to make the claim that the death of a single civilian individual – subject to the possible head of state exception, as discussed in the remains of this section and in Section 6.4.2 – in and of itself gives rise to the right of self-defence, although the overall 'scale and effects' of the attack in which that individual was killed may alter the way in which the attack is perceived.

Arguably in realisation of the potential controversies involved in relying on this single death as the basis for its action, the United States included in its justificatory discourse broader historical claims in regard to deaths and injuries to US nationals. Indeed, in addition to claiming that Soleimani was 'responsible for the deaths of hundreds of American and coalition service members and the wounding of thousands more',[410] the Trump administration also claimed it was acting to protect 'American diplomats and service members',[411] later claiming that the United States had more broadly 'protected and defended the American people'.[412] Yet, claims of such an historical and vague nature are arguably an insufficient basis upon which to make the case that the United States had been the victim of an armed attack or that one was forthcoming. In a similar fashion, as part of President Putin's speech upon the launching of the 'special military operation' against Ukraine in February 2022 the claim of individual self-defence was not only made in regards to the protection of Russian territory but also the protection of Russian nationals – or, at least, those provided with passports – abroad.[413] While there was evidence that serious human rights violations had been perpetrated in areas of eastern Ukraine by both sides to the conflict since 2014,[414] there was little evidence to suggest that Russian nationals had been

---

[409] For example, Secretary of State, Mike Pompeo, on 5 January, seemed to focus on 'recent deaths', in particular the 'recent killing on December 27th' which 'killed an American'. See U.S. Department of State, 'Secretary Michael R. Pompeo with Chuck Todd of NBC Meet the Press', 5 January 2020, available at: https://kr.usembassy.gov/010520-secretary-michael-r-pompeo-with-chuck-todd-of-nbc-meet-the-press/. See Julian E. Barnes, 'American Contractor Killed in Rocket Attack in Iraq', *New York Times*, 27 December 2019, available at: www.nytimes.com/2019/12/27/us/politics/american-rocket-attack-iraq.html.

[410] Presumably this latter claim was in relation to attacks that had occurred since the US presence in Iraq commenced in 2004, but it is not entirely clear, and such a brief press statement was not sufficient to support such a claim.

[411] See 'Statement by the Department of Defense', n. 400.

[412] U.S. Department of State, n. 409.

[413] See Address by the President of the Russian Federation', Office of the President of the Russian Federation, 24 February 2022, available at: http://en.kremlin.ru/events/president/transcripts/67843 (official English translation, as published by the Kremlin); Обращение Президента Российской Федерации, Президент России, 24 февраля 2022 года, available at: http://kremlin.ru/events/president/news/67843(original Russian text, as published by the Kremlin).

[414] See, for example, 'Report of the Special Rapporteur on Torture and Other Cruel, Inhuman or Degrading Treatment or Punishment on His Visit to Ukraine, Human Rights Council, UN Doc. A/HRC/40/59/Add.3, 17 January 2019.

specifically targeted or that such violations had occurred on a scale that could be equated to an armed attack.[415]

Questions also arise as to whether there are any limitations upon the *types* of nationals that may be the target of an armed attack thereby giving rise to the right of self-defence. It is hard to identify clear rules on this issue. State practice, however, would seem to suggest that attacks on certain individuals abroad may give rise to the right of self-defence, such as heads of state, given their symbolic affinity with the victim state.[416] Indeed, whether or not the action taken had a true defensive purpose, or whether it was taken more simply in retaliation or just for the US government to be seen to be doing something, the United States' invocation of the right of self-defence and subsequent military action in response to an assassination attempt on former President George H. W. Bush while on a visit to Kuwait in 1993 was widely supported by states.[417] Similarly, and as discussed in Section 6.2.2, the armed forces of a state can arguably be considered as a clear manifestation of a state for the purposes of the right of self-defence, meaning that an attack on them is likely to be seen as an attack on the state itself. Indeed, while 'armed attack' and 'aggression' are not necessarily synonymous, the Definition of Aggression includes as an act which qualifies as an act of aggression '[a]n attack by the armed forces of a State on land, sea or air forces, or marine and air fleets of another State'.[418] Yet, there is also nothing per se to exclude attacks on civilians as constituting an armed attack, providing the other requirements for a lawful invocation of the right of self-defence are satisfied. Indeed, if the protection of nationals is viewed as an action in self-defence, any action taken would need to satisfy the twin criteria of necessity and proportionality, in particular that any action is confined to defensive purposes.

### 6.4.2 Attacks or Threats to Nationals by a Foreign Government

In many cases those accused of harming or threatening the nationals concerned are members of the authorities within the state in which the nationals are located, giving rise to a *prima facie* necessity for their state of nationality to protect them as there would seem to be no one else to turn to within the state concerned to ensure their protection. Following a military coup in Grenada in 1983, the United States, along with small contingents of troops

---

[415] James A. Green, Christian Henderson and Tom Ruys, 'Russia's Attack on Ukraine and the *Jus ad Bellum*', (2022) 9 *Journal on the Use of Force and International Law* 4, at 15.
[416] Stuart Casey-Maslen, Jus ad Bellum: *The Law on Inter-State Use of Force* (Hart, 2020), at 59–60.
[417] Henderson, n. 310, at 251.
[418] Article 3(d), UNGA Res. 3314 (XXIX) (1974). Such a determination is reserved for 'the most serious and dangerous form of the illegal use of force'. Ibid., preamble.

from Jamaica and Barbados, forcibly intervened.[419] The United States justified its actions upon an invitation to intervene by the Governor-General of the island, an invitation to intervene by the Organization of Eastern Caribbean States and on the basis that it was intervening to protect, and facilitate the departure of, its nationals.[420] While the UN Security Council did not condemn the operation, due to the veto of the United States,[421] the debates that took place in the Council chamber were notable by their rejection of the assertion by the United States that there was a credible danger to US citizens and also by the general sense that the actions were taken for ulterior political motives, such as reversing the socialist military coup that had taken place.[422] The UN General Assembly did, however, adopt a resolution by an overwhelming majority that '*deeply deplore*[d]' the armed intervention as a 'flagrant violation of international law' and called for its immediate cessation.[423] While nothing was expressly mentioned in this resolution about either of the United States' justifications for its intervention in general, or specifically the necessity of the protection of nationals, the resolution recalled Article 2(4) of the UN Charter and '[c]*all*[ed] for an immediate cessation of the armed intervention and the immediate withdrawal of the foreign troops from Grenada'.[424]

Similarly, the United States intervened in Panama in 1989, following a disputed election result whereby General Manuel Noriega refused to stand down.[425] This began with an increased military presence by the United States at its bases within the Canal Zone but, subsequently, after Noriega had declared a 'state of war' with the United States and violence had occurred against some US nationals, the United States intervened more forcibly, invoking its 'inherent right of self-defence under international law'.[426]

However, in addition to safeguarding the lives of US citizens, the operation was also justified upon the basis of defending democracy in Panama, combatting drug trafficking by Noriega and in defence of the Panama Canal Treaties.[427] The operation received both limited support and condemnation within the debates of the Security Council, although a resolution condemning

---

[419] Thomas Franck, *Recourse to Force: State Action against Threats and Armed Attacks* (Cambridge University Press, 2002), at 86. See Levitin, n. 255, at 650.
[420] UN Doc. S/16076, 25 October 1983. See Chapter 9 for more on intervention by invitation.
[421] See (1983) *United Nations Yearbook* 211.
[422] UN Doc. S/PV.2487, 25 October 1983; UN Doc. S/PV. 2489, 26 October 1983; UN Doc. S/PV. 2491, 27 October 1983.
[423] UNGA Res. 38/7 (1983).   [424] Ibid., preamble and para. 4, respectively.
[425] Franck, n. 419, at 91. See Ved. P. Nanda, 'The Validity of United States Intervention in Panama under International Law' (1990) 84 *American Journal of International Law* 494; John Quigley, 'The Legality of the United States Invasion of Panama' (1990) 15 *Yale Journal of International Law* 287; Ruth Wedgwood, 'The Use of Armed Force in International Affairs: Self-Defence and the Panama Invasion' (1991) 29 *Columbia Journal of International Law* 609.
[426] UN Doc. S/PV. 2899, 20 December 1989, at 31.   [427] Ibid.

the action was not adopted due to the vetoes of the United States, France and the United Kingdom.[428] In a similar fashion to events in the UN following the intervention in Grenada, things shifted to the General Assembly which adopted a resolution condemning the action as a 'flagrant intervention of international law', although support for it was equivocal with seventy-five states voting in favour, twenty states against and forty states abstaining.[429] The operation was withdrawn after the elected president, Guillermo Endara, had taken power.

Interventions for the protection of nationals become more complicated and controversial from the perspective of both the necessity and proportionality when they are ostensibly taken to ensure the continued safety of the states' nationals. Any action taken must have a strictly confined defensive purpose, so that those taken with the aim of making life better for the nationals of the victim state residing there, or to achieve a political aim of the intervening state, are prohibited. In this respect, the proportionality of the US operation in Grenada was called into question given that over 7,000 troops were deployed to protect fewer than 1,000 nationals and with the actions of the United States going far beyond offering them protection, ultimately remaining to install a new government.[430] Indeed, much of the condemnation that the United States received for its operation was based on its disproportionate nature[431] and it is difficult to envisage a situation whereby regime change would be a proportionate response in the context of the protection of nationals abroad. Similarly, in Panama, the danger to US nationals appeared to be confined to threats to a few hundred nationals and the death of a US officer. In the light of the 10,000 troops that were deployed, accusations were, again, made that the operation was disproportionate.[432] In addition, the fact that the measures taken were far from strictly confined to the object of protecting the nationals against injury alluded to there being underlying ulterior motives.

While there was some debate as to whether the resolutions and the debates at the UN in connection with both the Grenada and Panama interventions represented a rejection of the right to intervene for the protection of nationals, or just a rejection of the particular interventions on their facts,[433] it is nonetheless difficult to see any precedential value in either intervention and, given the plurality of justification in both cases, it is difficult to say that the

---

[428] UN Doc. S/21048, 22 December 1989.   [429] UNGA Res. 44/240 (1989).
[430] William C. Gilmore, *The Grenada Intervention: Analysis and Documentation* (A. Spitz, 1984), at 55–64.
[431] The issue of proportionality was, for example, a key element of the statement made by Zimbabwe in the Security Council. See UN Doc. S/PV. 2491, n. 422, at 5.
[432] See, for example, UN Doc. S/PV. 2900, 21 December 1989, at 14–15 (Finland).
[433] See Franck, n. 419, at 88; Gray, n. 91, at 166–7.

general criticism was aimed specifically towards the protection of nationals element of the justifications.

The United States carried out more limited airstrikes in April 1986 against various Libyan military targets following a bomb attack at a Berlin nightclub that killed two Americans and injured seventy-nine.[434] In again invoking the right of self-defence under Article 51 of the UN Charter, the United States claimed that it launched the strikes in response to 'an ongoing pattern of attacks by the Government of Libya' against US nationals and installations,[435] thereby implicitly basing the action both on the protection of nationals and on the fact that there had been an accumulation of attacks against it.[436] Indeed, it was claimed that '[o]ver a considerable period of time Libya has openly targeted American citizens and U.S. installations.'[437] While the United States did not make claims that there were threats of further imminent attacks against US nationals, it justified the strikes as necessary to 'discourage' further attacks.[438] A draft UN Security Council resolution condemning the strikes received vetoes from the United States, the United Kingdom and France.[439] In justifying its actions, the United States was keen to stress that it 'had exercised great care in restricting its military response to terrorist-related targets ... which have enabled Libyan agents to carry out deadly missions against U.S. installations and innocent individuals' and that it had taken 'every possible precaution to avoid civilian casualties and to limit collateral damage', yet many states condemned the action,[440] with even those accepting that Libya was targeting US nationals also considering the strikes as disproportionate to any continuing threat posed.[441]

A similar bombing campaign was undertaken by the United States in June 1993, this time against an intelligence headquarters on the outskirts of Baghdad, Iraq, following an attempted assassination attempt on former US President George H. W. Bush while on a visit to Kuwait in 1993.[442] On this occasion, however, the United States, in again justifying its actions as self-defence under Article 51 of the UN Charter,[443] received considerable support from those within the Security Council[444] and the assassination attempt was considered sufficient to enable the United States to invoke its right of self-defence, although the positive reaction was arguably down to the target being a former head of state as opposed to it representing a general endorsement of the protection of nationals under the right of self-defence.

---

[434] Franck, ibid., at 89–91. See Greenwood, n. 405.   [435] See UN Doc. S/17990, 14 April 1986.
[436] See Sections 6.2.5.4 and 6.3.2.1 on the accumulation of events theory.
[437] UN Doc. S/17990, n. 435.   [438] Ibid.   [439] (1986) *United Nations Yearbook* 254.
[440] Ibid.
[441] UN Doc. S/17989, 14 April 1986; UN Doc. A/41/285; S/17996, 15 April 1986; UN Doc. A/41/287; S/17999, 15 April 1986.
[442] *Keesing's* (1993) 39531. See Kritsiotis, n. 136.   [443] UN Doc. S/26003, 26 June 1993.
[444] See UN Doc. S/5657, 27 June 1993.

In the case of the strike by the United States against General Soleimani in 2020, and perhaps in realisation that any military action purely in response to either the recent death of a single US contractor or the more historical claims, regardless of their gravity, might appear to have a purpose other than self-defence,[445] the justificatory discourse also appeared to focus on the *future* protection of US nationals, and in particular armed forces personnel present in Iraq and the region. In this respect, it was notable that while the United States has maintained the position that not only is self-defence available for the protection of nationals but in respect to *any* use of force, Secretary of State Mike Pompeo made the claim that the death of Soleimani prevented attacks that would have put 'dozens if not hundreds of American lives at risk'.[446] If true, and taking the gravity of this potential situation on its own to the exclusion of other relevant considerations, it might appear to be of sufficient 'gravity' for the invocation of the right of self-defence. This claim, however, 'generated doubts because no attack in the Middle East over the past two decades, even at the height of the Iraq war, has ever resulted in so many American casualties at once in part because embassies and bases have become so fortified',[447] thereby placing question marks over the United States' invocation of the right of self-defence and the necessity and proportionality of the action on this basis.

Finally, a central justification advanced by Russia for its interventions in the South Ossetian region of Georgia in 2008, in the Crimean region of Ukraine in early 2014 and in mainland Ukraine in 2022 was the protection of Russians and Russian-speaking individuals from attacks by the Georgian and Ukrainian authorities, respectively. The intervention in Georgia was justified on the basis of protecting Russian citizens,[448] who were, in actual fact, ethnic Ossetians that had been granted Russian passports. This aspect of the operation led to claims that Russia had 'manufactured nationals' to be used as a pretext for intervention.[449] No discussion took place in the Security Council on this issue, although Russia's actions received condemnation, mostly upon the basis of the suspected motive of Russia and the disproportionate nature of the operation.[450] Indeed, while Russia explicitly defended its actions as

---

[445] See, in particular, Section 6.2.

[446] Reuters, 'Pompeo Says U.S. Strike on Iranian Commander in Response to Imminent Attack', 3 January 2020, available at: www.reuters.com/article/iraq-security-blast-pompeo-update-1-pompeo-says-u-s-strike-on-iranian-commander-in-response-to-imminent-attack-idUSL1N298094.

[447] See Baker and Gibbons-Neff, n. 52.     [448] See UN Doc. S/2008/545, 11 August 2008.

[449] James A. Green, 'Passportisation, Peacekeepers and Proportionality: The Russian Claim of the Protection of Nationals Abroad in Self-Defence', in James A. Green and Christopher P. M. Waters (eds.), *Conflict in the Caucasus: Implications for International Legal Order* (Palgrave Macmillan, 2010), 54, at 66–7.

[450] Ibid., at 70.

proportionate,[451] the Russian intervention went far beyond simply protecting its nationals, with Russian forces entering Abkhazia and further into Georgian territory and remaining in the area long after the conflict had ended.

Somewhat similarly, in 2014 Russia claimed that persons of Russian ethnicity in Crimea were 'in distress' and were 'threatened with repression' as they had opposed President Viktor Yanukovych being removed from power,[452] while in 2022 President Putin claimed that given that Russian nationals in the Donbas region of Ukraine had been attacked by Ukrainian authorities and remained under threat of further attack there was not 'any other option for defending Russia and our people, other than the one we are forced to use today'.[453]

Russia therefore attempted again to rely on historical ethnic connections between it and the individuals concerned to justify its intervention, yet in both cases Russia had also been busy issuing passports prior to the interventions,[454] thus again appearing to manufacture nationals in order to provide the pretext for a protection of nationals justification. On this issue it has been said that

[l]egally, the status of such recently 'passportised' nationals is at least questionable, in terms of how real their connection to the state may be, and such mass passportisation could, in itself, amount to an act of unlawful intervention. In any event, it may be said that claiming to use force in self-defence to protect a large number of nationals who until recently were not nationals lacks credibility.[455]

The intervention and ultimate annexation of Crimea was met with widespread condemnation, with the UN General Assembly adopting a resolution on 1 April 2014 which not only recalled the obligation not to resort to force but also called upon states not to recognise the annexation,[456] while on 2 March 2022 the General Assembly adopted a resolution which '[d]*eplore*[d] in the strongest terms the aggression by the Russian Federation against Ukraine in violation of Article 2(4) of the Charter' and '[d]*emand*[ed] that the Russian Federation immediately cease its use of force against Ukraine and to refrain from any further unlawful threat or use of force against any Member State'.[457]

In both cases, and aside from any ulterior motives involved, it appeared that Russia was seeking the *future* protection of its 'nationals', rather than responding simply to a past attack or attempting to evacuate them from Ukrainian

---

[451] See UN Doc. S/2008/545, 11 August 2008: 'the use of force by the Russian side is strictly proportionate to the scale of the attack and pursues no other goal but to protect the Russian peacekeeping contingent and citizens of the Russian Federation'.
[452] See UN Doc. A/68/803-S/2014/202, 20 March 2014.
[453] 'Address by the President of the Russian Federation', n. 413 (emphasis added).
[454] See Fabian Burkhardt, 'Passports as Pretext: How Russia's Invasion of Ukraine Could Start', *War on the Rock*, 17 February 2022, available at: https://warontherocks.com/2022/02/passports-as-pretext-how-russias-war-on-ukraine-could-start/.
[455] Green, Henderson and Ruys, n. 415, at 16.
[456] UNGA Res. 68/262 (2014).
[457] UNGA Res. ES-11/1 (2022), paras. 2 and 3.

territory. Yet, the intervention in 2014 led ultimately to the annexation of a part of the state where the nationals were located, while the action in response to the threat allegedly posed by Ukraine to Russia in 2022 involved a full-scale invasion rather than a targeted operation into areas where Russian nationals were under threat with the aim of evacuating them to Russia. In this respect, both might be said to be 'lightyears removed' from satisfying the proportionality principle.[458] In addition, while another of President Putin's stated goals to 'demilitarize' Ukraine might plausibly be seen as a proportionate outcome if in response to a genuine threat of imminent armed attack,[459] the objective of 'denazifying' Ukraine 'equates to regime change, which is something that is plainly at odds with the purported aim of protecting nationals under imminent threat.'[460]

### 6.4.3 Attacks or Threats to Nationals that a Foreign Government Is Either Unwilling or Unable to Prevent

Self-defence has also been invoked in situations where harm to nationals has not been inflicted directly by the state, but action on its territory is deemed necessary due to the fact that the government is nonetheless perceived to be either unable or unwilling to prevent the harm from occurring.[461] A proponent of this interpretation of self-defence is the United Kingdom, with its 2004 Manual of the Law of Armed Conflict declaring that 'self-defence may include the rescue of nationals when the territorial state is unable or unwilling to do so'.[462]

However, it has been the United States that, again, has invoked it, either explicitly or implicitly, most frequently. For example, on 24 April 1980, in a limited military operation the United States sent a special unit to Iran to free fifty-three US nationals that were being held hostage by a group of Iranian students in the US embassy in Tehran.[463] No fighting ensued, and the operation ended in failure, with two helicopters crashing. The United States, in justifying the operation by invoking its right of self-defence under Article 51 of the UN Charter, attempted to portray the hostage-taking as an armed attack.[464] While the hostages were not taken by agents of the state, the Iranian authorities were clearly not willing to take any action to end the siege at the embassy – in fact

---

[458] Green, Henderson and Ruys, n. 415, at 16.   [459] Ibid.   [460] Ibid.
[461] See Section 8.4.2 for more on the 'unable or unwilling' doctrine in self-defence.
[462] UK Ministry of Defence, *Manual of the Law of Armed Conflict* (Oxford University Press, 2004), at 2. Humphrey Waldock stated the requirement to be 'a failure or an inability on the part of the territorial sovereign to protect them'. Waldock, n. 397, at 467.
[463] *Keesing's* (1980) 30531–3. See John R. D'Angelo, 'Resort to Force by States to Protect Nationals: The U.S. Rescue Mission to Iran and Its Legality under International Law' (1980–1) 21 *Virginia Journal of International Law* 485; Anthea Jeffery, 'The American Hostages in Tehran: The I.C.J. and the Legality of Rescue Missions' (1981) 30 *International & Comparative Law Quarterly* 717.
[464] UN Doc. S/13908, 25 April 1980.

subsequently expressing approval of the situation – and accused the United States of engaging in 'military aggression'.[465] In reacting to the situation there was a general lack of reference to international law. While some states expressed 'understanding' for the operation,[466] Italy stated its 'clear opposition to the recourse to action in force in any circumstances for the liberation of hostages'.[467] Other states similarly condemned the rescue operation.[468]

Arguably the archetypal example of self-defence for the protection of nationals is to be found in Israel's raid on Entebbe, Uganda, in July 1976.[469] A group of terrorists had hijacked an aircraft and diverted it to Entebbe airport in Uganda. Non-Israeli passengers were released and threats were made to kill the remaining passengers if Israel did not comply with the hijacker's demands. Israel subsequently launched a raid involving storming the aircraft, which resulted in the deaths of a small number of hostages and the hijackers, as well as injury to several Ugandan soldiers and the destruction of several Ugandan aircraft. Israel justified its actions in the Security Council as its 'right to take military action to protect its nationals in mortal danger'.[470]

International reaction to the operation appeared to be mixed. It was noticeable that, while some states rejected the use of force for the protection of nationals abroad in principle,[471] others were prepared to accept it.[472] Furthermore, while the operation was condemned in many respects and by many states,[473] most states took no position or objected to the operation on the basis that the necessity for self-defence had not been satisfied due to the fact that negotiations were in progress for the release of the hostages at the time the Israeli operation was launched.[474] The operation was also condemned on the basis that it had resulted in violence in the face of opposition to it by the Ugandan government,[475] although states refrained from expressly condemning it as disproportionate. Indeed, it was a relatively limited, or 'surgical', operation and was therefore perceived by many as being proportional.[476]

---

[465] UN Doc. S/13915, 29 April 1980.   [466] *Keesing's* (1980) 30534.   [467] Ibid.   [468] Ibid.
[469] See David J. Gordon, 'Use of Force for the Protection of Nationals Abroad: The Entebbe Incident' (1977) 9 *Case Western Reserve Journal of International Law* 117; Kristen E. Eichensehr, 'Defending Nationals Abroad: Assessing the Lawfulness of Forcible Hostage Rescues' (2007–8) 48 *Virginia Journal of International Law* 451.
[470] UN Doc. S/PV. 1939, 9 July 1976, at 105–21.
[471] See UN Doc. S/PV. 1943, 14 July 1976, at 11 (Cuba).
[472] See UN Doc. S/PV. 1941, 12 July 1976, at 8 (United States) and UN Doc. S/PV. 1943, ibid., at 7 (France).
[473] See UN Docs. S/PV. 1939–43, ibid.
[474] See, for example, UN Doc. S/PV. 1939, at 26 (Mauritania (on behalf of a group of African states)) and UN Doc. S/PV. 1940, at 6 (Mauritius).
[475] Ruys, n. 10, at 228.
[476] The United States, for example, was keen to point out that the 'Israeli military action was limited to the sole objective of extricating the passengers and crew and it terminated when the objective was accomplished.' UN Doc. S/PV. 1941, n. 472, at 8.

An interesting aspect of the US drone strike in 2020 that led to the death of General Soleimani was that, while the attacks against US nationals were claimed to have been undertaken by both Iranian forces and the Kata'ib Hezbollah group, the strike itself took place on Iraqi territory, in which the United States was operating with the consent of the Iraqi authorities against the so-called Islamic State. In this respect, any military operation on Iraqi territory not connected with the operation against the Islamic State, including one in the protection of nationals, required a separate justification.

It was somewhat surprising, therefore, that the United States did not attempt to justify this aspect of its operation, including through an invocation of the unable or unwilling doctrine of self-defence which it has been a leading proponent of.[477] This was particularly surprising in light of various claims made by the United States that appeared to warn the Iraqi government to take the necessary action to protect US personnel operating within Iraqi territory,[478] warnings that the Iraqi government had apparently not heeded, opening up a claim that it was either unable or unwilling to take the necessary action.[479] However, and as discussed further in Chapter 8,[480] the unable or unwilling doctrine remains controversial.

### 6.4.3.1 *Operations to Extract Nationals*

A distinction can arguably be made, however, between action in self-defence and the forcible extraction of nationals by a state from the territory of another state during, or following, times of widespread breakdown of law and order, serious civil disturbances, armed conflict or devastation caused by natural disaster. Such extraction operations can be seen in the United States operations in Liberia in 1990 and Haiti in 2004, on several occasions by France and Belgium in Rwanda in the early 1990s, by several states during the conflict in Lebanon in 2006 and in Sudan in 2023. At the time extraction operations take place there is often no effective government from whom to request consent, or there appears to be either consent or implied consent for the action taken. In any case, the interventions are not often raised or discussed in the UN, while the intervening states do not often provide a legal justification for their actions or report their actions under Article 51 to the UN Security Council, and neither the territorial state or other states protest at the interventions. For example, the United Kingdom's intervention in Libya in 2011 to extract some of its nationals in danger during the uprising and subsequent civil war in the country was

---

[477] See, further, Section 8.4.2.  [478] See Talmon and Heipertz, n. 133.  [479] Ibid.
[480] See Section 8.4.2.

not considered unlawful by other states,[481] and neither were the rescue missions carried out by various states in Sudan in April 2023 in the face of serious civil conflict between Sudan's army and a paramilitary group called the Rapid Support Forces.[482] Ultimately, '[i]t seems that third states [are] willing to acquiesce in the forcible evacuation of nationals; their concern is roused only with regard to those rescue missions where the territorial state objects to the intervention or where the protection of the nationals was just a pretext for an invasion with wider objectives',[483] as was arguably the case, for example, with the US interventions in Grenada and Panama, as discussed above in Section 6.4.2.

Ultimately, the use of force in self-defence for the protection of nationals remains something of a grey area. While clear and principled objections to the invocation of the right of self-defence for this purpose have been rare, it is difficult to discern from state practice clear guiding principles for such interventions.

## 6.5 THE RIGHT OF COLLECTIVE SELF-DEFENCE

In addition to the right of individual self-defence, Article 51 of the UN Charter makes express reference to the right of collective self-defence, which has been invoked on several occasions since 1945, perhaps most notably by the United States in Lebanon in 1958, the United States in Vietnam in 1961–75, the USSR in Czechoslovakia in 1968 and Afghanistan in 1979, various states after the attacks of 11 September 2001 and also by various states in Iraq in response to attacks by the Islamic State group from 2014. While much of what has been said already in this chapter – and what is said in Section 6.6 on the role of the UN Security Council – applies equally to both individual and collective self-defence, and there is nothing specifically within the UN Charter to distinguish the two forms of self-defence, the ICJ in the *Nicaragua* case provided 'separate and additional schemata for the regulation of the right of collective self-defence in international law'.[484] It is the purpose of this section of the chapter to examine this schemata, although the section will first look at the nature of collective self-defence more generally.

---

[481] See Francis Grimal and Graham Melling, 'The Protection of Nationals Abroad: Lawfulness or Toleration? A Commentary' (2011) 16 *Journal of Conflict & Security Law* 541.
[482] Eliza Mackintosh, Noon Salih, Sana Noor Haq, 'Foreign Powers Rescue Nationals whilst Sudanese Must Fend for Themselves', *CNN*, 24 April 2023, available at: https://edition.cnn.com/2023/04/23/europe/france-evacuates-citizens-sudan-hnk-intl/index.html.
[483] Gray, n. 91, at 169 (n. 243).
[484] Kritsiotis, n. 4, at 181. Elsewhere, Kritsiotis describes these as 'peculiarities of the law governing the exercise of the right of collective self-defence'. Ibid., at 182.

## 6.5.1 The Nature of Collective Self-Defence

The term 'collective self-defence' has been described by Josef Kunz as 'not a happy one' on the basis that '[i]t is not self-defense, but defense of another state'.[485] Similarly, Rosalyn Higgins has claimed that the term is 'inaccurate' due to the fact that '[d]efence of the self cannot be collective; though there may exist collective security or mutual aid'.[486] However, while these criticisms are valid, on the basis that perhaps the most appropriate way to view the right is as one permitting those who can exercise some means of defence to come to the aid of those who cannot, it is also possible to view an invocation of the right of collective self-defence as a demonstration of solidarity against the attacks and the perpetrators of them, or even as a defence against a threat to each state's own security, justifying the 'self' in collective self-defence.[487] Indeed, Judge Jennings claimed in his dissenting opinion in the *Nicaragua* case that:

> The assisting State surely must, by going to the victim State's assistance, be also, and in addition to other requirements, in some measure defending itself. There should even in 'collective self-defence' be some real element of self involved with the notion of defence. This is presumably also the philosophy which underlies mutual security arrangements, such as the system of the Organization of American States, for which indeed Article 51 was specifically designed.[488]

While the Organization of American States is mentioned here by Jennings,[489] there are, of course, other mutual security or collective defence organisations, such as the North Atlantic Treaty Organization,[490] the Warsaw

---

[485] Kunz, n. 102, at 875. In connection with the 'inherent' right of self-defence, Weightman notes that '[i]t is hardly possible to regard the right or duty of a state to go to the assistance of another state as "inherent", in a natural law sense'. Weightman, n. 5, at 1111.

[486] Rosalyn Higgins, *The Development of International Law through the Political Organs of the United Nations* (Oxford University Press, 1963), at 208–9.

[487] Derek W. Bowett, 'Collective Self-Defence under the Charter of the United Nations' (1955-6) 32 British Yearbook of International Law 130; Derek W. Bowett, 'The Interrelation of Theories of Intervention and Self-Defence', in John Norton Moore (ed.), *Law and Civil War in the Modern World* (Johns Hopkins University Press, 1974), 38, at 47; Dinstein, n. 3, at paras. 785–92. On the latter point, despite the occurrence of an armed attack against the victim state, it may mean that it is being invoked by other states as a form of preventative self-defence. For more on this doctrine, see Chapter 7.

[488] *Nicaragua* case, n. 6, Dissenting Opinion of Judge Jennings, at 545–6.

[489] See Article 3(h) of the Charter of the Organization of American States (1948), which provides that '[a]n act of aggression against one American State is an act of aggression against all other American States'.

[490] See Article 5 of the Washington Treaty (1949), which provides that 'an armed attack against one or more of [the parties] in Europe or North America shall be considered an attack against them all and consequently they agree that, if such an armed attack occurs, each of them, in exercise of the right of individual or collective self-defence recognized by Article 51 of the Charter of the United Nations, will assist the Party or Parties so attacked by taking forthwith,

Pact,[491] the Australia, New Zealand and United States Security Treaty (ANZUS),[492] the League of Arab States[493] and the South East Asia Collective Defence Treaty.[494] Such mutual security arrangements might appear to imply the need for a 'proximate relationship' between the defending states, not necessarily of a geographical nature, but perhaps of either a political, economic or cultural nature.[495] Yet, to require any sort of 'proximity criterion seems so vague and subjective that it can hardly be said to have any constraining effect at all'.[496] In addition, not only is there virtually no customary practice in support of it but state practice would on the contrary seem to directly counter this particular proposition. The US actions in Vietnam in 1965, the states invoking their right of collective self-defence in the light of the attacks of 11 September 2001, and the invocation of collective self-defence of Iraq by the United States and other states in 2014 against attacks by the so-called Islamic State are examples countering the proposition.

## 6.5.2 The Regulation of the Right of Collective Self-Defence

The ICJ in the *Nicaragua* case stated that three elements must exist before collective self-defence can be invoked by a state, something that Judge

---

individually and in concert with other Parties, such actions as it deems necessary, including the use of armed force, to restore and maintain the security of the North Atlantic area'.

[491] See Article 4 of the Treaty of Friendship, Cooperation and Mutual Assistance (1955), which provides that '[i]n the event of armed attack in Europe on one or more of the Parties to the Treaty by any state or group of states, each of the Parties to the Treaty, in the exercise of its right to individual or collective self-defence in accordance with Article 51 of the Charter of the United Nations Organization, shall immediately, either individually or in agreement with other Parties to the Treaty, come to the assistance of the state or states attacked with all such means as it deems necessary, including armed force'.

[492] See Article IV of the Security Treaty between Australia, New Zealand, and the United States of America (1951), which provides that '[e]ach Party recognizes that an armed attack in the Pacific Area on any of the Parties would be dangerous to its own peace and safety and declares that it would act to meet the common danger in accordance with its constitutional processes'.

[493] See Article 6 of the Pact of the League of Arab States (1945), which provides that '[i]n case of aggression or threat of aggression by a State against a member State, the State attacked or threatened with attack may request an immediate meeting of the Council'. See also Article 2 of the Treaty of Joint Defense and Economic Cooperation between the States of the Arab League (1950).

[494] See Article IV(1) of the South East Asia Collective Defence Treaty (1945), which provides that '[e]ach party recognizes that aggression by means of armed attack in the treaty area against any of the parties or against any state or territory which the parties by unanimous agreement may hereafter designate, would endanger its own peace and safety, and agrees that it will in that event act to meet the common danger'.

[495] Bowett, 'Collective Self-Defence', n. 487, at 133–4.

[496] Ruys, n. 10, at 87. Gray also rejects the need for a 'third state interest'. Gray, n. 91, at 18–9.

Jennings described as 'a somewhat formalistic view of the condition for the exercise of collective self-defence'.[497] Yet these were envisaged by the Court as operating as mechanisms to prevent abuse of the right. First, the Court noted, '[r]eliance on collective self-defence ... does not remove the need' for the state concerned to be a victim of an armed attack,[498] as this was 'the condition *sina qua non* required for the exercise of the right of collective self-defence'.[499] Secondly, the victim state must declare that it has been the victim of an armed attack. As the Court stated, 'it is to be expected, that the State for whose benefit this right [of collective self-defence] is used will have declared itself to be the victim of an armed attack'.[500] Indeed, 'there is no rule in customary international law permitting another State to exercise the right of collective self-defence on the basis of its own assessment of the situation'.[501]

Thirdly, and perhaps most importantly, the victim state must expressly request the assistance of the state claiming to act in collective self-defence. As the ICJ stated: 'there is no rule, permitting the exercise of collective self-defence in the absence of a request by the State which regards itself as the victim of an armed attack'.[502] The Court noted that it was evident that 'if the victim State wishes another State to come to its help in the exercise of the right of self-defence, it will normally make an express request to that effect'.[503] Such a declaration and request must be genuine and timely. For example, in the *Nicaragua* case the Court found that '[t]he declaration and the request of El-Salvador, made publicly for the first time in August 1984, do not support the contention that in 1981 there was an armed attack capable of serving as a legal foundation for United States activities which began in the second half of that year'.[504] Yet, it might be questioned whether such a request would always need to be expressed if it can be 'established in some other way, for example it is clear that the States' military actions are closely coordinated or if the States jointly submit a report to the Security Council'.[505]

However, these requirements have been criticised on the basis that the Court provided no evidence for their existence within international law.[506]

---

[497] *Nicaragua* case, n. 6, Dissenting Opinion of Judge Jennings, at 544.
[498] Ibid., Merits, at para. 195.　[499] Ibid., at para. 237.　[500] Ibid., at para. 195.　[501] Ibid.
[502] Ibid., at para. 199. The Court also stated that 'the requirement of a request by the State which is the victim of the alleged attack is additional to the requirement that such a State should have declared itself to have been attacked'. Ibid. See also *Oil Platforms* case, n. 11, at para. 51; *Armed Activities* case, n. 119, at para. 128.
[503] *Nicaragua* case, ibid., at para. 232. It is the victim state that must undertake the necessity and proportionality assessments. For more on these twin customary requirements see Section 6.3.
[504] Ibid., at para. 236.　[505] Ruys, n. 10, at 91.
[506] Donald W. Greig, 'Self-Defense and the Security Council: What Does Article 51 Require?' (1991) **40** *International & Comparative Law Quarterly* 366, at 375–6; Gray, n. 91, at 182.

As mentioned in Section 6.1, the right of collective self-defence was novel at the time of the adoption of the UN Charter, and in establishing these criteria the Court provided no evidence substantiating their customary status. In addition, they have been criticised on the basis that they provide 'unrealistic and undesirable bureaucracy' to the right of collective self-defence, particularly given the immediacy of certain actions in self-defence.[507] Indeed, Dino Kritsiotis is of the view that '[t]he appeal of such legal niceties might well not shine through the raw realities or emergencies of the application of force and the need for counter-force'.[508] Yet, he goes on to say that '[b]e that as it may, the obligations as recalled and outlined ... were no doubt indicators that the Court found useful in testing the veracity of claims made before it by states'.[509] They are also frequently referenced in the academic literature,[510] and serve the purpose of preventing states invoking the right of collective self-defence as a pretext for intervention for other purposes. Furthermore, and perhaps most importantly, 'in the main, states do not seem to have found these procedures to be either onerous or inconvenient to their actions'.[511]

Yet, there does appear to be only a partial application of them, in that while the request-for-assistance requirement is often witnessed in the practice of states, the requirement that a state declare itself the victim of an armed attack is not.[512] For example, since 2014, a number of states have intervened on behalf of Iraq in collective self-defence to fight so-called Islamic State forces in Syria. While the actions of the Islamic State had been horrific, in particular its attacks on the Yazidi and Christian populations, and the group had taken over parts of territory within both Iraq and Syria, it might be questioned whether the attacks, taken individually or cumulatively,[513] constituted an armed attack for the purposes of Article 51.

---

[507] Kritsiotis, n. 4, at 186. See also R. St J. Macdonald, 'The Nicaragua Case: New Answers to Old Questions?' (1986) 24 *Canadian Yearbook of International Law* 127, at 151; Moore, n. 109, at 155.

[508] Kritsiotis, ibid., at 186–7.   [509] Ibid.

[510] See, for example, Josef Mrazek, 'Prohibition of the Use and Threat of Force: Self-Defence and Self-Help in International Law' (1989) 27 *Canadian Yearbook of International Law* 81, at 93; Michael Wood, 'Self-Defence and Collective Security: Key Distinctions', in Marc Weller (ed.), *The Oxford Handbook of the Use of Force in International Law* (Oxford University Press, 2015), 649, at 654; Kritsiotis, n. 4 at 185–7. Gray also states that customary practice supports these requirements. See Gray, n. 91, at 185–8.

[511] Kritsiotis, n. 4, at 187.

[512] See James A. Green. 'The "Additional" Criteria for Collective Self-Defence: Request but Not Declaration' (2017) 4 *Journal on the Use of Force and International Law* 4. The ICJ in both the 2003 *Oil Platforms* and 2005 *Armed Activities* cases indicated that a request on the part of the victim state was required but made no mention of the requirement that the victim state declare itself the victim of an armed attack. See *Oil Platforms* case, n. 11, at para. 51 and *Armed Activities*, n. 119, at para. 128.

[513] See Sections 6.2.5.4 and 6.3.2.1 on the accumulation of events theory.

However, even if a certain 'gravity' is required of the attacks before constituting an armed attack, it is arguable that the actions of the so-called Islamic State in Iraq and through its operations against Iraq, which included the seizure of cities, towns and oil plants, had crossed this threshold.[514] It was, however, notable that Iraq did not claim, as the ICJ appeared to require in the *Nicaragua* case, that it had been the victim of an armed attack and neither did the defending states make the claim that Iraq had been the victim of such an attack. What was clear, however, was that there had been a clear request for assistance by Iraq.[515] Furthermore, in invoking the right of collective self-defence upon initiating its military action, the United States stated that 'the Government of Iraq ha[d] asked that the United States lead international efforts to strike [Islamic State] sites and military strongholds in Syria in order to end the continuing attacks on Iraq'.[516] The other states acting in collective self-defence were similarly explicit about the fact that they were acting upon the basis of Iraq's request for assistance.[517] Belgium, for example, in its letter to the UN Security Council, claimed that it was using force 'in Syria in the exercise of the right of collective self-defence, in response to the request from the Government of Iraq', although it did not also mention that Iraq had either declared itself to be the victim of an armed attack or that it should have done.[518]

Such a partial application of the ICJ's framework for the regulation of the right of self-defence can also be seen in other examples, such as the 1950 US intervention in support of South Korea against attacks by North Korea,[519] and the request for assistance by Kuwait following the invasion by Iraq in 1990,[520]

---

[514] Christian Henderson, 'The Use of Force and Islamic State' (2014) 1 *Journal on the Use of Force and International Law* 209, at 215.

[515] See UN Doc. S/2014/691, 22 September 2014. It was interesting that, as Ryan Goodman has suggested, if collective self-defence is relied upon then 'Iraq may thus also need to accept the doctrine of unwilling or unable and determine that Syria fails the test', given that other states acting in its defence justified their actions within Syria upon this basis. See Ryan Goodman, 'International Law on Airstrikes against ISIS in Syria', *Just Security*, 28 August 2014, available at: www.justsecurity.org/14414/international-law-airstrikes-isis-syria/. See Section 8.4.2 for more on the 'unable or unwilling' doctrine.

[516] UN Doc. S/2014/695, 23 September 2014. See, generally, Henderson, n. 514.

[517] Green, n. 512, at 9–10.

[518] See UN Doc. S/2016/523, 9 June 2016. See similar letters from Australia (UN Doc. S/2015/693, 9 September 2015); the Netherlands (UN Doc. S/2016/132, 10 February 2016); Norway (UN Doc. S/2016/513, 3 June 2016); and the United Kingdom (UN Doc. S/2014/841, 26 November 2014).

[519] See UN Doc. S/PV.473, 25 June 1950, at 8; UN Doc. S/PV.475, 30 June 1950, at 10.

[520] See UN Doc. S/21498, 13 August 1990, for Kuwait's letter to the UN Security Council in which assistance was requested. See UN Doc. S/21492, 10 August 1990, for the letter to the Security Council from the United States in which the US expressly related this request for assistance to Article 51 of the UN Charter (1945). However, while it is possible to view the military action that led to the eviction of Iraq from Kuwait as either one of collective self-

again in which a request for assistance was made but there was no declaration by the victim state that it had suffered an armed attack. Yet, the absence of the express declaration that an 'armed attack' has occurred is no different in the context of individual self-defence.[521] While a partial application of the requirements can also be seen in regard to the interventions undertaken by the Warsaw Pact states in Czechoslovakia in 1968, the issue in this case was more about the legitimacy of those issuing the request, rather than the request itself,[522] which raises issues of a factual nature.

The prominence of collective self-defence continues to persist in international affairs. While the Trump Administration's disdain for NATO was well-known, there was a stark shift in tone following the Biden Administration taking office, with President Biden stating that he regarded Article 5 of the North Atlantic Treaty on collective self-defence as a 'sacred commitment'.[523] Collective self-defence also provided a significant backdrop to the Ukraine crisis in 2022. Indeed, in addition to President Putin's claims regarding individual self-defence,[524] there was also a claim of collective self-defence. On 21 February 2022 Russia had rebranded and recognised the two separatist-leaning regions in the Donbas area of Ukraine of Donetsk and Luhansk as the sovereign states of the 'Donetsk People's Republic' and the 'Luhansk People's Republic',[525] a move which was widely condemned as a violation of international law.[526] These new 'states' immediately subsequently signed treaties of friendship and mutual assistance with Russia and proceeded to request its military aid.[527] Consequently, in his address on 24 February, President Putin claimed that '[t]he people's republics of Donbass ... asked Russia for help' and it responded 'in execution of the treaties of friendship and

---

defence or collective security, it is generally seen as an example of the latter. See further, Section 3.4.2.1.

[521] See Henderson, n. 129, at 62.   [522] See, in general, UN Doc. S/PV.1441, 21 August 1968.
[523] U.S. Department of Defense, 'NATO Stands Together as Biden Reaffirms U.S. Commitment to Alliance', 15 June 2021, available at: www.defense.gov/News/News-Stories/Article/Article/2658794/nato-stands-together-as-biden-reaffirms-us-commitment-to-alliance/.
[524] See, in particular, Section 6.4.1.
[525] See Presidential Decree of the Russian Federation, No 71, 'About recognition of the Donetsk People's Republic', 21 February 2022; Presidential Decree of the Russian Federation, No 72, 'About recognition of the Luhansk People's Republic', 21 February 2022.
[526] For example, the UN General Assembly '[d]*eplore*[d] the 21 February 2022 decision by the Russian Federation related to the status of certain areas of the Donetsk and Luhansk regions of Ukraine as a violation of the territorial integrity and sovereignty of Ukraine and inconsistent with the principles of the Charter'. See UNGA Res. ES-11/1 (2022), para. 5.
[527] Treaty of Friendship, Cooperation and Mutual Assistance between the Russian Federation and the Donetsk People's Republic, 21 February 2022; Treaty of Friendship, Cooperation and Mutual Assistance Between the Russian Federation and the Lugansk People's Republic, 21 February 2022. For the request for military assistance see: https://t.me/tass_agency/111840.

mutual assistance with the Donetsk People's Republic and the Lugansk People's Republic, ratified by the Federal Assembly on February 22'.[528] However, in addition to there being an absence of an armed attack against Russia, the conditions under which these 'states' were created and recognised meant that any request of assistance must be rendered invalid.[529]

Furthermore, a significant lingering issue over the crisis was Ukraine's possible membership of NATO. If Ukraine had been a member of NATO at the time of Russia's invasion there would have been an obligation upon the organisation to come to its defence and assist it in repelling the Russian armed attack. Of course, while Article 5 of the North Atlantic Treaty provides that 'an armed attack against one or more [NATO members] in Europe or North America shall be considered an attack against them all', there was nothing specifically preventing NATO or any of its member states to come to the defence of Ukraine in the absence of Ukraine's membership. Indeed, in addition to the clear armed attack that was in progress there were multiple requests for assistance by Ukraine.[530] Yet, broader strategic and security issues and concerns regarding the possibility of a wider – possibly world – war provided the stark reminder of the extent to which collective self-defence remains a right, and by no means an obligation.

## 6.6 THE ROLE OF THE UN SECURITY COUNCIL

The opening phrase of Article 51 – that '[n]othing in the present Charter shall impair the inherent right of individual or collective self-defence if an armed attack occurs against a Member of the United Nations' – appears clear that, should such an armed attack occur, nothing, at least within the Charter, should impair the 'inherent' right of self-defence. However, this guarantee of non-

---

[528] 'Address by the President of the Russian Federation', n. 413.
[529] This request for assistance could be seen as an invitation to Russia to intervene in a domestic situation. See further, Chapter 9 on interventions by invitation. Yet, seeing as Russia's military actions in response went beyond the territories of these proclaimed states they are arguably more appropriately assessed through the prism of collective self-defence.
[530] See Paul LeBlanc, 'Ukraine Has Requested Military Aid. Here's How Allies Are Providing Assistance', *CNN*, 18 March 2022, available at: https://edition.cnn.com/2022/03/18/politics/ukraine-military-weapons-javelin-stinger-s300-switchblade-drones/index.html.
Furthermore, the United Kingdom and Finland issued a joint declaration in May 2022 which stated that 'should either country suffer a disaster or an attack, the United Kingdom and Finland will, upon request from the affected country, assist each other in a variety of ways, which may include military means'. This was, however, described as a 'political declaration and not a legally binding commitment under international law'. See Prime Minister's Office, 10 Downing Street, 'United Kingdom–Finland statement', 11 May 2022, available at: www.gov.uk/government/publications/united-kingdom-finland-statement-11-may-2022/united-kingdom-finland-statement.

impairment appears to be qualified within the very same sentence, in that the guarantee was only to last 'until the Security Council has taken measures necessary to maintain international peace and security'. Indeed, Article 51 includes 'an institutional dimension' to the right of self-defence.[531]

In incorporating a prominent role for the UN Security Council in the exercise of the right of self-defence, Article 51 further makes clear that any measures taken in self-defence 'shall not in any way affect the authority and responsibility of the Security Council under the present Charter to take at any time such action as it deems necessary in order to maintain or restore international peace and security'. It would thus appear that the Council is free to take any measures it deems necessary, even if these contradict or interrupt the exercise of the right of self-defence. As will be discussed in this section, the 'until clause' has proved to be controversial, particularly in regard to when it can be said that 'necessary' measures have been taken by the Council, and who is to determine that this is the case. However, the Security Council has a role in self-defence even before taking any measures itself, in that Article 51 provides that '[m]easures taken by Members in the exercise of this right of self-defence shall be immediately reported to the Security Council'.[532] While this appears to be an obligatory requirement, with the use of the modal verb 'shall', there is some discussion around both the true nature of this requirement and the role of the Security Council more generally within actions taken in self-defence.

### 6.6.1 The Reporting Requirement

Although Article 51 stipulates that measures in self-defence should be reported to the Council, at no point does the UN Charter expand upon the purpose of this requirement or 'the actual form or contents that such a report should entail'.[533] The purpose seems to be 'to enable the Council to respond effectively to any threat that an attack (or forcible defensive response) may pose to international peace and security' as well as 'to provide the Council with information with which it could begin to assess the validity of a state's self-defense claim'.[534] The ICJ has discussed the purport of this particular obligation in the *Nicaragua* case. While the United States argued that its direct and indirect actions towards Nicaragua were lawful measures of self-defence, it nonetheless failed to report these to the Security Council as per Article 51. However, Article 51 was not directly relevant in the case as the Court was precluded from applying the Charter provisions as a result of the Vandenberg reservation, which meant that it was restricted to determining the case upon

---

[531] Kritsiotis, n. 4, at 219.
[532] See James A. Green, 'The Article 51 Reporting Requirement for Self-Defense Actions' (2015) 55 *Virginia Journal of International Law* 563.
[533] Kritsiotis, n. 4, at 224.     [534] Green, n. 532, at 568.

## 6.6 The Role of the UN Security Council

customary international law. In this respect, the Court stated that 'in customary international law it is not a condition of the lawfulness of the use of force in self-defence that a procedure so closely dependent on the content of a treaty commitment and of the institution established by it, should have been followed'.[535] The Court did not, therefore, treat the absence of a report by the United States 'as the breach of an undertaking forming part of the customary international law applicable to the present dispute'.[536]

Nonetheless, as Kritsiotis has noted:

these representations of the Court might well be taken to suggest that, as a matter of the strict letter of the law of the Charter as opposed to the position in custom, compliance with the reporting requirement *is* indeed very much indispensable to any successful claim of self-defence being made.[537]

Yet, in defining further the potential 'indispensability' of a report to the Security Council under Article 51, Tom Ruys has noted that:

[t]wo options can be distinguished. Either it could be considered a substantive precondition in the absence of which self-defence cannot be invoked; *or* it could be identified as a separate procedural obligation, the violation of which would also provide a rebuttable indication that the State did not consider itself to be acting in self-defence.[538]

The former of the two options indicated here would mean that a report constitutes an intrinsic part of an action in self-defence, while the latter presents us with the possibility that it is of mere probative value in assessing claims to be acting in self-defence. However, whereas Yoram Dinstein has claimed that 'the duty of reporting becomes a substantive condition and a limitation on the exercise of self-defence',[539] it is the duality of the source of the right of self-defence that perhaps leads to the latter of the two options posed by Ruys proving to be the more favourable.[540] For example, if the former of the two options was accepted – that is, that the submission of a report is a substantive precondition for the invocation of the right of self-defence – it would potentially present a situation in which an action in self-defence is lawful under customary international law while at the same time unlawful under the UN Charter. Such a discrepancy between the Charter and customary forms of the right of self-defence would not be consistent with how the ICJ viewed in general the treaty and customary forms of the rules

---

[535] *Nicaragua* case, n. 6, at para. 200. As Tom Ruys has pointed out, 'it could moreover be argued that the reporting requirement is admittedly not of a "fundamentally norm-creating character such as could be regarded as forming the basis of a general rule of law", in the sense of the *North Sea Continental Shelf* case'. Ruys, n. 10, at 69.
[536] *Nicaragua* case, n. 6, at para. 235.   [537] Kritsiotis, n. 4, at 226.   [538] Ruys, n. 10, at 68.
[539] Dinstein, n. 3, at para. 678.   [540] Greig, n. 506, at 380.

governing the use of force.[541] In addition, the sequence of events as set out in Article 51 would dictate that the obligation is of a procedural, as opposed to substantive, nature as members are only required to report measures after they have begun their acts in self-defence (although there is nothing to suggest that they may not do so beforehand) and it would, as such, be illogical to suggest that the legality of the entire operation, including its initiation, should rest upon compliance with this obligation.[542]

Lastly, and perhaps most importantly, state practice would seem to lend its support to the latter of the two options presented by Ruys. Indeed, not only does there appear to be an absence of express statements to the effect that failing to report makes unlawful an otherwise lawful invocation of self-defence,[543] but rather that the failure to file a report with the Security Council merely weakens, or at least raises question marks over, a claim to be acting in self-defence.[544] The report is, in this sense, merely of probative value. In the *Nicaragua* case, for example, the Court noted that 'in the Security Council, the United States has itself taken the view that failure to observe the requirement to make a report *contradicted* a State's claim to be acting on the basis of collective self-defence',[545] rather than entirely precluding it. Indeed, in 1980 the United States, in regard to the intervention by the Soviet Union in Afghanistan in November 1979, stated that the fact that 'neither the Soviet Union nor the puppet regime it has installed in Afghanistan has given the required notice to the Security Council under Article 51 is itself evidence of the hollowness of the Soviet Union's refuge in the Charter'.[546] Other states in other situations have also made a similar claim.[547]

The probative nature of the report also finds some support in the context of the killing of General Soleimani by the United States in 2020. While there were various statements from various individuals within the Trump administration, it was not until six days after the strike that the first invocation of the right of self-defence under Article 51 of the UN Charter was raised, and which was then subsequently referenced by the administration with some frequency. This initial invocation was in the form of the letter the United States submitted to the UN Security Council notifying it of its invocation of the right of self-

---

[541] See, for example, Section 1.3.
[542] Ruys, n. 10, at 70. The view that the reporting requirement is a procedural obligation of probative value, as opposed to a substantive precondition for the invocation of the right of self-defence, has also been supported by numerous scholars. See, for example Gray, n. 91, at 128–31; Higgins, n. 486, at 207; Green, n. 532, at 591–6; Greig, n. 506, at 384.
[543] Ruys, ibid., at 71.  [544] Gray, n. 91, at 128.
[545] *Nicaragua* case, n. 6, at para. 235 (emphasis added).
[546] UN Doc. S/PV.2187, 6 January 1980, at 3.
[547] For example, the USSR raised this issue in relation to the UK raid against Yemen in 1964. See (1964) *United Nations Yearbook* 184.

defence.[548] It could, of course, be questioned why it took so long for the administration to provide this. As Article 51 of the United Nations Charter clearly states, '[m]easures taken by Members in the exercise of this right of self-defence shall be *immediately* reported to the Security Council'. It might be questioned whether such a delay meant that the United States had violated this immediacy procedural obligation within the provision, given that six days between the action and the reporting is certainly not by any standards immediate, and raises the question as to the reason for this delay. Nonetheless, the delay was not seen by itself as precluding the United States' claim of self-defence on this occasion.

However, what is evident from the *Nicaragua* case is that, even in the context of the customary international law right of self-defence, the Court provided the reporting obligation with probative value by observing that the failure of the United States to provide a report to the Security Council 'hardly conforms with the [United States'] avowed conviction that it was acting in the context of collective self-defence as consecrated by Article 51 of the Charter'.[549] As Kritsiotis observes, '[f]or the Court, then, as for the United States, the *reporting* of the exercise of the right of self-defence to the Security Council had important probative value, quite apart from any substantive significance that one might wish to award it'.[550]

While the Court did not discuss whether there should be a specific form or content to the required reports,[551] it has been observed by certain scholars that the obligation to report is seldom observed in practice.[552] However, on the other hand, Christine Gray notes that, if not before then certainly after the *Nicaragua* judgment, it is, on the contrary, the case that the requirement is often complied with.[553] Despite the fact that there are observable occasions when there has been a failure to comply with the requirement, such as the

---

[548] Letter dated 8 January 2020 from the Permanent Representative of the United States of America to the United Nations addressed to the President of the Security Council, UN Doc. S/2020/20, 9 January 2020.

[549] *Nicaragua* case, n. 6, at para. 235. In the *Armed Activities* case the ICJ also 'observed that ... Uganda did not report to the Security Council events that it had regarded as requiring it to act in self-defence'. *Armed Activities* case, n. 118, at para. 145.

[550] Kritsiotis, n. 4, at 227. However, Judge Schwebel drew a distinction in the Court's treatment of the reporting requirement in the *Nicaragua* case between 'overt' and 'covert' defensive measures: 'it appears that, in resisting aggression, covert measures have been and legitimately may be used, which could not, by their nature, be reported to the Security Council without prejudicing the security and effectiveness of those measures'. *Nicaragua* case, n. 6, Separate Opinion of Judge Schwebel, at para. 223.

[551] In this respect Kritsiotis has observed that 'there is a marked variance in what states have chosen to report (and not to report) to the Council'. Kritsiotis, n. 4, at 224.

[552] See, for example, Jean Combacau, 'The Exception of Self-Defence in U.N. Practice', in Antonio Cassese (ed.), *The Current Legal Regulation of the Use of Force* (Martinus Nijhoff, 1986), 9, at 15–16; Ronzitti, n. 117, at 356.

[553] Gray, n. 91, at 129.

Turkish intervention in Northern Iraq in 2007–8,[554] the Colombian raid in Ecuador in 2008[555] and the Ethiopian intervention in Somalia in 2006,[556] on the whole states do report their actions, or at least bring the particular situation to the attention of the Security Council or put the Council on notice as to the possible future exercise of the right.[557]

Finally, Kritsiotis has observed that 'there is a marked variance in ... the *frequency* with which reports have made their way to the Council over the entire period of an operation undertaken in self-defence'.[558] States have often provided several reports to the Council over the course of an operation in self-defence, as the United Kingdom did during the course of the Falklands War. Yet, there is no need for constant updates as is, by contrast, often required of UN authorised forces during an operation.[559] In this sense, Gray is correct in observing a tendency to *over*-report, in that states often provide the Security Council with a separate report for each action taken in a prolonged conflict, instead of confining their reporting to one being provided at the initial opening of measures in self-defence.[560]

A separate issue to those of whether states provide reports and the legal value of them doing so is the way the Security Council receives, reacts to and shares these communications with other states both within and outside of the Council.[561] Neither the Council or the UN Secretariat publishes a comprehensive list of Article 51 notifications and these letters are not circulated efficiently or routinely discussed in the Council, which has been raised by certain scholars and practitioners as particularly problematic.[562] Indeed,

---

[554] See Tom Ruys, '*Quo Vadit Jus ad Bellum?*: A Legal Analysis of Turkey's Military Operations against the PKK in Northern Iraq' (2008) 9 *Melbourne Journal of International Law* 334, at 345.

[555] See Tatiana Waisberg, 'Columbia's Use of Force in Ecuador against a Terrorist Organization: International Law and the Use of Force against Non-State Actors', *ASIL Insights*, 22 August 2008, available at: www.asil.org/insights/volume/12/issue/17/colombias-use-force-ecuador-against-terrorist-organization-international.

[556] See Awol K. Allo, 'Ethiopia's Armed Intervention in Somalia: The Legality of Self-Defense in Response to the Threat of Terrorism' (2010) 39 *Denver Journal of International Law and Policy* 139, at 140.

[557] See Ruys, n. 10, at 73; Green, n. 532, at 573–87.

[558] Kritsiotis, n. 4, at 224 (emphasis added).  [559] See further, Chapters 3 and 4.

[560] Gray, n. 91, at 129–31.

[561] See Working paper submitted by the delegation of Mexico, UN Doc. A/AC.182/L.154, 7 February 2020.

[562] See, in particular, Pablo Arrocha Olabuenaga, 'An Insider's View of the Life-Cycle of Self-Defense Reports by U.N. Member States: Challenges Posed to the International Order', *Just Security*, 2 April 2019, available at: www.justsecurity.org/63415/an-insiders-view-of-the-life-cycle-of-self-defense-reports-by-u-n-member-states/

if a delegation is not a Security Council member, it is not actively part of a coalition using force to counter terrorism in other countries, and it doesn't have the time or human resources to track down these letters, it is almost impossible for it to take part in the discussion on the substantive legal terms that this practice entails. Most UN Member States are left in the dark.[563]

However, through certain initiatives to draw attention to this problem states have also been able to express their views on this, most notably during an Arria-formula meeting of the UN Security Council on 24 February 2021.[564] During the meeting the participants noted the importance of transparency regarding self-defence communications submitted under Article 51. In particular, it was generally agreed that even though these communications are ultimately made available to the public, the way in which they are processed and distributed makes it difficult to identify and search for them and to obtain them in a timely way, which is particularly important in the context of reacting both to any military action taken in self-defence and the justification provided for it. Being able to do so in a timely and efficient way may not only provide a restraint on state action in the circumstances, but having easy access to and being able to respond to such reports provides states more generally with the possibility to positively inform the future direction of the right of self-defence. Given the shared view within the Arria-formula meeting that this was particularly problematic it seems likely that options to ensure transparency and accessibility with respect to these communications will remain on the agenda of the Council.

### 6.6.2 The 'Until Clause'

Article 51 stipulates that the right of self-defence exists 'until the Security Council has taken measures necessary to maintain international peace and security' and that measures taken in self-defence 'shall not in any way affect the authority and responsibility of the Security Council under the present Charter to take at any time such action as it deems necessary in order to maintain or restore international peace and security'. Hans Kelsen defended this clause on the basis that:

---

[563] Ibid.
[564] Letter dated 8 March 2021 from the Permanent Representative of Mexico to the United Nations addressed to the Secretary-General and the President of the Security Council, UN Doc. A/75/993–S/2021/247, 16 March 2021. For an illuminating discussion see, also, Naz K. Modirzadeh and Pablo Arrocha Olabuenaga, 'A Conversation between Pablo Arrocha Olabuenaga and Naz Khatoon Modirzadeh on the Origins, Objectives, and Context of the 24 February 2021 "Arria-formula" Meeting Convened by Mexico' (2021) 8 *Journal on the Use of Force and International Law* 291.

[w]ithin a system of collective security organized on the basis of a complete centralization of the legitimate use of force, self-defense as a case of decentralized use of force is an exceptional and provisional interlude between an act of illegal use of force ... and the collective enforcement action which the community, through its central organ, is to take as a sanction against the illegal use of force.[565]

This 'complete centralization' that Kelsen speaks of can be witnessed in the fact that the constitutive instruments of the two prominent collective self-defence arrangements of the Cold War – that is, the Warsaw Pact and the North Atlantic Treaty Organization – as well as others such as ANZUS, all prominently include clauses of a virtually identical nature to that contained within Article 51, thereby emphasising the central role of the UN Security Council.[566] However, as Ruys explains, '[f]or most of the UN era the temporal limitation of Article 51 has been of little practical significance ... [as] the Cold War deadlock impeded the Security Council from taking any significant action in the overwhelming majority of cases.'[567] Ruys continues, however, by noting that '[t]he revitalization of the Council at the end of the twentieth century may have initiated a more frequent implementation of the "until clause"'.[568] In this respect, it is now, if not for most of the UN Charter era, important to understand how this clause operates.

Questions arise in determining what form such 'necessary' measures might take and who is to determine when the particular measures taken have proven effective so as to terminate the right of self-defence. It is maintained by some scholars that the right of self-defence ceases as soon as the Security Council becomes seized of an issue.[569] Such an interpretation is a difficult one to accept in a practical sense, however, as it is possible that an aggressor state could simply bring a situation to the attention of the Council and thus extinguish the victim state's right to defend itself. As such, it might be contended that the right of self-defence ceases upon the Security Council adopting a resolution in connection with

---

[565] Hans Kelsen, 'Collective Security and Collective Self-Defense under the Charter of the United Nations' (1948) 42 *American Journal of International Law* 783, at 785. Kritsiotis notes that, while the point of Article 51 'is to preserve the right of self-defence', it is also to 'adapt it to the modern context of the universal collective security system of which it forms so profound and fitting a part'. Kritsiotis, n. 4, at 227. This clause is not, therefore, a qualification of the right as it exists in customary international law.

[566] Article 4, Treaty of Friendship, Cooperation and Mutual Assistance (1954); Article 5, The North Atlantic Treaty (1949); Article V, Australia, New Zealand, United States Security Treaty (1951).

[567] Ruys, n. 10, at 74–5. See Section 3.4.1 for more on the activity of the Security Council during the Cold War.

[568] Ibid., at 75.

[569] See, for example, Eugene V. Rostow, 'Until What? Enforcement Action or Collective Self-Defense?' (1991) 86 *American Journal of International Law* 506, at 511 (quoting Professor Rein Müllerson).

the situation, regardless of whether it results in actually extinguishing the victim state's need to defend itself.[570]

While neither of these interpretations are attractive from the perspective of defending states, they are also possibly contradicted by the practice of the Security Council. In the context of Iraq's invasion of Kuwait in 1990, for example, the Security Council adopted Resolution 661 (1990) in which, while noting concern that its earlier demand in Resolution 660 (1990) that Iraq withdraw from Kuwait had not been complied with[571] – and, as a consequence, imposed various measures upon Iraq including sanctions[572] –it at the same time '[a]*ffirm*[ed] the inherent right of individual or collective self-defence, in response to the armed attack by Iraq against Kuwait, in accordance with Article 51 of the Charter'.[573] Similarly, in the aftermath of the attacks of 11 September 2001, the Security Council adopted various counter-terrorism measures in Resolution 1373 (2001), such as those to prevent acts of terrorism and targeted towards the prevention and suppression of terrorist financing, yet the preamble to the same resolution '[reaffirmed] the inherent right of individual or collection self-defence as recognized by the [UN] Charter'. These measures clearly did not affect the right of the United States to engage in self-defence[574] and suggest that the right of self-defence and collective security action by the Security Council may 'subsist in parallel'.[575] Yet, it might be said that these examples are *sui generis*, in that the Council explicitly reaffirmed the right of self-defence, leaving the question open as to the position of the victim state's right of self-defence if it had not done so.

It has been argued that measures adopted by the Council under Articles 41 and 42 of the Charter 'are by their nature considered to be "measures necessary" in the sense of Article 51'.[576] However, this perhaps overstates their role and authority in the context of the inherent right of self-defence. While economic sanctions under Article 41 of the Charter are often strong persuasive tools of the Security Council in guiding state behaviour, in the heat of the moment of an armed attack they are unlikely to be effective in and of themselves to cease the attack and will often not be conceived of as being 'necessary to maintain international peace and security', as was the case in

---

[570] See the discussion in W. Michael Reisman, 'Allocating Competences to Use Coercion in the Post–Cold War World: Practices, Conditions, and Prospects', in Lori F. Damrosch and David J. Scheffer (eds.), *Law and Force in the New International Order* (Westview Press, 1991), 26, at 43. See also Malvina Halberstam, 'The Right of Self-Defense Once the Security Council Takes Action' (1995-6) 17 *Michigan Journal of International Law* 229, at 234.

[571] UNSC Res. 661 (1990), para. 1. For the earlier demand see UNSC Res. 660 (1990), para. 2.

[572] UNSC Res. 661 (1990), paras. 2–10.   [573] Ibid., preamble.

[574] See, for example, Thomas M. Franck, 'Terrorism and the Right of Self-Defense' (2001) 95 *American Journal of International Law* 839, at 841–2.

[575] Wood, n. 510, at 656.   [576] Ruys, n. 10, at 82.

Kuwait in 1990.[577] Alternatively, given the forcible nature of measures taken in self-defence it is perhaps arguable that it is only when the Council takes measures of a comparable nature that the right of self-defence is no longer available. In this respect, while the Council's earlier resolutions on the situation in Kuwait in 1990 did not extinguish the right of self-defence, 'when the Council authorized the collective use of force under Resolution 678, this must surely be construed under Article 51 as "measures necessary to maintain international peace and security", which displaced the right to use force in self-defence'.[578]

Yet, it is arguably too categorical to state that 'it stands beyond doubt that the imposition of military enforcement measures in accordance with Article 42 UN Charter suspends the exercise of the right to self-defence'.[579] While the measures authorised by the Council in Kuwait in 1991 were effective, there will be occasions when similar measures will not have the same effect. In this respect, it could be argued that once the Council has become seized of a situation it is only those measures taken by it, whether of a forcible or non-forcible nature, which actually prove objectively effective in restoring international peace and security that extinguish the right of self-defence.[580] It would seem to be unfair to the victim state to suggest otherwise and the wording of the phrase 'measures *necessary* to maintain international peace and security' suggests effectiveness is key in halting the right of self-defence. It is possible, therefore, that the right of self-defence and measures taken in collective security may occur simultaneously, as the right of self-defence will remain alive until measures taken by the Council have proved effective in extinguishing the need to resort to self-defence.

As Kritsiotis points out, the formulation in Article 51 indicates that the Security Council may take measures that 'might well not coincide with the measures that are actually necessary for the purposes of interpreting or activating the until clause'.[581] Indeed, '[w]hile the Security Council might take measures which it regards as necessary to terminate the armed attack, whether they do have that effect only time will tell. If they do not have that consequence, then clearly additional measures are "necessary".'[582] In this

---

[577] Indeed, Christopher Greenwood has contended that '[i]t is very doubtful ... that economic measures will have the same effect [as the use of force]'. Christopher Greenwood, 'New World Order or Old?: The Invasion of Kuwait and the Rule of Law' (1992) 55 *Modern Law Review* 153, at 164.

[578] Frank Berman, 'The Authorization Model: Resolution 678 and its Effects', in David M. Malone (ed.), *The UN Security Council: From the Cold War to the 21st Century* (Lynne Rienner, 2004), 153, at 154.

[579] Ibid. Ruys notes that there is state practice providing evidence that 'Council measures, other than those provided for in Articles 41 and 42 UN Charter may call a halt to the exercise of self-defence *if* they are effective'. Ruys, n. 10, at 81 (original emphasis).

[580] See Greig, n. 506, at 389.   [581] Kritsiotis, n. 4, at 221.   [582] Greig, n. 506, at 389.

respect, '[t]he question of determining whether "the Security Council has taken the measures necessary to maintain international peace and security" is fact-specific and depends upon the circumstances of the case'.[583] However, until these are actually taken by the Council the right of self-defence, which inheres in each state, must be permitted to continue. This is supported by state practice, as on several occasions states have claimed that their right of self-defence only ceases when the Security Council has taken effective measures.[584] Of course, however, there will often be disagreement between a defending state and the UN Security Council (and, indeed, other states) as to what the result of any measures taken should be, that is, when it can be determined that they have proven effective. For example, defending states will often adopt a more expansive approach, often believing it is justified in taking extensive action to cease an attack or permanently put an end to a series of attacks, while the Council may take a more restrictive view of what is necessary in the circumstances.

In addition to any measures it may take under Articles 41 and 42 of the Charter, the Security Council may – alternatively or in addition to such measures – *demand* that a state ceases its military action in self-defence or order a *ceasefire* between the parties. However, the 'effect of each of these interventions is more uncertain in terms of any significance they yield for the purposes of the until clause of Article 51 of the Charter'.[585] Humphrey Waldock argued that '[o]nce action in self-defence is in motion', and in the absence of either the defending state or the Council having taken measures that have resulted in terminating the armed attack, 'it requires an affirmative decision of the Council, including the concurring votes of the Permanent Members, to order the cessation of defensive action'.[586] While the Security Council is able to adopt decisions binding upon member states of the UN and potentially other actors, it is not always clear when such a decision is binding. For example, it is not clear whether such binding decisions are restricted to resolutions adopted under Chapter VII or indeed whether there is a difference in the Security Council 'calling' for a ceasefire and 'demanding' one.[587]

The answer to this question will most likely be based upon a contextual analysis.[588] During the 1982 Falklands War, for example, the Security Council adopted Resolution 502 (1982) in which it demanded an immediate cessation of hostilities and an immediate withdrawal of all Argentine forces from the

---

[583] Wood, n. 510, at 656.
[584] As one example, Pakistan asserted in 1965 its right of self-defence 'until the Security Council took effective measures to vacate India's aggression against Pakistan and Jammy and Kashmir'. See (1965) *United Nations Yearbook* 164.
[585] Kritsiotis, n. 4, at 224.   [586] Waldock, n. 397, at 495–6.   [587] See Section 3.2.1.
[588] See Christian Henderson and Noam Lubell, 'The Contemporary Legal Nature of UN Security Council Ceasefire Resolutions' (2013) 26 *Leiden Journal of International Law* 369, at 381–8.

Falklands, and called upon the governments of Argentina and the United Kingdom to seek a diplomatic solution to their differences.[589] The United Kingdom claimed that its right of self-defence remained alive as Argentina had not withdrawn its forces, meaning that the decision of the Council had not, 'in fact, been effective to restore international peace and security because of Argentina's refusal to comply'.[590] The 'until clause' 'can only be taken to refer to measures which are actually effective to bring about the stated objective'.[591] So, while the ceasefire was arguably binding upon both parties, given the refusal of Argentina to comply it could hardly be said that in these circumstances the right of self-defence of the United Kingdom had been extinguished.[592]

Ultimately, while on the one hand a 'demand' by the Security Council that a particular state ceases its action is a legally binding obligation under Article 25 of the UN Charter, Article 51 is, on the other hand, relatively clear that '[n]*othing in the present Charter* shall impair the inherent right of individual or collective self-defence if an armed attack occurs against a Member of the United Nations'. As such, while Frank Berman has interpreted the 'until clause' in Article 51 as providing 'the Council [with an] unfettered right to assume control',[593] the better view would seem to be that an obligation to obey the demands of the Council or defer to action it has taken will not necessarily displace the right of states to continue their action in self-defence, particularly if any action taken or proposed by the Council is objectively ineffective or unnecessary in removing the need for the action in self-defence.

## 6.7 CONCLUSION

The right of self-defence, which is a mix of both treaty and customary elements, is one which exists to enable states to protect themselves in the face of an attack that requires an armed response. While on the face of it an invocation of the right hinges on the occurrence of an armed attack, and then any implementation of it has to be both necessary and proportionate, as this chapter has demonstrated these criteria are not easy to set out in the abstract, let alone apply in practice.

Although they have been consistently challenged, there appears little appetite for either formal reform of the rules or an extreme interpretation of them. For example, the issue of cyber-attacks is one that is clearly of growing prominence. Yet, while 'a system of law based in the cognitive shorthand of physical consequences may not pay sufficient due to the values of thoroughly wired societies' so that we might 'anticipate a fairly rapid evolution of state

---

[589] UNSC Res. 502 (1982), paras. 1–3.    [590] UN Doc. S/15017, 30 April 1982.
[591] UN Doc. S/15016, 30 April 1982.    [592] Gill, n. 13, at 749.    [593] Berman, n. 578, at 155.

interpretations of international law's prescriptive norms regarding the use of force when applied to cyberspace',[594] it is also the case that 'conduct in cyberspace does not require a reinvention of customary international law, nor does it render existing international norms obsolete'.[595] In this respect, '[l]ong-standing norms guiding state behaviour – in times of peace and conflict – also apply in cyberspace'.[596] Indeed, states and scholars seem content to apply the existing rules and norms to such a change in the way attacks take place and the responses to them.

However, given the perceived change in threats facing states, there have, in particular, been pressures put on the temporal restrictions on the right of self-defence. There has been, and continues to be, real debate as to the point at which self-defence may be resorted to in order to prevent an attack, or its effects, from materialising, which is the focus of the following Chapter 7. Furthermore, while the UN Charter was undoubtedly drafted with inter-state conflict in mind, the reality is that states are more likely today to invoke the right of self-defence in response to attacks by non-state actors rather than states. Chapter 8 proceeds to address if and how such action can be reconciled with the right of self-defence. Ultimately, while the law is far from perfect, these challenges have, and can be, dealt with within the realms of the existing rules, norms and institutions.

## QUESTIONS

1 What, if anything, distinguishes an 'armed attack' from a 'use of force'?

2 What does a state need to demonstrate before resorting to the use of force in self-defence?

3 It is often stated that 'armed reprisals' are unlawful. Does state practice confirm or contradict this statement?

4 To what extent does the right of self-defence incorporate the protection of nationals abroad?

5 To what extent have states affirmed that the right of self-defence applies in the context of cyber operations?

6 How, if at all, are the individual and collective forms of the right of self-defence distinguished?

7 What role does the UN Security Council have in the right of self-defence?

---

[594] Schmitt, n. 313, at 1130.   [595] Ibid.
[596] President of the United States of America, International Strategy for Cyberspace, May 2011, available at: https://obamawhitehouse.archives.gov/sites/default/files/rss_viewer/international_strategy_for_cyberspace.pdf.

## SUGGESTED FURTHER READING

Derek W. Bowett, 'Collective Self-Defence under the Charter of the United Nations' (1955–6) 32 *British Yearbook of International Law* 130

Derek W. Bowett, 'Reprisals Involving Recourse to Armed Force' (1972) 66 *American Journal of International Law* 1

James A. Green, *The International Court of Justice and Self-Defence in International Law* (Hart Publishing, 2009)

Donald W. Greig, 'Self-Defense and the Security Council: What Does Article 51 Require?' (1991) 40 *International & Comparative Law Quarterly* 366

Chris O'Meara, *Necessity and Proportionality and the Right of Self-Defence in International Law* (Oxford University Press, 2021)

Tadashi Mori, *Origins of the Right of Self-Defence in International Law* (Brill, 2018)

Natalino Ronzitti, *Rescuing Nationals Abroad through Military Coercion and Intervention on the Grounds of Humanity* (Martinus Nijhoff Publishers, 1985)

Tom Ruys, *'Armed Attack' and Article 51 of the UN Charter* (Cambridge University Press, 2010)

# 7 Preventative Self-Defence

## 7.1 INTRODUCTION

Article 51 of the United Nations (UN) Charter provides for the right of self-defence 'if an armed attack occurs'. There is nothing, however, in the Charter or in other documents to guide us specifically on the temporal meaning of this requirement. A literal reading of this phrase would suggest that an armed attack needs to be physically occurring or have perhaps occurred in the recent past with a continuing defensive necessity.[1] While not entirely novel, an issue that has come into sharp focus in recent years, and particularly in the aftermath of the attacks of 11 September 2001 (9/11), is whether the right of self-defence can be invoked *before* an armed attack has been launched or at least before the physical manifestations of one have begun to occur. Given that there have been no attempts at formal reform of Article 51, the question arises as to how, if at all, self-defence of a preventative nature might be reconciled with this key requirement of an armed attack.

This raises the question of when an armed attack can be said to have begun. Is it, for example, when the victim state begins to witness the physical manifestations of the effects of the armed attack, for example the destruction caused by a missile hitting a target, tanks rolling over the border, the explosion of a bomb or the mass destruction caused by a cyber-attack upon the computer systems operating a dam? Or, alternatively, is it when the aggressor state has completed the final step in the launching of the attack, for example the pressing of the trigger in launching a missile? However, could it be said that accepting either is counterintuitive in that they both favour the aggressor and potentially seal the fate of the victim state? In this respect, and going further back along the temporal spectrum, might an armed attack be said to occur before either of these stages have been reached? If so, at what point exactly? Might it be, for example, immediately before the taking of an irreversible step in launching an armed attack? Lastly, might it be said that an

---

[1] See Section 6.3.1 for more on the concept of 'armed attack'.

armed attack has begun to occur when plans are being drawn up or an aggressor is in the initial stages towards launching an armed attack? Most controversially, could it be said that an armed attack has begun to 'occur' when dark clouds begin to form, either through the alleged development of weapons of mass destruction by an unfriendly state or armed group or, still more controversially, when belligerent statements are made or there is an open display of general animosity? Might addressing any of these questions be entirely contextual and depend on the nature of the attacker and the means of attack being used, for example? As discussed in this chapter, rather than focusing upon the precise requirements of Article 51, focus has, instead, been placed on the 'inherent' or customary form of the right of self-defence and, in particular, the concept of 'imminence' in assessing threats of attack and when it might be said that self-defence has become necessary, taking into account the realities of contemporary adversaries, technology and threats.

The term 'preventative' self-defence is used here as an umbrella term for all forms of self-defence that have been employed in the various discussions on self-defence in preventing the physical manifestation of an armed attack from occurring – that is, interceptive, anticipatory and pre-emptive. However, and as Ashley Deeks notes, 'states and scholars use a variety of poorly defined terms to discuss acts of self-defence in advance of an attack'.[2] Indeed, these terms are rarely used consistently and 'confusion regarding the appropriate terms easily leads one to misinterpret the position of those using them as well as to misjudge the impact of customary practice'.[3] While the way in which this chapter (and book) uses the terms considered here is by no means universal, it arguably represents how they are most commonly employed by states and in the legal literature. As such, this chapter, and in building upon Chapter 6, provides an examination of the various forms of preventative self-defence.

It is, however, important to draw a distinction here between the notion of purely preventative action in the absence of a prior armed attack – which is the primary focus of this chapter and goes to the heart of the question as to when it can be said that an armed attack has begun or whether one is even necessary for the invocation of the right of self-defence – and a delayed response to an armed attack or a series of attacks that nonetheless has the ostensibly defensive element of preventing the occurrence of a further future attack. The latter of these two – which is more about the prolongation of an armed attack, when it might be said that an armed attack comes to an end, and whether the right of

---

[2] Ashley S. Deeks, 'Taming the Doctrine of Pre-Emption', in Marc Weller (ed.), *The Oxford Handbook of the Use of Force in International Law* (Oxford University Press, 2015), 661, at 661.

[3] Tom Ruys, *'Armed Attack' and Article 51 of the UN Charter: Evolutions in Customary Law and Practice* (Cambridge University Press, 2010), at 254. See also Christopher Greenwood, 'International Law and the Pre-Emptive Use of Force: Afghanistan, al Qaida and Iraq' (2003) 4 *San Diego International Law Journal* 7, at 9.

self-defence can be of a continuous nature – has been examined in Chapter 6,[4] although, as will be discussed in Section 7.5, a factor to be taken into account in the context of 'contextual imminence' is whether there has been a pattern of continuing armed activity.

## 7.2 INTERCEPTING AN ARMED ATTACK

'Interceptive' self-defence describes a form of self-defence that takes place after an attack has been launched but before it has reached its target or its effects have been felt. Upon this view, an armed attack occurs at the point an armed attack is launched and cannot be reversed, such as intercepting rockets in flight,[5] rather than when the final target has been reached. As Yoram Dinstein describes, it occurs when an 'apparently irreversible course of action, thereby crossing the legal Rubicon', has been embarked upon.[6] 'The concept', Noam Lubell explains, 'revolves around the possibility of defining the occurrence of an armed attack based on when it begins, rather than when the effect of the first strike is experienced'.[7] Israel's 'Iron Dome' missile defence system, which emerged in the light of the 2006 Israel–Hezbollah conflict and was first put into use in 2011, provides a good example,[8] whereby missiles are identified and destroyed before they land in Israeli territory.

It is the fact that the aggressor has engaged in an 'irreversible course of action' that distinguishes this form of self-defence from both anticipatory and pre-emptive self-defence (see Sections 7.3 and 7.4, respectively) as, while there may be some degree of doubt regarding the acceptability of both anticipatory self-defence (in response to a threat of an 'imminent' attack) and pre-emptive self-defence (in response to a perceived temporally remote threat of attack), it is incontrovertible that interceptive self-defence falls within the confines of Article 51's requirement of the occurrence of an armed attack,[9] with any

---

[4] See, in particular, Section 6.3.
[5] Ian Brownlie, *International Law and the Use of Force by States* (Oxford University Press, 1963), at 367–8.
[6] Yoram Dinstein, *War, Aggression and Self-Defence*, 6th ed. (Cambridge University Press, 2017), at para. 609. While not expressly advanced by Israel, Dinstein is of the view that Israel's actions in the Six Day War of 1967 could be legally justified as 'interceptive self-defence, in response to an incipient armed attack by Egypt'. Ibid., at para. 555.
[7] Noam Lubell, 'The Problem of Imminence in an Uncertain World', in Marc Weller (ed.), *The Oxford Handbook of the Use of Force in International Law* (Oxford University Press, 2015), 697, at 704.
[8] BBC News, 'Israel's Iron Dome Missile Shield', 18 November 2012, available at: www.bbc.co.uk/news/world-middle-east-20385306.
[9] Dinstein notes that '[i]nterceptive self-defence is lawful, even under Article 51 of the UN Charter, for it takes place after the other side has committed itself to an armed attack'. Dinstein, n. 6, at para. 610; James A. Green, 'The "*Ratione Temporis*" Elements of Self-Defence' (2015) 2

response being *prima facie* justifiable under the customary criterion of necessity.[10] Indeed, in this context we are no longer simply talking of threats of an armed attack, no matter how temporally imminent they appear to be. As Sir Humphrey Waldock put it in 1951, '[w]here there is convincing evidence not merely of threats and potential danger but of an attack being actually mounted, then an armed attack may be said to have begun to occur, though it has not passed the frontier'.[11]

## 7.3 ANTICIPATING AN ARMED ATTACK: THE CONCEPT OF 'IMMINENCE'

In contrast to interceptive self-defence, 'anticipatory' self-defence is employed to describe the taking of defensive military action at the point immediately preceding the physical launching of an armed attack. It is, in this sense, more difficult to reconcile with Article 51's 'if an armed attack occurs' stipulation. However, on the basis of the facts and correspondence of the *Caroline* incident and the 'Webster formula' – which required there to be 'a necessity of self-defence, instant, overwhelming, leaving no choice of means and no moment for deliberation'[12] – it is an increasingly accepted view that if self-defence is to be resorted to then the threatened armed attack would need to be 'imminent'.[13] Indeed, although not free from controversy and disagreement, the concept of 'imminence' that has emerged as a guiding principle from the *Caroline* incident has come to be of some utility during the UN Charter era in determining

---

*Journal on the Use of Force and International Law* 97, at 107–8; Ruys, n. 3, at 264–6; Lubell, n. 7, at 718.

[10] See Section 6.3.1 on the criterion of necessity, and in particular its twin requirements of force being the only reasonable option for the victim state and any military response taken by it having a defensive objective.

[11] Humphrey Waldock, 'The Regulation of the Use of Force by Individual States in International Law' (1951) **81** *Recueil des cours* 451, at 498.

[12] W. R. Manning, *Diplomatic Correspondence of the United States, Canadian Relations, 1784–1860, III: 1836–1848, Documents 1193–1853* (Carnegie Endowment for International Peace, 1943), at 145 (Doc. No. 1269) (letter of Daniel Webster, US Secretary of State, to Lord Ashburton, special envoy of Great Britain to the United States of 27 July 1842). See Section 6.3.

[13] See, for example, Rainer Hofmann, 'International Law and the Use of Military Force against Iraq' (2002) **45** *German Yearbook of International Law* 9, at 31; Alex Bellamy, 'International Law and the War with Iraq' (2003) **4** *Melbourne Journal of International Law* 497, at 515–17; Miriam Sapiro, 'Iraq: The Shifting Sands of Preemptive Self-Defense' (2003) **97** *American Journal of International Law* 599, at 601–4; Surya P. Sharma, 'The American Doctrine of "Pre-Emptive" Self-Defence' (2003) **43** *Indian Journal of International Law* 215, at 220–4; Stefan Talmon, 'Changing Views on the Use of Force: The German Position' (2005) **5** *Baltic Yearbook of International Law* 41, at 60–3; Jan Wouters, *International recht in kort bestek* (Intersentia, 2006), at 209. While many states still express reservations on this issue, other states have also expressed acceptance of it. See the discussion in Section 7.4.2.2.

at which point the right of self-defence might be resorted to and, by implication, when it might be said that an armed attack has begun to occur.

### 7.3.1 The Academic Debate: 'Expansionists' versus 'Restrictionists'

The debate as to the legality and logic of anticipatory self-defence has taken place between the so-called expansionists and those described as the 'restrictionists'. In essence, the expansionists take the position that Article 51 clearly states that self-defence is a right that 'nothing in the Charter shall impair'.[14] This includes Article 51 itself, so, while it expressly states that the right of self-defence arises 'if an armed attack occurs', this was declaratory as opposed to regulatory and it did not say that the right arises 'if, and only if, an armed attack occurs'.[15] In addition, Article 51 expressly labels the right of self-defence as an 'inherent right'. This, it is argued, is an express reference to pre-existing customary international law and the *Caroline* incident which permitted a limited preventative form of self-defence.[16] In any case, faced with the threat of immediate attack logic would dictate that states should not be expected to wait like 'sitting ducks' to become victims. Indeed, 'common sense cannot require one to interpret an ambiguous provision in a text in a way that requires a state passively to accept its fate before it can defend itself'.[17] This argument of the expansionists had particular poignancy during the Cold War when the UN Security Council, which had been provided with 'primary responsibility for the maintenance of international peace and security', was seen to operate in a state of partial paralysis.[18]

In response, however, the restrictionists argue that self-defence is permissible if, and only if, an armed attack occurs and imminent threats of attack are not covered by Article 51.[19] In particular, 'nothing in the records of the San Francisco Conference suggests that the phrase "if an armed attack occurs" was intended to be declaratory instead of regulatory'.[20] Indeed, '[t]here is no

---

[14] See, for example, Derek W. Bowett, *Self-Defence in International Law* (Manchester University Press, 1958), at 178–93; John Norton Moore, 'The Secret War in Central America and the Future World Order' (1986) 80 *American Journal of International Law* 43, at 83.

[15] *Case Concerning Military and Paramilitary Activities in and against Nicaragua (Nicaragua v. United States of America)*, Merits (1986) ICJ Reports 14, Separate Dissenting Opinion of Judge Schwebel, at para. 173.

[16] Bowett, n. 14, at 188–9.

[17] Rosalyn Higgins, *Problems and Process: International Law and How We Use It* (Clarendon Press, 1994), at 242.

[18] Nigel D. White, *Keeping the Peace: The United Nations and the Maintenance of International Peace and Security* (Manchester University Press, 1997), at 7. See, in general, Chapter 3.

[19] Josef Kunz, 'Individual and Collective Self-Defense in Article 51 of the Charter of the United Nations' (1947) 41 *American Journal of International Law* 872, at 878; Avra Constantinou, *The Right of Self-Defence under Customary International Law and Article 51 of the United Nations Charter* (Ant. N. Sakkoulas, 2000), at 114–15; Ruys, n. 3, at 266.

exception so the general rule is that United Nations Members are barred by the Charter from exercising self-defence in response to a mere threat of force'.[21] In addition, the word 'inherent' was included in Article 51 without any debate as to its meaning and, even if it is accepted that it provides a reference to broader pre-existing customary law, the principle *lex posterior derogate legi priori* would lead to the conclusion that the Charter and its stipulation for the occurrence of an armed attack takes precedence. While 'the Charter's aim is obviously not to favour the aggressor by forcing the defending State to wait until the armed attack has actually achieved its objective',[22] the restrictionists make the point that a potential victim state can take action to repel an attack once it is in progress and can take various measures prior to the launching of the attack, including non-forcible countermeasures, and resort to the UN Security Council. The UN Charter was not, therefore, a suicide pact, but rather one that sought to minimise the risk of tensions spiralling out of control.

However, even if it is conceded that prior customary international law survived the UN Charter intact, not only is it argued that the *Caroline* incident cannot be used as a precedent for purely preventative self-defence, as the ship had already been involved in previous military actions against Canadian territory,[23] but it was also argued by Ian Brownlie that the position of customary international law in the period preceding the adoption of the UN Charter was not so very different from the restrictive stipulations of Article 51.[24]

### 7.3.2 International Jurisprudence

Following the Second World War both the Nuremberg and Tokyo Military Tribunals implicitly accepted the 'Webster formula' and the notion of preventative self-defence. For example, the Nuremberg Tribunal stated that: 'It must be remembered that preventive action in foreign territory is justified only in case of "an instant and overwhelming necessity for self-defense, leaving no choice of means, and no moment of deliberation" (The Caroline case … )'.[25] It should be noted, however, that both Tribunals were dealing with the law as it stood prior to the adoption of the UN Charter and were pronouncing on matters of individual as opposed to state responsibility.[26]

---

[20] Ruys, n. 3, at 260.   [21] Dinstein, n. 6, at para. 592.   [22] Ruys, n. 3, at 266.
[23] Dinstein, n. 6, at para. 589; Chris O'Meara, *Necessity and Proportionality and the Right of Self-Defence in International Law* (Oxford University Press, 2021), at 61.
[24] Brownlie, n. 5, at 394.
[25] Judgment of the International Military Tribunal (Nuremberg), 1 October 1946, reproduced in (1947) 41 *American Journal of International Law* 172, at 205. See also Judgment of the International Military Tribunal (Tokyo), Cmd 6964, at 35.
[26] See Ruys, n. 3, at 261; Brownlie, n. 5, at 258.

In the *Nicaragua* case the International Court of Justice (ICJ) was keen to point out that '[t]here appears now to be general agreement on the nature of the acts which can be treated as constituting armed attacks'.[27] While the Court elaborated upon certain aspects of the nature of the 'armed attack' criterion, such as the gravity and attribution aspects,[28] it did not, however, provide a comprehensive definition of 'armed attack', including its temporal elements. Although the Court considered the description of the right as an 'inherent' one as being a reference to the customary nature of the right,[29] it did not link this back to the 'Webster formula' and steered well clear of pronouncing upon the legality of any form of preventative self-defence. This was perhaps for good reason; in that it really did not need to do so. Indeed, it simply stated that:

> reliance is placed by the Parties only on the right of self-defence in the case of an armed attack which has already occurred, and the issue of the lawfulness of a response to the imminent threat of armed attack has not been raised [so that] the Court expresses no view on that issue.[30]

The Court did not, however, expressly rule out the existence of a right of anticipatory self-defence, or the possible future development of such a right, although its insistence upon the need for an armed attack might arguably be seen as an implicit rejection.[31]

### 7.3.3 Cold War State Practice on the Right of Anticipatory Self-Defence: The 1967 Six-Day War

There is limited Cold War state practice on the concept of anticipatory self-defence, and that which does exist is ambiguous. Arguably the best example is to be found in the 1967 Six-Day War. In 1967, tensions begun to mount between Israel and several of its neighbours. During the course of the year, Egypt expelled the United Nations Emergency Force (UNEF) peacekeeping operation from Egyptian territory,[32] built up Egyptian troops on the Sinai border, dispatched troops to Jordan and closed the Straits of Tiran to Israeli

---

[27] *Nicaragua* case, n. 15, at para. 195.  [28] See Chapters 6 and 8, respectively.

[29] See, in general, Section 6.1.

[30] *Nicaragua* case, n. 15, at para. 194. As noted in Section 7.3.1, in the *Nicaragua* case, Judge Schwebel rejected a reading of Article 51 that would provide for a right of self-defence 'if, and only if, an armed attack occurs'.

[31] See Dino Kritsiotis, 'A Study of the Scope and Operation of the Rights of Individual and Collective Self-Defence under International Law', in Nigel D. White and Christian Henderson (eds.), *Research Handbook on International Conflict and Security Law: Jus ad Bellum, Jus in Bello and Jus post Bellum* (Edward Elgar, 2013), 170, at 188. Such an express rejection might have proved controversial given the security concerns of many states. In the same way, the ICJ could not rule out *in extremis* the legality of the threat or use of nuclear weapons in its *Nuclear Weapons* advisory opinion.

[32] See Section 5.5.1 for more on this operation.

shipping, which blocked the port of Eilat. This course of events took place amid statements by Egyptian President Nasser which indicated an intention to eliminate Israel.[33] Subsequently, on 5 June 1967, Israel launched a strike against Egypt's airbases which resulted in the complete destruction of the Egyptian air force. By 11 June, Israel had defeated Egypt and occupied Gaza, the West Bank, the Sinai and the Golan Heights.

In justifying its actions Israel appeared to swing between claiming that the actions of Egypt constituted an armed attack, that the Egyptian blockade was itself an act of war, and that it was acting in response to an 'imminent' threat caused by the transfer of large numbers of Egyptian forces to the 'very gates' of Israel.[34] Israel's actions which, regardless of how they were justified, resembled anticipatory self-defence, were not widely condemned. Indeed, draft resolutions holding Israel to be the aggressor state failed to receive sufficient votes in both the UN Security Council and General Assembly. While the incident arguably 'recognize[s] that, in demonstrable circumstances of extreme necessity, anticipatory self-defense may be a legitimate exercise of a State's right to ensure its survival',[35] it also does not 'amount to an open-ended endorsement of a general right of anticipatory self-defense'.[36] Indeed, no statements made in the UN fora during this incident expressly supported a right of preventative self-defence, while several states expressly adopted the position that '[t]he action taken by Israel was not legitimate self-defence ... because no armed attack on her territory had occurred'.[37] Ultimately, it is difficult to find support for a right of anticipatory self-defence either from Israel's justification or indeed the reaction to the incident.

## 7.4 PRE-EMPTING THE DEVELOPMENT OF A THREAT OF AN ARMED ATTACK: MOVING BEYOND 'IMMINENCE'?

Further down the temporal spectrum, during the Cold War the argument was occasionally made that the Webster formula was 'cast in language so

---

[33] Cited in UN Doc. S/PV. 1348, 6 June 1967, at para. 150.
[34] Ibid., at paras. 142–94. However, Christine Gray argues that Israel was not claiming to act in anticipatory self-defence. See Christine Gray, *International Law and the Use of Force*, 4th ed. (Oxford University Press, 2018), at 171. In contrast, Thomas Franck argues that Israel's 'words and actions clearly asserted a right of anticipatory self-defence against an imminent armed attack'. Thomas M. Franck, *Recourse to Force: State Action against Threats and Armed Attacks* (Cambridge University Press, 2002), at 103. See also Edward Miller, 'Self-Defence, International Law, and the Six Day War' (1985) 20 *Israel Law Review* 49.
[35] Franck, n. 34, at 105.   [36] Ibid.
[37] UN Doc. A/PV.1530, 12 June 1967, at para. 58 (Sudan). See also para. 153 (India); UN Doc. A/PV.1529, 21 June 1967, at para. 93 (Yugoslavia); UN Doc. A/PV.1538, 27 June 1967, at para. 84 (Zambia); UN Doc. A/PV. 1541, 29 June 1967, at para. 72 (Cyprus).

abstractly restrictive as almost, if read literally, to impose paralysis'.[38] There was, as such, some support for a broader doctrine of 'pre-emptive' self-defence; that is, armed forcible action taken to prevent more temporally remote threats of an armed attack from coming to fruition at some point in the future. Targeting the facilities of a hostile state that are believed to be developing a nuclear capability is an example of this form of self-defence. This argument had its proponents during the Cold War, in particular due to the threat posed by nuclear weapons. Indeed, the argument was made that '[t]he destructive potential of nuclear weapons is so enormous as to call into question any and all received rules of international law regarding the transboundary use of force'.[39] The restrictionists argued, however, that not only are the opportunities for abuse of such a broad interpretation too great to permit one from emerging, but that '[i]t is precisely in the age of the major deterrent that nations should not be encouraged to strike first under the pretext of prevention or pre-emption'.[40]

What is important to note here is that, while an argument can be made that the concept of self-defence against a temporally imminent threat – that is, one that is objectively highly likely to occur in the immediate future unless action is taken to prevent it – is reconcilable with the requirement for the occurrence of an armed attack in Article 51, the notion of self-defence against a temporally remote threat of an attack where there is little knowledge as to if, when, how and possibly against what or whom the attack may be launched, is not. Arguments in favour of pre-emptive self-defence were, therefore, a direct and open challenge to both the restrictions of the Webster formula and, more fundamentally, Article 51 of the UN Charter.

### 7.4.1 Cold War State Practice on the Right of Pre-emptive Self-Defence

#### 7.4.1.1 The 1962 Cuban Missile Crisis

In October 1962, Soviet ballistic missiles were installed in Cuba, an act which was perceived by the United States as posing a security risk to it. In response, US President John F. Kennedy imposed a naval quarantine on Cuba under which US forces were authorised to intercept and search, by force if necessary, any vessel proceeding towards Cuba. In justifying its actions, President Kennedy referred to a Joint Resolution of the US Congress of 3 October

---

[38] Myers S. McDougal and Florentino P. Feliciano, *Law and Minimum World Public Order: The Legal Regulation of International Coercion* (Yale University Press, 1961), at 217.
[39] Anthony D'Amato, 'Israel's Air Strike upon the Iraqi Nuclear Reactor' (1983) **77** *American Journal of International Law* 584, at 586. See also Bowett, n. 14, at 191–2; Higgins, n. 17, at 242.
[40] Louis Henkin, *How Nations Behave: Law and Foreign Policy*, 2nd ed. (Columbia University Press, 1979), at 142.

1962, which proclaimed that the United States would 'prevent by whatever means may be necessary, including the use of arms, ... the creation or use [in Cuba] of an externally supported military capability endangering the security of the United States',[41] and also to a decision of the Organization of American States (OAS) Council of 23 October 1962 which 'recommended that the Member States, in accordance with Articles 6 and 8 of the Inter-American Treaty of Reciprocal Assistance, take all measures, individually and collectively, including the use of armed force, which they may deem necessary' to ensure that Cuba no longer received military material from the Soviet Union and 'to prevent the missiles in Cuba ... from ever becoming an active threat to the peace and security of the Continent'.[42] There was no suggestion that an armed attack was imminent.

When the matter came before the UN Security Council, states were split along Cold War lines and the debate unfolded largely in political and strategic terms rather than legal ones.[43] The United States provided little in the way of legal justification but US Ambassador Adlai Stevenson instead stated that the United States and OAS responded to prevent 'this transformation of Cuba into a base for offensive weapons of sudden mass destruction' in pursuit of a Soviet 'policy of aggression'.[44] The crisis was ultimately resolved peacefully through negotiations between the United States and the Soviet Union, with the mediation efforts of the UN Secretary-General, which resulted in the removal of the Soviet missiles from Cuba in exchange for the removal of US missiles from Turkey. During the course of the crisis, neither Article 51, 'armed attack' nor self-defence were ever mentioned, with the operation not being perceived as falling within the purview of Article 51[45] but instead 'within a third category: action by regional organizations to preserve the peace' under Article 52 of the Charter.[46] The failure of the United States to rely on self-defence in this situation arguably alludes to its lack of belief in the existence of a right of pre-emptive self-defence and it is difficult to argue that any *opinio juris* in regard to the right of pre-emptive self-defence can be garnered from the statements of other states during the time of the crisis.[47]

---

[41] US President, Proclamation 3504, Interdiction of the delivery of offensive weapons to Cuba, 23 October 1962, reprinted in (1963) 57 *American Journal of International Law* 51.
[42] Ibid.   [43] UN Docs. S/PV.1022–5, 23–5 October 1962.
[44] UN Doc. S/PV. 1022, 23 October 1962, at paras. 14 and 29.
[45] See Quincy Wright, 'The Cuban Quarantine' (1963) 57 *American Journal of International Law* 546. Although, for an argument that the crisis should be viewed in the context of self-defence, see Myers S. McDougal, 'The Soviet-Cuban Quarantine and Self-Defense' (1963) 57 *American Journal of International Law* 597.
[46] Abram Chayes, 'Law and Quarantine of Cuba' (1962–3) 41 *Foreign Affairs* 550, at 554. For more on regional organisations and the use of force see Section 3.5.
[47] Although see the statement of Ghana which argued specifically that the invocation of the right of self-defence could not be reconciled with the Webster formula. See UN Doc. S/PV/1024, 24 October 1962, at para. 110.

### 7.4.1.2 *The 1981 Israeli Strike on the Osiraq Nuclear Reactor (Iraq)*

While Israel's actions at the outbreak of the 1967 Six-Day War resembled – if they were not expressly justified as – anticipatory self-defence,[48] Israel was again involved in what appeared to be more an action in pre-emptive self-defence when it attacked and destroyed the Osiraq nuclear reactor at the Tuwaitha research centre in Iraq in June 1981.[49] In justifying its attack, Israel claimed that '[a] threat of nuclear obliteration' was being developed against it by Iraq so that it 'was exercising its inherent right of self-defence as understood in general international law and as preserved in Article 51 of the [United Nations] Charter'.[50] In echoing arguments that had been made by some of the more expansionist academic scholars, it later added that the scope of the right of self-defence had taken on 'a new and far wider application with the advent of the nuclear era' and 'the concepts of "armed attack" and the threat of such an attack must be read in conjunction with, and are related to, the present-day criteria of speed and power'.[51]

The Israeli operation was heavily condemned, with all states participating in the UN debates condemning the strike.[52] Israel's actions were also condemned in UN Security Council Resolution 487 (1981) for being 'in clear violation of the Charter of the United Nations and the norms of international conduct'.[53] However, while none spoke out in favour of preventative action – and some, such as Algeria, specifically rejected the right of 'preventive' self-defence,[54] while Sweden took the position that pre-emptive self-defence could be extended 'almost limitlessly to include all conceivable future dangers, subjectively defined'[55] – most states appeared to be of the view that 'Israel had not satisfactorily discharged the argumentative or the evidential burden of

---

[48] See Section 7.3.3 for more on the 1967 Six Day War.
[49] W. Thomas Mallison and Sally V. Mallison, 'The Israeli Attack on June 7, 1981, upon the Iraqi Nuclear Reactor: Aggression or Self-Defense?' (1982) 15 *Vanderbilt Journal of Transnational Law* 417; John Quigley, 'Israel's Destruction of Iraq's Nuclear Reactor: A Reply' (1995) 9 *Temple International and Comparative Law Journal* 441; Anthony D'Amato, 'Israel's Air Strike against the Osiraq Reactor: A Retrospective' (1996) 10 *Temple International and Comparative Law Journal* 259; Timothy L. H. McCormack, *Self-Defense in International Law: The Israeli Raid on the Iraqi Nuclear Reactor* (Magnes Press, 1996).
[50] UN Doc. S/PV. 2280, 12 June 1981, at paras. 58–9.
[51] UN Doc. A/36/PV.52, 11 November 1981, at para. 63.
[52] See UN Docs. S/PV.2280-8, 12–19 June 1981; UN Docs. A/36/PV.52-5, 11–13 November 1981.
[53] See UNSC Res. 487 (1981). See also UNGA Res. 36/27 (1981) which, although by and large followed the findings of the Security Council resolution, also expressly condemned the Israeli aggression.
[54] UN Doc. S/PV. 2280, 12 June 1981, at paras. 78–80.
[55] UN Doc. A/36/PV.56, 13 November 1981, at para. 119.

proving *imminence* in its invocation of this right.'[56] In particular, although the United States joined in this condemnation, it did so on the basis that the attack was unnecessary due to Israel not having exhausted diplomatic means as opposed to being in opposition to the idea of pre-emptive self-defence.[57] Indeed, emphasis was placed on the failure to demonstrate the imminence of attack by Iraq or the necessity of a response in self-defence as opposed to rejecting in principle a right of pre-emptive self-defence.[58] As such, while state practice had not demonstrated any discernible *opinio juris* towards the acceptance of pre-emptive self-defence, it arguably demonstrated a 'crack' in the *opinio juris* against anticipatory self-defence in response to threats of imminent attack,[59] although this was not tested any further until after the events of 11 September 2001.

### 7.4.2 Attempts to Adapt the Concept of 'Imminence' in the Aftermath of 9/11: The 'Bush Doctrine'

At 8.46 a.m. on 11 September 2001, an American Airlines passenger plane crashed into the northern tower of the World Trade Center in New York City. Within the space of the next few hours, nearly 3,000 individuals had lost their lives as a result of a coordinated set of terrorist attacks involving passenger airline jets being used to target the second of the twin towers of the World Trade Center and the Pentagon in Washington DC, while another crashed in a field outside Pennsylvania.[60] The utter shock that this could happen upon the territory of the United States, along with the realisation that terrorism had taken a dramatic turn in terms of both sophistication and scale, were palpable.

The United States did not immediately respond with military action following the terrorist attacks. Instead, after identifying the perpetrators of the attacks and following attempts at engaging with the ruling Taliban regime in Afghanistan to hand over the leader of the al-Qaida terrorist group, Osama bin Laden, on 7 October 2001 it launched Operation Enduring Freedom. The initial phase of this operation consisted of a military intervention led by the United States and involved direct attacks against al-Qaida and Taliban targets as well as the provision of support to the Northern Alliance, which led to the ousting from power of the Taliban regime in November 2001.

---

[56] Kritsiotis, n. 31, at 191 (see, for example, the United Kingdom, which noted that 'there was no instant or overwhelming necessity for self-defence'. UN Doc. S/PV.2282, 15 June 1981, at para. 106).

[57] UN Doc. S/PV.2288, 19 June 1981, at para. 30. See Section 6.3.1.1 on the conception of necessity requiring a state to be without recourse to reasonable alternative non-forcible means.

[58] Heather Harrison Dinniss, *Cyber Warfare and the Laws of War* (Cambridge University Press, 2012), at 87. For more on necessity see Section 6.3.1.

[59] Ruys, n. 3, at 287.    [60] *Keesing's* (2001) 44333.

Upon launching this military action, the US ambassador to the UN, John Negroponte, informed the UN Security Council that the United States was invoking its right of self-defence.[61] The action and the justification for it appeared to be accepted by virtually the entire international community of states.[62] Indeed, the fact that non-state terrorist groups could perpetrate 'armed attacks', without them necessarily needing to be fully attributed to a state, was seemingly accepted.[63] Not only did the United States turn its sights towards taking the fight to those who perpetrated the attacks but also to terrorism more generally, to rogue states and the possible development, proliferation and future use of weapons of mass destruction (WMD) by America's enemies.

With these attacks, which were the first large-scale attack against US territory since the Japanese attack on Pearl Harbor in December 1941, a new era involving a so-called war on terror had seemingly commenced. This first manifested itself in the very same letter of the United States to the Security Council which was sent upon it commencing Operation Enduring Freedom, in that the United States did more than simply invoke the right of self-defence in direct response to the attacks of 9/11 in stating that: '[w]e may find that our self-defence requires further actions with respect to other organisations and other states'.[64] This might be seen as an attempt by the United States to elongate its right of self-defence which had arisen in respect to this particular armed attack, perhaps indefinitely, on the basis that it was now engaged in a 'war' on terror, thus casting its net wide as to where and who might be covered by the same armed response. Yet, with hindsight it is now clear that this part of the letter was also laying the groundwork for the Bush administration's subsequent attempts to expand the concept of necessity – and the temporal requirement of 'imminence' beyond any reasonable definition – so as to incorporate more temporally remote and uncertain threats of a future armed attack. While the essence of the argument was the same as asserted by Israel in 1981, this was the first time that a state had expressly elaborated upon and sustained such an argument.

After declaring in his January 2002 State of the Union Address that the greatest danger to the United States lay where terrorism, rogue states and WMD intersected and that an 'axis of evil' existed consisting of Iran, North Korea and Iraq,[65] President Bush went on in his June 2002 speech at the West Point military

---

[61] UN Doc. S/2001/946, 7 October 2001.

[62] See n. 27 of Chapter 6 for more on this reaction. See also Christian Henderson, *The Persistent Advocate and the Use of Force: The Impact of the United States upon the Jus ad Bellum in the Post-Cold War Era* (Ashgate, 2010), at 155.

[63] See Section 6.2.1 and, in general, Chapter 8.    [64] UN Doc. S/2001/946, 7 October 2001.

[65] President of the United States of America, 'State of the Union Address', 29 January 2002, available at: https://georgewbush-whitehouse.archives.gov/news/releases/2002/01/20020129-11.html.

academy to claim, for the first time, the right to launch pre-emptive strikes on states deemed a threat but before the United States itself had been attacked.[66] In particular, it was claimed that the United States must 'confront the worst threats before they emerge' and that it must 'be ready for pre-emptive action when necessary'.[67] In the United States' National Security Strategy (NSS) of 17 September 2002, however, the United States went further in explaining how, in its view, such action might be reconciled with existing legal doctrine:

> For centuries, international law recognized that nations need not suffer an attack before they can lawfully take action to defend themselves against forces that present an imminent danger of attack. Legal scholars and international jurists often conditioned the legitimacy of pre-emption on the existence of an imminent threat – most often a visible mobilization of armies, navies, and air forces preparing to attack.
>
> We must adapt the concept of imminent threat to the capabilities and objectives of today's adversaries. Rogue states and terrorists do not seek to attack us using conventional means. They know such attacks would fail. Instead, they rely on acts of terror and, potentially, the use of weapons of mass destruction – weapons that can be easily concealed, delivered covertly, and used without warning.
>
> ...
>
> The United States has long maintained the option of pre-emptive actions to counter a sufficient threat to our national security. The greater the threat ... the more compelling the case for taking anticipatory action to defend ourselves, even if uncertainty remains as to the time and place of the enemy's attack. To forestall or prevent such hostile acts ... the United States will, if necessary, act pre-emptively.
>
> The United States will not use force in all cases to pre-empt emerging threats, nor should nations use pre-emption as a pretext for aggression. Yet in an age where the enemies of civilization openly and actively seek the world's most destructive technologies, the United States cannot remain idle while dangers gather.
>
> We will always proceed deliberately, weighing the consequences of our actions.[68]

This was an extraordinary document and there are several notable points in its main proclamations. In particular, while it made no mention of Article 51 and the requirement for an 'armed attack', it expressly framed its argument in the context of customary international law governing the use of force, and it was not solely political or strategic in nature. In this respect it adopted the position that anticipatory self-defence was at that time recognised in international law, which, on the basis of what has already been set out in this chapter, was not the case. However, the Bush administration went further in

---

[66] President of the United States of America, 'Remarks by the President at 2002 Graduation Exercise of the United States Military Academy at West Point', 1 June 2002, available at: https://georgewbush-whitehouse.archives.gov/news/releases/2002/06/20020601-3.html.
[67] Ibid.
[68] The White House, The National Security Strategy of the United States of America, October 2002, at 15, available at:https://2009-2017.state.gov/documents/organization/63562.pdf.

making the argument that the concept of imminence must be adapted to meet 'the capabilities and objectives of today's adversaries'. This represented a sharp break from interpretations of imminence that had been witnessed in state practice, which were based almost exclusively upon the temporal nature of the threat, to talking of imminence 'even if uncertainty remains as to the time and place of the enemy's attack' so that action 'against ... *emerging threats* before they are fully formed' was now acceptable.[69]

There were also many absent details as to how this expanded concept of imminence – and, more generally, customary criterion of necessity and the broader right of self-defence – was to operate, in particular who was to judge whether an emerging threat constituted a sufficient threat for the purposes of the right of pre-emptive self-defence. However, in terms of the contemporary legality of this form of self-defence the United States appeared to contradict itself as, on the one hand, it was adamant that '[t]he United States has long maintained the option of pre-emptive actions to counter a sufficient threat to our national security' while on the other it seemed less sure of the legality of pre-emptive action in making the argument that '[w]e must adapt the concept of imminent threat to the capabilities and objectives of today's adversaries'. However, regardless of whether the United States was talking in terms of *lex lata* or *lex ferenda*, it remained to be seen whether the doctrine of pre-emptive self-defence would ultimately be utilised and how the international community would respond to the United States' vision for the future of the law of self-defence and, in particular, its apparent simultaneous attempted dismantling of the 'armed attack' requirement and loosening of the necessity criterion.[70]

### 7.4.2.1 Test Cases for the Bush Doctrine of Pre-emptive Self-Defence?

#### 7.4.2.1.1 Iraq (2003)

Given the extent of the political and legal rhetoric that had emanated from the United States during the course of the previous year regarding the doctrine of pre-emptive self-defence, the military action against Iraq in March 2003 would seem to have been an ideal test case for the doctrine of pre-emptive self-defence.[71] There was a 'rogue' state – indeed, one that formed a part of President Bush's 'axis of evil' – which even the less belligerent members of the international community believed possessed WMD and which was led by an individual who's 'sanity and restraint' could evidently not be trusted.[72]

---

[69] Ibid (emphasis added).
[70] See Section 6.2 on the Article 51 requirement of an armed attack and Section 6.3.1 on the customary criterion of necessity.
[71] See, for example, Christian Henderson, 'The Bush Doctrine: From Theory to Practice' (2004) **9** *Journal of Conflict & Security Law* 3.
[72] President of the United States of America, 'State of the Union Address', 28 January 2003, available at:https://georgewbush-whitehouse.archives.gov/stateoftheunion/2003/index.html.

Furthermore, upon the launching of military action against Iraq on 19 March 2003, while the United States dedicated the majority of its letter to the UN Security Council to setting out the 'revival' argument, as discussed and set out in Chapter 4,[73] the last few lines arguably indicated that the concept of pre-emption formed the underlying backdrop to the invasion: '[The actions undertaken] are necessary steps to defend the United States and the international community from the threat posed by Iraq and to restore international peace and security in the area. Further delay would simply allow Iraq to continue its unlawful and threatening conduct.'[74] Yet, while the intervention itself might be seen as a test case for how a doctrine of pre-emptive self-defence might operate in practice, there are various reasons why this intervention has not had an impact upon the legal status of the doctrine of pre-emption. For example, states will, of course, instinctively put forward the legal justification that is perceived as having the best chances of finding acceptance within the international community. Yet, given the bitter disagreements within the Security Council over the revival argument, it did not say a great deal about the United States' belief in the doctrine of pre-emptive self-defence that it appeared not to think that it would have had a better chance of finding acceptance. Indeed, the reference to self-defence in the letter can arguably be seen as no more than a 'rhetorical flourish'.[75]

Furthermore, if the incident was to prove a successful test case for the doctrine of pre-emptive self-defence in regard to its impact upon the law, the doctrine would need to be 'shared in principle by other States',[76] and it was not. Neither of the other two main states taking action on this occasion – the United Kingdom and Australia – included a similar reference to 'defence' within their respective letters to the UN Security Council, both relying fully upon the revival argument.[77] In addition, the military operation received heavy condemnation in general, as discussed in Section 4.3, and those third states that referred to self-defence did so in negative terms. Iran, for example, stated that the invasion was 'not waged in self-defence against any prior armed attack. Nor, even by any stretch of the imagination, could Iraq, after 12 years of comprehensive sanctions, be considered an imminent threat against the national security of the belligerent powers.'[78]

---

[73] See Section 4.3.   [74] UN Doc. S/2003/351, 20 March 2003.
[75] Dino Kritsiotis, 'Arguments of Mass Confusion' (2004) 15 *European Journal of International Law* 233, at 249.
[76] *Nicaragua* case, n. 15, at para. 202. See also 'Legal and Procedural Issues Associated with the *Jus ad Bellum*' in the Introduction.
[77] See UN Doc. S/2003/350, 20 March 2003 and UN Doc. S/2003/352, 20 March 2003, respectively.
[78] UN Doc. S/PV.4726, 26 March 2003, at 33. See also 8 (Malaysia), 10 (Algeria), 13 (Yemen) and 35 (Lebanon).

## 7.4 Pre-empting the Development of a Threat of an Armed Attack

The intervention also demonstrated all too clearly the key pitfalls in the practical implementation of such a doctrine. The practical frailties of relying on intelligence from even some of the most sophisticated intelligence services in the world,[79] and the devastation and lasting conflict caused by doing so, place serious question marks over whether such a doctrine could ever work in practice.

All of this might lead one to conclude that the Iraq debacle sounded the death knell for the doctrine of pre-emptive self-defence. Yet, the United States persisted with its belief in the doctrine. Indeed, while the 2002 NSS was published prior to the launching of Operation Iraqi Freedom, the following NSS of the Bush administration of March 2006, in which it openly pronounced that '[t]he place of pre-emption in our national security strategy remains the same',[80] came after the failures and controversy of this conflict had been witnessed.

### 7.4.2.1.2 Syria (2007)

The attack by Israel upon a Syrian nuclear plant, not long after the publication of the United States' 2006 NSS, provided an indication that, while the right of pre-emptive self-defence may not have found a place within international law, there might be occasions when states are prepared to overlook its use. On 6 September 2007, Israel fighter jets destroyed a target near al-Kibar in Syria in an operation that came to be known as Operation Orchard.[81] For weeks following this incident very little information emerged; Israel did not acknowledge the strike, let alone justify it, which in itself was perhaps telling as to its belief that a right of pre-emptive self-defence existed. Furthermore, while Syria protested about the incident on 9 September,[82] it did not confirm the target of the strike.

It was only in mid-October 2007 when reports began to appear suggesting that the site targeted had been a secret Syrian nuclear complex,[83] and then on

---

[79] Although the Iraq Inquiry Report, which was published in July 2016, arguably highlights that, at least in connection with the United Kingdom, the intelligence presented for public consumption may not have been an accurate reflection of the intelligence itself. See the Report of the Iraq Inquiry, 6 July 2016, vol. 4: Iraq's Weapons of Mass Destruction, available online at: www.iraqinquiry.org.uk/the-report/.

[80] Office of the White House, The National Security Strategy of the United States (2006), at 23, available at: https://georgewbush-whitehouse.archives.gov/nsc/nss/2006/. See, in general, Christine Gray, 'The Bush Doctrine Revisited: The 2006 National Security Strategy of the USA' (2006) 5 *Chinese Journal of International Law* 555; Christian Henderson, 'The 2006 National Security Strategy of the United States: The Pre-Emptive Use of Force and the Persistent Advocate' (2007) 15 *Tulsa Journal of Comparative and International Law* 1.

[81] See Andrew Garwood-Gowers, 'Israel's Airstrike on Syria's Al-Kibar Facility: A Test Case for the Doctrine of Pre-Emptive Self-Defence' (2011) 16 *Journal of Conflict & Security Law* 263.

[82] See UN Doc. S/2007/537, 9 September 2007.

[83] David E. Sanger and Mark Mazzetti, 'Israel Struck Syrian Nuclear Project, Analysts Say', *New York Times*, 14 October 2007, at 6.

24 April 2008 the United States released intelligence about the al-Kibar complex which stated that it was a nearly completed nuclear reactor which was intended to produce uranium for a weapons programme, and also confirmed that the reactor had been destroyed by Israel because it 'considered a Syrian nuclear capability to be an existential threat to the state of Israel'.[84] A further report by the International Atomic Energy Agency also confirmed that samples taken from the area contained weapons-grade uranium particles.[85] What is of some significance, and which throws hesitation over any arguments that the intervention in Iraq and the general reaction to the Bush doctrine had sounded the death knell for the doctrine of pre-emptive self-defence, is that there was virtually no condemnation of the strike. While this may have been for various reasons,[86] it does suggest that, although states do not wish to see pre-emptive self-defence take its place *lex lata* within the law of self-defence, there may be times when they wish to say nothing. However, given the lack of even any acknowledgement of the incident by Israel, let alone the advance of a legal justification of pre-emptive self-defence, it is difficult to read too much into, and draw firm conclusions from, the silence with which this particular incident was met.

### 7.4.2.2 General Reaction to the Bush Doctrine of Pre-emptive Self-Defence

Following the hugely controversial intervention in Iraq in 2003 there was significant activity within the United Nations as to how to repair the fissures that had become so clear within the international community. In September 2003 the UN Secretary-General, Kofi Annan, addressed the UN General Assembly and, in declaring that the UN and the international community more broadly had reached 'a fork in the road', went on to describe the situation:

Article 51 of the Charter prescribes that all States, if attacked, retain the inherent right of self-defence. But until now it has been understood that when States go beyond that ... they need the unique legitimacy provided by the United Nations. Now, some say this understanding is no longer tenable, since an 'armed attack' with weapons of mass destruction could be launched at any time, without warning, or by a clandestine group. Rather than wait for that to happen, they argue, States have the right and obligation to use force pre-emptively ... even while weapons systems that might be used to attack them are still being developed ... This logic represents a fundamental

---

[84] Office of the Director of National Intelligence, 'Background Briefing with Senior U.S. Officials on Syria's Covert Nuclear Reactor and North Korea's Involvement', 24 April 2008, at 8.
[85] International Atomic Energy Agency, 'Implementation of the NPT Safeguards Agreement in the Syrian Arab Republic', GOV/2010/11, at para. 2.
[86] See Garwood-Gowers, n. 81, at 282–5. See also 'Legal and Procedural Issues Associated with the *Jus ad Bellum*' in the Introduction.

## 7.4 Pre-empting the Development of a Threat of an Armed Attack

challenge to the principles on which, however imperfectly, world peace and stability have rested for the last fifty-eight years. My concern is that, if it were to be adopted, it could set precedents that resulted in a proliferation of the unilateral and lawless use of force, with or without justification.[87]

Following this, the High Level Panel on Threats, Challenges and Change was established and published its final report, 'A More Secure World: Our Shared Responsibility', in 2004.[88] On the issue of self-defence the report adopted the position that 'a threatened State, according to long established international law, can take military action as long as the threatened attack is *imminent*, no other means would deflect it and the action is proportionate'.[89] Notably, this was distinguished from a situation 'where the threat in question is not imminent but still claimed to be real: for example the acquisition, with allegedly hostile intent, of nuclear weapons-making capability'.[90] In these circumstances, the Panel noted:

if there are good arguments for preventive military action, with good evidence to support them, they should be put to the Security Council, which can authorize such an action if it chooses to. If it does not so choose, there will be, by definition, time to pursue other strategies, including persuasion, negotiation, deterrence and containment – and to visit again the military option.[91]

In justifying its position, the Panel was well aware of the potentially greater destructive effect of permitting such a doctrine:

For those impatient with such a response, the answer must be that, in a world full of perceived potential threats, the risk to the global order and the norm of non-intervention on which it continues to be based is simply too great for the legality of unilateral preventive action, as distinct from collectively endorsed action, to be accepted. Allowing one to so act is to allow all.[92]

Ultimately, the Panel was clear that it did not '*favour the rewriting or reinterpretation of Article 51*'.[93] In his follow-up report, 'In Larger Freedom: Towards Development, Security and Human Rights for All', in March 2005, the UN Secretary-General adopted a similar position,[94] concluding that '[i]mminent threats are fully covered by Article 51 [of the UN Charter], which

---

[87] UN Secretary-General Kofi Annan, Address to the General Assembly, New York, 23 September 2003, available at: www.un.org/webcast/ga/58/statements/sg2eng030923.htm.
[88] Report of the Secretary-General's High-Level Panel on Threats, Challenges and Change, A More Secure World: Our Shared Responsibility, UN Doc. A/59/565, 2 December 2004.
[89] Ibid., at para. 188. This was also a reference back to the principles of necessity and proportionality. See Section 6.3.
[90] Ibid.. [91] Ibid., at para. 190. [92] Ibid., at para. 191.
[93] Ibid., at para. 192 (emphasis in original).
[94] UN Secretary-General, In Larger Freedom: Towards Development, Security and Human Rights for All, UN Doc. A/59/2005, 21 March 2005, at para. 122. Further details of this report are available at: https://digitallibrary.un.org/record/550204?ln=en.

safeguards the inherent right of sovereign States to defend themselves against armed attack'.[95]

Both reports were, therefore, dismissive of the attempts by the Bush administration to broaden the meaning of imminence. Nonetheless, while they rejected 'the doctrine of pre-emption theorized by the US President George W. Bush in the 2002 National Security Strategy document'[96] they nonetheless interpreted the right of self-defence 'in a way that UN bodies have been loath to do until now' in supporting the taking of action against 'imminent' threats of armed attack.[97] However, and as Noam Lubell observes, '[w]hile it is the UN Charter's apparent renunciation of anticipatory self-defence which supplies the opponents of such action with their most potent ammunition, it is also through developments under the UN auspices which provide support for a limited form of anticipatory self-defence'.[98]

During the debates that ensued regarding the reports of the High-Level Panel and the UN Secretary-General within the UN,[99] the position taken in them on the issue of imminent threats was expressly accepted by many states,[100] while many other states condemned this very aspect of the reports.[101] Pakistan, for example, stated that Article 51 'provides for the use of force in self-defence only in case of an actual attack against a Member State'[102] while Vietnam was equally clear when it stated that

> Article 51 of the Charter is clear and restrictive in the sense that the inherent right of individual or collective self-defence can be employed only if an armed attack occurs against a Member State. We do not believe, therefore, that Article 51 provides an expanded scope for permitting States to take military action on the basis of a perceived imminent threat.[103]

The Non-Aligned Movement, representing 125 states, issued a position paper in 2005 emphasising the same point.[104] Subsequently, following the

---

[95] Ibid., at para. 124.
[96] Natalino Ronzitti, 'The Expanding Law of Self-Defence' (2006) 11 *Journal of Conflict & Security Law* 343, at 345. See also Christine Gray, 'A Crisis of Legitimacy for the UN Collective Security System?' (2007) 56 *International & Comparative Law Quarterly* 157, at 161.
[97] Ronzitti, ibid., at 346.    [98] Lubell, n. 7, at 699.
[99] For an account of these debates see Olivier Corten, *The Law against War: The Prohibition on the Use of Force in Contemporary International Law*, 2nd ed. (Hart, 2021), at 419–27; Ruys, n. 3, at 338–42; Gray, n. 96, at 160–4.
[100] These included, for example, the United States, United Kingdom, Australia, Israel, Germany, Liechtenstein, Singapore, Uganda, Switzerland and Republic of Korea.
[101] These included, for example, Turkey, Argentina, Mexico, Pakistan, Vietnam, Belarus, Bangladesh, Algeria, Iran, Cuba, Costa Rica, Egypt, China, India, Syria, Malaysia and Indonesia.
[102] See UN Doc. A/59/PV.86, 6 April 2005, at 4–7.
[103] See UN Doc. A/59/PV.89, 8 April 2005, at 22.
[104] See UN Doc. A/59/565 and A/59/565CORR.1, 28 February 2005, at paras. 23–4.

## 7.4 Pre-empting the Development of a Threat of an Armed Attack

2005 World Summit, and perhaps in recognition of the disagreement over the issue, the Outcome document of the Summit contained no mention of Article 51 or self-defence, let alone preventative self-defence, although perhaps one might be able to read an implicit rejection of pre-emptive self-defence in the document's conclusion that 'the relevant provisions of the Charter are sufficient to address the full range of threats to international peace and security'.[105] In any case, this appeared to reaffirm Article 51 and its 'if an armed attack occurs' pre-requisite for the invocation of the right of self-defence.

Outside of the UN, open support for the doctrine of pre-emptive self-defence was limited, with Australia expressing some support for the doctrine, particularly following the Bali bombings on 12 October 2002.[106] However, while through its use of the rhetoric of pre-emptive self-defence being employed against 'terrorists' and 'rogue states' the Bush administration perhaps thought that it was restricting by whom the right could be invoked, it is unlikely that it could have done so.[107] It was, in this sense, somewhat ironic that additional support for the doctrine was provided by Iran[108] and North Korea,[109] who were two of the three states that had constituted former President Bush's 'axis of evil'.

Even the United Kingdom, which has long claimed to have a 'special relationship' with the United States, did not accept a broad right of pre-emptive self-defence as set out by the Bush administration, although it arguably continues to accept a rather expansionist reading of 'imminence'. For example, in representing what is stated to be a 'consistent position of successive United Kingdom Governments',[110] the UK's former Attorney-General, Lord Goldsmith, provided a legal opinion to the former UK Prime Minister,

---

[105] 2005 World Summit Outcome, UN Doc. A/RES/60/1, 24 October 2005, at para. 79.

[106] BBC News, 'Australia Ready to Strike Abroad', 1 December 2002, available at: http://news.bbc.co.uk/1/hi/world/asia-pacific/2532443.stm. Despite apparent support for the Bush doctrine of pre-emptive self-defence following the Bali bombings, no mention was subsequently made of pre-emptive self-defence in Australia's National Security Strategy in either 2003 or 2005, perhaps indicating some ambivalence in its support. Although see Nicole Abadee and Donald R. Rothwell, 'The Howard Doctrine: Australia and Anticipatory Self-Defence against Terrorist Attacks' (2007) 26 *Australian Yearbook of International Law* 19, where it is argued that the Australian position is closer to the classic notion of anticipatory self-defence than to the Bush doctrine of pre-emptive self-defence.

[107] Robert Knox, 'Civilizing Interventions? Race, War and International Law' (2013) 26 *Cambridge Review of International Affairs* 111, at 114.

[108] Nazila Fathi, 'Iran Says It May Pre-Empt Attack against Its Nuclear Facilities', *New York Times*, 20 August 2004, available at: www.nytimes.com/2004/08/20/world/iran-says-it-may-pre-empt-attack-against-its-nuclear-facilities.html.

[109] UN Doc. S/2003/681, 1 July 2003; *Keesing's* (2003) 45238.

[110] Attorney-General, House of Lords, Hansard, 21 April 2004, col. 370.

Tony Blair, on 7 March 2003, in the lead up to the Iraq invasion, in which it was stated that:

> Force may be used in self-defence if there is an actual or imminent threat of an armed attack ... The concept of what is imminent may depend on the circumstances. Different considerations may apply, for example, where the risk is of attack from terrorists sponsored or harboured by a particular State, or where there is a threat of an attack by nuclear weapons. *However, in my opinion there must be some degree of imminence.* I am aware that the USA has been arguing for recognition of a broad doctrine of a right to use force to pre-empt danger in the future. If this means more than a right to respond proportionally to an imminent attack (and I understand that the doctrine is intended to carry that connotation) *this is not a doctrine which, in my opinion, exists or is recognized in international law.*[111]

Furthermore, it was noted in the European Union's Fact-Finding Mission on the Conflict in Georgia that self-defence cannot be taken to counter 'potential or abstract' threats but that there must be a 'concrete danger of an imminent attack' which is 'objectively verifiable'[112] and, with a few exceptions which include individuals mainly based within the United States,[113] 'legal scholars have almost in unison denounced the doctrine of [pre-emptive] self-defence' as presented by the Bush administration.[114]

### 7.4.2.3 *Pre-emptive Self-Defence and the International Court of Justice*

The ICJ had a further opportunity to pronounce on the issue of preventative self-defence following the events of 9/11 and the arguments of the United States regarding pre-emptive self-defence that were advanced subsequently. However, in the *Armed Activities* case the Court maintained the line it had taken on this issue in the *Nicaragua* case.[115] After noting that 'the position of

---

[111] The advice is available at: www.theguardian.com/politics/2005/apr/28/election2005.uk (emphases added).

[112] Report of the Independent International Fact-Finding Mission on the Conflict in Georgia, September 2009, vol. II, at paras. 254–6, available at: www.mpil.de/de/pub/publikationen/archiv/ independent_international_fact.cfm.

[113] See, for example, William H. Taft and Todd F. Buchwald, 'Preemption, Iraq, and International Law' (2003) 97 *American Journal of International Law* 557.

[114] Deeks, n. 2, at 663; Ruys, n. 3, at 322; Greenwood, n. 3, at 15 ('In so far as talk of a doctrine of "pre-emption" is intended to refer to a broader right of self-defence to respond to threats that might materialize at some time in the future, such a doctrine has no basis in law.'). Sean D. Murphy, 'The Doctrine of Pre-Emptive Self-Defense' (2005) 50 *Villanova Law Review* 699; Terry D. Gill, 'The Temporal Dimension of Self-Defense: Anticipation, Pre-Emption, Prevention and Immediacy', in Michael N. Schmitt and Jelena Pejic (eds.), *International Law and Armed Conflict: Exploring the Faultlines: Essays in Honour of Yoram Dinstein* (Martinus Nijhoff, 2007), 113.

[115] *Case Concerning Armed Activities on the Territory of the Congo (Democratic Republic of Congo v. Uganda)* (2005), Judgment ICJ Reports 168, at para. 143.

the [Ugandan] High Command is that it is necessary "to secure Uganda's legitimate security interests" ... [t]he specified security needs are essentially preventative',[116] it went on to state that:

> Article 51 of the Charter may justify a use of force in self-defence only within the strict confines there laid down. It does not allow the use of force by a State to protect perceived security interests beyond these parameters. Other means are available to a concerned State, including, in particular, recourse to the Security Council.[117]

While it has been commented that the Court has rather 'shied away' from addressing the issue,[118] this pronouncement of the Court can arguably be seen as a rather thinly veiled reference to – indeed, rejection of – the proposed right of pre-emptive self-defence.

### 7.4.3 The Obama Doctrine of 'Necessary Force'

During the presidency of US President Barack Obama, the United States attempted to move beyond – or at least blur the debate regarding – the doctrine of pre-emptive self-defence that was such a defining aspect of his predecessor's time in office and which was so associated with the catastrophic intervention in Iraq in 2003. Indeed, the US National Security Strategy of May 2010 struck a somewhat different tone:

> The United States must reserve the right to act unilaterally if necessary to defend our nation and our interests, yet we will also seek to adhere to standards that govern the use of force. Doing so strengthens those who act in line with international standards, while isolating and weakening those who do not. We will also outline a clear mandate and specific objectives and thoroughly consider the consequences – intended and unintended – of our actions.[119]

The document steered clear of the language of pre-emptive self-defence, yet this did not mean that the position of the United States on self-defence had become any more benign. On the contrary, while the 2010 NSS paid lip service to the 'standards that govern the use of force', no effort was even made to link what the current author has termed the Obama doctrine of 'necessary force' with these traditional standards, including the concept of an 'armed attack' or the imminent threat of one.[120] The Bush administration had, at least, made an

---

[116] Ibid.   [117] Ibid., at para. 148.
[118] Niaz A. Shah, 'Self-Defence, Anticipatory Self-Defence and Pre-Emption: International Law's Response to Terrorism' (2007) 12 *Journal of Conflict & Security Law* 95, at 100.
[119] The White House, The National Security Strategy of the United States, May 2010, at 22, available at:https://obamawhitehouse.archives.gov/sites/default/files/rss_viewer/national_security_strategy.pdf.
[120] See, in general, Christian Henderson, 'The 2010 National Security Strategy of the United States and the Obama Doctrine of "Necessary Force"' (2010) 15 *Journal of Conflict & Security*

effort to link its doctrine of pre-emptive self-defence with these traditional and generally accepted standards of international law. By contrast, the Obama administration's promises to adhere to the standards of international law, while reserving 'the right to act unilaterally if necessary to defend our nation' and, even more controversially, 'our interests',[121] is vague, uncertain and, some might say, more dangerous and threatening than the rhetoric and legal reasoning of its predecessor.

President Trump's isolationist and nationalistic approach towards the international community meant that there was little reference to international law, let alone the standards governing the resort to force, in his administration's 2017 National Security Strategy.[122] However, it was interesting, if not totally surprising given the political ties between the two administrations, that the Biden administration in the 2022 National Security Strategy stuck closely to the position set out previously by the Obama administration.[123] Indeed, the Strategy stated that:

America will not hesitate to use force when necessary to defend our national interests. But we will do so as the last resort and only when the objectives and mission are clear and achievable, consistent with our values and laws, alongside non-military tools, and the mission is undertaken with the informed consent of the American people.[124]

Yet, unlike with the Obama administration's strategy, except for the assertions that it would act 'consistent with domestic and international law' when using 'force to disrupt and degrade terrorist groups that are plotting attacks against the United States, our people, or our diplomatic and military facilities abroad',[125] and that it would 'limit the use of force to circumstances where it is necessary to protect our national security interests and consistent with

---

*Law* 403. See also Christine Gray, 'President Obama's 2010 United States National Security Strategy and International Law on the Use of Force' (2011) 10 *Chinese Journal of International Law* 35.

[121] See Section 6.2.2.2 on the targeting of a state's 'interests' as constituting an armed attack for the purposes of the right of self-defence.

[122] The White House, National Security Strategy of the United States of America, December 2017, available at: https://trumpwhitehouse.archives.gov/wp-content/uploads/2017/12/NSS-Final-12-18-2017-0905.pdf. It did say that '[w]e must also deter, disrupt, and defeat potential threats before they reach the United States. We will target jihadist terrorists and transnational criminal organizations at their source and dismantle their networks of support' (at 7) and that '[t]he U.S. military and other operating agencies will take direct action against terrorist networks and pursue terrorists who threaten the homeland and U.S. citizens regardless of where they are' (at 11). See, generally, Heike Krieger, 'Trumping International Law? Implication of the 2016 US Presidential Election for the International Legal Order', *EJIL Talk!*, 3 January 2017, available at www.ejiltalk.org/trumping-international-law-the-implications-of-the-2016-us-presidential-election-for-the-international-legal-order/.

[123] The White House, National Security Strategy of the United States of America, October 2022, available at: https://nssarchive.us/wp-content/uploads/2022/10/Biden-Harris-Administrations-National-Security-Strategy-10.2022.pdf.

[124] Ibid., at 20.  [125] Ibid., at 31.

international law',[126] there were no other references to the standards governing the use of force.

## 7.5 REASSESSING 'IMMINENCE' IN THE LIGHT OF CONTEMPORARY THREATS: THE 'BETHLEHEM PRINCIPLES' AND BEYOND

Emerging from the *Caroline* incident over 150 years ago, today '[t]he practice of states and views of commentators clearly demonstrate that the presence of imminence will often be a major factor in their position on anticipatory action'[127] and 'is, in fact, often the key factor upon which the legitimacy of such action will turn'.[128] However, there remains much uncertainty regarding the meaning of the notion of imminence. Dictionaries throw up definitions such as 'about to happen'[129] or 'coming or likely to happen very soon',[130] and it has been claimed that '[b]y definition, it relates to a future event'.[131] Yet, ultimately, and as Dinstein has pointed out, '[t]here is no authoritative definition of imminence in the context of an armed attack'.[132] In addition, or arguably as a result, 'imminence may mean different things to different people: either too little or too much. Hence, its usefulness is doubtful'.[133]

While there has been a general rejection of pre-emptive self-defence and an increased express acceptance of anticipatory self-defence, both implicit and explicit arguments have nonetheless begun to (re)emerge that existing doctrine and, in particular, the restrictive temporal conception of imminence, does not accord with the operational realities faced by states,[134] particularly in the context of attacks or threats of imminent attack by non-state actors.[135] It would seem that, given the *modus operandi* of these actors, while not going so far as to fully embrace pre-emptive self-defence against future threats and those responsible for them, a further attempted dismantling of the traditional conception of 'temporal imminence' towards what might be described as 'contextual imminence' has gathered some momentum. Indeed, as the Chatham House Principles of International Law on the Use of Force by States in Self-Defence, which were published in 2006, framed it: 'In the context of contemporary threats imminence cannot be construed by reference to a temporal criterion only, but must reflect the wider circumstances of the threat.'[136]

---

[126] Ibid., at 43.   [127] Lubell, n. 7, at 700.   [128] Ibid., at 701.
[129] *Oxford English Dictionary*.   [130] *Cambridge Dictionary*.   [131] Lubell, n. 7, at 699.
[132] Dinstein, n. 6, at para. 612.   [133] Ibid.
[134] Daniel Bethlehem, 'Principles Relevant to the Scope of a State's Right of Self-Defense against an Imminent or Actual Armed Attack by Nonstate Actors' (2012) **106** *American Journal of International Law* 769, at 772.
[135] See Chapter 8 for a general discussion on self-defence in the context of attacks by non-state actors.
[136] Elizabeth Wilmshurst, 'The Chatham House Principles of International Law on the Use of Force in Self-Defence' (2006) **55** *International & Comparative Law Quarterly* 963, at 967.

Firmly endorsing this view, and in attempting to take things forward from the Bush doctrine of pre-emptive self-defence, the UK Attorney-General, Jeremy Wright, made the argument in January 2017 that 'much has changed even since the immediate response to 9/11'.[137] Indeed, even as recently as 9/11 the technological advances that appear to be the driving force behind a further step in the attempted (d)evolution of the concept of imminence did not exist. As such, the UK government has taken the position that '[a]n effective concept of imminence cannot therefore be limited to be assessed solely on temporal factors. The Government must take a view on a broader range of indicators of the likelihood of an attack, whilst also applying the twin requirements of proportionality and necessity.'[138] Elaborating earlier upon this general position, in 2006 the Chatham House Principles stated that:

Whether the attack is imminent depends upon the nature of the threat and the possibility of dealing effectively with it at any given stage. Factors that may be taken into account include: the *gravity* of the threatened attack – whether what is threatened is a catastrophic use of Weapons of Mass Destruction (WMD); *capability* – for example, whether the relevant State or terrorist organization is in possession of WMD, or merely of material or component parts to be used in its manufacture; and the *nature* of the attack – including the possible risks of making a wrong assessment of the danger. Other factors may also be relevant, such as the geographical situation of the victim State, and the past record of attacks.[139]

In similar terms, the Leiden Policy Recommendations on Counter-Terrorism and International Law, which were published in 2010, stated that:

Whether an attack may be regarded as imminent falls to be assessed by reference to the immediacy of the attack, its nature, and gravity. There must be a reasonable and objective basis for concluding that an attack will be launched, while bearing in mind that terrorists typically rely on the unpredictability of attacks in order to spread terror among civilians. Armed force may be used only when it is anticipated that delay would result in an inability by the threatened state effectively to avert the attack.[140]

---

[137] United Kingdom Attorney-General Jeremy Wright, 'The Modern Law of Self-Defence', 11 January 2017, available at:https://assets.publishing.service.gov.uk/government/uploads/system/uploads/attachment_data/file/583171/170111_Imminence_Speech.pdf.

[138] House of Lords, House of Commons, Joint Committee on Human Rights, 'The Government's Policy on the Use of Drones for Targeted Killing: Government's Response to the Committee's Second Report of Session 2015–16', Fourth Report of Session 2016–17, HL Paper 49, HC 747, at para. 14. See Section 6.3 for more on the twin requirements of necessity and proportionality.

[139] Chatham House Principles, n. 136, at 967.

[140] 'Leiden Policy Recommendations on Counter-Terrorism and International Law', in Larissa Van Den Herik and Nico Schrijver (eds.), *Counter-Terrorism Strategies in a Fragmented Legal Order: Meeting the Challenges* (Cambridge University Press, 2013), 706, at para. 46.

However, and in a notable article published in 2012, Sir Daniel Bethlehem, a former Legal Adviser at the UK Foreign and Commonwealth Office, set out what have come to be known as the 'Bethlehem Principles' in which it was argued that there is 'little scholarly consensus on what is properly meant by "imminence" in the context of contemporary threats' and that 'the concept needs to be further refined and developed'.[141] In attempting to contribute to this development, Bethlehem advanced the relevant contextual factors that, in his view, should be taken into account in any assessment:

Whether an armed attack may be regarded as 'imminent' will fall to be assessed by reference to all relevant circumstances, including (a) the nature and immediacy of the threat, (b) the probability of an attack, (c) whether the anticipated attack is part of a concerted pattern of continuing armed activity, (d) the likely scale of the attack and the injury, loss, or damage likely to result therefrom in the absence of mitigating action, and (e) the likelihood that there will be other opportunities to undertake effective action in self-defense that may be expected to cause less serious collateral injury, loss, or damage.[142]

These contextual factors clearly played a role in the United Kingdom's decision to launch an RAF drone strike on 21 August 2015 which targeted and killed Reyaad Kahn, a British national who was located in Syria and who, it was claimed, was 'planning and directing armed attacks against the UK' which were 'part of a series of actual and foiled attempts to attack the UK and [its] allies'.[143] Indeed, a little over a year later, the UK Attorney-General, Jeremy Wright, who had provided the UK Prime Minister with the legal basis for the action, expressly endorsed the Bethlehem Principles.[144] These contextual factors, propounded by Daniel Bethlehem in 2012, were also expressly approved in a speech by Brian Egan, Legal Adviser to the US Department of State in 2016,[145] and by the Australian Attorney-General, George Brandis, in a speech on 11 April 2017.[146]

---

[141] Bethlehem, n. 134, at 773.   [142] Ibid., Principle 8.

[143] HC Deb, Hansard, 7 September 2015, col. 26, available at: https://publications.parliament.uk/pa/cm201516/cmhansrd/cm150907/debtext/150907-0001.htm. See Section 8.5 for more on targeted killings.

[144] In regard to the Bethlehem Principles: 'these are the right factors to consider in asking whether or not an armed attack by non-state actors is imminent and the UK Government follows and endorses that approach'. Wright, n. 137.

[145] Brian Egan, 'International Law, Legal Diplomacy, and the Counter-ISIL Campaign: Some Observations' (2016) 92 *International Law Studies* 234, at 239.

[146] Australian Attorney-General George Brandis, 'The Right of Self-Defence against Imminent Armed Attack in International Law', *EJIL Talk!*, 25 May 2017, available at www.ejiltalk.org/the-right-of-self-defence-against-imminent-armed-attack-in-international-law/.

## 7.5.1 From 'Temporal' to 'Contextual' Imminence

Questions thus arise as to how 'contextual' imminence is to be viewed and how it might operate in practice. Of course, by definition it inherently turns on the facts of each case, and is not argued to be based upon a single factor, but instead by several factors that are to be weighed together in any decision to resort to self-defence. In this respect, there appears to be several key factors that are of relevance.

### 7.5.1.1 The Expected Timing of the Attack

While the states that have endorsed the Bethlehem Principles have committed themselves to only taking action in the context of a threat that is 'imminent',[147] it is incorrect, or perhaps even disingenuous, given what has been discussed in this chapter on the temporality of a threat to use this term in these circumstances or, at least, its use needs explaining and qualifying. The Bethlehem Principles, which have, at least, been expressly accepted by the governments of the United Kingdom, the United States and Australia, claim that '[t]he absence of specific evidence of where an attack will take place or of the precise nature of an attack does not preclude a conclusion that an armed attack is imminent for purposes of the exercise of a right of self-defense, provided that there is a reasonable and objective basis for concluding that an armed attack is imminent'.[148] While this focused on the 'where' and 'how' of a future attack, the UK Attorney-General went further in saying that 'we will not always know where and *when* an attack will take place, or the precise nature of the attack. But where the evidence supports an assessment that an attack is imminent' action will be taken.[149]

This particular point prompted the UK Joint Parliamentary Committee on Human Rights to comment that 'the Attorney-General's continued reference to "imminence" shows that what the Government describes as "temporal factors" are still important. In other words, evidence of *when* an attack is likely to take place must still be relevant to any decision as to whether there is a right to use force in self-defence' although 'it is not clear what it considers to be the relevance of when a threatened attack might take place' or 'the relevance of the timing of any possible future attack when deciding whether the right to self-defence is triggered'.[150] It is, however, this very obfuscation that makes

---

[147] As Jeremy Wright, the UK Attorney-General, stated in setting out the UK's position on self-defence, 'this approach does not, however, in any way dispense with the concept of imminence'. As the Attorney-General continued, this position 'is a very long way from supporting any notion of a doctrine of pre-emptive strikes against threats that are more remote ... It is absolutely not the position of the UK Government that armed force may be used to prevent a threat from materialising in the first place'. Wright, n. 137.
[148] Bethlehem, n. 134, Principle 8.   [149] Wright, n. 137 (emphasis added).
[150] Joint Committee on Human Rights Report: Government's Response, n. 138, at para. 16.

contextual imminence such an attractive doctrine to states with the power and inclination to project their military forces abroad and, as discussed in Section 7.5.3, a concerning one for those who wish to preserve necessity as a restraining rather than enabling criterion in the law of self-defence.

### 7.5.1.2 Capabilities of the Potential Attacker

In his speech, Jeremy Wright also claimed that '[i]t is obvious that much has changed since 1837. We are a long way from being able to see troops massing on the horizon. The frontline has irretrievably altered.'[151] Contemporary attacks are often unpredictable, secretive and potentially instantaneous, thus meaning that where an opportunity to prevent a threat coming to fruition presents itself action should be taken, as it is often not possible for a state to know when it is faced with the last window of opportunity to take action.[152] This is particularly pertinent in the case of attacks of a terrorist or cyber nature, for example, but is also of relevance in the context of WMD, which can be developed covertly and launched at the touch of a button. In particular, the threat posed by contemporary potential attackers 'plays on the fear of the unknown, and raises the question of engaging in self-defence to prevent a possible future attack without knowledge of what it might be'.[153] As such, '[t]he challenge posed in the context of imminence is that, in effect, we are faced with a threat, for which we cannot positively identify how soon it might happen, where it will originate from, where it will strike, or even who precisely will be behind the attack'.[154]

However, as seen in Section 7.4.2, states have not, expressly at least, demonstrated a perceived need to stretch the concept of imminence to meet the contemporary threats set out by the Bush administration following the attacks of 9/11. Furthermore, while there is a good level of acceptance of the applicability in principle of the rules and principles of the *jus ad bellum* to cyber operations, there has, to date, been little appetite expressed for bending the rules to enable a broader concept of imminence in meeting the threat posed by this contemporary capability when in the hands of adversaries.[155]

### 7.5.1.3 Gravity of the Threatened Attack

The gravity or scale of the effects or consequences of a threatened attack should it materialise may permit a rethinking of the traditional temporal

---

[151] Wright, n. 137. See also Greenwood, n. 3, at 16.
[152] This is linked to the intention stated in the 2002 NSS that the United States would be prepared to act in certain circumstances 'even if uncertainty remains as to the time and place of the enemy's attack'. 2002 NSS, n. 68, at 15.
[153] Lubell, n. 7, at 707.   [154] Ibid.   [155] See, further, Sections 1.7.4 and 6.2.5.2.

requirement of imminence. In this respect, it has been argued that the prospect of such threats 'can reasonably be treated as imminent in circumstances where an attack by conventional means would not be so regarded'[156] and 'it is less about the source of the threat, and more about the gravity of its consequences should it materialize ... [a]ccordingly, it requires an examination of whether the scale of the threat might affect the understanding of imminence'.[157] Yet, while this is a 'seemingly realistic approach, precisely how this factor of gravity will in fact affect the imminence, is not always clear'.[158] For example, if we are to accept a gravity threshold for an armed attack in giving rise to the right of self-defence,[159] does this also apply to the taking of action against threats of attack under contextual imminence?[160] Will action be lawful if the gravity is deemed not to be significant but the other relevant factors of contextual imminence are otherwise satisfied? Furthermore, at what point exactly along the 'temporal continuum'[161] will action be deemed necessary? Given the gravity of the threat, is mere suspicion of the development of a threat sufficient or will a threat still need to be close to or at the time of potential launch? There is also an inherent difficulty in measuring and assessing the proportionality of any given action in self-defence against a threat when the gravity of the resulting armed attack is at that point uncertain.[162]

### 7.5.1.4 *Intent of the Potential Attacker*

The factors considered thus far cannot by themselves provide the basis for the launching of armed action in self-defence. Indeed, states may look around and perceive potential attacks with serious consequences emanating from many places and by various actors. What, however, may arguably change a potential threat into a potent one is the *intent* of the potential attacker.[163] Yet, determinations regarding the intent of a particular actor would need to be based upon more than general animosity and political rhetoric or subjective perceptions of the actor's intentions and aims. Claims that a group is 'terrorist' in nature, for example, will often be disputed and, in any case, terrorism is a concept that

---

[156] Greenwood, n. 3, at 16. As the 2002 NSS argued, the 'greater the threat, the greater the risk of inaction'. 2002 NSS, n. 68, at 15.
[157] Lubell, n. 7, at 708.  [158] Ibid., at 709–10.  [159] See Section 6.2.5.
[160] However, as Lubell notes, if one considers minor incidents as constituting armed attacks it may be prudent to require a higher threshold for anticipatory action in the light of threats of such attacks. Lubell, n. 7, at 708–9.
[161] Deeks, n. 2, at 663.
[162] Proportionality is a key limitation upon the right of self-defence as set out in Section 6.3.2.
[163] Chatham House Principles, n. 136, at 967. It has been argued that, while this hostile intent is necessary for a violation of the prohibition of the threat or use of force in Section 2.6, it is not for an armed attack in Section 6.2.4 as, faced with an actual armed attack, states may defend themselves without having to determine the intent of those carrying out the attack.

lacks a definition, which means that it is open to subjective interpretation as to whether a particular group is, or is not, terrorist in nature.[164]

Questions then arise as to how we might determine intent. Are specific plans required or do the preparations need to go beyond mere planning? In any case, it may be that general negative perceptions of a potential attacker combined with, for example, a developing capability to carry out a potentially serious attack may mean that a strike in self-defence is made more acceptable, as the Israeli attack on the al-Kibar site in Syria in 2007 perhaps demonstrates.[165] As the Chatham House Principles noted, '[w]hile the possession of WMD without a hostile intent to launch an attack does not in itself give rise to a right of self-defence, the difficulty of determining intent and the catastrophic consequences of making an error will be relevant factors in any determination of imminence made by another State'.[166]

### 7.5.1.5 The Occurrence of Previous Attacks

Although moving the issue outside of the realms of pure preventative self-defence, previous attacks from a state or group may, however, impact upon the perception of intent for the purposes of assessing contextual imminence in various ways. First, '[t]he difference is plain between self-defence after and in advance of an attack: in the former situation, the attacker has already demonstrated an intent and willingness to attack'.[167] While this may be demonstrable from a single attack, Bethlehem referred to a 'concerted pattern of continuing armed activity' in his Principles as being of relevance.[168] In this respect, a previous attack or 'a concerted pattern of continuing armed activity' might reasonably affect how a use of force taken ostensibly with a possible future attack in mind is perceived, in that not only will the armed attack criterion have been possibly satisfied[169] but it also 'allows a more reliable prediction that a threat within this pattern will materialize with sufficient gravity'.[170]

Secondly, however, it may also give rise to a situation of what might be described as 'permanent imminence'.[171] As questioned by the UK Joint

---

[164] For more on the attempts at defining terrorism and the problems in doing so see, in general, Ben Saul, *Defining Terrorism in International Law* (Oxford University Press, 2006). The questions regarding whether terrorists are able to perpetrate armed attacks and how a victim state may respond are addressed in Section 6.2.1 and, generally, in Chapter 8.

[165] See Section 7.4.2.1.2.   [166] Chatham House Principles, n. 136, at 968.

[167] Deeks, n. 2, at 664. See also Murphy, n. 114, at 735.   [168] Bethlehem, n. 134, Principle 4.

[169] See Section 6.2.5.4. on gravity and the accumulation of events theory.

[170] Dapo Akande and Thomas Liefländer, 'Clarifying Necessity, Imminence and Proportionality in the Law of Self-Defence' (2013) **107** *American Journal of International Law* 563, at 565.

[171] Marc Weller, 'Permanent Imminence of Armed Attacks: Resolution 2249 (2015) and the Right to Self-Defence against Designated Terrorist Groups', *EJIL Talk!*, 25 November 2015, available at: www.ejiltalk.org/permanent-imminence-of-armed-attacks-resolution-2249-2015-and-the-right-to-self-defence-against-designated-terrorist-groups/.

Parliamentary Committee on Human Rights, '[o]nce a specific individual has been identified as being involved in planning or directing attacks in the UK, does the wider meaning of imminence mean that an ongoing threat from that individual is, in effect, permanently imminent?'[172] Given that the authorisation for the UK's drone strike against Reyaad Khan had been given by the UK National Security Council in May 2015, with the eventual lethal strike only taking place on 21 August 2015, it is arguable that this was a reflection of the permanent imminence of the threat posed by that particular individual.[173]

The UN Security Council also appears to have alluded to the possibility of permanent imminence. Resolution 2249 (2015), which was adopted following the attacks in Sousse, in Ankara, over the Sinai, in Beirut, and in Paris in November 2015, confirmed that so-called Islamic State has 'the capability and the intention to carry out further attacks'.[174] By doing so the Council may have relieved states from having to demonstrate imminence before invoking their right of self-defence against this terrorist group.[175] Indeed, the Council had 'considered [Islamic State's] recent track record of attacks and concluded that it is safe to assume that there will be further such attacks, both in terms of capacity and intent'.[176]

Lastly, and alternatively, in the view of the United States:

once a State has lawfully resorted to force in self-defense against a particular armed group following an actual or imminent armed attack by that group, *it is not necessary as a matter of international law to reassess whether an armed attack is imminent prior to every subsequent action taken against that group, provided that hostilities have not ended.*[177]

This is a controversial and confusing position, in that it seems to do away with an assessment of the imminence of an attack if a prior attack, or even an 'imminent' one, has already been responded to. The reason for this appears to be that the state concerned is now considered a party to an armed conflict with the group, thus blurring the lines between the applicability of the *jus ad bellum* and *jus in bello*.[178] This apparent conflation of these legal frameworks, or,

---

[172] House of Lords, House of Commons, Joint Committee on Human Rights, 'The Government's Policy on the Use of Drones for Targeted Killing', Second Report of Session 2015–16, HL Paper 141, HC 574, at para. 3.39.

[173] For more on this incident, see Section 8.5.    [174] UNSC Res. 2249 (2015), para. 1.

[175] The Joint Parliamentary Committee on Human Rights also said that 'we note that the broader interpretation of "imminence" preferred by the Government appears to have the implicit support of the UN Security Council in its most recent resolution concerning ISIL/Da'esh in Syria and Iraq (UNSCR 2249 (2015))'. Joint Committee on Human Rights Report, n. 172, at 3.36.

[176] Weller, n. 171.    [177] Egan, n. 145, at 239 (emphasis added).

[178] See Section 8.5 on targeted killing.

more accurately, the squeezing of the former into the latter, is a misunderstanding of their relationship and not widely accepted. It is generally agreed that, for a non-international armed conflict to exist between a state and a non-state armed group, the armed hostilities need to be both protracted and of a particular intensity, with the armed group concerned also needing to be sufficiently organised.[179] So while an assessment of imminence would be necessary prior to the first military action taken in response, unless a non-international armed conflict can be observed upon this basis, further imminence assessments would be required prior to each subsequent response in self-defence, and particularly if the conflict is subsequently seen to be taking place on the territories of more than one state.

### 7.5.2 Imminence and the Drone Strike on Iranian General Soleimani (2020)

Immediately following the strike on General Soleimani in January 2020, the Trump administration in the United States – and without seemingly realising the legal distinctions involved, or at least fully appreciating their nuances – attempted to navigate its justificatory discourse between the two ends of the temporal spectrum of self-defence. This was done primarily by, on the one hand, and as discussed in Section 6.2, setting out and stressing previous attacks and incidents that had been perpetrated both by the Iranian state itself and the Qods Forces-backed militia groups and, on the other hand, making general and vague claims that the strike was necessary to prevent 'imminent' attacks. This was combined with mixed and confusing signals as to the relative importance placed on both. While there were no simple and clear-cut divisions between the various justifications, certain trends were discernible with the seeming emergence of two, often parallel, claims.

The idea that Soleimani posed a threat of 'imminent' attack was at the forefront of the initial justifications proffered by the Trump administration.[180] In his first comment on the strike on 2 January 2020 President Trump himself made the claim that 'Soleimani was plotting imminent and sinister attacks on American diplomats and military personnel, but we caught him in the act and terminated him'.[181] No indication was given as to what these attacks were or what meaning the Trump administration was giving to the concept of 'imminence'. Against this background, the Trump administration's claim of an

---

[179] See ibid.
[180] It might plausibly be claimed that the references to 'imminence' were for domestic purposes, given that this would be necessary under US constitutional law for the President to be able to authorise force without seeking Congressional approval. It is, of course, impossible to say for certain.
[181] The White House, 'Remarks by President Trump on the Killing of Qasem Soleimani', 3 January 2020, available at:https://trumpwhitehouse.archives.gov/briefings-statements/remarks-president-trump-killing-qasem-soleimani/.

'imminent' threat by Soleimani received significant attention both in the general media and in academic legal commentary, with the Trump administration consistently pressed on what was meant by its use on this occasion and on the existence of the evidence, if any, to support it. Yet, through suggesting that they had 'caught him in the act' the President appeared to be making the claim that Soleimani presented a temporally imminent threat, that is, it was of a more immediate rather than a temporally remote or contextual nature.

That – at least some within – the Trump administration were basing the claim on temporal imminence can be seen in the fact that on two occasions members of the administration ventured to provide a definition of imminence. On 5 January 2020, the Chairman of the Joint Chiefs of Staff, General Mark A. Milley, stated that imminence was taken to mean '[d]ays, weeks',[182] while on 12 January the National Security Adviser, Robert C. O'Brien, declared it meant 'soon, quickly, in progress'.[183] While these temporal limitations were not perhaps as strict as those found within the *Caroline* correspondence,[184] they at least gave the impression of some certainty that an attack was forthcoming within the near – temporal – future. Yet, the imminent claim continued to be the focus of attention and the claim by these Trump administration officials that an attack was to occur within these periods was reportedly disputed by military and intelligence officials, who were apparently of the view that there was not the level of certainty in the intelligence to be able to claim that a strike was imminent, even within these time frames.[185] Indeed, it was suggested that General Soleimani had not yet even received permission from Iran's supreme leader to carry out an attack,[186] let alone was one temporally imminent.

With the increased pressure on the Trump administration to justify and explain its claim that Soleimani had posed such an imminent threat of attack which they had halted, and with it being unable to provide a satisfactory response, there was a noticeable subsequent shift towards contextual imminence. Indeed, while the Trump administration continued to assert that the threat of attack was 'imminent' (presumably in the temporal sense) it also moved to suggest that in this instance imminence (again, presumably in the temporal sense) was not required due to the series of prior attacks against the United States.

---

[182] Helene Cooper et al., 'As Tensions with Iran Escalated, Trump Opted for Most Extreme Measure', *New York Times*, 7 January 2020, available at: www.nytimes.com/2020/01/04/us/politics/trump-suleimani.html.

[183] Cathy Burke, 'NSA O'Brien: "Exquisite Intelligence" Showing Iran Wanted to Kill Americans', *Newsmax*, 12 January 2020, available at: www.newsmax.com/politics/obrien-iran-intelligence-embassies/2020/01/12/id/949441/.

[184] See Section 6.3.   [185] Cooper et al., n. 182.   [186] Ibid.

## 7.5 Reassessing 'Imminence' in the Light of Contemporary Threats

With the administration now continuously being required to defend its 'imminence' claim in increasingly uncomfortable ways, it was noticeable that the concept of 'imminence' had been entirely dropped from its justificatory discourse in its formal letter to the UN Security Council on 8 January 2020, with the letter making no mention of it and instead focused and elaborated upon a host of previous attacks by both the armed forces of Iran and the Qods-backed militia forces.[187] However, while the focus shifted firmly to completed attacks, these attacks were placed in the context of a 'series' of such attacks, as discussed in Chapter 6.[188] With this shift in emphasis, the justificatory discourse appeared, on the one hand, to be attempting to portray the United States as the victim of a contemporaneous – albeit somewhat intermittent – armed attack. Indeed, the Trump administration painted the picture of a 'campaign' against the United States.[189] While there is some support for the 'accumulation of events' theory providing a basis for invocation of the right of self-defence,[190] this is also something that the United States has not needed to express a view on given its position that *any* use of force can justify the invocation of the right of self-defence.[191] However, in this instance it may be that the United States took to portraying Soleimani and Iran as responsible for a series of attacks in order to justify the proportionality of the response taken, that is, the targeting and killing a high-ranking state official of Iran.

This change in approach by the Trump administration was perhaps illustrated most vividly – and in typical style – by President Trump himself in the form of a Tweet on 13 January 2020 in which he declared, largely in response to the public debate in regards to the imminence claim that there was a prospective imminent attack by Soleimani, but that 'it [didn't] really matter because of his horrible past!'[192] This arguably destroyed any remaining vestiges of the defensive veil from the justificatory discourse and made it difficult to avoid clearly labelling the operation as one of punitive armed reprisal or targeted killing.[193]

---

[187] See, for example, Letter dated 8 January 2020 from the Permanent Representative of the United States of America to the United Nations addressed to the President of the Security Council, UN Doc. S/2020/20, 9 January 2020. Imminence was also absent from the speech by the US Ambassador to the UN, Kelly Craft, the following day. See United States Mission to the United Nations, Remarks at a UN Security Council Debate on Upholding the UN Charter, 9 January 202, available at: https://usun.usmission.gov/remarks-at-a-un-security-council-debate-on-upholding-the-un-charter/.

[188] See Section 6.2.5.4.

[189] Zachary Cohen, 'Barr and Pompeo Shift Justification for Iran Strike from 'Imminent' Threat to Deterrence', *CNN*, 14 January 2020, available at: https://edition.cnn.com/2020/01/13/politics/pompeo-barr-soleimani-strike-iran-rationale/index.html.

[190] See Sections 6.2.5.4 and 6.3.2.1.     [191] See Section 6.2.5.1.

[192] See https://twitter.com/realdonaldtrump/status/1216754098382524422?lang=en.

[193] See Section 6.3.1.2 on armed reprisals and Section 8.5 on targeted killings.

Nonetheless, a key element of the Trump administration's overall shift to contextual imminence was its underpinning by a gradual shift in focus from the threat of *certain* future attack by Soleimani, and the Iranian state in general, to the past attacks and generally bad behaviour being *indicative* of a further attack and, therefore, requiring a defensive response. For example, on 7 January 2020, the Secretary of State, Mike Pompeo stated, in reference to the incidences that took place at the end of December, that '[i]f you're looking for imminence, you need look no further than the days that led up to the strike that was taken against Suleimani'.[194] Furthermore, the Trump administration also pressed the case that the action in self-defence was being taken 'in response to an *escalating* series of armed attacks',[195] with it beginning to appear that prior attacks were being presented as evidence that further, and potentially more serious, attacks were forthcoming.

This distinction, the Trump administration appeared to argue, changed the assessment regarding 'if', 'when' and 'where' an attack is to take place. In this respect, and unlike with temporal imminence, the administration was claiming that *certainty* is not required regarding any prospective attack, but rather some grounds, perhaps objectively reasonable grounds, to suspect that one is forthcoming. Indeed, the administration pressed the idea that imminence was not required where armed attacks 'already had occurred and were expected to occur again'.[196] Without more – and the Trump administration offered us no more – it seemed in this situation as if past events were being used as a predictive tool for future events. Members of the Trump Administration expressed this in different ways, with it being claimed that the action it took was on the balance of risk, in that it was taken with 'full situational awareness of risk and analysis'[197] and that in these situations the United States does not 'deal in certainties' but rather in 'probabilities'.[198]

There was some support for this view from within the scholarly community. While some commentators appeared to be of the view that the prior attacks

---

[194] Paul D. Shinkman, 'U.S. Backs Away from Claim on "Imminent" Soleimani Attack', *U.S. News*, 7 January 2020, available at: www.usnews.com/news/national-news/articles/2020-01-07/mike-pompeo-backs-away-from-claim-on-imminent-soleimani-attack

[195] UN Doc. S/2020/20, n.187 (emphasis added).

[196] U.S. Department of Defense, 'DoD General Counsel Remarks at BYU Law School', 4 March 2020, available at: www.defense.gov/Newsroom/Speeches/Speech/Article/2181868/dod-general-counsel-remarks-at-byu-law-school/.

[197] U.S. Department of State, 'Secretary Michael R. Pompeo with Chuck Todd of NBC Meet the Press', 5 January 2020, available at:https://kr.usembassy.gov/010520-secretary-michael-r-pompeo-with-chuck-todd-of-nbc-meet-the-press/.

[198] U.S. Department of Defense, Press Gaggle with Secretary of Defense Dr. Mark T. Esper and Chairman of the Joint Chiefs of Staff General Mark A. Milley, 6 January 2020, available at: www.defense.gov/Newsroom/Transcripts/Transcript/Article/2051321/press-gaggle-with-secretary-of-defense-dr-mark-t-esper-and-chairman-of-the-join/.

## 7.5 Reassessing 'Imminence' in the Light of Contemporary Threats

*impacted upon the way the law is to be interpreted*,[199] others, in taking what appeared to be a more moderate position, claimed that the prior attacks rather had *probative value* in demonstrating the resolve and capabilities of the adversary as well as the likelihood of further attacks from it.[200] Indeed, while such prior attacks are 'relevant to assessing future intentions and capabilities, they [do] not, standing alone, provide a legal justification' for military action.[201] In other words, they are 'relevant, albeit not sufficient, in assessing necessity'.[202]

Furthermore, and again in contrast to temporal imminence, there is no requirement for *immediacy* in the threat of attack. Indeed, the contextual imminence standard that the Trump administration was operating under meant that the prior attacks were presented as altering not just the *knowledge* calculus but also the *temporal* calculus in determining the necessity for self-defence. While the Trump administration maintained the view that the first use of force in self-defence was permissible against the threat of a temporally imminent attack, something that it said was supported by other 'like-minded states',[203] it claimed on more than one occasion that a focus on temporal imminence was a 'red herring' in circumstances such as these in which a state has already suffered attacks.[204] Indeed, in these situations there is no longer a requirement of 'knowing the exact time and place of the next attack'.[205]

---

[199] This appeared to be the position of Stefan Talmon and Miriam Heipertz, 'The U.S. Killing of Iranian General Qasem Soleimani: Of Wrong Trees and Red Herrings, and Why the Killing May be Lawful After All', *German Practice in International Law*, 23 January 2020, available at:https://gpil.jura.uni-bonn.de/2020/01/the-u-s-killing-of-iranian-general-qasem-soleimani-of-wrong-trees-and-red-herrings-and-why-the-killing-may-be-lawful-after-all/.

[200] As Marty Lederman has argued, recent completed attacks demonstrate 'resolve, plan, capability, etc'. See comments in response to Marko Milanovic, 'The Soleimani Strike and Self-Defence against an Imminent Armed Attack', *EJIL Talk!*, 7 January 2020, available at: www.ejiltalk.org/the-soleimani-strike-and-self-defence-against-an-imminent-armed-attack/. Geoffrey Corn and Rachel VanLandingham have also argued that the record of previous attacks is 'relevant to the assessment of intelligence indicating an adversaries capabilities and whether more was about to come'. Geoffrey S. Corn and Rachel Van Landingham, 'Lawful Self-Defense vs. Revenge Strikes: Scrutinizing Iran and U.S. Uses of Force under International Law', *Just Security*, 8 January 2020, available at www.justsecurity.org/67970/lawful-self-defense-vs-revenge-strikes-scrutinizing-iran-and-u-s-uses-of-force-under-international-law/. See Section 7.5.1.5 on the relevance of previous attacks.

[201] Corn and VanLandingham, ibid. (although they also note that '[t]he one qualifier to this is the possibility that these attacks are occurring in the context of an ongoing armed conflict between the United States and Iran').

[202] See comments in response to Milanovic, n. 200.

[203] 'DoD General Counsel Remarks at BYU Law School', n. 196.

[204] Ibid. This phrase was also used by the Attorney General, William Barr. See Masood Farivar and Ken Bredemeier, 'US Attorney General Calls Imminence of Iranian Threat a "Red Herring"', *Voice of America*, 13 January 2020, available at: www.voanews.com/middle-east/voa-news-iran/us-attorney-general-calls-imminence-iranian-threat-red-herring.

[205] Philip Rucker, John Hudson, Shane Harris and Josh Dawsey, '"Four embassies": The Anatomy of Trump's Unfounded Claim about Iran', *The Philadelphia Inquirer*, 14 January 2020, available at: www.inquirer.com/politics/nation/four-embassies-trump-iran-

While several commentators expressed the view that the legality of the United States' strike against Soleimani was contingent on it preventing a temporally imminent armed attack,[206] which was not the case, others came out in support of the US government's view, with the argument being made that all the focus on temporal imminence misunderstood the situation from a legal perspective in the context of a series of attacks.[207] Indeed, those who required temporal imminence in these situations were, in the words of Stefan Talmon, 'barking up the wrong tree'.[208]

Lastly, while temporal imminence requires at least some knowledge of *if* and *when* an attack is to take place, the contextual imminence standard under which the Trump administration subsequently turned to not only dispensed with the need for knowledge of these but also any knowledge as to *where* an attack may take place. Indeed, while various members of the Trump administration were keen to stress that knowledge of where an attack was to take place, or against what, was unnecessary, President Trump, when pushed, waded in to claim that the target was four US embassies.[209] Not only did he not make this claim with a level of certainty, only claiming that he 'believed' it was four embassies, but qualified even this prediction by stating that the target 'could have been a lot of other things too'.[210] It spoke volumes that two days later the National Security Adviser watered down the 'four embassies' claim to say that it was probably US facilities in the region that were the likely target of

---

soleimani-20200114.html. On 9 January, Secretary of State Pompeo similarly stated, while maintaining that the US faced an 'imminent' attack, that the intelligence upon which this was based was not concrete, in his acknowledgement that '[w]e don't know precisely when and we don't know precisely where, but it was real'. Samuel Chamberlain and Charles Creitz, 'Pompeo responds to John Kerry on Iran: "It's a Fantasy to Think That the Iran Deal Was Good for the United States"', *Fox News*, 9 January, available at: www.foxnews.com/media/mike-pompeo-john-kerry-iran-qassem-soleimani-nuclear-deal.

[206] See, for example Adil Ahmad Haque, 'U.S. Legal Defense of the Soleimani Strike at the United Nations: A Critical Assessment', *Just Security*, 10 January 2020, available at: www.justsecurity.org/68008/u-s-legal-defense-of-the-soleimani-strike-at-the-united-nations-a-critical-assessment/; Milanovic, n. 200.

[207] See, for example, Robert Chesney, 'Targeting Shahla'I in Addition to Soleimani: Unpacking the Legal Questions', *Lawfare*, 10 January 2020, available at: www.lawfareblog.com/targeting-shahlai-addition-soleimani-unpacking-legal-questions.

[208] Talmon and Heipertz, n. 199.

[209] Shane Harris, Josh Dawsey and Seung Min Kim, 'Trump Now Claims Four Embassies Were under Threat from Iran, Raising Fresh Questions about Intelligence Reports', *The Washington Post*, 11 January 2020, available at: www.washingtonpost.com/national-security/trump-now-claims-four-embassies-were-under-threat-from-iran-raising-fresh-questions-about-intelligence-reports/2020/01/10/02f8d154-33e7-11ea-a053-dc6d944ba776_story.html.

[210] Martin Pengelly, 'Donald Trump's Iran Claims on Fox News Met with Skepticism and Complaint', *The Guardian*, 11 January 2020, available at: www.theguardian.com/us-news/2020/jan/11/trump-iran-fox-news-ingraham-suleimani.

the future attack but that, in any case, it is 'always difficult, even with exquisite intelligence, to know exactly what the targets are'.[211]

### 7.5.3 The Impact of 'Contextual Imminence' upon the Necessity Criterion

It is clear from what has been discussed in this chapter that some states and commentators remain of the view that an actual armed attack is required to have commenced or occurred before self-defence becomes permissible. Most who have accepted the right of self-defence in response to a threat of an 'imminent' attack have seen imminence in a temporal sense and have pushed back against any attempts to elongate it from permitting a response to an immediate threat to permitting a response to threats of a more temporally remote nature.[212]

The view of some that imminence should now be seen in a more contextual sense would therefore seem to provide a fundamental challenge to this traditional view of imminence, and to the necessity criterion more generally. Indeed, it forces us to alter our perspective from focusing on the *temporal nature* of the *threat* to the *necessity* of *any action taken in response* given the full array of circumstances prevailing at the time, with the temporal nature of the threat being just one factor among several for consideration. This then forces us to examine imminence and its relationship with the principle of necessity, and both theoretical and practical ways by which states are able to adequately defend themselves against contemporary security threats.

Given that imminence is a part of necessity, it stands to reason that any changes to the way it is understood through a broader and more widespread adoption of contextual imminence will inevitably have an impact upon – and a loosening of – the traditionally understood restraints provided by the necessity criterion.[213] However, contextual imminence can arguably be located within the *Caroline* correspondence of 1842 which is so often used to sustain a restrictive interpretation of imminence and the necessity and proportionality criteria. Indeed, several scholars have made the point that this conception of imminence is in fact supported by the *Caroline* correspondence, in that, while it is most often associated with the requirement for an impending attack to be temporally imminent before self-defence may be invoked, the correspondence actually referred to there being a 'necessity of self-defence'.[214] The requirement in the correspondence was not so much *if an*

---

[211] Peter Baker and Thomas Gibbons-Neff, 'Esper Says He Saw No Evidence Iran Targeted 4 Embassies, as Story Shifts Again', *The New York Times*, 12 January 2020, available at: www.nytimes.com/2020/01/12/us/politics/esper-iran-trump-embassies.html.
[212] See, in particular, Section 7.4.2.
[213] See, in general, Section 6.3.1 on the necessity criterion.
[214] See Marty Lederman, 'The Egan Speech and the Bush Doctrine: Immanence, Necessity and "First Use" in the *jus ad bellum*', *Just Security*, 11 April 2016, available at: www.justsecurity.org/30522/egan-speech-bush-doctrine-imminence-necessity-first-use-jus-ad-bellum/.

*attack is temporally imminent* but *if military action in self-defence is necessary at that point in time*.

However, given that beyond the Bethlehem Principles there are, as yet, no agreed upon prescriptive guidelines for states as to how these factors are to be assessed and weighed, contextual imminence can be seen as having the result of fundamentally shifting necessity from an essentially constraining criterion to an *enabling* one,[215] in that states have a greater array of bases upon which to locate the necessity for any military action in self-defence, thereby providing them with the possibility of highlighting and emphasising those that support their decision to resort to military action to the greatest extent. The danger is that self-defence consequently solidifies as a right that is no longer formally limited to those situations in which states *need* to resort to military force for immediate defensive purposes but also those in which they *wish* to resort to military action for just about any strategic or political reason. If this is accepted, states are not restricted to taking immediate action but are permitted greater temporal freedom in deciding when to act. Indeed, the United States has on more than one occasion claimed that it will respond in a time, manner and place of its choosing,[216] sweeping away any remnants of immediacy or lack of alternative non-forcible options encapsulated in the traditional form of necessity.[217]

Furthermore, it has evidential implications in that, whereas it is at least possible for claims of temporal imminence to be objectively verified, this will

---

As the Chatham House Principles stated, '[n]ecessity is a threshold, and the criterion of imminence can be seen to be an aspect of it, inasmuch as it requires that there be no time to pursue non-forcible measures with a reasonable chance of averting or stopping the attack'. Chatham House Principles, n. 136, at 967.

[215] See Christian Henderson, 'The 25 February 2021 Military Strikes and the "Armed Attack" Requirement of Self-Defence: from "sina qua non" to the Point of Vanishing?' (2022) 9 *Journal on the Use of Force and International Law* 55, at 68.

[216] U.S. Department of Defense, 'Statement of Secretary of Defense Dr. Mark T. Esper as Prepared', 2 January 2020, available at: www.defense.gov/Newsroom/Releases/Release/Article/2049227/statement-by-secretary-of-defense-dr-mark-t-esper-as-prepared/. This was encapsulated in the remarks by White House Press Secretary Psaki following the strikes by the United States in Syria in February 2021 in that 'when threats are posed, [the President] has the right to take an action at the time and in the manner of his choosing', The White House, 'Press Gaggle by Press Secretary Jen Psaki and Homeland Security Advisor and Deputy National Security Advisor Dr Elizabeth Sherwood-Randall', 26 February 2021, available at www.whitehouse.gov/briefing-room/statements-releases/2021/02/26/press-gaggle-by-press-secretary-jen-psaki-and-homeland-security-advisor-and-deputy-national-security-advisor-dr-elizabeth-sherwood-randall/. The State Department also said about the preceding rocket attack in Erbil that 'we will respond in a way that's calculated within our own timetable and using a mix of tools at a time and place of our choosing.' See 'U.S. Voices Outrage Over Rocket Attacks in Iraq But Will Not "Lash Out"', *Reuters*, 22 February 2021, available at: www.reuters.com/article/us-iraq-security-usa/u-s-voices-outrage-over-rocket-attacks-in-iraq-but-will-not-lash-out-idUSKBN2AM2F3. For more on this incident see Section 6.2.5.1.

[217] On these see Section 6.3.1.

not often be the case with invocations of contextual imminence. While under the Bethlehem Principles there is an apparent need to be able to demonstrate a 'reasonable and objective basis' that an armed attack is 'imminent', it ultimately comes down to what a state believes to be the case having taken into consideration 'all relevant circumstances' which will be supported (or not) by evidence and intelligence that the state will most often not be willing or able to divulge, thereby denying other states and relevant actors the possibility of providing an assessment as to whether it provided an objective necessity for an invocation of the right of self-defence. Even if states are willing to divulge such information, given the limited window that a state will claim was presented to it to act, any assessment would only be relevant *post facto*.

Whether or not one agrees that contextual imminence has an historical pedigree in the *Caroline* correspondence, one cannot overlook the fact that it has only been expressly accepted, to date, by the United States, the United Kingdom and Australia,[218] with other states having chosen to not, as yet, expressly follow suit,[219] or indeed to broadly express condemnation of the three states for having done so. On the one hand, this relative lack of reaction may be interpreted as acquiescence in the legal views of these three states, particularly when viewed in comparison to the volume of reaction generated to the attempted loosening of the constraints of imminence and necessity presented by the United States in 2002.[220] Yet, on the other hand, given the fact that so many states at that time were only prepared to stretch the necessity criterion to incorporate temporal imminence in the context of anticipatory self-defence, their silence or failure to react may be an indication of these states not feeling it necessary to express, or reiterate, their views on the issue. It also cannot necessarily be assumed that all states are cognisant of the views of these three states, or that the expression of views necessarily called for a specific response from other states.[221]

However, a third possibility that cannot be discounted is that the relative lack of reaction by other states is indicative of the fact that, while not wishing to see contextual imminence take a position as *lex lata*, they nonetheless see contextual imminence as often both operationally and practically necessary in that given contemporary threats and actors a focus solely on temporal factors

---

[218] These states may well be criticised for openly adopting a standard which would appear to be contrary to existing law and their positions 'remain open to varying interpretations' and raise 'as many questions as answers'. O'Meara, n. 23, at 63. Yet, O'Meara notes that these expressed positions 'are extremely valuable (if not entirely coherent) in terms of the detail that they provide for contemplation of the subject at hand'. Ibid.

[219] The UK Attorney General, Jeremy Wright, seemed to imply in 2017 that Canada and New Zealand, the remaining two of the so-called Five Eyes, might also have adopted it, although these two states have not expressly confirmed this. Wright, n. 137.

[220] See Section 7.4.2.2.

[221] See 'Legal and Procedural Issues Associated with the *Jus ad Bellum*' in the Introduction.

is both unworkable and fails to reflect the reality facing states when considering issues of defence.

## 7.6 CONCLUSION

Today, while there remains a divide between those who accept anticipatory self-defence against imminent threats and those that do not, an area of contemporary disagreement that has arisen is in regard to the breadth of the concept of anticipatory self-defence and, in particular, the concept of imminence and how it operates in the context of contemporary threats and actors. Indeed, while some are unable to accept that this right can be reconciled with Article 51, there has been a discernible rise in its acceptance, particularly since 9/11,[222] with some observing 'an obvious ideological slide towards a position more lenient to the use of force by States in international law',[223] particularly in cases 'where the force is intended to suppress terrorist acts or the proliferation of WMD'.[224] In this respect, the focus of discussion has often shifted from talking about *armed attacks* to *threats* of attack. However, even amongst states and scholars who accept anticipatory self-defence against threats of imminent attack, the contemporary disagreements are in regard to what is meant by 'imminence' and when it can be said that the use of force in self-defence is necessary. As such, the precise parameters remain, and look to continue to remain, unclear.

It is in the context of permissible actions in self-defence against threats and attacks by non-state actors where arguably the law is in the greatest state of flux. While there is a good deal of support for the notion that non-state actors are able to independently perpetrate armed attacks, when such a response may take place has been the focus of this chapter. There are, however, additional problems with resorting to the use of force against these actors in that they normally operate from the territory of another state. This issue, and the response in self-defence, is the central topic of Chapter 8, the next and final chapter of this Part of the book.

### QUESTIONS

1 What are the different forms of preventative self-defence and how are they distinguished?

2 Can preventative self-defence be reconciled with Article 51 of the UN Charter?

---

[222] Deeks, n. 2, at 663; Lubell, n. 7, at 701. One aspect of this apparent broadening of interpretation of Article 51 and the armed attack criterion that is often overlooked is how it can be reconciled with the correlating contraction of the breadth and scope of Article 2(4).

[223] Robert Kolb, 'Self-Defence and Preventive War at the Beginning of the New Millenium' (2004) 59 *Zeitschrift für offentliches Recht* 111, at 125–6.

[224] Deeks, n. 2, at 677.

3 To what extent, if any, can it be said that the Bush Doctrine of pre-emptive force has a place within international law?

4 Where does the concept of 'imminence' come from in gauging the legality of preventative force?

5 Can it still be said that 'imminence' is interpreted on a temporal basis? If not, is it possible to take other factors into account?

## SUGGESTED FURTHER READING

Michael Bothe, 'Terrorism and the Legality of Pre-Emptive Force' (2003) 14 *European Journal of International Law* 227

Christopher Greenwood, 'International Law and the Pre-Emptive Use of Force: Afghanistan, Al-Qaida, and Iraq' (2003) 4 *San Diego International Law Journal* 7

Christian Henderson, 'The 2010 National Security Strategy of the United States and the Obama Doctrine of "Necessary Force"' (2010) 15 *Journal of Conflict & Security Law* 403

Noam Lubell, 'The Problem of Imminence in an Uncertain World', in Marc Weller (ed.), *The Oxford Handbook of the Use of Force in International Law* (Oxford University Press, 2015), 697

Chris O'Meara, 'Reconceptualising the Right of Self-Defence against "Imminent" Armed Attacks' (2022) 9 *Journal on the Use of Force and International Law* 278

Kinga Tibori Szabó, *Anticipatory Action in Self-Defence: Essence and Limits under International Law* (Springer, 2011)

# 8 The Use of Force against Non-state Actors

## 8.1 INTRODUCTION

Responses to attacks by non-state actors is something that today, and in particular following the attacks of 11 September 2001 (9/11), is a central concern to the international community. This is, however, an issue of historical importance as it arose not only in the *Caroline* incident of the nineteenth century[1] but has also been a persistent one within the era of the United Nations (UN) Charter, as seen in the actions of South Africa in Botswana and other countries in southern Africa in the 1970s and 1980s, Israeli interventions in Lebanon in 1968 and Tunis in 1985 and Turkey's various interventions in northern Iraq against the PKK during the 1990s and 2000s. It was also a central aspect of the *Nicaragua* and *Armed Activities* cases before the International Court of Justice (ICJ), and in the *Wall* advisory opinion. As discussed in Chapter 6, today it is a widely held view that non-state actors are not excluded as the possible perpetrators of an armed attack. While not a point free from controversy, attacks by non-state actors are arguably within the purview of the right of self-defence, in particular in the light of the fact that the right arises in the face of an 'armed attack' and is not restricted to 'any particular kind of attacker'.[2] However, establishing that they may perpetrate an armed attack and, indeed, have perpetrated such attacks, is only one half of the equation.

Chapter 7 examined the issue of *when* it might be possible to respond to the threat of an armed attack, including from non-state actors. This chapter is more concerned with the fundamental questions of *if, how* and *where* to

---

[1] The *Caroline* incident of 1837, which has formed the backbone to the customary elements of the right of self-defence, involved the taking of action against the activities of non-state actors unsupported, let alone controlled, by a host state. See Section 6.3.

[2] See Thomas Franck, 'Terrorism and the Right of Self-Defense' (2001) 95 *American Journal of International Law* 839, at 840. See Section 6.2.1. See also Elizabeth Wilmshurst, 'The Chatham House Principles of International Law on the Use of Force in Self-Defence' (2006) 55 *International & Comparative Law Quarterly* 963, at 969–70; Noam Lubell, *Extraterritorial Use of Force against Non-State Actors* (Oxford University Press, 2010), at 31–2.

respond to such attacks. Measures in self-defence against an armed attack – or imminent threat thereof – from a state take the form of either repelling the armed attack in motion, and perhaps therefore take place upon the defending state's territory or, more often, striking targets within the attacking state's territory. Yet, non-state actors are not located on the high seas or in outer space but are rather normally located and operate within the territory of another state. As such, and given that the prohibition of the use of force concerns the 'international relations' between states, there are the rights and obligations of a third party – the territorial state – that also form part of the equation in determining the legality of measures in self-defence in response to an armed attack by a non-state actor. There is, in this sense, what might be described as the 'sovereignty barrier' to extraterritorial defensive force.[3] For example, if the non-state actors are now located in another state or a manifestation of that state, such as an embassy, then that state's sovereign rights and territorial integrity provide an initial barrier to the victim state invoking its right of self-defence in taking forcible actions within its territory. As such, it becomes necessary to explore whether, and if so, how the sovereignty barrier might be overcome.

This chapter seeks to untangle these issues in providing a picture as to the way in which the law operates in these circumstances. As such, Section 8.2 raises some important general considerations in relation to self-defence against non-state actors. Section 8.3 then looks at the situation of self-defence measures which target both the non-state actors and the host state, as was the case with the United States' response to the terrorist attacks of 9/11. A distinction needs to be made between self-defence against both the non-state actor perpetrators of the attack or those posing a threat *and* the state within which they are located, which is covered in Section 8.3, and those actions that are more limited in only specifically targeting the non-state actors, which are addressed in Section 8.4. Section 8.5 finally addresses the particular phenomenon of so-called targeted killings, which engage not only the *jus ad bellum* but also the legal frameworks of international human rights law and, potentially, international humanitarian law.

## 8.2 GENERAL CONSIDERATIONS OF THE RIGHT OF SELF-DEFENCE AGAINST NON-STATE ACTORS

It was discussed in Chapter 6 that the ICJ has held that in its view a use of force should be of a certain gravity before it can be said to constitute an 'armed

---

[3] Christian Henderson, 'Non-State Actors and the Use of Force', in Math Noortmann, August Reinisch and Cedric Ryngaert (eds.), *Non-State Actors in International Law* (Hart, 2015), 77, at 88.

attack' for the purposes of the right of self-defence.[4] Terrorist attacks would thus seem to pose a problem, in that, while the attacks of 9/11 appear to have been generally accepted as having the required 'scale and effects' of an armed attack, the *modus operandi* of terrorist groups is not, generally speaking, to launch attacks on such a scale.[5] Instead, due to their size, capabilities and covert nature, terrorist groups tend to perpetrate smaller attacks, perhaps on a more regular basis,[6] but with the aim of killing as many individuals as possible.

In this respect, there are three ways in which a response in self-defence might be legally justifiable. The first is by adopting the alternative view that no gravity threshold in fact exists and the legality of self-defence in response to an attack of whatever gravity is determined upon the basis of satisfying the twin principles of necessity and proportionality.[7] As such, if a terrorist attack is committed on a relatively minor scale and with relatively minor effects, if a defensive necessity can be demonstrated then a proportionate armed response would be permissible. Secondly, it is arguable that, under the 'accumulation of events' theory, a state is permitted at some point to equate an accumulation of these smaller attacks to an 'armed attack' and thereby justify a forcible response in self-defence.[8] Although controversial from many perspectives, Israel's various invasions into the Gaza Strip are arguably an example of this theory in action.[9] As discussed in Chapter 6, the theory, while perhaps seen to a limited extent in state practice and having received the support of certain scholars,[10] along with the fact that the ICJ has, perhaps unwittingly, given a

---

[4] See, in general, Section 6.2.5. See also Christine Gray, *International Law and the Use of Force*, 4th ed. (Oxford University Press, 2018), at 136.

[5] See Sean D. Murphy, 'Terrorism and the Concept of Armed Attack in Article 51 of the UN Charter' (2002) 43 *Harvard International Law Journal* 41, at 45–51; Constantine Antonopoulos, 'Force by Armed Groups as Armed Attack and the Broadening of Self-Defence' (2008) 55 *Netherlands International Law Review* 159, at 169. By recognising the right of self-defence in the aftermath of 9/11, the Security Council appeared to imply that this attack could be viewed as an armed attack in UNSC Res. 1368 (2001). However, the issue of the gravity of the attack was not referenced explicitly in the resolution.

[6] Christopher Greenwood, 'International Law and the United States' Air Operation against Libya' (1987) 89 *West Virginia Law Review* 933, at 955–6.

[7] On the gravity threshold of an armed attack see Section 6.2.5, whilst see Section 6.3 on the twin criteria of necessity and propotionality.

[8] See Sections 6.2.5.4 and 6.3.2.1.     [9] See ibid.

[10] See, for example, Theresa Reinold, 'State Weakness, Irregular Warfare, and the Right to Self-Defense Post-9/11' (2011) 105 *American Journal of International Law* 244, at 271 and 284. However, it has been rejected by many others on the basis that it possibly provides 'an open-ended licence to use force'. See Elizabeth Wilmshurst, 'Anticipatory Self-Defence against Terrorists', in Larissa Van Den Herik and Nico Schrijver (eds.), *Counter-Terrorism Strategies in a Fragmented Legal Order: Meeting the Challenges* (Cambridge University Press, 2013), 356, at 368; Nigel D. White, *Advanced Introduction to International Conflict and Security Law* (Edward Elgar, 2014), at 43.

certain nod to it,[11] has seemingly been rejected by the Security Council.[12] It is a doctrine that remains, as such, controversial and vague, to say the least.

The covert nature of terrorist groups and the surprise element of their attacks, combined with the need to obtain sufficient evidence in identifying the perpetrator[13] and then following the various preliminary issues that need to be addressed, such as attempting to engage the host state in taking the necessary action against the group, means that action in self-defence is most often likely to take place after the attack has come to an end, with the response to the 9/11 attacks, for example, coming several weeks after the attacks.[14] While it may be claimed that such actions taken ostensibly in self-defence are more akin to actions of armed reprisal,[15] as long as the response can be seen to have a clear and identifiable prospective defensive element to it, such a distinction has now become blurred almost to the point of extinction.[16] Indeed, as it will normally be possible to argue that following an attack from a terrorist group another will follow at some point, any action taken in self-defence will often be taken with the express aim of preventing further future attacks, which does not appear to prevent acceptance of the legality of the action. In its justification for Operation Enduring Freedom in 2001, for example, the United States responded to '[t]he attacks on 11 September 2001 and the ongoing threat to the United States and its nationals posed by the al-Qaeda organization' by taking action 'designed to prevent and deter further attacks on the United States'.[17]

If no prior attack from the particular terrorist group – either singularly or cumulatively – has been sustained, action in self-defence is difficult to reconcile with Article 51's requirement for the 'occurrence' of an armed attack and in this sense might appear to be of a purely anticipatory or pre-emptive nature.[18] Yet, as a third option and as discussed in Section 7.5, certain states have claimed the right to take action in self-defence against a threat of 'imminent' attack by non-state actors. While 'imminence' has traditionally been provided with a temporal meaning, these states argue that it is necessary to instead view imminence in a contextual sense, thereby permitting a range

---

[11] See, for example, *Case Concerning Oil Platforms (Islamic Republic of Iran v. United States of America)*, Judgment (2003) ICJ Reports 161, at para. 64.

[12] See UNSC Res. 188 (1964).

[13] See Mary Ellen O'Connell, 'Evidence of Terror' (2002) 7 *Journal of Conflict & Security Law* 19.

[14] After gathering evidence attributing the attacks to al-Qaida, the United States unsuccessfully requested the Taliban to unconditionally close al-Qaida training camps in Afghanistan, surrender Osama bin Laden to the United States and open Afghanistan to inspections. See *Keesing's* (2001) 44337.

[15] See Sections 6.3.1.2.1 and 6.3.1.2.2.      [16] Henderson, n. 3, at 87.

[17] See UN Doc. S/2001/946, 7 October 2001. See Section 6.3.1.

[18] See Niaz A. Shah, 'Self-Defence, Anticipatory Self-Defence and Pre-Emption: International Law's Response to Terrorism' (2007) 12 *Journal of Conflict & Security Law* 95. See, in general, Chapter 7.

of factors to be taken into account in determining whether it is necessary to take action in self-defence.[19] This might be seen as controversial, and, as discussed in Chapter 7, it cannot be said – at this stage at least – to represent the general view of the international community. Assuming, however, that one of these three possible ways arises to justify a response in self-defence, and is found acceptable to the broader international community, the next question, which is the focus of this chapter, is how one overcomes the barrier of the territorial sovereignty of the state within which the non-state actors are located at the time armed force is taken against them.

## 8.3 SELF-DEFENCE AGAINST NON-STATE ACTORS AND THEIR HOST STATE

### 8.3.1 The 'Effective Control' Standard of Attribution

In the *Nicaragua* case of 1986 the ICJ had to determine whether the actions of El Salvadorian rebels were attributable to the government of Nicaragua in order to justify the claim of the United States that it was acting in collective self-defence of El Salvador.[20] While the Court drew upon Article 3(g) of the Definition of Aggression in declaring that an armed attack might be perpetrated not only through the direct use of force by a state but also '[t]he sending by or on behalf of a State of armed bands, groups, irregulars or mercenaries, which carry out acts of armed force against another State of such gravity as to amount to the acts listed above, or its substantial involvement therein',[21] such acts could only be attributed to a state that was in 'effective control' of the non-state actors,[22] although the Court did not explain its reasoning for this test and it was the subject of criticism by some judges within the Court.[23] It was evident that in the Court's view such control was restricted to the 'sending' of non-state actors by a state who were under its direct control to commit such acts, while the provision of weapons or logistical or other support was insufficient.[24] In this sense, while the ICJ was not saying that an armed

---

[19] See Section 7.5.
[20] *Case Concerning Military and Paramilitary Activities in and against Nicaragua (Nicaragua v. United States of America)*, Merits (1986) ICJ Reports 14.
[21] Ibid., at para. 195. [22] Ibid., at para. 115.
[23] In particular, Judges Schwebel and Jennings. Ibid., Dissenting Opinion of Judge Schwebel, at para. 171; ibid., Dissenting Opinion of Judge Jennings, at para. 543. See, further, Section 6.2.5.
[24] Ibid., at para. 228. In this respect, '[t]he residual role of "substantial involvement" was clearly construed in a very limited fashion' by the Court, with it being difficult to see what meaning the Court provided to it outside of conditions of effective control. Tom Ruys, *'Armed Attack' and Article 51 of the UN Charter: Evolutions in Customary Law and Practice* (Cambridge University Press, 2010), at 418. See Section 6.2.5, see also Section 2.4.3 on the distinction the Court made between acts of intervention and uses of force.

attack had to be physically perpetrated by a state actor, it did appear to say that the right of self-defence would only become available if the host state was in effective control of the non-state actor perpetrators of the attack, thereby essentially making the actions of the non-state actors those of the state.

The Court's jurisprudence on this issue was subsequently interpreted by some scholars as firmly maintaining the right of self-defence within the inter-state context so that the actions of non-state actors, in the absence of direction or control by a state, regardless of whether they reached the threshold of an armed attack, could not be defended against through the invocation of self-defence.[25] But while there will be occasions when non-state actors indeed carry out armed attacks under the effective control of a state, it is difficult to find any examples of such 'effective control' in practice.[26] This standard is very difficult, or 'virtually impossible', to demonstrate,[27] meaning that the option of responding in self-defence would not arise in most cases if this standard of attribution was applied. Whether one agrees or not on a policy level that this is a positive thing, it does render the possibility of self-defence in most cases somewhat moot. Indeed, it is almost never the case that states exert such a high degree of control over non-state perpetrators of an armed attack or, if they do, it will rarely, if ever, be possible to prove. Furthermore, it is possible that the non-state actor is not, or is no longer, located within the territory of the state which has been effectively controlling it, but is instead within the territory of a third state. In this case, while a forcible response may be taken against the controlling state, the non-state actor would be effectively protected, seeing as it would be located in a third state thus potentially permitting it to operate with a degree of impunity, or at least with protection from military action by the defending state.[28]

It might, therefore, be argued that the 'overall control' test, as set out by the International Criminal Tribunal for the former Yugoslavia (ICTY) in the *Tadic* case of 1995, is more appropriate in this context.[29] Under this lower threshold of attribution, the activities of a non-state actor group would be attributable to a state if the state were to equip and finance the group and assist it in the coordination or planning of its activities, although it would seem to 'require[] more than mere assistance, providing a territorial base, or condoning its

---

[25] See, for example, Antonopoulos, n. 5, at 168; see also Shah, n. 18, at 108–11.

[26] Arguably an example of this standard of control in practice can be found in the attempted assassination of former US President George H. W. Bush in Kuwait in 1993 by Iraqi agents. See Dino Kritsiotis, 'The Legality of the 1993 US Missile Strike on Iraq and the Right of Self-Defence in International Law' (1996) 45 *International & Comparative Law Quarterly* 162, at 174.

[27] Antonio Cassese, 'The *Nicaragua* and *Tadic* Tests Revisited in Light of the ICJ Judgment on Genocide in Bosnia' (2007) 18 *European Journal of International Law* 649, at 666.

[28] Murphy, n. 5, at 66.

[29] *Prosecutor v. Tadic*, Case No. IT-94-1-A ICTY, Appeals Chamber, 1999, at para. 120.

actions'.[30] However, this test was employed by the ICTY in *Tadic* in examining whether an armed conflict was international or non-international in nature, and not in the specific context of self-defence, and, more broadly, was used in connection with determining individual criminal, as opposed to state, responsibility. It is also a test that the ICJ dismissed in the *Bosnia Genocide* case of 2007 in favour of the effective control standard,[31] a standard that has also been incorporated into the general rules regarding state responsibility.[32]

In this respect, it may be contended that the tests confuse either the law of state responsibility or the law of armed conflict with the *jus ad bellum* and that, rather than drawing upon these general tests, the *jus ad bellum* needs to develop its own bespoke standards.[33] Furthermore, and more significantly, while some have argued that the overall control test is more appropriate in the context of contemporary international terrorism,[34] in particular due to evidentiary problems in establishing effective control by states over the actions of non-state actors, it is the element of 'control' in both tests that is problematic. It is often the case that the terrorist actors conduct attacks in the absence of any state control and the states where the terrorist groups are located, and where the action in self-defence will take place, exercise no control over the groups. On the contrary, very often the host states will be actively opposed to the group, as Somalia is to the al-Shabaab group from whose territory it carries out its armed activities into Kenya, and both Iraq and Syria are to the so-called Islamic State, which based itself within these two states. The question thus arises as to if and how a state may invoke its right of self-defence after a non-state actor group has attacked it or poses a threat to the state concerned, is located within the territory of another state, and where it is not

---

[30] Lindsay Moir, 'Action against Host States of Terrorist Groups', in Marc Weller (ed.), *The Oxford Handbook of the Use of Force in International Law* (Oxford University Press, 2015), 720, at 723.

[31] *Case Concerning Application of the Convention on the Prevention and Punishment of the Crime of Genocide (Bosnia and Herzegovina v. Serbia and Montenegro)*, Judgment (2007) ICJ Reports 43, at paras. 402–6. However, see the Dissenting Opinions of Judge Al-Khasawneh, at 36–9, and Judge ad hoc Mahiou, at 113–17. See also Report of the Independent International Fact-Finding Mission on the Conflict in Georgia, September 2009, vol. II, at 260, in which it was stated that '[i]n the law governing state responsibility, and arguably also for identifying the responsibility for an armed attack, control means "effective control".' Available at: www.mpil.de/de/pub/publikationen/archiv/independent_international_fact.cfm.

[32] Article 8 of the International Law Commission's 2001 Draft Articles on the Responsibility of States for Internationally Wrongful Acts, which were adopted by the UN General Assembly in UNGA Res. 56/83 (2001), provides that: 'The conduct of a person or group of persons shall be considered an act of a State under international law if the person or group of persons is in fact acting on the instructions of, or under the direction or control of, that State in carrying out the conduct.'

[33] Although on this issue see Marko Milanovic, 'Special Rules of Attribution of Conduct in International Law' (2020) **96** *International Law Studies* 295, at 331–9.

[34] Cassese, n. 27, at 657–63, 665–7.

possible to demonstrate an element of control by the host state over the actions of the non-state actor. The attacks of 9/11 and the immediate aftermath have proved to be pivotal in this debate.

### 8.3.2 The 'Harbouring' Standard of Attribution

The day after the 9/11 attacks, the UN Security Council adopted Resolution 1368 (2001), which recognised the inherent right of individual or collective self-defence in accordance with the UN Charter. It is difficult to read too much into this recognition, and whether it was confirming that a right of self-defence against non-state actors existed in general or whether it existed in relation to these specific attacks, particularly as at that time it was not entirely clear who had perpetrated them. Nonetheless, following the attacks, clear, if implicit, attempts were made by the administration of President George W. Bush to lower the 'effective control' threshold of attribution, thus broadening the possibilities for invoking the right of self-defence in the face of attacks by non-state actors.[35] Indeed, President Bush stated that the United States would make 'no distinction between the terrorists who committed these acts and those who *harbor* them',[36] and in its letter to the UN Security Council upon the launching of Operation Enduring Freedom on 7 October 2001 the United States stated that the 9/11 attacks and the ongoing threat from al-Qaida resulted from 'the decision of the Taliban regime to allow parts of Afghanistan that it controls to be used by this organization as a base of operation'.[37]

Clear, if implicit, attempts were therefore made to lower the traditional standard of 'effective control' to a 'harbouring' standard of attribution. Subsequently, after failing to convince the Taliban regime in Afghanistan to hand over Osama bin Laden and to close terrorist training camps, the United States commenced Operation Enduring Freedom. During the course of the military action not only did the US coalition target al-Qaida but also Taliban locations and the state infrastructure of Afghanistan, leading to the eventual toppling of the Taliban regime. There was no suggestion that the Taliban regime in Afghanistan was in effective control of al-Qaida. Indeed, if anything, suggestions were made that it was more likely that al-Qaida in fact exerted an element of control, or at least substantial influence, over the Taliban.[38] In this

---

[35] This was in addition to attempts to develop a right of pre-emptive self-defence, on which see Section 7.4.2.

[36] President of the United States of America, 'Address to the Nation on the Terrorist Attacks', 11 September 2001, 37 *Weekly Compilation of Presidential Documents* 1301 (emphasis added).

[37] UN Doc. S/2001/946, 7 October 2001.

[38] See Michael N. Schmitt, 'Deconstructing October 7th: A Case Study in the Lawfulness of Counterterrorist Military Operations', in Michael N. Schmitt and Gian Luca Beruto (eds.),

respect, and without being able to legitimately claim effective control, the 'response was prima facie inconsistent with the prevailing rules'.[39]

However, the operation received general support within the international community. This was no doubt for a variety of reasons and cannot simply be attributed to an acceptance of the harbouring standard of attribution. Indeed, the reaction to 9/11 was most likely 'motivated by the emotional reaction to the horrific terrorist action of 11 September, [and] may not amount to the consistent practice and *opinio juris* required for a customary change'.[40] Furthermore, while claims of 'instant custom' were made following the action in self-defence by the United States and the reaction to this,[41] state practice in the years following this operation would, as highlighted in Section 8.4, appear to militate against a finding that the law had incorporated such a lowering of the standard of attribution.

Nonetheless, given that it is entirely conceivable that an armed attack may be perpetrated by a non-state actor acting entirely without any state support or acquiescence, the question arises as to whether the victim state in these situations is expected to have to endure the attack without being able to respond forcibly. Or, as examined next, might it be that the victim state has the possibility of taking action solely against the non-state actor perpetrators of the attack, whereby the sovereignty barrier may not be seen as causing an issue due to the fact that while force is to be used *within* a state it is not to be targeted specifically *against* it?[42]

## 8.4 MILITARY ACTION RESTRICTED TO THE NON-STATE ACTORS

A host state's effective control of non-state actors during the time they carry out attacks against a victim state may lead to its territorial sovereignty being sacrificed to the extent that action in self-defence becomes permissible in principle against both the host state and the non-state actors. But the question arises as to the rights, if any, of the victim state to take action in self-defence in situations where a state's involvement with the non-state actors does not meet the stringent 'effective control' standard, but where there is evidence of lesser control, substantial involvement, limited involvement, approval or even simple apathy towards the actions of the non-state actors or in those situations

---

*Terrorism and International Law: Challenges and Responses* (International Institute for International Humanitarian Law, 2003), 39, at 45–6.

[39] Moir, n. 30, at 727.
[40] Antonio Cassese, *International Law*, 2nd ed. (Oxford University Press, 2005), at 475.
[41] See, for example, Benjamin Langille, 'It's "Instant Custom": How the Bush Doctrine Became Law after the Terrorist Attacks of September 11, 2001' (2003) 26 *Boston College International and Comparative Law Review* 145.
[42] Henderson, n. 3, at 90.

## 8.4 Military Action Restricted to the Non-state Actors

where there is an inability on the part of a host state to do anything about the activities of the non-state group.

While some scholars have maintained a rigid state-centric view of the perpetrators of an armed attack and, thus, the targets of any action taken in self-defence, this appears to be based to a large degree upon the jurisprudence of the ICJ on this issue.[43] However, although the jurisprudence of the Court has been influential in determining and shaping the law in this area, a careful reading of it also demonstrates that limited action in self-defence solely against non-state actors was not precluded. Indeed, in both the *Nicaragua* and *Armed Activities* cases, which are the two main contentious cases in which the Court addressed claims to self-defence against attacks undertaken by non-state actors, the states claiming self-defence did not solely target non-state actors, *but also the host states* of Nicaragua and the Democratic Republic of Congo (DRC), respectively. This explains, in part, why a requirement of attribution of the actions of the non-state actors to the host state was deemed to be necessary by the Court.[44] Indeed, in taking action in collective self-defence of El Salvador, rather than directing measures solely against the non-state actors who were physically perpetrating the attacks, the United States both provided support to the *contras* in their operations against the Nicaraguan government *as well as* directly attacking Nicaragua in the form of the mining of ports and aerial incursions into Nicaraguan territory. It was, therefore, in this light 'far less incredible' that before accepting the United States' justification of self-defence on this occasion the ICJ required attribution to Nicaragua of the activities of the non-state actors attacking El Salvador.[45]

The *Armed Activities* case arose out of a complex conflict within central Africa.[46] Troops from Uganda were in the territory of the DRC initially with the government's consent. However, in August 1998 the troops began to operate in support of a number of rebel groups opposed to the president of the DRC, Laurent Kabila. At the same time, a number of rebel groups were operating from the territory of the DRC against Uganda, and a number of states were also intervening in support of Kabila. The DRC filed an application against Uganda, charging it with 'armed aggression'.[47] Uganda claimed in its defence that it had operated with the consent of the DRC until 11 September 1998 and after

---

[43] See Section 6.2.1.  [44] For more on the facts behind the *Nicaragua* case see Section 1.5.5.1.
[45] Kimberley N. Trapp, 'Back to Basics: Necessity, Proportionality, and the Right of Self-Defence against Non-State Terrorist Actors' (2007) 56 *International & Comparative Law Quarterly* 141, at 142.
[46] *Case Concerning Armed Activities on the Territory of the Congo (Democratic Republic of Congo v. Uganda)*, Judgment (2005) ICJ Reports 168.
[47] Ibid., Application: Instituting Proceedings, at 3. The DRC filed a linked application against Uganda, Rwanda and Burundi, charging them each with 'armed aggression' against it, although those against Rwanda and Burundi were subsequently withdrawn.

this date was acting in self-defence in response to attacks against it by rebel groups based within the DRC which, Uganda claimed, had been supported by the government of the DRC. In response, the DRC denied it was responsible for the activities of the rebel groups against Uganda and that it was, itself, entitled to respond in self-defence. However, of importance here is that, and in a similar vein to the *Nicaragua* case, Uganda attacked both the non-state actors *and* the government and infrastructure of the DRC, rather than limiting its actions to the non-state actors that were carrying out raids within its territory.

In this light it is, again, perhaps unsurprising that the Court was of the view that the conditions for self-defence against the DRC had not been satisfied as the attacks carried out by the rebel groups operating from the DRC's territory against Uganda were 'non-attributable to the DRC'.[48] The Court therefore left the question open as to 'whether and under what conditions contemporary international law provides for a right of self-defence against large-scale attacks by irregular forces'.[49] In this respect, while it may have avoided taking the opportunity to clarify an important and controversial aspect of the law, and received criticism for doing so,[50] it also did not, technically, need to do so.

However, the perception that armed attacks must be directed, or effectively controlled, by a state before the right of self-defence becomes available was also seen in earlier state practice. For example, following the death of three Israeli citizens in Cyprus in 1985, Israel targeted the Palestinian Liberation Organisation (PLO) headquarters in Tunis, Tunisia.[51] In invoking its right of self-defence, Israel claimed that '[i]t was against [the PLO] that our action was directed, not against their host country'.[52] In order to justify its violation of Tunisian territory, Israel nonetheless felt the need to state that 'the host country does bear considerable responsibility'.[53] In particular, 'Tunisia did not show an inkling of a desire or an intention to prevent the PLO from planning and initiating terrorist activities from its soil.'[54] Yet, in reaction, states focused upon the fact that Tunisia could not be held responsible for the conduct of the PLO and therefore condemned the actions of Israel.[55] As Kimberley Trapp notes, '[t]his line of argument is in line with some of the contemporaneous thinking on the right of self-defence',[56] coming as it did at around the time of the *Nicaragua* case, in that it was considered to be the case

---

[48] *Armed Activities* case, n. 46, at para. 146.
[49] Ibid., at para. 147. See Jörg Kammerhofer, 'The *Armed Activities* Case and Non-State Actors in Self-Defence Law' (2007) 20 *Leiden Journal of International Law* 89.
[50] See, for example, the Separate Opinion of Judge Kooijmans. *Armed Activities* case, n. 46, Separate Opinion of Judge Kooijmans, at paras. 16–35.
[51] UN Doc. A/40/688-S/17502, 27 September 1985.
[52] UN Doc. S/PV. 2611, 2 October 1985, at 22–5.    [53] Ibid.    [54] Ibid., at 26.
[55] See, for example, ibid., at 41 (UK). See also UN Doc. S/PV. 2613, 3 October 1985, at 11 (Madagascar).
[56] Trapp, n. 45, at 149.

that the right of self-defence could only be invoked in response to an armed attack by a state.

However, it is also apparent that, with the emergence of what might be described as 'global terrorism', the attitudes of states apparently began to shift. For example, the United States responded in self-defence to the bombing of its embassies in both Kenya and Tanzania in 1998 by bombing an al-Qaida training camp in Afghanistan and a pharmaceutical plant located within Sudan, which it claimed was being used by the terrorist group to manufacture biological weapons.[57] In partially echoing Israel's justification following its action in 1985, while claiming a limited form of responsibility on the part of the host states, in that the bombing was 'carried out only after repeated efforts to convince the Government of the Sudan and the Taliban regime in Afghanistan to shut these terrorist activities down and to cease their cooperation with the Bin Laden organization',[58] the United States, in invoking its right of self-defence, stated that it nonetheless had limited its actions to installations of al-Qaida and not the infrastructure of the states in which they were located. By contrast to the incident in 1985, however, condemnation was limited to the bombing of the pharmaceutical plant, in the absence of evidence to suggest that this had been used for anything other than civilian purposes.[59] There was little condemnation of the attack on the training camp in Afghanistan or the justification of self-defence in general,[60] although no state expressly approved of the legal argument advanced by the United States for the strikes.

It might be seen, therefore, as something of an anomaly that while the attacks against the United States on 11 September 2001 were undertaken by the al-Qaida group, the US actions in self-defence in response were directed against both al-Qaida *and* the *de facto* government of Afghanistan, the Taliban. Indeed, while only seemingly claiming a similar level of responsibility as Israel did in Tunisia in 1985 and the United States did in Sudan and Afghanistan in 1998, through its claims that the attacks of 11 September 2001 had 'been made possible by the decision of the Taliban regime to allow the parts of

---

[57] UN Doc. S/1998/780, 20 August 1998. See, in general, Jules Lobel, 'The Use of Force to Respond to Terrorist Attacks: The Bombing of Sudan and Afghanistan' (1999) 24 *Yale Journal of International Law* 537.

[58] UN Doc. S/1998/780, 20 August 1998.

[59] There was no meeting of the UN Security Council, although several states submitted letters in protest at the strikes. See UN Doc. S/1998/786, 21 August 1998 (Sudan); UN Doc. S/1998/789, 21 August 1998 (League of Arab States); UN Doc. S/1998/879, 21 August 1998 (Non-Aligned Movement). For academic condemnation of the strikes see Lobel, n. 57. Others, however, were more supportive. See, for example, Ruth Wedgwood, 'Responding to Terrorism: The Strikes against Bin Laden' (1999) 24 *Yale Journal of International Law* 559.

[60] Many states offered support, or at least understanding, for the strikes, such as Japan, Germany, France, the United Kingdom and Spain. See William Drozdiak, 'European Allies Back US Strikes: Japan Says It Understands', *Washington Post*, 21 August 1998, at A20.

Afghanistan that it controls to be used by this organisation as a base of operation', the United States nonetheless included 'measures against Al-Qaeda terrorist training camps *and* military installations of the Taliban regime in Afghanistan'.[61] This was, as noted elsewhere, widely accepted.

The 'harbouring' standard of attribution employed by the United States on this occasion to justify attacks within and against Afghanistan stood in marked contrast to the 'effective control' standard expressly adopted by the ICJ and seemingly witnessed in subsequent state practice.[62] However, while its invocation was accepted on this occasion, the harbouring standard has not been witnessed in state practice since.[63] Indeed, a discernible practice can be seen following Operation Enduring Freedom of states, again limiting their actions in self-defence to the targeting of non-state actors located in a host state while claiming at least some limited form of responsibility of the state for failing to put an end to the activities of the non-state actors. Examples of this practice can be found in Israel's use of force against Hezbollah in Lebanon in 2006,[64] Russia's use of force against Chechen rebels in Georgia in 2002,[65] Colombia's forcible actions against the Revolutionary Armed Forces of Colombia People's Army (FARC) in Ecuador in 2008,[66] Turkey's 2008 Operation Sun in northern Iraq[67] and, arguably, the US incursion into Pakistani territory in the raid which led to the death of Osama bin Laden in 2011.[68] Taken together, they paint a picture of states invoking 'self-defence against terrorist attacks not imputable to another state'.[69] The question

---

[61] UN Doc. S/2001/946, 7 October 2001 (emphasis added).

[62] See Christian Henderson, *The Persistent Advocate and the Use of Force: The Impact of the United States Upon the* Jus ad Bellum *in the Post–Cold War Era* (Ashgate Publishing, 2013), at 137–70.

[63] Ibid. Although for a relatively recent argument in favour of it, see Daniel Bethlehem, 'Self-Defense against an Imminent or Actual Armed Attack by Nonstate Actors' (2012) **106** *American Journal of International Law* 770, at Principle 11: 'In the case of a colluding or a harboring state, the extent of the responsibility of that state for aiding or assisting the nonstate actor in its armed activities may be relevant to considerations of the necessity to act in self-defense and the proportionality of such action, including against the colluding or harboring state.' (Bethlehem Principles).

[64] UN Doc. S/2006/560, 21 July 2006.

[65] UN Doc. S/2002/854, 31 July 2002; UN Doc. S/2002/1012, 11 September 2002.

[66] See Comunicado del Ministerio de Relaciones Exteriores de Colombia, 081, Bogotá, 2 March 2008, for the specifics of this self-defence claim.

[67] UN Doc. A/HRC/7/G/15, 28 March 2008.

[68] See Remarks by the President on Osama bin Laden, 'Osama bin Laden Dead', 2 May 2011, available at: https://obamawhitehouse.archives.gov/blog/2011/05/02/osama-bin-laden-dead. See Meagan S. Wong, 'Targeted Killings and the International Legal Framework: With Particular Reference to the US Operation against Osama Bin Laden' (2012) **11** *Chinese Journal of International Law* 127.

[69] Christian J. Tams, 'The Use of Force against Terrorists' (2009) **20** *European Journal of International Law* 359, at 381.

remains, however, as to how, if at all, we can legally rationalise what would appear to be a relatively consistent practice.

### 8.4.1 Lowering the Standard of Attribution

The first way of possibly legally rationalising this practice is through a lowering of the threshold for attribution. For example, as opposed to the need to demonstrate 'effective control' by the territorial state over the non-state actors, defending states arguably now only need to demonstrate that a state has 'aided and abetted' the non-state actors,[70] for example, or even been merely 'complicit'[71] or 'acquiescent' in their conduct[72] or having, as discussed in Section 8.3.2, 'harboured' them. Yet, while an attractive idea, in that it justifies a violation of state sovereignty through making the state responsible in some way, there are some notable problems. First, while effective control presents a high threshold for attributing the actions of a non-state actor to a state, albeit one which arguably does not fit the context of modern terrorism, it is far from clear and settled what types of support would satisfy the threshold for these various suggested standards. Furthermore, while they have all received at least some support, none have received widespread and settled support within either state practice or the academic literature.

However, the very notion of 'attribution' under these standards is somewhat artificial, in that, in reality, while a state may have been supportive of the non-state actor(s), it may also have not taken any positive action itself in connection with the commission of any attacks. It is, in this sense, detached from reality to say that the acts perpetrated by the non-state actors are those of the state – or, in other words, that they can be attributed to it – on the basis of this level of support. Furthermore, to say that the actions are in any way attributed to the state gives rise to the impression that action may be taken against the host state as well as the non-state actors, which lies in contrast to recent state practice. Christian Tams has stated that 'the underlying legal claim argument – that states aiding and abetting terrorists abuse their sovereignty and *must accept some form of counter-action* – has become a standard formula of modern debates and would probably meet with approval of some and tacit agreement of many states'.[73] This does, however, provide the impression that the action in self-defence is taken *against* the state itself as opposed to *upon* the state's territory, which is more reflective of recent state practice.

---

[70] Tom Ruys and Sten Verhoeven, 'Attacks by Private Actors and the Right of Self-Defence' (2005) 10 *Journal of Conflict & Security Law* 289, at 315.
[71] Tams, n. 69, at 385. See, in general, Miles Jackson, *Complicity in International Law* (Oxford University Press, 2015).
[72] Daniel Janse, 'International Terrorism and Self-Defence' (2006) 36 *Israel Yearbook of Human Rights* 149, at 168–9.
[73] Tams, n. 69, at 393 (emphasis added).

Finally, the attribution approach does not say what is to happen in cases where the state is simply unaware of the activities of the non-state group or simply unable to do anything about them. In this context, Tams notes that the attribution approach has limitations in that 'where a state is unaware of terrorist conduct it will not be exposed to forcible responses', although he does not then go on to say whether a victim state must simply sit and do nothing or whether it is able to take action which is then restricted to the non-state actors.[74] Kimberly Trapp, on the other hand, notes that, in these circumstances, 'the victim State is left with little choice. Either it respects the host State's territorial integrity at great risk to its own security, or it violates that State's territorial integrity in a limited and targeted fashion, using force against (and only against) the very source of the terrorist attack.'[75]

As such – and in maintaining the necessity for attribution under the effective control standard if the defending state wishes to extend its defensive actions *against*, as opposed to merely *within*, the host state and its infrastructure – another view is that attribution is not necessary if the victim state limits its response to action taken solely against the non-state actors. In this respect, '[b]eing an inherent right to repel or avert attacks, self-defence does not require that armed attacks by terrorists be attributable to the territorial state under the rules of state responsibility'.[76] It remains, however, that '[u]sing force against the base of operations of non-State terrorist actors within another State's territory ... amounts to a violation of that State's territorial integrity, even if the use of force is defensive and not targeted at the State's apparatus'.[77] The question thus becomes how, in the absence of attribution, a state might, if at all, overcome that violation of state territorial sovereignty.

### 8.4.2 The 'Unable or Unwilling' Doctrine

While some scholars have refrained from attempting to attribute the actions of non-state actors to a state for the purposes of invoking the right of self-defence, focus has remained upon the obligations that states are under in

---

[74] Ibid., at 386. [75] Trapp, n. 45, at 147.
[76] 'Leiden Policy Recommendations on Counter-Terrorism and International Law', in Larissa Van Den Herik and Nico Schrijver (eds.), *Counter-Terrorism Strategies in a Fragmented Legal Order: Meeting the Challenges* (Cambridge University Press, 2013), 706, at para. 42.
[77] Trapp, n. 45, at 145. See also Dapo Akande, 'Classification of Armed Conflicts: Relevant Legal Concepts', in Elizabeth Wilmshurst (ed.), *International Law and the Classification of Conflicts* (Oxford University Press, 2012), 32, at 73–4, where it is stated that 'the use of force by [a defending state against non-state actors] on the territory of the territorial State, without the consent of the latter, is a use of force *against* the territorial State. This is so even if the use of force is not directed against the government structures of the territorial State, or the purpose of the use of force is not to coerce the territorial State in any way.'

## 8.4 Military Action Restricted to the Non-state Actors

regard to the activities of non-state groups within their territory. Indeed, although the actions of the non-state actors may not be attributable to the state out of which they are operating, states are nonetheless legally obligated to not only refrain from providing positive assistance in support of the armed activities of non-state armed groups against other states[78] but also to take due diligence in ensuring that their territory is not used by non-state actors for such activities.[79] They have, in this sense, obligations of both a positive and a negative nature upon them. While a violation of these obligations does not *per se* provide states with a right to engage in self-defence against the non-state actors located within the violating state's territory, the situation has nonetheless given rise to what has become known as the 'unable or unwilling' doctrine.[80] Under this doctrine, forcible action in self-defence may be permissible if the host state is either *unable* or *unwilling* to take effective action against the non-state groups. In this respect, the host state would not be held responsible for the attack and could not, therefore, be directly targeted in response, but its inability or unwillingness to prevent the attacks would leave its territorial integrity susceptible to a limited breach by a defending state, with the defensive action restricted to targets of the non-state group.[81] For example, the Somalian authorities were *unable* to halt the activities of al-Shabaab in the border region with Kenya before Kenya invaded Somalian territory in 2011 and invoked its right of self-defence under Article 51,[82] while the international community appeared to accept that the Taliban regime was

---

[78] See Section 2.4.3 for more in the indirect use of force.

[79] It is an established principle of international law that a state has an obligation 'not to allow knowingly its territory to be used for acts contrary to the right of other states'. *Corfu Channel Case (United Kingdom v. Albania)*, Merits (1949) ICJ Reports 4, at 18–23. See also Declaration on Principles of International Law concerning Friendly Relations and Co-operation among States in Accordance with the Charter of the United Nations, UNGA Res. 2625 (XXV) (1970): 'States are required to take all reasonable steps to ensure that their territory is not used by non-state actors for purposes of armed activities – including planning, threatening, perpetrating, or providing material support for armed attacks – against other states and their interests.' See, in general, Joanna Kulesza, *Due Dilligence in International Law* (Brill, 2016).

[80] See, for example, Ashley S. Deeks, '"Unwilling or Unable": Toward a Normative Framework for Extraterritorial Self-Defense' (2012) 52 *Virginia Journal of International Law* 483; Paula Starski, 'Right to Self-Defense, Attribution and the Non-State Actor – Birth of the "Unable or Unwilling" Standard?' (2015) 75 *Heidelberg Journal of International Law* 455; Jutta Brunnée and Stephen J. Toope, 'Self-Defence against Non-State Actors: Are Powerful States Willing but Unable to Change International Law?' (2018) 67 *International & Comparative Law Quarterly* 263; Craig Martin, 'Challenging and Refining the "Unable or Unwilling" Doctrine' (2019) 52 *Vanderbilt Journal of Transnational Law* 387.

[81] Moir, n. 30, at 730.

[82] See Vidan Hadzi-Vidanovic, 'Kenya Invades Somalia Invoking the Right of Self-Defence', *EJIL Talk!*, 18 October 2011, available at: www.ejiltalk.org/kenya-invades-somalia-invoking-the-right-of-self-defence/.

*unwilling* (and potentially unable also) to take action against al-Qaida or permit the United States to do so in 2001.[83] Furthermore, this doctrine has been endorsed in the Chatham House Principles,[84] the Leiden Policy Recommendations,[85] and the so-called Bethlehem Principles,[86] and has also been an important part of the practice of some states, most notably the United States,[87] as well as having been expressly endorsed by the Attorney-Generals of both the United Kingdom and Australia[88] and as explicitly or implicitly witnessed in the practice of a number of other states.[89]

While a supporting legal basis has not always been provided for this doctrine, it appears to be based upon the customary principle of necessity.[90] In this respect, '[t]he requirement of necessity must first be assessed in the light of the actions of the state from the territory of which the terrorist acts emanate'.[91] Indeed:

[i]n the context of a use of force against a non-State group, it is suggested that the necessity condition would only be satisfied where the territorial State itself is either unable or unwilling to prevent continued attacks. It is worth emphasizing that this test of whether the territorial state is unable or unwilling to act is not an independent legal standard but merely an aspect of the application of the long-standing criterion of necessity.[92]

---

[83] See Section 8.3.2, although note that, despite an apparent acceptance that the Taliban was unwilling to take the required action against al-Qaida, the United States used this unwillingness to take action also against the Taliban regime.

[84] Chatham House Principles, n. 2, at 969.

[85] Leiden Policy Recommendations, n. 77, at para. 42.

[86] Bethlehem Principles, n. 63, at Principles 11 and 12.

[87] See, for example, its letter to the UN Security Council upon the launching of military action against the so-called Islamic State in Syria in 2014: UN Doc. S/2014/695, 23 September 2014.

[88] See UK Attorney-General Jeremy Wright, 'The Modern Law of Self-Defence', 11 January 2017, available at: www.gov.uk/government/uploads/system/uploads/attachment_data/file/583171/170111_Imminence_Speech_.pdf; Australian Attorney-General George Brandis, 'The Right of Self-Defence against Imminent Armed Attack in International Law', *EJIL Talk!*, 25 May 2017, available at: www.ejiltalk.org/the-right-of-self-defence-against-imminent-armed-attack-in-international-law/.

[89] According to one study, ten states have provided explicit endorsement of the doctrine (United States, United Kingdom, Germany, the Netherlands, Czech Republic, Canada, Australia, Russia, Turkey and Israel), three states have provided implicit endorsement (Belgium, South Africa and Iran), while ten states were ambiguous on the issue (France, Denmark, Norway, Portugal, Members of the GCC, Colombia, Uganda, Rwanda, Ethiopia and India), and then six objected (Syria, Ecuador, Venezuela, Cuba, Brazil and Mexico). See Elena Chachko and Ashley Deeks, 'Who Is on Board with "Unwilling or Unable"', *Lawfare*, 10 October 2016, available at: www.lawfareblog.com/who-board-unwilling-or-unable.

[90] See Section 6.3.1.  [91] Leiden Policy Recommendations, n. 76, at para. 42.

[92] Christof Heyns, Dapo Akande, Lawrence Hill-Cawthorne and Thompson Chengeta, 'The International Law Framework Regulating the Use of Armed Drones' (2016) 65 *International & Comparative Law Quarterly* 791, at 804.

## 8.4 Military Action Restricted to the Non-state Actors

More specifically, the 2006 Chatham House Principles stated:

If the right of self-defence ... is to be exercised in the territory of another State, it must be evident that that State is unable or unwilling to deal with the non-state actors itself, and that it is necessary to use force from outside to deal with the threat in circumstances where the consent of the territorial state cannot be obtained.[93]

While, in broadly similar terms, the 2010 Leiden Policy Recommendations frame the doctrine slightly differently:

Where a state is itself supporting or encouraging the actions of terrorists on its territory, it may well be unwilling to avert or repel the attack and action in self-defence may be necessary. Self-defence may also be necessary if the armed attack *cannot* be repelled or averted by the territorial state. States relying on self-defence therefore must show that the territorial state's action is not effective in countering the terrorist threat.[94]

As such, before an action in self-defence can be justified under the doctrine as necessary, a solution via the host state should normally be explored first, either through a request to the host state to take the appropriate action – whether or not of a forcible nature – or through a request for its consent to permit the defending state to take the necessary action itself. If after having done so it is clear that the host state is either unable or unwilling to take effective measures against the non-state actors to disrupt their activities and any plans for attack, then a right of self-defence will arise. Depending upon the circumstances this may be after the victim state has first approached the UN Security Council to take or authorise appropriate action.

The doctrine has been employed on several occasions. For example, in invoking its right of self-defence against terrorist attacks by Chechen rebels in the Pankisi Gorge border area of Georgia, Russia claimed that Georgia was 'unable or unwilling to counter the terrorist threat' posed to Russia by the rebels operating from its territory.[95] However, the doctrine arguably received most attention when the United States and a coalition of other states launched military action against the so-called Islamic State group within Syria in September 2014 in order to, in the words of former US President Obama, 'degrade and ultimately destroy' the group.[96] In her letter to the UN Secretary-General upon the launching of the strikes, the US ambassador to the United Nations, Samantha Power, stated that 'the Government of Iraq has asked that

---

[93] The Chatham House Principles, n. 2, at 969.
[94] Leiden Policy Recommendations, n. 76, at para. 42.
[95] See UN Doc. S/2002/1012, 12 September 2002.
[96] The White House, 'We Will Degrade and Ultimately Destroy ISIL', 10 September 2014, available at: https://obamawhitehouse.archives.gov/blog/2014/09/10/president-obama-we-will-degrade-and-ultimately-destroy-isil.

the United States lead international efforts to strike ISIL sites and military strongholds in Syria' and that:

> States must be able to defend themselves, in accordance with the inherent right of individual and collective self-defense, as reflected in Article 51 of the UN Charter, when, as is the case here, the government of the State where the threat is located is *unwilling or unable* to prevent the use of its territory for such attacks. The Syrian regime has shown that it cannot and will not confront these safe-havens effectively itself. Accordingly, the United States has initiated necessary and proportionate military actions in Syria in order to eliminate the ongoing ISIL threat.[97]

However, although the original coalition included, in addition to the United States, the states of Bahrain, Qatar, Saudi Arabia, Jordan and the United Arab Emirates, several of the coalition states who employed force within the territory of Iraq at the request of the Iraqi government refrained from extending action into Syrian territory. For example, Australian Prime Minister Tony Abbott stated that 'the legalities of operating inside Syria ... are quite different from the legalities of operating inside Iraq at the request and in support of the Iraqi government'.[98] However, many of these states that had initially refrained from extending military action into Syria against Islamic State subsequently joined the coalition in doing so. Nonetheless, it was notable that while several states expressly referred to the fact that Syria had no effective control over the part of Syrian territory that Islamic State had occupied,[99] only a few made express reference to the 'unable or unwilling' doctrine.[100]

Furthermore, while it was arguably not possible to clearly attribute to Iraq any of the attacks that were used to justify the killing of Iranian General Qassem Soleimani in January 2020,[101] this may not have been fatal to the US's claim of self-defence upon Iraqi territory as the claim may have been made that Iraq had been either unable or unwilling to take the necessary action to halt the series of attacks by Kata'ib Hezbollah which, in turn, permitted the United States to take the necessary action. However, despite the fact that the United States has been a leading proponent of the unable or unwilling doctrine it was of significance that it did not expressly choose to invoke it on this occasion to justify the killing of

---

[97] UN Doc. S/2014/695, 23 September 2014. See Jens David Ohlin, 'The Unwilling or Unable Doctrine Comes to Life', *Opinio Juris*, 23 September 2014, available at: http://opiniojuris.org/2014/09/23/unwilling-unable-doctrine-comes-life/.

[98] Prime Minister of Australia, 'Interview with Fran Kelly', *ABC Radio National*, 16 September 2014, available at: www.abc.net.au/radionational/programs/breakfast/tony-abbott/5746376.

[99] See, for example the letter from Germany to the UN Security Council (UN Doc. S/2015/946, 10 December 2015) and the letter from Belgium to the UN Security Council (UN Doc. S/2016/523, 9 June 2016).

[100] See UN Doc. S/2015/221, 31 March 2015 (Canada); UN Doc. S/2015/693, 9 September 2015 (Australia); UN Doc. S/2015/563, 24 July 2015 (Turkey).

[101] This incident is discussed in Chapters 6 and 7.

Soleimani. This was particularly surprising given that claims were made that the United States had issued warnings to the Iraqi government to take action to halt the attacks.[102] For example, in a special briefing by the US State Department following military strikes that the United Sthates had undertaken on 29 December 2019 against Kata'ib Hezbollah positions within the Iraqi–Syrian border it was claimed that the United States had 'warned the Iraqi Government many times ... to carry out their responsibility to protect [it] as their invited guests ... and *they have not taken the appropriate steps to do so*'.[103] Similarly, not long before the Soleimani strike, US Secretary of Defence Mark Esper again stated that the US had repeatedly 'urged the Iraqi government to take all necessary steps to protect American forces in their country' in light of attacks that had taken place during November and December 2019.[104]

These statements potentially could have been used to support a claim that Iraq had been both unwilling *and* unable to take the necessary action. Indeed, as Scott Anderson argued, the fact that 'the United States repeatedly complained to Iraqi officials about ongoing rocket attacks against U.S. facilities over an extended period of time without successful resolution may give it a reasonable argument for necessity under either standard'.[105] However, the focus here was arguably on Iraq's inability to take the necessary action given that the United States ultimately took action *on* Iraqi territory rather than specifically *against* Iraq.

Although the 'unable or unwilling' doctrine is now a fairly well settled part of the US government's legal position, and also appears to be creeping into the justificatory discourse and general rhetoric of other states, it nonetheless remains controversial under international law, with various theoretical and practical problems surrounding its emergence.[106]

---

[102] There is a further aspect of the application of the unable or unwilling doctrine to this situation which arguably distinguishes it from those situations in which it is normally applied, in that rather than the focus of the use of force being non-state actors it was, instead, a state actor (Iran). As such, in addition to a determination that Iraq is either unable or unwilling to take action to cease the attacks/threat, the United States was also arguably under an obligation to make such a request to the state of Iran in satisfying the criterion of necessity, although there is no specific evidence to suggest that it had done so.

[103] US Department of State, Senior State Department Officials On U.S. Airstrikes in Iraq and Syria, Special Briefing, Office of the Spokesperson, 30 December 2019, available at: https://2017-2021.state.gov/senior-state-department-officials-on-u-s-airstrikes-in-iraq-and-syria/ (emphasis added).

[104] US Department of Defense, Statement by U.S. Secretary of Defense Dr. Mark T. Esper as Prepared, 2 January 2020, available at: www.defense.gov/News/Releases/Release/Article/2049227/statement-by-secretary-of-defense-dr-mark-t-esper-as-prepared/.

[105] Scott R. Anderson, 'The Law and Consequences of the Recent Airstrike in Iraq', *Lawfare*, 1 January 2020, available at: www.lawfareblog.com/law-and-consequences-recent-airstrikes-iraq.

[106] See Ryan Goodman, 'International Law on Airstrikes against ISIS in Syria', *Just Security*, 28 August 2014, available at: www.justsecurity.org/14414/international-law-airstrikes-isis-syria/.

### 8.4.2.1 Theoretical and Practical Problems of the Doctrine

In satisfying the necessity requirement of self-defence, reasonable non-forcible courses of action should either not be available to the defending state or there should exist, at least, a reasonable expectation that any recourse to them would be ineffective.[107] Yet, there appears to be little agreement as to what this might entail. Given that for the most part the action under the unable or unwilling doctrine is not ostensibly taken *against* the host state itself, but against non-state actors operating from within it, the principle of state sovereignty would seem to dictate that the defending state should either approach the host state to take the required action or at least coordinate with it in doing so. If military action is deemed necessary, either taken jointly with the host state or solely by the defending state, this should be with the consent of the host state.[108] However, the unable or unwilling doctrine appears to throw some doubt on this position.

#### 8.4.2.1.1 Unable (and Unwilling?) States

While the Leiden Policy Recommendations proclaim that a state '*unable* to avert or halt a non-state armed attack ought to consent to forcible action by other states to act in its place' and '[i]f it does not do so, action may be taken in self-defence',[109] on the basis that it can then presumably be certified to be an unwilling state, the Bethlehem Principles appear to go further in proclaiming that:

> [t]he *requirement for consent does not operate* in circumstances in which there is a *reasonable and objective basis* for concluding that the third state is *unable* to effectively restrain the armed activities of the non-state actor such as to leave the state that has a necessity to act in self-defense with no other reasonably available effective means to address an imminent or actual armed attack.[110]

In other words, under the Bethlehem Principles – which, as noted in Section 8.4.2, have been expressly adopted, at least, by the United States, United

---

[107] See Section 6.3.1.1. [108] See Chapter 9 on the general issue of consent to intervention.
[109] Leiden Policy Recommendations, n. 76, at Principle 50.
[110] Bethlehem Principles, n. 63, at Principle 12 (emphasis added). For an argument against such a broad interpretation of the right of self-defence see 'A Plea against the Abusive Invocation of Self-Defence as a Response to Terrorism' (2016) 1 *Revue Belge De Droit International* 31, which is a document published in 2016 and signed by 242 leading experts on the *jus ad bellum*: 'the mere fact that, despite its efforts, a State is unable to put an end to terrorist activities on its territory is insufficient to justify bombing that State's territory without its consent. Such an argument finds no support either in existing legal instruments or in the case law of the International Court of Justice. Accepting this argument entails a risk of grave abuse in that military action may henceforth be conducted against the will of a great number of States under the sole pretext that, in the intervening State's view, they were not sufficiently effective in fighting terrorism.'

Kingdom and Australia – a perceived inability of the host state to be able to effectively deal with the non-state actors seemingly removes even the requirement of seeking consent. Yet, it is not clear how a 'reasonable and objective' determination is to be reached that a state is unable to restrain the activities of the non-state actors. Similarly, it is unclear how it is to be determined whether any action taken by the territorial state has proven to be ineffective or likely to be ineffective. For example, what is the situation if the host state is taking action but not in a way or to an extent that is acceptable to the defending state? Does this then trigger the 'unable' element of the doctrine (or even, perhaps, the 'unwilling' element)? An acting state may not be in the best position to be able to make such an objective determination, with it perhaps more appropriately being left to a body such as the UN Security Council to make. Yet, given that the unable or unwilling doctrine falls for consideration under the right of self-defence this would arguably be seen by advocates of the doctrine as going too far and depriving states of their 'inherent' right.

In the context of the conflict in Syria from 2014, it was not entirely clear whether the Assad regime was able to prevent Islamic State from operating and continuing to carry out attacks from its soil against Iraq,[111] although given the regime's continued military action against the group it would appear that it was not. US President Obama was seemingly clear that he did not 'see *any scenario* in which Assad is *able* to bring peace and stability' to areas controlled by Islamic State in Syria,[112] although he provided no supporting reasoning or evidence for this conclusion. By contrast, in invoking the right of self-defence to strike Islamic State in Syria a number of states also expressly included in their justification the existence of Security Council Resolution 2249 (2015), which '[d]*etermin*[ed]' that the Islamic State 'constitutes a global and unprecedented threat to international peace and security' and '[n]ot[ed] the letters ... from the Iraqi authorities which state[d] that Da'esh has established a safe haven outside Iraq's borders that is a direct threat to the security of the Iraqi people and territory'.[113] It is at least arguable, then, that the acting states felt compelled to rely on these determinations made by the Security Council, rather than on their own or any other state's determination of the ability of the Assad regime in Syria to take the required action, in establishing

---

[111] See, for example, Michael Lewis, 'What Does the "Unwilling or Unable" Standard Mean in the Context of Syria?', *Just Security*, 12 September 2014, available at: www.justsecurity.org/14903/unwilling-unable-standard-context-syria/.

[112] See Colum Lynch, 'Obama Hints at Legal Rationale for Airstrikes in Syria', *Foreign Policy*, 28 August 2014, available at: http://foreignpolicy.com/2014/08/28/obama-hints-at-legal-rationale-for-airstrikes-in-syria/ (emphasis added).

[113] UNSC Res. 2249 (2015), preamble.

that the pre-conditions for the invocation of the doctrine were met in this case.[114]

### 8.4.2.1.2 Failed States

Further questions regarding the 'ability' aspect of the doctrine arise in the context of so-called failed or failing states (that is, states without a functioning government in all, or at least in large, parts of the state). While a failed state does not mean a loss of statehood, and '[t]he territory and the population of that state will continue to be protected by the prohibition of the use of force',[115] it is arguably more reasonable to assume that there is an inability under these circumstances. In such cases, questions arise in regard to whether action is only permissible in regions of the host state where it is no longer in effective control, or whether it may equally be taken in areas in which the host state is in control but simply unable to quell the threat presented by the group. While the Assad regime, with the direct assistance of Russian armed forces,[116] has been able to regain control of areas previously controlled by rebel groups and the Islamic State, the regime was not for many years in control of large parts of Syrian territory. This lack of full control by the Assad regime was, as noted in Section 8.4.2, a key element in the decision of many states to join the military action,[117] as well as being something referenced by the UN Secretary-General in what appeared to be an implicit blessing of the strikes shortly after they were launched when he noted 'that the strikes took place in areas no longer under the effective control of that Government.'[118]

As a further example, on 16 October 2011, Kenya invoked its right of self-defence in sending ground troops into Somalia and carrying out airstrikes in response to attacks by the al-Shabaab terrorist group which were not only located there but which also controlled large portions of territory outside of the capital, Mogadishu.[119] Although at the time Somalia was not quite the failed state it had been,[120] it was clear that governmental control was limited.

---

[114] Monika Hakimi and Jacob Katz Cogan, 'A Role for the Security Council on Defensive Force?', *EJIL Talk!*, 21 October 2016, available at: www.ejiltalk.org/a-role-for-the-security-council-on-defensive-force/. See Section 8.4.2.

[115] Leiden Policy Recommendations, n. 76, at 50.

[116] Support that was not, in and of itself, claimed to be unlawful by other states. See Tom Ruys, 'Of Arms, Funding and "Non-Lethal" Assistance: Issues Surrounding Third-State Intervention in the Syrian Civil War' (2014) 13 *Chinese Journal of International Law* 13, at 16–17.

[117] See, for example, UN Doc. S/2015/946, 10 December 2015 (Germany); UN Doc. S/2016/523, 9 June 2016 (Belgium).

[118] Ryan Goodman and Sarah Knuckley, 'Remarkable Statement by UN Secretary General on US Airstrike in Syria', *Just Security*, 23 September 2014, available at: www.justsecurity.org/15456/remarkable-statement-secretary-general-airstrikes-syria/.

[119] UN Doc. S/2011/646, 18 October 2011.    [120] See Sections 3.4.2.2 and 5.6.2.

Kenya did not request Somalia's consent to the intervention and appeared to assume, perhaps reasonably, that the Transitional Federal Government was unable to take effective action against the group. While the president of Somalia initially rejected the intervention, claiming that 'Somalia's government and its people will not allow forces entering its soil without prior agreement', there was a generally muted reaction to the intervention.[121] On the basis of these incidents it might appear, therefore, that a lack of effective control by a government over its territory justifying the conclusion that seeking consent is not required, at least for strikes within the areas of territory over which the host state does not exert control. Yet, the muted reaction in relation to Kenya's intervention in Somalia, at least, may equally have been due to a subsequent declaration that the action was taken with the concurrence of the authorities in Mogadishu and a joint communiqué issued at the conclusion of a meeting between the government of Kenya and the Transitional Federal Government of Somalia, which focused on the breakdown of governance within the country which had given rise to the prevalence of threats and attacks by al-Shabaab.[122]

### 8.4.2.1.3 Unable Yet Willing States

Issues also arise in the context of a state that is *willing* to take military action against the non-state groups operating from within its territory, regardless of the fact that it is ultimately unable to do so. Despite the animosity between the Assad regime in Syria and the intervening states in 2014, the Assad regime was, for example, clearly willing to take action against so-called Islamic State. It should not, in this respect, necessarily be assumed that it was hostile to the US-led coalition taking action upon its territory. Indeed, Syrian Foreign Minister, Walid al Moallem, stated that 'Syria is ready to cooperate and coordinate on the regional and international level in the war on terror ... But any effort to combat terrorism should come in coordination with the Syrian government.'[123]

However, in these circumstances the willingness element of the doctrine would seem to be somewhat redundant, in that if the host state is perceived to be unable to take effective action against the non-state group then whether it is willing to take action or not is irrelevant in that action will be initiated by the defending state regardless. Indeed, either the host state consents to the

---

[121] Mike Pflanz, 'Somalia's President Questions Kenya's Al-Shabaab Mission', *The Telegraph*, 25 October 2011, available at: www.telegraph.co.uk/news/worldnews/africaandindianocean/kenya/8848537/Somalias-president-questions-Kenyas-al-Shabaab-mission.html.
[122] Ibid.
[123] Justin Sink, 'White House Won't Commit to Asking Congress for Syria Strike', *The Hill*, 25 August 2014, available at: http://thehill.com/policy/defense/215905-white-house-wont-commit-to-asking-congress-for-syria-strike.

defending state taking action upon its territory or it does not, in which case it also becomes an unwilling state. In this respect it has been observed, that under the doctrine, given that 'Syria [was] unable to prevent its territory from being used by [Islamic State] to plan, prepare and execute attacks against targets in Iraq ... Whether they are willing to cooperate with the US strikes against ISIS is irrelevant to this analysis.'[124]

Others, however, have questioned this, in particular the motive of a defending state which is not willing to cooperate with an unable yet willing territorial state.[125] It was of significance then, and a clear rebuke to any potential willingness on the part of the Syrian regime, that the Obama administration expressly stated, in the light of President Obama's comments regarding the inability of the regime to deal with the group, that it was 'not looking for the approval of the Syrian regime' in launching action against Islamic State on Syrian territory.[126] It was not clear, however, whether and on what basis Syria was still deemed an unwilling state, given its clear expression of willingness to cooperate and coordinate action against the Islamic State upon its territory. In the future, as with determinations regarding the *ability* of a state, it remains to be seen whether the *willingness* of a state is something that will only be determined unilaterally or whether states will seek to rely on a UN Security Council determination, for example, that this is the case.

### 8.4.2.1.4 Able Yet Unwilling States

Further questions arise in regard to states that are able, yet unwilling. The Bethlehem Principles assert that '[t]he failure or refusal to agree to a reasonable and effective plan of action, and to take such action, may support a conclusion that the state in question is to be regarded as a colluding or a harboring state',[127] thereby permitting action also to be taken against it. This is significant in light of the fact that there are few indications in state practice that the 'effective control' test of attribution no longer governs situations where action is to be taken against both the non-state actors and the host state.[128] Indeed, the Bethlehem Principles, in their conception of the 'unwilling or unable' doctrine, appear to be of the view that the standard of attribution should be lowered so as to permit action against a 'colluding' or 'harbouring' state:

In the case of a colluding or a harboring state, the extent of the responsibility of that state for aiding or assisting the non-state actor in its armed activities may be relevant

---

[124] Lewis, n. 112.
[125] Ryan Goodman, 'International Law – and the Unwilling and Unable Test – for US Military Operations in Syria', *Just Security*, 12 September 2014, available at: www.justsecurity.org/14949/ international-law-unwilling-unable-test-military-operations-syria/.
[126] As stated by State Department spokeswoman Jen Psaki. Quoted in Sink, n. 124.
[127] Bethlehem Principles, n. 63, at Principle 12.   [128] See Section 8.3.

to considerations of the necessity to act in self-defense and the proportionality of such action, *including against the colluding or harboring state.*[129]

It is, of course, quite a leap between a state not agreeing to – perhaps extensive and destructive – military action upon its territory, albeit that which may be limited to targeting non-state actors located there, and that state being held effectively responsible for the actions of the non-state actors and thus subject to being directly targeted. In any case, however, it would appear, again, that:

> [t]he requirement for consent does not operate in circumstances in which there is a reasonable and objective basis for concluding that the third state is *colluding* with the non-state actor or is otherwise unwilling to effectively restrain the armed activities of the non-state actor such as to leave the state that has a necessity to act in self-defense with no other reasonably available effective means to address an imminent or actual armed attack.[130]

While there was nothing to suggest that the Assad regime in Syria was colluding with the Islamic State – indeed, it appeared to be actively fighting against it – it appears that if there is evidence to suggest that a host state is colluding with a non-state group, then unwillingness can therefore be presumed, thereby rendering any questions regarding the ability of the state to take action unnecessary. It does, however, again raise the question as to how a 'reasonable and objective' determination is to be made, this time in relation to whether the host state is, in fact, colluding with the non-state group, as opposed to whether it is able to take the required action against it, and what is to fall within the parameters of 'collusion'.

Furthermore, if action is permitted against not just *harbouring* but also *colluding* states, it is possible that action might be taken against neither the non-state actors who perpetrated the attack nor the host state where the non-state actors are located, but instead against one or more other states that have 'colluded' in some way with the non-state group. Even more broadly, however, under the Bethlehem Principles the use of armed force may also seemingly be taken against any *entity* responsible for the 'provision of material support essential to the attacks'.[131] This is particularly concerning as it potentially 'puts banks and other financial institutions in the firing line'.[132]

---

[129] Bethlehem Principles, n. 63, at Principle 4 (emphasis added).
[130] Ibid., at Principle 11. See Section 7.5 for more on self-defence in response to imminent threats.
[131] Ibid., at Principle 7.
[132] Elizabeth Wilmshurst and Michael Wood, 'Self-Defense against Non-State Actors: Reflections on the "Bethlehem Principles"' (2013) **107** *American Journal of International Law* 390, at 394. By contrast, the Leiden Policy Recommendations provide for a more limited version of the 'unable or unwilling' doctrine in stating that the proportionality requirement of self-defence 'will normally mean that measures of self-defence against suspected terrorists must be directed primarily against the terrorist groups responsible for the armed attack in

### 8.4.2.1.5 Other Relevant Factors

In addition to the inability of a state to take the necessary action against the non-state groups, or its collusion with them, there are other factors that might be relevant in determining whether the seeking of consent is necessary under the unable or unwilling doctrine. Indeed, the Bethlehem Principles suggest that making efforts to obtain consent is unnecessary in circumstances where the state is either able or willing, albeit this time if there is:

> a strong, reasonable, and objective basis for concluding that the seeking of consent would be likely to *materially undermine the effectiveness of action in self-defense*, whether for reasons of disclosure, delay, incapacity to act, or otherwise, or would increase the risk of armed attack, vulnerability to future attacks, or other development that would give rise to an independent imperative to act in self-defense.[133]

On the one hand this would seem to be a reasonable qualification on the need to obtain consent, as it would be futile to require such an approach for consent to be made if this would ultimately jeopardise the defensive action undertaken. Yet, on the other hand, it might appear to be the final nail in the coffin in terms of any requirement to obtain consent, as it would appear to provide a limitless discretion to states to take action for virtually any reason without seeking consent. In this respect, if the unable or unwilling doctrine is located within the principle of necessity, rather than providing a restraint upon the actions of states the principle would, instead, seem to constitute an *enabler* of action in providing a broad freedom in determining where to focus the justificatory discourse.

However, in avoiding seeking consent the defending state's concerns would arguably need to be directly in regard to the effectiveness of any prospective military action. In this respect, the existence of any recent or historical animosity between a state and the defending state is, by itself, arguably insufficient to indicate unwillingness or collusion. In these circumstances an alternative justification – outside of the bounds of self-defence, including the 'unable or unwilling' doctrine – would be required for the proposed military action.[134] Yet, if such animosity, or indeed any other factor, gives rise to clear

---

question or their facilities. Only in exceptional circumstances will self-defence justify the use of force against the armed forces or facilities of the territorial state, for example, in circumstances where the territorial state is *supporting* suspected terrorists, as in Afghanistan in 2001.' Leiden Policy Recommendations, n. 76, at para. 43. Yet, no information is provided as to the level of 'support' which it would be necessary to demonstrate in taking action against the host state and it seems to be, again, a significant departure from the 'effective control' standard of attribution for action to be taken against a host state (on which see Section 8.3.1).

[133] Bethlehem Principles, n. 63, at Principle 12 (emphasis added).
[134] Goodman, n. 126. See Section 6.3.1.2 on the requirement that any action in self-defence be for the obtainment of defensive objectives.

and legitimate concerns regarding the effectiveness of the proposed course of action, then this perhaps might be perceived as altering the situation.

### 8.4.2.1.6 The Legal Status of the Doctrine

While the Bethlehem Principles provide but one version of the 'unable or unwilling' doctrine, it is significant – not to mention arguably concerning, given the latitude for action which they provide – that three of the leading proponents of the doctrine (United States, United Kingdom and Australia) have expressly endorsed these principles.[135] However, in addition to the theoretical and practical issues discussed in the preceding sections that arise in its application, there remain significant question marks over the international legal status of the doctrine. Even academic proponents of it struggle to argue that it exists as an established legal doctrine. For example, while setting out how as a normative doctrine it might operate, an extensive study on the topic by Ashley Deeks in 2012 'found no cases in which states clearly assert that they follow the test out of a sense of legal obligation'.[136] While some scholars have argued that despite the apparent invocation by a number of states the doctrine was far from accepted by the international community of states as a whole in the context of the US-led intervention in Syria in 2014,[137] others have argued that there is a more general lack of state practice and *opinio juris* in favour of it.[138] Yet, whereas states have not directly engaged in debate regarding the doctrine and the issues it gives rise to and have neither clearly accepted or rejected it, a small number of states have, either explicitly or implicitly, provided support to the doctrine,[139] meaning that, at present, it would appear that 'the precise parameters of the right to respond to an armed

---

[135] The UK Attorney General, Jeremy Wright, seemed to imply in 2017 that Canada and New Zealand, the remaining two of the so-called Five Eyes, might also have adopted them, although these two states have not expressly confirmed this. See UK Attorney-General Jeremy Wright, 'The Modern Law of Self-Defence', 11 January 2017, available at: https://assets.publishing.service.gov.uk/government/uploads/system/uploads/attachment_data/file/583171/170111_Imminence_Speech_.pdf.

[136] Deeks, n. 81, at 503. See also Laurie O'Connor, 'Legality of the Use of Force in Syria against Islamic State and the Khorasan Group' (2016) 3 *Journal on the Use of Force and International Law* 70, at 95; Christine Gray, 'Targeted Killings: Recent US Attempts to Create a Legal Framework' (2013) 66 *Current Legal Problems* 75, at 86.

[137] See, in general, Olivier Corten, 'The 'Unwilling or Unable' Test: Has It Been, and Could It Be, Accepted?' (2016) 29 *Leiden Journal of International Law* 777.

[138] See, in particular, Kevin Jon Heller, 'The Absence of Practice Supporting the "Unwilling or Unable" Test', *Opinio Juris*, 17 February 2015, available at: http://opiniojuris.org/2015/02/17/unable-unwilling-test-unstoppable-scholarly-imagination/; Kevin Jon Heller, 'The Seemingly Inexorable March of "Unwilling or Unable" through the Academy', *Opinio Juris*, 6 March 2015, available at: http://opiniojuris.org/2015/03/06/the-seemingly-inexorable-march-of-unwilling-or-unable-through-the-academy/.

[139] See Chachko and Deeks, n. 90.

attack by [non-state actors] with a use of force in foreign territory are still being worked out in practice'.[140]

## 8.5 TARGETED KILLINGS

The final section in this chapter takes a dedicated look at so-called targeted killings.[141] There is no generally accepted definition of targeted killings, although they can be understood as the extrajudicial use of force with lethal effect against a specific individual located in the territory of another state. There have been several prominent instances of targeted killings in recent years, most notably the operation which led to the death of the al-Qaida leader, Osama bin Laden, in 2011 in Pakistan, as well as, more recently, the drone strike which led to the death of Iranian General Qassem Soleimani in 2020 in Iraq, both of which were conducted by the United States.

There are several legal frameworks that regulate such killings. The *jus ad bellum*, as the focus of this book, is a key legal regime in assessing the legality of the practice of targeted killings given their extraterritorial element. Yet, the legal regimes of the law of armed conflict (LOAC) and international human rights law (IHRL) are also relevant in the assessment depending upon the circumstances in which the individual is located and targeted.[142] A *jus ad bellum* justification of self-defence is often advanced as the main justification for these killings. Yet, given that it is the extrajudicial targeted killing of a particular individual that is under consideration, human rights considerations are particularly significant in the assessment of their legality. Furthermore, these types of killings have often been seen in situations where a state is in a continuous armed conflict with the group of whom the individual is affiliated, or at least declares it is at war with the group, meaning that LOAC is also of some relevance. Given that there is an interaction between these different relevant legal regimes, a holistic approach must be taken in examining the

---

[140] Kimberley N. Trapp, 'Can Non-State Actors Mount an Armed Attack?', in Marc Weller (ed.), *The Oxford Handbook of the Use of Force in International Law* (Oxford University Press, 2015), 679, at 696.

[141] See, in general, Nils Melzer, *Targeted Killings in International Law* (Oxford University Press, 2008); Claire Finkelstein, Jens David Ohlin and Andrew Altman (eds.), *Targeted Killings: Law and Morality in an Asymmetrical World* (Oxford University Press, 2012).

[142] These frameworks are, of course, potentially applicable in the context of *all* uses of force, and are not restricted to those constituting acts of targeted killing. See Section 1.6 on the emerging recognition of a 'human element' to the *jus ad bellum*. While not all may agree that international human rights law should be a prominent consideration when a state resorts to military action against another state, the fact that targeted killings involve the specific killing of an individual means that one cannot escape the relevance of this branch of law.

legality of the practice in general, and in any examination of a particular incident.[143]

The first port of call in assessing the legality of targeted killings is the *jus ad bellum* framework in that it is concerned with, as discussed in the previous sections of this chapter, as well as throughout this book, the issue of if and how one state may enter the territory of another state in employing armed force. If an identifiable necessity arises for the use of force against a specific individual within another state, the acting state would first need to request the consent of the territorial state concerned for it to use force within its territory.[144] While controversial in many respects, consent has been provided by Pakistan, Yemen and Somalia at various points for the use of drones by the United States within their respective territories which have been utilised for targeted killings.[145] If such consent is clearly and freely granted, and subject to what has been discussed in Section 8.4.2 in connection with consent in the context of the 'unable or unwilling' doctrine, then the prohibition of the threat or use of force would not be engaged.[146]

However, if consent is denied or withdrawn, or is not sought, then a state's use of lethal armed force upon the territory of another state would need to be legally grounded elsewhere, most obviously upon the right of self-defence. The immediate problem facing such a justification is whether the action in self-defence has been preceded by an attack of sufficient gravity to constitute an 'armed attack' for the purposes of Article 51 of the UN Charter[147] or the imminent threat thereof.[148] While Chapter 6 highlighted the difficulties regarding attaching such a threshold to armed attacks, it is a requirement that is consistently raised by scholars for a use of force to constitute an armed attack.[149]

---

[143] See, for example, Nigel D. White and Lydia Davies-Bright, 'Drone Strikes: A Remote Form of Self-Defence?', in Jens David Ohlin (ed.), *Research Handbook on Remote Warfare* (Edward Elgar, 2017), 213, at 235–44.

[144] While the issue of state consent is addressed more fully in Chapter 9, and so will not be explored in any depth here, it should be noted that consent would need to be obtained from the highest levels of government and not, for example, a regional authority within the state. It also would need to be provided in advance of or at the time that the action is taken and be clearly expressed and established and have been provided freely and without coercion. Any force taken upon the basis of consent must remain within the limits of the consent provided and if it is withdrawn by the territorial state any forcible measures would need to cease.

[145] See, in general, Max Byrne, 'Consent and the Use of Force: An Examination of "Intervention by Invitation" as a Basis for US Drone Strikes in Pakistan, Somalia and Yemen' (2016) 3 *Journal on the Use of Force and International Law* 97.

[146] See, in general, Chapter 9 on the issue of consent to intervention.

[147] For an extensive discussion on this issue, see Section 6.2.5.

[148] See, further, Section 7.5 on the concept of imminence.

[149] See, as an example of this in the context of targeted killings, White and Davies-Bright, n. 144, at 230. During these incidents, the host state is not usually directly targeted, meaning

In this respect, although it is perhaps arguable that the killing of Osama bin Laden was in response to the armed attack against the United States that took place on 9/11,[150] it is difficult to see how the killing of Reyaad Khan by the United Kingdom in 2015 in Syria may be said to be in response to an actual or imminent threat of an armed attack. Indeed, in what was seen as 'a new departure' for the United Kingdom,[151] a British RAF drone carried out the strike against the British national, Reyaad Khan, on 21 August 2015,[152] which was the first such targeted killing by the United Kingdom outside of an armed conflict. While the killing of bin Laden had occurred after an armed attack, albeit one that took place ten years previously, the targeted killing of Reyaad Kahn seemingly did not. Indeed, the strike appeared to ostensibly be in response to plans for attacks against the United Kingdom and British citizens.[153] The United Kingdom informed the UN Security Council of its actions, as required by Article 51 of the UN Charter,[154] and merely stated that '[t]here was clear evidence of [him] planning and directing armed attacks against the UK. These were part of a series of actual and foiled attempts to attack the UK and our allies',[155] although no evidence or further information was provided on the nature of these. The drone attack that led to the death of Iranian General Qassem Soleimani in January 2020 was, as discussed in Chapters 6 and 7, based upon both past attacks as well as the generally perceived bad behaviour of both Iran and the Iranian supported group Kata'ib Hezbollah, neither of which by themselves would seem to constitute an armed attack, or the temporally imminent threat of one.[156] Yet, as discussed in Chapter 7, certain states, including the United Kingdom, no longer assess imminence upon the basis of the temporal proximity of an armed attack, but rather on the existence of contextual factors regarding a perceived threat,[157] and it

---

that states do not often attempt to fully attribute the actions of the individuals to the host state

[150] It is also arguable that the killing took place as part of the conflict against al-Qaida in Afghanistan that had 'spilled over' into Pakistan. See Marko Milanovic and Vidan Hadzi-Vidanovic, 'A Taxonomy of Armed Conflict', in Nigel D. White and Christian Henderson (eds.), *Research Handbook on International Conflict and Security Law:* Jus ad Bellum, Jus in Bello *and* Jus post Bellum (Edward Elgar, 2013), 256, at 292.

[151] Christine Gray, 'Targeted Killing Outside Armed Conflict: A New Departure for the UK?' (2016) 3 *Journal on the Use of Force and International Law* 198.

[152] See BBC News, 'Cardiff Jihadist Reyaad Khan, 21, Killed by RAF Drone', 7 September 2015, available at: www.bbc.co.uk/news/uk-wales-34176790.

[153] See House of Commons Debates, Hansard, 7 September 2015, col. 26, available at: https://publications.parliament.uk/pa/cm201516/cmhansrd/cm150907/debtext/150907-0001.htm.

[154] See UN Doc. S/2015/688, 8 September 2015, in which the United Kingdom claimed to be acting in the context of its inherent right of both individual *and* collective self-defence, thereby also linking it to the armed conflict it was involved in with ISIS in Iraq. See Section 6.6.1 for more on the reporting requirement under the right of self-defence.

[155] Hansard, n. 153.   [156] See Section 6.2 for more on this incident.   [157] See Section 7.5.

appeared to be this version of imminence and necessity that was employed by the United Kingdom and United States on these occasions.[158]

More broadly, the necessity and proportionality criteria of self-defence require a state to restrict its actions to those with a defensive objective.[159] Not only would these seem to rule out any military action taken in punishment or simple retaliation for a prior attack, but question marks are also raised over whether the elimination of an enemy, whether an entire group or an individual, could be said to have a sufficiently specific defensive objective, as well as whether such an action would be proportionate to it.

A clear engagement and application of the relevant international legal regimes is not always apparent in either the practice of states or the work of scholars, and such targeted killing operations and the associated justifications tend to blur the boundaries between them.[160] The blurring of the distinction between the law on the use of force and LOAC can in certain respects also be seen following the killing of Reyaad Khan by the United Kingdom. The Prime Minister David Cameron clearly stated 'that the strike was not part of coalition military action against ISIL in Syria; it was a targeted strike to deal with a clear, credible and specific terrorist threat to our country at home'.[161] Indeed, the UK Parliament had only provided the green light for the United Kingdom to join the military campaign against Islamic State in Syria on 2 December 2015, sometime after the strike had taken place. Yet, it was somewhat ironic that with self-defence as the legal justification for the strike a subsequent report by the Human Rights Committee of the UK's Parliament that addressed the UK's policy on the use of drones for targeted killings adopted the view 'that the drone strike in Syria was part of [the] wider armed conflict in which the UK was already engaged, to which the Law of War applies, and that the Government therefore did not use lethal force outside of armed conflict when it targeted and killed Reyaad Khan on 21 August'.[162] Nonetheless, given that

---

[158] See, in particular, the discussion in Section 7.5.2.
[159] See Section 6.3 on the twin requirements of necessity and proportionality.
[160] This was apparent, for example, in a speech on the topic of the 'Obama Administration and International Law' given by former Legal Advisor to the US Department of State, Harold Koh, on 25 March 2010. In his speech, Koh appeared to set out two underlying legal bases for targeted killings in the fight against al-Qaida but did not elaborate on the distinction and relationship between them: 'the United States is in an armed conflict with Al Qaeda, as well as the Taliban and associated forces, in response to the horrific 9/11 attacks, and may use force consistent with its right to self-defense under international law'. Harold H. Koh, 'The Obama Administration and International Law', 25 March 2010, available at: https://2009-2017.state.gov/s/l/releases/remarks/139119.htm. Koh therefore identifies the two legal regimes of the *jus ad bellum* and international humanitarian law but does not refer to international human rights law.
[161] Hansard, n. 153.
[162] See House of Lords, House of Commons, Joint Committee on Human Rights, 'The Government's Policy on the Use of Drones for Targeted Killing', Second Report of Session

the strike was presented as a 'new departure' by the UK government the report focused upon the general issue of the United Kingdom using lethal force *outside* of an armed conflict.

This blurring of the *jus ad bellum* and the LOAC was also clearly seen in the killing of Osama bin Laden. On 2 May 2011, a team of US Special Forces entered his compound in Abbottabad, Pakistan, and carried out an operation which resulted in his death.[163] The operation was justified in the following way:

> Given bin Laden's unquestioned leadership position within al Qaeda and his clear continuing operational role, there can be no question that he was the leader of an enemy force and a legitimate target in our armed conflict with al Qaeda. In addition, bin Laden continued to pose an imminent threat to the United States that engaged our right to use force, a threat that materials seized during the raid have only further documented. Under these circumstances, there is no question that he presented a lawful target for the use of lethal force.[164]

Whether or not bin Laden actually posed an 'imminent' threat under the *jus ad bellum*, thereby justifying the incursion into Pakistani territory to conduct the operation that led to his killing, it is clear that the US also perceived the LOAC as providing a basis in the justification. This branch of law does not govern if and when a military operation is legally permissible but how armed conflicts may be fought, in particular who and what may be targeted, and it only applies if the conditions for an armed conflict exist.[165]

---

2015–16, HL Paper 141, HC 574, at 7. See, also, the series of *op-eds* on the Committee's report in (2016) 3 *Journal on the Use of Force and International Law* 194–233.

[163] BBC News, 'Osama Bin Laden's Death: How It Happened', 7 June 2011, available at: www.bbc.co.uk/news/world-south-asia-13257330. See, in general, Wong, n. 68. The domestic legal basis assumed by the United States for operations such as these stem from the Authorization for Use of Military Force in which, on 14 September 2001, the US Congress expressly authorised the president 'to use all necessary and appropriate force against those nations, organizations, *or persons* he determines planned, authorized, committed, or aided the terrorist attacks that occurred on September 11, 2001, or harbored such organizations or persons, in order to prevent any future acts of international terrorism against the United States by such nations, organizations, *or persons*.' See www.gpo.gov/fdsys/pkg/PLAW-107publ40/pdf/PLAW-107publ40.pdf (emphasis added). This was subsequently interpreted in 2016 to also include other Islamic militant groups. See the White House, 'Report on the Legal and Policy Frameworks Guiding the United States' Use of Military Force and Related National Security Operations', December 2016, available at: www.justsecurity.org/wp-content/uploads/2016/12/framework.Report_Final.pdf

[164] Harold H. Koh, 'The Lawfulness of the U.S. Operation against Osama bin Laden', *Opinio Juris*, 19 May 2011, available at: http://opiniojuris.org/2011/05/19/the-lawfulness-of-the-us-operation-against-osama-bin-laden/.

[165] Milanovic and Hadzi-Vidanovic, n. 151, at 256. While there is a wealth of literature on international humanitarian law, for a comprehensive work on the subject see Andrew Clapham and Paola Gaeta (eds.), *The Oxford Handbook of International Law in Armed Conflict* (Oxford University Press, 2015).

It is generally recognised that there are two types of armed conflict: international and non-international. While the parties to an international armed conflict will be two or more states,[166] it will normally be the case that a targeted killing will take place in the context of a non-international armed conflict occurring between the armed forces of the government of a state and non-state actors or between two or more groups of non-state actors. Indeed, it is arguable that 'non-international' refers to the status of the parties rather than the territorial scope of the conflict and therefore such a conflict may take place across state borders.[167] Somewhat problematic, however, was the position of the United States that there was a single 'global' non-international armed conflict against al-Qaida with the relatively permissive rules of LOAC targeting applying at all times and wherever elements of the group may be located. An example of this approach can be seen in a speech made by John Brennan, President Obama's advisor on Homeland Security and Counterterrorism, when he stated that:

An area in which there is some disagreement is the geographic scope of the conflict. The United States does not view our authority to use military force against al-Qaida as being restricted solely to hot battlefields like Afghanistan. Because we are engaged in an armed conflict with al-Qaida, the United States takes the legal position that – in accordance with international law – we have the authority to take action against al-Qaida and its associated forces without doing a separate self-defense analysis each time. And as President Obama has stated on numerous occasions, we reserve the right to take unilateral action if or when other governments are unwilling or unable to take the necessary action themselves.[168]

---

[166] Common Article 2 of the Geneva Conventions of 1949 states: 'the present Convention shall apply to all cases of declared war or of any other armed conflict which may arise between two or more of the High Contracting Parties, even if the state of war is not recognized by one of them'. Furthermore, in commenting upon this provision, Jean Pictet has stated that 'any difference arising between two States and leading to the intervention of armed forces is an armed conflict within the meaning of Article 2, even if one of the Parties denies the existence of a state of war. It makes no difference how long the conflict lasts, or how much slaughter takes place'. Jean Pictet, *Commentary on the Geneva Convention for the Amelioration of the Condition of the Wounded and Sick in Armed Forces in the Field* (ICRC, 1952), at 32.

[167] See Heyns *et al.*, n. 92, at 805. The wording of Common Article 3 to the Geneva Conventions of 1949 merely refers to 'the case of armed conflict not of an international character occurring in the territory of one of the High Contracting Parties', which is widely regarded as requiring only that the fighting takes place at least on the territory of one party to the Geneva Conventions. See Noam Lubell, 'The War (?) against Al-Qaeda', in Elizabeth Wilmshurst (ed.), *International Law and the Classification of Armed Conflicts* (Oxford University Press, 2012), 421, at 432–3.

[168] Remarks of John O'Brennan, 'Strengthening our Security by Adhering to our Values and Laws', as delivered to the Program on Law and Security, Harvard Law School, 16 September 2011, available at: https://obamawhitehouse.archives.gov/the-press-office/2011/09/16/remarks-john-o-brennan-strengthening-our-security-adhering-our-values-an.

Yet, even if one accepts the idea that the US was in a non-international armed conflict with al-Qaida, this is arguably geographically limited to bordering or geographically proximate states to where the conflict began in Afghanistan, such as Pakistan where bin Laden was ultimately located and killed.[169] Broadening it out to a global conflict and beyond 'hot' battlefields presents a situation whereby any state could be subject to military action taking place upon its territory at any time without the acting state having to do 'a separate self-defense analysis each time'. The implications of this for global security and the security of relatively weaker states were stark, and found little support.[170]

In any case, whether an armed conflict exists is an objective reality, as opposed to something to be determined by the belligerent parties, and a non-international armed conflict is generally said to exist where there is 'protracted armed violence between governmental authorities and organized armed groups or between such groups within a State'.[171] The two elements are thus the intensity of the conflict and the organisation of the respective parties.[172]

Whether a particular situation satisfies the intensity requirement will depend upon the particular facts, but it is clear that there must be more than a riot, a mere internal disturbance, or minor attacks[173] and it must be protracted in nature. Given the general nature of attacks by terrorist groups, in meeting the intensity requirement the individual acts of violence by the group would therefore arguably require aggregating to meet such a threshold, and if the armed group is spread across several states it may raise further question marks over whether any attacks possess the required intensity.

Furthermore, whether a group of which the individual is a part is sufficiently organised to meet the threshold is, again, to be determined on a case-by-case basis, yet relevant factors will include, *inter alia*, whether the group has a command structure, headquarters and the ability to plan and carry out military operations.[174]

If these two threshold elements are met, however, the question then becomes who may be targeted with lethal force under LOAC, and in what circumstances.

---

[169] Milanovic and Hadzi-Vidanovic, n. 151.

[170] As the Leiden Policy Recommendations note, '[w]here the terrorist attacks emanate from more than one state [the conditions of necessity and proportionality] must be assessed *in relation to each state*'. Leiden Policy Recommendations, n. 77, at para. 40 (emphasis added).

[171] *Prosecutor v. Tadic*, Case No. IT-94-1, ICTY, Decision on the Defence Motion for Interlocutory Appeal on Jurisdiction, 1995, at para. 70.

[172] *Prosector v. Tadic*, Case No. IT-94-1, ICTY, Trial Judgment, 1997, at para. 562.

[173] Article 1(2), Additional Protocol I to the Geneva Conventions of 1949 (1977).

[174] *Prosecutor v. Limaj and others*, Case No. IT-03-66, ICTY, Trial Judgment, 30 November 2005, at paras. 94–134; *Prosecutor v. Lubanga*, Case No. ICC-01/04-. 01/06, ICTY, Judgment Pursuant to Article 74 of the Statute, 14 March 2012, at paras. 536–8.

## 8.5 Targeted Killings

The cardinal principle of distinction within this branch of international law provides that a state must not intentionally target civilians or civilian objects.[175] While civilians are not defined in the law of non-international armed conflict, such individuals who are not members of a state's armed forces may lose their protection if, and for such time as, they take a direct part in hostilities,[176] which is narrowly interpreted to mean the commission of a direct act[177] and for a short period immediately before and after the commission of that act.[178] However, an individual may also be part of an organised armed group and 'whose continuous function it is to take a direct part in hostilities' – that is, they have a 'continuous combat function' which leads to them losing their protected status.[179] The individuals must be members of the same armed group involved in the armed conflict and not some vaguely connected group based on ideological grounds, for example, as well as directly participating in the hostilities, not merely aiding the war effort in a more peripheral role.[180] In other words, there must be direct causation of harm.[181] If there is any doubt, however, the presumption is that the individual is protected from being targeted.[182]

Yet, while an individual may be directly participating in hostilities when they are targeted, or alternatively they are identified as having a 'continuous combat function', there is some debate as to whether there is an obligation upon the acting state to first attempt to capture the individual before resorting to lethal force. Some have maintained that the status or conduct of an individual alone justifies the use of lethal armed force against them, so if they are a member of a state's armed forces, a member of an armed group in a non-international armed conflict or a civilian directly participating in hostilities, they may be targeted with lethal force.[183] On the other hand, others, and most notably the International Committee of the Red Cross, have taken the view that 'it would defy the basic notions of humanity to kill an adversary or to refrain

---

[175] Article 48, Additional Protocol I to the Geneva Conventions of 1949 (1977).

[176] See Article 13(2) and (3), Additional Protocol I to the Geneva Conventions of 1949 (1977). See also Jean-Marie Henckaerts and Louise Doswald-Beck, *Customary International Humanitarian Law*, vol. I: *Rules* (Cambridge University Press, 2005), Rule 6.

[177] The ICRC's Interpretive Guidance on this issue states that 'the harm in question must be brought about in one causal step'. ICRC, *Interpretive Guidance on the Notion of Direct Participation in Hostilities under International Humanitarian Law* (ICRC, 2009), at 53.

[178] The ICRC's Interpretive Guidance highlights that '[m]easures preparatory to the execution of a specific act of direct participation in hostilities, as well as the deployment to and the return from the location of its execution, constitute an integral part of that act'. Ibid., at 65.

[179] Ibid., at 27.   [180] Ibid., at 53.   [181] Ibid., at 53.

[182] Article 50(1), Additional Protocol I to the Geneva Conventions of 1949 (1977).

[183] See Michael N. Schmitt, 'The Interpretive Guidance on the Notion of Direct Participation in Hostilities: A Critical Analysis' (2010) 1 *Harvard National Security Journal* 5, at 39–43. See also Dapo Akande, 'Clearing the Fog of War? The ICRC's Interpretive Guidance on Direct Participation in Hostilities' (2010) **59** *International & Comparative Law Quarterly* 180, at 191.

from giving him or her an opportunity to surrender where there manifestly is no necessity for the use of lethal force'.[184] While, ultimately, this remains an unresolved issue, and 'it should be remembered that drones by their very nature will in most cases not allow capture',[185] the United States has, for one, stated that it will not immediately resort to lethal force where it is possible to capture a terrorist suspect.[186] While it is unclear as to whether this was the case in the situation of bin Laden's death, this seems to have been borne out with the capture of Abu Anas al-Liby, on 5 October 2013 in Libya, who was a suspect in the bombing of the US embassies in Tanzania and Kenya in 1998.[187]

Whether or not an armed conflict can be said to exist, however, the rules of IHRL are relevant in the assessment of the legality of any targeted killing operation,[188] in particular the right to life, which is protected in various international and regional human rights treaties and in customary international law.[189] Some have relied exclusively on the right of self-defence to justify targeted killings outside of an armed conflict.[190] Yet, while self-defence may preclude the wrongfulness of the violation of the state's sovereignty where the individual is located, it does not, and cannot, preclude the wrongfulness that arises in violating the right to life of the individual concerned.[191]

There are, however, two issues that arise in connection with the protection of the right to life in these situations. The first is that, while Article 6(1) of the International Convention on Civil and Political Rights (1966) (ICCPR) provides that 'every human being has the inherent right to life ... No one shall be

---

[184] Interpretive Guidance, n. 178, at 82    [185] Heyns *et al.*, n. 92, at 817.

[186] White House, Fact Sheet: U.S. Policy Standards and Procedures for the Use of Force in Counterterrorism Operations Outside the United States and Areas of Active Hostilities, 23 May 2013, available at: https://obamawhitehouse.archives.gov/the-press-office/2013/05/23/fact-sheet-us-policy-standards-and-procedures-use-force-counterterrorism.

[187] See Christian Henderson, 'The Extraterritorial Seizure of Individuals under International Law – The Case of al-Liby: Part I', *EJIL Talk!*, 6 November 2013, available at: www.ejiltalk.org/the-extraterritorial-seizure-of-individuals-under-international-law-the-case-of-al-liby-part-one/; Christian Henderson, 'The Extraterritorial Seizure of Individuals under International Law – The Case of al-Liby: Part II', *EJIL Talk!*, 7 November 2013, available at: www.ejiltalk.org/the-extraterritorial-seizure-of-individuals-under-international-law-the-case-of-al-liby-part-two/.

[188] See, further, Section 1.6. That IHRL applies in times of armed conflict can be inferred from the fact that several human rights treaties provide for the possibility of derogation from certain human rights during times of war or times of public emergency.

[189] UNHRC, General Comment No. 24, CCPR/C/21/Rev.1/Add.6, 4 November 1994, at 10.

[190] See, for example, Kenneth Anderson, 'More Predator Drone Debate, in the Wall Street Journal, and What the Obama Administration Should Do as a Public Legal Position', *The Volokh Conspiracy*, 9 January 2010, available at: http://volokh.com/2010/01/09/more-predator-drone-debate-in-the-wall-street-journal-and-what-the-obama-administration-should-do-as-a-public-legal-position/.

[191] Marko Milanovic, 'Drones and Targeted Killings: Can Self-Defence Preclude Their Wrongfulness?' *EJIL Talk!*, 10 January 2010, available at: www.ejiltalk.org/drones-and-targeted-killings-can-self-defense-preclude-their-wrongfulness/.

arbitrarily deprived of his life',[192] under what circumstances may an individual's life be taken so that it is not 'arbitrary'? In short, lawful action that is taken with the result of depriving someone of their life must be a last resort in response to the imminent threat of harm to another person's life.[193] In this respect, while in the context of an armed conflict an individual may arguably be targeted with lethal force on the basis of their status, as discussed above in this section, outside of an armed conflict the possibility of capturing the individual needs to be fully considered and explored before lethal force may be discharged. The problem is that several states have a 'kill list' of individuals to be targeted.[194] This is where more serious problems arise, as 'a targeted killing in the sense of an intentional, premeditated and deliberate killing ... cannot be legal because, unlike in armed conflict, it is never permissible for killing to be the sole objective of an operation'.[195]

However, a second, and arguably even more controversial, issue is whether a state's human rights obligations apply to its actions outside of its territory or, in other words, whether human rights obligations apply extraterritorially. Article 2(1) of the ICCPR states that '[e]ach State Party to the present Covenant undertakes to respect and to ensure to all individuals within its territory *and subject to its jurisdiction* the rights recognized in the present Covenant' (emphasis added). In its General Comment 31, the Human Rights Committee was of the view that, under this obligation, each state party must respect and ensure the rights laid down in the Covenant 'to anyone within the power or *effective control* of that State Party, *even if not situated within the territory of the State party*'.[196]

Although the United States has always denied the extraterritorial application of its human rights obligations in times of peace or armed conflict,[197] this position of the Human Rights Committee, which accepts the extraterritorial application of

---

[192] By contrast, Article 2(2) of the European Convention on Human Rights (1950) provides an exhaustive list of permissible grounds upon which lethal force may be used.

[193] 'The non-arbitrariness standard defining the scope of the right to life has generally been interpreted in human rights jurisprudence to require that intentional lethal force be used only as a last resort in order to *protect* life.' Heyns et al., n. 92, at 819, and see 820. See also Principle 9 of the UN Basic Principles on the Use of Force and Firearms by Law Enforcement Officials (1990).

[194] See Ian Cobain, 'Obama's Secret Kill List – The Disposition Matrix', *The Guardian*, 14 July 2013, available at: www.theguardian.com/world/2013/jul/14/obama-secret-kill-list-disposition-matrix.

[195] Philip Alston, Report of the Special Rapporteur on extrajudicial, summary or arbitrary executions, UN Doc. A/HRC/14/24/Add.6, 28 May 2010, at para. 33. As discussed in Section 6.3.1.2, under the right of self-defence any use of armed force must be undertaken with a defensive objective.

[196] Human Rights Committee, General Comment 31, Nature of the General Legal Obligation on States Parties to the Covenant, 29 March 2004 (emphasis added).

[197] Milanovic and Hadzi-Vidanovic, n. 151, at 310.

human rights, does raise the question of the meaning of 'effective control' or 'authority or control'.[198] While some have taken the position that this would only apply if an individual is within the physical custody of state officials,[199] others have argued that an individual comes within the effective control of officials of a state if the officials have control over whether that individual lives or dies.[200] Given the prevalence of the use of armed drones in targeted killings, for example in strikes against Reyaad Khan and General Soleimani, the latter position is arguably more favourable as '[o]ne of the key difficulties posed by drones is that the attacking State can engage in targeted killing without exercising effective control over territory or without having the individual in custody'.[201]

Although the possession or use of drones – or 'unmanned aerial vehicles' – is not in itself unlawful, '[t]he attraction of drones is clear – in particular, they provide a strategic advantage of the deployment of deadly force against a remote target without exposing one's own forces to risks'.[202] In this respect, while they have been described as potentially 'the future of warfare',[203] their deployment by the United States, United Kingdom, Israel and NATO in countries such as Afghanistan, Pakistan, Yemen, Libya, Iraq, Somalia, Gaza and Syria has been accompanied by a significant death toll amongst the civilian population which has proved controversial and a real cause for continuing concern.[204] Furthermore:

[o]ne of the most important consequences of the expanding use of drones is that targeted killing across borders appears to be easier than in the past. This creates the potential for undermining the role that State sovereignty, irrespective of the controversies that admittedly surround this concept, plays in sustaining the international security system.[205]

As such, while drones are not *per se* unlawful weapons,[206] in that there exists no treaty or customary international law prohibiting their possession, and

---

[198] *Ocalam v. Turkey*, App. No. 46221/99, Judgment, 12 March 2003, para. 93.
[199] Jordan J. Paust, 'Self-Defence Targetings of Non-State Actors and Permissibility of U.S. Use of Drones in Pakistan' (2010) 19 *Journal of Transnational Law and Policy* 237, at 265.
[200] See Lubell, n. 2, at 227–31; Marko Milanovic, *Extraterritorial Application of Human Rights Treaties: Law, Principles and Policy* (Oxford University Press, 2011), at 209–21.
[201] Heyns et al., n. 92, at 824.   [202] Ibid., at 792.   [203] Ibid., at 793.
[204] See, for example, Susan Breau, 'Civilian Casualties and Drone Attacks: Issues in International Humanitarian Law', in Robert P. Barnidge (ed.), *The Liberal Way of War* (Ashgate, 2013), 115.
[205] Heyns et al., n. 92, at 793. See also Jordan J. Paust, 'Remotely Piloted Warfare as a Challenge to the *Jus ad Bellum*', in Marc Weller (ed.), *The Oxford Handbook of the Use of Force in International Law* (Oxford University Press, 2015), 1095, at 1100–1; and generally, Noam Lubell and Nathan Derejko, 'A Global Battlefield? Drones and the Geographical Scope of Armed Conflict' (2013) 11 *Journal of International Criminal Justice* 65.
[206] See, in general, Mary Ellen O'Connell, 'The Resort to Drones under International Law' (2011) 39 *Denver Journal of International Law and Policy* 585.

their use does not appear to necessitate any change in the law governing the use of force,[207] their proliferation in use is accompanied by legal and humanitarian concerns.[208] These are particularly acute given that the proliferation in ownership of armed drones means that they are also already within the arsenal of some non-state actors.[209]

## 8.6 CONCLUSION

Actions in self-defence against non-state actors are now more prevalent than those of an inter-state nature. While some maintain a right to self-defence in the context of attacks by non-state actors may only arise if the actions of the non-state actors have been effectively controlled by a state,[210] others take the polar opposite view that there is now a right of self-defence against attacks by non-state actors regardless of any state involvement.[211] However, both of these positions throw up problems in that, while the former means that non-state actors can often effectively act with impunity, the latter fails to show any respect towards preserving the sovereignty of states.

It is true that whether or not '[t]he traditional approach requiring "effective state control" may have become accepted over time ... it was a standard developed by the [ICJ], not God-given',[212] and 'the [ICJ] has yet to engage recent State practice of using defensive force against non-State actors in reliance on Article 51 of the UN Charter'.[213] One should also not jump to the conclusion that it is no longer necessary to establish 'effective control' by a host state over the actions of a non-state actor. As was demonstrated in the *Nicaragua* and *Armed Activities* cases, this is arguably still required if forcible measures in self-defence extend beyond action against the non-state actors to directly against the state concerned.

There have been no formal calls for reform of the law in this area, beyond a rather isolated and short-lived attempt to bring in the 'harbouring' standard of attribution by the United States, as well as general calls

---

[207] Paust, n. 206, at 1096; O'Connell, n. 207, at 599. See also Marie Aronsson, 'Remote Law-Making? US Drone Strikes and the Development of *Jus ad Bellum*' (2014) 1 *Journal on the Use of Force and International Law* 273; Alejandro Chehtman, 'The Ad Bellum Challenge of Drones: Recalibrating Permissible Use of Force' (2017) 28 *European Journal of International Law* 173.
[208] See Breau, n. 205.  [209] Heyns *et al.*, n. 92, at 793.
[210] See, for example Antonio Cassese, 'The International Community's Legal Response to Terrorism' (1989) 38 *International & Comparative Law Quarterly* 589, at 596–7.
[211] See, for example, Dieter Janssen, 'International Terrorism and Self-Defence' (2006) 36 *Israel Yearbook of Human Rights* 149, at 170–1.
[212] Tams, n. 69, at 386.  [213] Trapp, n. 45, at 150.

from scholars to lower the threshold of attribution to permit action to be taken against non-state actors. Question marks remain, nonetheless, as to if and how the law permits a breach of a state's sovereign territorial rights in order that an effective response in self-defence might be taken against non-state actors responsible for an attack, or a threat of one, from its territory. For example, what standard of attribution, if any, is required before action can be taken against a non-state group upon a state's territory, or – as seems, on one view, to be increasingly the case – does it boil down to a question of demonstrating necessity through the 'unable or unwilling' doctrine? While far from universally accepted – although seemingly a firm part of the stated position of certain states – the possible development and refinement of this doctrine might mean that not only is the use-of-force regime still seen through the prism of state sovereignty but non-state actors are less able to act with impunity. It might, of course, also mean that states feel liberated or enabled to act with freedom and impunity themselves upon, and sometimes against, any state which it concludes is colluding with the enemy.

Furthermore, the law governing the specific targeting of individuals in particular involves an assessment of three branches of international law. While these three branches are complementary and can work together to provide a clear picture of if, when and how such action might be taken, they are restrictive and it appears that only by conflating them can states find a way to make the law more permissive to suit the lethal actions they wish to take. Ultimately, while the law is not, and should not be, infinitely malleable, in particular to suit the perceived needs of a handful of states, it does need to maintain its relevancy and effectiveness. And the future challenge is to ensure that the appropriate balance is struck.

### QUESTIONS

1 Are non-state actors able to perpetrate an 'armed attack' for the purposes of Article 51 of the UN Charter?

2 Are states able to act in self-defence against another state in response to attacks by non-state actors?

3 Explain and critique the 'effective control' standard of attribution.

4 In what circumstances has the 'unable or unwilling' doctrine been applied? Is this a doctrine that exists as a rule under international law?

5 What are 'targeted killings'? In what circumstances, if any, might they be lawful?

## SUGGESTED FURTHER READING

Noam Lubell, *Extraterritorial Use of Force against Non-State Actors* (Oxford University Press, 2010)

Nils Melzer, *Targeted Killing in International Law* (Oxford University Press, 2008)

Lindsay Moir, *Reappraising the Resort to Force: International Law, Jus ad Bellum and the War on Terror* (Hart, 2010)

Mary Ellen O'Connell, Christian J. Tams, and Dire Tladi, *Self-Defence against Non-State Actors* (Cambridge University Press, 2019)

Carsten Stahn, 'Terrorist Attacks as "Armed Attack": The Right to Self-Defense, Article 51(1/2) of the UN Charter, and International Terrorism' (2003) **27** *Fletcher Forum of World Affairs* 35

Kimberley N. Trapp, 'Actor Pluralism, the "Turn to Responsibility" and the *Jus ad Bellum*: "Unwilling or Unable" in Context' (2015) **2** *Journal on the Use of Force and International Law* 199

Part IV

# Forcible Intervention in Situations of Civil Unrest

# 9 Consent to Intervention and Intervention in Civil Wars

## 9.1 INTRODUCTION

While authorisation by the United Nations (UN) Security Council and self-defence are two clear exceptions to the prohibition of the use of force, even if their application is often mired in controversy, it might plausibly be contended that there is a further exception to the prohibition: consent by a state to the forces of another state operating upon its territory.[1] Although on the one hand the coercive nature of the force used under Security Council authorisation or in self-defence remains a violation – albeit, a justified violation – of state sovereignty, a state's use of force upon the territory of another state with its consent, on the other hand, involves no violation of state sovereignty *ab initio*. If the deployment of the military personnel of one state upon the territory of another is undertaken with the valid consent of the latter there is no use of force resulting in a violation of its territorial integrity or political

---

[1] Despite the prevalence with which consensual interventions have taken place, and the controversy which they have often given rise to, there has been until recently relatively little academic international legal literature on this topic. Some notable contributions include 'The Principle of Non-Intervention in Civil Wars', Institut de droit international, Session of Wiesbaden, Resolution (1975); Lousie Doswald-Beck, 'The Legal Validity of Military Intervention by Invitation of the Government' (1985) 56 *British Yearbook of International Law* 189; 'Present Problems of the Use of Force in International Law: Military Assistance on Request', Institut de droit international, Session of Rhodes, Resolution (2011); Eliav Lieblich, *International Law and Civil Wars: Intervention and Consent* (Routledge, 2013); Gregory H. Fox, 'Intervention by Invitation', in Marc Weller (ed.), *The Oxford Handbook of the Use of Force in International Law* (Oxford University Press, 2015), 816; Erika de Wet, *Military Assistance on Request and the Use of Force* (Oxford University Press, 2020); Olivier Corten, Gregory Fox and Dino Kritsiotis, *Armed Intervention and Consent* (Cambridge University Press, 2023). The *Journal on the Use of Force and International Law* held a conference on the topic of 'Military Assistance on Request' in December 2019, with many of the contributions published over three special issues of the journal (see issues 7(1) (2020), 7(2) (2020) and 8(1) (2021)). The International Law Association's Committee on the Use of Force has also recently turned its attention to this topic: International Law Association, Use of Force – Military Assistance on Request, available at: www.ila-hq.org/en_GB/committees/use-of-force-military-assistance-on-request.

independence. Consent in this context should not, therefore, be considered as an exception to the prohibition of the use of force.[2] This appears to be a widely shared view of consent to intervention. It is, for example, the view of the United Kingdom that 'in the case of consent validly given, there is no violation of international law, and therefore no question of wrongfulness should arise',[3] and it is arguable that 'the majority of doctrine has come down on this side'.[4]

Yet, this apparently clear position regarding the legality of consent to intervention assumes 'clarity in the status of actors and the nature of the consent that is often lacking'.[5] Force is employed in these situations most often against non-state actors present and operating within a state's territory, who may be a perceived enemy of either the acting state, the territorial state or both. A specific request was thus made to the United States and other states by Iraq in 2014 to take action upon its territory in the battle against so-called Islamic State.[6] Yet, what happens in cases where it is not clear which entity represents, or has come to represent, the 'state'? For example, a full-blown civil war may have become identifiable with both sides controlling a portion of state territory, as was witnessed at times during the Syrian civil war that began in 2011. Alternatively, an elected leader who is unable to take his or her seat in office (or perhaps even be present within the state) due to a former leader refusing to step down may invite outside intervention to aid the transition to power. This was the situation, for example, in the Gambia in 2017, when the sitting president, Yahya Jemmeh, refused to leave office and with the president-elect, Adama Barrow, immediately calling for assistance to enforce his electoral win after having been sworn into office.[7] What this demonstrates

---

[2] Consent is included as a circumstance precluding wrongfulness in the International Law Commission's 2001 Draft Articles on State Responsibility for Internationally Wrongful Acts. Article 20 states that '[v]alid consent by a State to the commission of a given act by another State precludes the wrongfulness of that act in relation to the former State to the extent that the act remains within the limits of that consent'. In earlier elaborating upon this, the International Law Commission (ILC) noted that to produce legal effects: 'the consent of the State must be valid in international law, clearly established, really expressed (which precludes merely presumed consent), internationally attributable to the State and anterior to the commission of the act to which it refers. Moreover, consent can be invoked as precluding the wrongfulness of an act by another State only within the limits which the State expressing the consent intends with respect to its scope and duration.' (1979) 2 (Part II) *Yearbook of the International Law Commission* 112.

[3] UN Doc. A/CN.4/488, 25 March 1998.

[4] Olivier Corten, *The Law Against War: The Prohibition on the Use of Force in Contemporary International Law*, 2nd ed. (Hart, 2021), at 250. Similarly, Gregory Fox has noted that '[i]f a target state holds rights against foreign intervention and that state, through its government, waives those rights by consenting to the presence of foreign troops on its territory, *no claim remains* that a right against intervention has been violated'. Fox, n. 1, at 816 (emphasis added).

[5] Fox, ibid., at 816.   [6] See UN Doc. S/2014/691, 22 September 2014.

[7] See, in general, Claus Kreß and Benjamin Nußberger, 'Pro-Democratic Intervention in Current International Law: The Case of The Gambia in January 2017' (2017) 4 *Journal on the Use of Force and International Law* 239.

is that, while the rules are not in themselves controversial, their application to concrete situations can often prove to be so.

This chapter will examine the elements of a 'valid' consent to the use of force.[8] Section 9.2 sets out the ways in which those with authority to consent to intervention might be identified. While this has traditionally been reserved for governments of states, clarity in this respect is, as noted, often lacking, meaning that issues such as effective control, recognition and the principle of self-determination all have relevance in providing a broad picture of this issue. Section 9.3 then examines consent to intervention specifically within the context of a civil war and the various issues to which this gives rise. Section 9.4 addresses the form that consent might take, while Section 9.5 takes a look at the express and implied limits upon the provision of consent to intervention.

## 9.2 IDENTIFYING AUTHORITY TO CONSENT

International law historically had, in general, relatively little to say on questions of who might govern a state, how a government might come to power and who might lawfully sacrifice – even just temporarily – sovereign aspects of the state concerned. In addition, the question of if and how regimes might defend themselves against domestic uprisings, and whether internal groups had the right to depose regimes in power, were not directly regulated by international law, and were seen more as issues of a domestic, as opposed to an international, nature. In this respect, '[g]overnments faced no limitations on their ability to quell internal uprisings and anti-government rebels held no international legal entitlement to displace incumbent governments (with a limited and controversial exception for self-determination conflicts)'.[9] While international law still arguably maintains a limited distance on these issues, they are no longer outside of its reach and, in particular, come under sharp focus in the consideration of military intervention by consent or invitation.

---

[8] The notion of a 'consent' to intervention is also often referred to as 'intervention by invitation' and 'military assistance on request'. The latter has been favoured in recent academic work on the topic, primarily on the basis that 'intervention by invitation' might be seen as an oxymoron given that if a state has received an invitation then it will not be *intervening* within the state. See de Wet, n. 1, at 16. This chapter adopts the notion of consent, primarily on the basis that the notions of 'invitation' and 'request' both seem to imply that the initiative, at least, has been taken by the *assisted* state with a formal and positive request for assistance, whereas often the initiative is taken by the *assisting* or *intervening* state(s) or organisation and in situations where there is no request or invitation to speak of, or at least one that has emerged without some form of pressure or coercion thereby vitiating the consent provided. In any case, and as de Wet herself notes, 'the terms "request" and "consent" can be used interchangeably, as two sides of the same coin'. Ibid., at 1.

[9] Fox, n. 1, at 819. See also Section 9.2.4 on self-determination.

This section examines the issues in identifying those entities or individuals with authority to provide consent or extend an invitation to intervene.

### 9.2.1 The General Framework: Governments and Non-state Actors

The most fundamental, not to mention controversial, question in examining the issue of the validity of consent to intervention is who is entitled to provide it. The obvious answer would be that it is the government of the state concerned. On the possibility of consent or invitation to intervene, the International Court of Justice (ICJ) in the *Nicaragua* case merely alluded to 'intervention, which is already allowable at the request of the government'.[10] In general, states are permitted to resort to forcible measures within the territorial confines of another state in principle, so long as it is at the invitation or with the consent of the *government* of that state.

History is replete with examples of states intervening upon the justification that there has been an invitation to intervene by the government of a state. During the Cold War, the United States chose to rely upon this justification in its interventions in Colombia (1960), the Dominican Republic (1965), Grenada (1983) and Panama (1989). Similarly, the USSR justified its interventions in Hungary (1956) and Czechoslovakia (1968) upon this basis. This justification was also employed during many of the conflicts that have troubled Africa, in particular in Sierra Leone (1997) and the Democratic Republic of the Congo (DRC). Former colonial powers have also sought to rely on it in intervening in former colonies, with France relying upon it in Gabon (1964), Chad (1968), Central African Republic (CAR) (1979), Côte d'Ivoire (2002) and Mali (2013); and the United Kingdom in Tanganyika (1964), Uganda (1964), Kenya (1964) and Sierra Leone (2000). More recently, we have witnessed consent by the government of a state concerned being advanced as the justification for action by several states in their interventions in Iraq (2014–21), by Russia in its interventions in Ukraine (2014 (in relation to an invitation by deposed President Yanukovych which led to the annexation of Crimea and intervention in parts of the Donbas) and 2022 (in relation to a request from the so-called Donetsk People's Republic and Luhansk People's Republic which had been recognized by Russia)) and in Syria (2015–), and by Saudi Arabia for its military action in Yemen (2015–). Indeed, these interventions were not generally condemned upon the basis that the governments did not *per se* possess the right to issue an invitation.

---

[10] *Case Concerning Military and Paramilitary Activities in and against Nicaragua (Nicaragua v. United States of America)* (1986) ICJ Reports 14, at para. 246. Yet, as Fox points out, this is a 'remarkably blunt statement' as it 'can be read to hold in all cases'. Fox, n. 1, at 820. Indeed, the Court failed to qualify it.

Yet this relatively simple statement of the law masks a plethora of problematic issues regarding the identity, status and legitimacy of those providing consent, which will be addressed throughout this chapter. Furthermore, within the government itself there is a 'sliding scale of authority' in terms of those in a position to be able to issue invitations.[11] While in the context of certain activities of a state, such as the adoption of a treaty, authority is delegated to a number of different individuals,[12] only the highest authorities within a state, such as the president or prime minister, are able to provide consent in the case of military intervention.[13] In the case of the intervention by the United States in Grenada in 1983, for example, the individual allegedly providing the consent was the Governor-General of Grenada, somebody without the requisite powers to consent to such an act, which was the basis for much of the condemnation of the intervention.[14]

From this it might be thought that elected individuals that are yet to take up office are unable to invite outside intervention. Indeed, the 1989 US invasion of Panama, which was taken 'after consultation with' the democratically-elected – although yet to be sworn-in – president, Guillermo Endara, is a case in point.[15] The intervention, which resulted in the ousting of the incumbent President Manuel Noriega, was broadly condemned.[16] Yet, and by contrast, in January 2017 Senegalese troops entered the Gambia as part of an Economic Community of West African States (ECOWAS) intervention after President Yahya Jammeh had refused to accept the results of the presidential elections in

---

[11] Fox, n. 1, at 818.

[12] Article 7 of the Vienna Convention of the Law of Treaties (VCLT) (1969) expresses authority in the context of the formation of treaties as those with 'full powers'.

[13] Corten, n. 4, at 256. In her study on the topic, de Wet concludes that this is one of only two requirements found in customary international law limiting direct military assistance upon request. Indeed, 'in international law there is a strong presumption that consent to direct military assistance has to be issued by the highest officials of a state. This presumption can only be rebutted by clear evidence of a lower-ranked official's competence to consent to forcible measures, for example in the form of domestic legislation to this effect.' De Wet, n. 1, at 155.

[14] See UN Doc. S/PV.2487, 25 October 1983; UN Doc. S/PV. 2489, 26 October 1983; UN Doc. S/PV. 2491, 27 October 1983.

[15] In its letter to the UN Security Council the US justified the intervention as self-defence in protection of US nationals located there and to protect the integrity of the Panama Canal Treaty. See UN Doc. S/21035, 20 December 1989. See also UN Doc. S/PV. 2902, 23 December 1989.

[16] However, while the intervention received broad condemnation, it was not generally targeted towards this aspect of the intervention, but rather towards the invocation by the US of the Panama Canal Treaties to justify the intervention. See UNGA Res. 44/240 (1989), para. 3. The resolution only passed with 75 states in support, with 20 voting against and 40 abstaining, which was arguably a sign of general disdain for Noriega. The OAS also condemned the intervention. See *Keesing's* (1989) 37113. See, further, Section 6.4.2. where this incident is discussed in the context of self-defence for the protection of nationals abroad.

December 2016.[17] The newly-elected president, Adama Barrow, had issued an invitation,[18] and his claim to take up office and the Senegalese operation was welcomed, including by the Security Council in Resolution 2337.[19] The contrast in reaction to that of the US intervention in Panama may be due to a number of reasons, including the collective nature of the ECOWAS operation, the fact that ulterior motives or broader aims were not apparent or that, while there has not been the development of a right of pro-democratic intervention, the role and prevalence of democratic considerations in determining legitimacy has arguably become more prominent since the end of the Cold War.

However, and in contrast to the right of states to intervene with the consent or invitation of the government of a state, there is no generally recognized 'right for States to intervene, directly or indirectly, with or without armed force, in support of an internal opposition in another State'.[20] More specifically, states have recognized that 'no State shall organize, assist, foment, finance, incite or tolerate subversive, terrorist or armed activities directed towards the violent overthrow of the regime of another State, or interfere in civil strife in another State'.[21] In other words, states are not permitted to respond to consensual invitations by non-governmental forces to intervene or assist with their activities or operations, although there is no obligation upon the non-state actors under international law to refrain from issuing such invitations.[22]

---

[17] 'Gambian President Yahya Jammeh Rejects Election Results', *The Guardian*, 10 December 2016, available at: www.theguardian.com/world/2016/dec/10/gambian-president-rejects-election-results-yahya-jammeh-adama-barrow.

[18] Ruth Maclean, 'Troops Enter the Gambia after Adama Barrow Is Inaugurated in Senegal', *The Guardian*, 19 January 2017, available at: www.theguardian.com/world/2017/jan/19/new-gambian-leader-adama-barrow-sworn-in-at-ceremony-in-senegal.

[19] UNSC Res. 2337 (2017), preamble. In this resolution, the Security Council did not specifically and expressly endorse military action, but rather '[e]xpresse[d] its full support to the ECOWAS in its commitment to ensure, *by political means first*, the respect of the will of the people of The Gambia as expressed in the results of 1st December elections' (para. 6, emphasis added). In the Council debate that followed the adoption of the resolution some states also expressed their concerns regarding the use of force to resolve the situation. See UN Doc. S/PV.7866, 19 January 2017 (Uruguay (3); Bolivia (3); Egypt (6); Russia (3)). However, the fact that Barrow may request intervention was expressed in comments by Russia and the United Kingdom following the vote. See Edith M. Lederer, 'UN Adopts Resolution Backing Gambia's New President Barrow', *AP News*, 19 January 2017, available at: https://apnews.com/article/44fe8d11a7134ad084794fb450c95556.

[20] *Nicaragua* case, n. 10, at paras. 206–9; *Armed Activities on the Territory of the Congo (Democratic Republic of the Congo v. Uganda)*, Judgment (2005) ICJ Reports 168, at para. 164. See also Draft Declaration on the Rights and Duties of States, UNGA Res. 375 (1949), Articles 3 and 4. For more on the distinction between direct and indirect intervention, see Section 2.4.3.

[21] Declaration on the Inadmissibility of Intervention in the Domestic Affairs of States and the Protection of Their Independence and Sovereignty, UNGA Res. 2131 (1965), para. 2.

[22] This can perhaps be surmised from the 2010 Kosovo advisory opinion in which the ICJ found that a declaration of independence by the autonomous region of Kosovo on 17 February 2008

States do not often expressly claim to be supporting non-governmental forces against the government of a state, and when such support is provided it is rarely through the direct use of force by the intervening state's armed forces but rather through indirect means and often covertly, as was the case for much of the Cold War.[23] In addition, the intervening states often claim to be acting in individual or collective self-defence. For example, in the *Nicaragua* case the United States argued that its support for the *contras* who were acting within Nicaragua and against the government was in collective self-defence of Honduras, Costa Rica and El Salvador.[24] Similarly, in the *Armed Activities* case Uganda claimed that its support for the Movement for the Liberation of the Congo (MLC), which was operating in the DRC and against the government, was an act of self-defence.[25] In both cases, the Court held that there had been a violation of the principle of non-intervention and the prohibition of the use of force, regardless of whether the intervening states had intended to overthrow the government of the states concerned.[26]

States have not attempted to develop a general right to assist non-governmental forces. Indeed, neither of the acting states in the *Nicaragua* or *Armed Activities* cases claimed to have been acting under, or to have developed, such a right. It was upon this basis, and an examination of general state practice, that the Court in the *Nicaragua* case found that 'no such general right of intervention in support of an opposition within another State exists in contemporary international law'.[27] However, there was also an overt policy element to the Court's finding here as, in elaborating upon this point, the ICJ stated that the principle of non-intervention:

would certainly lose its effectiveness as a principle of law if intervention were to be justified by a mere request for assistance made by an opposition group in another State ... Indeed, it is difficult to see what would remain of the principle of non-intervention in international law if intervention, which is already allowable at the request of the government of a State, were also to be allowed at the request of the opposition. This would permit any State to intervene at any moment in the internal affairs of another State, whether at the request of the government or at the request of its opposition. Such a situation does not in the Court's view correspond to the present state of international law.[28]

did not violate international law. *Accordance with International Law of the Unilateral Declaration of Independence in Respect of Kosovo*, Advisory Opinion (2010) ICJ Reports 403.
[23] See Section 2.4.3 on the indirect use of force.  [24] *Nicaragua* case, n. 10, at para. 228.
[25] See *Armed Activities* case, CR/2005/16, at 3–18, available at: www.icj-cij.org/files/case-related/116/116-20050429-ORA-01-01-BI.pdf.
[26] *Nicaragua* case, n. 10, at para. 241; *Armed Activities* case, n. 20, at para. 163.
[27] *Nicaragua* case, ibid., at para. 209.
[28] Ibid., at para. 246. For more on the principle of non-intervention, see Section 2.2.

There is, however, ambiguity in these broad statements of the ICJ. Indeed, questions immediately arise regarding the point at which a non-governmental force ceases being a mere rebel group and begins to look like it is exercising governmental powers and/or are in control of the state or a portion of it. Indeed, what factors are relevant, if any, in making an assessment as to whether it is now lawful to intervene at their request? Furthermore, while making this statement in 1986 the Court appeared to be open to the idea that its adopted position on this point was subject to change over time. There have, in this sense, been some discernible general shifts within the international community and incidences of state practice which have muddied the traditional conceptual waters, which shall be addressed next.

### 9.2.2 Effective Control

In connection with the question as to who may invite outside assistance it was traditionally the case that '[t]he answer turned ... on wholly pragmatic questions of effective control over territory. A government in control of its territory could invite outside assistance to counter a rebel movement and the rebels could not.'[29] So the right of a government to invite outside intervention to support it in its efforts to quell a domestic disturbance or fight a civil war turned on whether it was in *de facto* 'effective control' of its territory, or at least the majority of it. Indeed, '[w]hether or not a regime is in effective control has traditionally been the most important factor in the law of recognition and so it is not surprising that the idea was incorporated wholesale into this aspect of the *jus ad bellum*'.[30]

While as a matter of international law *de facto* effective control was arguably the determinative factor for governmental authority, no generally accepted definition of what this meant emerged. In the 1923 *Tinoco Concessions* arbitral decision, however, it was 'independence and control' that entitled an entity to be classed as a national personality.[31] James Crawford has also noted, in reference to this decision, that '[i]n the case of governments, the "standard set by international law" is so far the standard of *secure* de facto *control of all or most of the state territory*'.[32]

---

[29] Fox, n. 1, at 817. See, in general, Christopher J. Le Mon, 'Unilateral Intervention by Invitation in Civil Wars: The Effective Control Test Tested' (2002–3) 35 *New York University Journal of International Law and Politics* 741.

[30] Fox, n. 1, at 833. As de Wet also notes, '[t]raditionally, the key constraint imposed by customary international law is that of effective control, which served as the point of departure for identifying the recognized de jure government of a state'. De Wet, n. 1, at 31.

[31] See (1923) 1 *RIAA* 369, at 381.

[32] James Crawford, *Brownlie's Principles of Public International Law*, 8th ed. (Oxford University Press, 2012), at 152 (emphasis added).

Yet, while on this basis the requirement of effective control might appear to be firmly grounded within international law there are numerous contemporary examples of governments providing consent despite controlling only a portion – or, at least, not 'all or most' – of the territory of the state concerned. There was apparent acceptance by the international community of the legality of French military intervention in support of the beleaguered Malian government in 2013, regardless of the fact that Islamist rebels controlled the north of the country and were moving in on the capital of the country.[33] Many states were also prepared to intervene, or support the intervention of others, within Iraq in 2014 at the request of the Iraqi government to fight the Islamic State group, which at the time exercised control over a significant proportion of Iraqi territory.[34]

Furthermore, as was the case in the Gambia in 2017 and Côte d'Ivoire in 2011, a leader who is not yet even in office, let alone in effective control of the country, might issue an invitation to intervene if they have been elected through a constitutional democratic process.[35] Consent or invitations to intervene from members of a government no longer in office may not be perceived as legitimate, however, and will depend on the mode by which they have been removed from office. On the one hand, a leader who has been removed through an internal political process may no longer be seen as possessing the requisite authority to extend an invitation to intervene. For example, Russia intervened in Ukraine in 2014 at the request of former democratically elected President Viktor Yanukovych.[36] The request was made on 1 March 2014, although the Ukrainian parliament had voted to remove Yanukovych from power on 22 February 2014.[37] Yanukovych had also left

---

[33] This is based on the fact that ECOWAS thanked the French government for its operation in Mali (Statement of the President of ECOWAS Commission on the Situation in Mali, 12 January 2013, available at: https://reliefweb.int/report/mali/statement-president-ecowas-commission-situation-mali) and that the UN Security Council welcomed France's intervention at the request of the government of Mali to deter the terrorist threat to the north of the country (see UNSC Res. 2100 (2013), preamble; UNSC Res. 2227 (2015), preamble). See also Dapo Akande and Zachary Vermeer, 'The Airstrikes against Islamic State in Iraq and the Alleged Prohibition on Military Assistance to Governments in Civil Wars', *EJIL Talk!*, 2 February 2015, available at: www.ejiltalk.org/the-airstrikes-against-islamic-state-in-iraq-and-the-alleged-prohibition-on-military-assistance-to-governments-in-civil-wars/.

[34] States directly participating in the air strikes following the request of the Iraqi government included the United States, the United Kingdom, the Netherlands, Belgium, Denmark, Jordan, Australia, France and Canada. Furthermore, and as de Wet has observed, '[n]o state has thus far challenged the validity of US-led air strikes against [Islamic State] in Iraq'. de Wet, n. 1, at 99.

[35] See Section 9.2.1. See also Kreß and Nußberger, n. 7, at 248.

[36] See Zachery Vermeer, 'Intervention with the Consent of a Deposed (but Legitimate) Government? Playing the Sierra Leone Card', *EJIL Talk!*, 6 March 2014, available at: www.ejiltalk.org/intervention-with-the-consent-of-a-deposed-but-legitimate-government-playing-the-sierra-leone-card/.

[37] It has been claimed, however, that this vote may have been unconstitutional, as it did not meet the two-thirds majority required by the Ukrainian Constitution. Vermeer, ibid.

the country and been replaced by an interim government.[38] In this respect, he arguably 'no longer had authority to represent Ukraine in relation to the use of force',[39] so that 'any consent he might have provided for the Russian action is unlikely to have been valid because he was no longer effectively acting as president of Ukraine'.[40]

However, if the leader has been forcibly removed by an armed group then this may mean that the leader retains their right to invite outside assistance. President Abdo Rabbo Mansour Hadi of Yemen, who was elected into office in 2012, resigned alongside members of his cabinet in early 2015 and fled to the city of Aden after coming under pressure from the Houthi militia which was based in the north-west of the country but which had captured the capital Sana'a in September 2014.[41] In February 2015 the Houthis released a declaration which effectively dissolved parliament and established a Presidential Council and a Supreme Revolutionary Committee.[42] Hadi, who had escaped house arrest, subsequently rescinded his resignation and stated Aden to be the temporary capital of Yemen.[43] However, on 24 March 2015 he also issued an intervention to the Cooperation Council for the Arab States of the Gulf and the League of Arab States to intervene and oust the Houthi rebels and fled to Saudi Arabia.[44] The Saudi Arabian-led intervention (Operation Decisive Storm) commenced on 26 March 2015 with the objective of 'protect[ing] the people of Yemen and its legitimate government from a takeover by the Houthis'.[45]

---

[38] See UN Doc. S/PV. 7125, 3 March 2014, at 3–4.
[39] Marc Weller, 'The Shadow of the Gun' (2014) **164** (7599) *New Law Journal* 164.
[40] James A. Green, 'The Annexation of Crimea: Russia, Passportisation and the Protection of Nationals Revisited' (2014) 1 *Journal on the Use of Force and International Law* 3, at 7. It may also be possible to read this conclusion into the fact that UNGA Res. 262 (2014), which rejected the change status of Crimea, was supported by 100 states (with 11 states voting against and 58 states abstaining).
[41] Final Report of the Panel of Experts on Yemen Established Pursuant to Security Council Committee Resolution 2140 (2014), UN Doc. S/2015/125, 20 February 2015, at paras. 32 and 130ff.
[42] 'Yemen's Houthis Form Own Government in Sana'a', *Al Jazeera*, 6 February 2015, available at: www.aljazeera.com/news/2015/2/6/yemens-houthis-form-own-government-in-sanaa.
[43] Mohamed Ghobari and Mohammed Mukhashaf, 'Yemen's Hadi Flees to Aden and Says He Is Still President', *Reuters*, 21 February 2015, available at: www.reuters.com/article/us-yemen-security-idUSKBN0LP08F20150221; 'Yemen President Considers "Aden country's capital"', *Al Jazeera*, 7 March 2015, available at: www.aljazeera.com/news/2015/3/7/yemen-president-considers-aden-countrys-capital.
[44] Statement Issued by the Kingdom of Saudi Arabia, the United Arab Emirates, the Kingdom of Bahrain, the State of Qatar and the State of Kuwait, Enclosure to Annex of Identical Letters Dated 26 March 2015 from the Permanent Representative of Qatar to the United Nations Addressed to the Secretary-General and the President of the Security Council, UN Doc. S/2015/21, 27 March 2015.
[45] See Statement by Saudi Ambassador Al-Jubeir on Military Operations in Yemen, 25 March 2015, available at: www.operationrenewalofhope.com/#sthash.SD7Kc2OI.dpbs. Given the external support for the Houthis by Iran the operation was also based upon

By contrast to Russia's intervention in Ukraine, however, Saudi Arabia's intervention at the request of President Hadi received general support. The UN Security Council condemned the actions of the Houthis while expressing its support for President Hadi.[46] In Resolution 2216 (2015) the Council 'took note' of Hadi's request for intervention.[47] There was also broader support for the operation, with the only notable dissent to its legal basis being expressed by Iran,[48] although the operation subsequently received broad criticism for the ways in which it was conducted, in particular for violations of international humanitarian law and international human rights law.[49]

The difference between the two cases in terms of the reaction to the legality of the respective interventions is arguably explained by the fact that, while Hadi had lost effective control over the territory of Yemen, he remained and was recognized both internally and externally as the undisputed legitimate president of the country, whereas Yanukovych, who had similarly fled the territory of his country, had lost any legitimate claim to the presidency. In this respect, while the notion of effective control comprises control of territory and state machinery, it also 'requires a certain amount of acquiescence on the part of the civilian population, which has to show an habitual obedience to the regime's authority'.[50] These various elements of 'control' will feature to greater or lesser degrees in any determination regarding the extent to which an individual or regime possesses the authority to consent to external intervention. What is clear, however, is that broad international recognition of the person or regime will effectively compensate to a large extent for any lack of effective control over territory.[51]

### 9.2.3 Recognition

In Section 9.2.2 it was concluded that, while providing a legal basis for invitations or consent to intervene, control of the territory of a state by a particular regime is not determinative of the issue. Rather, it would appear to

---

collective self-defence. The operation continues at the time of writing (although on 21 April 2015 was replaced by Operation Renewal of Hope) but has failed to reverse the Houthis control of Sana'a and much of Yemeni territory and the population of the country.

[46] UNSC Res. 2201 (2015), paras 1ff.   [47] UNSC Res. 2216 (2015), preamble.

[48] Annex to the Letter Dated 17 April 2015 from the Permanent Representative of the Islamic Republic of Iran to the United Nations Addressed to the Security Council, UN Doc. S/2015/263, 17 April 2015.

[49] See Final Report of the Panel of Experts on Yemen, n. 41, paras. 119 and 126ff.

[50] de Wet, n. 1, at 32.

[51] Tom Ruys and Luca Ferro, 'Weathering the Storm: Legality and Legal Implications of the Saudi-Led Military Intervention in Yemen' (2016) 65 *International & Comparative Law Quarterly* 61, at 85. See also Benjamin Nußberger, 'Military Strikes in Yemen in 2015: Intervention by Invitation and Self-Defence in the Course of Yemen's "Model Transitional Process"' (2017) 4 *Journal on the Use of Force and International Law* 110.

more often be based upon whether the regime can demonstrate external recognition by other states, in turn affecting its ability to consent to the use of force upon the territory concerned.[52]

States have not historically offered – and do not today generally offer – express recognition to governments, which is something normally left to be implicitly determined upon the basis of their interaction with the regime concerned.[53] Yet, today there are many examples of states, often through the collective voice of the Security Council, expressly recognising entities as the rightful government of a state, notably in the context of civil wars or disturbances, in particular those that have arisen following an election. For example, during the political turmoil in Côte d'Ivoire in 2011 following the disputed election there between Alassane Ouattara and Laurent Gbagbo, the Security Council '*Urge*[d] all the Ivorian parties and other stakeholders to respect the will of the people and the election of Alassane Dramane Ouattara as President of Côte d'Ivoire'.[54]

In this regard, it is notable that '[i]n the post-Cold War era ... international law in a variety of areas has begun to develop qualitative criteria on questions of governance. These developments pose a challenge for rules on intervention by invitation.'[55] For example, there has undoubtedly been a gradual increase in the attention paid to democratic governance, with some having termed this an emerging 'right' of populations.[56] A notable example of focus being placed upon democratic governance, although not in the *jus ad bellum* context, can be found in the European Community 'Guidelines on the Recognition of New States in Eastern Europe and in the Soviet Union' which were issued in December 1991 following the break-up of the Soviet Union and Yugoslavia, in which the democratic credentials of the emerging states were given

---

[52] See Malcolm Shaw, *International Law*, 6th ed. (Cambridge University Press, 2008), at 454, 459.

[53] See Stefan Talmon, *Recognition of Governments in International Law: With Particular Reference to Governments in Exile* (Oxford University Press, 1998), at 3ff. During the late twentieth century many states adopted the position of non-recognition of governments, primarily due to the perception that the provision of recognition equated to approval, which often proved embarrassing, for example where the governmental regime concerned was involved in human rights violations. For a discussion of this policy in connection with the recognition of the National Transitional Council in Libya, see Dapo Akande, 'Which Entity Is the Government of Libya and Why Does It Matter', *EJIL Talk!*, 16 June 2011, available at: www.ejiltalk.org/which-entity-is-the-government-of-libya-and-why-does-it-matter/.

[54] UNSC Res. 1975 (2011), para. 1. See Jean d'Aspremont, 'Duality of Government in Côte d'Ivoire', *EJIL Talk!*, 4 January 2011, available at: www.ejiltalk.org/duality-of-government-in-cote-divoire/#more-2898.

[55] Fox, n. 1, at 817.

[56] See Thomas M. Franck, 'The Emerging Right to Democratic Governance' (1992) **86** *American Journal of International Law* 46. See, in general, de Wet, n. 1, at 31–8.

emphasis.[57] As such, while it might be argued that the 'effective control' test continues to hold sway in theory, 'since the end of the Cold War, questions of recognition have increasingly revolved around democratic criteria, specifically whether a regime has been chosen in free and fair elections',[58] and this has impacted upon the right of an entity to invite intervention by third states. For example, and as discussed in Section 9.2.2, this move clearly has the power to 'validate an invitation to intervene by a government in exile that controls no territory'.[59]

Further still, although far more controversially, it might even 'validate requests by rebel factions that have never held power, but which promise a democratic future for the state, or at least one that is less undemocratic than the prospects under the incumbent regime'.[60] Indeed, arguably a way to circumvent the general rules on invitation to intervene as set out already in this chapter is through the recognition of an opposition group as the government of a state. For example, during the popular uprising that took place against the regime of Colonel Gaddafi in Libya from February 2011, many states recognised the Libyan National Transitional Council (NTC) as the government of Libya.[61] While this represented recognition in the context of the violent overthrow of a formerly recognised government by a rebel group, it was on the back of what was a widespread and popular revolt against the Gaddafi regime which had itself engaged in a violent crackdown against those protesting against it. This recognition had various legal consequences, such as the release of assets held in various states to the opposition forces.[62] But it also raised questions as to whether and, if so, the extent to which states may offer military assistance in response to a request from the NTC.

Some have suggested that recognition of the NTC occurred while the regime of Colonel Gaddafi continued to effectively control much of the state, particularly territory in the west of the country.[63] Indeed, it has been argued that

---

[57] Reproduced in (1993) 4 *European Journal of International Law* 72.    [58] Fox, n. 1, at 833–4.
[59] Ibid.    [60] Ibid.
[61] The NTC was recognised as the legitimate governing authority of Libya, and the Gaddafi regime was expressly derecognised by thirty-two states on 15 July 2011. See Fourth Meeting of the Libya Contact Group, Chair's Statement, 15 July 2011, at para. 4, available at: www.nato.int/nato_static/assets/pdf/pdf_2011_07/20110926_110715-Libya-Contact-Group-Istanbul.pdf. The UN accepted the credentials of the NTC on 16 September 2011. See UN Doc. A/RES/66/1 A, 16 September 2011. In October 2011 the African Union recognised the NTC as the legitimate government of Libya. See AUPSC, Communiqué of the 297th Meeting, PSC/PR/COMM/2 (CCXCVII), 20 October 2011, at para. 4, available at: www.peaceau.org/uploads/297thpsccommuniqueen.pdf.
[62] See Dapo Akande, 'Recognition of Libyan National Transitional Council as Government of Libya', *EJIL Talk!*, 23 July 2011, available at: www.ejiltalk.org/recognition-of-libyan-national-transitional-council-as-government-of-libya/.
[63] See Stefan Talmon, 'Recognition of the Libyan National Transitional Council', *ASIL Insights*, 16 June 2011, available at: www.asil.org/insights/volume/15/issue/16/recognition-libyan-national-transitional-council.

recognition of the NTC as the government of Libya 'when it did not have effective control of most of Libya was premature and therefore of dubious legality'.[64] As such, it might also be argued that the provision of arms or non-lethal assistance to the NTC that took place after this recognition had been provided may well have been unlawful.[65] Yet, while others acknowledge the doubt over the extent of the NTC's control over Libyan territory,[66] effective territorial control is, as discussed previously, but one element in any determination regarding recognition, and with that the extent to which an individual, regime or group possesses the authority to consent to external intervention. In the case of Libya, however, the supply of arms and training into the territory of the state was prohibited under the arms embargo contained in Resolution 1970 (2011) – except, perhaps, in the context of the protection of civilians[67] – meaning that, even if the NTC was lawfully recognised as the government of Libya, arguably this did not in this case have an impact upon the legality of the provision of arms and non-lethal assistance to it.

Alternatively, an opposition group may be recognised as the 'legitimate representative' of the people of a state. For example, while in 2012 the Syrian National Council (SNC) called on states to recognise it as the 'transitional government', specifically so as to permit states to provide it with weapons in its struggle against the Assad regime,[68] a move that arguably would have been premature at the time, states instead restricted their recognition of the SNC to 'the legitimate representatives of the Syrian people'.[69] It might be argued that despite the recognising states refraining from using the word 'government' in their statements of recognition, governmental recognition was nonetheless their intention.[70] However, '[t]he legal effect of these statements is unclear. The historical antecedents are so sparse that it may be that we are witnessing the emergence of a new category of quasi-state entities. But some of the states made clear that their statements were intended for political rather than legal purposes.'[71] Indeed, that governmental recognition was not the intention of the states seemed to be generally clear in this instance. The United States was clear, for example, that it was not prepared to recognise the Syrian National Council as a 'government-in-exile' but only, and in joining other states, as 'the

---

[64] Dapo Akande, 'Would It Be Lawful for European (or other) States to Provide Arms to the Syrian Opposition?', *EJIL Talk!*, 17 January 2013, available at: www.ejiltalk.org/would-it-be-lawful-for-european-or-other-states-to-provide-arms-to-the-syrian-opposition/.
[65] Ibid.   [66] de Wet, n. 1, at 61 (n. 267).   [67] See Section 4.4.1.
[68] The head of the Coalition, Mouaz Alkhatib, stated that '[w]hen we get political recognition, this will allow the Coalition to act as a government and hence acquire weapons and this will solve our problems'. BBC News, 'Syria: France Backs Anti-Assad Coalition', 13 November 2012, available at: www.bbc.co.uk/news/world-middle-east-20319787.
[69] BBC News, 'Syria Conflict: UK Recognises Opposition, says William Hague', 20 November 2012, available at: www.bbc.co.uk/news/uk-politics-20406562.
[70] See Talmon, n. 53, on the importance of intention in these matters.   [71] Fox, n. 1, at 838.

legitimate representative of the Syrian people'.[72] France also appeared to choose its words carefully in not recognising it as the government of Syria, but rather as 'the *future* government of a democratic Syria',[73] thus making any provision of arms and non-lethal assistance under such a recognition unlawful while perhaps providing some legitimacy to the SNC's claim of self-determination.[74]

An invitation to intervene has inherent overlaps with so-called pro-democratic intervention.[75] However, while 'the political goals underlying the use of force may include the re-establishment of "democratic" government', for example the ECOWAS intervention in the Gambia in January 2017, and, more controversially, the US intervention in Panama in 1989, this has 'not led states to espouse a legal doctrine of "pro-democratic" invasion without UN authority'.[76] Indeed, a right of pro-democratic intervention has been absent from state practice and is very rarely advanced as a discrete legal basis for intervention. Instead, interventions with a pro-democratic flavour have normally taken place with Security Council authorisation, such as that in Côte d'Ivoire in 2011, or been based upon consent or invitation to intervene, such as that in the Gambia in 2017. The existence of such a right also arguably remains a minority view amongst scholars and commentators.[77]

### 9.2.4 The Principle of Self-Determination

During the Cold War, resolutions were adopted by the UN General Assembly in which national liberation movements such as the Palestinian Liberation Organization and the African National Congress were recognised as having the right to 'struggle' for self-determination,[78] in particular to be able 'freely to determine, without external interference, their political status and to pursue their economic, social and cultural development'.[79] Although some have questioned whether the use of the ambiguous term 'struggle' included the use of force,[80] there nonetheless appeared to be a consensus within the UN

---

[72] BBC News, n. 68.   [73] Ibid. (emphasis added).
[74] See Section 9.2.4 on self-determination.
[75] See, in general, David Wippman, 'Pro-Democratic Intervention', in Marc Weller (ed.), *The Oxford Handbook of the Use of Force in International Law* (Oxford University Press, 2015), 797.
[76] Christine Gray, *International Law and the Use of Force*, 4th ed. (Oxford University Press, 2018), at 64.
[77] See, for example, Oscar Schachter, 'The Legality of Pro-Democratic Invasion' (1984) **78** *American Journal of International Law* 645; Kreß and Nußberger, n. 7; Wippman, n. 75.
[78] See, for example, Definition of Aggression, UNGA Res. 3314 (XXIX), 14 December 1974, Article 7.
[79] Declaration on Principles of International Law Concerning Friendly Relations and Co-operation among States (1970), UNGA Res. 2625 (XXV), 24 October 1970.
[80] See, for example, Gray, n. 76, at 71.

General Assembly that 'armed struggle' by self-determination movements was envisaged.[81]

Importantly, however, the 1970 Declaration on Principles of International Law Concerning Friendly Relations and Co-operation among States declared that '[e]very State has the duty to refrain from *any forcible action* which deprives peoples ... of their right to self-determination and freedom and independence',[82] with states being in addition not permitted to support a state suppressing this right. It further declared that '[i]n their actions against, and resistance to, such forcible action in pursuit of the exercise of their right to self-determination, such peoples are entitled to *seek and to receive support* in accordance with the purposes and principles of the Charter'.[83] In addition, the 1972 Implementation of the Declaration on the Granting of Independence to Colonial Countries and Peoples 'urges all States ... to provide moral and *material* assistance to all peoples struggling for their freedom and independence'.[84] There is, however, little support for the proposition that the intention was for this 'material assistance' to go beyond the provision of indirect military assistance, in particular so as to permit states to directly militarily intervene for the liberation of a territory from colonial, alien or racist rule.[85]

Despite the right of self-determination existing in the context of a 'people' there is no objective definition of the nature of a 'people' for the purposes of the right.[86] However, the elaboration of the rights and obligations regarding

---

[81] See, for example, Declaration on the Inadmissibility of Intervention and Interference in the Internal Affairs of States, UNGA Res. 36/103, 9 December 1981, para. 3(b) (which was adopted 120-22-6).

[82] Friendly Relations Declaration, n. 79 (emphasis added).   [83] Ibid (emphasis added).

[84] Implementation of the Declaration on the Granting of Independence to Colonial Countries and Peoples, UNGA Res. 2908 (XXVII), 2 November 1972, para. 8 (emphasis added). de Wet notes that '[t]hese resolutions were not in themselves binding and were opposed by Western states ... socialist and developing countries consistently supported these resolutions and their foreign assistance to anti-colonial armed struggles in Africa became an open and established practice. In addition, no international body ever claimed that such support was illegal. In light of the extent of third state military support for liberation movements, as well as the absence of practice condemning such support as illegal, it is fair to conclude that indirect military support to liberation movements constituted an exception to the prohibition of the use of force in international relations.' de Wet, n. 1, at 25. Gray, however, notes that 'this deliberately does not unequivocally set out any right of national liberation movements or of sympathetic states to use force'. Gray, n. 76, at 70. See, in general, Heather A. Wilson, *International Law and the Use of Force by National Liberation Movements* (Oxford University Press, 1988).

[85] Brad Roth, *Governmental Illegitimacy in International Law* (Oxford University Press, 2000), at 215-16; de Wet, n. 1, at 26. See Section 2.4.3 on the indirect use of armed force.

[86] Robert McCorquodale and Kristin Hausler, 'Caucuses in the Caucasus: The Application of the Right of Self-Determination', in James A. Green and Christopher P. M. Waters (eds.), *Conflict in the Caucasus: Implications for International Legal Order* (Palgrave, 2010), 26, at 29. Both the International Covenant on Civil and Political Rights (1966) and the International

'material support' in the 'struggle' for self-determination occurred during the decolonisation era of the twentieth century and, as such, are arguably limited to national liberation movements battling against colonialism, occupation and racist rule. Indeed, there does not appear to be any 'support for the right to use force to attain self-determination outside of the context of decolonization or illegal occupation'.[87] It is, therefore, questionable whether 'peoples' in other contexts who potentially possess a right of self-determination also possess a similar right to engage in – and be supported by – armed force to achieve it,[88] if the people concerned have been denied the right to political, social and cultural development within the borders of the state in question or been subjected to extreme oppression at the hands of the state authorities.[89] It is, therefore, also doubtful whether a state could forcibly intervene on behalf of – or provide arms and non-lethal assistance to – opposition forces operating within another state upon the legal basis of supporting a self-determination movement.[90]

## 9.3 INTERVENTION IN CIVIL WARS

While arguably the first thing that one thinks of when the words 'civil war' are uttered is a conflict occurring within the territorial confines of a state between governmental and rebel forces, such conflicts are rarely as straightforward as this and often involve at least some form of outside intervention. Indeed, interventions, and the provision of consent to intervene, normally arise in the context of civil wars, whereby a state intervenes in support of one of the opposing parties with the aim normally of assisting them to either remain in power, in the case of a government, or with the means to be able to effectively challenge for governmental authority, in the case of opposition forces.

There is extensive literature examining civil wars and the legal issues involved.[91] However, this section restricts itself to an examination of the

---

Covenant on Economic, Social and Cultural Rights (1966) provide, in Article 1(1) of each instrument, that '[a]ll peoples have the right of self-determination'. Yet, neither document goes into any further detail as to who might represent a 'people' for this purpose.

[87] Gray, n. 76, at 73.

[88] The ICJ in the *Nicaragua* case did not address the question of the use of force by national liberation movements. *Nicaragua* case, n. 10, at para. 206.

[89] Report of the Independent International Fact-Finding Mission on the Conflict in Georgia, September 2009, vol. II, at 136, available at: www.mpil.de/de/pub/publikationen/archiv/independent_international_fact.cfm.

[90] de Wet, n. 1, at 26.

[91] See, in general, Richard A. Falk (ed.), *The International Law of Civil War* (Johns Hopkins Press, 1971); Lindsay Moir, *The Law of Internal Armed Conflict* (Cambridge University Press, 2003); Anthony Cullen, *The Concept of Non-International Armed Conflict in International Humanitarian Law* (Cambridge University Press, 2010); Sandesh Sivakumaran, *The Law of*

legality of outside intervention, in particular if and when it might be permitted. Indeed, there is much debate as to whether the principles set out earlier on the rights of governments to invite outside intervention – which are, in turn, denied in principle to opposition and rebel groups – apply in the context of civil wars.

### 9.3.1 The 'Negative Equality' Principle

Connected with the principle of self-determination, which has been discussed in Section 9.2.4, is what has been coined the 'negative equality' principle.[92] This principle provides that, during a civil war – that is, an internal armed struggle for power within a state the outcome of which is uncertain – states are under a legal obligation to refrain from intervening in support of *either* side, whether the belligerent parties happen to be two non-governmental forces or the governmental forces of the state concerned and an opposition force. The underlying basis for this principle is that in such a situation the people of a state should be permitted to determine their political future independently and without outside intervention, which may prove influential or decisive in determining the outcome. In other words, 'where a society is fully divided about its political future, meaning that the government cannot plausibly claim to represent the entire population, external assistance on the government's behalf would interfere with the people's right to determine their own future'.[93] In the context of the conflict in Syria between the Assad government and the various groups that have risen up against it since 2011, this would mean that, once it had been determined that the uprising against President Assad was of the nature of a civil war, outside intervention on behalf of either side would have been prohibited.

The report of the 2009 Independent International Fact-Finding Mission on the Conflict in Georgia described the 'negative equality' principle as 'the most recent trend in scholarship'.[94] It is true, as Fox notes, that '[m]any contemporary scholars argue that if a conflict has reached the level of a civil war, intervention on the government side, permitted without qualification by the *Nicaragua* case, is in fact prohibited'.[95] However, support for this principle is not entirely new,

---

*Non-International Armed Conflict* (Oxford University Press, 2012); Yoram Dinstein, *Non-International Armed Conflicts in International Law*, 2nd ed. (Cambridge University Press, 2021).

[92] See Fox, n. 1, at 827–9.   [93] Ibid., at 827.
[94] See *Independent International Fact-Finding Mission on the Conflict in Georgia*, n. 89, at 277.
[95] Fox, n. 1, at 827. See, for example, Doswald-Beck, n. 1, at 196; Derek W. Bowett, 'The Interrelation of Theories of Intervention and Self-Defense', in John N. Moore (ed.), *Law and Civil War in the Modern World* (Johns Hopkins University Press, 1974), 38, at 41; Corten, n. 4, at 277–8; in general, Luca Ferro, 'The Doctrine of "Negative Equality" and the Silent Majority of States' (2021) 8 *Journal on the Use of Force and International Law* 4.

with the Institut de Droit International stating in 1975 that 'third states shall refrain from giving assistance to parties in a civil war which is being fought in the territory of another state'.[96] Even earlier, the 1965 Declaration on the Inadmissibility of Intervention in the Domestic Affairs of States declared that 'no state shall ... interfere in civil strife in another state'.[97]

There are several factors that exist in support of this principle. For example, identifying those with authority to consent may be difficult during a civil war.[98] It also avoids the question of whether any invitation has been validly issued[99] and can help avoid escalating what is at the point of intervention a civil war into an international armed conflict. There are, however, also identifiable problems with the principle and, in general, to attaching a different set of rules to civil wars to those that apply during peace time. First, there is a distinct lack of clarity over what constitutes a 'civil war' for the purposes of applying these rules and '[n]o generally accepted definition exists, largely because "civil war" is not a critical term of art in international instruments'.[100] An analogy could, of course, be made with the law of armed conflict so that a civil war is equated with a non-international armed conflict which can be defined, in general, as 'protracted armed confrontations occurring between governmental armed forces and the forces of one or more armed groups, or between such groups arising on the territory of a State [party to the Geneva Conventions]' with '[t]he armed confrontation ... reach[ing] a minimum level of intensity and the parties involved in the conflict ... show[ing] a minimum of organization',[101] thereby excluding less serious forms of violence, such as internal disturbances and tensions, riots or acts of banditry. While the Security Council does not normally use the phrase 'civil war' in its resolutions dealing with internal conflict, a civil war can perhaps normally be observed when the Council begins to talk about the necessity of both parties to a conflict complying with, or of seriously violating, international humanitarian law, which can be taken as implying that a non-international armed conflict, and by analogy a civil war, is occurring.[102]

---

[96] Institut de droit International, Resolution, 'The Principle of Non-Intervention in Civil Wars' (1975) 56 *Annuaire de l'Institut de droit international* 545, at 547.

[97] UNGA Res. 2131 (1965), para. 2. See also the 1970 Friendly Relations Declaration, n. 79, at para. 3(2).

[98] See Section 9.2.   [99] See Section 9.4.   [100] Fox, n. 1, at 827.

[101] See International Committee of the Red Cross, 'How Is the Term "Armed Conflict" Defined in International Humanitarian Law?', Opinion Paper, March 2008, available at: www.icrc.org/eng/assets/ files/other/opinion-paper-armed-conflict.pdf. See also Common Article 3 to the Geneva Conventions (1949); *The Prosecutor* v. *Dusko Tadic*, Case No. IT-94-1, ICTY, Decision on the Defence Motion for Interlocutory Appeal on Jurisdiction, 1995, at para. 70; *The Prosecutor* v. *Dusko Tadic*, Case No. IT-94-1, ICTY, Judgment, 1997, at paras. 561–8; Article 1, Additional Protocol II to the Geneva Conventions of 1949 (1977).

[102] For example, in the context of the conflict in Libya in 2011, see UNSC Res. 1970 (2011), preamble.

Using the concept of a non-international armed conflict might appear to be a good starting point in defining when the 'negative equality' principle becomes applicable. There are, however, certain problems in doing so and it is not altogether clear whether it is entirely appropriate to apply rules on non-intervention in this context. It has, for example, been correctly observed that the definition of non-international armed conflict encompasses 'only the most intense and large-scale conflicts'.[103] Yet, the required degree of protraction and intensity of conflict, as well as the required degree of organisation of the parties involved, and whether this is met in each case, is something that is open to interpretation.[104] However, not only is the definition of a non-international armed conflict somewhat vague and difficult to apply in practice, and open to subjectivity, it might be argued that, given that the negative equality principle is based upon not impeding the right of self-determination, it should also be applied beyond full-blown civil wars to situations of domestic political unrest.[105] Indeed, if we accept this principle as existing to prevent outside states determining the future destiny of the people within a state then it may legitimately be questioned whether it should be restricted to applying only during civil wars. To do so might appear to simply provide a greater right of self-determination to those with greater capabilities to fight.

A second identifiable problem with the negative equality principle is that normally 'a prohibition on aid to both sides necessarily benefits the stronger party, which is in almost all cases the incumbent regime',[106] thus supporting the *status quo*. Nevertheless, one might conversely argue that this is the lesser of two evils, given that any intervention under the traditional position set out above would, in any case, be at the invitation, and in support, of the incumbent regime.

Thirdly, there is no universal consensus on the validity of the principle within the scholarly community.[107] As Fox notes:

> [n]egative equality has not yet attracted a consensus among scholars and indeed remains controversial, for it is vulnerable to the same criticism of disjunction from state practice used to criticize pre-Charter belligerency doctrine. Governments that have lost substantial portions of their territory to rebel insurgencies have continued to receive external assistance.[108]

Indeed, the final identifiable problem, and perhaps the one most damaging for the prospects of the 'negative equality' principle, is that it is not 'at all clear that the view that international law (the *jus ad bellum*) treats interventions in

---

[103] Moir, n. 91, at 101.   [104] See Section 8.5 for more on these issues.
[105] Quincy Wright has argued that this principle extends also to 'rebellion, insurrection, or civil war. Since international law recognises the right of revolution, it cannot permit other states to interfere to prevent it.' Quincy Wright, 'Subversive Intervention' (1960) **54** *American Journal of International Law* 521, at 529.
[106] Fox, n. 1, at 829.   [107] Akande and Vermeer, n. 33.   [108] Fox, n. 1, at 828.

civil war differently from any other situation has support in State practice'.[109] Although the United Kingdom provided some support to the principle in 1984,[110] there does not seem to be much evidence on the whole that states accept that they are legally obliged to refrain from supporting governments in a civil war situation.[111] Instead, there are many examples within contemporary international practice where armed forces have been sent by one state to another, at the latter's request in what could be described as a civil war. France's intervention in Mali in 2013 at the request of the government to fight against violent non-state actors in its territory commenced and appeared to be generally accepted after the non-state actors had captured and controlled the entire northern part of the state and were less than 300 miles from the capital.[112] It was notable, however, that 'no state raised the "negative equality" principle or spoke in opposition to the French intervention'.[113] The Russian supply of arms and subsequent deployment of forces to the Assad regime during the protracted civil war in Syria that began in 2011 provides another example.[114] Concerns were clearly expressed by several Western and Arab states, as well as some international organisations, regarding the righteousness of this assistance and the continuation of the situation. Yet, this condemnation appeared to be targeted towards the risks regarding 'prolonging the conflict, undermining a political process, aggravating the humanitarian situation and increasing radicalization'[115] or that 'attacks against the Syrian moderate opposition ... benefit so-called ISIL (Daesh) and other terrorist groups, such as Al-Nusrah Front, and contribute to a further deterioration of the humanitarian situation'.[116] There was little apparent, at least express, accusation that such intervention at the request of the Syrian government was in and of itself unlawful.

---

[109] Akande, n. 53. See also James W. Garner, 'Questions of International Law in the Spanish Civil War' (1937) 31 *American Journal of International Law* 66, at 67–9.
[110] UK Foreign Policy Document No. 148, 'UK Materials on International Law' (1986) 57 *British Yearbook of International Law* 614.
[111] See Akande, n. 53.
[112] See n. 33. See also BBC News, 'Mali: France Pledges "Short" Campaign against Islamists', 14 January 2013, available at: www.bbc.co.uk/news/world-europe-21007517.
[113] Fox, n. 1, at 828.
[114] See, in general, Tom Ruys, 'Of Arms, Funding and "Non-Lethal" Assistance": Issues Surrounding Third-State Intervention in the Syrian Civil War' (2014) 13 *Chinese Journal of International Law* 13.
[115] Council of the European Union, 'Council Conclusions on Syria', 12 October 2015, available at: www.consilium.europa.eu/en/press/press-releases/2015/10/12/fac-conclusions-syria/.
[116] UN Third Committee, 'Situation of human rights in the Syrian Arab Republic', UN Doc. A/C.3/70/L.47, 2 November 2015, at para. 15.

### 9.3.2 The Purpose-Based Approach

It is noticeable that several scholars have adopted what has been described as a 'purpose-based approach' to the legality of intervention in support of a government during a civil war, or what might be seen as a qualified version of the 'negative equality' principle. Those accepting this position deny the legality of intervention which aims to aid government forces in the context of a civil war, and thus potentially interfere with the right of self-determination, although accept that intervention with the government's invitation or consent for other specific purposes, such as fighting terrorism, may be permissible. As a leading proponent of this approach has argued:

> If the *purpose* of the intervention on request of the government does not violate the principle of self-determination, then normally such intervention is legal. A purpose-based approach is thus necessary. State practice shows that the legality of intervention by invitation (even in cases of civil war) has never raised problems when the purpose of such consensual intervention was clearly limited to the realization of other objectives, such as, the fight against terrorism; the fight against rebels who use the territory of the neighbouring state as 'safe haven' to launch attacks against the intervening state; the protection of nationals abroad; the liberation of hostages; the protection of crucial infrastructure; the joint fight against drug smugglers and other criminals; and more generally, support to the government to maintain law and order, and the deployment of 'peacekeeping operations'.[117]

This approach gives rise to the problem of identifying and confirming the legitimacy of the proclaimed purpose of an intervention. For example, in the fight against terrorism, and without a definition of terrorism in international law, there is scope for a large degree of subjectivity, and issues arise as to who exactly is able to determine that a group is, in fact, 'terrorist' in nature.[118] This might not be so much of a problem if a particular group has been preordained by the Security Council as a terrorist group. In the context of France's intervention in Mali in 2013, for example, all three groups that were targeted by France were depicted as 'terrorist' by the Council.[119] Similarly, in the context of the civil wars taking place in Syria, Iraq and Libya, the Council has clearly categorised Islamic State, al-Nusrah Front and al-Qaida as terrorist groups. Yet, the conflict in Syria also highlights the problem of such a determination being made by states. Indeed, while the Security Council categorised some of the groups fighting in Syria as terrorist, the Syrian government appeared to seek to characterise virtually all groups opposing the government in this way.[120]

---

[117] Karine Bannelier-Christakis, 'Military Interventions against ISIL in Iraq, Syria and Libya, and the Legal Basis of Consent' (2016) 29 *Leiden Journal of International Law* 743, at 747.
[118] Ibid.   [119] See UNSC Res. 2100 (2013), para. 4.
[120] See UN Doc. S/2016/80, 28 January 2016 ('Islamic State in Iraq and the Levant (ISIL), the Nusrah Front, the Army of Islam, the Islamic Front, the Army of Conquest, Ahrar al-Sham and the Free Army').

This approach has also been challenged by some scholars who claim that arguments that there is a prohibition on intervention by invitation of a government in a civil war, and therefore that a 'negative equality' principle exists, are, as discussed in the previous section, 'inconsistent with state practice',[121] and in the absence of the 'negative equality' principle there is no need to look for a legitimate purpose for the issuing of a consent or invitation to intervene.[122] However, Karine Bannelier-Christakis argues that '[m]ore generally, the argument of "invitation" or "consent" has been used dozens of times in state practice in order to provide legal justification to various external interventions', yet 'in the overwhelming majority of cases, states which carry out such military interventions take all necessary precautions to convince others that their action should not be regarded as an intervention in a civil war'.[123]

There are indeed instances of states intervening for a stated purpose rather than upon the basis of intervening in a civil conflict. For example, following its armed intervention in Chad in 1978 France was accused of having intervened in the civil war that was taking place there in support of the government.[124] Yet, France expressly rejected this and argued instead that it was there for the protection of its nationals and in order to train the army of Chad.[125] More recently, the Gulf Cooperation Council (GCC) intervened in Bahrain in March 2011, principally on the grounds of 'contribut[ing] to the maintenance of order and stability' following an uprising in the state.[126] However, it later transpired that '[t]he [Government of Bahrain] [had] expressed its concerns about a possible Iranian armed intervention in Bahrain' and 'that these concerns were *among the principal reasons* that it requested the deployment of GCC forces in Bahrain starting on 14 March 2011'.[127] Although there was some doubt as to the reality of the Iranian intervention, the fact remains that neither Bahrain or the GCC appeared to feel able to rely solely on the ground of invitation by the Government of Bahrain to quell civil unrest, but rather attempted to frame it more as a counter-intervention.[128]

---

[121] Akande and Vermeer, n. 33.    [122] See Fox, n. 1, at 828.
[123] Bannelier-Christakis, n. 117, at 749.    [124] *Keesing's* (1978) 28976.    [125] Ibid.
[126] Gulf Cooperation Council, Secretary-General of the Cooperation Council, 'Notes and supports the positions of the GCC countries to contribute to the preservation of order and security in the Kingdom of Bahrain' (Riyadh, 15 March 2011), at para. 1. It might be questioned, however, whether the unrest had reached the level of a civil war.
[127] Bahrain Independent Commission of Inquiry, 'Report of the Bahrain Independent Commission of Inquiry', 10 December 2011, Chapter IV, at para. 1575 (emphasis added), available at: www.bici.org.bh/BICIreportEN.pdf.
[128] Agatha Verdebout, 'The Intervention of the Gulf Cooperation Council in Bahrain: 2011', in Tom Ruys, Olivier Corten and Alexander Hofer (eds.), *The Use of Force in International Law* (Oxford University Press, 2018), 795, at 801. The doctrine of counter-intervention is addressed in Section 9.3.3.

Similarly, in intervening during the civil war in Mali in 2013, France denied that it was intervening in the war between the government and the Tuareg rebels of Le Mouvement national de libération de l'Azawad (MLNA), but was instead acting against Islamist terrorist groups which were partly composed of foreign fighters.[129] And in its intervention in support of the Assad regime during the Syrian civil war, Russian President Putin was keen to stress that '[t]he country's only goal is to combat the international terrorists of ISIL' and other terrorist groups.[130]

In addition, the Saudi-led coalition intervention in Yemen – Operation Decisive Storm – that commenced on 26 March 2015 in response to armed activity by Yemen's Houthi movement could be seen as intervention in a civil war in response to an invitation by Yemen's president.[131] Indeed, it was launched to 'protect the people of Yemen and its legitimate government from a takeover by the Houthis'[132] and received much support within the international community.[133] Yet, in its letter to the Security Council, Saudi Arabia placed clear focus, not upon consent or invitation to intervene in the civil war,

---

[129] See UN Doc. S/2013/17, 14 January 2013. See Theodore Christakis and Karine Bannelier, 'French Military Intervention in Mali: It's Legal but ... Why? Part I: The Argument of Collective Self-Defense', *EJIL Talk!*, 24 January 2013, available at: www.ejiltalk.org/french-military-intervention-in-mali-its-legal-but-why-part-i/; Theodore Christakis and Karine Bannelier, 'French Military Intervention in Mali: It's Legal but ... Why? Part II: Consent and UNSC Authorisation', *EJIL Talk!*, 25 January 2013, available at: www.ejiltalk.org/french-military-intervention-in-mali-its-legal-but-why-part-2-consent-and-unsc-authorisation/.

[130] 'Syria Crisis: Vladimir Putin Insists Russia Is Only Bombing Isis as Critics Say He Is "the Anti-Christ for Sunni Muslims"', *The Independent*, 12 October 2015, available at: www.independent.co.uk/news/world/middle-east/syria-crisis-vladimir-putin-says-russia-only-wants-to-bomb-isis-as-critics-say-he-is-becoming-a6690346.html. See also, 'Russia Rejects Criticism of Air Strikes in Syria', *Aljazeera*, 1 October 2015, available at: www.aljazeera.com/news/2015/10/russia-rejects-criticism-air-strikes-syria-151001173827826.html.

[131] See Section 9.2.2.

[132] 'Statement by Saudi Ambassador al-Jubeir on Military Operations in Yemen', 25 March 2015, available at: www.operationrenewalofhope.com/statement-by-saudi-ambassador-al-jubeir-on-military-operations-in-yemen/#sthash.E7gLWUDk.dpbs.

[133] For example, the League of Arab States 'fully welcome[d] and support[ed] the military operations in defence of legitimate authority in Yemen'. Note Verbale Dated 2 April 2015 from the Permanent Observer of the League of Arab States to the United Nations Addressed to the President of the Security Council, UN Doc. S/2015/232, 15 April 2015. While some caution was expressed by UN Secretary-General Ban Ki-Moon and the EU High Representative for Foreign Affairs, Federica Mogherini, as well as some states such as China and Oman, barring a few exceptions (such as Iran and Russia) there was an absence of express condemnation of the operation. See Luca Ferro and Tom Ruys, 'The Saudi-led Military Intervention in Yemen's Civil War: 2015', in Tom Ruys, Olivier Corten and Alexander Hofer (eds.), *The Use of Force in International Law* (Oxford University Press, 2018), 899, at 902–4. During the debate at which UNSC Resolution 2216 (2015) was adopted, which merely noted the letter of request for assistance by President Hadi and the letters of the states responding to this request, no state questioned the legality of the operation. See UN Doc. S/PV.7426, 14 April 2015.

but on the fact that the Houthi rebels were 'supported by regional forces' and 'had always been a tool of outside forces' and therefore there had been an act of 'aggression' against Yemen.[134] While it has been argued that 'the coalition's efforts were without a doubt primarily aimed at repelling the "internal" Houthi militias' and 'the fight against recognized terrorist groups such as Al-Qaida and Islamic State was not at the forefront of the military operations',[135] consent in the context of a civil war was still nonetheless not considered sufficient by itself, and reliance was instead placed again upon 'counter-intervention'.[136]

Ultimately, it is arguably true, as Olivier Corten has observed, that 'no State has claimed a right to help a government having allegedly made an appeal for the purpose of putting down a rebel movement' and they 'never ... assume a right to intervene in any purely internal conflict'.[137] While Akande and Vermeer have argued, on the other hand, that the justifications offered on these occasions seem 'to refer more to the *motivations or reasons* for which states provide military assistance to other states, as opposed to the *legal justification* for intervention' and that 'it would be wrong to think that the motivation or reason equates to the legal justification as that would misunderstand the *opinio juris* element of custom',[138] the problem is, of course, and as is clear in the justifications advanced on these occasions, that it is not often easy to distinguish between the two.

### 9.3.3 Counter-Intervention

Although the 'negative equality' principle is far from universally accepted, it does command a good deal of support within the scholarly community and, as set out in Section 9.3.2, states generally refrain from justifying interventions in times of civil war upon the basis of consent without declaring that they are doing so for reasons other than pure support for a government in the context of a civil crisis. However, those that subscribe to the position of strict non-interference during a civil war do often accept that there is an exception to the principle in the form of counter-intervention, or, in other words, it is argued that outside interference in favour of one party to the struggle permits counter-intervention on behalf of the other.[139] Under this view, prior intervention on behalf of one side to the conflict internationalises the conflict,

---

[134] UN Doc. S/2015/217, 27 March 2015, at 5 (Saudi Arabia).
[135] Ruys and Ferro, n. 51, at 92.
[136] Ferro and Ruys, n. 133, at 910. The doctrine of counter-intervention is addressed in Section 9.3.3.
[137] Corten, n. 4, at 277 and 306.  [138] Akande and Vermeer, n. 33.
[139] See Wright, n. 105. See, generally, John A. Perkins, 'The Right of Counter-Intervention' (1986) **17** *Georgia Journal of International and Comparative Law* 171.

meaning that the 'negative equality' principle, which only applies to *civil* or *domestic* wars, loses its relevance.[140] In this respect, as Fox has pointed out, 'external intervention in civil wars internationalizes the conflict for the purposes of international law, even though the dominant players and issues at stake may remain primarily domestic'.[141]

While this is a position with significant scholarly support,[142] it is also one that several states have apparently adopted. For example, in 1986, the UK Foreign Office stated that:

any form of interference or assistance is prohibited (except possibly of a humanitarian kind) when a civil war is taking place and control of the State's territory is divided between warring parties. But it is widely accepted that outside interference in favour of one party to the struggle permits counter-intervention on behalf of the other.[143]

In addition, during the long-running civil war in Chad that began in 1975, France and Libya intervened on opposite sides of the conflict while claiming to be doing so in support of the legitimate government in response to prior intervention by the other state.[144] More recently, as discussed in Section 9.3.2, prior intervention by Iran on behalf of the Houthi rebels played a central role in Saudi Arabia's justification for its intervention in Yemen and was not subject to any notable or sustained criticism,[145] although whether, and if so to what extent, Iran was in fact supporting the Houthi rebels on this occasion was unclear.[146]

However, claims of prior intervention, and thus implementation of the counter-intervention doctrine, have been abused in the past.[147] Indeed, while it has been said that counter-intervention 'is the best established exception to the prohibition of intervention' it is also 'possibly the most abused'.[148] Arguably the most infamous examples of abuse can be found in the interventions by the USSR in Czechoslovakia in 1968 and in Afghanistan in 1979. With collective self-defence being implicitly claimed by the USSR in each case,

---

[140] If the activities of the non-state armed group are characterised as an 'armed attack' for the purposes of Article 51 and outside state support for the non-state armed group reaches the level of effective control then an armed response may be taken by the territorial state against the intervening state in collective self-defence. See, further, Chapter 6 on the right of self-defence and Chapter 8 specifically on the question of the right of self-defence against non-state actors.

[141] Fox, n. 1, at 820.

[142] Doswald-Beck, n. 1, at 251; Gray, n. 76, at 95–100; Bannelier-Christakis, n. 117, at 747 ('The legality of *counter-intervention* when the rebels receive substantial outside support is also generally recognized.' (emphasis added)).

[143] 'Is Intervention Ever Justified?' (1986) 57 *British Yearbook of International Law* 616.

[144] See A. Mark Weisburd, *Use of Force: The Practice of States since World War II* (The Pennsylvania State University Press, 1997), at 188–96.

[145] See n. 133 and accompanying text.   [146] Ruys and Ferro, n. 51, at 75–6.

[147] Gray, n. 76, at 95.   [148] Ibid.

it also stated that it had been invited by the respective governments to repel outside threats and interference,[149] although the government of Czechoslovakia later denied this,[150] while the government in Afghanistan had been recently installed by the USSR. Both interventions received widespread condemnation,[151] with the intervention in Afghanistan being expressly condemned by the UN General Assembly.[152] Of course, abuse of rights is, unfortunately, a fact of life, including for the established right of self-defence, and so should not, by itself, be seen to preclude the existence of a right of counter-intervention.

The required *degree* of prior outside intervention to justify counter-intervention is, however, not clear,[153] as well as whether there is a requirement for proportionality between the prior intervention and the counter-intervention,[154] as is the case both in the context of self-defence and the taking of countermeasures, and, if so, whether this is of a qualitative or quantitative nature. Neither of these questions can be affirmatively answered through an examination of state practice, the jurisprudence of the ICJ or scholarly contributions,[155] although it is admittedly difficult to square the existence of a proportionality test in this context with the state practice that exists. For example, Saudi Arabia's direct intervention in Yemen in 2015, which involved approximately 200 aircraft, 18 warships and over 15,000 troops along the border,[156] was clearly disproportionate (regardless of whether one measures it in quantitative or qualitative terms or through the aims of the acting state) to the provision of arms and military training that was alleged to have been provided by Iran to the Houthi rebels. Yet, the operation was not heavily objected to[157] and, while the Saudi-led operation has been criticised for violations of international humanitarian law and the dire humanitarian situation on the ground,[158] claims that the actions were disproportionate have been relatively muted.

---

[149] UN Doc. S/PV. 1441, 21 August 1968, at paras. 3, 75, 104 and 216; UN Doc. S/PV. 2185, 5 January 1980, at para. 13, and UN Doc. S/PV. 2186, 5 January 1980, at para. 22.

[150] UN Doc. S/PV. 1441, ibid., at para. 133

[151] See, respectively, the statements made during the meetings of the Security Council on 21 August 1968 (UN Doc. S/PV. 1441, n. 149) and 5 January 1980 (UN Doc. S/PV. 2185, n. 149, and UN Doc. S/PV. 2186, n. 149).

[152] UNGA Res. 40/12 (1984).    [153] Ruys and Ferro, n. 51, at 93.    [154] Ibid.

[155] Ibid. See also Zachary Vermeer, 'The *Jus ad Bellum* and the Airstrikes in Yemen: Double Standards for Decamping Presidents?', *EJIL Talk!*, 30 April 2015, available at: www.ejiltalk.org/the-jus-ad-bellum-and-the-airstrikes-in-yemen-double-standards-for-decamping-presidents/.

[156] Katherine Zimmerman, '2015 Yemen Intervention Map', *American Enterprise Institute Critical Threats Project*, 23 April 2015, available at: www.aei.org/multimedia/2015-yemen-intervention-map/.

[157] See n. 133.

[158] Edith M. Lederer, 'UN Experts Say Saudi Coalition Violated International Humanitarian Law in Yemen Attack', *The Independent*, 21 October 2016, available at: www.independent.co.uk/

It is possible to conceive of such a right of counter-intervention as supporting the principle of self-determination and the rights of a people to freely determine their own political status. In this respect, if the starting point is that during a civil war outside intervention in support of either party is prohibited, it is possible to view the right of counter-intervention to permit the provision of counter-support upon the basis of the principle of self-determination. Yet, while it has been stated that 'counter-intervention should be about undoing the impact of the original intervention' on the other side as well as 'evening the odds, not tilting the balance in favour' of the supported party,[159] it is difficult to see this implemented in practice. Indeed, it is clear that Russian support for the Assad regime in the Syrian civil war has not, and will not, cease until the rebels have either surrendered or, more likely, been crushed and the war won, despite the rebels merely being supplied with arms, training and non-lethal supplies. There are also occasions when the right to counter-intervention will presumably not be available. For example, it has been argued that where the state has plunged into 'chaotic turbulence, with several claimants to constitutional legality or none at all' the 'negative equality' principle should be strictly maintained as it may simply not be possible to identify 'any remnants of the central Government and determin[e] who has rebelled against whom'.[160]

## 9.4 THE FORM OF THE CONSENT OR INVITATION TO INTERVENE

If the legality of an intervention is based upon the consent of the territorial state, then questions arise as to the form of the consent or invitation and whether it can be considered to be valid. In this respect, the International Law Commission has noted that 'the consent of the State must be valid in international law, clearly established, really expressed (which precludes merely presumed consent), internationally attributable to the State and anterior to the commission of the act to which it refers'.[161] While the issue of the individuals within a government who possess the authority to issue consent has been addressed in Section 9.2, there are certain identifiable elements that make a particular consent or invitation valid, and which have also given rise to some controversy.

In assessing the validity of a consent or invitation to intervene it is important to examine the form that it has taken, although consent does not appear to

---

news/world/middle-east/un-saudi-arabia-yemen-air-strikes-violated-international-law-a7372936.html.

[159] Ruys and Ferro, n. 51, at 93–4.

[160] Yoram Dinstein, *War, Aggression and Self-Defence*, 6th ed. (Cambridge University Press, 2017), at para. 341.

[161] See n. 2.

need to follow any particular formalities. In this respect, although it is arguably necessary for consent to be clearly established, there does not appear to be a requirement for it to necessarily be in written form or publicly stated,[162] although the consenting state will usually make it public, for example in a letter to the UN Security Council, a statement before the Security Council, a public address, or in the form of a 'memorandum of understanding'.[163] Various examples exist of one state expressly inviting another state to intervene, for example the request of the king of Bahrain, Hamad Bin Issa Al-Khalifa, to the GCC in 2011,[164] Yemeni President Hadi's request also to the GCC to intervene in 2015,[165] and Iraq's invitation to the United States in 2014.[166] While these interventions may be criticised upon other grounds, they were all examples of the government of a state clearly expressly consenting to the intervention of another state to engage in military action upon its territory, although such statements of consent 'rarely contain the details regarding the scope and the duration of the military mandate agreed to between the countries in question'.[167] Consent may also be established implicitly, for example 'if it is clear that the States' military actions are closely coordinated'.[168] Yet, it is important that the consent of the territorial state is neither constructed nor presumed to exist by the intervening state. Indeed, there must be objective indicators regarding the validity of the consent. In this respect, despite a lack of protest by the Syrian government when airstrikes by the United States commenced upon its territory in September 2014 against the so-called Islamic State, this should not be taken as tacit consent to them. On the contrary, the United States neither sought or gave the Syrian government the chance to consent to the airstrikes beforehand and,[169] in any case, prior to their commencement in August 2014 the Syrian government stated that any

---

[162] de Wet, n. 1, at 161. It has been argued that there is a need for 'express *public* consent'. See Mary Ellen O'Connell, 'Unlawful Killing with Combat Drones' *Notre Dame Law School Research Paper* (2010), at 18 (emphasis added). It is not clear, however, where the need for 'publicity' comes from. Indeed, Sean Murphy has argued, by contrast, that consent may be adduced in 'whatever venue is necessary' to confirm its existence. See Sean D. Murphy, 'The International Legality of US Military Cross-Border Operations from Afghanistan into Pakistan' (2009) 85 *International Legal Studies* 109, at 188.

[163] See, for example, Memorandum of Understanding between the Government of the Republic of South Africa and the Government of the Central African Republic Concerning Defence Cooperation, 11 February 2007, available at: www.politicsweb.co.za/documents/sas-2007-mou-with-car-on-defence-cooperation.

[164] See Section 9.3.2.     [165] See Section 9.2.2.     [166] See Section 9.1.

[167] de Wet, n. 1, at 161. This may have implications for determining whether the assisting state has gone beyond the limits of what was consented to by the territorial state. See, further, Section 9.5.

[168] Tom Ruys, *'Armed Attack' and Article 51 of the UN Charter: Evolutions in Customary Law and Practice* (Cambridge University Press, 2010), at 91.

[169] Anne Gearan, 'US Rules-Out Coordinating with Assad on Airstrikes against Islamists in Syria', *Washington Post*, 26 August 2014, available at: www.washingtonpost.com/world/

airstrikes launched in the absence of its consent would constitute an act of aggression and a violation of Syrian sovereignty.[170] A year later, in September 2015, Syria again expressly objected to the fact that the military action had occurred in the absence of any coordination with it.[171]

Not only must the consent not be implied or presumed, it must also not be provided retrospectively but rather before, or at least at the time, the intervention commences.[172] On several occasions alleged retrospective invitations have been equated to the manufacturing of consent by the intervening state. For example, consent for the Soviet Union's intervention in Afghanistan in 1979 was seemingly provided after the intervention had begun.[173] On 25 December 1979 Soviet troops entered Afghanistan, two days later the incumbent government was overthrown and on 28 December the press reported an appeal from the Afghan government to intervene, a chronological problem that was highlighted in the criticism that the USSR faced for this operation.[174] An invitation to intervene was also part of the justification advanced by Iraq for its intervention in Kuwait in 1990, whereby it was subsequently claimed in 1991 that it had been provided with a request to intervene from the Free Provisional Government of Kuwait.[175] No evidence was provided for this and it appeared to be manufactured, although, in any case, the Free Provisional Government of Kuwait lacked the authority to invite outside intervention.[176]

It is apparent, then, that a central problem with consent being provided, or coming to light, after an intervention has commenced is the possibility for coercion into accepting the troops of one state upon the territory of another. Indeed, as an expression of a state's will, valid consent is also that which is

---

national-security/us-rules-out-coordinating-with-assad-on-airstrikes-against-islamists-in-syria/2014/08/26/cda02e0e-2d2e-11e4-9b98-848790384093_story.html.

[170] 'US Air Strikes on Syrian ISIS Targets Need Permission: Syria', *CBC News*, 25 August 2014, available at: www.cbc.ca/news/world/u-s-airstrikes-on-syrian-isis-targets-need-permission-syria-1.2745775.

[171] See Identical Letters dated 16 September 2015 from the Permanent Representative of the Syrian Arab Republic to the United Nations Addressed to the Secretary-General and the President of the Security Council, UN Doc. S/2015/718, 17 September 2015; Identical Letters dated 17 September 2015 from the Permanent Representative of the Syrian Arab Republic to the United Nations Addressed to the Secretary-General and the President of the Security Council, UN Doc. S/2015/719, 21 September 2015.

[172] Draft Articles on Responsibility of States for Internationally Wrongful Acts, with commentaries (2001), Article 20, para. 3. If it is provided during or after the action it might constitute 'a form of waiver or acquiescence, leading to loss of the right to invoke responsibility' although the wrongfulness of the prior action would remain. Ibid. See Corten, n. 4, at 264.

[173] Corten, ibid., at 265.   [174] See UN Doc. S/PV. 2185, 5 January 1980.

[175] See UN Doc. S/PV. 2932, 2 August 1990, at 11 (Iraq).

[176] The argument based upon an invitation to intervene 'was soon abandoned because of the survival of the Emir of Kuwait and the strong negative reaction to the invasion both from Kuwaitis and the international community'. Weisburd, n. 144, at 56.

## 9.4 The Form of the Consent or Invitation to Intervene

provided freely and in the absence of any coercion, meaning that expression of a state's consent to intervention which has been procured by coercion is without legal effect.[177] In other words, coercion vitiates consent. Such a state of affairs can be seen, again, in the intervention by Warsaw Pact states in Czechoslovakia in 1968, which was based upon an invitation by local authorities under apparent intense pressure from Moscow.[178] The coercive pressure imposed formed the basis for several states' criticism of the intervention.[179] That said, the validity of consent has not often been an issue in the context of military operations in the post–Cold War era. Indeed, '[e]ven in protracted conflicts with overwhelming military involvement by states, such as Russia (in Syria), Saudi Arabia (in Yemen), and the United States (in Afghanistan), the validity of the consent issued by the recognized government has not been questioned'.[180]

Situations may also arise where there is an apparent contradiction between, on the one hand, public denial of consent by the government of the territorial state and, on the other, apparent secret approval by the same government. The United States, for example, notified Pakistan about its drone strikes against al-Qaida members located within its territory[181] and Pakistan's failure to respond to these was interpreted as tacit consent.[182] However, following the raid against the compound of Osama bin Laden in 2011,[183] Pakistan subsequently expressed its 'deep concerns and reservations' over the drone strikes which, it

---

[177] See Articles 51 and 52 of the Vienna Convention on the Law of Treaties (1969). Article 51 concerns the coercion of the representative of the state and Article 52 concerns coercion of the state itself through the threat or use of force. These articles have been held to constitute customary international law. See *Fisheries Jurisdiction (UK v. Iceland)* (Jurisdiction of the Court) (1973) ICJ Rep. 3, at para. 24. While these are in relation to coercion in the context of consent to the conclusion of a treaty rather than consent to military assistance on request, de Wet concludes that in both contexts the 'causal and probative threshold' is high. de Wet, n. 1, at 159. In this respect, the coercion must have been directly responsible for the consent, must have clearly extended beyond persuasion, influence or advice, must not have been vague or general and must not have been based on the fact that the assisting state had previously used force in the territory of the requesting state or because the assisting state is the dominant partner between the two states or is seen to be directing the military operations. Ibid., at 158–60.

[178] Corten, n. 4, at 266.

[179] See, for example, the statement of the United States, UN Doc. S/PV. 1441, 21 August 1968, at para. 41.

[180] de Wet, n. 1, at 160.

[181] Adam Entous, Siobhan Gorman and Even Perez, 'U.S. Unease over Drone Strikes: Obama Administration Charts Delicate Legal Path Defending Controversial Weapons', *Wall Street Journal*, 26 September 2012, available at: www.wsj.com/articles/SB10000872396390444100404577641520858011452.

[182] Ibid; Max Byrne, 'Consent and the Use of Force: An Examination of "Intervention by Invitation" as a Basis for US Drone Strikes in Pakistan, Somalia and Yemen' (2016) 3 *Journal on the Use of Force and International Law* 97, at 104.

[183] See Section 8.5.

alleged, were carried out 'without Pakistan's knowledge or permission'.[184] Yet, while Pakistan continued to publicly condemn the strikes,[185] secret memos allegedly existed showing that Pakistan in fact endorsed them.[186] In these contexts, determining the validity of the claimed consent is a matter for evidentiary proceedings, although any confusion as to the existence of consent by the territorial state is a sign that any consent provided was, at best, fragile, if it was provided at all.

Lastly, questions arise in respect to the distinction, if any, between ad hoc consent to intervention and prior or ex ante treaty-based consent for another state or organisation to intervene should the circumstances arise, despite the territorial state possibly protesting against the intervention at the time. Indeed, while Iraq was a member of the UN and bound by the UN Charter during its invasion of Kuwait in 1990–1, and protested against intervention by the Security Council-backed forces in 1991 to evict it from Kuwait, it had provided prior consent to the possibility that the Security Council might authorise force against it by signing and ratifying the text of the UN Charter.[187]

However, while in the context of the Security Council the ex-ante consent to intervention provided to the Council by members of the UN does not need to be supplemented with any subsequent ad hoc consent by the government of the territorial state concerned, this is not the same in the context of other organisations or in the relationships between states.[188] Indeed, in the post–Cold War era the practice of states and regional organisations supports the view that any ex ante consent to forcible measures should be complemented either by additional ad hoc consent or authorisation by the UNSC under either Chapter VII or VIII. A certain amount of controversy has arisen, for example, in the context of Article 4(h) of the African Union's (AU) Constitutive Act of 2000 which appeared to provide for a competing regional treaty-based intervention through its provision of 'the right of the Union to intervene in a Member State pursuant to a decision of the Assembly in respect of grave circumstances, namely: war crimes, genocide and crimes against humanity'.[189] It is notable that this 'makes no reference to the

---

[184] Karin Brulliard and Karen DeYoung, 'Pakistani Military, Government Warn U.S. against Future Raids', *Washington Post*, 6 May 2011, available at: www.washingtonpost.com/world/pakistan-questions-legality-of-us-operation-that-killed-bin-laden/2011/05/05/AFM2l0wF_story.html.

[185] See, for example, 'Pakistan Summons US Ambassador to Protest against the Latest Drone Killing', *The Guardian*, 8 June 2013, available at: www.theguardian.com/world/2013/jun/08/pakistan-us-drone-killings.

[186] Olivia Flasch, 'The Legality of the Air Strikes against ISIL in Syria: New Insights on the Extraterritorial Use of Force against Non-State Actors' (2016) 3 *Journal on the Use of Force and International Law* 37, at 42; Byrne, n. 182, at 106.

[187] See Chapters 3 and 4 for more on the use of force under the authority of the United Nations.

[188] See further, Section 3.5 on regional organisations.

[189] Article 4(h), Constitutive Act of the African Union (2000). This was provided for in the Constitutive Act due to the inability of the AU's predecessor, the Organization of African

need for prior authorization by the UNSC in terms of Article 53(1) of the UN Charter when invoking article 4(h)',[190] suggesting that it is not regarded as a legal requirement.[191] However, while opinions have differed in regard to the true meaning of, and possibilities for, intervention contained within Article 4(h), the fact is that in 'the still embryonic practice' of the AU it has not yet been invoked by the African Union to intervene either without the prior ad hoc consent of a member state or the authorisation of the UNSC. The AU was not, for example, willing to use military intervention in the situation in Darfur on the basis of Article 4(h) and in the absence of consent by the government of Sudan.

Furthermore, on the one occasion (at the time of writing) that it has attempted to intervene militarily on the basis of Article 4(h), that is, in the context of the widespread conflict in Burundi in 2015 following the announcement of President Pierre Nkurunziza that he would seek a third term in office,[192] the AU Peace and Security Council combined its invocation of Article 4(h) with an appeal to the UNSC to endorse the deployment.[193] This, along with the fact that the President and Foreign Minister of Burundi compared the deployment to an 'attack on' and 'invasion of' Burundi, respectively,[194] while various member states expressed reservations about the deployment,[195] indicated that such a deployment in the absence of specific, ad hoc consent by the government of Burundi would have constituted 'enforcement action' in terms of Article 53(1) of the UN Charter.

Outside of the context of the AU, Article 52 of the Protocol Relating to the Mechanism for Conflict Prevention, Management, Resolution, Peace-Keeping and

---

Unity, to respond to atrocities that took place in the 1990s, notably those in Rwanda and Sierra Leone. This should be contrasted with Article 4(j) of the same Act, in that while Article 4(h) appeared to provide for a form of treaty-based consent, Article 4(j) provides for 'the right of Member States to request intervention from the Union in order to restore peace and security' on an *ad hoc* basis. See Gabriel Amvane, 'Intervention Pursuant to Article 4(h) of the Constitutive Act of the African Union without United Nations Security Council Authorisation' (2015) 15 *African Human Rights Law Journal* 282.

[190] de Wet, n. 1, at 172.

[191] Anel Ferreira-Snyman, 'Intervention with Specific Reference to the Relationship between the United Nations Security Council and the African Union' (2010) 63 *Comparative and International Law Journal of Southern Africa* 160.

[192] 'Burundi President Pierre Nkurunziza Confirms Third-Term Bid', *BBC News*, 25 April 2015, available at: www.bbc.co.uk/news/world-africa-32464054.

[193] AU Peace and Security Council, Communiqué, 571st Meeting at the Level of Heads of State and Government, PSC/AHG/COMM.3(DLXXI), 29 January 2016, at para. 11, available at: http://afripol.peaceau.org/uploads/571-psc-com-burundi-29-1-2016.pdf.

[194] See Nina Wilén and Paul D. Williams, 'The African Union and Coercive Diplomacy: The Case of Burundi', (2018) 4 *The Journal of Modern African Studies* 677, at 687.

[195] See Solomon Dersso, 'To Intervene or Not to Intervene? An Inside View of the AU's Decision Making on Article 4(h) and Burundi', *World Peace Foundation*, 26 February 2016, 7, available at: https://sites.tufts.edu/wpf/files/2017/05/AU-Decision-Making-on-Burundi_Dersso.pdf.

Security of 1999 of ECOWAS provides for the deployment of ECOMOG troops in a member state without the specific, ad hoc consent of the recognized government, as well as an ambivalence as to whether UNSC authorisation is required, merely requiring that it will 'inform' the UN of any military intervention undertaken, rather than request prior authorization.[196] However, 'since the adoption of the 1999 Protocol, ECOWAS has consistently deployed ECOMOG forces only after having obtained the additional, ad hoc consent of the recognized government, or with prior UNSC authorization under Chapter VII or VIII of the UN Charter (or both)'.[197] Indeed, as discussed in Section 9.2.1, ECOWAS forces were only deployed within the Gambia on the basis of a request for assistance from the new president.

Furthermore, the Protocol on Politics, Defence and Security Operation of 2001 of the Southern African Development Community, which solidified the jurisdiction and competencies of the organisation in relation to security matters, gave the organisation jurisdiction in a wide range of circumstances.[198] However, Article 11(3)(d) provides that it 'shall resort to enforcement action only as a last resort, and in accordance with Article 53 of the United Nations Charter, only with the authorization of the United Nations Security Council', while Article 11(4)(a) determines that '[i]n respect of both inter–intra-state conflicts, the Organ shall seek to obtain the consent of the disputant parties to its peacemaking efforts'. The only military operation authorised by the SADC since this Protocol was adopted was deployed in Lesotho in 2017 following the breakdown of the rule of law after a commander of the defence force had been assassinated.[199] This mission, however, which was formed with the aim of creating a secure and stable environment necessary for implementing a series of political and judicial reforms,[200] was deployed with the ad hoc consent of the government.[201]

---

[196] See Article 52, Protocol Relating to the Mechanism for Conflict Prevention, Management, Resolution, Peace-Keeping and Security, 10 December 1999, available at: https://amaniafrica-et.org/wp-content/uploads/2021/04/Protocol-Relating-to-the-Mechanism-for-Conflict-Prevention-Management-Resolution-Peace-Keeping-and-Security-1999.pdf.

[197] de Wet, n. 1, at 176.

[198] See Article 11(2), Protocol on Politics, Defence and Security Operation, 14 August 2001, available at: www.sadc.int/sites/default/files/2021-08/Protocol_on_Politics_Defence_and_Security20001.pdf.

[199] SADC Secretariat, 'SADC Secretariat Briefs African Union Peace and Security Council on the Contingent Force Deployed in Lesotho', 25 January 2018, available at: www.sadc.int/latest-news/sadc-secretariat-briefs-african-union-peace-and-security-council-contingent-force.

[200] Peter Fabricius, 'Lesotho: Seven-Nation SADC Force Deployed to "Establish Secure, Stable Environment" in Mountain Kingdom', *Daily Maverick*, 3 December 2017, available at: www.dailymaverick.co.za/article/2017-12-03-lesotho-seven-nation-sadc-force-deployed-to-establish-secure-stable-environment-in-mountain-kingdom/.

[201] SADC Secretariat, n. 199.

## 9.5 THE LIMITS OF THE CONSENT OR INVITATION TO INTERVENE

There may be circumstances where, despite prior consent having been provided, a violation of international law nevertheless arises. First, if consent has been given by the territorial state but is then subsequently withdrawn, failure by the sending state to remove its armed forces will constitute a violation of international law.[202] Indeed, just as a state is free to provide consent or an invitation to intervene, it is similarly free to withdraw it and, as the ICJ stated in the *Armed Activities* case, a state may withdraw its consent at any time and with 'no particular formalities'.[203] In this case, Uganda had argued that any withdrawal of consent by the DRC to the presence of Ugandan troops within its territory would only be through a formal denunciation of the 1998 Protocol in regards to the control of the common border between the two states.[204] The ICJ noted that a statement made by DRC President Kabila on 28 July 1998 that the Rwandan military operation within the territory of the DRC had been terminated and that '[t]his mark[ed] the end of the presence of *all* foreign military forces in the Congo'[205] was ambiguous as to whether it also constituted a revocation of consent to the continued presence of Ugandan troops on its territory.[206] Yet, the Court nonetheless concluded that the withdrawal of consent in regards to both Rwanda *and* Uganda had occurred at the latest by 8 August 1998 when the DRC accused both states of 'invading its territory'.[207] Similarly, Iraq's protest against the operations of Turkey's armed troops in its territory in December 2015 can be seen as constituting a revocation of its consent in regard to Turkey's use of force within its territory.[208] In addition, the fact that the Trump administration failed to offer a legal rationale for the killing of General Soleimani in January 2020 taking place on Iraqi territory may have been due to the fact that US forces were at the time stationed in Iraq with its consent.[209] Yet, the clear protest against the strike by the Iraqi government and its subsequent demand that the United States withdraw from

---

[202] That is, unless the intervening state can base its continued presence within the territorial state upon another legal justification, most notably that its presence is necessary in self-defence or that it has been authorised by the UNSC.

[203] *Armed Activities* case, n. 20, at paras 47 and 51.    [204] Ibid., at para. 50.

[205] Ibid., at para. 49.    [206] Ibid., at para. 51.    [207] Ibid., at para. 53.

[208] Al Jazeera, 'Iraq Summons Turkey Ambassador over Troop "Incursion"', 5 December 2015, available at: www.aljazeera.com/news/2015/12/iraq-demands-withdrawal-turkish-troops-mosul-151205061510572.html.

[209] See UN Doc. S/2014/695, 23 September 2014.

Iraqi territory meant that any consent had been withdrawn.[210] Ultimately, there is nothing to suggest that consent cannot be withdrawn at any time and in any manner so long as the withdrawal is clear from the context.[211]

Furthermore, a violation of the non-intervention principle and the prohibition of the use of force may occur if the sending state uses force in a manner going beyond either the *scope* or any *period of time* attached to the consent by the state providing it.[212] However, the scope of the consent or any time limits provided to it may not always be easy to discern. The letter from Syria to the UN Security Council in October 2015, for example, in which it reported its request to Russia to 'cooperate in countering terrorism' was broad and general, only focusing on the air support provided by Russia rather than the ground offensives, and made no mention of the period for which such consent was provided.[213] Given the often lack of details,

the reaction of the consenting (territorial) state to the particular military conduct by the assisting state on its territory will be decisive for determining whether the assisting state has remained within its mandate. If the territorial state does not publicly object to the military conduct, it would be fair to assume that it was tacitly or implicitly consenting to it.[214]

Yet, consent can also be provided in more formal agreements, in particular so-called status of forces agreements, which are agreements regarding the stationing of the military forces of a state or organisation within the territory of a host state, and which primarily establish the rights and duties of the stationed troops and personnel. For example, in May 1997 an agreement was formed permitting Russian military forces to be located within various bases in Crimea.[215] On 28 February 2014 the forces strayed beyond these bases in

---

[210] Edward Wong and Megan Specia, 'U.S. Says It Won't Discuss Withdrawing Troops from Iraq, Defying Baghdad's Request', *The New York Times*, 10 January 2020, available at: www.nytimes.com/2020/01/10/world/middleeast/us-troops.html.

[211] de Wet, n. 1, at 165.

[212] Article 20 of the ARSIWA states that '[v]alid consent by a state to the commission of a given act by another state precludes the wrongfulness of that act in relation to the former state *to the extent that the act remains within the limits of that consent*' (emphasis added).

[213] See Identical Letters dated 14 October 2015 from the Permanent Representative of the Syrian Arab Republic to the United Nations Addressed to Secretary-General and the President of the Security Council, UN Doc. A/70/429-S/2015/789, 16 October 2015.

[214] de Wet, n. 1, at 162–3.

[215] See 1997 Russia–Ukraine Partition Treaty on the Status and Conditions of the Black Sea Fleet (which refers to three separate bilateral treaties between Russia and Ukraine). Under the treaty Ukraine agreed to lease Crimean naval bases for 20 years until 2017 and allowed Russia to maintain up to 25,000 troops, 24 artillery systems, 132 armoured vehicles and 22 military planes on the Crimean Peninsula. The Kharkiv Pact, which was signed on 21 April 2010, extended the lease until 2042.

defiance of the consent that had been provided by Ukraine.[216] One of the clear examples of aggression provided in the Definition of Aggression is '[t]he use of armed forces of one State which are within the territory of another State with the agreement of the receiving State, in contravention of the conditions provided for in the agreement or any extension of their presence in such territory beyond the termination of the agreement'.[217] While it might be argued that under this provision the Russian forces would have needed to have been 'used' to constitute an act of aggression, as opposed to simply straying beyond their bases or staying beyond the time agreed upon, in the case of Crimea the Russian forces stationed there ultimately assisted in the unlawful forcible secession and subsequent annexation by Russia of Crimea from Ukraine,[218] thereby answering any questions regarding the illegality of their actions.

Furthermore, the breadth of the consent with which the United States was operating under on Iraqi territory in January 2020 at the time it targeted and killed General Soleimani only stretched to combating the so-called Islamic State.[219] Simply because the armed forces of a state happen to be located upon the territory of another state with the consent of its government does not mean that the state is able to take any desired military action it deems necessary, including through a determination that the territorial state is in any way unable or unwilling to take action which the acting state deems necessary.[220] Otherwise, and as Labuda has articulated, '[t]he result is that [the unable or unwilling doctrine], applied in a context where the territorial State has already provided consent to the presence of the intervening State, effectively hollows out the *jus ad bellum* notion of consent. A deeply contested doctrine, such as [unable or unwilling], makes consent, a universally recognized exception to the Charter's prohibition of use of force, irrelevant.'[221] In addition, and as a

---

[216] *Keesing's* (2014) 53188, 53242. The stationing rules were contained in the Agreement between Ukraine and the Russian Federation on the Status and Conditions of the Stationing of the Black Sea Fleet on the Territory of Ukraine. On the basis of this Russian forces could operate 'beyond their deployment sites' only after 'coordination with the competent authorities of Ukraine'. See Spencer Kimball, 'Bound by Treaty: Russia, Ukraine and Crimea', *DW*, 11 March 2014, available at: www.dw.com/en/bound-by-treaty-russia-ukraine-and-crimea/a-17487632. See also Thomas D. Grant, 'Current Developments: Annexation of Crimea' (2015) **109** *American Journal of International Law* 68, at 78–80; Green, n. 40, at 6.

[217] Definition of Aggression, n. 78, Article 3(e).

[218] The UNGA '[c]all[ed] upon all States to desist and refrain from actions aimed at the partial or total disruption of the national unity and territorial integrity of Ukraine, including any attempts to modify Ukraine's borders through the threat or use of force or other unlawful means'. See UNGA Res 68/262, 27 March 2014, para. 2. The vote was 100 to 11 with 58 abstentions.

[219] See UN Doc. S/2014/695, 23 September 2014.   [220] See Section 8.4.2.

[221] Patryk I. Labuda, 'The Killing of Soleimani, the Use of Force against Iraq and Overlooked *Ius ad Bellum* Questions', *EJIL Talk!*, 13 January 2020, available at:

further consequence of this, if the state goes beyond the boundaries of consent, it is arguable, as noted in this section, that its military action would constitute an act of aggression.[222] While one may nonetheless argue that a valid claim of self-defence, including on the basis of the unable or unwilling doctrine, nullifies any accusation of aggression, given not only that the United States in Iraq in 2020 used force beyond the breadth and scope of the consent provided but then refused to withdraw its troops in light of the revocation of consent from Iraq,[223] it is difficult to escape the conclusion that this was 'a textbook case of aggression'.[224]

However, while these are limitations concerning the scope of the consent provided and the circumstances in which it may be vitiated, questions also arise as to whether there are any legal limitations upon the ability of a third state to intervene, or which affect the scope of any intervention, which are *external* to the specific agreement between the intervening and consenting parties. For example, it might be considered that the 'international law pedigree' of the consenting territorial state has an impact upon the validity of any consent provided, or that states are prohibited from sending their armed forces to consenting states implicated in widespread violations of international humanitarian and human rights law.[225] Yet, although the consenting state may be perpetrating violations of international law, and the intervening state may be legally responsible for 'aiding and assisting' those violations through the supply of military personnel, arms, intelligence, financial resources or training,[226] and may as such be under a legal obligation to alter or cease such assistance,[227] this does not appear to impact upon the validity of the consent itself. Indeed, state practice 'does not support the conclusions that the human rights record of the inviting government (or that of the invited state) would in and of itself form a legal barrier under international law to extending or accepting an invitation for forcible intervention'.[228]

This point is arguably demonstrated in Russia's military intervention in Syria that begin in 2015.[229] Despite the widespread repression of human rights and violations of international humanitarian law that the Assad regime in Syria was engaged in, as well as several notable incidences of suspected

---

www.ejiltalk.org/the-killing-of-soleimani-the-use-of-force-against-iraq-and-overlooked-ius-ad-bellum-questions/.

[222] Definition of Aggression, n. 78, Article 3(e). See also Labuda, ibid.
[223] Wong and Specia, n. 210.   [224] Labuda, n. 221.
[225] A phrase used by de Wet. See de Wet, n. 1, at 125.
[226] Article 16, Draft Articles on Responsibility of States for Internationally Wrongful Acts (2001).
[227] Article 30(a), ibid.
[228] de Wet, n. 1, at 135. Furthermore, '[t]his remains the case even where such violations amounted to serious violations of peremptory norms of international law'. Ibid., at 152.
[229] See Section 9.3.1.

violation of international humanitarian law by the Russian military,[230] the consent to the intervention by the Assad regime itself was not questioned. Furthermore, Saudi Arabia's claim to have been invited by exiled President Hadi for its intervention to combat the advance of the Houthi rebels in Yemen appeared to have received widespread acceptance by the international community.[231] Yet, there has also been widespread concern regarding violations of international humanitarian law perpetrated by the Saudi-led coalition since 2015.[232] Thousands of individuals have died as a result of the fighting and the campaign has been criticised for the level of civilian casualties and the widespread destruction of civilian infrastructure that have resulted, including the bombing of a funeral in Sana'a in October 2016 that resulted in the deaths of 140 civilians.[233] Despite these clear violations of international humanitarian law, the High Court in the United Kingdom refused to halt arms sales by the United Kingdom to Saudi Arabia on the basis that Yemen was committed to upholding international law and in that light there was no 'real risk' of 'serious violations' of it, with the UK government, rather than the courts, being best placed to determine if and when such a risk might exist.[234]

Finally, any direct military assistance upon request or with consent would be limited to the territory of the consenting state. This is unless a case for collective self-defence could be made, including that an 'armed attack' has occurred against the inviting state which has either been launched from outside of the territory of the consenting state or within the territory of the consenting state but under the control of the state upon whose territory the military action has been extended to.[235] For example, in 2014 Iraq invited the US-led coalition to use force upon its territory against the so-called Islamic State,[236] and could do so regardless of whether the attacks it was suffering were 'armed attacks'. By contrast, its invitation to assist with taking action

---

[230] See, for example, Amnesty International, '"Nowhere Is Safe for Us": Unlawful Attacks and Mass Displacement in North-West Syria', 11 May 2020, available at: www.amnesty.org/en/documents/mde24/2089/2020/en/.

[231] See Section 9.2.2.

[232] Final Report of the Panel of Experts on Yemen, UN Doc. S/2017/81, 31 January 2017, available at: www.securitycouncilreport.org/atf/cf/%7B65BFCF9B-6D27-4E9C-8CD3-CF6E4FF96FF9%7D/s_2017_81.pdf.

[233] 'Saudi-Led Coalition Admits to Bombing Yemen Funeral', *The Guardian*, 15 October 2016, available at: www.theguardian.com/world/2016/oct/15/saudi-led-coalition-admits-to-bombing-yemen-funeral.

[234] Alice Ross, 'UK Arms Exports to Saudi Arabia Can Continue, High Court Rules', *The Guardian*, 10 July 2017, available at: www.theguardian.com/world/2017/jul/10/uk-arms-exports-to-saudi-arabia-can-continue-high-court-rules.

[235] See Section 6.5 for more on collective self-defence. See, in general, Laura Visser, 'Intervention by Invitation and Collective Self-Defence: Two Sides of the Same Coin?' (2020) 7 *Journal on the Use of Force and International Law* 292.

[236] See, for example, UN Doc. S/2014/695, 23 September 2014.

against Islamic State bases in Syria could not be covered by the same invitation, as the strikes were to take place upon the territory of another state (Syria) and so a legal justification of collective self-defence was required.[237] In this respect, in addition to the request for assistance, an armed attack would need to have occurred, or be imminent,[238] and the action would need to satisfy the twin requirements of necessity and proportionality.[239]

## 9.6 CONCLUSION

While this is arguably true for most areas of the *jus ad bellum*, in the case of consent to intervention, perhaps more than any other area, the disputes 'mostly involve wildly divergent versions of the facts involved, rather than disagreements over legal standards'.[240] Indeed, disputes and disagreements are more about the validity of consent and the circumstances in which it is said to exist rather than about the principles regarding consent to intervention themselves.

Consent to intervention is generally given by those with governmental authority to do so, and does not, in this respect, engage the prohibition of the use of force. However, questions might be asked as to whether outside states are permitted to intervene *against* the government to cease or suppress human rights violations that are being perpetrated by it. In other words, and more generally, the question arises as to whether intervention is ever permitted in the protection, or furtherance, of human rights? Indeed, while forcible intervention for political and ideological purposes has never been permitted, and support of self-determination movements is no longer permitted in today's context, an enduring debate is whether forcible intervention is lawful when taken in the extreme circumstances of a humanitarian catastrophe within another state, which the governmental authorities are either unable to prevent or are actively perpetrating. Given that interventions have taken place ostensibly upon this basis in the post–Cold War period, and with the emergence of the Responsibility to Protect concept in 2001,[241] the possibility that such a situation provides an independent legal basis for forcible intervention will be discussed in the next, and final, chapter of the book.

---

[237] See for a discussion on this, Claus Kreß, 'The Fine Line between Collective Self-Defence and Intervention by Invitation: Reflections on the Use of Force against "IS" in Syria', *Just Security*, 17 February 2015, available at: www.justsecurity.org/20118/claus-kreb-force-isil-syria/. See Chapter 8 for more on the right of self-defence against non-state actors situated in another state.

[238] See Section 6.2 for more on the requirement for an armed attack and Section 7.5 for more on the concept of imminence.

[239] See Section 6.3 on these twin requirements of self-defence.   [240] Fox, n. 1, at 830.

[241] See Section 4.6 for more on the Responsibility to Protect concept.

## QUESTIONS

1 Upon what basis are we able to identify those possessing authority to consent to intervention?

2 Explain and critically assess, with reference to examples of state practice:
  - the 'negative equality' principle
  - the 'purpose-based' approach to intervention
  - the right of counter-intervention.

3 Is there a particular form that consent to intervention must take?

4 Are there any limits upon what actions consent to intervention may be provided for?

5 Was the intervention in Iraq by the US-led coalition in 2014 in response to attacks by the so-called Islamic State a consent to intervention or an invocation of the right of collective self-defence?

## SUGGESTED FURTHER READING

Olivier Corten, Gregory Fox and Dino Kritsiotis, *Armed Intervention and Consent* (Cambridge University Press, 2023)

Erika de Wet, *Military Assistance on Request and the Use of Force* (Oxford University Press, 2020)

Louise Doswald-Beck, 'The Legal Validity of Military Intervention by Invitation of the Government' (1986) 56 *British Yearbook of International Law* 189

Eliav Lieblich, *International Law and Civil Wars: Intervention and Consent* (Routledge, 2013)

Chiara Radaelli, *Intervention in Civil Wars: Effectiveness, Legitimacy and Human Rights* (Hart Publishing, 2021)

# 10 The Doctrine of Humanitarian Intervention

## 10.1 INTRODUCTION

The term 'humanitarian intervention' might be taken to mean simply one state criticising the human rights record of another with the aim of influencing the latter state's treatment of individuals within its territory.[1] Such a practice is common today and when it occurs does not normally attract stinging rebukes, and neither is it described as a violation of international law.[2] Of course, whether it is politically or economically wise for a state to engage in commenting on the affairs occurring within another state is a separate issue. The term 'humanitarian intervention' is instead employed in the common parlance of international lawyers as referring to the use of *armed force* in the absence of the authorisation of the United Nations (UN) Security Council for humanitarian purposes – that is, the use of armed force to intervene in another state to prevent or end a humanitarian crisis.[3]

---

[1] See Section 2.2 for more on the prohibition of intervention.
[2] See, in general, Myers S. McDougal and W. Michael Reisman, 'Rhodesia and the United Nations: The Lawfulness of International Concern' (1968) 62 *American Journal of International Law* 1.
[3] For an example of the literature on humanitarian intervention in the sense employed in this chapter, see Jean-Pierre L. Fonteyne, 'The Customary International Law Doctrine of Humanitarian Intervention: Its Current Validity under the U.N. Charter' (1974) 4 *California Western International Law Journal* 203; Sean Murphy, *Humanitarian Intervention: The United Nations in an Evolving World Order* (University of Pennsylvania Press, 1996); Christopher Greenwood, 'Humanitarian Intervention: The Case of Kosovo' (1999) 10 *Finnish Yearbook of International Law* 141; Christine Gray, 'The Legality of NATO's Military Action in Kosovo: Is There a Right of Humanitarian Intervention', in Wang Tieva and Sinenho Yee (eds.), *International Law in the Post-Cold War World* (Routledge, 2000), 240; Peter Hilpold, 'Humanitarian Intervention: Is There a Need for a Legal Reappraisal?' (2001) 12 *European Journal of International Law* 437; Nico Krisch, 'Review Essay: Legality, Morality and the Dilemma of Humanitarian Intervention after Kosovo' (2002) 13 *European Journal of International Law* 323; Anne Orford, *Reading Humanitarian Intervention: Human Rights and the Use of Force in International Law* (Cambridge University Press, 2003); Christine Gray, 'The Use of Force for Humanitarian Purposes', in Nigel D. White and Christian Henderson (eds.), *Research Handbook on International Conflict and Security Law:* Jus ad Bellum, Jus in Bello *and*

Although there are examples of what might be described as humanitarian interventions in the pre-UN Charter era,[4] in 1945 the UN Charter prohibited all uses of force except those taken under the auspices of the UN Security Council or in self-defence.[5] In assessing the current status of the doctrine, the focus of this chapter will be on post-1945 practice. In this respect, in Section 10.2, the focus is placed upon assessing if the doctrine can be reconciled with the UN Charter, while Section 10.3 looks at Cold War and post-Cold War practice in assessing the position of the doctrine during the UN era. Given that the forcible entry by the North Atlantic Treaty Organization (NATO) in the Kosovo crisis in 1999 proved something of a landmark in terms of events that have shaped the path of the modern doctrine of humanitarian intervention, the status of the doctrine in the immediate aftermath of this intervention will be given particular attention, as well as whether more recent events in Ukraine have had any impact, while Section 10.4 looks at the Syrian civil war and the relevance of the doctrine of humanitarian intervention to that particularly tragic conflict, which continues at the time of writing. Finally, a conception of humanitarian intervention that has come to dominate contemporary debates on the issue is that of the 'Responsibility to Protect' (R2P). Given its rise to prominence, Section 10.5 will assess its impact upon the doctrine of humanitarian intervention.

## 10.2 THE UN CHARTER AND HUMANITARIAN INTERVENTION

As highlighted in Chapter 1, the contemporary prohibition of the threat or use of force is contained both within Article 2(4) of the UN Charter and customary international law and has been held by some to constitute a *jus cogens* norm.[6]

---

Jus post Bellum (Edward Elgar, 2013), 229; Nigel Rodley, 'Humanitarian Intervention', in Marc Weller (ed.), *The Oxford Handbook of the Use of Force in International Law* (Oxford University Press, 2015), 775; 'Symposium on Unauthorized Interventions for the Public Good' (2017) 111 *AJIL Unbound* 284; Kevin Jon Heller, 'The Illegality of "Genuine" Humanitarian Intervention' (2021) 32 *European Journal of International Law* 613; Federica I. Paddeu, 'Humanitarian Intervention and the Law of State Responsibility' (2021) 32 *European Journal of International Law* 649; Natasha Kuhrt, 'Russia, the Responsibility to Protect and Intervention', in Daniel Fiott and Joachim Koops (eds.), *The Responsibility to Protect and the Third Pillar: Legitimacy and Operationalization* (Springer, 2015), 97. For a particularly good set of essays on humanitarian intervention, see J. L. Holzgrefe and Robert O. Keohane, *Humanitarian Intervention: Ethical, Legal and Political Dilemmas* (Cambridge University Press, 2003).

[4] For example, some of the interventions which took place in the nineteenth century in the former Turkish Empire might be considered as such. See, in general, Davide Rodongo, *Against Massacre: Humanitarian Interventions in the Ottoman Empire* (Princeton University Press, 2011).

[5] See Chapters 3–5 and 6–8, respectively.

[6] See Section 1.3 on the sources of the prohibition of the threat or use of force. See also 'The Sources of the Law on the Use of Force and the Question of Methodology' in the Introduction.

While the treaty source of the prohibition does not, strictly speaking, take priority over its customary form, this section will solely address the Charter prohibition. Not only does it possess a tangible textual nature but virtually the entire international community of states is a party to it. Additionally, although the two sources of the obligation are not necessarily identical,[7] there is nothing to indicate they are, or have been at any point since 1945, different to any significant degree. Furthermore, the emergence of a right of humanitarian intervention would mean that states would *prima facie* be acting in direct contravention of their UN Charter obligation to refrain from the threat or use of force. Therefore, in the absence of states taking the unlikely step of expressly rescinding their obligations under the UN Charter, Article 2(4) would have either been reinterpreted to permit such a practice or it would lay in desuetude.[8] Given that no change in the law can emerge without primary consideration being given to Article 2(4), it will be given particular attention here.

This assumes, of course, that the use of force for humanitarian purposes cannot be reconciled with the provisions of the UN Charter. There are two well-established express exceptions to the prohibition found within the UN Charter: the use of force under the auspices of the Security Council and self-defence under Article 51. There is no express exception to Article 2(4) of humanitarian intervention contained within the Charter, which might seem surprising given that the UN Charter was drafted at the time of the horrors of the Holocaust. This does not mean, however, that the UN Charter puts responding to humanitarian crises beyond the reach of the international community. On the contrary, as Chapter 3 demonstrated, the Security Council is able to take appropriate action, including through the use of force, in response to such crises.[9] Although the UN General Assembly has a certain competence in this field, in that it may discuss situations and the actions of other UN organs, it has not developed the competence to authorise states and organisations to take forcible action.[10] The fact that the Security Council can today determine that a humanitarian crisis constitutes a threat to the peace and thus employ enforcement measures against either the government of the

---

[7] See *Case Concerning Military and Paramilitary Activities in and against Nicaragua* (*Nicaragua v. United States of America*), Merits (1986) ICJ Reports 14, at para. 176.
[8] For an argument that the latter has occurred, see Michael J. Glennon, 'How International Rules Die' (2005) 83 *Georgetown Law Journal* 939.
[9] See Section 3.4.2.2. While Article 2(7) of the UN Charter prohibits the intervention of the UN into the internal or domestic affairs of a member state this does not apply in the context of Chapter VII enforcement measures.
[10] See Sections 3.4.1 and 3.4.2.4. See also Christian Henderson, 'The Centrality of the UN Security Council in the Legal Regime Governing the Use of Force', in Nigel D. White and Christian Henderson (eds.), *Research Handbook on International Conflict and Security Law: Jus ad Bellum, Jus in Bello and Jus post Bellum* (Edward Elgar, 2013), 120, at 132–3.

state concerned or groups of individuals within the state, or both, rarely draws criticism and concern in and of itself from states. This is not to say that disagreements do not arise in the context of such authorisations,[11] rather it is to say that the central area of concern in regard to legality *ab initio* is the use of force undertaken by one or more states, perhaps acting under the umbrella of a regional organisation, in the absence of authorisation of the Security Council.

One may also question, however, whether the exception of self-defence provides for a right of intervention by states for the protection of individuals located within another state. If the individuals concerned are entirely, or predominantly, nationals of the intervening state, the state would more likely be intervening under the justification of protecting its nationals abroad, a notion which many argue comes under the right of self-defence.[12] It has, however, been argued that non-nationals located in another state who are suffering at the hands of the government might also be protected by states through the invocation of Article 51 of the UN Charter.[13] George Fletcher and Jens David Ohlin argue that the equally authoritative French version of Article 51 uses the term 'légitime défense' in place of self-defence, which in domestic contexts incorporates the defence of others.[14] This is used to argue that Article 51 provides a right to intervene in other states to protect individuals located there. However, while an interesting argument, it is, in this author's view, ultimately unpersuasive as it overlooks the inter-state context in which these rules were devised. While it might be said that the invocation of the right of self-defence in this context is more akin to the intervening state acting in collective self-defence of the individuals concerned, collective self-defence remains very much within the inter-state context in which a request for assistance by a victim state is required.[15] Similarly, for the right of self-defence to be invoked there must be an 'armed attack' or the imminent threat of one. In this respect, '[w]hilst the meaning of "armed attack" is disputed in international jurisprudence, the notion that such an attack can be carried out by a state on its own people thus triggering an external right to defence of others is one that falls outside of even the widest definitions'.[16]

---

[11] See, in general, Chapter 4.

[12] Richard B. Lillich, 'Forcible Self-Help by States to Protect Human Rights' (1967) 53 *Iowa Law Review* 325, at 332, who claims that if the human rights violations are connected with citizens of the intervening states this more appropriately comes under the conceptual heading of self-defence. For more on the protection of nationals abroad, see Section 6.4.

[13] See George P. Fletcher and Jens D. Ohlin, *Defending Humanity: When Force Is Justified and Why* (Oxford University Press, 2008).

[14] Ibid., at 76.   [15] See Section 6.5.

[16] Christian Henderson, 'Review of G. P. Fletcher and J. D. Ohlin, *Defending Humanity: When Force is Justified and Why*' (2009) 14 *Journal of Conflict & Security Law* 529, at 533. For more on the notion of 'armed attack', see Section 6.2.

Nonetheless, whilst authorisation by the Security Council and self-defence are firmly established as the key exceptions to the prohibition of the use of force it is also notable that Article 2(4) itself does not expressly allude to any exceptions, which at least raises the possibility that humanitarian intervention is, or could be, an 'implied' exception to it. The provision simply prohibits threats or uses of force that are 'against the territorial integrity or political independence of any state, or in any other manner inconsistent with the Purposes of the United Nations'. This has led to claims that force that does not result in the seizure of either the whole or a part of another state's territory, and does not result in a change of government, is not prohibited.[17] Although it did not arise in connection with a use of force for humanitarian purposes, in the *Corfu Channel* case of 1949 the United Kingdom advanced the argument that its military action to retrieve evidence from Albania's territorial waters was lawful in that it did not threaten the territorial integrity or political independence of Albania.[18] However, the International Court of Justice (ICJ) did not accept this argument and was of the opinion that the UK's arguments were based upon a policy of force

such as has, in the past, given rise to most serious abuses and such as cannot, whatever be the present defects in international organization, find a place in international law ... from the nature of things, it would be reserved for the most powerful States, and might easily lead to perverting the administration of international justice itself.[19]

In the *Legality of Use of Force* case of 1999, which involved Serbia and Montenegro bringing a claim against various NATO states for the Kosovo bombing campaign, Belgium made a similar argument in the ICJ to that relied upon by the United Kingdom in the *Corfu Channel* case, albeit this time in the context of humanitarian intervention.[20] It argued that NATO's intervention in Kosovo was lawful on the basis that it 'never questioned the political independence and the territorial integrity of the Federal Republic of Yugoslavia' and was, as such, an 'armed humanitarian intervention, compatible with Article 2, paragraph 4, of the Charter, which covers only intervention against the territorial integrity or political independence of a State'.[21] However, Belgium was relatively isolated in making this argument and it was not one that the Court had the opportunity to express its opinion on as it did not ultimately hear the case for jurisdictional reasons, most notably Serbia and Montenegro's lack of *locus standi* before the Court. Furthermore, while the

---

[17] See, for example, Anthony D'Amato, 'Israel's Air Strike upon the Iraqi Nuclear Reactor' (1983) 77 *American Journal of International Law* 584, at 585. See also Section 1.3.1.2.
[18] *Corfu Channel Case (United Kingdom v. Albania)*, Merits (1949) ICJ Reports 4.
[19] Ibid., at 35. See, further, Section 2.5.2.
[20] *Legality of Use of Force (Serbia and Montenegro v. Belgium)*, Oral Proceedings, Public Sitting, International Court of Justice, 10 May 1999, 12.
[21] Ibid.

## 10.2 The UN Charter and Humanitarian Intervention

prohibition prohibits force which is 'inconsistent with the purposes of the United Nations', some have taken the position that, given that the protection of human rights has a place within the UN Charter, in particular within Articles 55 and 56, the use of force with the aim of protecting human rights is not prohibited.[22] Along similar lines some argued during the Cold War that, due to the fact that the UN collective security system as contained in Chapter VII of the Charter was not operating Article 2(4), it should be interpreted to permit forcible measures that furthered the purposes of the UN, with the protection of human rights being one of them.[23]

By contrast, others have taken the position that the prohibition as contained in Article 2(4) only permits the narrowly construed exceptions of self-defence and collective security as contained in the Charter. It is argued that the wording of Article 2(4) does not permit the use of force solely for humanitarian purposes,[24] and the reference to 'territorial integrity and political independence' is included to specifically highlight these for protection rather than provide them as the exclusive focus of the prohibition, something which is confirmed as being the case in the *travaux préparatoires*.[25] While human rights are promoted within the Charter, this stands in contrast with the obligatory language of Article 2(4). Indeed '[t]he avoidance and repression of international armed conflict was the dominant gene in the UN's genetic code'.[26] Such a restrictive interpretation of Article 2(4) also finds support in the Declaration on Friendly Relations, which in many respects elaborates upon this relatively brief provision.[27] In connection with the prohibition of force it states that '[n]o State or group of States has the right to intervene, directly or indirectly, *for any reason whatever*, in the internal or external affairs of any other State', thus apparently offering confirmation that it does not provide for a right of unilateral humanitarian intervention.[28] The reference here to 'direct'

---

[22] See, for example, Fernando R. Teson, *Humanitarian Intervention: An Inquiry into Law and Morality*, 2nd ed. (Transnational Publishers, 1997), at 151.

[23] See, generally, W. Michael Reisman, 'Coercion and Self-Determination' (1984) 78 *American Journal of International Law* 642. See also Section 1.7.

[24] Ian Brownlie, *International Law and the Use of Force by States* (Oxford University Press, 1963), at 267; Oliver Corten, *The Law against War: The Prohibition of the Use of Force in Contemporary International Law*, 2nd ed. (Hart, 2021), at 493–503.

[25] See Albrecht Randelzhofer, 'Article 2(4)', in Bruno Simma (ed.), *The Charter of the United Nations: A Commentary*, 2nd ed. (Oxford University Press, 2002), 112, at paras. 37–9.

[26] Rodley, n. 3, at 778.

[27] Declaration on Principles of International Law Concerning Friendly Relations and Cooperation among States in Accordance with the Charter of the United Nations, UNGA Res. 2625 (XXV), 24 October 1970.

[28] Ibid. (emphasis added). In similar terms, the Definition of Aggression provides that '[n]o consideration of whatever nature, whether political, economic, military or otherwise, may serve as a justification for aggression'. Definition of Aggression, UNGA Res. 3314 (XXIX) (1974), 14 December 1974.

and 'indirect' intervention also raises the question as to the types of intervention that states might take in carrying out humanitarian interventions. Forcible intervention, as the ICJ highlighted in the *Nicaragua* case, need not be of a direct nature to constitute a violation of the prohibition of the use of force.[29] Indeed, a state may still be held responsible for a use of force by providing weapons to individuals or groups in another state who are fighting against the oppressive actions of their government, as the ICJ set out in the *Nicaragua* case.[30] That is, *indirect* armed force is equally covered by the prohibition.[31]

Finally, the International Law Commission's Draft Articles on State Responsibility of 2001 include certain circumstances which preclude the wrongfulness of a state's actions that are not in conformity with an international obligation.[32] In particular, Article 24 provides that 'distress' may constitute such a circumstance if there is 'no other reasonable way ... of saving the [life of the author of the act in question] or the lives of other persons', while Article 25 provides that 'necessity' may, if the action taken '[i]s the only way for the State to safeguard an essential interest against a grave and imminent peril', preclude wrongfulness.[33] Some focus has been placed on these, and, in particular on necessity, as possibly precluding the wrongfulness of a humanitarian intervention. A central problem with invoking necessity in this context, however, is that it cannot be invoked if the action would 'seriously impair an essential interest of the State or States towards which the obligation exists, or of the international community as a whole'.[34] It is difficult to see how the territorial integrity or sovereignty of the state concerned – which would, if only temporarily, be compromised during a humanitarian intervention operation – are not 'essential interests' in the context under focus. Furthermore, Article 26 is clear that these circumstances cannot preclude 'the wrongfulness of any act of a State which is not in conformity

---

[29] *Nicaragua* case, n. 7, at para. 205.  [30] Ibid., at para. 228.  [31] See Section 2.4.3.

[32] International Law Commission, Draft Articles on the Responsibility of States for Internationally Wrongful Acts (2001) (DARSIWA). See, in general, Katja Creutz, *State Responsibility in the International Legal Order: A Critical Appraisal* (Cambridge University Press, 2020).

[33] On the use of necessity as a justification, exception, excuse or circumstance precluding wrongfulness, see Nicholas Tsagourias, 'Necessity and the Use of Force: A Special Regime' (2010) **41** *Netherlands Yearbook of International Law* 11; Robert D. Sloane, 'On the Use and Abuse of Necessity in the Law of State Responsibility' (2012) **106** *American Journal of International Law* 447; Olivier Corten, 'Necessity', in Marc Weller (ed.) *The Oxford Handbook of the Use of Force in International Law* (Oxford University Press, 2015), 861; Jens David Ohlin and Larry May, *Necessity in International Law* (Oxford University Press, 2016).

[34] Article 25(1)(b), DARSIWA, n. 32.

## 10.2 The UN Charter and Humanitarian Intervention

with an obligation arising under a peremptory norm of general international law'. While the debate is somewhat open as to whether it is force or only force of a particularly aggressive nature which is prohibited as a peremptory or *jus cogens* norm,[35] the pronouncements of the ICJ in the *Nicaragua* case would seem to suggest it may be the former, thus precluding any action taken under the banner of necessity which involves the use of force.[36] Consequently, and as Corten notes, '[a]s a *jus cogens* rule, the prohibition of the use of force cannot be circumvented ... by references to exceptional circumstances other than those envisaged in the primary rule'.[37]

However, the Draft Articles also state that 'necessity may not be invoked by a State as a ground for precluding wrongfulness if ... the international obligation in question excludes the possibility of invoking necessity'.[38] While Article 2(4) of the UN Charter does not expressly exclude the invocation of necessity in precluding any wrongfulness under it, 'considerations akin to those underlying article 25', as discussed in the above paragraph, should be 'taken into account in the context of the formulation and interpretation of the primary obligations', in this case the prohibition of force and the UN Charter in general.[39] As such, Corten is arguably correct in observing that '[a]n interpretation of the Charter itself, as it was devised and then construed by several General Assembly resolutions, shows that the prohibition of the use of force represents a legal regime from where there is no way out'.[40]

However, although the debate has been somewhat heated amongst scholars as to the permissibility of unilateral humanitarian intervention under the UN Charter, the formation and modification of international law is ultimately a consensual enterprise amongst states. Consequently, this chapter will turn to examine state practice on the concept of unilateral humanitarian intervention to see if it has had an impact upon the interpretation of the Charter provided in this section.

---

[35] See Section 1.3.2.
[36] The Court pronounced that: '[a] further confirmation of the validity as customary international law of the principle of the prohibition of the use of force expressed in Article 2, paragraph 4, of the Charter of the United Nations may be found in the fact that it is frequently referred to in statements by State representatives as being not only a principle of customary international law but also a fundamental or cardinal principle of such law. The International Law Commission, in the course of its work on the codification of the law of treaties, expressed the view that "the law of the Charter concerning the prohibition of the use of force in itself constitutes a conspicuous example of a rule in international law having the character of *jus cogens*".' See *Nicaragua* case, n. 7, at para. 190.
[37] Corten, n. 24, at 246.   [38] Article 25(2)(a), DARSIWA, n. 32.
[39] International Law Commission, Draft Articles on the Responsibility of States for Internationally Wrongful Acts, with commentaries (2001), at 84.
[40] Corten, n. 24, at 246.

## 10.3 HUMANITARIAN INTERVENTION IN THE PRACTICE OF STATES

Following on from the analysis in Section 10.2 of the prohibition of the use of force as found within Article 2(4) of the UN Charter, this section examines the practice of states. This practice will provide the basis for determining if – and if so, how – the prohibition has been modified so as to permit the use of forcible measures for humanitarian purposes not under the authorisation of the Security Council. The practice can be seen as not only possibly providing 'subsequent agreement' or 'subsequent practice' for the purposes of interpreting Article 2 (4),[41] but also the state practice and *opinio juris* necessary for a modification of the customary form of the prohibition of the threat or use of force.[42] While, as discussed in Section 1.3.2, there is at least some disagreement as to the status of the prohibition as a *jus cogens* norm, it is nonetheless undeniably a fundamental norm within the international system, arguably meaning that if a modification is to occur this will need to be supported by a clear and widespread acceptance within the international community as a whole.[43]

Given that there have been differences of both a qualitative and quantitative nature in the practice of states between the Cold War and the post–Cold War periods, this section will separate discussion between these two periods.

### 10.3.1 Cold War

During the Cold War (1945–89) three main incidences occurred where states used force ostensibly for humanitarian purposes: India's intervention in East Pakistan in 1971, Vietnam's intervention in Cambodia (Kampuchea) in 1978–9 and Tanzania's intervention in Uganda in 1979.[44] Peter Hilpold has stated that '[o]f all the interventions after 1945 that could be qualified with the epithet

---

[41] Both possibilities are contained within the Vienna Convention on the Law of Treaties (1969) (VCLT). See Section 31(3)(a) and (b), respectively. See also 'The Sources of the Law on the Use of Force and the Question of Methodology' in the Introduction.

[42] In particular, Article 38(1)(b) of the Statute of the International Court of Justice (1945) describes international customary law as 'a general practice accepted as law'.

[43] See 'The Sources of the Law on the Use of Force and the Question of Methodology' and 'Legal and Procedural Issues Associated with the *Jus ad Bellum*' in the Introduction.

[44] A comprehensive analysis of these three incidences can be found in Nicholas J. Wheeler, *Saving Strangers: Humanitarian Intervention in International Society* (Oxford University Press, 2000), at 55–136. See also Thomas M. Franck and Nigel S. Rodley, 'After Bangladesh: The Law of Humanitarian Intervention by Military Force' (1973) **67** *American Journal of International Law* 275; Farooq Hassan, 'Realpolitik in International Law: After Tanzanian–Ugandan Conflict "Humanitarian Intervention" Reexamined' (1981) **17** *Willamette Law Review* 859; Michael J. Bazyler, 'Reexamining the Doctrine of Humanitarian Intervention in Light of the Atrocities in Kampuchea and Ethopia' (1987) **23** *Stanford Journal of International Law* 547.

"humanitarian" those of the 1970s stand out'.[45] In each of the cases, while it is undeniable that an oppressed people received humanitarian assistance through the particular intervention, it is also of significance that in each case a legal right of humanitarian intervention was not advanced in justification, with each of the intervening states preferring to rely on self-defence.[46] It is, therefore, not possible to attribute any specific belief in the existence of a right of humanitarian intervention to the intervening states, or any desire to create one. Despite the humanitarian outcomes of these interventions, the states' justifications instead provide 'evidence of the fact that none of these countries attributed much standing to the concept of humanitarian intervention in modern international law'.[47] Furthermore, states generally showed sympathy for the human suffering involved in each of the incidences[48] and the Tanzanian intervention was accompanied by a general lack of international condemnation,[49] leading some to claim a general acquiescence in the interventions and therefore the possible development of a legal right of humanitarian intervention.[50] However, this overlooks not only the lack of justification upon the basis of humanitarian intervention but also the fact that the reaction to the interventions was, on the whole, negative.[51]

---

[45] Peter Hilpold, 'Intervening in the Name of Humanity: R2P and the Power of Ideas' (2012) 17 *Journal of Conflict & Security Law* 49, at 62.

[46] India appeared to legally base its actions on responding to 'refugee aggression' as well as military aggression from Pakistan. See UN Doc. S/PV. 1606, 4 December 1971, at 15–17; Vietnam declared that it was 'determined to repel aggression and to punish the aggressors, to put down the forces that unleashed this war of aggression against it ... That is the sacred right of self-defence of peoples in the face of aggression'. See UN Doc. S/PV. 2108, 11 January 1979, at 13; Tanzania advanced several justifications for its incursion into Uganda, although the one most resembling one of a legal nature was that it was acting to protect its territorial integrity and to prevent further aggression from Uganda. See Africa Contemporary Record 178–89: B396.

[47] Hilpold, n. 45, at 62.    [48] See Wheeler, n. 44.

[49] Indeed, both the UN General Assembly and the UN Security Council refused to debate the situation, while the Organisation of African Unity was unwilling to condemn Tanzania. The most vocal criticism came from Kenya and Libya, indicating that the 'intervention was supported by the vast majority of states'. Kenneth Chan, 'The Ugandan-Tanzanian War – 1978-79', in Tom Ruys, Olivier Corten and Alexandra Hofer (eds.), *The Use of Force in International Law: A Case-Based Approach* (Oxford University Press, 2018), 255, at 263.

[50] See, in general, Thomas M. Franck, 'Interpretation and Change in the Law of Humanitarian Intervention', in J. L. Holzgrefe and Robert O. Keohane (eds.), *Humanitarian Intervention: Ethical, Legal and Political Dilemmas* (Cambridge University Press, 2003), 204.

[51] With regards to India's intervention in East Pakistan, see UN Doc. S/PV. 1606, 4 December 1971, UN Doc. S/PV. 1607, 5 December 1971, and UN Doc. S/PV. 1608, 6 December 1971. On Vietnam's intervention in Cambodia, see UNGA Res. 34/22 (1979), which called for an 'immediate withdrawal of all foreign forces from [Cambodia]' (although the resolution passed eighty-five votes in favour, thirty-two against and with twenty-three abstentions.). The ASEAN also 'deplored the armed intervention against the independence, sovereignty and territorial integrity of [Cambodia]' as well as having 'called for the immediate and total withdrawal of the foreign forces from [Cambodian] territory'. See Joint Statement of the

These episodes of state practice were ultimately a good reflection of the fact that a right of unilateral humanitarian intervention could not be said to exist at this time. Indeed, in the light of this practice a notable statement by the UK Foreign Office in 1986 arguably summarises the position of the international community towards the end of the Cold War:

> the overwhelming majority of contemporary legal opinion comes down against the existence of a right of humanitarian intervention, for three main reasons: first, the UN Charter and the corpus of modern international law do not seem specifically to incorporate such a right; secondly, state practice in the past two centuries, and especially since 1945, at best provides only a handful of genuine cases of humanitarian intervention, and, on most assessments, none at all; and finally, on prudential grounds, that the scope for abusing such a right argues strongly against its creation ... In essence, therefore, the case against making humanitarian intervention an exception to the principle of non-intervention is that its doubtful benefits would be heavily outweighed by its costs in terms of respect for international law ... the best case that can be made in support of humanitarian intervention is that it cannot be said to be unambiguously illegal.[52]

The United Kingdom's concern for 'respect for international law' was shared by certain scholars at the time. Oscar Schachter, for example, noted that '[t]he reluctance of governments to legitimise foreign invasion in the interest of humanitarianism is understandable in the light of past abuses by powerful states'.[53] Yet Rosalyn Higgins responded to this by claiming that those that argue against the lawfulness of humanitarian intervention 'make much of the fact that in the past the right has been abused. It undoubtedly has. But then so have there been countless abusive claims of the right of self-defence. This does not lead us to say that there should be no right of self-defence'.[54] However, those wishing to resort to force for humanitarian purposes today first have to demonstrate that a right exists, before then claiming that the facts provide for an appropriate invocation of it. It is arguable that if a right existed, the removal of this first step would increase the possibilities for abuse.

In the *Nicaragua* case within the ICJ, while the United States did not expressly put forward the doctrine of humanitarian intervention to justify its

---

Special Meeting of the ASEAN Foreign Ministers held on 12–13 January 1979 in Bangkok (1979), UN Doc. S/13025, Annex. While, as noted above (see n. 49), Tanzania's intervention in Uganda was accompanied by a general lack of condemnation, a few states offered condemnation.

[52] UK Foreign Office Policy Document No. 148. See 'UK Materials on International Law' (1986) 57 *British Yearbook of International Law* 614, at 619. See Section 10.3.2 on how the United Kingdom's position changed in the post-Cold War period.

[53] Oscar Schachter, 'The Right of States to Use Armed Force' (1984) 82 *Michigan Law Review* 1620, at 1629.

[54] Rosalyn Higgins, 'International Law and the Avoidance, Containment and Resolution of Disputes' (1991) 230 *Recueil des Cours de l'Académie de Droit International* 9, at 313–16.

support for the armed opposition *contra* forces in their attempt to overthrow the government of Nicaragua, the Court nonetheless considered whether the actions of the United States could be legally justified in the context of the protection of human rights and concluded that:[55]

> the use of force could not be the appropriate method to monitor or ensure such respect. With regard to the steps actually taken, the protection of human rights, a strictly humanitarian objective, cannot be compatible with the mining of ports, the destruction of oil installations, or again with the training, arming and equipping of the *contras*.[56]

Thus, while drawing a distinction between humanitarian intervention and the strict provision of humanitarian aid,[57] the Court seemed to affirm a restrictive interpretation of Article 2(4) in the light of the US actions. Ultimately, by the time the Cold War drew to an end in 1989 it is difficult to claim that a right of humanitarian intervention existed in international law. Those that claim that state practice supports such a right fail to explain how, in particular, such a claim can be reconciled with the clear lack of support for one from both the acting and reacting states. However, things were to take an interesting turn in the post–Cold War era.

### 10.3.2 Post–Cold War: From Iraq to Kosovo

At the end of the Cold War era, and with the easing of East–West tensions, changes were discernible within the international community. These manifested themselves most notably in the authorisation provided by the Security Council for the US-led coalition to evict Iraq from Kuwait in 1990–1.[58] However, these changes also had consequences for the way in which humanitarian intervention was viewed, in the sense of both intervention with and without authorisation by the Council. In this respect, there are a number of specific incidents and events that are necessary to address in some detail.

#### 10.3.2.1 *Iraq (1991–2002)*

In the aftermath of the successful eviction of Iraq from Kuwait by the US-led coalition acting under the authority of UN Security Council Resolution 678 (1990) in February 1991,[59] Saddam Hussein remained in power and violently suppressed the Shiites in the south of Iraq and the Kurds in the north who had risen up against him.[60] The Security Council consequently adopted Resolution

---

[55] See *Nicaragua* case, n. 7, at para. 202.   [56] Ibid., at para. 268.
[57] The Court drew a distinction between forcible humanitarian intervention and humanitarian assistance, with the latter not being 'regarded as unlawful intervention, or as in any other way contrary to international law' if delivered without discrimination to alleviate suffering. Ibid., at para. 242.
[58] See Section 3.4.2.1.   [59] Ibid.   [60] *Keesing's* (1991) 38981.

688 (1991) on 5 April 1991 which '[c]*ondemn*[ed] the repression of the Iraqi civilian population ..., the consequences of which threaten international peace and security in the region'.[61] In this light it '[d]*emand*[ed] that Iraq ... immediately end this repression'[62] and '[i]*nsist*[ed] that Iraq allow immediate access by international humanitarian organizations'.[63] In contrast to Resolution 678 (1990), however, no state or organisation was authorised to use 'all necessary means' to put an end to the repression or protect those sections of the population who were the targets of it.

However, the United Kingdom, United States, France and Russia went on to establish safe havens and then no-fly zones over the north, ostensibly to protect the Kurds, and then subsequently did the same in 1992 in the south to protect the Shiites and enforced these through patrolling Iraqi airspace.[64] Those states acting did not provide a justification, or at least not one of a legal nature, for these actions. However, in addition to claiming that there existed support by the UNSC for the action in Resolution 688 (1991),[65] in 1992, in what was one of the more express justifications for the actions, the United Kingdom claimed that it 'believe[d] that international intervention without the invitation of the country concerned can be justified in cases of extreme humanitarian need'.[66] This was quite a turnaround from its previously expressed position in 1986 in which it denied the existence of a right of humanitarian intervention and argued against the creation of one.[67]

While it has to be acknowledged that these actions and associated justifications did not prove at first to attract a significant amount of controversy, although there was similarly no discernible *opinio juris* for a right of humanitarian intervention, the acting states began to lose the support of the international community when the United States, in particular, began to expand its rules of engagement and, consequently, permissible targets for the use of force.[68] This led to France and Russia retracting their active support for the

---

[61] UNSC Res. 678 (1990), para. 1. It is notable that while it made such a determination, which for all intents and purposes is what is required to open up the range of enforcement powers at its disposal under Chapter VII, it did not expressly state it was adopting the resolution under that Chapter of the Charter.
[62] Ibid., para. 2.   [63] Ibid., para. 3.
[64] *Keesing's* (1991) 38127; 'US Press Release: Coalition to Impose "No-Fly" Zone in Southern Iraq' (26 August 1992), quoted in Marc Weller (ed.), *Iraq and Kuwait: The Hostilities and Their Aftermath* (Grotius, 1993), at 724–5.
[65] See Section 4.5.1.1 on implied authorisation.
[66] 'UK Materials on International Law' (1992) 63 *British Yearbook of International Law* 824. See Chapter 9 on intervention by invitation.
[67] See Section 10.3.1 of this chapter.
[68] This was first through the United States' attack on Iraqi military targets in the south after Iraqi forces had entered the northern no-fly zones (see *Keesing's* (1996) 41246 and 41296–7) and then extending the southern no-fly zone (ibid., 41297).

operations,[69] as well as condemnation from other states, many of whom were allies of the United States.[70] The enforcement of the no-fly zones over Iraq continued for over a decade.[71] In the months preceding Operation Iraqi Freedom in March 2003, the operations of the United States and United Kingdom in enforcing the no-fly zones appeared to have the aim of destroying Iraqi air defences in preparation for the large-scale invasion of Iraq that was to follow, as opposed to defending the Iraqi population.[72]

### 10.3.2.2 ECOWAS Intervention in Liberia (1990)

On 24 August 1990 the Economic Community of West African States (ECOWAS) entered Liberia in the absence of the authorisation of the Security Council and conducted an operation which had the appearance of being for humanitarian purposes.[73] Prior to this, in December 1989, rebels led by Charles Taylor from across the border in Côte d'Ivoire had entered Liberia, causing a civil war, and committed massive atrocities which resulted in thousands of deaths and widespread displacement.[74] While the president of Liberia at the time, Samuel Doe, had requested ECOWAS to send a peacekeeping force to help re-establish control, ECOWAS instead sent in the neutral Ceasefire Monitoring Group (ECOMOG) to enforce peace and, ultimately, a truce between the parties.[75] Given that such an operation had not been requested by President Doe, nor was it subsequently approved by the president or the leader of the main rebel group, Charles Taylor, it is difficult to see this intervention as one based upon consent.[76] Furthermore, ECOWAS itself justified the action upon humanitarian grounds, through its claims of 'going to Liberia first and foremost to stop the senseless killing of innocent civilian nationals and foreigners, and to help the Liberian people to restore their

---

[69] See UN Doc. S/1996/712, 3 September 1996; Ben MacIntyre, 'France Refuses to Patrol Widened No-Fly Zone: Split Allies', *The Times*, 6 September 1996, at 15.

[70] Craig R. Whitney, 'From Allies, U.S. Hear Mild Applause or Silence', *New York Times*, 4 September 1996, at A1; Dania Darwish, 'Arabs Refuse to Back US Strike', *The Independent*, 4 September 1996, at 22. For condemnation by the Arab League of the extension of the no-fly zone, see UN Doc. S/1996/796, 26 September 1996.

[71] See, in general, Michael Byers, 'The Shifting Foundations of International Law: A Decade of Forceful Measures Against Iraq' (2002) 13 *European Journal of International Law* 21.

[72] Christine Gray, *International Law and the Use of Force*, 4th ed. (Oxford University Press, 2018), at 44.

[73] See, in general, Anthony Chukwuka Ofodile, 'The Legality of ECOWAS Intervention in Liberia' (1994) 32 *Columbia Journal of Transnational Law* 381.

[74] *Keesing's* (1990) 37644; Thomas Franck, *Recourse to Force: State Action against Threats and Armed Attack* (Cambridge University Press, 2002), at 155.

[75] Franck, ibid., at 156.

[76] See Chapter 9 for more on interventions with the consent of the territorial state.

democratic institutions'.[77] What is interesting about this intervention, given that it was undertaken without Security Council authorisation,[78] is that, later, in January 1991 the Security Council itself issued a Presidential Statement in which it 'commend[ed] the efforts made by the ECOWAS Heads of State and Government to promote peace and normalcy in Liberia'[79] and 'to bring the Liberian conflict to a speedy conclusion'.[80] Whatever the reasons for this support, it is difficult to avoid the conclusion that the Security Council appeared 'willing not only to tolerate but to support a considerable degree of intervention in internal conflicts when necessary to restore order and save lives'.[81]

### 10.3.2.3 ECOWAS Intervention in Sierra Leone (1997-8)

While the civil war in Sierra Leone had begun in 1991, on 25 May 1997 a military coup ousted newly chosen President Ahmad Tejan Kabbah.[82] The Organization of African Unity requested that ECOWAS engage in mediation efforts in the country.[83] ECOWAS, however, ultimately went beyond this and in August 1997 sent a military contingent of ECOMOG troops to occupy the capital city, Freetown, and later enforce ECOWAS sanctions against Sierra Leone.[84] The UN Security Council did not authorise this enforcement action at the time it commenced, as might have been expected from a reading of Chapter VIII of the UN Charter,[85] but instead in a Presidential Statement expressed its 'support for the objectives of these efforts ...'.[86] Later ECOWAS went even further and ousted the military junta, invited President Kabbah to return and seized control of Freetown.[87] The Security Council again appeared to welcome the unauthorised actions, or at least the result created by them, and even

---

[77] UN Doc. S/21485, 10 August 1990.    [78] See Section 4.5.2.
[79] UN Doc. S/22133, 22 January 1991.    [80] UN Doc. S/23886, 7 May 1992.
[81] David Wippman, 'Enforcing the Peace: ECOWAS and the Liberian Civil War', in Lori F. Damrosch (ed.), *Enforcing Restraints: Collective Intervention in Internal Conflicts* (Council on Foreign Relations Press, 1993), 157.
[82] See, in general, Karsten Nowrot and Emily W. Schabacker, 'The Use of Force to Restore Democracy: International Legal Implications of the ECOWAS Intervention in Sierra Leone' (1998) 14 *American University International Law Review* 321.
[83] Franck, n. 74, at 159.
[84] In UN Doc. S/PRST/1997/42 of 6 August 1997 the Council 'took note' of the decision by ECOWAS to impose sanctions while it was only in UNSC Res. 1132 (1997) of 8 October 1997 that the Council 'authorize[d] ECOWAS ... to ensure [their] strict implementation'.
[85] Article 53(1) of the UN Charter clearly states: 'no enforcement action shall be taken under regional arrangements or by regional agencies without the authorization of the Security Council'. See Section 3.5 for more on the authorisation of regional organisations.
[86] UN Doc. S/PRST/1997/36, 11 July 1997.
[87] See UN Doc. S/1998/249, 18 March 1998, at 2.

joined them by deploying UN personnel to coordinate closely with ECOMOG.[88] This incident differed from the Liberian intervention in that there appeared to be a clearer request for direct assistance witnessed from President Kabbah. Nonetheless, while it is a bit of a stretch to claim that these two incidents 'effectively reinterpret[ed] the text of Article 53'[89] they do nonetheless show a certain propensity of the Security Council to retrospectively welcome forcible interventions which have resulted in a positive humanitarian outcome,[90] something which was arguably seen again in the form of NATO's use of force in regard to the situation in Kosovo in 1999.

### 10.3.2.4 Kosovo (1999)

By the late 1990s tensions had existed between the semi-autonomous province of Kosovo and Serbian authorities for many years.[91] However, in 1998–9 the federal government of Yugoslavia under President Slobodan Milošević increased its repression of the Kosovo Albanians, with the final trigger being the killing of four Serb police officers by the Kosovo Liberation Army (KLA) in the disputed province in February 1998.[92] Many civilians died or were made to flee their homes by the federal government, which also used violent measures against the KLA which had taken up arms against it.

In response to the events in Kosovo, the Security Council adopted three resolutions in 1998: 1160, 1199 and 1203.[93] These, in particular, expressed concern regarding the intense fighting, the flow of refugees, the humanitarian situation, the impending humanitarian catastrophe and the increasing violations of human rights and international humanitarian law.[94] They also made a determination that the deterioration of the situation in Kosovo constituted a threat to peace and security in the region,[95] demanded an end to hostilities[96] and set out measures for Yugoslavia to take,[97] whereby a failure would lead to the consideration of further action and additional measures.[98] Although the last two of the resolutions were adopted under Chapter VII of the UN Charter, none authorised the use of 'all necessary means' to halt the humanitarian catastrophe that was undoubtedly unfolding in the province of Kosovo. It was interesting that, despite this lack of authorisation, the United Kingdom, United States and NATO nonetheless issued threats to use force against the federal

---

[88] See, respectively, UNSC Res. 1156 (1998), para. 1 and UNSC Res. 1162 (1998), para. 5.
[89] Franck, n. 74, at 162.   [90] See Section 4.5.2 on retrospective authorisation.
[91] For some of the background to this conflict, see Ruth Wedgwood, 'NATO's Campaign in Yugoslavia' (1999) 93 *American Journal of International Law* 828, at 828–9.
[92] *Keesing's* (1998) 42156–7.
[93] UNSC Res. 1160 (1998); UNSC Res. 1199 (1998); UNSC Res. 1203 (1998).
[94] See UNSC Res. 1199 (1998), preamble; UNSC Res. 1203 (1998), preamble.
[95] See UNSC Res. 1199 (1998), preamble; UNSC Res. 1203 (1998), preamble.
[96] UNSC Res. 1199 (1998), para. 1.   [97] Ibid., para. 4.   [98] Ibid., para. 16.

authorities throughout 1998 and early 1999.[99] Furthermore, on 13 October 1998 the North Atlantic Council, NATO's decision-making body, issued activation orders for a phased air campaign in the Federal Republic of Yugoslavia (FRY) and limited air operations.[100]

Following the Serbian authorities' refusal to accept the Rambouillet Agreement[101] and after the 'final warning bell'[102] in the market town of Raçak, when forty-five civilians were killed and 5,500 fled,[103] NATO launched Operation Allied Force on 24 March 1999. This was a seventy-eight-day aerial bombing campaign against military targets within the FRY which had the ostensible aim of halting the humanitarian catastrophe that was unfolding.[104] It was also clear that, given the aerial nature of the intervention by NATO, the Yugoslavian authorities were able to, at least initially, increase their repressive actions on the ground, resulting in what can only be described as a massive increase in the displacement of Kosovo Albanians.[105] No ground troops were ever deployed. Once Milošević had accepted a proposed peace plan by the European Union (EU) on 4 June 1999,[106] which involved the withdrawal of troops from Kosovo, NATO Secretary-General Javier Solana announced a suspension of the operation on 10 June.[107]

What was significant, however, was that, despite not having express authorisation from the Security Council for its actions,[108] NATO itself did not expressly rely on a doctrine of humanitarian intervention to justify its use

---

[99] See Dino Kritsiotis, 'The Kosovo Crisis and NATO's Application of Armed Force against the Federal Republic of Yugoslavia' (2000) 49 *International & Comparative Law Quarterly* 330, at 330-1. See Section 1.4 for more on threats to use force.

[100] See the statement made to the press by the NATO Secretary-General, available at: www.nato.int/docu/speech/1998/s981013a.htm. See also www.nato.int/docu/speech/1999/s990130a.htm.

[101] See (1999) United Nations Yearbook 340. However, Gray remarks that '[t]his refusal by Yugoslavia was understandable given the terms of the proposed agreement; Yugoslavia would have been required to concede almost unlimited autonomy to Kosovo and to allow free movement for NATO troops throughout the whole of Yugoslavia'. Gray, 'The Use of Force for Humanitarian Purposes', n. 3, at 233.

[102] Richard A. Falk, 'Kosovo, World Order, and the Future of International Law' (1999) 93 *American Journal of International Law* 847, at 849.

[103] Raymond Whitaker, 'Belgrade's Link to Massacre', *The Independent*, 29 January 1999, at 13.

[104] It used 1,000 aircraft in 38,000 combat missions. See UK House of Commons Defence Committee, 'Fourteenth Report – Lessons of Kosovo', Session 1999-2000, at Section III: The Conduct of the Campaign, available at: www.publications.parliament.uk/pa/cm199900/cmselect/cmdfence/347/34702.htm.

[105] The International Criminal Tribunal for the Former Yugoslavia (ICTY) found that the deliberate actions of the Yugoslav forces caused the departure of at least 700,000 Kosovo Albanians from Kosovo during the conflict. See *Prosecutor* v. *Milutinovic et al.*, Case No. IT-05-87-T, ICTY, Trial Chamber Judgment, 2009.

[106] *Keesing's* (1999) 43007. For the acceptance letter, see UN Doc. S/1999/646, 4 June 1999.

[107] UN Doc. S/1999/663, 10 June 1999; *Keesing's* (1999) 43013.    [108] See Section 4.5.1.2.

of force. In fact, it offered no clear legal explanation or justification as an organisation and neither did any of its member states. Instead, it justified its resort to force on this occasion as intended simply to halt the violence and bring an end to the humanitarian catastrophe.[109] The same could be said of the acting states themselves, with none offering an express legal justification but instead arguing that action had to be taken to avert a humanitarian catastrophe.[110] At the Security Council meeting held on the day Operation Allied Force commenced, while only two of the acting or supporting states expressly claimed that the action was legal,[111] most deemed it 'necessary'[112] either to avert a 'humanitarian catastrophe'[113] or because of the FRY's refusal to act in compliance with Security Council resolutions.[114] As with the acting states, those supporting the action did not offer any unequivocal support for the doctrine of humanitarian intervention as the legal basis for the use of force in such circumstances.

By contrast, many states opposing the intervention did so upon legal grounds, asserting that a violation of the UN Charter had occurred. Indeed, some opposed the action and condemned it as 'aggression',[115] 'completely illegal'[116] and 'unlawful'.[117] Russia stated that it was 'profoundly outraged' at Operation Allied Force which was 'carried out in violation of the Charter of the United Nations and without the authorization of the Security Council',[118] while China, which was 'strongly opposed' to the action, also clearly stated

---

[109] NATO Press Release 99/12, 30 January 1999, available at: www.nato.int/docu/pr/1999/p99-012e.htm.

[110] For example, the United States justified the action as averting a humanitarian catastrophe. See UN Doc. S/PV. 3988, 24 March 1999, at 4.

[111] Ibid. The Netherlands noted that 'the legal basis ... we have available in this case is more than adequate'. Ibid., Netherlands (8); the UK also stated that '[t]he action being taken is legal. It is justified as an exceptional measure to prevent an overwhelming humanitarian catastrophe'. Ibid., United Kingdom (12).

[112] For example, the United Kingdom claimed that 'on the grounds of overwhelming humanitarian necessity, military intervention is legally justifiable'. Ibid., United Kingdom (12). See also United States (4), Slovenia (6), Gambia (7), Netherlands (8), France (9), Malaysia (10), Argentina (11) and Slovenia (19).

[113] The United States claimed that '[w]e have begun today's action to avert this humanitarian catastrophe and to deter further aggression and repression in Kosovo'. Ibid., United States (3). See also Canada (6), Bahrain (7), Netherlands (8), Malaysia (9), Argentina (11), Slovenia (6), United Kingdom (12), EU (16) and Albania (18).

[114] A leading proponent of this basis was France, which stated that '[t]he actions that have been decided upon are a response to the violation by Belgrade of its international obligations, which stem in particular from the Security Council resolutions adopted under Chapter VII of the United Nations Charter'. Ibid., France (9). See also Canada (5), Slovenia (6) and United Kingdom (11). Furthermore, Slovenia claimed that 'the action which is being undertaken will be carried out strictly within the substantive parameters established by the relevant Security Council resolutions'. Ibid., Slovenia (7).

[115] Ibid., Serbia (13) and Belarus (15). [116] Ibid., India (16) and Russia (3).

[117] Ibid., Belarus (15). [118] Ibid., Russia (2).

it viewed the action as 'a blatant violation of the United Nations Charter and of the accepted norms of international law'.[119] Nonetheless, a Russian draft Security Council resolution which condemned the intervention as a 'flagrant violation' of the UN Charter, in particular Articles 2(4) and Article 24, was heavily defeated.[120] While this might be interpreted as support for the existence or emergence of a doctrine of humanitarian intervention under international law, it was significant that those voting against did not frame their objections in legal terms. Similarly, after the intervention had ended the Security Council adopted Resolution 1244 (1999). Despite it not using any language which could be interpreted as endorsing the intervention, some commentators nonetheless interpreted this as retrospective endorsement of Operation Allied Force.[121] However, what is significant is that none of the acting or supporting states within the Security Council at the time of its adoption made such an argument.

Although up until this stage the legal issues did not appear to have been fully addressed, the incident came before the ICJ in the *Legality of Use of Force* cases in which Yugoslavia brought actions against ten NATO member states.[122] The argument of Yugoslavia essentially consisted of two elements. First, it argued that there was no right of humanitarian intervention in international law. Secondly, it argued that, even if there were such a right, NATO's aerial assault would not qualify. Nonetheless, both the United Kingdom and Belgium responded to Yugoslavia's legal arguments by claiming that there was such a right.[123] In particular, they claimed that the action was not a violation of Article 2(4) of the UN Charter as NATO's intervention had not violated Yugoslavia's territorial integrity or political independence, but rather had the intention of saving lives, as well as making reference as precedents to the interventions in Bangladesh, Uganda and Cambodia.[124] Ultimately, however, as noted in Section 10.2, Yugoslavia's request for provisional measures was refused on the ground of a lack of *prima facie* jurisdiction on the merits of the case.

### 10.3.2.5 Humanitarian Intervention in the Aftermath of Operation Allied Force

After the controversies of NATO's intervention in Kosovo, the doctrine of humanitarian intervention was at something of a crossroads. Although an

---

[119] Ibid., China (12).
[120] See UN Doc. S/1999/328, 26 March 1999. There were three states that voted for the resolution (China, Namibia, Russia) and twelve that voted against (Argentina, Bahrain, Brazil, Canada, France, Gabon, Gambia, Malaysia, Netherlands, Slovenia, United Kingdom, United States).
[121] See, for example, Franck, n. 50, at 204.
[122] *Legality of Use of Force*, Provisional Measures, Order of 2 June 1999 (1999) ICJ Reports 124.
[123] *Legality of Use of Force (Serbia and Montenegro v. Belgium)*, Preliminary Objections, Judgment (1999) ICJ Reports 279.
[124] See Section 10.3.1 for more on these incidents.

intervention had occurred which many of the acting and supporting states deemed to be necessary, attempts to locate a legal basis for such an intervention were futile. As set out in Section 10.2, no exception for a use of force for humanitarian purposes undertaken in the absence of authorisation by the Security Council exists under the contemporary prohibition of the use of force and neither could one be said to have arisen from the limited incidents that had occurred up to that point. No doubt for this reason, the majority of the acting states themselves, as noted in Section 10.3.2.4, were not prepared to justify and defend the intervention upon legal grounds.

States have not adopted the view that the prohibition of the use of force no longer exists. This has, instead, been a view restricted to certain scholars,[125] and in the aftermath of the Kosovo intervention a minority of scholars were willing to proclaim the legality of the intervention on this basis.[126] However, following the intervention most international law scholars perceived the intervention as a violation of international law,[127] and there was also a distinct lack of support within the international community for its legality, or that of a right of humanitarian intervention more generally.[128] For example, on 24 September 1999, just a few months after Operation Allied Force had come to an end, a Ministerial Declaration was produced by the meeting of Foreign Ministers of the Group of 77 in New York.[129] Paragraph 54 of this Declaration stated that the Ministers 'stress[ed] the need to maintain clear distinctions between humanitarian assistance and other activities of the United Nations. We reject the so-called "right" of humanitarian intervention, which has no basis in the United Nations Charter or in the general principles of international law.'[130] This statement was particularly significant in that the Group of 77 represents the opinion of 134 developing states, including 23 Asian states, 51 African states, 22 Latin American states and 13 Arab states. Such a large and representative rejection of the doctrine presents a high hurdle to claim that either agreement regarding the interpretation of Article 2(4) or a general *opinio juris* had formed as a result of the muscular humanitarianism that had occurred in Kosovo.

---

[125] See, further, Section 1.7. See, in general, Thomas M. Franck, 'Who Killed Article 2(4) or: Changing Norms Governing the Use of Force by States' (1970) **64** *American Journal of International Law* 809.

[126] Perhaps the leading proponent of this view is Michael Glennon. See Michael J. Glennon, *Limits of Law, Prerogatives of Power: Interventionism after Kosovo* (Palgrave, 2001).

[127] See, for example, Ian Brownlie and Christine J. Appleby, 'Kosovo Crisis Inquiry: Memorandum on International Law Aspects' (2000) **49** *International & Comparative Law Quarterly* 904.

[128] Although, see discussion in Section 3.5.1 on the African Union's Constitutive Act of 2000, which could be perceived as providing such a right.

[129] Group of 77 South Summit, 'Declaration of the South Summit' (Havana, Cuba, 10–14 April 2000).

[130] Ibid., at para. 54.

### 10.3.2.5.1 Humanitarian Intervention and the 'Thin Red Line' from Legality

Many scholars were prepared, however, to look beyond the view of the Kosovo intervention as a violation *simpliciter* of Article 2(4). A dominant approach that was discernible, arguably reflecting the positions of the acting states themselves, was that, while unlawful *stricto sensu*, the intervention in Kosovo should not be seen in such a narrow manner. For example, shortly following the intervention, Bruno Simma published an article in which it was argued that, while the intervention was unlawful, it was only separated from legality by 'a thin red line'.[131] This was due to, *inter alia*, the overall circumstances surrounding the intervention, including the various Security Council resolutions on the situation in Kosovo, and the *erga omnes* nature of the obligation of states to respect human rights.[132] The argument made seemed to share notable similarities with the views of many of the intervening states that it was a *sui generis* intervention justified by the specific circumstances, but that it was not to set a precedent for future similar forcible interventions for humanitarian purposes.[133] Thomas Franck, in addition, made an analogy with mitigating circumstances in domestic criminal law in claiming that no change in the law was required, but that in exceptional circumstances a violation which resulted in the saving of lives in this way might give rise to mitigating circumstances.[134]

Reflecting this view the Independent International Commission on Kosovo concluded that, while the Kosovo intervention was 'unlawful' based upon the law at the time, it was nonetheless 'legitimate'.[135] Similarly, although the UK Foreign Affairs Committee concluded in its report on the Kosovo intervention that the NATO operation was contrary to the specific terms of the UN Charter and that the doctrine of humanitarian intervention had a tenuous basis in

---

[131] Bruno Simma, 'NATO, the UN and the Use of Force: Legal Aspects' (1999) 10 *European Journal of International Law* 1.

[132] The ICJ described an obligation *erga omnes* as one which 'all states can be held to have an interest [in] protecting'. See *Barcelona Traction, Light and Power Company, Limited (Belgium v. Spain)*, Judgment (1970) ICJ Reports 3, at para. 33.

[133] For example, US Secretary of State, Madeleine Albright, asserted during a press conference that the situation in Kosovo was 'a unique situation *sui generis* in the region of the Balkans' and that it was important 'not to overdraw the various lessons that come out of it'. US Secretary of State Madeleine Albright, Press Conference with Russian Foreign Minister Igor Ivanov, Singapore, 26 July 1999, available at: https://1997-2001.state.gov/statements/1999/990726b.html. See Michael Byers and Simon Chesterman, 'Changing the Rules about Rules? Unilateral Humanitarian Intervention', in J. L. Holzgrefe and Robert O. Keohane (eds.), *Humanitarian Intervention: Ethical, Legal and Political Dilemmas* (Cambridge University Press, 2003), 177, at 199; Stefan Talmon, 'Changing Views on the Use of Force: The German Position' (2005) 5 *Baltic Yearbook of International Law* 41.

[134] See, for example, Franck, n. 74, at 174–91.

[135] Independent International Commission on Kosovo, Kosovo Report: Conflict, International Response, Lessons Learned (2000), at 164.

current international customary law, thus rendering the NATO action at best legally questionable,[136] it was also of the view that the military action was justified on moral grounds.[137]

Looking at the possible future consequences of the NATO intervention in Kosovo, Antonio Cassese took the position that neither sufficient state practice nor *opinio juris* existed to bring about a radical modification to the prohibition of the use of force.[138] Yet, he identified what was termed '*opinio necessitatis*' for the intervention on this occasion, in that, while there was a lack of belief in the legality of the operation, there was a general feeling that it was necessary nonetheless, which if witnessed again in the future might have implications for the legality of the doctrine of humanitarian intervention.

However, if such a position of relative legality arose in the law where notions of *legitimacy* impacted upon how the *legality* of a particular action was viewed, or what the repercussions were for the actors involved, it might, as Anthea Roberts has highlighted, have the consequence of undermining the coherence of international law.[139] In addition, if such an approach was to be adopted, the question arises as to how long such interventions can remain *sui generis*. If enough Kosovo-like interventions were to take place, how long would it be before a right of intervention might begin to form? Or if the law was to remain the same, would its credibility not be drawn into question given the number of violations that would be seen to be occurring?

### 10.3.2.5.2 Justified by a Failure of the UN Security Council?

Under the system as it stands, which arguably prioritises peace over justice, interventions for humanitarian purposes may be undertaken by the Security Council. Yet, the crux of the problem lies in the fact that it has proven inconsistent in taking such action. Whether this is a 'failure' on the part of the Security Council, or whether it is simply acting as was originally intended, is debatable. Nonetheless, Michael Reisman has argued that:

[w]hen human rights enforcement by military means is required, it should, indeed, be the responsibility of the Security Council acting under the Charter. But when the Council cannot act, the legal requirement continues to be to save lives, however one can and as quickly as one can, for each passing day, each passing hour, means more

---

[136] UK House of Commons Foreign Affairs Committee, 'Fourth Report – Kosovo', Session 1999–2000, available at: www.publications.parliament.uk/pa/cm199900/cmselect/cmfaff/28/2802.htm.
[137] Ibid., at para. 138.
[138] Antonio Cassese, 'A Follow-Up: Forcible Humanitarian Countermeasures and *Opinio Necessitatis*' (1999) 10 *European Journal of International Law* 791.
[139] Anthea Roberts, 'Legality vs Legitimacy: Can Uses of Force be Illegal but Justified?', in Philip Alston and Euan Macdonald (eds.), *Human Rights, Intervention and the Use of Force* (Oxford University Press, 2009), 179.

murders, rapes, mutilations and dismemberments – violations of human beings that no prosecution will expunge nor remedy or repair.[140]

In attempting to get over the hurdle of Security Council inaction, but keeping the solution within the UN, some scholars have raised the prospect of utilising the Uniting for Peace resolution of the UN General Assembly, an organ of the UN which, given its representative composition, arguably possesses greater legitimacy than the Security Council.[141] However, a potential problem with this procedure in these circumstances is that the General Assembly may only recommend the use of forcible measures in the context of a 'breach of a peace' or an 'act of aggression'.[142] The Security Council has consistently characterised situations in which it has intervened for humanitarian purposes as lesser 'threats to the peace',[143] which may pose problems for those claiming that the General Assembly has the jurisdiction to recommend forcible measures in similar situations.

### 10.3.2.5.3 Genocide: A Legal Requirement to Save Lives?

Reisman's reference to 'the legal requirement ... to save lives' set out in the preceding section deserves further attention. While the prominence of human rights, and the importance of their protection, has undoubtedly increased since the drafting of the Charter, there is, as discussed in Section 10.2, insufficient evidence at present to support the claim that there is a legal obligation to 'save lives', let alone one that has displaced the legal obligation to refrain from non-defensive use of force.

A possible exception might be seen to exist in the context of acts of genocide. In particular, in Article I of the Convention on the Prevention and Punishment of the Crime of Genocide (1948) state parties agree to 'undertake to prevent and to punish' acts of genocide. Following the invasion of Ukraine by Russia that commenced on 24 February 2022,[144] the question promptly

---

[140] W. Michael Reisman, 'Kosovo's Antinomies' (1999) 93 *American Journal of International Law* 860, at 862.
[141] See Nigel D. White, 'The Legality of Bombing in the Name of Humanity' (2000) 5 *Journal of Conflict & Security Law* 27.
[142] See Sections 3.4.1 and 3.4.2.4.
[143] For example, in Resolution 794 (1992) the Security Council '[d]etermin[ed] that the magnitude of the human tragedy caused by the conflict in Somalia, further exacerbated by the obstacles being created to the distribution of humanitarian assistance, constitutes a threat to international peace and security'. UNSC Res. 794 (1992), preamble.
[144] 'Russian forces launch full-scale invasion of Ukraine', *Al Jazeera*, 24 February 2022, available at: www.aljazeera.com/news/2022/2/24/putin-orders-military-operations-in-eastern-ukraine-as-un-meets. This invasion was euphemistically framed by President Putin as a 'special military operation'.

came before the International Court of Justice as to whether such acts of 'prevention and punishment' under the Convention may entail the use of military force.[145]

In a speech shortly before the invasion commenced on 24 February 2022, President Putin had asserted that – amongst other pretextual justifications – '[t]he purpose of [the] operation [was] to protect people who, for eight years now, have been facing humiliation and genocide perpetrated by the Kiev [Kyiv] regime', mainly people in the Ukrainian territories of Donetsk and Luhansk.[146] Ukraine subsequently made a request to the Court on 27 February 2022 for provisional measures ordering Russia to cease its military action.[147] In particular, it asserted, and the Court accepted, that two rights existed under the Convention; 'not to be subject to a false claim of genocide, and not to be subjected to another State's military operations on its territory based on a brazen abuse of Article I of the Genocide Convention'.[148]

In its order granting provisional measures the Court stated that it could 'only take a decision on [Ukraine's] claims if the case proceeds to the merits' although at the time of the request for provisional measures it was 'not in possession of evidence substantiating the allegation of the Russian Federation that genocide ha[d] been committed on Ukrainian territory'.[149] Importantly, however, and in light of the fact that the use of force is not expressly mentioned in the Genocide Convention, something that both Russia and Ukraine acknowledged, it also pronounced that 'it is doubtful that the

---

[145] International Court of Justice, *Allegations of Genocide under the Convention on the Prevention and Punishment of the Crime of Genocide (Ukraine v. Russian Federation)*, Request for the Indication of Provisional Measures, Order, 16 March 2022, available at www.icj-cij.org/public/files/case-related/182/182-20220316-ORD-01-00-EN.pdf.

[146] Office of the President of the Russian Federation, 'Address by the President of the Russian Federation', 24 February 2022, available at: http://en.kremlin.ru/events/president/transcripts/67843 (official English translation, as published by the Kremlin); Обращение Президента Российской Федерации, *Президент России*, 24 февраля 2022 года,, available at: http://kremlin.ru/events/president/news/67843 (original Russian text, as published by the Kremlin). As Milanovic noted, Russia appeared to be invoking 'something like a humanitarian intervention argument'. Marko Milanovic, 'What Is Russia's Legal Justification for Using Force against Ukraine?', *EJIL Talk!*, 24 February 2022, available at: www.ejiltalk.org/what-is-russias-legal-justification-for-using-force-against-ukraine.

[147] International Court of Justice, *Dispute Relating to Allegations of Genocide (Ukraine v. Russian Federation)*, Application Instituting Proceedings, 26 February 2022, available at: www.icj-cij.org/public/files/case-related/182/182-20220227-APP-01-00-EN.pdf.

[148] International Court of Justice, *Dispute Relating to Allegations of Genocide (Ukraine v. Russian Federation)*, Request for the Indication of Provisional Measures Submitted by Ukraine, 27 February 2022, at para. 12, available at: www.icj-cij.org/public/files/case-related/182/182-20220227-WRI-01-00-EN.pdf. In this respect, Ukraine argued that there was a duty to implement treaty obligations in good faith.

[149] *Allegations of Genocide under the Convention on the Prevention and Punishment of the Crime of Genocide*, n. 145, at para. 59.

Convention, in light of its object and purpose, authorizes a Contracting Party's unilateral use of force in the territory of another State for the purpose of preventing or punishing an alleged genocide'.[150]

Russia had argued that, given that the Genocide Convention does not provide for one party to use force on the territory of another party to prevent and punish genocide, Ukraine could not consequently invoke the Convention as a legal basis for its right to be free from Russia's use of force.[151] In any case, it argued, the Genocide Convention was inapplicable and the Court without jurisdiction, because Russia's formal basis for using force was self-defence under Article 51 of the Charter.[152] Nonetheless, and in light of Putin's assertions regarding the purpose of the military action being in response to the perpetration of genocide, on 16 March 2022 the Court concluded that '[u]nder these circumstances, [it] considers that Ukraine has a plausible right not to be subjected to military operations by the Russian Federation for the purpose of preventing and punishing an alleged genocide in the territory of Ukraine'[153] and ordered Russia to cease its military operations in order to preserve Ukraine's asserted rights pending resolution of the legal dispute on the merits.[154]

---

[150] Ibid. As Keitner and Tatarsky note, '[t]he qualifier "doubtful" could be read as an attempt not to prejudge the United Kingdom's doctrine of humanitarian intervention, although there is not currently a UK judge on the Court. In any event, at the provisional measures stage, the Court is not being called upon to interpret the Convention definitively, so there is no reason for it to phrase its observations conclusively.' See Chimène Keitner and Zoe Tatarsky, 'Q&A: The ICJ's Order on Provisional Measures in Ukraine v. Russian Federation', *Just Security*, 16 March 2022, available at: www.justsecurity.org/80703/qa-icj-order-on-provisional-measures-ukraine-russia/. The Court here reiterated its prior view that in meeting the Genocide Convention duty of prevention 'every State may only act within the limits permitted by international law', that is, that the use of force is not permitted beyond the confines of the UN Charter. This was stated in a previous case brought under the Convention. See *Application of the Convention on the Prevention and Punishment of the Crime of Genocide (Bosnia and Herzegovina v. Serbia and Montenegro)*, Judgment (2007) ICJ Reports 43, at para. 430.

[151] Russia did not appear before the Court but issued a submission to the Court. See International Court of Justice, *Dispute Relating to Allegations of Genocide (Ukraine v. Russian Federation)*, Document (with annexes) from the Russian Federation setting out its position regarding the alleged 'lack of jurisdiction' of the Court in the case, 7 March 2022, at paras. 12–14, available at: www.icj-cij.org/public/files/case-related/182/182-20220307-OTH-01-00-EN.pdf.

[152] Ibid., at paras. 15–16. See 'Address by the President of the Russian Federation', Office of the President of the Russian Federation, 24 February 2022, available at: http://en.kremlin.ru/events/president/transcripts/67843 (official English translation, as published by the Kremlin); Обращение Президента Российской Федерации, Президент России, 24 февраля 2022 года, available at: http://kremlin.ru/events/president/news/67843 (original Russian text, as published by the Kremlin).

[153] *Allegations of Genocide under the Convention on the Prevention and Punishment of the Crime of Genocide*, n. 145, at para. 60.

[154] Ibid., at paras. 78–86. The measures were adopted by thirteen votes to two (Judges Gevorgian (Russia) and Xue (China)), although the measure that '[b]oth Parties shall refrain from any

### 10.3.2.5.4 The Operation of a Possible Right of Humanitarian Intervention in Practice

Even if a standalone right of humanitarian intervention by states was to emerge in international law, various issues would open up as to its operation in practice. For example, states, as well as the Security Council, do not have the right to forcibly intervene in another country simply upon the basis of making life better for those within its territory. This being the case, where does the legal threshold lie in permitting a possible response? Could we say that just as a simple use of force does not constitute an 'armed attack' and thus give rise to the right of self-defence,[155] there should similarly and presumably be a certain threshold of harm before the right of intervention would become permissible or, to use the words of the ICJ in the *Nicaragua* case, must the harm to individuals be particularly 'grave'?[156] Would the international community have to wait until a full-scale humanitarian crisis was under way, or would imminent or more temporally remote 'threats' of grave harm to individuals be sufficient to justify a response, perhaps giving rise to a doctrine of anticipatory or pre-emptive humanitarian intervention?[157] If so, when can such a catastrophe or crisis be said to exist? Can their occurrence be objectively determined? Or is it purely based upon the subjective perceptions of states? Regarding the type of humanitarian situation, would a humanitarian catastrophe need to be caused by humans, such as that occurring in Darfur (Sudan), or would states be able to intervene in another state in the context of natural disasters, such as that which became all too evident in the light of Cyclone Nargis in Burma in 2008? Lastly, in the context of the use of armed force for humanitarian purposes, are there specific means by which the force must be employed? In other words, would ground troops be necessary or could more imprecise air power – similar to that used in Kosovo – be the sole means for responding to a humanitarian crisis, despite the almost certain collateral civilian casualties that would result?

---

action which might aggravate or extend the dispute before the Court or make it more difficult to resolve' (ibid., at para. 86(3)) was adopted unanimously. A notable aspect of the measures indicated by the Court was that, while Ukraine had requested that the Court indicate the measure that Russia cease all military activities 'which have as their stated purpose and objective preventing or punishing Ukraine for committing genocide' (see ibid., at para. 5), the Court went further and instead ordered Russia to 'immediately suspend the military operations that it commenced on 24 February 2022 in the territory of Ukraine' (see ibid., at paras. 86 (1) and (2)). This reformulation of the measure was arguably to 'avoid[] creating an abusive escape valve by which Russia could say that no military operations are being conducted that have as their "stated purpose and objective" the prevention of genocide'. See Marko Milanovic, 'ICJ Indicates Provisional Measures against Russia, in a Near Total Win for Ukraine; Russia Expelled from the Council of Europe', *EJIL Talk!*, 16 March 2022, available at: www.ejiltalk.org/icj-indicatesprovisional-measures-against-russia-in-a-near-total-win-for-ukraine-russia-expelled-from-the-council-ofeurope/.

[155] See Section 6.2.5 on the distinction between use of force and armed attacks.
[156] See *Nicaragua* case, n. 7, at para. 191.
[157] On the doctrine of preventative self-defence, see Chapter 7.

In aiming to mend the fissure between law and legitimacy, and in attempting to take a pragmatic and progressive approach, criteria and frameworks to govern decision-making in the case of future humanitarian situations have been proposed. For example, in a speech on 28 January 2000, UK Foreign Secretary Robin Cook stated that the United Kingdom had submitted to the UN Secretary-General:

> a set of ideas to help the international community decide when it is right to act: first, any intervention is by definition a failure of prevention. Force should always be the last resort; second, the immediate responsibility for halting violence rests with the state in which it occurs; but, third, when faced with an overwhelming humanitarian catastrophe and a government that has demonstrated itself unwilling or unable to halt or prevent it, the international community should act; and finally, any use of force in this context should be collective, proportionate, likely to achieve its objective, and carried out in accordance with international law.[158]

However, none of the various criteria that have been advanced have to date been taken up by states (with the exception of the United Kingdom, as discussed in Sections 10.4.1 and 10.4.3) or the Security Council and seemingly played very little part in the way states and the international community responded to the atrocity unfolding in Syria.

## 10.4 THE CIVIL WAR IN SYRIA AND HUMANITARIAN INTERVENTION

At the time of writing in 2023 the civil war in Syria continues. Both Russia and Iran initiated their involvement in the conflict by providing weapons to the Assad regime in Syria. As discussed in Chapter 9, this was arguably not unlawful under the *jus ad bellum* and few accusations of illegality were made against these two states on this basis, despite concerns being raised over the dire situation on the ground in Syria.[159] However, this led to several states supplying (in particular Qatar and Saudi Arabia) or proposing to supply (in particular France, the United Kingdom and the United States) arms and 'non-lethal' military assistance to the opposition forces fighting the Assad regime. Although European Union states were initially prohibited from doing so through an arms embargo,[160] this was subsequently lifted.[161] While no longer

---

[158] See (2000) 71 *British Yearbook of International Law* 646.

[159] See, in particular, Section 9.3.1.

[160] Regulation (EU) No. 442/2011 of 9 May 2011 Concerning Restrictive Measures in View of the Situation in Syria [2011] OJ L 121/1, Article 2(1)(a). See also 'EU Imposes Arms Embargo on Syria', *The Guardian*, 10 May 2011, available at: www.guardian.co.uk/world/2011/may/09/syria-european-union-arms-embargo.

[161] 'EU Arms Embargo on Syrian Opposition Not Extended', *The Guardian*, 28 May 2013, available at: www.guardian.co.uk/world/2013/may/27/eu-arms-embargo-syrian-opposition.

unlawful under EU law, whether the provision of such arms would still have potentially constituted a prohibited forcible intervention under international law, or a legitimate implementation of the doctrine of counter-intervention, was seemingly overlooked.[162] However, in August 2012, US President Barack Obama stated that the use of chemical weapons in Syria constituted a 'red line' which would affect his calculations as to the extent that the United States would be prepared to intervene.[163] The horrific August 2013 chemical attack in Ghouta represented a crossing of this line[164] and placed the possibility of direct forcible intervention on the table.

### 10.4.1 The Debate Regarding Air Strikes in 2013

The possibility of forcible intervention had been discussed prior to the Ghouta attacks,[165] but had not been agreed upon. What was notable following the attacks, however, was that, while several states were discussing intervention in the absence of authorisation by the Security Council, only the United Kingdom was unequivocal in stating in a memorandum of 29 August 2013 that 'the legal basis for military action would be humanitarian intervention'.[166] Since the end of the Cold War, the United Kingdom has been a leading proponent of

---

[162] See Section 2.4.3 on indirect force and the discussion in general in Chapter 9 on military assistance on request.

[163] James Ball, 'Obama Issues Syria a "Red Line" Warning on Chemical Weapons', *The Washington Post*, 21 August 2012, available at: www.washingtonpost.com/world/national-security/obama-issues-syria-red-line-warning-on-chemical-weapons/2012/08/20/ba5d26ec-eaf7-11e1-b811-09036bcb182b_story.html.

[164] See Haroon Siddique, 'Syria Crisis: Rebels Claim Hundreds Killed in Government Chemical Weapons Attack', *The Guardian*, 21 August 2013, available at: www.theguardian.com/world/2013/aug/21/syria-crisis-rebels-claim-hundreds-killed-government-chemical-weapons-attack-live.

[165] For example, US Senator John McCain called for US-led air strikes for humanitarian purposes in the light of the prolonged attacks on civilians by the Assad regime. See BBC News, 'US Senator John McCain Calls for Air Strikes on Syria', 6 March 2012, available at: www.bbc.co.uk/news/world-us-canada-17266798. The United Kingdom claimed that its military might be deployed into the region in the case of a worsening humanitarian situation. Andy McSmith, 'UK Troops "May Be Sent to Syrian Borders"', *The Independent*, 11 November 2012, available at: www.independent.co.uk/news/world/middle-east/uk-troops-may-be-sent-to-syrian-borders-8305055.html.

[166] *Chemical Weapon Use by Syrian Regime – UK Government Legal Position*, 29 August 2013, available at: www.gov.uk/government/publications/chemical-weapon-use-by-syrian-regime-uk-government-legal-position/chemical-weapon-use-by-syrian-regime-uk-government-legal-position-html-version. See, in general, Christian Henderson, 'The UK Government's Legal Opinion on Forcible Measures in Response to the Use of Chemical Weapons by the Syrian Government' (2015) **64** *International & Comparative Law Quarterly* 179.

such a right, although this was the first time it had relied on it in such an unequivocal way. While R2P was raised by various Members of Parliament when the issue was discussed[167] it was interesting that no mention was made of the concept in the memorandum itself. This was arguably a consequence of the development of the 'responsibility-to-react' element of R2P thus far having been firmly located within the realms of Security Council authorisation.[168] What was also notable was the lack of support that the invocation of humanitarian intervention generated, with only Denmark seemingly following suit in claiming a similar right to the United Kingdom.[169] The United States, rather equivocally, took the position that, while any forcible action against Syria without authorisation by the Security Council would not fit 'a traditionally recognized legal basis under international law', it would still be 'justified and legitimate under international law'.[170] The United States did not set out exactly how any prospective military action would be so justified, with President Obama just a few days later stating that any action would be focused upon deterring further attacks, protecting allies in the region and enforcing the norm against the use of chemical weapons,[171] none of which represent such a legal justification.

However, shortly after the publication of the UK's memorandum in August 2013, the UK Parliament voted against military action against Syria.[172] In this respect, it seemed that not only did other states who were in favour of taking action not share the United Kingdom's legal justification of humanitarian intervention, but it was not one that even the UK Parliament could collectively agree on. While other states, notably the United States and France, continued to discuss action in the absence of United Kingdom participation, this was shelved due to the adoption of a plan between the United States and Russia to dispose of Syria's chemical weapons.[173]

---

[167] House of Commons Daily Debates, 29 August 2013, available at: https://publications.parliament.uk/pa/cm201314/cmhansrd/cm130829/debtext/130829-0001.htm.

[168] See Section 4.6.

[169] Danish Military of Foreign Affairs, 'General Principled Considerations on the Legal Basis for a Possible Military Operation in Syria', UPN Alm.del Bilag 298, 30 August 2013, available at: www.ft.dk/samling/20121/almdel/upn/bilag/298/1276299/index.htm.

[170] Charlie Savage, 'Obama Tests Limits of Power in Syria Conflict', *New York Times*, 8 September 2013, available at: www.nytimes.com/2013/09/09/world/middleeast/obama-tests-limits-of-power-in-syrian-conflict.html?pagewanted=all&_r=0.

[171] The White House, Remarks by the President in Address to the Nation on Syria, 10 September 2013, available at: https://obamawhitehouse.archives.gov/the-press-office/2013/09/10/remarks-president-address-nation-syria. See also Section 6.4 on armed reprisals.

[172] BBC News, 'Syria Crisis: Cameron Loses Commons Vote on Syria Action', 30 August 2013, available at: www.bbc.co.uk/news/uk-politics-23892783.

[173] UNSC Res. 2118 (2013), paras. 4, 6 and 7.

## 10.4.2 The April 2017 Air Strikes

Humanitarian intervention was not subsequently the subject of discussion by states, yet, on 7 April 2017, the United States fired fifty-nine Tomahawk missiles on a Syrian government airbase at Shayrat, near Homs, in response to the alleged use of chemical weapons by the Assad regime against civilians.[174] No express legal justification was advanced by the United States, although President Trump claimed the missiles were launched to prevent 'the spread and use of deadly chemical weapons' after previous efforts to change Assad's behaviour 'had failed, and failed very dramatically', while calling upon the international community to 'join [it] in seeking to end the slaughter and bloodshed in Syria and also to end terrorism of all kinds and all types'.[175] The Department of Defense stated it 'was intended to deter the regime from using chemical weapons again'.[176] While the strikes were condemned by Russia as 'aggression against a sovereign state in violation of international law',[177] they also did not appear to receive widespread condemnation as being unlawful,[178] with some states, such as the United Kingdom, coming out in clear support.[179] It is difficult to find a legal basis for this strike and the United States did not advance a justification of humanitarian intervention, although one might attempt to read this into its general claim to be deterring the future use of chemical weapons.

In the aftermath of the 2017 strikes some commentators described them as 'clearly illegal',[180] and an armed reprisal.[181] The argument was, however, raised that the fact that the United States did not even try to bring this action within the ambit of the Charter rules on the use of force might, on the one hand, be a positive thing as it had the effect of preserving the strength of Article 2(4). If the

---

[174] Spencer Ackerman, Ed Pilkington, Ben Jacobs and Julian Borger, 'Syria Missile Strikes: US Launches First Direct Military Action against Assad', *The Guardian*, 7 April 2017, available at: www.theguardian.com/world/2017/apr/06/trump-syria-missiles-assad-chemical-weapons.

[175] Ibid.    [176] Ibid.

[177] 'Russia Condemns US Strikes on Syria as a "Violation of International Law"', *France24*, 7 April 2017, available at: www.france24.com/en/20170407-russia-iran-condemns-usa-strikes-syria-violation-international-law.

[178] See, in general, UN Doc. S/PV.7919, 7 April 2017. For a summary of the reactions to the strikes see: www.nytimes.com/interactive/2017/04/07/world/middleeast/world-reactions-syria-strike.html.

[179] BBC News, 'UK Government "Fully Supports" US Airstrike in Syria', 7 April 2017, available at: www.bbc.co.uk/news/uk-39524685.

[180] Marko Milanovic, 'The Clearly Illegal Missile Strike in Syria', *EJIL Talk!*, 7 April 2017, available at: www.ejiltalk.org/the-clearly-illegal-us-missile-strike-in-syria/.

[181] Aldo Zammit Borda, 'The Precedent Set by the US Reprisal against the Use of Chemical Weapons in Syria', *EJIL Talk!*, 1 May 2017, available at: www.ejiltalk.org/the-precedent-set-by-the-us-reprisal-against-the-use-of-chemical-weapons-in-syria/; Monika Hakimi, 'Macron's Threat of Reprisals and the *Jus ad Bellum*', *EJIL Talk!*, 2 June 2017, available at: www.ejiltalk.org/macrons-threat-of-reprisals-and-the-jus-ad-bellum/.

international community had been presented with a clearly articulated legal justification, this would have 'serve[d] certain interests that are associated with the rule of law, like transparency and the articulation of generally applicable legal standards', yet at the same time it would have 'advanc[ed] a novel legal claim to permit more unilateral force' and that '[e]ven if other states do not accept that claim at the moment, they or the United States could more easily invoke it to justify future actions. After all, the United States would have said that such actions are, in its view, lawful.'[182] In a similar fashion, others took the view that keeping the Charter-based rules and justifications separate from extra-Charter excuses 'would at least keep us paddling in the already dangerous but probably inevitable waters of "illegal but legitimate"',[183] as was witnessed in the aftermath of NATO's bombing in response to events in Kosovo in 1999.

While some appeared to be willing to attempt to contain this as a 'one-off incident' with relatively little impact upon the *jus ad bellum*,[184] others were more concerned with the (potential) precedent set by it, as singular 'exceptional' cases, regardless of the justification or excuse advanced, may result in a pattern with equally harmful potential for the prohibition of the use of force.[185] Even further, it might be argued that 'just ignoring the *jus ad bellum* risks conveying a total disregard for the law. It risks suggesting that the United States does not view the *jus ad bellum*, and maybe international law more generally, as normatively relevant in the global order.'[186] What is clear, though, is that, while this represented another example of state practice that could, at least, be interpreted as a humanitarian intervention, it is difficult to observe any decisive shifts in the legality of the doctrine in the absence of any further *opinio juris* either firmly in favour or against from either the acting or reacting states on this occasion.

### 10.4.3 The April 2018 Air Strikes

Almost exactly a year later the doctrine of humanitarian intervention was to come into more direct focus. On 14 April 2018 the United States, United Kingdom and France launched more than 100 missiles against three sites in Syria (a scientific research centre in Damascus, a chemical weapons storage

---

[182] Monika Hakimi, 'US Strikes against Syria and the Implications for the *Jus ad Bellum*', *EJIL Talk!*, 7 April 2017, available at: www.ejiltalk.org/us-strikes-against-syria-and-the-implications-for-the-jus-ad-bellum/#more-15138.

[183] Jure Vidmar, 'Excusing Illegal Use of Force: From Illegal But Legitimate to Legal Because It Is Legitimate?', *EJIL Talk!*, 14 April 2017, available at: www.ejiltalk.org/excusing-illegal-use-of-force-from-illegal-but-legitimate-to-legal-because-it-is-legitimate/.

[184] Hakimi, n. 181.

[185] Anthea Roberts, 'Syrian Strikes: Singular Exception or a Pattern and a Precedent?', *EJIL Talk!*, 10 April 2017, available at: www.ejiltalk.org/syrian-strikes-a-singular-exception-or-a-pattern-and-a-precedent/.

[186] Hakimi, n. 181.

facility west of Homs and another storage site and command post nearby) in response to a chemical weapons attack in Douma on 7 April which killed dozens of civilians and which the acting states attributed to the Syrian government.[187] As the United States did in the 2017 strikes, all three states made strong reference to the strikes being a response to the chemical weapons attack, in particular 'to establish a strong deterrent against the production, spread, and use of chemical weapons',[188] 'to degrade and deter the use of chemical weapons by the Syrian Regime'[189] and to avoid 'the normalization of the employment of chemical weapons, which is an immediate danger to the Syrian people and to our collective security'.[190] While neither the United States, United Kingdom or France justified the actions expressly as such, the strikes therefore had the flavour of armed reprisals, that is, the use of limited force with the aim of coercing a state into complying with its international legal obligations, a basis for the use of force which is widely regarded as unlawful.[191] Most clearly in this respect France stated that it had acted 'in line with the objectives and values proclaimed from the outset by the Charter of the United Nations' and that the action was 'necessary in order to address the repeated violations by the Syrian regime of its obligations – obligations stemming from the law, treaties and its own commitments'.[192]

The United Kingdom, however, went further and clearly asserted that its actions were based on a legal right of humanitarian intervention.[193] In particular:

[187] Julian Borger and Peter Beaumont, 'Syria: US, UK and France Launch Strikes in Response to Chemical Attack', *The Guardian*, 14 April 2018, available at: www.theguardian.com/world/2018/apr/14/syria-air-strikes-us-uk-and-france-launch-attack-on-assad-regime.

[188] Quinta Jurecic, 'Transcript: President Trump's Remarks on Syria Airstrikes', *Lawfare*, 13 April 2018, available at: www.lawfareblog.com/transcript-president-trumps-remarks-syria-airstrikes.

[189] Prime Minister's Office, 10 Downing Street, 'PM Statement on Syria: 14 April 2018', *GOV.UK*, available at: www.gov.uk/government/news/pm-statement-on-syria-14-april-2018.

[190] Press statement by the President of the French Republic on the intervention of the French armed forces in response to the use of chemical weapons in Syria, *ÉLYSÉE*, 14 April 2018, available at: www.elysee.fr/en/emmanuel-macron/2018/04/14/press-statement-by-the-president-of-the-french-republic-on-the-intervention-of-the-french-armed-forces-in-response-to-the-use-of-chemical-weapons-in-syria-1.

[191] See Section 6.3.1.2.1. See also Mary Ellen O'Connell, 'Unlawful Reprisals to the Rescue against Chemical Attacks', *EJIL Talk!*, 12 April 2018, available at: www.ejiltalk.org/unlawful-reprisals-to-the-rescue-against-chemical-attacks/.

[192] UN Doc. S/PV.8233, 14 April 2018, at 9. While the use of chemical weapons in both international and non-international armed conflicts is prohibited under customary international law, in a deal struck between the United States, Russia and Syria in September 2013 Syria acceded to the Chemical Weapons Convention (1997) which, amongst other things, prohibits the use of such weapons. See n. 173.

[193] Prime Minister's Office, 10 Downing Street, 'Syria action – UK government legal position', 14 April 2018, available at: www.gov.uk/government/publications/syria-action-uk-government-legal-position/syria-action-uk-government-legal-position.

The UK is permitted under international law, on an exceptional basis, to take measures in order to alleviate overwhelming humanitarian suffering. The legal basis for the use of force is humanitarian intervention, which requires three conditions to be met:

(i) there is convincing evidence, generally accepted by the international community as a whole, of extreme humanitarian distress on a large scale, requiring immediate and urgent relief;
(ii) it must be objectively clear that there is no practicable alternative to the use of force if lives are to be saved; and
(iii) the proposed use of force must be necessary and proportionate to the aim of relief of humanitarian suffering and must be strictly limited in time and in scope to this aim (i.e. the minimum necessary to achieve that end and for no other purpose).[194]

It is, on the basis of what has been covered in this chapter, unclear as to how the UK government could be so certain that a right of humanitarian intervention existed under international law. Yet, the conditions provided for action and the way they were applied on this occasion give rise to further questions.[195] It is, for example, unclear how such 'convincing evidence' of humanitarian distress is to be certified as such, particularly given that it has, in the United Kingdom's view, to be 'accepted by the international community as a whole'. The international community is rarely united on such issues and even when it is there are divisions as to what form a response should take. Indeed, such 'objective' clarity 'that there is no practicable alternative to the use of force' will rarely be found, with such clarity more often than not seen through the subjective eyes of the acting states.

However, given the circumstances in 2018 '[t]he UK consider[ed] that military action met the requirements of humanitarian intervention'.[196] In particular, 'the Syrian regime's pattern of use of chemical weapons to date' meant that 'it was highly likely that the regime would seek to use chemical weapons again',[197] and the '[a]ctions by the UK and its international partners to alleviate the humanitarian suffering caused by the use of chemical weapons' had either not proved to have been effective, as was the case with the April 2017 US strikes, or had been blocked by the Syrian regime and its allies.[198] As such, '[i]n these circumstances, and as an exceptional measure on grounds of overwhelming humanitarian necessity, military intervention to strike carefully considered, specifically identified targets in order effectively

---

[194] Ibid., at para. 3.
[195] See, in general, House of Commons Foreign Affairs Select Committee, *Global Britain: The Responsibility to Protect and Humanitarian Intervention*, 10 September 2018, available at: https://publications.parliament.uk/pa/cm201719/cmselect/cmfaff/1005/1005.pdf.
[196] 'Syria action – UK government legal position', n. 193, para. 4.   [197] Ibid., at para. 4(i).
[198] Ibid., at para. 4(ii).

to alleviate humanitarian distress by degrading the Syrian regime's chemical weapons capability and deterring further chemical weapons attacks was necessary and proportionate and therefore legally justifiable.'[199] It was not at all clear at the time that such a limited strike would positively contribute to the 'relief of humanitarian suffering' or that it would do so through the deterrence of the further use of chemical weapons, particularly given that the 2017 strikes had so clearly not had that effect.

While the United Kingdom might, on the one hand, be commended for making such an attempt at providing transparency and clarity as to its legal justification, it might, on the other hand, be condemned for proffering and acting upon a doctrine that clearly did not exist in international law. Putting aside the fact that any emerging right of humanitarian intervention would need to be squared with the text of the Charter,[200] the inherent chronological paradox within customary international law means that states need to believe that a right exists in customary international law before it can actually become such a *lex lata* right. However, while one might ponder over whether the United Kingdom offered and acted upon the doctrine on this occasion under a firm belief that it existed as a justification *lex lata*, or whether it offered it more in the hope that it would catch on, what was clear was that although the strikes in themselves received some notable political and moral support within the international community,[201] no state, including the other acting states, came out in support of its legal position regarding humanitarian intervention. In this respect, the United Kingdom's claim can be seen as rather isolated, meaning that its invocation on this occasion arguably did the chances of a right of humanitarian intervention emerging as a distinct legal justification within the *jus ad bellum* more harm than good.

---

[199] Ibid., at para. 4(iii).    [200] See Section 10.2.
[201] See, in general, UN Doc. S/PV.8233, n. 192. At this meeting of the UN Security Council member states rejected a proposed resolution by Russia which would have condemned the military strikes as aggression. The draft resolution – which was defeated by a recorded vote of eight against (Côte d'Ivoire, France, Kuwait, Netherlands, Poland, Sweden, United Kingdom, United States) to three in favour (Bolivia, China, Russian Federation), with four abstentions (Equatorial Guinea, Ethiopia, Kazakhstan, Peru) – would have demanded the United States and its allies immediately cease such actions and refrain from any further use of force in violation of international law. For a comprehensive assessment of the position of states in response to this incident, see Alonso Gurmendi Dunkelberg, Rebecca Ingber, Priya Pillai and Elvina Pothelet, 'Mapping States' Reactions to the U.S. Strikes against Syria of April 2018 – A Comprehensive Guide', *Just Security*, 7 May 2018, available at: www.justsecurity.org/55835/mapping-states-reactions-syria-strikes-april-2018-a-comprehensive-guide/.

## 10.5 HUMANITARIAN INTERVENTION AND THE RESPONSIBILITY TO PROTECT

This chapter has demonstrated that the doctrine of humanitarian intervention has never achieved a settled place within the international legal system. While it is now well accepted that the Security Council can authorise military action for humanitarian purposes – indeed, this is arguably where the contemporary focus of such authorisations lies – the notion of unilateral humanitarian intervention runs directly counter to its multilateral relation and has, as such, been controversial. As both the Cold War and post–Cold War interventions illustrated, acting states have been careful not to invoke it in justifying their actions, either due to its illegality or concerns regarding the precedent that would be set by doing so.

The R2P doctrine has not changed things in this respect.[202] While there were concerns that such a doctrine would encourage unilateral actions, this has not proved to be the case. This is not to say, however, that it has not proved controversial. Indeed, the NATO intervention in Libya demonstrates that states have very different views on the extent of the actions that can be taken when acting under a secondary responsibility to protect, and in the UN General Assembly's 2011 informal debate on R2P several states voiced their doubts regarding the manner in which NATO was implementing Resolution 1973 (2011) in Libya.[203] During this debate some states questioned whether it might be possible to develop criteria to determine when it was justified to resort to the use of force.[204] However, the success of any such criteria is doubtful as on each occasion those criteria and their application to the facts of the particular situation would need to be interpreted, thus potentially leading to further disagreement. Furthermore, concerns were expressed regarding selectivity in the application of the R2P doctrine.[205]

Ultimately, while it cannot be said that the R2P doctrine has reached the stage in its normative development to be described a legal norm, it has nonetheless cemented a limited place in the rhetoric of states and organisations. This, as was the case with self-determination, is an important step in the normative development of such a concept. Yet, if it is to reach the stage of

---

[202] See further, Section 4.6. For a symposium on Latin American perspectives on the Responsibility to Protect, see (2015) 41 *Pensamiento Propio* 7–286, available at: www.cries.org/wp-content/uploads/2015/09/pp41-web-FINAL-Corr.pdf. See also Vladimir Baranovsky and Anatoly Mateiko, 'Responsibility to Protect: Russia's Approaches' (2016) 51 *The International Spectator* 49.

[203] International Coalition for the Responsibility to Protect, 'Interactive Dialogue of the UNGA on the Regional and Sub-regional Arrangements in Implementing the RtoP', August 2011; UN Press Release GA/11112, 12 July 2011.

[204] Ibid.   [205] Ibid.

development so as to be recognised as a legal norm there are issues that will have to resolved first, not least of all what is to happen if the Security Council does not authorise military action when there is an apparent need for such action to prevent or halt a humanitarian catastrophe. If, and if so how, these are resolved will arguably form the next chapter in the life of the doctrine of humanitarian intervention.

## 10.6 CONCLUSION

This chapter has demonstrated that, while there is no right of humanitarian intervention in the absence of an authorisation by the Security Council, it is difficult to say that this is entirely unqualified. ECOWAS's intervention in Liberia and Sierra Leone demonstrated that the Security Council is willing to provide approval of humanitarian action that it did not authorise. Furthermore, both during and in the aftermath of NATO's intervention in Kosovo it has been shown that the issue is still very much a live one. Just a few years later, the UK Attorney-General in his Memorandum on the 2003 use of force against Iraq stated that: '[t]he use of force to avert an overwhelming humanitarian catastrophe has been emerging as a further, and exceptional, basis for the use of force', although it was acknowledged that '[t]he doctrine remains controversial'.[206] This seemed to echo a statement by the UN Secretary-General Kofi Annan, in an address to the Commission on Human Rights in Geneva on 7 April 1999: 'Emerging slowly, but I believe surely, is an international norm against the violent repression of minorities that will and must take precedence over concerns of sovereignty' and that the UN Charter should 'never [be] the source of comfort or justification' for 'those guilty of gross and shocking violations of human rights'.[207] It is also, as discussed in Section 1.5.5.2, not entirely clear whether a humanitarian intervention would be seen by the International Criminal Court as a 'manifest violation' of the UN Charter in terms of determining whether the crime of aggression has been committed.

It was against this background that attempts have been made to ignite a revolution, at least in a terminological sense, in the form of the 'Responsibility to Protect' doctrine. Yet, rather than increasing the moral and legal currency of arguments regarding the existence of a right of unilateral humanitarian intervention, this concept has, instead, simply dampened, if not entirely halted, any prospects for a right to emerge. Furthermore, while *opinio necessitatis* has clearly been present in regard to particular interventions taken for

---

[206] 'Attorney-General's Advice on the Iraq War: Resolution 1441' (2005) 54 *International & Comparative Law Quarterly* 767, at para. 4.

[207] See UN Press Release SG/SM/6949 and HR/CN/89, 7 April 1999, available at: https://press.un.org/en/1999/19990407.sgsm6949.html.

humanitarian purposes,[208] and it is possible to at least identify certain threads of a 'tapestry of argument' in favour of a right of humanitarian intervention,[209] any form of consensus regarding the existence of a right has, as yet, far from clearly established itself.

## QUESTIONS

1 Does the UN Charter provide for a right of 'humanitarian intervention'?

2 To what extent can it be said that state practice since 1945 has developed a right of humanitarian intervention?

3 Was humanitarian intervention relied upon in:
   - Kosovo (1999)?
   - Syria (2014–)?

4 What are the possibilities for reconciling the law and legitimacy of the use of force in the context of humanitarian crises?

5 To what extent has the doctrine of Responsibility to Protect impacted upon the doctrine of humanitarian intervention?

## SUGGESTED FURTHER READING

AJIL Editorial Comments, 'NATO's Kosovo Intervention' (1999) 93 *American Journal of International Law* 824 (consists of several articles by leading scholars of international law)

Simon Chesterman, *Just War or Just Peace? Humanitarian Intervention and International Law* (Oxford University Press, 2001)

Thomas Franck and Nigel Rodley, 'After Bangladesh: The Law of Humanitarian Intervention by Military Force' (1973) 67 *American Journal of International Law* 297

Christopher Greenwood, 'Humanitarian Intervention: The Case of Kosovo' (1999) 10 *Finnish Yearbook of International Law* 141

Anders Henriksen and Marc Schack, 'The Crisis in Syria and Humanitarian Intervention' (2014) 1 *Journal on the Use of Force and International Law* 132

Mark Swatek-Evenstein, *A History of Humanitarian Intervention* (Cambridge University Press, 2020)

Jennifer Trahan, 'Defining the "Grey Area" Where Humanitarian Intervention May Not be Fully Legal, But Is Not the Crime of Aggression' (2015) 2 *Journal on the Use of Force and International Law* 42

---

[208] Cassese, n. 138.
[209] Daniel Bethlehem, 'Stepping Back a Moment – The Legal Basis in Favour of a Principle of Humanitarian Intervention', *EJIL Talk!*, 12 September 2013, available at: www.ejiltalk.org/stepping-back-a-moment-the-legal-basis-in-favour-of-a-principle-of-humanitarian-intervention/.

# CONCLUDING REMARKS

One theme that it is hoped emerges from this book is that the law governing the use of force is not purely epiphenomenal. It is possible to suggest that as states on the whole refrain from resorting to the use of armed force the law clearly has a restraining influence upon their actions. However, such assumptions must give way to the reality that the law actually has a far more subtle influence over the actions of states. There can be no escaping the fact that states, and some more often than others, resort to force in their international affairs. Yet, at the same time, states, in general, often engage with the law in justifying their actions, as well as in responding to the actions of other states, and in attempting to shape the contours of the law through interpretation and practice. While there are occasions when states use force without offering a legal justification for doing so, as was the case with the US strikes against Syria in April 2017, it is more often the case that states engage in justificatory discourse of a legal nature which is indicative that they consider the law to be at least of some relevance, even if violations of its strictures are not supported by clear and reliable enforcement mechanisms. It arguably follows, then, that if they feel compelled to offer at least a justification, they feel similarly compelled to adjust their actions to make them at least plausible within the substantive rules and procedures that exist. Furthermore, the law in this area, if nothing else – as is arguably the case with much of international law – provides a language and framework through which discursive intercourse between states and other actors can occur.

A further theme that hopefully emerges through the chapters of this book is that there exists no general appetite amongst states for either the scrapping, rewriting or radical reinterpretation of the rules within the UN Charter and customary principles governing the use of force which both enable and restrain state action. That is not to say, however, that the rules have not been constantly challenged and, in some cases, interpreted and adapted with the ostensible aim of meeting contemporary threats and challenges. Yet, state reactions to contemporary challenges do not generally appear – yet, at least – to allude to a deep dissatisfaction with the rules, at least to the point that it would be better to not have them at all. While there are question marks over the peremptory status of the prohibition of the threat or use of force, with even the continued existence of this norm a subject for scholars on occasion, we have not witnessed the same challenges being made by states.

This is not to say, of course, that the law in this area and the way that it operates in practice is without its problems. Indeed, arguably the clearest theme that emerges through this book is that, while there is broad agreement regarding the *existence* of the rules and procedures, their breadth and scope, as well as their operation in practice, often remain unclear and subject sometimes to broad disagreement between both states and scholars. Part II of the book highlighted that the UN has broad powers in meeting its responsibility to maintain international peace and security, including through the use of armed force in both peace enforcement and peacekeeping operations. Yet, as a clear example of where law meets politics, this system has either not functioned or it has functioned but only partially. The 'authorisation method' is an example of the UN Charter being provided with a gloss of effectiveness through interpretation, without the need to formally modify the Charter. However, while this has provided the UN with a new lease of life in the post–Cold War era, there have been notable problems with it in practice, in particular in terms of existing authorisations or resolutions of the Council being abused or through the Council being selective in utilising its powers of enforcement. These problems ultimately come down to divisions between states and underlying great-power politics and it is difficult to see how these might be overcome with the body existing and functioning as it does. Reform of the UN, and in particular the Security Council, has long been on the agenda, but with no agreement as to a way forward. The conflict in Ukraine, which was aggressively initiated by a permanent member of the Council, has reignited these debates, but we will have to wait to see if reform proposals are seriously considered, and, if so, how they will affect the composition, powers and functioning of this body in implementing its mandate for the maintenance of international peace and security.

Arguably the greatest controversies, however, have arisen in the context of the right of self-defence. Conventional wisdom dictated that an 'armed attack' had to occur prior to, or at the time of, the right becoming available. Question marks remain, however, over fundamental issues in connection with this right, such as whether there is a gravity threshold between a use of force and an armed attack and, if there is one, how it is determined, both in the abstract and in the context of particular incidences. For example, while the 'accumulation of events theory' has gained some traction in recent years, it appears to remain just that, a theory, with few conceptual guidelines as to how it might operate in practice. The doctrine of pre-emption, as so famously peddled by United States President George W. Bush after the attacks of 9/11, appears to have been widely rejected amongst states. Yet, incidents such as the Israeli attack on the al-Kibar site in Syria in 2007 – and, in particular, the general silence towards it – demonstrate that it is an issue that has still not been completely laid to rest, and its acceptability may still be said to depend upon the circumstances. However, while a degree of acceptance of anticipatory self-defence seems to have been the result of the discernible widespread rejection of pre-emptive self-defence, the limits of this more limited form of preventative self-defence have only become less clear, with certain states resting on the uncertainty of contemporary threats to argue for a shift from a temporal reading of 'imminence' to one focusing upon the broader – and arguably more subjectively determined – context of the individual threat, leaving states to determine which element in the assessment of the threat is of most significance and thus providing them with the greatest freedom of action. On the basis of the contemporary positions of certain states and scholars, the requirement for an armed attack has been, in the context of contemporary threats, all but eliminated from the equation.

There is now widespread, although far from universal, agreement that non-state actors may perpetrate armed attacks and that states may respond to them. Disagreements remain, however, as to how, and in what circumstances, such a response may take place. For example, in restricting its response to the non-state actor perpetrators of the armed attack, do the actions of the non-state actors still need to be attributed to the state in which they reside or can the defending state's response be based purely on the concept of the customary criterion of necessity and, in particular, the so-called 'unable or unwilling' doctrine? Yet, even if one accepts the 'unable or unwilling' doctrine, there are question marks over how it operates in practice. No matter how well these issues may be established in principle in the abstract, all will nonetheless depend upon states implementing them in good faith which also can never be guaranteed.

The absence of clarity is not restricted to issues of self-defence and extends to the issue of consent to intervention. While not providing an exception to the prohibition of the use of force, as such, consent nonetheless provides a lawful means in principle for a state to use force upon the territory of another state. Yet, there is always subjectivity in making assessments as to who is entitled to request assistance or provide consent, and questions arise as to how this concept operates during times of civil crisis.

Finally, while the UN Security Council has the right to intervene within a state to prevent or halt a humanitarian catastrophe, this is a right that states – individually or collectively – do not, as yet, possess. Indeed, the emergence of the Responsibility to Protect (R2P) doctrine has, if anything, only highlighted this further, as forcible implementation of R2P has continuously been asserted as a prerogative restricted to the Council and not individual states. This point was highlighted only too well in the context of the United Kingdom's justification for its proposed military intervention in Syria in 2013, which omitted to make any mention of the doctrine. Yet, while the initial excitement regarding

R2P has in some ways fizzled out, interventions for humanitarian purposes, albeit without necessarily being justified upon a legal doctrine, continue to occur and debate continues within the academic community regarding the wisdom of the development of a legal right of humanitarian intervention. An aspect of this debate that often seems to be overlooked is that the addition of new exceptions to the prohibition such as this, or any broadening of existing rights to use force such as self-defence, leads to a contraction in the breadth and scope of the prohibition or force, something that many deny as even possible without broad and clear agreement amongst the international community of states.

While uncertainty in the application of the law has arisen, the law has been viewed on the whole as being able to accommodate new and emerging threats and challenges, such as the destructive potential of cyber-attacks. It remains to be seen if this trend continues in regard to challenges that look set to become prominent in the future, such as the inevitable emergence of fully autonomous weapons systems as well as the potential for conflict caused by climate change and disputes over diminishing land and resources. Indeed, while it is a depressing reality, business looks set to continue for the use of force lawyer for the foreseeable future.

# INDEX

Abass, Ademola, 169
Abbott, Tony, 418
Abductions as law enforcement actions, 113–14
Abyssinia, Italian conquest of, 29
Accumulation of events theory, 290–6
　cyber attacks and, 294
　determination of threshold, 295
　ICJ and, 291, 402–3
　*lex lata*, not deemed, 295
　necessity principle and, 263–312
　non-state actors, self-defence against, 402–3
　proportionality principle and, 295–6, 321–2
　Soleimani drone strike and, 293–4
　in state practice, 291–4
　temporal frequency and, 295
Act of Chapultepec, 259
Afghanistan
　al-Qaida in, 313, 415–16
　collective self-defence and, 336
　consent to intervention and, 474
　drones, use in, 438
　NATO intervention in, 172
　Northern Alliance, 368
　Operation Enduring Freedom, 313, 368, 403, 407–8
　Soviet intervention in, 73, 346, 470–1, 474
　Taliban, 313, 320–1, 368, 403, 407–8, 411–12, 415–16
　"unable or unwilling" doctrine and, 415–16
　US and
　　air strikes by, 309, 310, 411
　　attack on al-Qaida by as self-defence, 266, 273, 310, 313, 320–1, 368–9, 407–8, 411–12
African National Congress, 459
African Union (AU)
　African Union Transition Mission in Somalia (ATMIS), 237–8
　African Union/United Nations Force in Somalia (AMISOM), 237–8
　African Union/United Nations Force in Sudan (UNAMID), 239–40
　authorisation of use of force by, 169–70
　Burundi, intervention in, 477
　consent to intervention and, 476–7
　Constitutive Act (2000), 169–70, 213, 214, 476–7
　Darfur, intervention in, 170, 213
　Libya and
　　authorisation of force by Security Council, 191
　　Responsibility to Protect, 214
　peacekeeping by, 221
　UN Charter, conflict with, 169–70
Agenda for Peace, 142–3
Aggression, crime of
　generally, 5
　defined, 57–8
　Definition of Aggression (1974) (*See* Definition of Aggression (1974))
　historical background, 55–7
　humanitarian intervention versus, 59–60, 61
　ICC and
　　defined, 57–8
　　humanitarian intervention and, 59–60
　　inclusion of, 57
　　jurisdiction, impact of, 61–4
　　use of force distinguished, 107, 108
　ICJ and, 108
　ILC on, 56–7
　Kellogg-Briand Pact not recognising, 56
　as "manifest" violation of UN Charter, 58–60
　*mens rea* element, 60–1
　mistake of law and, 61
　Security Council and
　　generally, 138, 143–4
　　determinations by, 70, 147–8
　self-defence versus, 59, 60–1
　specific gravity element, 62
　UN Charter and, 57–8
　use of force distinguished, 107–9

Ago, Robert, 300, 319
Aideed, Mohamed Farrah, 237
Aircraft
　foreign civil aircraft, law enforcement actions against, 118
　as weapons, 96
Akande, Dapo, 414, 469
Akehurst, Michael, 34
al-Assad, Bashar, 216, 315, 421, 422, 423, 425, 458, 462, 512–13, 515–16
Albania
　authorisation of force by Security Council in, 159, 178
　*Corfu Channel* case and (*See Corfu Channel* case (ICJ 1949))
Albright, Madeleine, 284, 506
Algeria on pre-emptive self-defence, 367–8
Alkhatib, Mouaz, 458
Allen, Jonathan, 115
al-Liby, Abu Anas, 114–20, 436
"All necessary means"
　generally, 225
　authorisation of use of force by Security Council and, 158–61, 175
　China and, 42
　Côte d'Ivoire and, 195–6
　Gulf War and, 41, 157–8, 201
　Iraq and, 179, 180, 497–8
　Kosovo and, 501–2
　Libya and, 215
　Mali and, 242–3
　peacekeeping and, 234
　Somalia and, 237–8
　use of force versus, 189
al Moallem, Walid, 423
al-Mouhandis, Abu Mahdi, 267–8
al-Nusrah Front, 465, 466
al-Qaida
　in Afghanistan, 313, 415–16
　armed attacks by, 264–5
　non-state actors, self-defence against, 2, 403
　self-defence and, 266, 273, 313, 320–1
　targeted killings of, 114–17, 431
　as terrorist group, 466
　US and
　　Afghanistan, intervention in, 368, 403
　　attack by as self-defence, 266, 273, 310, 313, 320–1, 368–9, 407–8
　　US embassies, armed attacks on, 273, 411
　　US attack on as self-defence, 411–12
　in Yemen, 469
al-Qaida in the Islamic Maghreb (AQIM), 242

al-Shabaab, 237–8, 406, 415–16
al-Wazir, Khalil Ibrahim, 114–17
Angola
　Lusaka Ceasefire Agreement (1999), 240
　South African aggression against, 147
Annan, Kofi, 48, 142–3, 374–5
Anticipatory self-defence
　generally, 360–1, 398
　expansionist approach, 361
　ICJ and, 362–3
　international jurisprudence, 362–3
　restrictionist approach, 361–2
　Six Day War and, 363–4
Aquinas, Thomas, 24–5
Arab League
　Iraq, opposition to intervention in, 198–9
　Libya, authorisation of force by Security Council and, 191
　Security Council, relation to, 169
　Syria and, 217
Arab Spring (2011), 37
Argentina
　abductions in, 113–20
　Falkland Islands, seizure of, 35, 147, 302, 353–4 (*See also* Falklands War (1982))
*Armed Activities* case (ICJ 2005)
　accumulation of events theory and, 291
　consent to intervention and, 451
　non-state actors, self-defence against, 400, 409–10, 439
　pre-emptive self-defence and, 378–9
Armed attack
　assassination attempts as, 98, 283–4
　collective self-defence, required for, 339
　determining when begins, 357–8
　ICJ and
　　generally, 285
　　issues of proof, 272–3
　　*mens rea* element, 274
　　military vessels, 268
　　non-state actors as perpetrators, 262, 263
　　proportional forcible countermeasures, 290
　　scale and effects test, 286
　　use of force distinguished, 106, 107, 276–81, 290
　interception of, 359–60
　9/11 attacks as, 401–2
　non-state actors, self-defence against distinguished, 403
　self-defence, required for
　　generally, 105–6, 261–2
　　cyber attacks, 265–6, 271–2

embassies, 269–71
hostile intent, 275
"interests," 269–70
issues of proof, 272–3
*mens rea* element, 274–6
military vessels, 268
non-state actors as perpetrators, 263–6
perpetrators of, 262–6
targets of, 267–72
use of force in territory of other states, 266
Soleimani drone strike and, 267–8
use of force distinguished
generally, 105–6
accumulation of events theory, 290–6 (*See also* Accumulation of events theory)
assassination attempts, 98, 283–4
assisting rebels, 277
border incidents, 277, 285
criticism of distinction, 278, 279–80
cyber attacks and, 285–9
*de miminis* threshold, 276–7
difficulty in drawing distinction, 280–1
ICJ and, 278–81, 290
proportional forcible countermeasures, 290
in state practice, 281–5
supply of arms, 279
third state involvement, attempts to limit, 278
Armed force
generally, 94
actual use of weapons not required, 96–7
aircraft as weapons, 96
as covered by UN Charter, 93–4
cyber attacks as, 96
cyber operations as, 98–102
effects created, 96–102
harm to persons or property not required, 97–8
ICJ and, 95–6, 99, 102–4
indirect use of, 102–5
means used, 95–6
non-state actors and, 104–5
scale and effects test, 98–9, 286
targeted killings as, 96
types of weapons used, 95–6
UN Charter Article 2(4) and, 93–4, 95
Armed reprisals
generally, 261
credibility gap regarding, 313–15
defined, 306–7
delay, relevance of, 310–14
ICJ and, 308

ILC on, 308–9
necessity principle and, 307
non-state actors, self-defence against distinguished, 403
prohibition on, 307–8
proportionality principle and, 307
purpose of, 306–7
self-defence distinguished, 291–310, 313–15
Special Arbitral Tribunal and, 307
UN Charter and, 307–8
Armenia
Bishkek Protocol (1994), 303–4
Nagorno-Karabakh, dispute with Azerbaijan regarding, 302–4
Arms embargoes
Iran, 160–1
Libya, 190, 192, 458
Sierra Leone, 204–5
Southern Rhodesia, 156
Ashburton, Lord (Alexander Baring), 296
Assassination attempts
as armed attack, 98, 283–4
armed reprisals in response to, 310
necessity principle and, 283–312
non-state actors, self-defence against, 405
protection of nationals abroad and, 327, 330
Association of Southeast Asian Nations (ASEAN)
cyber operations and, 84–5
on humanitarian intervention, 495–6
Augustine, 24–5
Australia
Bali bombings (2002), 377
on imminence, 384
Iraq, air strikes in, 453
Iraq War and, 1, 180
on pre-emptive self-defence, 372, 377
"unable or unwilling" doctrine and, 416, 420–1, 427
Australia, New Zealand and United States Security Treaty (ANZUS) (1951), 337–8, 350
Authorisation of use of force by Security Council. *See also specific country*
generally, 1, 18, 135–7, 175
"all necessary means" and, 158–61, 175
authorisation model generally, 136, 172–3, 217–18
breadth and scope of authorisation
generally, 175, 189
Côte d'Ivoire, 195–6
Libya (*See* Libya)
civilians, protection of, 160

530  Index

Authorisation of use of force by Security Council. (cont.)
  Cold War, during, 153-6
  concerns regarding authorisation model, 161-5
  development of authorisation method, 156-8
  domestic matters, applicability to, 164-5
  embargoes, 160
  historical background, 136, 153
  humanitarian aid, 158-60
  ICJ and, 162
  implied authorisation
    generally, 175, 196
    Iraq, 197-9
    Kosovo, 199-201
    Liberia, 203-4
    retrospective authorisation or approval, 202-7
    Sierra Leone, 204-5
    unilateral enforcement of collective will, 197-202
  implied powers doctrine and, 162-3
  internal matters, applicability to, 164-5
  multilateralism versus unilateralism, 175, 176-9
  no-fly zones, 160
  peacekeeping (*See* Peacekeeping)
  practice in authorisation model, 158-61
  privatisation of collective security, danger of, 162-3
  problems with authorisation model, 524
  proportionality principle and, 316-17
  recommendation versus authorisation, 166
  Responsibility to Protect (*See* Responsibility to Protect)
  revival of past authorisations
    generally, 175, 179-82
    authority to determine material breach, 185-7
    Iraq (*See* Iraq)
    legacy of revival argument, 187-9
    material breach, 183-5
    weapons of mass destruction (WMD) and, 183
Autonomous weapons, 526
"Axis of evil," 42-3, 179, 369-70, 371
Azerbaijan
  Bishkek Protocol (1994), 303-4
  Nagorno-Karabakh, dispute with Armenia regarding, 302-4

Bahrain
  consent to intervention and, 473
  GCC intervention in, 467
  Iranian intervention in, 467

Bahrain, Islamic State and, 418
Baker, James, 183
Bali bombings (2002), 377
Bangladesh, humanitarian intervention in, 494-5
Ban Ki-moon, 142-3
Bannelier-Christakis, Karine, 466-7
Barbados, intervention in Grenada, 327-8
Barrow, Adama, 446, 449-50
Basic Principles on the Use of Force and Firearms by Law Enforcement Officials, 99-117
Belgium
  collective self-defence and, 341
  Congo and, 232
  extraction of nationals by, 335
  on humanitarian intervention, 490-1, 504
  Iraq, air strikes in, 453
  Libya, intervention in, 190-1
  Rome Statute and, 63
  "unable or unwilling" doctrine and, 416
*Bellum justum*, 24-6
Bentwich, Norman, 94
Berman, Frank, 354
Bethlehem, Daniel, 383, 387, 412
Bethlehem Principles
  imminence and, 383, 384, 397
  non-state actors, self-defence against, 412
  "unable or unwilling" doctrine and, 416, 418-21, 424-5, 426
Bianchi, Andrea, 6, 7
Biden, Joe, 45, 281-2, 294, 295, 342
Bingham, Tom (Lord), 57
Bin Issa Al-Khalifa, Hamad, 473
bin Laden, Osama, 114-17, 313, 368, 403, 411, 412, 429-32, 434-8
Bishkek Protocol (1994), 303-4
Blair, Tony, 180, 377-8
Blockades, 148
Blokker, Niels M., 178
Bocoum, Marie-Thérèse Keita, 245
Border incidents, 277, 285
Bosnia and Herzegovina
  Dayton Peace Agreement (1995), 236
  NATO intervention in, 236
  non-state actors in, 249-50
  Security Council Resolution 807 (1993), 235
  Security Council Resolution 836 (1993), 235
  Serbian intransigence in, 235-6
  Srebrenica massacre (1995), 236
  United Nations Protection Force (UNPROFOR), 235-6, 247-8
Botswana, South African intervention in, 400
Boutros-Ghali, Boutros, 142-3

Bowett, Derek, 307-8, 315
Brahimi Report (2000), 246-7, 254
Brandis, George, 383
Brazil
  Security Council, consideration for permanent member status, 138
  on use of force in self-defence in territory of other states, 266
Breaches of peace
  generally, 138, 143-4
  determinations, 147-8
Brennan, John, 433
Brothers to the Rescue, 118
Brownlie, Ian, 30, 98, 280, 362
Bryan Treaties (1913-1914), 65
Buchan, Russell, 99
Buchwald, Todd, 184
Budapest Convention (2001), 79
Burundi, AU intervention in, 477
Bush, George H.W., 197-8
Bush, George H.W., assassination attempt (1993)
  as armed attack, 98, 283-4
  armed reprisals in response to, 310
  necessity principle and, 283-312
  non-state actors, self-defence against, 405
  protection of nationals abroad and, 327, 330
Bush, George W., 42-3, 179-80, 187, 369-70, 371, 376, 407, 433, 524. *See also* Bush Doctrine
Bush Doctrine
  generally, 179-80
  contradictions in, 371
  international reaction to, 374-8
  Iraq War and, 371-3
  Obama Doctrine compared, 379-81
  pre-emptive self-defence and, 369-71
  in Syria, 373-4
Butler, Richard, 184-5

Cambodia, humanitarian intervention in, 494-5
Cameron, David, 193, 430-1
Canada
  foreign vessels, law enforcement actions against, 118
  Iraq, air strikes in, 453
  Libya, intervention in, 190-1
  "unable or unwilling" doctrine and, 416
Capstone Doctrine, 223
*Caroline* incident (1837)
  generally, 400
  anticipatory self-defence and, 360, 361, 362
  necessity principle and, 260-1, 297, 299, 300

non-state actors as perpetrators, 263, 400
proportionality principle and, 260-1, 297
self-defence and, 26, 296-7
Cassese, Antonio, 307, 507
Catholic Church, 25
Central African Republic
  African-led International Support Mission in the Central African Republic (MISCA), 244
  authorisation of force by Security Council in, 178
  consent to intervention and, 448
  EU intervention in, 159
  Operation Bepka, 244
  stabilisation missions in, 248
  United Nations Multidimensional Integrated Stabilization Mission in the Central African Republic (MINUSCA), 243-5, 247
Chad
  civil war in, 467, 470
  EU intervention in, 159
  French intervention in, 467, 470
  Libyan intervention in, 470
Chad, consent to intervention and, 448
Charter Article 2(4). *See* Prohibition on use of force
Chatham House Principles of International Law on the Use of Force by States in Self-Defence
  imminence and, 278, 381-96
  "unable or unwilling" doctrine and, 416-17
Chemical weapons
  Novichok poisoning, 114-15
  in Syria, 41-2, 315, 513, 514, 515-17
Chemical Weapons Convention (1997), 517
Chesterman, Simon, 163
Chicago Convention on International Civil Aviation (1944), 118
China
  "all necessary means" and, 42
  DRC, opposition to intervention in, 241
  India, border incidents with, 277
  Iraq, opposition to intervention in, 198-9
  Kosovo, opposition to intervention in, 199, 200-1
  Libya, authorisation of force by Security Council and, 191
  Manchuria, Japanese invasion of, 29, 49
  on NATO intervention in Yugoslavia, 503-4
  Rome Statute and, 63
  Serbia, NATO bombing of Chinese embassy in, 128
  Taiwan and, 42, 155

China (cont.)
  threat of force and, 42
  on use of force in self-defence in territory of other states, 266
Churchill, Winston, 29–30
Cicero, 24–5
Civilians, protection of
  authorisation of use of force by Security Council, 160
  international humanitarian law (IHL), 153, 434–5
  peacekeeping and, 247
  targeted killings and, 434–5
Civil wars, intervention in
  generally, 447, 461–2
  counterintervention, 469–72
  difficulty in defining civil war, 463
  negative equality principle, 462–5
    generally, 462–5
    defined, 462–5
    identifying authority to consent, 463
    lack of consensus regarding, 464
    non-international armed conflict and, 463–4
    in state practice, 464–5
    status quo, as supporting, 464
  purpose-based approach, 466–9
    consent to intervention and, 466–7
    legitimacy of intervention, 466
Clinton, Bill, 284
Clinton, Hillary, 91
"Coalitions of the willing," 163–4, 189, 218
Coercion
  consent to intervention, coercion negating, 474–5
  cyber operations, coercion versus influence, 83
  use of force, coercion as basis of *mens rea* requirement, 125–6
  VCLT and, 475
Cold War
  authorisation of use of force by Security Council during, 153–6
  nuclear weapons and, 46–54
  peacekeeping during, 230–4
Collective security
  failures of, 75–6
  League of Nations and, 135
  NATO and, 171
  peacekeeping emerging in failures of, 220
  privatisation of, danger of, 162–3
  prohibition on use of force and, 27
  UN Charter and, 135
Collective self-defence
  generally, 261, 336

armed attack requirement, 339
cyber attacks and, 343
ICJ and, 336, 337, 338–9
Korean War and, 341–2
League of Arab States and, 338
NATO and, 337–8, 342
nature of, 337–8
9/11 attacks and, 336, 338
partial application of ICJ framework, 340–2
regulation of, 338–43
request requirement, 339
in state practice, 340–2
UN Charter and, 336
Colombia
  consent to intervention and, 448
  Ecuador, intervention in, 347–8, 412
  Revolutionary Armed Forces of Colombia People's Army (FARC), 412
Commissions of inquiry (CoI)
  Iraq War, 14, 66, 151–3, 186, 188, 373
  prohibition on use of force and, 65–6
  Security Council and, 14
Commonwealth, cyber operations and, 84–5
Complementarity, 62
Concert of Europe, 27, 135
Conference on Security and Cooperation in Europe, 308
Congo. *See also* Democratic Republic of the Congo (DRC)
  Belgium and, 232
  Katanga province, 232
  peacekeeping in, 221
  stabilisation missions in, 248
  United Nations Operation in the Congo (ONUC), 232–3, 248
  Uniting for Peace (UfP) process and, 166–7
Consent to intervention
  generally, 445–6, 447, 484
  civil wars and, 466–7
  form of consent
    generally, 447, 472
    *ad hoc* versus *ex ante* consent, 476–7
    coercion negating consent, 474–5
    express consent, 473
    implicit consent, 473–4
    informal requests, 472–3
    retrospective consent not recognised, 474
    secret consent, 475–6
    treaty-based consent, 476–7
  ICJ and, 448, 450–2, 479
  identifying authority to consent
    generally, 447–8

civil wars and, 463
effective control test, 452–5
elected officials unable to take office, 449–50, 453
recognition and, 455–9
self-determination and, 459–61
sliding scale of authority, 449
VCLT and, 449
ILC on, 472
invitation versus, 447
lack of clarity regarding, 525
limitations on consent
generally, 447
actions external to consent agreement, 482
international humanitarian law (IHL) and, 470–83
international human rights law (IHRL) and, 470–83
peremptory norms, 483
scope or time frame of consent, actions exceeding, 480
self-determination, suppression of, 475–84
status of forces agreements and, 480–1
territorial limits, 483–4
withdrawal of consent, 479–80
no generally recognised right, 450, 451–2
non-state actors, use of force against, 446
peacekeeping and
generally, 226–7
as basic principle, 227
evolution of, 249–50
non-state actors and, 249–50
stabilisation missions and, 250
withdrawal of consent, 249
self-defence and, 450–1
status of forces agreements and, 480–1
targeted killings and, 429
"unable or unwilling" doctrine and, 426–7
uncertainty regarding entity authorised to consent, 446–7
Contextual imminence
capabilities of potential attacker and, 385
evolution from temporal imminence, 381, 384
expected timing of attack and, 384–5
gravity of threatened attack and, 385–6
intent of potential attacker and, 386–7
as *lex lata*, 397–8
necessity principle and, 381–97
previous attacks and, 387–9
probative value of previous attacks, 392–3
Soleimani drone strike and, 389–95

Convention on the Prevention and Punishment of the Crime of Genocide (1948), 508–10
Cook, Robin, 512
Cooperation Council for the Arab States of the Gulf, 454
*Corfu Channel* case (ICJ 1949)
*de minimis* threshold for use of force and, 110–11
humanitarian intervention and, 490
*mens rea* element of use of force and, 127
prohibition on use of force and, 34–5
Corn, Geoffrey, 393
Corten, Olivier, 109, 118, 125, 126, 161–2, 163, 276, 469
Côte d'Ivoire
"all necessary means" and, 195–6
authorisation of force by Security Council in, 160, 178, 195–6, 459
consent to intervention and, 448, 453, 456
French intervention in, 160, 195, 196
Security Council Resolution 1975 (2011), 195–6
uncertainty regarding leadership in, 456, 160, 195–6, 453, 456
United Nations Operation in Côte d'Ivoire (UNOCI), 160, 178, 195, 196
Cotonou Peace Agreement (1993), 203
Council of Europe, Convention on Cybercrime (Budapest Convention) (2001), 79
Countermeasures
prohibition on use of force and, 51–2
proportional forcible countermeasures, 290
proportionality principle and, 51
sanctions as, 52
Craft, Kelly, 267–8, 324
Crawford, James, 452
Crimea, Russian annexation of, 45, 49, 73, 332
Crimean War, 27
Croatia, independence of, 235
Cruz Report (2017), 255
Cuba
on authorisation of force by Security Council, 176
Cuban Missile Crisis (1962) and, 365–6
foreign civil aircraft, law enforcement actions against, 118
Soviet missiles, removal of, 366
"unable or unwilling" doctrine and, 416
Cummings, Dominic, 74–5
Customary international law
extensive versus restrictive approach, 10
ILC on, 9, 10

Customary international law (cont.)
  interpretation of *jus ad bellum* and, 6
  lack of appetite for changing, 523-4
  non-intervention principle in, 90
  objections of states, 9-10
  *opinio juris*
    humanitarian intervention and, 494, 507, 521
    ICJ Statute Article 38 and, 31
    interpretation of *jus ad bellum* and, 9-10
    non-state actors, self-defence against, 408
    pre-emptive self-defence and, 368
  pre-emptive self-defence and, 370
  prohibition on use of force as, 31-2, 75
  self-defence in, 32, 260-1
  state practice (*See* State practice)
  UN Charter, relation to, 32
Cyber attacks
  accumulation of events theory and, 294
  armed attack, use of force distinguished, 285-9
  as armed force, 96
  collective self-defence and, 343
  cyber operations and, 79-80
  hostile intent, 129
  indirect and long-term impacts of, 288
  non-physical effects of, 288-9
  proportionality principle and, 318-19
  self-defence and, 265-6, 271-2, 354-5
Cyber operations
  generally, 79
  as armed force, 98-102
  coercion versus influence, 83
  cyber attacks and, 79-80
  disagreement regarding, 83-4
  due diligence and, 83-4
  EU and, 84-5
  GGE process and, 81-3, 84, 271
  historical background, 81
  NATO and, 84
  OEWG and, 82-3
  "scholarly interventionism" and, 86
  as self-defence, 82, 84
  sovereignty and, 83
  suitability of existing rules, 80
  *Tallinn Manual*, 84, 86, 98, 101, 102, 286, 294
Cyprus
  Turkish invasion of, 49
  United Nations Peacekeeping Force in Cyprus (UNFICYP), 233
Czechoslovakia
  collective self-defence and, 336
  consent to intervention and, 448
  Soviet intervention in, 73, 342, 470-1
  Warsaw Pact intervention in, 475
Czech Republic, "unable or unwilling" doctrine and, 416

D'Amato, Anthony, 34
Dannenbaum, Tom, 70-1
Darfur
  African Union intervention in, 170, 213
  Janjaweed militia, 212
  peacekeeping in, 253-4
  Responsibility to Protect and, 212-13
  Security Council Resolution 1706 (2006), 213
  Security Council Resolution 2559 (2020), 239-40
Dayton Peace Agreement (1995), 236
Declaration on Principles of International Law Concerning Friendly Relations and Co-operation among States (1970)
  armed force and, 93, 102
  armed reprisals and, 308
  crime of aggression and, 56
  humanitarian intervention and, 491
  non-state actors, self-defence against, 415
  prohibition on use of force and, 31
  self-determination and, 460
Declaration on the Enhancement of the Effectiveness of the Principle of Refraining from the Threat or Use of Force in International Relations (1987), 126
Declaration on the Inadmissibility of Intervention in the Domestic Affairs of States (1965), 463
Declaration on the Non-Use of Force (1987), 93-4
Deeks, Ashley, 358, 427, 484
Definition of Aggression (1974)
  armed attack and, 108-9, 262, 267, 278-9, 327
  armed force and, 93, 102, 481
  crime of aggression and, 39-58, 107
  hostile intent and, 274-5
  humanitarian intervention and, 491
  Kampala Amendments, 59-60
  prohibition on use of force and, 31, 39
  Security Council and, 147-8
Democratic Republic of the Congo (DRC). *See also* Congo
  *Armed Activities* case (*See Armed Activities* case (ICJ 2005))
  attacks on peacekeepers in, 252-3
  consent to intervention and, 448
  EU intervention in, 240
  French intervention in, 241

Intervention Brigade, 241–2, 252
Lusaka Ceasefire Agreement (1999), 240
Movement for the Liberation of the Congo (MLC), 451
M23 rebel group, 241
non-state actors in, 249–50
Operation Artemis, 240
Security Council Resolution 2277 (2016), 241
Security Council Resolution 2502 (2019), 241
stabilisation missions in, 248
Ugandan intervention in, 409–10, 451, 479
UK intervention in, 241
United Nations Observer Mission in the DRC (MONUC), 240–1, 252–3
United Nations Stabilization Mission in the Democratic Republic of the Congo (MONUSCO), 241–2, 247, 250, 251, 252
Denmark
humanitarian intervention in Syria and, 514
Iraq, air strikes in, 453
Libya, intervention in, 190–1
De Wet, Erika, 449, 452, 453, 460
Dinniss, Harrison, 286
Dinstein, Yoram, 30, 44, 151, 201, 278, 284, 315, 345, 359–60, 381, 465
Distinction principle, 4–5
Doe, Samuel, 203, 499
*Dogger Bank* inquiry (1904), 65
Domestic courts, interpretation of *jus ad bellum* and, 14
Dominican Republic, consent to intervention and, 448
Drones. *See also specific country*
Soleimani drone strike (*See* Soleimani, Qassem, targeted killing of (2020))
targeted killings, use in, 429, 433, 438–9

East Pakistan, humanitarian intervention in, 494–5
East Timor, authorisation of force by Security Council in, 178
Economic Community of West African States (ECOWAS)
generally, 203
authorisation of use of force by, 169
consent to intervention and, 477–8
ECOWAS Monitoring Group (ECOMOG), 203–4, 205, 238–9, 477–8
Gambia, intervention in, 449–50, 459, 478
Liberia, intervention in, 169, 203–4, 499–500, 520–1
peacekeeping by, 221

Sierra Leone, intervention in, 169, 205, 238–9, 500–1, 520–1
Ecuador
Colombian intervention in, 347–8, 412
"unable or unwilling" doctrine and, 416
Effective control standard of attribution, 404–13
Egan, Brian, 383
Egypt
Iraq, opposition to intervention in, 198–9
Six Day War, 363–4
United Nations Emergency Force (UNEF I), 224, 226, 230–2, 246, 249, 363–4
United Nations Emergency Force (UNEF II), 233–4
Eichmann, Adolf, 113–20
El Salvador, Nicaragua assisting rebels in, 277, 310–39, 404–5, 409
Endara, Guillermo, 329, 449
Entebbe hostage crisis (1976), 334
Erdogan, Recep Tayyip, 50
Eritrea-Ethiopia Claims Commission, 51, 55, 277
Esper, Mark, 270, 335
Estonia
on armed force, 100
cyber attacks and, 79, 100–1, 260–343
cyber operations and, 85–6
Ethiopia
Eritrea-Ethiopia Claims Commission, 51, 55, 277
Italian conquest of, 29
Somalia, intervention in, 347–8
European Convention of Human Rights (ECHR) (1950)
*jus ad bellum* and, 71
right to life and, 437
European Court of Justice, 151
European Union
Central African Republic, intervention in, 159
Chad, intervention in, 159
commissions of inquiry (CoI) and, 65–6
cyber operations and, 84–5
DRC, intervention in, 240
Guidelines on the Recognition of New States in Eastern Europe and in the Soviet Union, 456
Independent International Fact-Finding Mission on the Conflict in Georgia, 65–6, 109–10, 129, 378, 462
Lisbon Treaty (1999), 169
on pre-emptive self-defence, 377–8
Security Council, relation to, 169
Extraction of nationals, 335–6

## Index

Falklands War (1982)
  breach of peace and, 147, 302
  recovery of territory and, 35
  self-defence and, 302, 353–4
Findlay, Trevor, 228–9
Fink, Jonathan, 253
Finland
  on armed attack by non-state actors, 265–6
  on armed force, 98, 99
  collective self-defence and, 343
  cyber attacks and, 263–88, 318–19
  cyber operations and, 85–6
  NATO and, 343
First World War, 27
Fletcher, George, 489
Focarelli, Carlo, 217
Foreign civil aircraft, law enforcement actions against, 118
Foreign individuals or groups, law enforcement actions against, 116–17
Foreign vessels, law enforcement actions against, 118
Fox, Gregory, 446, 462, 464, 470
France
  accumulation of events theory and, 294
  on armed attack by non-state actors, 266
  Chad, intervention in, 467, 470
  consent to intervention and, 448, 453
  Côte d'Ivoire, intervention in, 160, 195, 196
  cyber attacks and, 289
  DRC, intervention in, 241
  extraction of nationals by, 335
  humanitarian intervention in Syria and, 512, 514
  Iraq and
    air strikes in, 453
    intervention in, 197–8
    no-fly zones, 498–9
  on Kosovo intervention, 200
  Libya, intervention in, 190–1
  Mali, intervention in, 242–3, 453, 465, 466, 467–8
  on NATO intervention in Yugoslavia, 503
  Rwanda, intervention in, 177–8
  Suez crisis and, 230–1
  Syria and, 458–9, 512, 514, 516–17
Franck, Thomas, 72–3, 204, 364, 506

Gabon, consent to intervention and, 448
Gaddafi, Muammar, 145, 189–90, 191, 193, 194, 457–8

Gambia
  authorisation of force by Security Council in, 459
  consent to intervention and, 449–50, 453, 459
  ECOMOG, participation in, 203
  ECOWAS intervention in, 449–50, 459, 478
  Security Council Resolution 2337 (2017), 449–50
  Senegalese intervention in, 449–50
  uncertainty regarding leadership in, 446, 449–50, 453
Gbagbo, Laurent, 195–6, 456
Geneva Conventions (1949)
  Common Article 2, 433
  Common Article 3, 433
Geneva Protocol on the Pacific Settlement of International Disputes (1924), 55
Genocide
  humanitarian intervention to prevent, 508–10
  ICJ and, 510–11
Georgia
  Abkhazia region, 331–2
  Chechen rebels in, 412, 417
  cyber attacks and, 100–1, 287
  Independent International Fact-Finding Mission on the Conflict in Georgia, 65–6, 109–10, 129, 378, 462
  Russian intervention in, 65–6, 79–80, 317, 325, 331–2
  South Ossetia region, 325, 331–2
Germany
  on armed attack by non-state actors, 265
  Security Council, consideration for permanent member status, 138
  Special Arbitral Tribunal and, 307
  "unable or unwilling" doctrine and, 416
Ghana, participation in ECOMOG, 203
Ghouta chemical weapons attack (2013), 41–2, 216, 513
Glennon, Michael, 72–3, 74, 76
Global war on terror, 433–6
Goldsmith, Peter (Lord), 377–8
Goodman, Ryan, 333–41
Gravity element of use of force, 105, 123–4
Gray, Christine, 77, 169, 194, 209, 213, 214, 249, 253, 278, 279, 347, 348, 364, 502
Green, James A., 275–6, 297, 318, 320
Greenwood, Christopher, 324–5
Grenada
  Barbadian intervention in, 327–8
  consent to intervention and, 448
  extraction of nationals from, 336

Jamaican intervention in, 327-8
US intervention in, 73, 327-30, 449
Grigsby, Alex, 82
Grotius, Hugo, 25
Group of Governmental Experts on Advancing Responsible State Behaviour in Cyberspace in the Context of International Security (GGE), 81-3, 84, 271
Group of 77, 505
Guaidó, Juan, 44-56
Guinea, participation in ECOMOG, 203
Gulf Cooperation Council (GCC), 214, 467, 473
Gulf War (1991)
  "all necessary means" and, 41, 157-8, 201
  authorisation of force by Security Council in, 157-8
  collective self-defence and, 341-2
  Operation Desert Storm, 157, 176, 182, 316-17
  proportionality principle and, 316-17
  Security Council involvement in, 53-4
  self-defence and, 349-51, 352
  threat of force and, 41
  US and, 41, 53-4, 157
Guterres, António, 142-3, 173
Guyana, proxy law enforcement actions and, 122-3

Hadi, Abdo Rabbo Mansour, 454-5, 468, 470-83
Hague Convention III Relative to the Opening of Hostilities (1907), 27
Hague Convention I on the Pacific Settlement of International Disputes (1899), 27, 65
Haiti
  authorisation of force by Security Council in, 147, 159-60, 164, 178
  extraction of nationals from, 335
  Governors Island Agreement, 159-60
Hamas, 292, 295
Hammarskjöld, Dag, 226, 231
Harbouring standard of attribution, 407-8
Helsinki Final Act, 31
Henkin, Louis, 74, 76
Heyns, Christof, 416, 438
Hezbollah, 285, 319, 359, 412
Higgins, Rosalyn (ICJ Judge), 263, 279-80, 337, 496
High-Level Panel on Threats, Challenges and Change, 187-8, 208, 209-10, 375
Hilpold, Peter, 211-12
Holy Roman Empire, 25
Hostile intent, 129, 274-5

Humanitarian intervention
  generally, 486-7
  as circumstance precluding wrongfulness, 487, 492-3
  crime of aggression versus, 59-60, 61
  failure of Security Council as justification for, 507-8
  genocide, to prevent, 508-10
  ICJ and, 490-1, 492, 493, 496-7, 504
  interpretation of *jus ad bellum* and, 8-9
  in Iraq, 497-9, 521
  *jus cogens* and, 493, 494
  in Kosovo, 501-4
    generally, 487, 521
    criticism of, 503-4, 505
    ICJ and, 504
    Operation Allied Force, 502-4
    as *sui generis* case, 506
    UN Charter and, 490-1
  as *lex lata*, 519
  in Liberia, 499-500, 520-1
  muscular humanitarianism, 505
  *opinio juris* and, 494, 507
  peremptory norms and, 493
  Responsibility to Protect and, 487, 520-1, 525-6
  self-defence versus, 494-5
  in Sierra Leone, 500-1, 520-1
  in state practice generally, 487, 494, 511-12
  in Syria
    generally, 487, 512-13
    debate regarding air strikes, 513-14
    Responsibility to Protect and, 514
  "thin red line" and, 506-7
  UN Charter and
    generally, 487
    authorisation of use of force by Security Council and, 488-9
    General Assembly and, 488
    implied exception to prohibition on use of force, 489-91
    Kosovo and, 490-1
    prohibition on use of force and, 487-8
    restrictive interpretation of, 491-2
    self-defence and, 489
    Uniting for Peace (UfP) process and, 508
    violation of international law, viewed as, 504-5
Hungary
  on authorisation of force by Security Council, 177
  consent to intervention and, 448
  Soviet intervention in, 73
Hussein, Saddam, 41, 180, 197, 497

ICJ. *See* International Court of Justice (ICJ)
IHL. *See* International humanitarian law (IHL)
IHRL. *See* International human rights law (IHRL)
ILC. *See* International Law Commission (ILC)
Imminence
   anticipatory self-defence and
      generally, 360–1
      expansionist approach, 361
      ICJ and, 362–3
      international jurisprudence, 362–3
      restrictionist approach, 361–2
      Six Day War and, 363–4
   Bethlehem Principles and, 383, 384, 397
   Chatham House Principles and, 278, 381–96
   contextual imminence (*See* Contextual imminence)
   defining, 381
   expansion of, 370–1
   Leiden Policy Recommendations and, 382
   non-state actors, self-defence against, 403–4
   permanent imminence, 387–8
   pre-emptive self-defence (*See* Pre-emptive self-defence)
   targeted killings and, 383, 388
   terrorism and, 388
Implementation of the Declaration on the Granting of Independence to Colonial Countries and Peoples (1972), 460
Implied powers doctrine, 162–3
Independent International Commission on Kosovo, 506
India
   China, border incidents with, 277
   Goa, invasion of, 35
   humanitarian intervention by, 494–5
   Pakistan and, 353
   Security Council, consideration for permanent member status, 138
Indonesia, United Nations Security Force (UNSF), 224
In Larger Freedom, 208, 210, 375–6
Institut de Droit International, 462–3
Inter-American Treaty of Reciprocal Assistance (1947), 169
Interception of armed attack, 359–60
International Atomic Energy Agency (IAEA), 180, 186, 374
International Commission on Intervention and State Sovereignty (ICISS), 207, 209–10
International Committee of the Red Cross (ICRC), 435–6

International Court of Justice (ICJ)
   accumulation of events theory and, 291, 402–3
   advisory opinions, 11
   anticipatory self-defence and, 362–3
   *Armed Activities* case (*See Armed Activities* case (ICJ 2005))
   armed attack and (*See* Armed attack)
   armed force and, 95–6, 99, 102–4
   armed reprisals and, 308
   authorisation of use of force by Security Council and, 162
   collective self-defence and, 336, 337, 338–9
   consent to intervention and, 448, 450–2, 479
   *Corfu Channel* case (*See Corfu Channel* case (ICJ 1949))
   crime of aggression and, 108
   *Fisheries Jurisdiction* case (1998), 118
   foreign vessels, law enforcement actions against and, 118
   General Assembly and, 140–1, 142
   genocide and, 510–11
   humanitarian intervention and, 490–1, 492, 493, 496–7, 504
   ICJ Statute Article 38
      interpretation of *jus ad bellum* and, 6
      *opinio juris* and, 31
      state practice and, 31
   *Legality of Use of Force* case (1999), 490–1, 504
   *mens rea* element of use of force and, 103–26
   necessity principle and, 297, 301–10
   *Nicaragua* case (*See Nicaragua* case (ICJ 1986))
   non-intervention principle and, 91–2
   non-state actors, self-defence against, 400, 404–5, 409–10, 439
   *Nuclear Weapons* advisory opinion (*See Nuclear Weapons* advisory opinion (ICJ 1996))
   *Oil Platforms* case (*See Oil Platforms* case (ICJ 2003))
   peacekeeping and, 225
   pre-emptive self-defence and, 378–9
   prohibition on use of force and, 39, 75, 77
   proportional forcible countermeasures, 290
   proportionality principle and, 297, 320
   *Reparations for Injuries* advisory opinion (1949), 162
   reporting requirement for self-defence and, 344–5, 346, 347
   Security Council and, 139–40, 151
   self-defence and, 260
   threat of force and, 40–1, 44, 46–7, 54–5
   *Wall* advisory opinion (2004), 263, 400

## Index

International Covenant on Civil and Political
    Rights (ICCPR) (1966)
  extraterritoriality and, 437
  right to life and, 68, 436-7
  self-determination and, 460-1
International Covenant on Economic, Social and
    Cultural Rights (1966), 460-1
International Criminal Court (ICC)
  complementarity and, 62
  crime of aggression and
    defined, 57-8
    humanitarian intervention and, 59-60
    inclusion of, 57
    jurisdiction, impact of, 61-4
    use of force distinguished, 107, 108
  generally, 5
  jurisdiction
    crime of aggression, impact on, 61-4
    *ratione personae*, 61
    *ratione temporis*, 62
  Kampala Conference (2010), 57, 59-60
  Libya and, 190, 214
  prosecutorial policy, 61-2
  Rome Statute, 31, 48, 57-60, 107, 108
  states not accepting amendments to Rome
    Statute, 63
  threat of force and, 48
International criminal law, relation to *jus ad*
    *bellum*, 5
International Criminal Tribunal for the former
    Yugoslavia (ICTY)
  non-state actors, self-defence against, 405-6
  Security Council compared, 149
  *Tadic* case (1995), 405-6
  use of force and, 14
International humanitarian law (IHL)
  civilians, protection of, 153
  consent to intervention and, 470-83
  international human rights law, relation to, 66-7
  necessity principle in *jus ad bellum* compared,
    4-5, 299
  proportionality principle in *jus ad bellum*
    compared, 4-5
  Security Council subject to, 151-3
  targeted killings and
    generally, 428, 432
    civilians, protection of, 434-5
    continuous combat function, 434-5
    duty to capture, 435-6
    intensity requirement, 433-4
    in non-international armed conflict, 433-4
    organization requirement, 433-4
International human rights law (IHRL)
  armed conflict, applicability to, 436
  consent to intervention and, 470-83
  international humanitarian law, relation to,
    66-7
  prohibition on use of force, relation to, 67
    generally, 5, 24
    aggression, determinations of, 70
    implications of, 70-2
    jurisdiction of human rights bodies and, 71
    positive obligations of states and, 71-2
    right to life and, 68-9, 71
  rightslessness, 70
  right to life
    ECHR and, 437
    HRC and, 68-9, 71, 418-38
    ICCPR and, 68, 436-7
    non-arbitrariness standard, 437
    targeted killings and, 436-7
  Soleimani drone strike and, 71
  targeted killings and
    generally, 71, 428, 436
    extraterritoriality and, 437-9
    right to life and, 436-7
International Law Association, 445
International Law Commission (ILC)
  on armed reprisals, 308-9
  on consent to intervention, 472
  on countermeasures, 52
  on crime of aggression, 56-7
  on customary international law, 9, 10
  Draft Articles on Responsibility of States for
    Internationally Wrongful Acts
    (DARSIWA) (2001), 48-9, 52, 53, 299,
    308-9, 446, 492
  Draft Articles on the Responsibility of
    International Organisations, 38, 151, 152-3
  Draft Code of Offences against the Peace and
    Security of Mankind, 56-7
  on prohibition on use of force, 38-9
  on self-defence, 53
International Military Tribunal (Nuremberg
    Tribunal), 55-6, 57, 362
Interpretation of *jus ad bellum*
  customary international law and, 6
  disagreement regarding, 7
  domestic courts and, 14
  humanitarian intervention and, 8-9
  ICJ and
    advisory opinions, 11
    decisions, 14-15
    ICJ Statute Article 38, 6

Interpretation of *jus ad bellum* (cont.)
  justifications for use of force, 10–11
  legal scholars and, 15–18
  NGOs and, 16
  *opinio juris* and, 9–10
  refraining from use of force, 12
  Security Council commissions of inquiry and, 14
  self-defence and, 8
  silence versus acquiescence, 13
  state practice and, 9–10
  subsidiary means, 14–15
  treaties and, 6
  UN Charter, 7
  unilateral statements of states, 11–12
  VCLT and, 7–8
Iran
  arms embargo, 160–1
  in "axis of evil," 42–3, 179, 369–70, 377
  Bahrain, intervention in, 467
  Islamic Revolutionary Guard Corps (IRGC), 267–8
  Joint Comprehensive Plan of Action, 43
  *Oil Platforms* case (*See Oil Platforms* case (ICJ 2003))
  on pre-emptive self-defence, 372, 377
  Quds force, 267–8, 293, 389, 391
  sanctions, 160–1
  Security Council Resolution 1929 (2010), 160–1
  Soleimani drone strike (*See* Soleimani, Qassem, targeted killing of (2020))
  Stuxnet cyber attack, 79–80, 96, 97–8, 100–1, 160–1, 287
  Syria and, 512
  "unable or unwilling" doctrine and, 416
  US and
    armed attack on embassy of, 271
    attempted rescue of hostages by, 333–4
    downing of civil aircraft, 122, 127
    "Eagle Claw" mission, 271
    oil platforms, armed attack on, 274, 301–10, 317–18
    proportionality principle and, 317–18
    threat of force by, 43
    threat to military vessels of, 268, 293
    use of armed force by, 97–112
  Yemen, intervention in, 455, 470, 471
Iran-Iraq War, 274
Iraq. *See also* Iraq War (2003)
  "all necessary means" and, 179, 180, 497–8
  in "axis of evil," 42–3, 179, 369–70, 371

  collective self-defence and, 336, 338, 340–1
  Compensation Commission, 50–1
  Compensation Fund, 50–1
  consent to intervention and, 473, 474, 479, 481, 482, 483
  drones, use in, 438
  France and
    air strikes in, 453
    intervention in, 197–8
    no-fly zones, 498–9
  humanitarian intervention in, 497–9, 521
  implied authorisation of use of force by Security Council, 197–9
  Islamic State in, 406, 418, 421–2, 446, 483
  Israeli missile strike on nuclear plant in (*See* Osiraq nuclear power plant missile strike (1981))
  Kuwait, invasion of, 35, 41, 50–1, 129, 157, 341–2, 474, 476 (*See also* Gulf War (1991))
  no-fly zones in, 197–9, 498–9
  Operation Desert Fox, 184–5
  Operation Desert Strike, 198
  Operation Poised Hammer, 198
  Operation Provide Comfort, 198
  Operation Southern Watch, 198
  opposition to intervention in, 198–9
  revival of past authorisations of use of force by Security Council
    generally, 179–82, 371–2
    authority to determine material breach, 185–7
    legacy of revival argument, 187–9
    material breach, 183–5
    Resolution 678 (1990), 179, 180–5
  Russia and
    no-fly zones, 498–9
    opposition to intervention in, 198
  safe havens in, 197–8
  sanctions, 156–7, 351–2, 372
  Security Council Resolution 660 (1990), 179, 182
  Security Council Resolution 661 (1990), 351
  Security Council Resolution 678 (1990)
    generally, 175
    breadth and scope of authorisation, 189
    development of authorisation method and, 157
    humanitarian intervention and, 497–8
    mandate of, 182–3
    multilateralism versus unilateralism, 176–9
    proportionality principle and, 316–17
    revival of, 179, 180–5

## Index

Security Council Resolution 687 (1991)
  cease fire under, 187
  Compensation Fund, 50-1
  material breach of, 183-5
  revival of past authorisations and, 179, 180-2
Security Council Resolution 688 (1991), 145, 197-8, 497-8
Security Council Resolution 692 (1991), 50-1
Security Council Resolution 707 (1993), 184
Security Council Resolution 1441 (2002)
  material breach and, 180, 185-7
  poor drafting of, 188
  revival of authorisations and, 180-2
Turkish intervention in, 347-8, 400, 412, 479-80
UK and
  intervention in, 197-8, 453
  no-fly zones, 498-9
United Nations Monitoring, Verification and Inspection Commission (UNMOVIC), 180, 186
United Nations Special Commission (UNSCOM), 184-5
US and
  air strikes by, 309, 330, 453
  embassy, armed attack on, 269, 281
  intervention in, 197-8
  Islamic State, action against, 483-4
  no-fly zones, 498-9
  targeted killings by, 334-5
  weapons of mass destruction (WMD) and, 371
Iraq War (2003)
  generally, 1
  Bush Doctrine and, 371-3
  commissions of inquiry (CoI), 14, 66, 151-3, 186, 188, 373
  conventional weapons in, 2
  debate regarding, 49
  Operation Iraqi Freedom, 180, 185, 187, 194
  pre-emptive self-defence and, 371-3
  Secretariat and, 143
  as violation of prohibition on use of force, 73
Islamic State
  collective self-defence and, 336, 338, 340-1
  imminence and, 388
  in Iraq, 406, 418, 421-2, 446, 483
  non-state actors, self-defence against, 406
  protection of nationals abroad and, 334-5
  Saudi Arabia and, 418
  Security Council Resolution 2249 (2015), 388, 421
  self-defence and, 266
  in Syria, 406, 416, 417-18, 421-4, 425, 465
  as terrorist group, 466
  UK action against, 430-1
  US action against, 416, 417-18
  in Yemen, 469
Israel
  abductions by, 113-20
  accumulation of events theory and, 292-3
  on armed attack by non-state actors, 265
  on armed force, 100, 101
  cyber attacks and, 318-19
  cyber operations and, 85-6
  drones, use of, 438
  Gaza, raids in, 292, 319, 321-2, 402-3, 438
  Hezbollah and, 359
  interception of armed attack and, 359
  Iraq, missile strike on nuclear plant in (See Osiraq nuclear power plant missile strike (1981))
  "Iron Dome," 359
  Lebanon, intervention in, 285, 309, 400, 412
  Operation Cast Lead, 292, 321-2
  Operation Change Direction, 319
  Operation Guardian of the Walls, 292, 322
  Operation Orchard, 373
  Operation Pillar of Defense, 292
  Operation Protective Edge, 292, 321, 322
  protection of nationals abroad and, 333-4
  Rome Statute and, 63
  self-defence and, 285
  Six Day War, 363-4
  Syria, air strikes in, 292-3, 373-4, 387, 524-5
  targeted killings by, 114-17, 428
  Tunisia, intervention in, 147, 400, 410, 411-12
  Uganda, rescue of hostages in, 334
  "unable or unwilling" doctrine and, 416
  United Nations Emergency Force (UNEF I), 224, 226, 230-2, 246
  United Nations Emergency Force (UNEF II), 233-4
Italy
  Abyssinia, conquest of, 29
  Libya, intervention in, 190-1
  on protection of nationals abroad, 334

Jamaica, intervention in Grenada, 327-8
Jammeh, Yahya, 446, 449-50
Japan
  Manchuria, invasion of, 29, 49
  Security Council, consideration for permanent member status, 138
Jennings, Robert Yewdall (ICJ Judge), 279, 337, 338-9

Jordan
    air strikes in Iraq, 453
    Islamic State and, 418
    opposition to intervention in Iraq, 198-9
Joyner, Christopher, 97-8
*Jus ad bellum*
    conceptual approach, 6-17
    ECHR and, 71
    epiphenomenal nature of, 523
    failures of, 3
    goals of, 2-3
    international criminal law, relation to, 5
    interpretation of (*See* Interpretation of *jus ad bellum*)
    *jus in bello*, relation to, 4-5, 388-9
    as *lex specialis*, 5, 66-7, 69, 71
    necessity principle, international humanitarian law (IHL) compared, 299
    protection of nationals abroad and, 323
    weapons of mass destruction (WMD) and, 2
*Jus cogens*
    *de minimis* threshold for use of force and, 111
    humanitarian intervention and, 493, 494
    prohibition on use of force as, 24, 38-40, 111
    Security Council subject to, 151
    threat of force, prohibition not deemed, 48
*Jus in bello*
    *jus ad bellum*, relation to, 4-5, 388-9
    proportionality principle in, 316
Justifications for use of force
    interpretation of *jus ad bellum*, 10-11
    prohibition on use of force and, 76-8
    self-defence, 11
Just war doctrine, 24-6

Kabbah, Ahmad Tejan, 204, 500-1
Kabila, Laurent, 240, 409, 479
Kata'ib Hezbollah, 74-5, 267-8, 281, 293, 327, 334-5
Kellogg-Briand Pact (1928)
    generally, 1
    adoption of, 28-9
    contracting parties, limitation to, 29
    crime of aggression not recognised, 56
    forcible measures short of war, omission of, 29
    possibility of war as policy, 29
    self-defence, omission of, 29, 259
    weaknesses of, 29
Kelsen, Hans, 140, 144, 349-50
Kennedy, John F., 365-6
Kenya
    al-Shabaab in, 406, 415-16, 422-3
    consent to intervention and, 448
    on humanitarian intervention, 495
    self-defence and, 415-16, 422-3
    Somalia, intervention in, 415-16, 422-3
    "unable or unwilling" doctrine and, 422-3
    US embassy, armed attack on, 270-1, 273, 283-312, 411, 436
Khan, Reyaad, 96, 114-17, 383, 388, 392-8, 429-38
Kim Jong-nam, 115
Koh, Harold, 431, 432
Kohen, Marcelo, 163
Korean War (1950-1953)
    generally, 147
    collective self-defence and, 341-2
    General Assembly and, 155-6
    Security Council and, 154-6
    Uniting for Peace (UfP) process and, 155-6
Kosovo
    "all necessary means" and, 501-2
    humanitarian intervention in, 501-4
        generally, 487, 521
        criticism of, 503-4, 505
        ICJ and, 504
        Operation Allied Force, 502-4
        as *sui generis* case, 506
        UN Charter and, 490-1
    implied authorisation of use of force by Security Council, 199-201
    independence of, 450-1
    Independent International Commission on Kosovo, 506
    Kosovo Liberation Army (KLA), 199, 501
    NATO intervention in, 36, 48, 73, 127, 199-201, 207, 223
    Operation Allied Force, 200
    peacekeeping in, 223
    Security Council Resolution 1160 (1998), 501-2
    Security Council Resolution 1199 (1998), 199-200, 501-2
    Security Council Resolution 1203 (1998), 199-200, 501-2
    Uniting for Peace (UfP) process and, 166-7
Kretzmer, David, 309-10
Kritsiotis, Dino, 316, 340, 345, 347, 348, 350, 352
Kunz, Joseph L., 278, 337
Kuwait
    consent to intervention and, 474
    Iraqi invasion of, 35, 41, 50-1, 129, 157, 341-2, 474, 476 (*See also* Gulf War (1991))

Ladsous, Hervé, 243
Lavrov, Sergei, 192
Law enforcement actions, use of force distinguished, 112–18. *See also* Use of force
League of Arab States
  collective self-defence and, 337–8
  Libya and, 214
  Yemen and, 454
League of Nations
  collective security and, 135
  Covenant, 1, 28
  creation of, 28
  League Council, 28
  self-defence, omission of, 259
Lebanon
  collective self-defence and, 336
  extraction of nationals from, 335
  Israeli intervention in, 285, 309, 400, 412
  Security Council Resolution 467 (1980), 228
  United Nations Interim Force in Lebanon (UNIFIL), 228, 233–4, 247
Lederman, Marty, 393
Legal scholars, interpretation of *jus ad bellum* and, 15–18
Leiden Policy Recommendations on Counter-Terrorism and International Law
  imminence and, 382
  terrorism and, 436
  "unable or unwilling" doctrine and, 416, 417, 418–20, 425–6
Lesaffer, Randall, 27–8, 30
Lesotho, SADC intervention in, 478
*Lex ferenda*
  generally, 17
  pre-emptive self-defence as, 371
*Lex lata*
  generally, 17
  accumulation of events theory not deemed, 295
  contextual imminence as, 397–8
  humanitarian intervention as, 519
  pre-emptive self-defence as, 371, 374
*Lex specialis*, *jus ad bellum* as, 5, 66–7, 69, 71
Liberia
  authorisation of force by Security Council in, 178
  Cotonou Peace Agreement (1993), 203
  ECOWAS intervention in, 169, 203–4, 499–500, 520–1
  extraction of nationals from, 335
  humanitarian intervention in, 499–500, 520–1

implied authorisation of use of force by Security Council, 203–4
Libya
  abductions in, 114–20
  "all necessary means" and, 215
  arms embargo, 190, 192, 458
  authorisation of force by Security Council in
    generally, 160, 189–91
    disputes regarding, 191
    opposition forces, assisting, 191–3
    regime change and, 194–5
  Chad, intervention in, 470
  drones, use in, 438
  extraction of nationals from, 335–6
  French intervention in, 190–1
  on humanitarian intervention, 495
  Human Rights Council and, 190
  ICC and, 190, 214
  National Transitional Council (NTC), 457–8
  NATO intervention in, 172, 190–2, 193, 194, 213–14, 520
  no-fly zones in, 214
  Responsibility to Protect and, 213–15, 520
  Security Council and, 145
  Security Council Resolution 1970 (2011)
    generally, 190
    arms embargo, 458
    opposition forces, assisting, 192
    Responsibility to Protect and, 213
    threats to peace and, 145
  Security Council Resolution 1973 (2011)
    generally, 190
    opposition forces, assisting, 192, 193
    regime change and, 194–5
    Responsibility to Protect and, 214–15, 520
    threats to peace and, 145
  Security Council Resolution 2016 (2011), 191
  Transitional National Council, 191
  US air strikes in, 309, 310, 330
Lieblich, Eliav, 69–70
Lillilch, Richard B., 489
Lisbon Treaty (1999), 169
Lobel, Jules, 183
Lotrionte, Catherine, 97–8
Lubell, Noam, 359, 376, 386
Luck, Edward, 211
Lusaka Ceasefire Agreement (1999), 240

Maduro, Nicolás, 44–56
Mali
  African-led International Support Mission to Mali (AFISMA), 242–3

Mali (cont.)
  Agreement for Peace and Reconciliation in Mali, 243
  "all necessary means" and, 242–3
  civil war in, 465, 466, 467–8
  consent to intervention and, 448, 453
  French intervention in, 242–3, 453, 465, 466, 467–8
  Le Mouvement national de libération de l'Azawad (MLNA), 467–8
  Security Council Resolution 2085 (2012), 242
  Security Council Resolution 2100 (2013), 242
  Security Council Resolution 2584 (2021), 243
  stabilisation missions in, 248
  United Nations Peacekeeping Mission in Mali (MINUSMA), 242–3, 247, 250
Martin, Andrew, 94
Material breach
  authority to determine, 185–7
  revival of past authorisations and, 183–5
McCain, John, 513
Menezes, Jean Charles da Silva e de, 113–29
*Mens rea*
  armed attack
    ICJ and, 274
    self-defence, required for, 274–6
  crime of aggression, 60–1
  use of force
    generally, 125–6
    coercion as basis of requirement, 125–6
    hostile intent, 128–9
    ICJ and, 103–26
    intention versus general motives for action, 126–7
    mistake and, 127–8
Mexico on use of force in self-defence in territory of other states, 266
Milanovic, Marko, 509
Milley, Mark A., 390
Milošević, Slobodan, 200, 501, 502
Multilateralism, 175, 176–9
Murphy, Sean D., 378, 473

Nagorno-Karabakh dispute, 302–4
Namibia
  Kosovo, opposition to intervention in, 200–1
  Lusaka Ceasefire Agreement (1999), 240
Napoleon, 27
Nasser, Gamel Abdel, 363–4
Nationals abroad, protection of
  generally, 261, 322–4
  armed attack, attacks on nationals as, 324–7

  assassination attempts and, 327, 330
  extraction of nationals, 335–6
  foreign governments
    attacks or threats to nationals by, 327–33
    "unable or unwilling" doctrine and, 333–5
  future harm, prevention of, 330–3
  Islamic State and, 334–5
  limitations on, 327
  proportionality principle and, 329
  as self-defence, 325
  Soleimani drone strike and, 323–6, 330–1, 334–5
  targeted killings as, 323–6, 330–1, 334–5
  UN Charter Article 51, 324–5
NATO. *See* North Atlantic Treaty Organization (NATO)
Natural disasters, 212
*Naulilaa* case (1928), 27
Navalny, Alexei, 45
Necessity principle
  accumulation of events theory and, 263–312
  armed reprisals and, 307
  assassination attempts and, 283–312
  border disputes and, 305
  contextual imminence and, 381–97
  delay in response, effect of, 301–2
  dual role of, 298
  as enabling actions in self-defence, 261–98
  further attacks, prevention of, 286–312
  ICJ and, 297, 301–10
  identity of perpetrator, relevance of, 312–13
  immediacy requirement, 301–2, 304
  imminent threat of further attacks, 286–312
  international humanitarian law (IHL) compared, 4–5, 299
  lack of alternatives required, 299–300
  lack of direct references to, 316
  merger with proportionality principle, 320
  nature of weapons used, relevance of, 313
  9/11 attacks and, 283–312
  non-state actors, self-defence against, 312–13, 402
  reasonableness requirement, 300–2
  recovery of territory and, 302–5
  Security Council and, 151
  self-defence generally, 260–1
  in state practice, 297–8
  targeted killings and, 430–1
Negative equality principle, 462–5. *See also* Civil wars, intervention in
Negroponte, John, 369
Netanyahu, Benjamin, 292–3

Netherlands
  armed attack, use of force distinguished, 285-6
  on armed attack by non-state actors, 265
  on armed force, 93-101, 102
  commissions of inquiry (CoI) and, 66
  cyber attacks and, 288, 289
  Iraq, air strikes in, 453
  on NATO intervention in Yugoslavia, 503
  Rome Statute and, 63
  "unable or unwilling" doctrine and, 416
New Zealand
  on armed force, 99-100, 101
  cyber attacks and, 286
  cyber operations and, 85-6
Nicaragua
  *contras* in, 55, 102-26, 451, 496-7
  El Salvador, assisting rebels in, 277, 310-39, 404-5, 409
  US intervention in, 55, 91-2, 102-3, 344-5, 451, 496-7
*Nicaragua* case (ICJ 1986)
  accumulation of events theory and, 291
  anticipatory self-defence and, 362-3
  armed force and, 99, 102-4
  armed reprisals and, 308
  collective self-defence and, 336, 337, 338-9
  consent to intervention and, 448, 451
  crime of aggression and, 108
  humanitarian intervention and, 492, 493, 496-7
  *mens rea* element of use of force and, 103-26
  necessity principle and, 297
  non-intervention principle and, 91-2
  non-state actors, self-defence against, 400, 404-5, 409, 439
  pre-emptive self-defence and, 378-9
  prohibition on use of force and, 39, 75, 77
  proportional forcible countermeasures, 290
  proportionality principle and, 297
  reporting requirement for self-defence and, 344-5, 346, 347
  self-defence and, 260
  threat of force and, 55
Nigeria, participation in ECOMOG, 203
9/11 attacks
  generally, 368
  as armed attack, 401-2
  collective self-defence and, 336, 338
  emotional response to, 408
  NATO and, 264
  necessity principle and, 283-312
  non-state actors, self-defence against, 2, 400, 401

pre-emptive self-defence and, 369
preventative self-defence and, 357
Security Council Resolution 1368 (2001), 264-5, 407
Security Council Resolution 1373 (2001), 264-5, 351
self-defence and, 96, 264-5, 266, 283-312, 398, 403
Nkurunziza, Pierre, 477
No-fly zones, 160, 197-9, 214, 498-9
Non-Aligned Movement on pre-emptive self-defence, 376-7
Non-governmental organisations (NGOs), Interpretation of *jus ad bellum* and, 16
Non-international armed conflict
  negative equality principle and, 463-4
  targeted killings in, 433-4
Non-intervention principle
  in customary international law, 90
  ICJ and, 91-2
  interference distinguished, 90-1
  UN Charter and, 90
Non-recognition of governments, 49, 456
Non-state actors, self-defence against
  generally, 2, 18, 261, 398, 400-1
  accumulation of events theory and, 402-3
  armed reprisals distinguished, 403
  assassination attempts and, 405
  Bethlehem Principles and, 412
  calls for reform, 439-40
  consent to intervention and, 446
  effective control standard of attribution, 404-13
  harbouring standard of attribution, 407-8
  host states and non-state actors
    generally, 401
    effective control standard of attribution, 404-7
    harbouring standard of attribution, 407-8
    overall control test, 405-6
  ICJ and, 400, 404-5, 409-10, 439
  imminence and, 403-4
  lack of clarity regarding, 525
  necessity principle and, 312-13, 402
  9/11 attacks and, 2, 400, 401
  non-state actors only
    generally, 401
    effective control standard, 408-13
    lower standard of attribution, 413-14
  *opinio juris* and, 408
  overall control test, 405-6
  proportionality principle and, 402

Non-state actors, self-defence against (cont.)
  state sovereignty barrier, 401
  targeted killings (*See* Targeted killings)
  "unable or unwilling" doctrine (*See* "Unable or unwilling" doctrine)
Noriega, Manuel, 328–9, 449
North Atlantic Treaty Organization (NATO)
  Afghanistan, intervention in, 172
  authorisation of use of force by, 171–2
  Bosnia and Herzegovina, intervention in, 236
  collective security and, 171
  collective self-defence and, 337–8, 342
  Cooperative Cyber Defence Centre of Excellence, 84
  cyber operations and, 84
  drones, use of, 438
  emergence of, 153
  Finland and, 343
  internal crisis management, expansion of mandate to include, 171–2
  International Group of Experts, 84, 86
  Kosovo, intervention in, 36, 48, 73, 127, 199–201, 207, 223
  Libya, intervention in, 172, 190–2, 193, 194, 213–14, 520
  9/11 attacks and, 264
  Operation Allied Force, 502–4
  Security Council, relation to, 171–2
  self-defence and, 171, 264, 350
  Serbia, bombing of Chinese embassy in, 128
  Serbia and Montenegro, humanitarian intervention in, 490–1
  Strategic Concept (2010), 171–2
  Sweden and, 343
  Syria and, 216
  *Tallinn Manual*, 84, 86, 98, 101, 102, 286, 294
  Ukraine and, 43–6, 343
  Washington Treaty (1949), 337
  Yugoslavia, attacks in, 200, 502–4
North Korea
  in "axis of evil," 42–3, 179, 369–70, 377
  nuclear program in, 147, 188
  on pre-emptive self-defence, 377
  Rome Statute and, 63
  sanctions, 147
  Security Council and, 147, 188
  Security Council Resolution 1718 (2006), 188
  South Korea, invasion of, 147, 154–6, 341–2 (*See also* Korean War (1950-1953))
  threat of force and, 45, 47
Norway, intervention in Libya, 190–1
Novichok poisoning, 114–15

Nuclear weapons
  Cold War and, 46–54
  North Korea and, 147, 188
  Osiraq nuclear power plant missile strike (1981) (*See* Osiraq nuclear power plant missile strike (1981))
  pre-emptive self-defence and, 365
  proportionality principle and, 320
  threat of force and, 47
  Treaty on the Non-Proliferation of Nuclear Weapons (1968), 46
  Treaty on the Prohibition of Nuclear Weapons (2017), 46
*Nuclear Weapons* advisory opinion (ICJ 1996)
  armed force and, 95–6
  armed reprisals and, 308
  proportionality principle and, 320
  threat of force and, 40–1, 44, 47
Nuremberg Military Tribunal. *See* International Military Tribunal (Nuremberg Tribunal)

Obama, Barack, 43, 299–300, 379–81, 417, 421, 424, 433–6, 513, 514
Obama Doctrine, 379–81
O'Brien, Robert C., 390
O'Connell, Mary Ellen, 109
Ohlin, Jens David, 489
*Oil Platforms* case (ICJ 2003)
  armed attack and, 106, 268, 272–3, 274, 280–1, 290, 291
  necessity principle and, 301–10
  proportionality principle and, 317–18
Open-Ended Working Group on Developments in the field of Information and Telecommunications in the Context of International Security (OEWG), 82–3
*Opinio juris*
  humanitarian intervention and, 494, 507, 521
  ICJ Statute Article 38 and, 31
  interpretation of *jus ad bellum* and, 9–10
  non-state actors, self-defence against, 408
  pre-emptive self-defence and, 368
*Opinio necessitatis*, 507, 521
Orakhelashvili, Alexander, 162, 171
Organization for the Prohibition of Chemical Weapons, 114–15
Organization of African Unity (OAU)
  on consent to intervention, 476–7
  on humanitarian intervention, 495
Organization of American States (OAS)
  collective self-defence and, 337–8
  Cuban Missile Crisis (1962) and, 365–6

## Index

cyber operations and, 84–5
9/11 attacks and, 264
Security Council, relation to, 169
self-defence and, 264
Organization of Eastern Caribbean States, 328
Organization of the Islamic Conference, 214
Osiraq nuclear power plant missile strike (1981)
  necessity principle and, 312, 313–34
  pre-emptive self-defence and, 367–8
  Security Council and, 53
  Security Council Resolution 487 (1981), 367
  as use of force, 34
Ouattara, Alassane, 195, 196, 456
Overall control test, 405–6

Pakistan
  bin Laden, killing of, 412
  consent to intervention and, 475–6
  drones, use in, 429, 438
  India and, 353
  on pre-emptive self-defence, 376
  self-defence and, 353
  US intervention in, 412, 475–6
Palestinian Liberation Organization (PLO), 114–17, 309, 410, 459
Panama
  consent to intervention and, 448, 449–50
  extraction of nationals from, 336
  Panama Canal Treaty (1977), 328–9, 449
  US intervention in, 73, 328–30, 449–50, 459
Peacekeeping. *See also specific country or mission*
  generally, 18, 222
  by African Union (AU), 221
  "all necessary means" and, 234
  Brahimi Report (2000), 246–7, 254
  Capstone Doctrine, 223
  civilians, protection of, 247
  Cold War, during, 230–4
  collective security, origins in failures of, 220
  consent of parties
    generally, 226–7
    as basic principle, 227
    evolution of, 249–50
    non-state actors and, 249–50
    stabilisation missions and, 250
    withdrawal of consent, 249
  Cruz Report (2017), 255
  defining, 222–4
  early challenges, 220–1
  effective equipping of peacekeepers, 254
  evolution of
    generally, 245–6
    consent of parties, 249–50
    impartiality, 250–1
    self-defence, use of force limited to, 246–9
  General Assembly and, 224
  ICJ and, 225
  impartiality
    generally, 226–7
    as basic principle, 227–8
    deviations from, 253
    evolution of, 250–1
    stabilisation missions and, 251
  increased risks to peacekeepers, 253
  legal basis for
    UN Charter Article 1, 224
    UN Charter Chapter VI, 225
    UN Charter Chapter VII, 225–6
  muscular peacekeeping, 136–7, 160, 221, 248, 249
  parties to conflict, peacekeepers becoming, 252–3
  peace enforcement distinguished, 221, 254–5
  peace observation distinguished, 223
  Secretariat and, 222–3
  Security Council, origins in failures of, 220
  self-defence, use of force limited to
    generally, 226–7
    as basic principle, 228–30
    civilians, protection of, 247
    deviations from, 253
    evolution of, 246–9
    expansion of use of force, 246–7
    individuals, right to self-defence, 228–9
    lack of clarity, 247–8, 254
    narrow interpretation of, 229–30
    resistance to attempts to prevent implementation of peacekeeping, 246
    stabilisation missions, 248
    states, right to self-defence, 228–9
    UN, right to self-defence, 229
    UN Charter Chapter VII mandates, 248–9, 254
  stabilisation missions
    consent of parties and, 250
    impartiality and, 251
    self-defence, use of force limited to, 248
  Uniting our Strengths for Peace Report (2015), 246–7, 254–5
  use of force in, 221–4
  war fighting versus, 252, 253
Peace of Westphalia (1648), 25

Pence, Mike, 44–56
Peremptory norms
    consent to intervention and, 483
    humanitarian intervention and, 493
    prohibition on use of force as, 38–40
    Security Council subject to, 151
    VCLT, under, 38
Permanent imminence, 387–8
Poland, Rome Statute and, 63
Pompeo, Mike, 326, 331, 392, 393–4
Portugal, Special Arbitral Tribunal and, 307
Power, Samantha, 417–18
Precautionary principle, 4–5
Pre-emptive self-defence
    generally, 364–5
    Bush Doctrine and, 369–71
    Cuban Missile Crisis (1962) and, 365–6
    customary international law and, 370
    ICJ and, 378–9
    imminence, expansion of, 370–1
    international reaction to, 374–8
    Iraq War and, 371–3
    as *lex ferenda*, 371
    as *lex lata*, 371, 374
    "necessary force" and, 379–81
    9/11 attacks and, 369
    nuclear weapons and, 365
    Obama Doctrine, 379–81
    *opinio juris* and, 368
    problems of implementation, 373
    in Syria, 373–4
    weapons of mass destruction (WMD) and, 369
Preventative self-defence
    generally, 18, 261, 355, 357
    anticipatory self-defence
        generally, 360–1
        expansionist approach, 361
        ICJ and, 362–3
        international jurisprudence, 362–3
        restrictionist approach, 361–2
        Six Day War and, 363–4
    armed attack, determining when begins, 357–8
    confusion regarding, 358
    delay in responding distinguished, 358–9
    interception of armed attack, 359–60
    9/11 attacks and, 357
    pre-emptive self-defence (*See* Pre-emptive self-defence)
    use of term, 358
Prohibition on use of force
    generally, 1, 18, 23–4, 86–7
    accountability
        generally, 24, 48–50
        commissions of inquiry (CoI), 65–6
        countermeasures, 51–2
        crime of aggression (*See* Aggression, crime of)
        regional organisations, involvement of, 53–4
        reparations, 50–1
        Security Council, involvement of, 53–4
        self-defence, 52–3
    collective security and, 27
    commissions of inquiry (CoI) and, 65–6
    continued relevance of
        generally, 24
        collective security failures and, 75–6
        cyber operations and (*See* Cyber operations)
        international law, role of, 74–5
        justifications for use of force and, 76–8
        other causes for decline in war, 74–5
        purported demise of, 72–3
    countermeasures and, 51–2
    crime of aggression (*See* Aggression, crime of)
    as customary international law, 31–2, 75
    cyber operations and (*See* Cyber operations)
    force versus war, 30
    historical background, 24–30
        generally, 23–4
        collective security and, 27
        formal rules of war, 26–7
        just war doctrine, 24–6
        legal institution, war as, 26–7
    ICJ and, 39, 75, 77
    ILC on, 38–9
    international human rights law, relation to, 67
        generally, 5, 24
        aggression, determinations of, 70
        implications of, 70–2
        jurisdiction of human rights bodies and, 71
        positive obligations of states and, 71–2
        right to life and, 68–9, 71
    as *jus cogens*, 24, 38–40, 111
    as peremptory norm, 38–40
    reaffirmation of, 78–9
    recovery of territory and, 35
    sources of generally, 24
    targeted killings and, 429
    threat of force (*See* Threat of force)
    Ukraine War as violation of, 73
    UN Charter Article 2(4)
        generally, 30
        "against the territorial integrity or political independence of any state," 33–5

armed force as covered by, 93-4, 95
as "cornerstone," 3-4, 31
domestic situations, exclusion of, 37
exceptions, lack of express mention of, 33
"in any other manner inconsistent with the purposes of the United Nations," 35-6
international relations, limitation to, 36-8
regional organisations, applicability to, 37-8
Security Council, applicability to, 38
text of, 31, 32-3
*travaux préparatoires*, 34, 92-3, 94
types of force covered by, 92-4
violations of, 73
Proportional forcible countermeasures, 290
Proportionality principle
accumulation of events theory and, 295-6, 321-2
armed reprisals and, 307
authorisation of use of force by Security Council versus self-defence, 316-17
contextual nature of, 321
countermeasures and, 51
cyber attacks and, 318-19
dual role of, 298
further attacks, prevention of, 320-1
ICJ and, 297, 317-18, 320
international humanitarian law (IHL) compared, 4-5
*jus in bello* compared, 316
merger with necessity principle, 320
non-state actors, self-defence against, 402
nuclear weapons and, 320
protection of nationals abroad and, 329
qualitative proportionality, 318-19
quantitative proportionality, 317-18
Security Council and, 151
self-defence and
generally, 260-1
as enabling actions in, 261-98
specific objective of defence and, 319-21
in state practice, 297-8, 319
targeted killings and, 430-1
Proxy, threat of force by, 41
Psaki, Jen, 396
Putin, Vladimir, 45-6, 50, 91, 275, 332, 333, 342-3, 468, 509-10

Qatar
humanitarian intervention in Syria and, 512
Islamic State and, 418
Qualitative proportionality, 318-19
Quantitative proportionality, 317-18
Quigley, John, 176

Rambouillet Agreement (1999), 502
Rasmussen, Anders Fogh, 213-14
Ratner, Michael, 183
Ratner, Steven, 270
*Rebus sic stantibus*, 75-6
Recognition
consent to intervention and, 455-9
non-recognition of governments, 49, 456
Regional organisations. *See also specific organisation*
accountability for use of force, involvement as, 53-4
authorisation of use of force by
generally, 136
competence allocation, 167-9
concurrent competences, 168
exclusive competence of Security Council, 168-9
Security Council, relation to, 138, 153-4, 168-9
UN Charter Article 2(4), applicability of, 38
Reisman, Michael, 507-8
Reparations, 50-1
Reporting requirement for self-defence, 344-9. *See also* Self-defence
Reprisals. *See* Armed reprisals
Responsibility to Protect
generally, 175-6
Darfur and, 212-13
enforcement of secondary responsibility, 208-11
General Assembly and, 209
High-Level Panel and, 208, 209-10
humanitarian intervention and, 487, 520-1, 525-6
ICISS and, 207, 209-10
Kosovo situation as impetus for, 207
Libya and, 213-15, 520
natural disasters and, 212
normative legal status of, 211-12
Rwanda situation as impetus for, 207
Secretariat and, 208, 210
Security Council and, 208-9, 212
Somalia situation as impetus for, 207
sovereignty, relation to, 207-8
Syria and, 216-17
World Summit Outcome Document and, 208, 210-11
Rightslessness, 70
Right to life
ECHR and, 437
HRC and, 68-9, 71, 418-38

## 550  Index

Right to life (cont.)
  ICCPR and, 68, 436–7
  non-arbitrariness standard, 437
  prohibition on use of force and, 68–9, 71
  targeted killings and, 436–7
Rio de Janeiro Inter-American Treaty of Reciprocal Assistance (1947), 31
Roberts, Anthea, 507
Roosevelt, Franklin D., 29–30
Roscini, Marco, 126
Rose, Michael, 237
Rouhani, Hassan, 43
R2P. *See* Responsibility to Protect
Russia. *See also* Soviet Union
  on air strikes in Syria, 515
  Chechen rebels and, 412, 417
  commissions of inquiry (CoI) and, 65
  consent to intervention and, 448, 453–4
  Crimea, annexation of, 45, 49, 73, 332
  cyber attacks and, 79
  cyber operations and, 81, 82
  DRC, opposition to intervention in, 241
  genocide, allegations against Ukraine, 509–11
  Georgia, intervention in, 65–6, 79–80, 317, 325, 331–2
  Iraq and
    no-fly zones, 498–9
    opposition to intervention in, 198
  Kosovo, opposition to intervention in, 199, 200–1
  Libya, authorisation of force by Security Council and, 191
  Mali, opposition to intervention in, 243
  Nagorno-Karabakh dispute and, 303
  on NATO intervention in Yugoslavia, 503–4
  Novichok poisoning by, 114–15
  protection of nationals abroad and, 325, 326–7, 331–3
  Rome Statute and, 63
  sanctions against, 52
  self-defence and, 284–5
  status of forces agreements and, 480–1
  Syria and, 216, 465, 468, 480, 512, 514
  threat of force and, 45–6
  Turkish downing of Russian fighter jet, 50
  Ukraine War and (*See* Ukraine War)
  "unable or unwilling" doctrine and, 416
  US elections, interference in, 91
  use of armed force in Ukraine, 97–103
Russia-Ukraine Partition Treaty on the Status and Conditions of the Black Sea Fleet (1997), 480

Ruys, Tom, 109, 110, 129, 290, 300, 315, 345, 346, 350
Rwanda
  authorisation of force by Security Council in, 177–8
  extraction of nationals from, 335
  French intervention in, 177–8
  Lusaka Ceasefire Agreement (1999), 240
  Organization of African Unity and, 476–7
  Security Council Resolution 918 (1994), 228
  Security Council Resolution 929 (1994), 177–8
  Senegalese intervention in, 177–8
  United Nations Assistance Mission for Rwanda (UNAMIR), 228, 237

Sana'a funeral bombing (2016), 483
Sanctions
  as countermeasures, 52
  Iran, 160–1
  Iraq, 156–7, 351–2, 372
  as non-forcible measures, 53–4
  North Korea, 147
  Sierra Leone, 205, 500–1
  Southern Rhodesia, 156
  Syria, 216
San Francisco Conference (1945), 29–30, 361
Saudi Arabia
  consent to intervention and, 448
  humanitarian intervention in Syria and, 512
  Iraq, opposition to intervention in, 198–9
  Islamic State and, 418
  Operation Decisive Storm, 454–5, 468–9
  Operation Renewal of Hope, 454–5
  UK arms sales to, 483
  Yemen, intervention in, 454–5, 468–83
Scale and effects test, 98–9, 286, 401–2
Schabas, William A., 66–7, 71
Schachter, Oscar, 34, 496
Schmitt, Michael N., 271–2, 289
Schwarzenberger, Georg, 307
Schwebel, Stephen M. (ICJ Judge), 278–9, 347, 363
Second World War, 29
Self-defence
  generally, 18, 259, 261, 354
  accountability for use of force and, 52–3
  anticipatory self-defence
    generally, 360–1, 398
    expansionist approach, 361
    ICJ and, 362–3
    international jurisprudence, 362–3
    restrictionist approach, 361–2
    Six Day War and, 363–4

armed attack required for (*See* Armed attack)
armed reprisals distinguished, 291–310, 313–15
collective self-defence (*See* Collective self-defence)
consent to intervention and, 450–1
crime of aggression versus, 59, 60–1
in customary international law, 32, 260–1
cyber attacks and, 265–6, 271–2, 354–5
cyber operations as, 82, 84
*de minimis* threshold for use of force and, 111–12
extinguishment of right
  demand for cessation by Security Council, 353–4
  forcible measures by Security Council, 352
  sanctions and, 351–2
  seizing of issue by Security Council, 350–1
  "until clause," 349–54
humanitarian intervention versus, 494–5
ICJ and, 260
ILC on, 53
imminence (*See* Imminence)
interpretation of *jus ad bellum* and, 8
justifications for use of force, 11
Kellogg–Briand Pact, omission in, 29
lack of clarity regarding, 524–5
League of Nations, omission by, 259
NATO and, 171, 264, 350
necessity principle and (*See* Necessity principle)
9/11 attacks and, 96, 264–5, 266, 283–312, 398, 403
non-state actors, against (*See* Non-state actors, self-defence against)
novel right versus pre-existing right, 259–60
peacekeeping, use of force limited to self-defence (*See* Peacekeeping)
pre-emptive self-defence (*See* Pre-emptive self-defence)
preventative self-defence (*See* Preventative self-defence)
proportionality principle and (*See* Proportionality principle)
protection of nationals abroad (*See* Nationals abroad, protection of)
reporting requirement, 344–9
  generally, 10–11
  frequency of, 348
  ICJ and, 344–5, 346, 347
  as precondition to acts in self-defence, 345
  probative value of, 347
  as separate procedural obligation, 345–6
  Soleimani drone strike and, 346–7
  in state practice, 346–8
  transparency of, 349
Security Council, role of
  generally, 135–6, 343
  reporting requirement, 344–9
  "until clause," 349–54
targeted killings as, 267–8, 283, 293–4, 429–30, 433
temporal restrictions on right of, 355
textual source of right, 259–60
threat of force and, 40
UN Charter Article 51
  armed attack under, 261–2
  perpetrators of armed attack, 262–3
  protection of nationals abroad, 324–5
  targets of armed attack, 267
  text of, 259–60
weapons of mass destruction (WMD) and, 313, 398
Webster formula, 296, 307, 360, 364–5
Self-determination, consent to intervention and, 459–61, 475–84
Senegal
  Gambia, intervention in, 449–50
  Rwanda, intervention in, 177–8
Serbia, NATO bombing of Chinese embassy in, 128
Serbia and Montenegro, humanitarian intervention in, 490–1
Shalev, Gabriela, 292
Sharp, Walter, 99
Sheeran, Scott, 229
Siad Barre, Mohamed, 158
Sierra Leone
  Armed Force Revolutionary Council (AFRC), 204–5
  arms embargo, 204–5
  attacks on peacekeepers in, 252–3
  consent to intervention and, 448
  ECOMOG, participation in, 203
  ECOWAS intervention in, 169, 205, 238–9, 500–1, 520–1
  humanitarian intervention in, 500–1, 520–1
  implied authorisation of use of force by Security Council, 204–5
  Organization of African Unity and, 476–7
  sanctions, 205, 500–1
  UK intervention in, 238–9
  United Nations Mission in Sierra Leone (UNAMSIL), 238–9, 247
  United Nations Observer Mission in Sierra Leone (UNOMSIL), 238

Simma, Bruno (ICJ Judge), 290, 506
Six Day War (1967), 231
Skripal, Sergei, 112–16
Skripal, Yulia, 112–16
Sloan, James, 225, 252
Slovenia
  independence of, 235
  on Kosovo intervention, 200
  on regional organisations, 172
Smith, Ian, 156
Solana, Javier, 502
SolarWinds cyber attack, 79–80
Soleimani, Qassem, targeted killing of (2020)
  accumulation of events theory and, 293–4
  armed attack and, 267–8
  contextual imminence and, 389–95
  criticism of, 283
  international human rights law and, 71
  as law enforcement action, 114–17
  protection of nationals abroad and, 323–6, 330–1, 334–5
  reporting requirement for self-defence and, 346–7
Somalia
  African Union Transition Mission in Somalia (ATMIS), 237–8
  African Union/United Nations Force in Somalia (AMISOM), 237–8
  "all necessary means" and, 237–8
  attacks on peacekeepers in, 252–3
  authorisation of force by Security Council in, 158–9, 176–7, 178
  drones, use in, 429, 438
  Ethiopian intervention in, 347–8
  Kenyan intervention in, 415–16, 422–3
  "Mogadishu line," 237
  Security Council Resolution 794 (1992), 158, 176–7, 189, 508
  Transitional Federal Government, 422–3
  "unable or unwilling" doctrine and, 415–16
  Unified Task Force (UNITAF), 158–9, 189
  United Nations Operation in Somalia (UNOSOM I), 158–9, 251
  United Nations Operation in Somalia (UNOSOM II), 158–9, 236–7
  UNOSOM I, 158
  US intervention in, 158–9, 207, 237
Somoza, Anastasio, 55
Sony Pictures malware, 79–80
South Africa
  African National Congress, 459
  Angola, aggression against, 147
  Botswana, intervention in, 400
  "unable or unwilling" doctrine and, 416
South East Asia Collective Defence Treaty (1945), 337–8
Southern African Development Community (SADC), 478
Southern Arab Federation (SAF), 291–2
Southern Rhodesia. *See also* Zimbabwe
  arms embargo, 156
  sanctions, 156
  Security Council and, 156
  Zambia, aggression against, 147
South Korea, North Korean invasion of, 147, 154–6, 341–2. *See also* Korean War (1950–1953)
South Sudan
  United Nations Interim Security Force for Abyei (UNISFA), 247
  United Nations Mission in South Sudan (UNMISS), 247
Sovereignty
  cyber operations and, 83
  Responsibility to Protect, relation to, 207–8
Soviet Union. *See also* Russia
  Afghanistan, intervention in, 73, 346, 470–1, 474
  breakup of, 456
  collective self-defence and, 336
  consent to intervention and, 448, 474
  Cuba, removal of missiles from, 366
  Cuban Missile Crisis (1962) and, 365–6
  Czechoslovakia, intervention in, 73, 342, 470–1
  Hungary, intervention in, 73
Spain
  commissions of inquiry (CoI) and, 65
  foreign vessels, law enforcement actions against, 118
  Libya, intervention in, 190–1
  Rome Statute and, 63
Sri Lanka on use of force in self-defence in territory of other states, 266
Stabilisation missions
  consent of parties and, 250
  impartiality and, 251
  self-defence, use of force limited to, 248
Stahn, Carsten, 209
Stalin, Joseph, 29–30
State practice
  accumulation of events theory in, 291–4
  armed attack, use of force distinguished, 281–5
  collective self-defence in, 340–2

## Index

humanitarian intervention generally, 487, 494, 511–12
ICJ Statute Article 38 and, 31
interpretation of *jus ad bellum* and, 9–10
necessity principle in, 297–8
negative equality principle in, 464–5
proportionality principle in, 297–8, 319
reporting requirement for self-defence in, 346–8
Status of forces agreements, 480–1
Stevenson, Adlai, 366
Sthoeger, Eran, 165
Stimson Doctrine, 49
Stoltenberg, Jens, 343
Stuxnet cyber attack, 79–80, 96, 97–8, 100–1, 160–1, 287
Sudan
  African Union/United Nations Force in Sudan (UNAMID), 239–40, 247
  Darfur
    African Union intervention in, 170, 213
    Janjaweed militia, 212
    peacekeeping in, 253–4
    Responsibility to Protect and, 212–13
    Security Council Resolution 1706 (2006), 213
    Security Council Resolution 2559 (2020), 239–40
  Janjaweed militia, 212
  United Nations Interim Security Force for Abyei (UNISFA), 247
  United Nations Mission in Sudan (UNMIS), 239
  US air strikes in, 309, 310, 411
Suez crisis (1956)
  United Nations Emergency Force (UNEF I), 230–2, 246
  Uniting for Peace (UfP) process and, 166–7
Suicide bombers, 2
Suriname
  oil rig dispute (2000), 122–3
  proxy law enforcement actions and, 122–3
Sweden
  NATO and, 343
  on pre-emptive self-defence, 367–8
Syria
  Arab League and, 217
  Bush Doctrine in, 373–4
  chemical weapons in, 41–2, 315, 513, 514, 515–17
  civil war in, 446, 462, 465, 468
  collective self-defence and, 340–1
  drones, use in, 438

  France and, 458–9, 512, 514, 516–17
  General Assembly and, 150–1, 165–6
  humanitarian intervention in
    generally, 487, 512–13
    debate regarding air strikes, 513–14
    Responsibility to Protect and, 514
  Iran and, 512
  Islamic State in, 406, 416, 417–18, 421–4, 425, 465
  Israeli air strikes in, 292–3, 373–4, 387, 524–5
  NATO and, 216
  pre-emptive self-defence in, 373–4
  Responsibility to Protect and, 216–17
  Russia and, 216, 465, 468, 480, 512, 514
  sanctions, 216
  Security Council and, 216
  supply of arms by, 279
  Syrian National Council (SNC), 458–9
  UK air strikes on, 516–19
  "unable or unwilling" doctrine and, 416
  Uniting for Peace (UfP) process and, 166–7
  US and
    air strikes by, 315, 396, 515–17
    consent to intervention and, 473–4
    humanitarian intervention by, 512
    Responsibility to Protect and, 216
    Syrian National Council (SNC), 458–9

Taft, William, 184
Taiwan, China and, 42, 155
*Tallinn Manual on the International Law Applicable to Cyber Warfare*, 84, 86, 98, 101, 102, 286, 294
Talmon, Stefan, 394
Tams, Christian, 413, 414
Tanganyika, consent to intervention and, 448
Tanzania
  humanitarian intervention by, 494–5
  Tanganyika, consent to intervention and, 448
  US embassy, armed attack on, 270–1, 273, 283–312, 411, 436
Targeted killings
  generally, 401, 428
  of al-Qaida, 114–17, 431
  as armed force, 96
  consent to intervention and, 429
  *de minimis* threshold for use of force and, 112–16
  drones, use of, 429, 433, 438–9
  imminence and, 383, 388
  international humanitarian law (IHL) and
    generally, 428, 432

Targeted killings (cont.)
　civilians, protection of, 434–5
　continuous combat function, 434–5
　duty to capture, 435–6
　intensity requirement, 433–4
　in non-international armed conflict, 433–4
　organization requirement, 433–4
　international human rights law (IHRL) and
　　generally, 71, 428, 436
　　extraterritoriality and, 437–9
　　right to life and, 436–7
　as law enforcement actions, 114–17
　necessity principle and, 430–1
　prohibition on use of force and, 429
　proportionality principle and, 430–1
　as protection of nationals abroad, 323–6, 330–1, 334–5
　as self-defence, 267–8, 283, 293–4, 346–7, 429–30, 433
　Soleimani drone strike (*See* Soleimani, Qassem, targeted killing of (2020))
Targeted killings generally, 440
Taylor, Charles, 203–4, 499–500
Terrorism. *See also specific group or person*
　generally, 2
　global war on terror, 433–6
　imminence and, 388
　Leiden Policy Recommendations and, 436
　scale and effects test and, 401–2
　self-defence and (*See* Non-state actors, self-defence against)
　suicide bombers, 2
Thakur, Ramesh, 137–8
"Thin red line," 506–7
Thirty Years War, 25
Threat of force
　generally, 24, 40–1
　aggression, crime of (*See* Aggression, crime of)
　communicative nature of, 42–4
　credibility of, 47
　demand or ultimatum requirement, 41–2
　ICC and, 48
　ICJ and, 40–1, 44, 46–7, 54–5
　*jus cogens*, prohibition not deemed, 48
　non-verbal or written threats, 44–7
　nuclear weapons and, 47
　by proxy, 41
　self-defence and, 40
　use of force versus, 48
Threats to peace
　generally, 138, 143–4
　cyber attacks as, 145–6

　determinations, 144–7
　discretion regarding determinations, 144–5
　forcible measures in response to, 146–7
　threat of use of force and, 146
*Tinoco Concessions* arbitration (1923), 452
Tokyo Military Tribunal, 362
*Torrey Canyon* shipwreck bombing (1967), 118
Trapp, Kimberley, 410–11, 414
Treaties. *See also specific treaty*
　consent to intervention and, 476–7
　interpretation of *jus ad bellum* and, 6
Treaty of Amity, Economic Relations and Consular Rights between the United States and Iran (1955), 274
Treaty of Versailles (1919), 50
Treaty on the Non-Proliferation of Nuclear Weapons (1968), 46
Treaty on the Prohibition of Nuclear Weapons (2017), 46
Trump, Donald, 43–4, 47, 74–5, 267–70, 281, 282, 293–4, 295, 317, 323–6, 342, 346–7, 381–6, 389–95, 515–16
Tsagourias, Nicholas, 152–3, 161, 249, 287
Tunisia, Israeli intervention in, 147, 400, 410, 411–12
Turkey
　Cyprus, invasion of, 49
　Iraq, intervention in, 347–8, 400, 412, 479–80
　Russian fighter jet, downing of, 50
　"unable or unwilling" doctrine and, 416
　US missiles, removal of, 366
Turkish Republic of Northern Cyprus, non-recognition of, 49

Uganda
　*Armed Activities* case (*See Armed Activities* case (ICJ 2005))
　consent to intervention and, 448
　DRC, intervention in, 409–10, 451, 479
　Entebbe hostage crisis (1976), 334
　humanitarian intervention in, 494–5
　Israeli rescue of hostages in, 334
　Lusaka Ceasefire Agreement (1999), 240
　pre-emptive self-defence and, 378–9
Ukraine. *See also* Ukraine War
　consent to intervention and, 448, 453–4
　Constitution, 453
　Crimea, Russian annexation of, 45, 49, 73, 332
　Donetsk People's Republic, 49, 342–3, 448, 509
　genocide, allegations by Russia, 509–11
　Lugansk People's Republic, 49, 342–3, 448, 509
　NATO and, 43–6, 343

## Index

status of forces agreements and, 480-1
use of armed force by Russia in, 97-103
Ukraine War
  generally, 1-2
  collective self-defence and, 342-3
  conventional weapons in, 2
  nuclear power plants and, 343
  protection of nationals abroad and, 326-7, 332-3
  Secretariat and, 143
  Security Council involvement in, 53, 173
  self-defence and, 275
  threat of force and, 45-6
  Uniting for Peace (UfP) process and, 167
  as violation of prohibition on use of force, 73
"Unable or unwilling" doctrine
  generally, 414-19
  able but unwilling states and, 424-5
  Bethlehem Principles and, 416, 418-21, 424-5, 426
  Chatham House Principles and, 416-17
  consent and, 426-7
  failed states and, 422-3
  lack of clarity regarding, 525
  legal status of, 427-8
  Leiden Policy Recommendations and, 416, 417, 418-20, 425-6
  problems with, 420-8
  protection of nationals abroad and, 333-5
  unable and unwilling states and, 418-21
  unable but willing states and, 423-4
Unilateralism, 175, 176-9
United Arab Emirates, Islamic State and, 418
United Kingdom
  accumulation of events theory and, 291-2
  on armed attack by non-state actors, 265
  Brexit, 79-80
  *Caroline* incident (1837) (*See Caroline* incident (1837))
  collective self-defence and, 343
  commissions of inquiry (CoI) and, 65, 66
  on consent to intervention, 446
  consent to intervention and, 448
  *Corfu Channel* case and (*See Corfu Channel* case (ICJ 1949))
  on counterintervention, 470-6
  cyber attacks and, 79-80, 286-7
  cyber operations and, 83
  DRC, intervention in, 241
  drones, use of, 438
  extraction of nationals by, 333, 335-6
  Falkland Islands, response to seizure of, 302, 348, 353-4 (*See also* Falklands War (1982))

Foreign Affairs Committee, 506-7
foreign vessels, law enforcement actions against, 118
on humanitarian intervention, 496, 504, 512
humanitarian intervention in Syria and, 512, 513-14
on imminence, 381-2, 384
Iraq and
  intervention in, 197-8, 453
  no-fly zones, 498-9
Iraq Inquiry, 186, 188, 373
Iraq War and, 1, 53, 180
Islamic State, action against, 430-1
Joint Parliamentary Committee on Human Rights, 384, 387-8, 431-2
law enforcement actions in, 113-29
Libya, intervention in, 190-1
Manual of the Law of Armed Conflict (2004), 333
on NATO intervention in Yugoslavia, 503, 506-7
on negative equality principle, 465
on pre-emptive self-defence, 372, 377-8
Saudi Arabia, arms sales to, 483
Sierra Leone, intervention in, 238-9
Southern Arab Federation (SAF) and, 291-2
Suez crisis and, 230-1
Syria, air strikes on, 516-19
targeted killings by, 114-17, 383, 388, 428, 429-38
threat of force and, 41-2
"unable or unwilling" doctrine and, 416, 420-1, 427
Yemen, air strikes in, 291-2, 308, 309, 310
United Nations Charter
  absence of states withdrawing from, 76
  adoption of, 1, 29-30
  armed reprisals and, 307-8
  Article 1, 224
  Article 2(4) (*See* Prohibition on use of force)
  Article 39 (*See also* United Nations Security Council)acts of aggression, 147-8
    breaches of peace, 147-8
    threats to peace, 144-7
  Article 41, 148
  Article 42, 148 (*See also* United Nations Security Council)
  Article 43, 148-9
  Article 51 (*See* Self-defence)
  Article 52, 167 (*See also* Regional organisations)
  Article 53, 168 (*See also* Regional organisations)

556  Index

United Nations Charter (cont.)
  Chapter VI, 225
  Chapter VII (*See specific topic*)
  collective security and, 135
  collective self-defence and, 336
  crime of aggression and, 57–8
  customary international law, relation to, 32
  force versus war, 30
  humanitarian intervention and (*See Humanitarian intervention*)
  interpretation of *jus ad bellum* and, 7
  lack of appetite for changing, 523–4
  maintenance of peace and security, 135
  non-intervention principle and, 90
  prohibition on use of force (*See* Prohibition on use of force)
  Security Council, forcible measures in accordance with, 150
  self-defence (*See* Self-defence)
  *travaux préparatoires*, 491
  VCLT and, 7–8
United Nations Convention on the Law of the Sea (UNCLOS) (1982), 31, 118
United Nations Department of Peacekeeping (DPK), 222
United Nations General Assembly
  generally, 136
  authorisation of use of force by, 165–7
  commissions of inquiry (CoI), 65
  Declaration on Friendly Relations (*See* Declaration on Principles of International Law Concerning Friendly Relations and Co-operation among States (1970))
  Declaration on the Inadmissibility of Intervention in the Domestic Affairs of States (1965), 463
  Declaration on the Non-Use of Force (1987), 93–4
  Definition of Aggression (1974) (*See* Definition of Aggression (1974))
  ICJ and, 140–1, 142
  Implementation of the Declaration on the Granting of Independence to Colonial Countries and Peoples (1972), 460
  Interpretation of *jus ad bellum* and, 16
  Korean War and, 155–6
  limitations on, 141–2
  peacekeeping and, 224
  powers of, 141
  recommendations, 141
  recommendation versus authorisation, 166
  Responsibility to Protect and, 209
  Security Council, relation to, 141–2, 150–1, 165

United Nations Human Rights Committee
  objections to approach, 69–70
  rightslessness and, 70
  right to life and, 68–9, 71, 418–38
United Nations Human Rights Council, 65
United Nations Office of Legal Affairs, 229
United Nations Secretariat
  generally, 136
  Agenda for Peace, 142–3
  High-Level Panel on Threats, Challenges and Change, 187–8, 208, 209–10, 375
  In Larger Freedom, 208, 210, 375–6
  peacekeeping and, 222–3
  powers of, 142–3
  Responsibility to Protect and, 208, 210
  Security Council, relation to, 142–3
United Nations Security Council
  generally, 136
  abductions and, 113–20
  accountability for use of force, involvement as, 53–4
  acts of aggression and
    generally, 138, 143–4
    determinations, 70, 147–8
  authorisation of use of force by (*See* Authorisation of use of force by Security Council)
  breaches of peace
    generally, 138, 143–4
    determinations, 147–8
  commissions of inquiry (CoI), 14, 65
  debates regarding membership, 137–8
  failures of, 75–6
  peacekeeping emerging from, 220
  forcible measures
    generally, 138, 143, 148
    inadequacy of non-forcible measures, 300
    international humanitarian law, subject to, 151–3
    *jus cogens*, subject to, 151
    *legibus solutus* not applicable, 149
    limitations on, 149–53
    necessity principle and, 151
    peremptory norms, subject to, 151
    proportionality principle and, 151
    threats to peace, in response to, 146–7
    UN Charter, acts in accordance with, 150
  foreign civil aircraft, law enforcement actions against and, 118
  General Assembly, relation to, 141–2, 150–1, 165
  humanitarian intervention justified by failure of, 507–8

557  Index

ICJ and, 139-40, 151
ICTY compared, 149
Interpretation of *jus ad bellum* and, 16
Korean War and, 154-6
legally binding nature of decisions, 139-40
limited membership, 137
maintenance of peace and security, 137
Military Staff Committee, 149, 153
non-forcible measures, 138, 148
pacific settlement of disputes, 138, 225, 492
peacekeeping and (*See* Peacekeeping)
permanent members, 3, 137
powers of, 138
primacy of decisions, 139
regional organisations, relation to, 138, 153-4, 168-9
Resolutions (*See specific country*)
Responsibility to Protect and, 208-9, 212
Secretariat, relation to, 142-3
self-defence, role in
  generally, 135-6, 343
  reporting requirement, 344-9
  "until clause," 349-54
threats to peace
  generally, 138, 143-4
  cyber attacks as, 145-6
  determinations, 144-7
  discretion regarding determinations, 144-5
  forcible measures in response to, 146-7
  threat of use of force and, 146
troops supplied by member states, 148-9
UN Charter Article 2(4), applicability of, 38
Uniting for Peace (UfP) Resolution, 155-6, 166-7, 173, 209, 508
veto power, 3, 137-8
United States
  abductions by, 114-20
  accumulation of events theory and, 293-4
  Afghanistan and
    air strikes by, 309, 310, 411
    attack on al-Qaida in as self-defence, 266, 273, 310, 313, 320-1, 368-9, 407-8, 411-12
  al-Qaida and
    Afghanistan, intervention in, 368, 403
    attack by as self-defence, 266, 273, 310, 313, 320-1, 368-9, 407-8
    US embassies, armed attacks on, 273, 411
  Authorization for Use of Military Force (2001), 429-32
  *Caroline* incident (1837) (*See Caroline* incident (1837))
  collective self-defence and, 336, 338, 341
  commissions of inquiry (CoI) and, 65
  consent to intervention and, 448, 449-50, 473, 475-6, 479, 481, 482
  Cuban Missile Crisis (1962) and, 365-6
  cyber attacks and, 79-80, 318, 319
  cyber operations and, 81, 85-6
  drones, use of, 438
  extraction of nationals by, 335, 336
  Grenada, intervention in, 73, 327-30, 449
  Gulf War and, 41, 53-4, 157
  on imminence, 384, 388
  Iran and
    armed attack on embassy by, 271
    attempted rescue of hostages in, 333-4
    downing of civil aircraft, 122, 127
    "Eagle Claw" mission, 271
    oil platforms, armed attack on, 274, 301-10, 317-18
    proportionality principle and, 317-18
    threat of force against, 43
    threat to military vessels by, 268, 293
    use of armed force in, 97-112
  Iraq and
    air strikes in, 309, 330, 453
    embassy, armed attack on, 269, 281
    intervention in, 197-8
    Islamic State, action against, 483-4
    no-fly zones, 498-9
    targeted killings in, 334-5
  Iraq War and, 1, 53, 73, 180, 185, 187
  Islamic State, action against, 416, 417-18
  Kenya, armed attack on US embassy in, 270-1, 273, 283-312, 411, 436
  on Kosovo intervention, 199
  Libya, intervention in, 190-1
  National Security Strategy (NSS) (2002), 370, 376, 385
  National Security Strategy (NSS) (2006), 373
  National Security Strategy (NSS) (2010), 379
  on NATO intervention in Yugoslavia, 503
  Nicaragua, intervention in, 55, 91-2, 102-3, 344-5, 451, 496-7
  9/11 attacks (*See* 9/11 attacks)
  *Oil Platforms* case (*See Oil Platforms* case (ICJ 2003))
  Operation Desert Fox, 184-5
  Pakistan, intervention in, 412, 475-6
  Panama, intervention in, 73, 328-30, 449-50, 459
  on pre-emptive self-defence, 368

United States (cont.)
  protection of nationals abroad and, 324, 325–31, 333–5
  on Responsibility to Protect and, 215
  Rome Statute and, 63
  Russian interference in elections, 91
  self-defence and
    Afghanistan, attack on al-Qaida in as, 266, 273, 310, 313, 320–1, 368–9, 407–8, 411–12
    9/11 attacks and, 96, 264–5, 266, 283–312, 320–1, 398, 403, 407–8
    state practice regarding, 281–4
    targeted killings as, 267–8, 283, 293–4, 346–7, 433
  Soleimani drone strike (See Soleimani, Qassem, targeted killing of (2020))
  Somalia, intervention in, 158–9, 207, 237
  Sudan, air strikes in, 309, 310, 411
  Syria and
    air strikes on, 315, 396, 515–17
    consent to intervention and, 473–4
    humanitarian intervention in, 512, 514
    Responsibility to Protect and, 216
    Syrian National Council (SNC), 458–9
  Tanzania, armed attack on US embassy in, 270–1, 273, 283–312, 411, 436
  targeted killings by, 96, 114–17, 267–8, 283, 293–4, 324, 325–6, 330–1, 334–5, 346–7, 428, 429–31 (See also Soleimani, Qassem, targeted killing of (2020))
  threat of force and, 41, 43–4
  Turkey, removal of missiles from, 366
  "unable or unwilling" doctrine and, 416, 418–22, 427
  Venezuela and, 44–56
Uniting for Peace (UfP) process, 155–6, 166–7, 173, 209, 508
Uniting our Strengths for Peace Report (2015), 246–7, 254–5
Urquhart, Brian, 252
Use of force
  generally, 18, 89, 130
  accumulation of events theory, 290–6 (See also Accumulation of events theory)
  aggression distinguished, 107–9
  "all necessary means" versus, 189
  armed attack distinguished (See Armed attack)
  armed force (See Armed force)
  de minimis threshold
    generally, 109
    acts falling below, 110
  importance of establishing, 111–12
  jus cogens and, 111
  law enforcement actions distinguished, 112–18
  self-defence and, 111–12
  targeted killings and, 112–16
  General Assembly, authorisation by, 165–7
  gravity element generally, 105, 123–4
  law enforcement actions distinguished, 112–18
    generally, 112–13
    abductions, 113–14
    foreign civil aircraft, against, 118
    foreign individuals or groups, against, 116–17
    foreign vessels, against, 118
    proxy actions, 121–3
    Soleimani drone strike and, 114–17
    targeted killings, 114–17
  mens rea element
    generally, 125–6
    coercion as basis of requirement, 125–6
    hostile intent, 128–9
    ICJ and, 103–26
    intention versus general motives for action, 126–7
    mistake and, 127–8
  non-intervention principle
    in customary international law, 90
    ICJ and, 91–2
    interference distinguished, 90–1
    UN Charter and, 90
  non-state actors, self defence against (See Non-state actors, self-defence against)
  in peacekeeping, 221–4
  prohibition on (See Prohibition on use of force)
  regional organisations, authorisation by
    generally, 136
    competence allocation, 167–9
    concurrent competences, 168
    exclusive competence of Security Council, 168–9
  Security Council, authorisation by (See Authorisation of use of force by Security Council)
  self-defence (See Self-defence)
  threat of force versus, 48
  types of force covered by UN Charter, 92–4

VanLandingham, Rachel, 393
Vattel, Emer de, 25
Venezuela
  "unable or unwilling" doctrine and, 416
  United States and, 44–56

Vermeer, Zachary, 469
Vienna Convention on Diplomatic Relations (1961), 128
Vienna Convention on the Law of Treaties (VCLT) (1969)
  coercion and, 475
  consent to intervention and, 449
  interpretation of *jus ad bellum* and, 7-8
  peremptory norms under, 38
  UN Charter and, 7-8
Vietnam
  collective self-defence and, 336, 338
  humanitarian intervention by, 494-5
  on pre-emptive self-defence, 376

Waldheim, Kurt, 233-4, 246
Waldock, Humphrey, 322-3, 333, 353, 360
WannaCry ransomware, 79-80
Warsaw Pact
  collective self-defence and, 337-8, 342
  Czechoslovakia, intervention in, 475
  emergence of, 153
  self-defence and, 350
Weapons
  aircraft as, 96
  armed force, types of weapons used in, 95-6
  autonomous weapons, 526
  cyber attacks and, 96
  defined, 96
  evolution of, 2
  kinetic force, 95
  necessity principle, relevance of nature of weapons used to, 313
  WMD (*See* Weapons of mass destruction (WMD))
Weapons of mass destruction (WMD)
  authorisation of use of force by Security Council and, 183
  chemical weapons
    Novichok poisoning, 114-15
    in Syria, 41-2, 315, 513, 514, 515-17
  Cuban Missile Crisis (1962) and, 366
  Iraq and, 371
  *jus ad bellum* and, 2
  nuclear weapons (*See* Nuclear weapons)
  pre-emptive self-defence and, 369
  self-defence and, 313, 398
Webster, Daniel, 296

Webster formula, 296, 307, 360, 364-5
Weightman, M.A., 337
West Irian, United Nations Security Force (UNSF), 224
Weston, Berns, 176
White, Nigel D., 146, 150, 152-3, 156-7, 165, 166, 229, 247
Wilson, Woodrow, 27-8
Wippman, David, 205
WMD. *See* Weapons of mass destruction (WMD)
Wood, Michael, 165, 202
World Summit Outcome Document (2005), 78, 208, 210-11
Wright, Jeremy, 381-2, 383, 384, 385, 397
Wright, Quincy, 464

Xi Jinping, 42

Yanukovych, Viktor, 332, 448, 453-4, 455
Yemen
  al-Qaida in, 469
  armed attacks by, 291-2
  on authorisation of force by Security Council, 176
  civil war in, 468-9
  consent to intervention and, 448, 454-5, 473
  drones, use in, 429, 438
  Houthis in, 454-5, 468-83
  Iranian intervention in, 455, 470, 471
  Islamic State in, 469
  Sana'a funeral bombing (2016), 483
  Saudi intervention in, 454-5, 468-83
  Security Council Resolution 2216 (2015), 455
  UK air strikes in, 291-2, 308, 309, 310
Yugoslavia. *See also specific country*
  attacks on peacekeepers in, 252-3
  breakup of, 456
  Kosovo Albanians, repression of, 501
  NATO attacks in, 200, 502-4
  United Nations Protection Force (UNPROFOR), 235-6, 247-8

Zambia, Southern Rhodesian aggression against, 147
Zimbabwe. *See also* Southern Rhodesia
  on authorisation of force by Security Council, 176-7
  Lusaka Ceasefire Agreement (1999), 240

For EU product safety concerns, contact us at Calle de José Abascal, 56–1°, 28003 Madrid, Spain or eugpsr@cambridge.org.